FEEDING THE FLOCK

Feeding the Flock

THE FOUNDATIONS OF MORMON THOUGHT: CHURCH AND PRAXIS

Terryl L. Givens

OXFORD
UNIVERSITY PRESS

OXFORD
UNIVERSITY PRESS

Oxford University Press is a department of the University of Oxford. It furthers the University's objective of excellence in research, scholarship, and education by publishing worldwide. Oxford is a registered trade mark of Oxford University Press in the UK and certain other countries.

Published in the United States of America by Oxford University Press
198 Madison Avenue, New York, NY 10016, United States of America.

© Oxford University Press 2017

Library of Congress Cataloging-in-Publication Data
Names: Givens, Terryl, author.
Title: Feeding the flock : the foundations of Mormon thought : church and praxis / Terryl L. Givens.
Description: Oxford, New York : Oxford University Press, [2017] |
Includes bibliographical references and index.
Identifiers: LCCN 2016042506 (print) | LCCN 2016043760 (ebook) |
ISBN 9780199794935 (cloth) | ISBN 9780199795000 (updf) |
ISBN 9780190657864 (oso) | ISBN 9780190657857 (epub)
Subjects: LCSH: Sacraments—Church of Jesus Christ of Latter-day Saints. |
Sacraments—Mormon Church. | Church of Jesus Christ of Latter-day
Saints—Doctrines. | Mormon Church—Doctrines.
Classification: LCC BX8655 .G58 2017 (print) | LCC BX8655 (ebook) |
DDC 289.3/32—dc23
LC record available at https://lccn.loc.gov/2016042506

9 8 7 6 5 4 3 2 1
Printed by Sheridan Books, Inc., United States of America

To Philip and Deborah

How good and glorious it has seemed unto me, to find pure and holy friends, who are faithful, just, and true.

— JOSEPH SMITH

Contents

Preface

IN VOLUME 1 of my history of Mormon thought I chose "Wrestling the Angel" to designate the metaphorical struggle to articulate in human terms the key ideas pertaining to the nature of God, the human, and their relationship. (I use "Mormon" as a simpler and interchangeable term for "the Church of Jesus Christ of Latter-day Saints," the formal designation for the faith tradition.) In this, the second volume, I chose "Feeding the Flock," as it is the metaphorical expression the resurrected Savior used to refer to the work of the ministry, executed in and through his church by his delegated servants.[1] I intend those words to convey the general scheme of organization, offices, authority, and practices that God designed to bring to fruition his ultimate intentions for the human family discussed in that first volume. This is a book, simply put, about the church, or what religious scholars call ecclesiology. In referring to a history of Mormon practice, I do not mean to present a sociology of Mormonism, or a history of Mormon culture. I mean only to contrast the study of Mormon theology, or Mormon thought as a system of ideas and doctrines, with Mormon ecclesiology, that is, the study of how those ideas and doctrines have been formally implemented through an ecclesiastical structure and modes of worship. In one volume, I cannot hope to cover the entire range of the institutional church, historically or organizationally. So while important, many aspects of the institutional church (like auxiliary organizations and educational systems) I have had to neglect or pass over lightly as being less central to the study of ecclesiology as historically understood.

The same caveats apply to this volume as they did with the first. I make no claims to either a comprehensive or authoritative presentation and have selected for treatment those aspects of Mormon ecclesiology that strike me as most useful in answering the fundamental question of ecclesiology: what did Joseph Smith and his successors understand the purpose of the church to be, and how did the resultant structure and forms of practice evolve over time?

Mormon ecclesiology in my experience has proven more complicated to arrange topically than theology, because of the complex interconnectedness of all the parts: sacraments are inseparable from questions of authority; authority has both institutional and soteriological roles; in addition, authority is both evidenced in and a precondition for certain spiritual gifts; some spiritual gifts are hard to distinguish from sacraments (healing, for example); some sacraments are central to temple theology but some are part of the order of worship (the Lord's Supper), and some are performed independently. A patriarch holds a priesthood office, but his work is to pronounce blessings, which are a form of sacrament. Seventies formed part of the church hierarchy, became a ward-level priesthood office, then reverted to part of the leadership structure, and so forth. Therefore, liberal use of the index may be the best way to ensure that one has access to all the angles from which a given topic may be discussed in this volume. For readability, most spelling from original sources has been modernized.

Acknowledgments

MANY OF THE questions this volume tackles were raised in the Mormon Scholars Foundation Summer Seminar of 2015, "Organizing the Kingdom: Priesthood, Church Government, and the Forms of LDS Worship." I thank the donors of the MSF for their support and the participants for their contributions. Several scholars have reviewed various drafts of this work and made helpful criticisms, especially Matthew Bowman, Benjamin Huff, Michael MacKay, Gerald Smith, and Joseph Spencer. Jed Woodworth's critiques have been crucial, and Jonathan Stapley's work on priesthood has been invaluable. A work of this nature would be much more difficult if not for the world-class editing of the Joseph Smith Papers editors, making available to this generation an unprecedented bonanza of readily accessible source materials, and I am grateful to the entire team of editors for their contributions to the field of Mormon Studies. I also express appreciation to the University of Richmond Faculty Research Committee and the Neal A. Maxwell Institute for Religious Scholarship for generous support in bringing this project to fruition. Finally, a thank you to my colleagues at Harris Manchester College, Oxford University, where I completed the manuscript as a Visiting Fellow in 2016.

FEEDING THE FLOCK

1

What Is the Church, and Why Is One Necessary?

IN MORMON THEOLOGY, human anthropology is traceable to a premortal sphere in which God the Eternal Father invited into eternal relationship with himself and a Heavenly Mother an innumerable host of those immortal human spirits by which they found themselves surrounded.[1] Rather than forming humans for their own glory, the Divine Parents choose to nurture these souls toward godliness so that these their children, women and men, "might have joy."[2] It is at this moment, before the earth is created or the first person formed, that grace—God's freely given offering of love—irrupts into the universe. In a seventeenth-century sermon, the English Puritan Thomas Watson asks, "What is the chief end of man," and replies, "Man's chief end is to glorify God."[3] A historian of theology writes that according to the great American divine Jonathan Edwards, God "always acts for his own glory and honor. Why did God create anything outside himself? . . . God's only motive was self-glory."[4] The first lesson of the Catholic Baltimore Catechism asked, "Why did God make you?" The answer: "God made me to know him, to love him, and to serve him."[5] One of the most popular preachers of the twenty-first century writes, "You were made for God's glory."[6] Mormon scripture challenges such orthodoxy, asserting, on the contrary, that humans were not created to serve as instruments of God's glory but that he has made it *his* project and purpose to create the conditions for *our* happiness, by bringing "to pass the immortality and eternal life of man."[7]

God, being perfectly and supremely joyful, wished the same condition to be shared by the human race and made provision—at his unfathomable personal cost—for this to be so. Embodiment for billions of spirits, the travails of mortality, and the educative experiences of pain and pleasure, dissolution, and death—all are orchestrated to effect the eventual incorporation of these numberless multitudes into a celestial family. Full communion with God, partaking of the divine nature by immersion in an eternal web of loving relationships, is the purpose and project of human existence. A mortal sphere exposing humans to the formative crucible of experiences and choices defines as much as refines our nature and propels the process onward. The crowning culmination is achieved when sanctified individuals are assimilated into eternal union with each other and with heavenly parents, in a divine family. Such ends are achieved through belief in God and his providence, and faith in an atoning sacrifice of God the Son that makes repentance, sanctification, and resurrection possible. This is the fundamental framework of Mormon thought.

The contrast with orthodox conceptions of human existence and redemption is profound. "God's purpose and goal in redemption," writes one religious historian, "is to reverse the sin, corruption and death introduced into humanity by Adam."[8] Mormons, on the other hand, do not see God's primary work as recuperative or restorative but as progressive and additive. They see the Fall as part of God's plan from the beginning, a prelude to a mortal experience that is educative, formative, and ennobling, linking an eternal, premortal past with post-resurrection future. As Smith would say in one of his last sermons, at some moment in a distant, primeval past, "God Himself found Himself in the midst of spirits and glory. Because He was greater He saw proper to institute laws whereby the rest, who were less in intelligence, could have a privilege to advance like Himself *and be exalted with Him*."[9] This conception of a covenant that precedes the world's existence, wherein a divine being (and a feminine divine companion) invites humans to participate in the divine nature and enter into eternal relation with them, with that human family reciprocally committing to the terms and conditions of such an outcome, is the governing paradigm of Mormon soteriology. This is the covenantal relationship that underlies and encompasses all other covenants. Smith is a long time unfolding the full cosmic narrative, but he finds the principal impetus with his translation of the Book of Mormon and its radical reworking of covenant theology, aided by revelations in the months following that detail premortal councils and human participation in the grand design. Mormon ecclesiology is best understood—indeed, it can only be understood—insofar as it is situated within this underlying covenantal framework.

Why, we might ask to begin with, is a church even necessary in such a bold scheme? A world of independent agents, exercising faith and living virtuous lives as

motivated or drawn by the clarion call of a heavenly love is a powerful point of departure. The comforting, fortifying, and instructing divine Spirit guides in the journey.
Is an actual church necessary in the process? Certain functions of the church are
neatly laid out in the letter to the Ephesians: ministering, edifying, and teaching
until the imitation of Christ is fully achieved.[10] But is the church thus alluded to
essential and indispensable or merely helpful? "Without religion," one literary character claims, "you *cannot* make the will equal to its tasks."[11] As fallen, self-interested
creatures with "willing spirits but weak flesh," outside aid is critical.[12] A church, from
this perspective, serves as spiritual reinforcement, a catalyst or facilitator of moral
betterment. In a related way, the collectivist model of public worship and religious
affiliation can provide a kind of spiritual as well as material synergy, transforming
the good intentions of solitary efforts into both personal transformation and public
impact. Not only are "two or three . . . gathered in [his] name" the guarantee of
God's presence,[13] but large-scale dilemmas require concerted action that charities
and orders and congregations moving in concert are better prepared to address than
individuals. But are such rationales sufficient explanation?

At the same time, institutional religion comes at a cost. Once a formal institution
enters the religious picture, a critical Rubicon in the call of faith has been crossed, and
a whole series of dichotomies complicate the life of discipleship. Belief and practice,
orthodoxy and orthopraxis, inward faith and outward performance, private conscience and organizational affiliation—such distinctions are useful labels, organizing categories we have come to employ in the study of religion. These dichotomies,
however, can also suggest a rupture that portends a crisis, if not a catastrophic failure, of the animating imperative at the core of Christianity: pure and uncalculating
love, leading to the holiness that fits one for full communion with God. The moral
philosopher and theologian Kenneth Kirk considers that the institutionalization of
the Christian church itself threatens to undermine its own avowed purpose, as faith,
yearning, love, and loyalty become overwhelmed by forms, rules, and procedures.

Such a dilemma manifested itself almost immediately in the Christian church, he
believes: "with the Apostolic Fathers . . . the actions and dispositions are [already]
wholly confused,—actions right and wrong pushing their way more and more into
the foreground of the code, and obedience and conformity taking the place of
enthusiastic loyalty as the basis of Christian life."[14] The problem, in other words,
is that moving from spontaneous love of God as a natural response, to creeds and
practices as prescribed belief and performance, would seem to turn religion into
the self-conscious pursuit of a goal. Selfless response becomes self-interested quest.
"If my aim in life is to attain a specified standard," notes Kirk, "or to live according
to a defined code, I am bound continually to be considering myself, and measuring
the distance between my actual attainment and the ideal. It is impossible by such

a road to attain the self-forgetfulness which we believe to be the essence of sanctity."[15] One remedy suggests itself: "How is disinterestedness, unselfishness, to be attained? Once grant that moralism, or formalism, cannot bring the soul nearer to it, and there remains only one way—the way of worship. Worship lifts the soul out of its preoccupation with itself and its activities, and centers its aspirations entirely on God."[16]

Worship is, as James White notes, "an exasperatingly difficult word to pin down."[17] Luther saw worship in terms of communion through "prayer and the song of praise," Calvin saw its end as union with God, while Archbishop Thomas Cranmer said worship was "directed to God's glory and human rectitude."[18] In Kirk's view, worship in its pure form is what saves us from preoccupation with self and turns our hearts and minds upward—enhancing a "stream of new life" that characterizes "this primary bond set up between God and the soul."[19] Most conceptions of worship, then, emphasize interaction, reciprocity, praise given, and God's spirit felt, "the glorification of God and the sanctification of humanity" in the Catholic view.[20] In what follows, I will treat the broad theme of Mormon worship in a similar way but extending Kirk's emphasis on how believers develop to fruition "this primary bond set up between God and the soul." Geoffrey Wainwright is correct that "the proper relationship between creature and Creator is ... the relationship of worship,"[21] but Mormons construe this "proper relationship" rather differently from other Christians. As I have suggested above and explicated at length elsewhere, Latter-day Saints interpret that bond "between God and the soul" as a literal kinship, a version of theosis more robust and more literal than other Christian versions of the doctrine. Given Mormonism's reading of that bond as one that is unimpeded by an "infinite qualitative divide,"[22] worship entails adoration and praise but also the forging of an eternal, familial relationality.

In addition, worship is not a solitary act—it is communal, an activity expressed in solidarity with others. "To S. Paul and S. John," notes Kirk, "it could have no other context than that of the Church."[23] As White quotes the Russian Orthodox theologian George Florovsky, "Christian existence is essentially corporate; to be a Christian means to be in the community."[24] Theologians like Wainwright have also emphasized worship's community-building and unifying function.[25] Latter-day Saints in particular emphasize the communal nature of religion but as much more than an assist to compensate for the human frailty of solitary devotion, or for purposes of establishing communities of merely provisional duration. Mormons construe salvation as eternal relationality with other human beings as well as with God, or what Joseph Smith called a "sociality" with friends and family "coupled with glory."[26] (In this volume, I am using salvation to refer to the Mormon conception of the highest degree of glory, the celestial kingdom or "exaltation." Mormons—confusingly—also use the term to refer to the state that virtually the entirety of the human race will inherit, excepting only the "sons of perdition.")

The philosopher Charles Taylor sees secularism as following upon a great cosmic reorientation in the Western world—an "anthropocentric shift," or a substitution of man for God at the center of ultimate concern. This anthropocentrism, he writes, replaces theocentrism as a consequence of Enlightenment thought.[27] Mormonism refuses this either/or split and reconstitutes heaven as a matrix of eternal relationships that are horizontal as well as vertical. Rather than transcending human relationships in a beatific vision, Mormonism sacralizes them and incorporates them into a divine family of which God (as Eternal Father united with an Eternal Mother) is the head. In both these ways, as celebration of God's invitation to participate in his heavenly family and as the work of forging a heavenly community here and now, Mormon worship seeks to reverse the direction of religious concern from self to other. More than this, however, the church exists as an indispensable means for developing communities of sanctified individuals that can endure eternally. This requires particularly robust means of shaping character and solidifying durable relationships, means that require covenants and sacraments.

THE PROTESTANT RUPTURE

Jesus launched true Christianity, the saying goes; humans invented churches. Such a wry remark only has resonance among Christians in a modern age, where the value of a formal institution through which to worship God has been called into question. In earlier Christian eras, the indispensability of the church was too obvious to doubt. Before the era of organized, institutional churches, religion was inseparable from culture. The Old Testament uses the Hebrew term qahal (ἐκκλησία or *ekklesia* in the Septuagint) to signify a convocation for civil or religious purposes. By the New Testament era, writers employ the term *ekklesia* to refer most commonly to organized congregations of Christian disciples in specific locales ("the church at Antioch"; "the churches of Asia"), though it can also indicate a more universal body of believers ("I will build my church"; "as Christ loved the church").[28]

The basis of Israel's religion was covenant; Jon Levenson wrote that Israel "was called into existence at a moment in ordinary time and at a specifiable place,"[29] but in other Jewish thought, God's covenant with humankind dates to the very creation of the heavens and the earth; "All the souls which existed from Adam onward," wrote Menasseh ben Israel, citing the Tanhuma, "and which will exist until the end of the world, all these were created in the six days of creation, and they were all in the garden of Eden." And, he added, they were all present at Sinai and participated in the reaffirmation of the covenant. This last assertion he found attested by the verse in Deuteronomy 29:14, "I make this covenant to those who are standing here, and with those who are not here with us today."[30] Its earliest biblical expression was in Abraham, where God defines his relationship with his covenant or "chosen" people as one that is passed on hereditarily, an "unconditional" gift, "valid forever."[31]

As Christianity grew out of Jewish roots, the principal mode of affiliation—of belonging—continued to be covenantal. However, in the new trans-ethnic community and amid Christianity's universal claims, the covenant was construed in terms of adoption rather than inheritance, and new institutional forms with affiliation open to all became fundamental to religious identity. This was because the church that Jesus was seen to have inaugurated, as locus of the new covenant, became an inescapable conduit to the salvation believers sought, effecting the purposes enumerated in the letter to the Ephesians: ministering, edifying, and teaching until the imitation of Christ was fully achieved. For centuries, the most emphatic rationale the church provided for its existence was simple and convincing; the principle "extra Ecclesiam nulla salus" ("outside the Church there is no salvation") was unquestioned at least from the third century, when it was first expressed by Bishop Cyprian of Carthage. Or, "whoever wishes to be saved, needs above all to hold the Catholic faith," as the Athanasian Creed put forth.[32] This was thought to be the case because the Fall of Adam immersed his posterity in a blanket condemnation from which none could escape through their own merits.

The underlying logic of this indispensability of the church was based on notions of divine authority, which Christ was believed to have bestowed on his apostles and their successors, and which was employed in administering the church sacraments, those "instrumental channels of God's grace to humanity," the indispensable conduits through which saving power was transferred to fallen humans.[33] Such sacraments were necessary to salvation, and only the Mother Church has the Christ-given authority to administer them. As the Council of Trent reaffirmed in response to challenges to this position, those (Protestants) who claimed that sacraments "have been instituted for the nourishing of faith alone" were profoundly wrong, and they were anathematized accordingly. Sacraments were not merely "outward signs of grace"; they were that, but they also "contain the grace which they signify" and "confer that grace" on the faithful.[34]

With the sixteenth-century Reformation, a major sticking point to separation from Rome was this perceived impossibility of finding salvation outside the formal church organization—of which there was only one plausible candidate in most eyes. Thus the objection of the Catholic cardinal Jacopo Sadoleto to Reformer John Calvin was typical: Sadoleto "rejected the Protestant teaching of salvation by faith alone and repeatedly emphasized the role of the institutional church."[35] A break with the Roman Catholic Church could only be justified, in this light, by an entirely new conceptualization of the church. Most specifically, as Horton Davies writes, Protestants would have to redefine the "authority of the ministry and the nature of the sacraments."[36] For the most part, Protestants redefined a church sacrament as a sign rather than a channel of grace. "Signs and seals of the covenant of grace," according to the Westminster Confession; "signs" of "divine promises," according to Melanchthon.[37] In Calvin's most authoritative work, *The Institutes*, he calls sacraments "useful helps in fostering and confirming our faith."[38] They were not the means of grace; Protestants came to use "sacraments" instead to refer to "those duties we perform for the purpose of improving our minds, affecting our hearts, and of obtaining spiritual blessings," activities like "hearing the Gospel, reading the Scriptures . . . [and] prayer."[39]

For Protestants, then, faith was the determinant of salvation, a faith that relied entirely upon the grace of Christ. But this proposition raised a critical problem. If, as the Reformers argued, salvation was truly by grace alone, and the word of God as a rule of faith trumped human councils or authorities, then neither the church nor its sacraments were the exclusive mediators of salvation. (As early as the fourth century an influential text had expressly called the bishop "the mediator between God and you," and another affirmed that priests are necessary "mediators between God and humanity" in the twentieth.)[40] Once this break with clerical authority occurred, it was not unreasonable to question the need for any institutional church at all. Initially, Reformers resisted that possibility.

Although Luther protested corruptions in the church that reached to the pope, he nonetheless affirmed his belief that the visible church was the institution in which that spiritual congregation could alone flourish, just as the human body is the proper abode in which the human spirit resides.[41] John Calvin at first justified his break with Rome by claiming individuals found salvation through personal encounter with the Word, not through institutional authority. However, he, like Luther, found it necessary to develop a rationale for the continued existence of a formally structured church, which he had done by the 1543 revision of his *Institutes*.[42] As a consequence of "human ignorance, sloth, and vanity of mind," he writes, we "stand in need of eternal helps." In generous "accommodation to our capacity," therefore, "God has provided a method by which, though widely separated, we might still draw near to him." However, what sounds here like merely useful assistance, a "method," he insists is an institution just as indispensable as ever the Catholic Church was to its adherents. Referring to the "visible church" in particular, he declares: "beyond the pale of the church no forgiveness of sins, no salvation, can be hoped for. . . . The abandonment of the church is always fatal."[43]

Early Methodism shifted through various phases. Wesley came to emphasize authority and correct doctrine less and less, though he valued his connection to the established church; eventually he lamented that he had not preached from the beginning that "every one who feareth God and worketh righteousness is accepted of him."[44] The church, in this expansive vision, encompassed "all the Christians under heaven," or "all the persons in the universe whom God hath so called out of the world."[45] And in his generosity, Wesley "dare[d] not exclude from the church catholic all those congregations in which any unscriptural doctrines . . . are sometimes, yea, frequently, preached."[46] However, participation in *some* visible church was in his view indispensable. Not for any sacraments performed or authority represented, but because Christians are called upon to constitute a community, a fellowship, and summoned as they are "to live the life that is hid with Christ in God, then [we must] take care how [we] rend the body of Christ by separating from [our] brethren."[47]

Others justified more radical responses to the collapse of sacramentalism. (Five years after launching his attack on medieval sacraments, notes Brooks Holifield, Luther was "struggling to save the sacraments themselves.")[48] In England, for instance, Benjamin Hoadly argued that individual "conscience" and "sincerity" trumped apostolic authority and "external communion"; in so doing he ignited a debate involving fifty churchmen and seventy-four pamphlets in 1714 alone. Anxious fellow Protestants correctly perceived that his argument would effectively "dissolve the Church as a *Society*."[49] In America a century later, the young Abraham Lincoln drew the same logical inference from Reformation thought as did numbers of Protestants: Lincoln embraced the Bible but felt no need for any formal religious affiliation whatsoever. "I am not a member of any Christian church, but I have never denied the truth of the Scriptures." In Nathan Hatch's words, such reasoning in effect calls "for a Christianity exclusively biblical that had no place for clergy, denominations, confessions or creed. What [Lincoln and others] came to affirm was a faith drawn from the Scriptures without human mediation."[50] The position was eminently reasonable: if essential sacraments administered by virtue of apostolic authority were not unequivocally requisite to salvation, of what necessity was any church at all?

Like other Christian thinkers, Joseph Smith did not believe the saved were limited to one institutional church. "The church of the Lamb of God" consists of "those who will have [the Lord] to be their God," in the words of the Book of Mormon, and an 1829 revelation had God declaring "whosoever repenteth and cometh unto me, the same is my church."[51] Yet another scripture produced by Smith held that some of "his [the Lord's] people" include many of the righteous who coexist *alongside* the Restored church.[52] All this only makes the question even more emphatic; *why* should Mormons believe the institutional church to have a vital— or even indispensable—role in human salvation? Why the necessity of a formal incorporation and organization? From Smith's own reminiscences of his youth, it is clear that the first function that he sought in religion was spiritual and emotional, and it is to those motives that we may trace the origins of the system he would shape. His personal faith journey gives important historical context to Mormonism's foundations in covenant theology, even as it establishes an enduring theme in LDS ecclesiology—the quest for assurance of salvation.

ANXIETY, CERTITUDE, AND COVENANT THEOLOGY

The intense human craving for relief from the fears of death and damnation has given rise to many cataclysms and innovations in the history of Christianity. In the Catholic soteriology, assurance of salvation can only come when an imperfect faith is supplemented, as Adolf von Harnack long ago characterized the principle, "by the doctrinal authority of the Church on the one side and by the Sacramental Church institution on the other, and yet in such a way that it is obtained only approximately."[53] In other words, salvation comes from belonging to the true church and receiving its sacraments by authorized administrators. Those conditions provide a degree of assurance that may fall short of absolute certitude but is as close to a guarantee as is possible in this world. Providing such assurance was a conspicuous function of the church. It may be true that Church Fathers professed a theological rationale for the indispensability of the church to human salvation; but the church had also provided a critical psychological role in assuaging a human fear of the hell that perpetually threatened in the background. That role was radically undermined with the Reformation critique of sacramental efficacy. Without those visible instruments of salvation, how does one know one is saved? Clearly, in light of the Reformation critique of Catholicism, the doctrine of the church would itself have to change if it were to maintain its relevance and value. The church would have to find an alternate means of satisfying the human craving for an antidote to the anxiety of damnation, and a firm theological basis as well.

Institutional abuses and purgatorial practices aside, Luther's unease with Catholic doctrine itself was precipitated in large measure because of the spiritual insecurity he found in his life of monastic commitment. No matter how devoutly he observed the rules and commandments of his faith and his order, he found himself incapable of confidence in his spiritual standing and future. "My situation was that, although an impeccable monk, I stood before God as a sinner troubled in conscience, and I had no assurance that my merit would assuage him."[54] "Assurance" emerges here as a critical preoccupation in Luther's mind, and it will assume paramount importance in the theological systems of most Protestant forms that follow in his wake.

Luther found Catholic sacramentalism insufficient as a basis for spiritual peace. And as Protestants came to deny that salvation comes through sacraments administered by an elect class of mediators, they entirely demolished the principal hedge against the personal dread of damnation that had for so many centuries been a constant in the Christian mind. If innate guilt and depravity are our natural inheritance and eternal torment our fitting destiny, then where is the balm of Gilead to be found, if not in Mother Church and her saving sacraments and commandments, faithfully upheld? Protestants had to necessarily supply a new answer to the age-old question: what constitutes the *certitudo salutis* (personal assurance of salvation), and how is it to be secured? The fear of damnation, soon reinforced by Calvinist preaching that emphasized human depravity and a fully merited eternal punishment, drove thousands and eventually millions to seek spiritual relief. A popular eighteenth-century schoolbook, *Collection of English Prose and Verse* captured the religious terrors that had become increasingly normalized. One writer in the anthology agonized over "the vast uncertainty I am struggling with . . . the force and vivacity of my apprehensions; every doubt wears the face of horror, and would perfectly overwhelm me, but for some faint gleams of hope, which dart across the tremendous gloom. What tongue can utter the anguish of a soul suspended between the extremes of infinite joy or eternal misery. . . . I tremble and shudder."[55]

The solution to this hunger for assurance, Luther held, was to repose trust in God's faithfulness rather than in his own. When Paul said "the just shall live by his faith," Luther took this to mean not that we live in a constant state of hopeful uncertainty. The power of faith did not for him refer to a human capacity for or exercise of simple trust. Rather, the righteous should live by confidence in Christ's promises. And given the fact that the *object* of that faith is certain and steadfast, being Jesus Christ himself, *his* reliability was of such perfection as to ground incontestably the confidence we repose in him. Our faith can relieve us of the purgatory of uncertainty, not because our mind is firm but because our foundation is Christ's faithfulness, not ours. The object, not the practitioner, of faith endows faith with its saving power but also confers its fruits: confidence and spiritual tranquility. "I grasped that the justice of God is that righteousness by which through grace and sheer mercy God justifies us through faith. Thereupon I felt myself to be reborn."[56] Luther's self-diagnosis for spiritual anxiety—and the prescribed cure—resonated through much of the continent and across the channel.

As the idea would be canonized by Anglicans in the Westminster Confession, "such as truly believe in the Lord Jesus, and love him in sincerity, endeavoring to walk in all good conscience before him, may in this life be *certainly assured* that they are in a state of grace" (emphasis mine). Furthermore, "this certainty is not a bare conjectural and probable persuasion, . . . but an infallible assurance of faith."[57] And this assurance, or "calling and election made sure," is one that all may obtain "without extraordinary revelation."[58] To the Protestants, writes one historian of theology, "the test of the Christian was not that he was so living as to secure the promise, but that he had experienced in himself the certain conviction that the promise was indefectibly his. This conviction—the 'assurance' of a status that cannot be lost—. . . is the palladium of orthodox Protestantism."[59]

This assurance the church offered, made available through the grace of Christ, took the form of a highly developed theology—Protestant covenant theology. As dissenters migrated to America especially, in the words of John von Rohr, "the often anguished Puritan search for personal assurance of salvation found substantial assuagement in covenantal certainty."[60] The general view was that God had established a covenant of works with Adam (the covenant made with Moses at Sinai, wrote Charles Buck's editor, was "merely a republication" of the original).[61] In the aftermath of Adam's (and Israel's) failure to fulfill his obligation of perfect obedience, God made provision for a new covenant—the covenant of grace, inaugurated by Christ's atoning sacrifice. Covenant theology was derived from the New Testament's express differentiation of Christ's sacrifice and the gospel it inaugurated from the Mosaic code and sacrifices which preceded it. Jesus himself referred to the Eucharistic wine as emblem of a new covenant,[62] and the author of Hebrews called Christ the "mediator of the new covenant," the "law [being] only a shadow of the good things to come."[63]

Covenant theology continued to evolve in the eighteenth century. The most substantive reworking of the idea would be in response to the emphasis of Jacob Arminius on the role of human agency in salvation. For Arminius, "inclusion in the covenant of grace is not determined solely by God but by the free response of the human person to God's imitative in Christ."[64] Herein, the door is again opened to that very anxiety that covenant theology was meant to alleviate. With John Wesley, the whole program of salvational assurance is once again thrown into radical doubt. In his "Call to Backsliders," Wesley obliterated any hope of an abiding spiritual security: even those "sanctified" in "the blood of the covenant" may indeed "fall away from sanctifying grace."[65] Is, then, no greater assurance possible? A limited one at best, opines Wesley. Like God's pledge to Abraham, the archetypal covenant, "though *everlasting, was conditional.*"[66] Wesley's critique reveals how unstable the solution of the *certitudo salutis*, or assurance of salvation, had become in the years leading up to Joseph Smith. It is no overstatement to say the religious world of antebellum America continued to be the story of personal quests for salvational assurance writ large. And covenant theology was the framework in which seekers found and secured that *certitudo salutis*. Covenant theology is the framework on which Mormonism, too, erects its ecclesiology—but it is a covenant theology radically transformed.

LUTHER, WESLEY, SMITH

Mormonism's beginnings connect the movement's founder—and founding vision—to Protestant predecessors in crucial ways. For many decades, Latter-day Saints (LDS) believers have dated the origins of Mormonism to the fourteen-year old Smith's remarkable theophany in an upstate New York grove of trees. Recent historians have pointed out that the event was of an almost exclusively personal nature.[67] In actual fact, both the historical revisionists and the Mormon laity are correct; Smith's experience in the upstate New York woods in 1820 was an intensely personal experience that neither involved nor intimated any commission to inaugurate a new religious tradition. At the same time, the particular motives and outcomes behind that spring theophany situate Smith firmly within a long-standing Protestant narrative, and connect the Mormon church's founding to an ongoing history of anxiety about salvation and covenant theology—just as Lutheranism and Wesleyanism were.

The typical Protestant conversion story occurring at the intersection of salvational anxiety and covenant theology was of the form we saw above with Martin Luther—and it appears again in the conversion of John Wesley. He found his spiritual quest one of perpetual anxiety until a decisive moment when, he recorded, "I felt that I did trust in Christ, Christ alone for salvation, and an assurance was given me, that he had taken away my sins, even mine, and saved me from the law of sin and death."[68] Out of Wesley's personal experience and entrepreneurial religiosity, Methodism was born. Joseph Smith's personal journey and religion-making career began in very similar circumstances (and indeed, Smith was long inclined toward Methodism and greatly influenced by it). The cause of his prayerful quest was—as the case with countless others before and since—spiritual unease. "I [had] become convicted of my sins," he recorded of his early adolescence, "therefore I cried unto the Lord for mercy for there was none else to whom I could go." (His later words, spoken out of personal experience, tie him even more closely to the pattern of Protestant terror about one's prospects of salvation: "There is no pain so awful as the pain of suspense.")[69] With telling language, Oliver Cowdery, in his account of Smith's First Vision (compiled, he said with Smith's assistance), referred specifically to the boy's yearning for "that *assurance* which the Lord Jesus has so freely offered" (emphasis in original).[70] In the ensuing 1820 theophany, Smith heard the sought-after words that firmly place him within the tradition of the Protestant conversion narrative: "Joseph my son thy sins are forgiven thee."[71]

The divine words of comfort, however, proved to be no enduring balm; forgiveness of sins gave no lasting assurance of salvation. Three years later Smith was haunted anew by the specter of damnation, and eternal torment again plagued his mind. So once more "I betook myself to prayer and supplication," seeking "a manifestation of my state and standing before him."[72] Smith's spiritual odyssey was to this point but one example of the familiar pattern: an anxious individual, conscience-plagued by introspection and chastened by hellfire sermons, seeking solace and tokens of grace.[73] However, Smith's case was complicated to some extent by the fact that remedies available to the spiritual heirs of Puritanism were not available to him. By personal inclination on the one hand and Methodist influence on the other, he was averse to the two preconditions of Puritan covenantal theology: "piety and predestination." Smith was famously disinclined to both evidence and claims of personal piety. Three years after his First Vision he lapsed into "sins and follies," and later frankly admitted, "I am not so much of a christian as many suppose I am."[74] Months later, he repeated the point: "I do not want you to think that I am very righteous, for I am not."[75] At the same time, his early partiality to Methodism equally rendered any Calvinist version of covenant assurance impossible. "I abhor the doctrine of predestination,"[76] thundered Wesley, and Smith followed suit: "God did not elect or predestinate."[77]

However, on the occasion of Smith's second spiritual quest, something more durable resulted from this heavenly encounter than a transient absolution from sin. This second vision, which Smith described as a visitation from the angel Moroni, laid the foundation for the production of the Book of Mormon, and it was to the receipt of this record that Smith dated his ministry.[78] This record—and the church that arose out of its pages—were both consequences of Smith's personal quest for salvational assurance, and both satisfy that quest in a manner analogous to the *certitudo salutis* fashioned by the Protestant theologians. In his project of Restoration, Smith effectively reworks the Protestant model of the covenant of grace—appropriating the language, modifying the form, and accomplishing the same ends. The theology Smith developed supplied an emotional and spiritual surrogate for the consoling balm of that covenant framework—one with a language familiar to a nineteenth-century Protestant audience—and it would effect the same assurance, without relying upon either piety or predestination. The Book of Mormon, subsequent revelations, and Smith's rhetoric of restoration were all replete with allusions to and explications of God's covenant with Israel. The Book of Mormon in particular served to radically reconstitute covenant theology: it replaced its dichotomies of old and new, law and grace, historic and spiritual, with an unparalleled synthesis of them all, even as it exploited and literalized the earliest conceptions of covenantal history to create a people with a rare spiritual cohesion; and it provided a concrete nexus for experiential religion that was a remarkably successful surrogate for the covenant of grace, channeling as it does a comparable effect of salvational assurance. Most important, in the newly reconstituted covenant theology that emerges from the Book of Mormon we find the outlines of a comprehensive rationale for the church that Smith organized immediately thereafter.

2

Latter-day Saint Covenant Theology

THE BOOK OF MORMON—"THE NEW COVENANT"

One contemporary remembered Joseph Smith relating a crucial detail about his First Vision: according to Levi Richards, Smith said that on that occasion, the Lord had confirmed to him that "all the sects" were "wrong, & that the Everlasting covenant was broken."[1] That phrase—the everlasting covenant—became central to Smith's understanding of his prophetic calling and the massive project of "restoration" to which he devoted his life. Translating the Book of Mormon, Smith found its prophets confirming that "many covenants of the Lord" had been corrupted or removed from the biblical text.[2] When Smith published the Book of Mormon seven years after Moroni's first visitation, the scripture's title page heralded a new version of covenant theology, with an emphatic declaration of salvational assurance: the Book of Mormon's very purpose, its final editor tells readers on the title page itself, is "to show unto the remnant of the House of Israel that they are not cast off forever." In fact, in an 1832 pronouncement Smith records the Lord's reference to the Book of Mormon as itself "*the* new covenant."[3] So how does the Book of Mormon reconstitute Christian understanding of covenant theology?

Protestant covenant theology is predicated on the radical opposition between the old and the new. As outlined above, the premise of covenant theology is that the original covenant given the human race in the Garden of Eden was a covenant of works, of obedience. But disobedience on Adam and Eve's part ruptured their relationship with God and incurred divine wrath and condemnation. Incapable of rising from the ashes of the perdition they had incurred and the state of sin to which humans would naturally and inevitably revert, Adam and Eve and their posterity could only be rescued by the intervention of a Savior, and a reconstituted relationship to God predicated on Christ's righteousness, rather than their own. This new covenantal relationship was built on the foundation of grace—and being founded on Christ's faithfulness rather than human obedience, the covenant was secure and absolutely reliable. All that was necessary was for the sinner to know that he or she fell under the covenant's provisions, as one of the elect.

This binary opposition between works and grace in covenant thought is paralleled at many related levels of Christian understanding. Spiritual Israel—those who constitute the body of Christ—takes the place of historic Israel—the biblical people of the covenant. The New Testament (New Covenant) supplants the Old Testament (Old Covenant). The qualifiers "Old" and "New" seem self-evidently instituted as emphatic differentiators of covenants, dispensations, even churches in Thomas Campbell's formulation: "Although the Scriptures of the Old and New Testaments are inseparably connected," he writes, "yet as to what directly and properly belongs to their immediate object, the New Testament is as perfect a constitution for the worship, discipline, and government of the New Testament Church, and as perfect a rule for the particular duties of its members, as the Old Testament was for the worship, discipline, and government of the Old Testament Church, and the particular duties of its members."[4] In the new gospel dispensation, salvation is experienced as an individual relationship, in distinction from the collective redemption associated with Israel. Finally, the gospel supplants the law ("no two words are more distinct in their signification than law and gospel," wrote Alexander Campbell).[5]

The essence of Joseph Smith's theology represents a rejection of such polarities, as portended by the Book of Mormon itself. Rather than reaffirm the supplanting of historical Israel by spiritual Israel, the Old by the New Testament, a national by a personal covenant, or the Mosaic Law by the Law of the Gospel, the Book of Mormon instead fully encompasses and unifies the diverse strands of history, scripture, and gospel dispensations into one. In so doing, the Book of Mormon prepares the ground for the church Smith was about to found, providing the rationale and theological base for its establishment. No other Christian tradition so conflates the two covenantal theologies into one covenant that precedes and encompasses both.[6]

Literal and Spiritual Israel

As early as the *Epistle of Barnabas*, written in approximately AD 100, Christians were arguing that they had replaced the Hebrews as God's covenant people and the practice was soon entrenched of reading the historic entity as "type of the people that should come afterwards," the true, spiritual body of believers.[7] So in Ambrose Serle's 1793 *Church of God*, we read how God's choosing of the people of Israel was "prophetic and emblematic . . . of his conduct towards the true and spiritual Israel," and "God's true and *spiritual* people are partakers of a better covenant," that is, the covenant of grace.[8] Or in Matthew Henry's *Exposition of the Old and New Testament*, we find God's "everlasting covenant . . . of grace" pertains to "all God's *spiritual* Israel."[9] Again in Isaac Penington's 1761 works, Moses led literal Israel by the "outward" law, as God's spirit would later lead "*spiritual* Israel" according to his "inward law"; God's "statutes and ordinances" conveyed on Mt. Sinai were "but a shadow of the inward and *spiritual* covenant, the new and everlasting covenant, which God makes with his inward and spiritual people in the latter days" (all above emphases mine).[10] These fixed polarities between historic and spiritual Israel collapse in the Book of Mormon's pages.

Here, historic Israel is not supplanted in God's eyes by spiritual Israel as was the case with supercessionist thought. Rather, historic Israel is revealed to be present in the ongoing work of gathering, literally rather than figuratively—in the form of both Native Americans and converts to the gospel. Amos had referred anciently to God's future mercy toward "the remnant of Joseph," meaning descendants of Ephraim and/or Manasseh, and Ezekiel had similarly intimated their eventual restoration.[11] The principal antagonists in the Book of Mormon narrative, the "Lamanites"—or American Indians in whole or in part[12]—are from "the house of Israel," tracing their literal descent from a Manassehite exile from sixth-century Jerusalem.[13] These people, descendants of one Lehi, self-identify as that remnant who would be preserved and later gathered by the Lord.[14] Though the narrative ends with the fratricidal elimination of the book's protagonists, the promise is made to the recordkeepers that "a mixture of [their] seed" will survive to find redemption in a future day.[15] How? The Book of Mormon prophesied its own transmission through "Gentiles," and the work of the Gentiles in bringing "the remnant" of Joseph to a knowledge and enjoyment of the covenant made to Abraham.[16]

In other words, the work predicts that in the modern era, a cadre of God's elect (whom Smith will later identify as scattered and now recovered Israelites) from a great Gentile nation will successfully evangelize New World descendants of the House of Israel (Native American descendants of historic Israel). And early Mormons thought they were living in the very moment of its prophesied fulfillment. For example, for Native Americans, the Indian Removal Act signed into law by Andrew Jackson was an unmitigated tragedy. For settlers on the frontier it was a welcome prelude to even more dramatic expansion into the frontier. But for Mormons, the (forced) relocation of scattered southern tribes to a designated federal territory represented the latest iteration of an ongoing fulfillment of Israel's covenantal history. The church paper proclaimed in 1832 that it was "marvelous, to witness the gathering of the Indians."[17] The first LDS missionaries, who were sent to the Indian Territory, saw those Delaware and Shawnee they visited as living emblems not of brutal government policies but of God's mercy and providential designs. As the *Evening and Morning Star* opined, "What a beauty it is to see the prophecies fulfilling so exactly," then quoted Nephi that the Lord "shall bring them again out of captivity, and they shall be gathered together to the lands of their inheritance, and they shall be brought out of obscurity and darkness."[18]

As Smith develops his understanding of covenant Israel, he will enfold the membership of the church as well in that same vision of a literal Israel restored to their birthright. For the Book of Mormon prophesied that not only Nephi's posterity but "all the house of Israel" were heirs to the promise that through Abraham's seed, "all the kindreds of the earth shall be blessed."[19] By baptism into the restored church, Smith will teach, those living remnants of historic Israel scattered among the Gentiles are gathered in, or the non-Israelite converts are adopted into the fold.

Old and New Testaments

A second, more conspicuous collapse of the divide between old and new, biblical Israel and adopted Israel, was the Book of Mormon itself, constituting a scriptural synthesis of Old and New World texts. The narrative begins in the Old World, in the city of Jerusalem, "in the reign of King Zedekiah, king of Judah."[20] The narrator tells us Jeremiah has been cast into prison,[21] and the prophecies of Isaiah are quoted liberally. But this seamless record chronicles an Israelite remnant's exodus under the leadership of one Lehi to the Western hemisphere, and six centuries later, describes the preaching of a New World John the Baptist (Samuel the Lamanite, a descendant of Lehi) on the eve of the Messiah's birth. Then, recapitulating the Gospels in this New World setting, the chroniclers describe the visit and ministry of a resurrected Christ, his ordination and commission to twelve disciples, and the institution of church sacraments. It is as if the Book of Mormon rewrites the Old/New Testament records into a holistic gospel narrative in which Christ is the fulcrum rather than the culmination of Christian history, with both sides of the historical divide equally Christocentric. Prophets actually date their years in anticipation of the Incarnation,[22] and rather than Old Testament writings merely foreshadowing the Christ, we find this volume quoting ancient texts that detail his death and resurrection.[23] In one remarkable passage, pre-Christian prophets demand the right to celebrate his nativity years before the fact: "Is it not as easy at this time for the Lord to send his angel to declare these glad tidings unto us as unto our children, or as after the time of his coming?" asks Alma,[24] while others "testified of the coming of Christ, and have looked forward, and have rejoiced in his day which is to come."[25]

The volume further disrupts any simple scriptural dichotomies by replacing Old and New Testaments, not with Old and New World canons, but with endlessly proliferating scriptures that erase any temporal or geographical divides. The Lord insists that "Wherefore, because that ye have a Bible ye need not suppose that it contains all my words; neither need ye suppose that I have not caused more to be written. For I command all men, both in the east and in the west, and in the north, and in the south, and in the islands of the sea, that they shall write the words which I speak unto them."[26]

National versus Individual

A third conflation of covenantal theology blends the communal and the individual. Jon D. Levenson points out that unlike Christian conceptions of salvation, "deliverance in the Hebrew Bible is in the main collective and historical, not individual."[27] ("The idea of a covenant between a deity and a people is unknown from other religions and cultures," notes the *Encyclopedia Judaica*.)[28] By contrast, Paul admonished Christians to "work out your own salvation with fear and trembling."[29] Even granting the "New Perspective on Paul,"[30] with its critique of an overly individualistic soteriology, Protestants have historically conceived conversion and adoption into the new covenant in intensely individualistic terms. In the Puritan covenant theology as articulated by Peter Bulkeley, the unconditional nature of Christ's gift did not negate the crucial fact that one "must enter into a particular covenant with God."[31] In the Book of Mormon, covenantal relationships blend the individual and the communal. "It portrays two distinct types of salvation working in harmony," Grant Hardy notes. "Nephite writers are deeply concerned with salvation history, that is, with God's intervention in the rise and fall of entire nations and peoples—Nephites and Lamanites, Jews and Gentiles—yet those same writers also repeatedly address individual sinners in need of the 'atoning blood of Christ.'"[32]

Often, covenants in the Book of Mormon operate in an intermediate way, made by small communities of the faithful—like the spiritually transformed people of King Benjamin who "enter into a [collectively administered] covenant with our God to do his will" and the little band of converts baptized by the missionary Alma—all of whom signal their covenant by individual attestation.[33] The most beautiful illustration in the Book of Mormon of a covenantal understanding that blends the preoccupation with a national or tribal salvation and an individual experience of healing grace is Enos's dialogic encounter with God. Hungering for personal relief from sin and guilt, Enos cries unto the Lord "all the day long" and into the night, before receiving a promise of his own blessedness. He is then moved by compassion to pray for the spiritual welfare of his brethren, the Nephites. He is assured by the voice of the Lord that according to the covenant made with "thy fathers," provision would be made for their salvation. Receiving assurance of both the covenant made with the fathers and of "the covenant which [God] had made" with Enos, his "soul did rest."[34] The exchange, and the thematic blending of individual and communal incorporation into covenant relationship with God, anticipates Smith's fuller exposition of a communal salvation—one in which neither blanket blessedness nor atomistic salvation is possible.

Old and New Gospels

Fourth and more profoundly, the Book of Mormon enacted the collapse into one of old and new covenants, the laws of Moses and of Christ. It does not, in other words, recapitulate the contrast between the old covenant of works and the Protestant covenant of grace; it reconstitutes covenant theology into something rather new. It does this by refusing to recognize the gospel of Jesus Christ as entirely supplanting or displacing an earlier covenant of works. For instance, in the Book of Mormon, the New World Christians, "notwithstanding [they] believe in Christ, [they] keep the law of Moses" centuries before his birth.[35] A later prophet notes that "the law of Moses did strengthen their faith in Christ."[36] Clearly, the law of Moses and the new covenant of the gospel co-exist harmoniously in the religious world described in the Book of Mormon. We read, for instance, that the ancient writers of the Book of Mormon "had a hope of [Christ's] glory many hundred years before his coming," and "keep the law of Moses" even as they "look forward with steadfastness unto Christ."[37] In a telescoping of the old and the new, righteous Nephites believed "in him to come as though he already was" and were taught faith, repentance, baptism, and reception of the Holy Ghost.[38] At the same time, the Book of Mormon invokes a central image of Mosaic religion and covenant Israel, the temple, and describes its replication and dispersion in the New World: a pattern that foreshadows Smith's erection of temples in the early nineteenth century, merging even Old Testament and New Testament worship forms.

The Book of Mormon, as the extra-biblical text most used by Mormons, and employed by the hundreds (and then thousands) to disseminate their message, was the principal conduit for a view of ecclesiastical and covenant history that minimized the transition from the Judaism of the prophets to the gospel of the apostles. Before Smith ever organized the first branch of the church, he was steeped in a text that depicted a pre-Christian people worshipping Christ, and a tribe of Hebrews making a covenant to be called "the children of Christ, his sons and his daughters."[39]

All of what we have said about Smith's conflating of old and new covenantal theology is merely prologue to his final vision of what God's covenant with his people actually entails, and where and how it originated. Months after publishing the Book of Mormon, Smith pushes the scope of the everlasting covenant even further back in time. Working on a new translation of the Bible, Smith makes critical revisions to Exodus 34. In his redacted text, Smith clarifies that what was originally given to Moses on Mt. Sinai was the fullness of the gospel; in Moses's first mountaintop encounter with Jehovah, he received the higher priesthood, Christ's "holy order" and "the ordinances thereof." Only after the apostate episode of the golden calf were those gifts withdrawn and replaced with a lesser version.[40] The preparatory law in this version, the "schoolmaster" or "disciplinarian until Christ came,"[41] is a temporary intervention bridging ancient privileges and Latter-day Restoration—not a crude first stage in a linear process of developing fullness. The resultant theology is one mired in paradox: the "new and everlasting covenant" which the church was restored to reestablish is actually "that which was from the beginning."[42]

Those readers accustomed to accepting the new covenant as a total displacement of the failed Adamic law of works would see in this revision the most radical reconstitution imaginable of the covenant of grace—one that collapses into one not just Old and New Testaments, but all of dispensational history itself. Indeed, Smith propounds not just an ancient American Christianity, nor does he stop at a Mosaic possession of gospel fulness, but reconstructs a gospel that dates back to Father Adam himself. In 1833 Smith published in the church newspaper the shocking claim that "Adam was the first member of the church of Christ on earth." "The plan of salvation was revealed to Adam," noted a subsequent treatment of his biblical revisions.[43] Indeed, Smith's interpolations in the Genesis account (as part of his Bible retranslation project) even has Adam learning about the atonement, experiencing baptism for the remission of sins, and the gift of the Holy Ghost.[44] As Smith's popularizer Parley Pratt put it with his typical self-assurance, "We have only the old thing. It was old in Adams day it was old in Mormons day & hid up in the earth & it was old in 1830 when we first began to preach it."[45] This perspective of a Christ-centered gospel dating in its fullness to Eden contrasts vividly with a Protestant theologian's casual comment that thinking to find a correct understanding of the Trinity in the *Shepherd of Hermas* is "expecting far too much from a second-century church father."[46]

Reassurance

Even as it reconstituted covenant theology, the Book of Mormon effectively promised the same salvational assurance that the Puritan covenant theology had so successfully grounded. This was in the direct access the Book of Mormon gave and modeled of a personal, dialogic encounter with Deity, situating the reader firmly in a covenant relationship with God; and through the artifactual concreteness of the gold plates at the story's core, which possessed an iconic status that pointedly heralded an open heaven. Thematically, a most consistent focus in the Book of Mormon is the means by which individuals engage in a direct, literal, dialogic encounter with God. The first Book of Mormon chronicler introduces this motif, pursuing his own visionary experience of Christ full of confidence that "I might see, and hear, and know of these things, by the power of the Holy Ghost, which is the gift of God unto all those who diligently seek him, as well in times of old as in the time that he should manifest himself unto the children of men."[47] As the narrative virtually opens with this theme, so does it conclude. The final editor, Moroni, offers a concluding promise of spiritual certainty so unequivocal and literal that it elicited cries of blasphemy in 1831 to the present day.[48] After reading the Book of Mormon, he directs, "If ye shall ask with a sincere heart, with real intent, having faith in Christ, he will manifest the truth of it unto you, by the power of the Holy Ghost. And by the power of the Holy Ghost ye may know the truth of all things."[49]

This theme of spiritual certitude is apparent in the reconstituted language of Mormon conversion, and in its pervasive rhetoric of certainty. The salvific, transformative encounter with the God of Protestantism results in an affective experience of grace. For Protestants, *personal* "assurance must come through personal awareness of the inner presence of that saving faith which is election's sign."[50] In Mormon culture, the private, experiential aspect of conversion becomes radically transposed into an affirmation of historical truths rooted in tangible artifacts, generally centering on the Book of Mormon. Still, the new scripture approaches through artifactual concreteness and the allure of individualized revelation what covenant theology achieved through contractual obligation, that is, confidence in one's hope of salvation. The Book of Mormon at one and the same time is a catalyst to personal adoption into a covenantal relationship with Christ, even as it serves as the instrument to redirect and repair the covenantal history of a wayward Israel and provide assurance that "I the Lord have not forgotten my people."[51]

As Smith organizes and develops the church, the New and Everlasting Covenant will find full exposition as a covenant made in premortal worlds, before the earth was created. In its final form, the church will provide the structures, principles, and practices that provide concrete preparation for, and assurance of, integration into an eternal heavenly family according to God's primordial designs. But the beginnings of that church are present in the Book of Mormon, and from its pages a reconceived church quickly emerges.

THE CHURCH OF CHRIST—"THE NEW AND
EVERLASTING COVENANT"

The Book of Mormon came off the press and began circulation in March 1830. Its purpose in laying out the fundamental framework of a new covenant theology that would justify a formal reestablishment of the church is evident in one simple fact—Smith organized a church mere days after its publication. It is not known when Joseph first conceived the project of a formal church organization. No such plan was indicated in his boyhood visions of the Father and Son, or the subsequent visitations of Moroni.[52] For some years, Smith clearly believed he had been called to translate and disseminate the Book of Mormon, not found a new religious tradition. Only in March 1829 was Smith given to know that God planned to again "establish [his] church."[53] Weeks later, as the translation raced to completion with Oliver Cowdery's help, the word came again that the Lord would "establish my church among [this generation]."[54] Then, as Smith finished laboring on the translation in June 1829 he received a specific command to "build up [the Lord's] church."[55] He was destitute, pilloried in the press, had suffered assault, and was alienated from his in-laws as his long and fraught project came to a conclusion. It is unlikely he anticipated this new commission to found a formal church under his leadership with eagerness.

Some followers, like David Whitmer, insisted that believers in the Book of Mormon and Smith's prophetic authority were already "fully organized—spiritually—before" any formal process took place. And indeed, Oliver Cowdery, in June 1829, prepared under Smith's direction an "Articles of the Church of Christ,"[56] which included instructions for baptism, ordaining teachers and priests, and administering the sacrament. (Those articles, however, were never ratified by the membership.) After formal organization of the church took place, Whitmer insisted it only occurred in response to criticisms that they had no clerical rights without legal standing.[57] And indeed, missionaries had been going abroad to share the news of the Book of Mormon before its pages were even bound into final form, but not to baptize. Unwilling to wait for the finished volumes, Christian Whitmer, David's brother, "copied from the manuscript the teachings and the doctrine of Christ, being the things which we were commanded to preach." Others took printed portions fresh from the press to do the same.[58] Once the manuscript was delivered to the printer in summer 1829, Smith recorded in his history, "We still continued to bear testimony and give information."[59] Smith, however, understood the formal incorporation as divinely mandated, whether those promptings constituted his interpretation of prior revelation or an unrecorded new one. He wrote simply that in this period, they "had received commandment to organize the church."[60] Accordingly

Smith and five others, to comply with state law, met in the home of Peter Whitmer and incorporated as the Church of Christ on April 6, 1830.

The most direct evidence that Smith connected church organization directly to a new covenant theology was the explicit rationale published in the first collection of the revelations given to him (*The Book of Commandments*, 1833). As his First Vision had revealed "that the Everlasting covenant was broken,"[61] so do the introductory verses given in the voice of God proclaim that Smith has been commanded to (re)institute the church so "that mine everlasting covenant might be established."[62] Some time earlier a slightly different designation had been assigned the restoration, in the form of a paradox: the Lord explained "all old covenants have I caused to be done away in this thing; and this is a *new* and an everlasting covenant, even that which was from the beginning."[63] What was new, in other words, was the understanding that the new covenant *was* the original covenant (or, "we have only the old thing," in Pratt's words). But how far back did this "beginning" reach?

The New and Everlasting Covenant, Smith came to understand, encompassed more, far more, than a conflation of Old and New Testament conceptions and histories, more even than promises made to New World Israelites, the prophet Moses, or Adam himself. In an 1835 text that Smith produced, known as the Book of Abraham, he depicted the inauguration of the everlasting covenant in premortal councils, where Abraham and many of God's "noble and great ones" were promised "an earth whereon [to] dwell," a probationary "first estate," and the promise of further "glory added upon their heads forever and ever."[64] As Smith gradually unfolded the portent of those words, a new conception of the nature of the divine and of the human, of their relationship before the Fall, and the possibilities of that relationship in the hereafter took shape in a way that utterly broke with contemporary Christian paradigms. The *Hymn of the Pearl*, a Gnostic text from the early Christian era that allegorizes the human descent into the world, describes heavenly parents who

> sent me on a mission
> from our home in the east. . . .
> They took off my bright robe of glory,
> which they had made for me out of love,
> and took away my purple toga,
> which was woven to fit my stature.
> They made a covenant with me
> and wrote it in my heart so I would not forget.[65]

So, too, in Smith's thought does a salvational scheme develop that was rooted in heavenly councils before the earth's creation and had as its design the incorporation of an innumerable host of premortal souls into an eternal family presided over by heavenly parents. This is the foundation for Mormonism's view of salvation history as a narrative of ascent from primeval intelligence through mortal embodiment toward eventual theosis, rather than as a story that is primarily about recuperation, repair, and rehabilitation.

Meanwhile, Smith was coming to develop his understanding of what constitutes that heavenly family. Smith noted of Moroni's 1823 appearance that the angel related to him "many" passages of scripture, from both the Old and New Testaments.[66] In one of his earlier recitations, however, it was only one biblical text he recalled being quoted, one of such importance it would appear in all four of Mormonism's standard works,[67] and which would become a point of orientation for Smith's entire ministry and life: Malachi 4. These last passages from the Old Testament, slightly modified from its King James rendering, Smith recorded as follows: "I will reveal unto you the Priesthood, by the hand of Elijah the prophet, before the coming of the great and dreadful day of the Lord. . . . And he shall plant in the hearts of the children the promises made to the fathers, and the hearts of the children shall turn to their fathers. If it were not so, the whole earth would be utterly wasted at his coming."[68]

Smith would be decades fathoming the implications of Moroni's slight modification. In its eventual form, the most robust version of theosis in the Christian tradition, that covenant portends the linking of the human family into an eternal chain of belonging that culminates with a Heavenly Father and Mother themselves. In its most essential form, *that* invitation, with *that* destiny, was the essence of the New and Everlasting Covenant. And that perspective and setting and compass changed everything for Smith. First, because it collapsed the radical ontological divide between the divine and the human, it intimated that in some way, more than metaphorical, "God, angels, and humans" are all of one species.[69] It made the human soul eternal rather than created and contingent. It transposed mortality from an experiment gone horribly awry to an educative process that from the inception anticipated sin, pain, and the resultant growth. It made the human family co-participants in a long-conceived plan rather than hapless victims of primeval wrongdoing. And it meant that God's intentions and human striving were to be directed not at recuperation of a lost paradise but at the ongoing emulation of divine parents, the development and sanctifying of relationships constitutive of eternal bonds extending both horizontally as well as vertically.

If this context, this premortal, cosmic narrative, constituted the "old thing" that was lost, then Smith had come at last to understand the burden of the Lord's words to him in his 1820 theophany that other religious traditions were "all wrong." This was why he could write a friend in 1833 that there was no question that what he called "an apostasy . . . from the Apostolic platform" had occurred.[70] A church newspaper article employed the term "Great Apostasy" shortly thereafter, though with reference to Jews, not Christians.[71] Smith's radical take on apostasy was the inference that given the covenant's antiquity, a longer gospel prehistory must have been lost than New Testament church forms and gifts alone, as other Restorationists claimed. The absence of spiritual gifts was evidence of a diminished church, but the most important loss, he wrote, involved much more ancient "Laws," "ordinances," and "covenants" of the gospel.[72] The word "ordinances," which figures so prominently in Mormon thought, has been variously understood as a religious term. Consistent with period usage, Smith originally used it in a generic way to denote God's laws and statutes as well as divinely prescribed rites and ceremonies. Low-church Protestants had long ago begun to employ the term in place of the Catholic terminology. "Instead of 'sacraments,' we prefer *ordinances*," noted Alexander Campbell.[73] Charles Buck defined ordinance more broadly as "an institution of divine authority relating to the worship of God; such as baptism, . . . [or]the Lord's supper" but also including "preaching and reading the word" and "singing of psalms."[74] Sidney Rigdon had been a disciple of Campbell, and Smith read Buck. Mormons initially used the term in the same way, but soon, as Ryan Tobler has detailed, they came to use "ordinance" with the primarily Catholic sense of "sacrament," that is, a saving ritual.[75] I will be using the terms "ordinance" and "sacrament" as equivalent expressions, though, as we will see, not all sacraments in Mormonism are essential or saving ordinances. Sacrament, in my usage, refers primarily to the rituals by which covenantal relationships are established, developed, and secured through the medium of authoritative representatives of God.

A crucial aspect of this new (restored) covenantal understanding was its universal scope. Understanding the work of evangelizing to be tantamount to gathering scattered Israel was a Christian commonplace. Jesus had reinterpreted the "seed of Abraham" in an expansive way when he denied that being descended of Abraham made one his seed.[76] For that matter, God was able "from these stones to raise up children to Abraham," the Baptist had said.[77] Abraham's seed were in fact "the dispersed children of God," according to the gospel of John, and the task of evangelizing was to gather them to the church.[78] Since the Abrahamic text Smith translated averred that the gospel commission would devolve upon Abraham's "literal seed,"[79] Smith drew the conclusion that Latter-day Saints missionaries and converts were, by and large, Israelite by blood, even if the Book of Mormon referred to the generality of European Americans as Gentiles. (Richard Brothers had similarly taught that the Jews were scattered among the population of Great Britain in the 1790s, and British Israelism later developed out of ideas like those of Brothers.)[80]

In one typical sermon of 1834, Rigdon discoursed on "the former covenants to Abraham, Isaac, Jacob & others of the ancients, which were to be realized in the last days."[81] Several revelations seemed to confirm that this "realization" entailed gathering in real descendants of scattered Israel. Smith and his fellow Saints were "to recover my people, who are of the house of Israel."[82] As Brigham Young explained the principle, "God has had regard to the blood of the covenant for his oath's sake. That promised blood has trickled down through our parents until now we are here. . . . Those who have the right will redeem the nations of the Earth."[83]

Mormons were here moving well beyond the language of New England Puritans, who taught that God sent his elect into the world "through the loyns of godly parents," and referred to America as the "New Israel."[84] Aboard the New World–bound *Arabella*, for instance, John Cotton took as his sermon text the words from Samuel: "I will appoint a place for my people Israel, and will plant them, that they may dwell in a place of their own."[85] But the Latter-day Saints went further, believing that the blood of Israel literally flowed in their missionaries—and in their converts as well. In an 1841 sermon, Smith taught that in the last days, "the Lord will begin by revealing the House of Israel among the gentiles."[86] This "revealing" was largely effected by their receptivity to the gospel—those who accepted the message of the restoration thereby identified themselves as true Israelites. And as for converts who were not literally of Israel, Smith taught, "the effect of the Holy Ghost upon a Gentile is to purge out the old blood & make him actually of the seed of Abraham. That man that has none of the blood of Abraham [naturally] must have a new creation by the Holy Ghost."[87] In other words, the Abrahamic covenant is limited to Abraham's seed, but the Holy Ghost can make anyone literally an Israelite. The covenant is therefore effectually universal.

God's invitation was extended to the entire human family but required for its fruition the resources and power of correct understanding, mutual reinforcement, and specific, essential salvific ordinances available only through an established body of disciples organized into communities. And taken as a whole, there are far more dead than living. Far more who died unbaptized than baptized. Far more who will necessarily be catechized in the world of spirits than here, if they are to be made participants in this scheme whose original conception, Smith would later teach, they witnessed and assented to. Therefore, the New and Everlasting Covenant, to be genuinely efficacious, must take within its purview the entire span of the human soul, from premortal beginnings to future participation in the divine nature and family; and it must encompass within its saving terms the entire range of humanity, living and dead, including those who lived and passed before, outside, and unknowing of the Savior's mission.

With these considerations in mind, Smith's conceptions of apostasy and restoration find very particular shades of meaning. In premortal councils, God recognized that a binding together of the human family had to occur, and he established laws and instituted ordinances, along with a mortal educative process, for the purpose of concretizing, formalizing, and metaphysically or morally grounding an endless web of eternal relationships. Mormons, in fact, believe the earth was created for this very purpose: to place the human family into eternal order. Marriage was ordained and families established "that the earth might answer the end of its creation; and that it might be filled with the measure of man, according to his creation before the world was made."[88] But through historical processes and corruptions willful and inadvertent, the larger cosmic context for this project was lost (after Christ's death, but recurrently in prior ages as well), the consummation toward which all was tending was diminished, and hence fallible humans and their institutions reconfigured the covenant in a tragically attenuated form, of limited prehistory, extent, and impact. Whereas Jon Levenson insists that Israel's "identity is not cosmic and primordial,"[89] Mormonism asserts it is both.

So in Mormon conception, the apostasy does not represent some minor corruptions of sacramental words or ritual forms. It is *not* about supposedly wicked priests whom God punished by removing their priesthood. (Mormons are not Donatists; unworthy administrators do not invalidate the ordinance.)[90] It *is* about a fundamental misapprehension of the background and purpose and extent of the covenant (premortal origins, mortal incarnation, and eventual theosis and sealing into eternal families) and the mode by which it is executed (temple covenants that effect the constituting of those chains of belonging, completing our journey from intelligence to deity). The apostasy did not consist of overly pessimistic accounts of human depravity and a universal fall but of losing sight of the Fall itself as a necessary and pre-meditated immersion of humankind into the crucible of experience, suffering, and schooling in the practice of love. Apostasy was not about baptizing at the wrong age or in the wrong medium. It was about not knowing that baptism makes us—all of us eventually—literally of Christ's family and his co-heirs. It was not about simple difference in standards of sexual practice or marriage's purpose per se. It is about failing to see marriage as a key mode of eternal association, associations that are at the very heart of what heaven is. In sum, Smith's "Restoration" is not about correcting particular doctrines or practices as much as it is about restoring their cosmic context. Consequently, Mormon emphasis on proper priestly administrators is not about authority for authority's sake. It is about officiators who understand the origins of that authority and the purposes for which priestly authority is to be exercised, and who can perform those sacred sacraments under God's immediate direction, according to his original intentions and designs.

It would appear that in Smith's understanding, the apostasy resulted from a critically impoverished account of God's everlasting covenant, one that rendered all sacraments and ordinances ineffectual not through wickedness but through loss of understanding of their scope and purpose—to constitute the human family into a durable, eternal, heavenly association. It is possible, on the principle of *lex orandi, lex credendi* (the rule of prayer determines the rule of belief) that the direction of influence was the reverse: if it is liturgy that fosters theology, then changes in the original sacraments would have produced the altered and diminished theological framework.[91] Whether the theological underpinnings were lost, and ordinances altered and given new meaning as a consequence, or the changes in sacraments and liturgy provoked new theological formulations, the result was the same from the LDS perspective—a critically impoverished understanding of God's everlasting covenant.

One historical narrative especially amenable to this reading of apostasy is summarized by Peter Leithard, who writes that in the century before Constantine, "persecutors targeted bishops and priests, and bishops who capitulated survived to rule the church once the persecution ended. It is hardly surprising that, with a few exceptions like Athanasius, the church leaders of the early fourth century were not men of the strongest character."[92] Mormons generally point to this period of creedal formation as decisive in Christian history—to the detriment of a theological grasp of human origins and of God's design for their future. This was the era, held Joseph F. Smith, in which the "true order of God was lost." By "about six hundred years after Christ," opined B. H. Roberts, "the gospel laws and ordinances had become so completely warped that it was as if the Church had departed from the earth."[93] So not a malicious desire to pervert as much as a culling of the most committed leaders may have led to the loss of sound understanding and spiritual discernment necessary to keep the larger gospel vision intact. Clearly, Smith envisioned his mission as that of reconstituting the full meaning of the original covenant with its accompanying panoply of uncorrupted gospel ordinances.

The language of religious exceptionalism is rarely heard today even among those traditions theologically committed to the principle. (Catholicism is one exception; as recently as 2007, the Congregation for the Doctrine of the Faith reaffirmed that the Church of Christ "subsists" in "only one Church . . . as a visible and spiritual community, viz, the Catholic Church.")[94] Mormonism, too, is scripturally bound to its claim to be "the only true and living church upon the face of the whole earth."[95] A seeming exclusivist, elitist, chauvinistic claim actually acquires, within the framework of Mormonism's program of universal vicarious outreach, precisely the opposite signification. The claim is best understood in light of what Mormons consider to be their unique grasp of the human soul's origins and destiny, and their sacred stewardship over the earthly ordinances that effect the necessary bridge between the two. Obviously, salvation is not confined to members of the institutional church, or the entire mammoth program of vicarious ordinance work for the dead performed by Mormons would be meaningless. That is why Smith's reply to a Washington crowd "that all who would follow the precepts of the Bible, whether Mormon or not, would assuredly be saved,"[96] finds corroboration in LDS scripture: "whosoever repenteth and cometh unto me, the same is my church," and in Smith's declared commission to bring an invisible church long "nourished in the wilderness" out of "obscurity and darkness."[97]

Mormonism thus forges a synthesis of exceptionalism and pluralism when it comes to the question of human salvation. Mormonism maintains that without the sacraments of the church, salvation is impossible. At the same time, its conception of both evangelization of, and vicarious ordinance work on behalf of, the dead means that "Mormonism" is the name for an epiphenomenal institution whose reach is universal and timeless. In this sense, for Mormons the meaning of "the church" as a historical institution founded in 1830 blurs into the meaning of "church" as the body of the faithful, living and dead, who at any time now or in the eons of time to come, receive the ordinances of salvation and abide their corresponding covenants. The Mormon apostle Henry Eyring explained the case simply: "This is the true Church, the only true Church, because in it are the keys of the priesthood" but also because "through the Church and the ordinances which are in it . . . the blessings of the sealing power reach into the spirit world."[98] In this view, the Church of Jesus Christ of Latter-day Saints is a portal of salvation, not the reservoir of the righteous or the domain of the saved.

In Mormon thought, then, participation in the church, that is, in the formal, visible institution, gives one access to knowledge of the full scope of human origins and futures, along with those powers and prerogatives that have the effect of integrating the individual into relationship with God and into eternal relationship with other humans—the essence of Mormon salvation and their version of covenant theology. Joseph Smith's status as restorer of the New and Everlasting Covenant, the Book of Mormon's place as principal evidence of his divine calling and priesthood authority, and the Mormon temples as the locus of those ordinances[99] that save, exalt, and bind together—all these components function to convey the emphatic assurance of salvation sought by Luther, Wesley, and multitudes of other seekers. That the form this complex of mutual commitments, promises, and sealing powers assumes is called "the New and Everlasting Covenant" is more than a token nod to its Puritan antecedents; it fulfills the same spiritual and theological functions for Latter-day Saints as the covenant of grace has for generations of fellow Christians: it provides both the means and the possibility of an assurance of salvation. It also appropriates, but extends in significant ways, the Christian meaning of the adoption—essential nucleus of that salvation—effected through sacramental forms and covenantal bonds.

ADOPTION AND THE FAMILY OF GOD

The church, in simplest terms, is the vehicle by which we come to be fully integrated into eternal relationship with a heavenly family. One must "subscribe [to] the articles of adoption to enter . . . the kingdom of God," said Smith.[100] But what exactly does adoption mean in Mormon thought? The term "adoption," first used by Paul in writing to the Romans, indicated a new and personal covenantal relationship to God that was symbolized by baptism, as contrasted with the old covenant of blood filiation, signified by circumcision.[101] Being born again as children of Christ, we feel to "cry, Abba! Father!"[102] Calvin is fairly representative in calling baptism "the symbol of adoption," which "has been substituted for circumcision and performs the same office."[103] If Jehovah's Old Testament promise was "to be God to you and to your offspring," the New Testament promise was seen as portending an even more intimate association, as converts were likened to children of a heavenly father, destined to be co-inheritors with God's son.[104] "We are adopted into the kingdom of God . . . as his creatures and offspring," wrote Augustine.[105] "Thus Christ leads his fellow heirs not only into a part of the inheritance but into a sharing of his power," wrote Origen.[106] Not "simple heirs," agreed Chrysostom; "we are 'fellow heirs with Christ.' See how concerned Paul is to bring us ever nearer to the Son!"[107] Calvin had seen in the sacraments God's promise "that he will be our God and we will be his people."[108] For Wesley, the truly converted, moved by the "spirit of adoption," are motivated by love rather than fear, and look upon God "no more as an angry Judge, but as a loving Father."[109]

Mormon understanding of adoption, like the New Testament version, builds on its Old and New Testament precedents, but it does so by concretizing rather than spiritualizing the nature of covenant relationships with the Divine. Against the turn toward figurative scriptural readings, Smith reemphasizes the early Hebraic literalism of God's passibility, anthropomorphism, and personhood. Not only did the creeds explicitly deny to God "body, parts or passions," but the church relegated the implication that the Father suffered the pains of the atonement and crucifixion to the category of heresy (patripassianism). By contrast, in the Book of Mormon, and again in the prophecy of Enoch, Smith locates God's essential nature in his choice to embrace the vulnerability and pain that interpersonal love entails. Not just the incarnate Son but the Eternal Father is depicted in two Mormon scriptural works as weeping over the misery and loss of his children.[110] Smith's God is the one Abraham Heschel finds in Exodus. This is the God who says of sorrowing Israel, not simply "I *know* their sufferings," as the inadequate translation renders it, but "I *have sympathy for*, I *am affected by*, their sufferings," in Heschel's version.[111]

This is the weeping God, the groom of an unfaithful bride, whose first great explicator, according to Heschel, is the prophet Hosea. Heschel finds in this prophet a poignant account of God's relationship to his people, one filled with "love, tenderness, and nostalgia." The covenant that God established with Abraham and reaffirmed through Moses, Heschel notes, is a concept that conveys "the permanence, steadfastness, and mutuality . . . of that relationship."[112] In Hosea's hands, the personal depth of God's relation to his people is its supernal component. That aspect is affirmed and emphasized through the addition of that most powerful of images: marriage. For "the most powerful reality is love between man and woman." This is why Hosea chooses marriage to characterize the nature of the covenantal relationship between God and humans, "one of the boldest conceptions of religious thinking."[113] In Smith's recuperation of the theophany of Enoch the prophet, Mormonism further develops this conception of God the Father's personal and passional investment in the human family.

> And Enoch said unto the Lord: How is it that thou canst weep, seeing thou art holy, and from all eternity to all eternity? And were it possible that man could number the particles of the earth, yea, millions of earths like this, it would not be a beginning to the number of thy creations; . . . how is it thou canst weep? The Lord said unto Enoch: Behold these thy brethren; they are the workmanship of mine own hands, and I gave unto them their knowledge, in the day I created them; and in the Garden of Eden, gave I unto man his agency; And unto thy brethren have I said, and also given commandment, that they should love one another, and that they should choose me, their Father; but behold, they are without affection, and they hate their own blood; . . . and among all the workmanship of mine hands there has not been so great wickedness as among thy brethren. . . . wherefore should not the heavens weep, seeing these shall suffer? . . . And it came to pass that the Lord spake unto Enoch, and told Enoch all the doings of the children of men; wherefore Enoch knew, and looked upon their wickedness, and their misery, and wept and stretched forth his arms, and his heart swelled wide as eternity; and his bowels yearned; and all eternity shook.[114]

In this scenario, we find a God fully susceptible to emotional pain and suffering on behalf of his human family. And in Enoch's moment of fully felt and fully shared divine empathy, the reverse condition, human participation in the divine, is realized as well. The distance separating God from man, and man from God, simultaneously collapses. This is the most explicit rendering in Mormonism of the full meaning of God's parenthood.

In Smith's early thought, though of God's "species" as co-eternal intelligences, humans were invited into eternal relation with God through adoption. As the editor of the church newspaper wrote in 1840, explicating Pauline teachings on the subject, before the world was even created, the Father chose his premortal children unto himself and put in place a plan whereby—through Jesus Christ—"mankind should become his sons [and daughters] through adoption."[115] By the time of Smith's death, a Father and Mother in heaven were coming to be understood as divine parents who had created or engendered spirit children from pre-existing "intelligence" or "intelligences." (In an 1845 article, W. W. Phelps refers to Adam's premortal existence as "a child with his father and mother in heaven.")[116] With this development, kinship to God became more emphatically literal.[117] Before Smith, perhaps only the mystic Meister Eckhart had "taken this idea of 'blood relationship' to God so seriously or followed its consequences so radically." He seemed to believe that "God's blood flows in our veins," in one editor's words, that "we are really in God's family." His words that "something in man . . . is of God's order, . . . by which man is of the genus and species of God," precisely anticipate those of Parley Pratt, who held that "God, angels and men are all of one species."[118] As eternal intelligence, Smith taught, humans are co-eternal with God.[119] In such a conception, Mormons are not being figurative when they hold, as they have from their beginnings, that the point of the gospel is to prepare us for "adoption into [God's] own family as lawful heirs."[120]

In Smith's lifetime, Mormon editors noted "the greatest importance" assumed by the "great law of adoption," and commented on its promulgation to the point of "weary[ing] the people by the monotony of the subject."[121] The question, then, is what role can adoption have when for Mormons the human race is already the literal, spiritual, posterity of God, and Christ our Savior but also our "elder brother"?[122] For Latter-day Saints insist adoption was not a metaphorical incorporation of a son of Adam into the family of Christ. The answer, writes Parley Pratt, is that we have lost our position as "children beloved, approved," with "claims to the heritage and glory of their parent."

Recognizing the reality of our alienation from our heavenly parents as a consequence of the veil occasioned by mortal birth and compounded by personal sin, adoption became for early Saints a *re-incorporation* into a binding and eternal relationship, after a temporary alienation consequent to the events in Eden. Following "alienation of our race from God," we have "lost all claim" to be heirs. That is why one must be spiritually reborn, and receive "the spirit of adoption, whereby he can call Abba, Father."[123] Adoption as *re*-integration was already being expressed in Smith's lifetime. Hence Pratt wrote in the *Millennial Star* that God's purpose was "to bring us back from that state of alienation into his own family."[124] Repairing our "state of alienation," we can re-cross "the very threshold of his house, . . . having a legal claim, by the laws of heaven, on the privileges of sonship."[125] The influential Orson Spencer wrote that adoption by baptism remedies our condition of "rebellion against the laws of Christ."[126] B. H. Roberts reaffirmed the seeming paradox: "It is chiefly through adoption, through obedience to the Gospel of Christ, that man in the scripture is spoken of as being a son of God"; at the same time, humans are literally "by nature the [children] of God," and human destiny portends an eventual, full likeness to God. But that process, given human alienation from God through personal sin, requires spiritual rebirth, and hence "'adoption' into the heavenly kingdom, and into sonship with God."[127]

Mormonism's rewriting of the Fall and its story of Enoch's encounter with God in fact place adoption at the very heart of its theology, making temporary alienation rather than sin the principal culprit, and proper relation rather than righteousness the remedy. As Kathleen Flake writes, in Smith's redaction of Genesis, Adam and Eve are pointedly given their agency before the world is created, "and placed in an environment that requires them to choose between manifest options. The choice is one of affiliation, of whom to love in an environment that makes one free to choose." Later in the same narrative, God laments to Enoch humankind's failure to "choose me their Father."[128]

Adoption is therefore renewal of a natural relationship after our estrangement and disqualification from a life of holy and eternal relationship through personal, not inherited, sin. Parley Pratt, early expositor of Mormonism, in a move typical of nineteenth-century Mormonism, saw the family of God in dynastic terms, likening our membership in that family to citizenship in a kingdom. In reference to the Kingdom of God referred to by Christ, Pratt wrote in one of Mormonism's founding treatises, "It happened that there were no natural born subjects of that kingdom, for both Jew and Gentile were included in sin and unbelief; and none could be citizens without the law of adoption." And in one of the clearest pronouncements on the place of sacraments in Mormon thought, Pratt explained that one attained to such membership in God's kingdom or family through the administration of "certain laws and ordinances, which were invariably the laws of adoption."[129]

The process of preparation and sanctification that underlie the pursuit of salvation, culminating in "the seal of adoption," are predicated upon Christ's atonement, his supernal grace, and human faith, repentance, and conformity to eternal law, and have been dealt with elsewhere.[130] The question at hand concerns the role of the institutional church in that process, and more particularly, the logic of the sacraments that do not merely signify or commemorate but actually constitute the individual's full adoption into the family of God. Those sacraments, as we will see, culminate in temple ordinances that have for their purpose the literal incorporation of the human family into an eternal family headed by Heavenly Parents. At this point, we have a tentative answer to the question, why does Mormonism believe a church is absolutely essential? It serves a twofold purpose. First, the church provides the context, resources, and aids for the sanctification of individuals. In this sense, Mormon theology is in accord with C. S. Lewis, who wrote, "The church exists to make us little Christs."[131] Ultimately, however, Mormons reject a salvation constructed on atomistic individualism. Hence the second aspect of Mormon ecclesiology, which is more transparently a function of Mormonism's ritualistic dimension: the church exists as a steward over the authority and ordinances which both foster and constitute a relationality between humans and God on the one hand, and humans with humans on the other. *In sum, the church exists to create the kind of persons, in the kinds of relationships, that constitute the divine nature.* The climax of this process is represented and effected through the sacraments of the Mormon temple.

CONCEPTUALIZING ZION

The challenge Mormon ecclesiology must address, then, is how best to structure a church so as to perfect and eternalize our human identity as children of Heavenly Parents, which I have referred to as religion's vertical dimension, while sanctifying and reifying participation in the larger human family now and hereafter, which I refer to as its horizontal dimension. If adoption into the divine family characterizes the vertical dimension of salvation, Zion is the name given its horizontal counterpart. Mormons push the logic of Zion to far horizons, providing a robust rationale behind the church as corporeal entity. The church is to *be* Zion, enfolding us in a society that merges seamlessly with a communal heaven. Zion was the name the Puritans gave to their New World aspirations for a godly society, based on the term first used in the Bible to designate the Jerusalem stronghold captured by David.[132] Philosophers and reformers from Plato to Thomas More to Robert Owen dreamed of earthly Utopias, and religious innovators like John Hartwick, Jemima Wilkinson ("the Publick Universal Friend"), and Robert Matthews ("Matthias") all attempted heavenly New Jerusalems in the nineteenth century. The quest for a literal Zion by these dreamers and eccentrics, on the one hand, and the persistent invocation of the word in church hymns, religious newspapers, and Sunday sermons, on the other, reveal something of the idea's powerful and enduring appeal in America's religious history. For most Christians, the New Jerusalem, Zion, and the Heavenly City all reflect men and women's deepest spiritual yearning. This longing takes many forms: the repair of a damaged relationship with God, the healing of a sick and sinful society, the dramatic triumph of good over evil, or the transition into the eternal of all that is mortal, transient, and temporary. The idea of Zion thus mingles concrete enactment with an aspiration that hovers at the borders of a mythic future never yet realized. It is heaven in its social dimension—and therefore of dubious possibility to some Christians. Like the invisible church, Zion has been easier to envision as a figurative conglomeration of celestial individuals—"every holy and godly person" who "is lifted above this life," according to the Church Fathers.[133]

But Mormonism's conception of heaven is radically social, and so Zion for them cannot be reduced to a metaphor. By mid-century, other Christians were also articulating heaven in terms of domestic circles.[134] Mormons, however, wedded the ideal to a covenant theology and conceived of family not as a Victorian scene of domesticity, but as an expansive, intergenerational web that extended back to Adam and forward into lines yet unborn. It is the fullest form of the covenant relationship that the church aspires to realize, a divine society, centering on family relations but radiating far beyond. That is one of the essential distinctives of Mormon soteriology. Salvation is a communal enterprise. Though Mormons embrace a robust concept of theosis, it is a social heaven they envision—and so the church must do more than cultivate individual models of sanctity. The church must function as the model, the catalyst, and the schoolmaster for the City of God. Another way of saying this is that the church exists to implement the everlasting covenant, which designates the character of an eternal relatedness to heavenly parents and the human family. And the template that foreshadows and characterizes such glorious sociality, to use Smith's language, is Zion. Zion-building is not *preparation* for heaven. It *is* heaven, in embryo.

The "great mission" of the Saints was to "organize a nucleus of Heaven," Smith preached.[135] Zion, then, is the ideal which the church aspires to create in tangible form. The biblical term has particular meaning in Mormonism, since LDS scripture builds on the ancient Enoch literature by providing an account of the patriarch (father of Methuselah) and his city which attained such righteousness that the entire community, and not just its leader, was taken up to heaven by God. (One ancient Jewish version has over 800,000 followers disappearing along with Enoch at his ascension.)[136] As Smith's version describes the process,

> Enoch continued his preaching in righteousness unto the people of God. And it came to pass in his days, that he built a city that was called the City of Holiness, even Zion. And it came to pass that Enoch talked with the Lord; and he said unto the Lord: Surely Zion shall dwell in safety forever . . . and lo, Zion, in process of time, was taken up into heaven. And the Lord said unto Enoch: Behold mine abode forever.[137]

The challenge of the earthly church is to replicate the city Enoch perfected. The book of Hebrews, after referring to Enoch's ascension, relates that Abraham "looked forward to the city . . . whose architect and builder is God."[138] Then, the epistle's author declares that Christians are even now drawing near to union with it. "But you have come to Mount Zion and to the city of the living God, the heavenly Jerusalem, and to innumerable angels in festal gathering, and to the assembly of the firstborn who are enrolled in heaven."[139] LDS scripture casts the merging of the earthly Zion and its heavenly counterpart as a literal event yet to unfold: at a future day, God's righteousness will "sweep the earth as with a flood, to gather out" those that will have Him to be their God. Then, as the Lord promised Enoch, "thou and all thy city [shall] meet them there, and we will receive them into our bosom, and they shall see us; and we will fall upon their necks, and they shall fall upon our necks, and we will kiss each other; And there shall be mine abode, and it shall be Zion."[140]

Smith's identification of his own restoration project with Enoch's was abundantly evident. Enoch represented the possibility of something more durable than a loose agglomeration of the righteous or of another in a version of ecclesiastical institutions. Enoch embodied the idea of a covenant people. "It is the testimony that I want," Joseph said, "that I am God's servant, and this people his people." Or, as he told a group in March 1842, he would succeed where Moses and other prophets had failed: "He was going to make of this society a kingdom of priests—as in Enoch's day." The forging of this community was his true prophetic task. When Mormon leaders chose code names for themselves in certain revelation texts, Smith's choice was virtually inevitable. Enoch, he was called.[141] The gesture was more than historical nostalgia. "The building up of Zion is a cause that has interested the people of God in every age; it is a theme upon which prophets, priests and kings have dwelt with peculiar delight; they have looked forward with joyful anticipation to the day in which we live; and fired with heavenly and joyful anticipations they have sung and written and prophesied of this our day; but they died without the sight; we are the favored people that God has made choice of to bring about the Latter-day glory."[142]

Mormons, then, take the project of Zion-building literally, believing that the church must build a community prepared to meet the Lord and join the heavenly community of the righteous. The process of sanctifying disciples of Christ, and constituting them into a community of love and harmony, does not *qualify* individuals for heaven; sanctification and celestial relationality *are* the essence of heaven. Zion, in this conception, is both an ideal and a transitional stage into the salvation toward which all Christians strive. In the history of Mormon ecclesiology, the church-as-Zion has had two overlapping phases: gathering and stake-building.

Populating Zion (The Gathering)

The invisible church may be a collection of the pure in heart however dispersed, but a literal Zion required a literal gathering of the Saints in compact society. Smith had determined to move the church westward soon after founding. But the decision was more than a simple relocation under the pressures of persecution. Smith had produced a revelation in September 1831 in which the Lord told him he was "called to bring to pass the gathering of mine elect; for mine elect hear my voice and harden not their hearts."[143] In fact, Smith learned, "it was the design in the Councils of heaven before the world was that the principles & law of that priesthood was predicated upon the gathering of the people in every age of the world."[144] Gathering, or the restoration of Israel, was an Old Testament motif. Like the building of Zion itself, it was generally held to have spiritual, rather than literal meaning, at least in the case of most Christian believers. But here again, Smith was literally reenacting, rather than rhetorically appropriating, prophetic patterns relating to covenant Israel.

Soon after establishing initial branches of the church in Colesville and Palmyra, New York, and Harmony, Pennsylvania, Smith received a revelation designating a place of gathering—initially called a "city," but soon to acquire the name of Zion.[145] As a journal edited by Charles Dickens would remark of the Mormons a few decades later, "It sounds strange to hear of a church having a 'location.' But a 'location' was the term they applied to their place of settlement."[146] The location was "on the borders of the Lamanites," that is, of the Indian Territory, a shifting land area that demarcated the boundary between white settlement and Native American resettlement— an appropriate location for a people who believed they would be pivotal in bridging the Israel-Gentile divide. Meanwhile, a provisional place of assembly was designated in Kirtland, Ohio. Soon the church operated from two central locations in Missouri and Ohio, but by 1837, the convert base had grown enough and shifted sufficiently westward that Smith set out to organize another dozen units in Missouri.[147]

Gathering was taught as part of the gospel, and most converts responded to the call. An 1842 church article considered "members scattered abroad," who refuse "to gather together to the body," as so many "dead branches." Heber C. Kimball explained that "as the branch of the vine cannot gather sap and nourishment from the body when separated from it, so the members of the church abroad, when commanded to gather to the body, cannot receive life and intelligence away from it, nor grow in the things of the kingdom of God."[148] Gathering furthered the project of Zion-building in two particular ways. Facilitating education was the first. "Intelligence is the great object of our holy religion," Joseph declared. And intelligence, he continued, "is the result of education, and education can only be obtained by living in compact society; One of the [principal] objects, then, of our coming together, is to obtain the advantages of education; and in order to do this, compact society is absolutely necessary."[149] Indeed, seven years earlier, as the gathering in Missouri began, the Saints laid the first log of a schoolhouse in Jackson County "as a foundation of Zion," even as Sidney Rigdon consecrated that land of Zion by prayer.[150] The ambitious educational agenda of the young church took the form of a "School of the Prophets" in

Kirtland, an "Elders School" in Kirtland and Missouri, and in Nauvoo, a Hebrew School, common schools, and a university.

The second and principal reason for the physical congregating of the Saints was to assemble sufficient collective resources to construct holy edifices where the New and Everlasting Covenant would find its full expression. As Joseph Smith would later teach, the object of gathering was precisely this, "to build unto the Lord an house whereby he could reveal unto his people the ordinances" of his temple.[151] Smith laid the cornerstone for a temple in Jackson County, Missouri, in August 1831, then prepared a plat for the City of Zion to be built there, with twenty-four temples at its center ("the Church of Christ's first organized efforts to physically build the kingdom of God through urban development," note several LDS historians).[152] Then, in the summer of 1833, plans proceeded for the construction of a temple in Kirtland, and the cornerstones were laid on July 23. Though it was not entirely clear in the first years, the temple and the full range of sacraments that would eventually be administered therein would become by the 1840s the very raison d'etre of the Restoration.

Populating Zion (Colonization)

Initially, the gathering had unfolded in response to revelations that put the Latter-day Saints in the prophetic role of Israel. The gathering was the coming out of the world and back into covenant relationship with God as foretold by Isaiah, Jeremiah, and other Old Testament prophets. As Smith wrote in the fall of 1835, he "used every influence and argument, that lay in my power, to get those who believe in the everlasting covenant, . . . to remove to the place which I now designated to be the land of Zion."[153] After the debacle in Missouri, where the gathering at times proceeded, Smith acknowledged, in a manner "derogatory to the genuine character and principles of the church,"[154] the Saints considered abandoning the practice of gathering that had cost them so dearly. Myriad reasons combined to create friction, hostility, violence, and expulsions of the Mormons in their first fifteen years of existence, but certainly their practice of sudden concentration of alarming numbers in areas long settled by others was a principal culprit—as well as proclaiming the land their spiritual inheritance. A document produced by the citizenry of Jackson County, Missouri, justified their forcible eviction of Mormons as a response to "swarms" of invading Mormons who threatened to appropriate the whole area to their theocratic kingdom.[155] Giving reasonable and well-intentioned counsel after subsequent expulsion from the entire state, the ranking militia general who oversaw their expulsion from the state advised the Saints to "scatter abroad, and never again organize yourselves with Bishops, Presidents, etc., lest you excite the jealousies of the people, and subject yourselves to the same calamities that have now come upon you."[156] But with Smith in jail, the Kirtland Temple in dissenters' hands, and a fractured, impoverished membership, consolidation rather than dispersal was seen as the only way forward. So they regrouped in Illinois, for a respite of a few years. Then, driven out of Nauvoo after Smith's assassination, they spent their final weeks diverting scarce resources of time and material to complete the temple there, even as they prepared to abandon it for the Rocky Mountains. No greater evidence could so illustrate the indispensable centrality of the temple to the Mormon sense of the Restoration's cardinal purposes and the continuing need to muster resources to renew temple construction in each place of gathering.

Once in Utah, Brigham Young colonized more than 300 towns and cities, compared to Smith's handful; he governed a cultural region larger than Texas and a church that comprised in excess of 100,000 Saints at his death in 1877. The church now had deep roots in many locations outside the United States, and other imperatives were coming to shift the scales away from a gathering that had become isolationist in the face of years of persecution and marginalization. "It is not the gathering of the people alone" we are called to accomplish, said George Q. Cannon in 1878. "Teaching the world," and serving as "leavening" among the nations was a heavenly mandate, he urged, portending a momentous shift in policy.[157]

By the close of the nineteenth century, leaders were already dampening the command to gather to Utah. Apostle James Talmage noted in 1900 that "the practice of gathering its proselytes into one place prevents the building up and strengthening of foreign branches."[158] In 1902, President Joseph F. Smith enumerated the blessings of the gathering and the consequent "force that has bound the Saints together."[159] He repeated in a May 1907 address "adopted by vote of the Church" in General Conference that "the gathering of scattered Israel" was a principal object of the church.[160] That December, however, the First Presidency chose the occasion of a Christmas greeting to Dutch Latter-day Saints to dramatically redefine the concept of gathering in terms that prevail to this day in the church. Henceforth, they announced simply and abruptly, "The policy of the Church is not to entice or encourage people to leave their native lands; but to remain faithful and true in their allegiance to their governments, and to be good citizens."[161] The shift did not mean the purposes of gathering—temple-building and "compact society"—had waned. Only that the great era of western colonization was past, that a millennialism deferred mitigated the urgency of millennial preparation, and the practice of widespread stake-building provided an effective surrogate model for geographical gathering. Clearly, the ideal of Zion and the work of the church in its building was shifting.

Millennialism Deferred

Mormonism emerged against a background of fervent millennialism. Whether anticipating Christ's Second Coming as the culmination of spiritual preparations and/or progressive moral and material improvements (postmillennialism) or expecting a dramatic arrival of Jesus in the midst of tribulations to inaugurate a thousand-year era of peace (premillennialism), wide swaths of nineteenth-century Christians expected the imminent arrival of the day of judgment. The publication of the Book of Mormon, the physical gathering of dispersed covenant Israel (converts), the physical gathering of a remnant of Israel (the removal of the American Indians to the Indian Territory), and the formal restoration of the "true and living Church," all unfolding in the year 1830, buttressed by the dozen revelations produced by Smith in which the Lord warned, "I come quickly,"[162] combined to convince Mormons in powerful fashion that the Second Coming was at the very door.

Such expectation had given special urgency to the Mormon project of Zion-building. Gathering in Missouri, a physical plat for the city of the New Jerusalem in hand, practicing a law of consecration to shape a New Testament–inspired communalism, and indefatigably evangelizing domestically and abroad even in the midst of penury, pogroms, and expulsions, Mormon hopes took emphatic and costly form. Shortly before his death, Smith even went so far as to organize a Council of Fifty, mostly composed of members of the Mormon ecclesiastical elite along with three sympathetic outsiders. The full name of the Council suggests a mix of political purpose and religious symbolism: "The Kingdom of God and His Laws with the Keys and Power[s] thereof, and Judgment in the Hands of His Servants, Ahman Christ."[163] Parley Pratt called it "the most exalted Council with which our earth is at present dignified."[164] He and other participants apparently saw it as the beginnings of a government that would rule the earth during the anticipated millennium.

At the height of the Saints' Zion-building euphoria, mobs had violently expelled the Saints from their settlements in Jackson County, Missouri, appropriating homes, possessions, and lands amounting to thousands of acres. "The situation of the saints, as scattered, is dubious, and affords a gloomy prospect." Until "God or the president" intervened, William W. Phelps recognized, "we shall not be able to live again in Zion."[165] The next year, Smith had mounted a paramilitary expedition with 200 volunteers—called Zion's Camp—to reclaim the land of Zion. Arriving on the banks of Fishing River, Missouri, riders brought word that the Governor of Missouri had reneged on this pledge of assistance. Meanwhile, hundreds of armed and alarmed Missouri citizens converged on the Saints' camp. A sudden storm surge separated the attackers from their main camp, soaked men and powder, and sent the Missourians and Mormons scurrying for shelter. One would-be assailant fell dead, struck by lightning. Nature's intervention prevented a conflict that would have been catastrophic for the outnumbered and outgunned Mormons. But the respite left the essential issue of Zion's "redemption" unresolved.[166]

Smith retired with his followers a few miles to the north and sought a revelation—as he customarily did in such moments of crisis and uncertainty—to guide his next steps. What followed shattered the Mormons' short-term hopes and confounded their expectations. But the revelation also provided crucial clarification regarding their identity and destiny as a church, causing the Saints to reconsider the foundations of a Zion society. Now, they learned after the encounter at Fishing River, they would have to "wait for a little season for the redemption of Zion." In the meantime, they would need to submit themselves to further refining and preparation. Zion, the revelation indicated, "cannot be built up unless it is by the principles of the law of the celestial kingdom." And there was only one place where they could learn the lessons and principles that would suit them to live this celestial law:

> That they themselves may be prepared, and that my people may be taught more perfectly, and have experience, and know more perfectly concerning their duty, and the things which I require at their hands. And this cannot be brought to pass until mine elders are endowed with power from on high. For behold, I have prepared a great endowment and blessing to be poured out upon them.[167]

The "great endowment," as they had been told in 1831 and now learned in earnest, could only take place in the Kirtland Temple, still years from completion.[168] The quest for Zion, the grand project of building and sanctifying a godly people in preparation for the Savior's return, could not be accomplished in isolation from the sacrifice, worship, and ordinances associated with the temple. An earlier revelation had anticipated such a rendering of Zion as a spiritual rather than temporal enterprise: "Verily, thus saith the Lord, let Zion rejoice, for this is Zion—THE PURE IN HEART."[169]

Five years into Utah settlement, Young was framing the enterprise of Zion-building in terms of personal rather than political or social organization. "The more purity that exists, the less is the strife," he told a congregation. "If the people will not serve the devil another moment whilst they live, if this congregation is possessed of that spirit and resolution, here in this house is the Millennium. Let the inhabitants of this city be possessed of that spirit, let the people of the territory be possessed of that spirit, and here is the Millennium. Let the whole people of the United States be possessed of that spirit, and here is the Millennium, and so will it spread over all the world."[170] The expectation of an imminent inheritance of Zion receded, and the work of its spiritual construction had begun in earnest. Though Christ's return and his thousand-year reign remain real hopes, the labor of preparation is now seen as generations long. You have time to have "children and grandchildren, maybe even great-grandchildren," apostle Boyd K. Packer told LDS youth in a widely disseminated 2011 message.[171]

Mormonism has gone through several wrenching transitions and phases, involving persecutions, expulsions, the martyrdom of Smith, polygamy (implementing then abruptly abandoning the practice)—but it is arguable that nothing so profoundly redefined Mormon self-understanding and reoriented its institutional forms as this devastating failure to realize Zion in the way and timetable anticipated. "The idea of being driven away from the land of Zion pained their very souls," reported two members of the exodus from Missouri.[172] A church that had aspired to embody in concrete form a modern version of Enoch's holy city on the cusp of Christ's return now prepared for the long haul, working with a globally dispersed citizenry. In remarks lauded by the church president in 1977, Bruce R. McConkie reaffirmed the expectation of a literal advent of Christ with a literal "restoration of the ten tribes" and "New Jerusalem . . . built upon [the American] continent." And like Young, he urged, "Each one of us can build up Zion in our own lives by being pure in heart," even as he affirmed that to get us there, "[God] has ordained and established the system which is now in operation."[173] So Zion persists as an idea that blends commitment to a literal brick and mortar fulfillment, with the spiritual preparation aided by the resources of the temple and its sacraments. In this regard, Hugh Nibley's depiction is still apt. "Zion is the great moment of transition, the bridge between the world as it is and the world as God designed it and meant it to be."[174] Certainly this is true of most Christian churches to some degree. Worship, writes Geoffrey Wainwright, "point[s] the historical Church towards a closer approximation to the Church as it is meant to be."[175]

In the case of Mormonism, that ideal has had two distinct phases, described by Bruce McConkie. First was the physical gathering, which allowed for assembled "congregations strong enough for the Saints to strengthen each other. There alone were the temples of the Most High where the fulness of the ordinances of exaltation are performed." With the millennium deferred, and the global spread of the LDS faith Young predicted come to pass, Mormonism has entered what McConkie calls its second phase, extending from "the creation of stakes of Zion in overseas areas . . . to the second coming of the Son of Man."[176] For the second phase to effect the purposes of the first, stakes (diocese-sized units) would have to fulfill the same functions of edification and temple access that centralized gathering did in the church's first decades.

Stake-Building

Isaiah had likened Zion to a tabernacle, a sacred tent supported by stakes. "Look upon Zion, the city of our solemnities," he had declared, "thine eyes shall see

Jerusalem a quiet habitation, a tabernacle that shall not be taken down; not one of the stakes thereof shall ever be removed." And in a prophecy of Latter-day expansion, the Lord had made the extension of stakes the key to growth and strength. "Enlarge the place of thy tent," he had admonished, "and let them stretch forth the curtains of thine habitations: spare not, lengthen thy cords, and strengthen thy stakes."[177] So under Joseph Smith, stakes already began to spread beyond the immediate areas of gathering to become the de facto version of a gathering that was still literal, but local and multiple in execution. What this means is that the concept of Zion has not faded from Mormon consciousness—it has just been transferred to dispersed local forums rather than a stage occupied by thousands gathered to a central location. In this new multiplex Zion, the two rationales for gathering articulated by Joseph Smith find as much relevance and studied implementation today as they did in Kirtland or Nauvoo. A church educational system enrolls some 400,000 high-school-age students in 150 countries in a four-year course of religious instruction.[178] The majority of students in the program attend an hour of religious schooling every weekday before school. A slightly smaller number of young adults attend church-staffed weekday religious classes in over 2,500 locations.[179] As for concentrating the resources necessary for temple-building, the church of the twenty-first century has the means, increasingly, to bring the temple and its sacramental opportunities to the far-flung members across the globe.

Temples Dot the Earth

Brigham Young had launched the construction of four temples in Utah (Salt Lake, St. George, Manti, and Logan), presided over the completion and dedication of only one (St. George, 1877), but had predicted that to accomplish the purposes of the Restoration "there will have to be not only one temple but thousands of them."[180] (They will come to "dot the earth," affirmed Bruce McConkie more than a century later.)[181] After all, with the gospel now restored through Joseph Smith, essentially all that remained to do was to "preach the gospel and build temples."[182] A century and a half after the church's founding, a mere nineteen temples were in operation.[183] Thereafter, during the presidency of Gordon B. Hinckley the pace of temple-building became almost a frenzy, averaging two per month. At the beginning of his tenure in 1995, forty-seven temples were in operation. "We are determined, brethren, to take the temple to the people," he announced in 1997.[184] By his death in 2008 there were an additional seventy-seven, and a decade later the number was climbing toward 200.

In the context of Mormon ecclesiology as we have outlined it, such proliferation of temples must be seen as far more than a construction project on steroids.

Putting temples within easy access of the majority of the Mormon population (over 85 percent are within 200 miles)[185] means that a principal rationale for gathering has been largely satisfied through such localized temple access. At the same time, the unprecedented access to, and emphasis on, temples has reinforced sacramentalism as the heart and soul of Mormon ecclesiology. While the cultural and organizational transformations of Mormonism have created an institution very different from its nineteenth-century counterpart, the late twentieth-century turn toward a temple-centric faith restores the church to the heart of Joseph Smith's vision, which placed sacramentalism, "the ordinances of salvation," at the heart of the New and Everlasting Covenant.

3

Sacramental Theology

AS WE HAVE seen, the Reformation represented a reconceptualization of the role of sacraments in salvation theology. The break was not in every case clear and definitive. Reformers and their followers differed on the degree to which their sacramental theology (especially as it concerned the Eucharist) departed from the Catholic: the semi-sacramental Luther affirmed a modified form of real presence in the bread and wine ("this is my body," as Luther doggedly insisted); Calvin believed Christ was present only in a "spiritual way"; "sacramentarians" like Zwingli disliked the term "sacrament" and considered sacraments forms of pledges or oaths made by congregants, devoid of inherent efficacy; later Quakers rejected all sacraments as unnecessary. In all these cases, however, the important thread was insistence that the priest was no longer the mediator of salvation. Salvation was personal, experiential, *sola gratia* and *sola fide* (by grace and faith alone) in the words adopted by so many Reformers.

Some nineteenth-century Protestants, though not usually viewing sacraments as indispensable channels of grace, lamented their "corruption" at the hands of the Catholic Church. In 1795, the Scottish minister Alexander Fraser published his *Key to the Prophecies*, which included a gloss of a passage from the book of Revelation: "And the woman fled into the wilderness, where she has a place prepared by God, . . . where she is nourished for a time."[1] Fraser took this passage to refer to the time when, "as the visible church declined from the doctrines and precepts of Christianity, the true Church of Christ gradually retired from the view of men, till at length, . . .

the true church of Christ, considered as a community, wholly disappeared." Fraser believed this allegory described a crucial distinction between an invisible church that persists, "fed by the word and Spirit of God," and a legitimate institution that disappears because it is no longer in possession of "*the outward ordinances, . . . which . . . were defiled*" (my emphasis).[2] (As we noted above, though often employed by Smith and his contemporaries in the generic sense to denote God's laws and statutes as well as divinely prescribed rites and ceremonies, ordinances gradually came to signify for Mormons—as for low-church Protestants—what other Christians would call sacraments.) Thomas Campbell, in his *Declaration and Address*, pointed to one "evil . . . of a very awful nature" that resulted from Christian apostasy from the church's "original unity, peace, and purity": "the Lord withholds his gracious influential presence from his ordinances."[3]

There is no ambiguity about the status of sacraments—or ordinances—in Mormon thought. Joseph Smith reinstated ordinances as absolutely indispensable. "[Baptism] is a sign, and commandment which God has set for man to enter into his Kingdom. Those who seek to enter in any other way will seek in vain; and God will not receive them, neither will the angels acknowledge their works as accepted; for they have not obeyed the ordinances, nor attended to the signs which God ordained for the salvation of man."[4] "Without the ordinances," he insisted, "no man can see the face of God."[5] This was swimming against the tide, and Mormons knew it. As Ryan Tobler has written, Mormons noted the prevalence of contemporary preachers calling baptism "non-essential," and they wrote articles and pamphlets defending their return to sacramentally based religion.[6] Once again, we see a blending in Mormon rhetoric of Catholic and Reformation language: baptism is a *sign*, but an *essential* sign, one of "certain decrees which are fixed, and immovable" in Smith's words.[7] As we saw in the effectual manifesto produced at the time of the Mormon church's organization, Smith summarized the rationale for restoration in language that would have been familiar to contemporaries like Frazer: in simplest terms, Christians "have strayed from mine ordinances."[8] Contrary to a common impression in Mormon culture that Smith's principal task was to restore "truth" to the earth, he saw his commission as tied more centrally to the reinstitution of legitimate authority and uncorrupted ordinances. At the same time, those ordinances certainly had renewed meaning and efficacy within a vastly enlarged cosmic vision, one that saw salvation as a linear ascent from premortal spirit beings to exalted humans incorporated into the family of God, rather than as a recuperative work repairing an Adamic catastrophe. This is why, in Smith's thought and language, ordinances essential to salvation were always associated with covenant-making. It is very much to the point that, according to the *Oxford English Dictionary*, "sacrament" derives from the Latin *sacramentum*, meaning "solemn oath." This connection is especially true of the "New and Everlasting Covenant"—which effected sacred and reciprocal bonds of belonging through sacramental rites.

Accordingly, the central purpose of the gathering and temple-building, Smith clearly stated in an 1841 revelation, was "that [God] may [again] reveal mine ordinances therein, unto my people,"[9] all within a restored framework in which such ordinances effected relationships of eternal duration. "All the known world have been left for centuries without . . . a priesthood authorized of God to administer ordinances," as Orson Pratt summarized, writing in 1840 that this belief in "a general and awful apostasy from the religion of the New Testament" was a core principle of the LDS Church.[10] If Mormons found in the Book of Mormon a partial solution to the problem of salvational certitude, then an emphatic theology of sacramentalism, culminating in temple rituals and assurances of salvation, was the full fruit arising out of the New and Everlasting Covenant as Mormons understood it.

This position of the Mormon church on the indispensability of the sacraments, and of their restitution as the principal reason for the Restoration so called, is perhaps the most emphatic differentiator of Mormonism from its Protestant peer groups. In Charles Taylor's analysis, the enchanted world of premodern Christendom is full of unseen forces and powers and agencies that are nonetheless real and impinge on human bodies and minds alike. In this universe, "the porous self is vulnerable: to spirits, demons, cosmic forces."[11] In Catholic doctrine, sacraments are the principal means by which heavenly powers are controlled, channeled, or administered. The central principle in this regard is "*ex opere operato*," meaning grace is conveyed by the very act of receiving the sacrament, and is inherently effective unless it meets "the resisting obstacle of a contrary will."[12] It is true that Catholicism teaches that "grace is . . . conferred from the work," that is, the sacrament.[13] At the same time, the Catholic Church has taught for centuries (as do Mormons) that although redemption depends upon the sacraments, sacramental efficacy is "dependent upon truth itself and sincerity."[14] A papal bull also stipulated that sacraments would only "confer [grace] upon those who receive them worthily."[15]

Challenges to orthodox Christianity, which emerge already in the early medieval period, were in Taylor's view powered by a sense that priests and sacraments amounted to "an illegitimate claim to control the power of God." In the view of Reformers, the inherent power of authoritative sacraments to convey grace "by the instrumentality of the ordinances themselves" was "not only false but repugnant," as Calvin protested.[16] Consequently, those agencies mediated by the clergy find replacement in the Protestant worldview by individual salvation through faith alone.[17] An abiding sacramentalism, or belief that sacraments are both essential to salvation and inherently efficacious, was challenged for the same reasons magic was in this new disenchanted universe. Still, Taylor notes in the nineteenth century "frequent attempts to 're-enchant' the world, or at least admonitions and invitations to do so."[18]

One way to characterize Smith's program is as an unabashed reversion to (or retention of) just such an enchanted worldview, involving an emphatic reassertion of sacramentalism and apostolic authority, and a rejection of Protestantism's *sola fide*. For such reasons, it is abundantly clear that Mormonism is more nearly aligned with Catholic than with Protestant soteriology and ecclesiology, in its deep structure. (Mormonism also shares with Catholicism a view of human nature and sin that Niebuhr condemned as semi-Pelagianism, i.e., rejection of the "enslaved will," and an insistence that "actual sins cannot be regarded as sinful or as involving guilt if they do not proceed from a will which is essentially free.")[19] Twentieth-century Mormon narratives tended to emphasize Reformation as a prelude to Restoration; being mostly Protestant in background, Mormon converts were much more likely to identify Protestant than Catholic commonalities: Mormonism emphasized a personal, unmediated relationship to God, Methodist forms of worship and conferencing, and low-church liturgy; in addition, influential Protestant depictions of the "Great Apostasy" with its emphasis on papal abuses and lay idolatry, infiltrated Mormon perceptions of the Roman church. For all these reasons, Mormonism has long felt greater affinity with the Protestant past, while the faith's far more substantive congruences with Catholicism have been largely overlooked. However, in light of Mormonism's sacramentalism, view of priesthood, and liturgical preoccupation with the departed, Stephen Webb's assessment is correct: Joseph Smith "was, in a way, reinventing Catholicism for a time and a place that did not have access to a truly Catholic presence."[20]

As we saw, Mormonism's version of covenant theology pushed the gospel narrative into primordial beginnings, and it sees saving sacraments as correspondingly rooted in antiquity. Consistent with Mormonism's vision of a gospel that preceded Christ's coming, Smith taught that the ordinances of the gospel were of eternal origin. In particular, Smith referred to Adam as the supreme priesthood authority in the human family holding "the keys of the universe," who would personally deliver up his stewardship to Christ preparatory to the second coming.[21] Adam, in other words, possessed the fullness of priesthood keys (or authority) to administer the ordinances of salvation. And to him was given responsibility to reveal to humankind those ordinances of salvation at the appointed times, either in his angelic role as Michael or through the intermediary of other celestial messengers. These ordinances God had "set . . . to be the same for Ever and ever."[22] Ordinances (or sacraments), in other words, are of divine origin and constituted the principal raison d'etre for the Restoration. They are non-negotiable, eternal, and the sine qua non of God's true church. There is, however, not a great deal of clarity about why that is so—other than the not insignificant reason that Mormons believe God has so dictated. Still, at least three explanations are implicit in Mormon scripture and Mormon pronouncements over time. Each constitutes a distinct rationale for the indispensability of the covenants effected through priesthood authority, which covenants are intrinsically bound up with salvific priesthood ordinances.

SACRAMENTS AS MORAL REINFORCEMENT

The Protestant explanation for the indispensability of sacraments is human weakness. In the Protestant conception, sacraments serve not as vehicles of grace but as facilitators of grace. They are not so much the channels through which divine power and mercy are transmitted to a fallen and morally weakened humanity as they are visible signs and aids. As Calvin wrote simply, "We have another help to our faith in the sacraments."[23] Charles Buck had pointed out that a sacrament originally meant an "oath," and the term continued in religious usage to denote "those ordinances of religion by which Christians came under an obligation" that was "equally sacred with that of an oath."[24] Melanchton, we noted, taught that sacraments were closely related to promises.[25] Calvin agreed that "there never is a sacrament without an antecedent promise"; hence, sacraments are "signs of the covenants."[26] Consistent with these conceptions, Mormons also hold saving ordinances—like baptism, priesthood ordination, endowment, and temple sealing—to be inextricably bound up with covenant-making, or reciprocal promises. Sacraments are seen as ways of confirming the believer in faith, strengthening the will, and empowering the spirit.

In the Old Testament, covenants affirm God's faithfulness and mercy; so, too, Mormon scripture indicates that after the expulsion from Eden, the gospel of repentance is preached to the first couple, and "all things were confirmed unto Adam, by an holy ordinance."[27] Ritualized covenants, in other words, reaffirm comforting pledges the Lord has made to a vulnerable and suffering humanity. In the Book of Mormon, the devout enter into covenants as a way of bolstering memory of reciprocal obligations.[28] The people of King Benjamin, as one example, make a covenant to be God's people, pledging to "remember to retain the name [of Christ] written always in your hearts." Mormons today partake of the Lord's Supper, in an ordinance that uses a form of "remember" four times.[29]

In this particular understanding of covenants, whether the efficacy associated with them derives from heavenly power or renewed commitment, ordinances are largely fortifying. Baptism, for example, does not itself supernaturally effect a remission of sins; it dramatically embodies a moment of profound commitment and catalyzes the repentance process that precedes and accompanies it. Similarly, a marriage sealing does not in this interpretation endow the relationship with special durability; the temple rituals simply formalize a relationship that must be renewed volitionally every day. Nothing keeps a couple eternally married except a commitment to fidelity and unity they daily confirm through love. In such a view, these rituals are not really binding or metaphysically grounded; they simply signify, embody, remind, and mentally and emotionally empower. "We are naturally forgetful," noted Brigham Young, "naturally prone to wander from that which is good." And "the gospel of salvation," steeped in covenants from birth through marriage till death, "is expressly for the purpose of changing" our inconstant disposition.[30]

SACRAMENTS AS THE COUNTER TO COSMIC ENTROPY

For Catholics, the sacraments are the vehicle God has chosen whereby his redemptive power and dominion over all things effect a saving transformation in the soul of the fallen individual. Paul writes, reassuringly, that "neither death, nor life, nor angels, nor rulers, nor things present, nor things to come, nor powers, nor height, nor depth, nor anything else in all creation, will be able to separate us from the love of God in Christ Jesus our Lord."[31] But something, apparently, can separate us from his presence—else salvation would be both universal and automatic. One could posit that only sin alienates humankind from a God "who cannot look upon sin with the least degree of allowance."[32] If so, then the ordinances are, as Protestants largely hold, signs of grace but not indispensable requirements; only righteousness, earned or imputed, is essential.

Mormons—like Catholics—are committed to the assertion that something more *is* required, that is, the performance of saving ordinances such as baptism. If these requirements are not mere caprice on God's part, then something else must be impeding the reunion of the repentant sinner with his God, something that those ordinances correct or compensate. By this logic, asking why God would separate families from each other, or children from God's presence, merely because they neglected to perform a ritual may be the wrong question. The more reasonable query would be, what is intrinsic to the structure of reality here or hereafter that will naturally disrupt harmony and associations and relationships, unless certain precautions are taken or remedies effected? Smith's own life was marred by tragedy and frequent loss. He came to feel through personal experience that the vicissitudes of mortality and the powers of darkness tend toward chaos, entropy, and disintegration. Sealing powers may here be seen as real ways of manipulating and controlling actual powers or forces that counteract those effects, forming durable bonds that connect individuals to each other and to God. In spite of the best efforts of the most earnest human individuals, marriages fail, friendships fade, and family ties falter.

For Smith, the priesthood provided access to real heavenly powers that effected powerful connections durable enough to survive the deleterious results of sin, of death, or of time. He repeatedly referred to the most important aspect of the priesthood as its "sealing powers," agencies that unite loved ones to each other and to God eternally.[33] That these are more than figurative powers is suggested by Smith's reference to metaphysical capabilities associated with the priesthood: "translation [as of Elijah] is a power which belongs to this priesthood"; so is resurrection,[34] the capacity to expel demons and cure sickness,[35] the power to generate "endless lives" (a post-resurrection posterity),[36] and the need to "handle or control" such priesthood powers in righteousness.[37] In sum, the priesthood consists of such "mystery, power, and glory . . . that the angels desired to understand it and cannot."[38] His confidence in the strength and efficacy of these God-dispensed powers was most evident in his assertion, probably said with deliberate overstatement, "If you have power to seal on earth & in heaven then we should be Crafty, the first thing you do go & seal on earth your sons & daughters unto yourself, & yourself unto your fathers in eternal glory, & go ahead and not go back, but use a little Craftiness & seal all you can. . . . I will walk through the gate of heaven and Claim what I seal."[39] Within this framework, ordinances would operate as the channels through which priesthood power is operative, and by which it overcomes or resists forces and processes that divide, fracture, and alienate humans from God and from each other.

SACRAMENTAL COVENANTS AS CONSTITUTIVE OF HEAVEN

Elements of both those paradigms outlined above find a place in Mormon thinking about sacraments. But in addition to borrowings from both Protestant and Catholic sacramental theology, Mormonism stakes out a third foundation on which to erect its own conception of covenants and ordinances, one that gives special emphasis to the performative power of ritual itself. And this emphasis derives from a particular Mormon theology of embodiment and the nature of heavenly existence.

It may be true, as Catherine Bell argues, that "there is no clear and widely shared explanation of what constitutes ritual or how to understand it."[40] However, most theory of ritual recognizes the primacy of the body as "embodied existence," "the fundamental means of human presence," "the fundamental sign for human communication."[41] Also in distinction from those theorists who depict ritual as symbolic, or "a vehicle . . . for sustaining a particular culture's root metaphor," other critics like Talal Asad emphasize the instrumental value of bodily ritual as "parts of a Christian program for creating in its performers, by means of regulated practice, the 'mental and moral dispositions' appropriate to Christians."[42] This follows from a covenantal sacrament being the physical enactment of a moral decision made in a deliberative ritualistic manner. The bodily dimension to ritual gives the action a particular efficacy insofar as it concretizes deliberate choice; it transforms inchoate desire into somatic form. Covenant is the verbal, and ritual the performative, recognition of law's benevolent dominion. Given the premises of Mormon theology, however, sacraments do more than just shape character and instill virtuous dispositions.

J. L. Austin long ago pointed out that some verbal actions are "performative," that is, their utterance can actually change or introduce new realities.[43] "I promise," "I now pronounce you man and wife," "we declare ourselves free and independent"—all such utterances bring into existence a new condition or state of affairs: a promise, a marriage, or an independent country. In an analogous way, covenantal pronouncements, spoken under the right conditions of priesthood authority, personal worthiness, and the confirmatory sanction of the Holy Spirit, become an enacted form of love that constitutes a new eternal reality. The Catholic theologian Dietrich von Hildebrand was emphatic in asserting the objective reality of bonds that are called into being by volitional acts. Specifically, the liability that is called into being by making a promise, he argues, cannot be reduced to a mere, subjective sense of obligation. A debt or obligation predicated on a personal promise or assurance is not simply a feeling. It is a "perversion" to reduce "to an affective state something which is not in the affective state at all, or which by its very nature cannot be a feeling. . . . It is a degradation and a desubstantialization for an objective bond to be reduced to mere feeling."[44] As he argues, covenants, as a type of promise with particular potency, undergirded by profound love, create durable interpersonal realities. Jonathan Stapley finds an analogy in the Catholic Eucharist. "As the priest who holds the host at the altar to materialize the flesh of Christ, the Mormon priest materialized heaven at his altar, sealing wife to husband and child to parent. Where these linkages did not exist, there was simply no heaven; where they did exist, so did heaven."[45]

Mormonism makes of this relational heaven more than metaphor or vague analogy. Mormon belief in a continuity between embodied relationality in this world and embodied relationality in the next is why Mormon conceptions of embodiedness constitute a new kind of sacramentalism. Brooks Holifield has noted, "Reformed sacramental doctrine . . . rested on the supposition that matter and spirit were fundamentally antithetical, a conviction that rendered problematic any profoundly sacramental understanding of Christian religion. How after all could corporeal elements and visible actions convey spiritual life and grace?"[46] Mormons deny such an opposition as a first principle. "The earthly is the image of the Heavenly," Smith said.[47] By this he meant "that which is earthly conform[s] to that which is heavenly," or "that which is temporal [is] in the likeness of that which is spiritual."[48] This may have been what Brigham Young referred to a few years later, preaching that "all things were created spiritual, then temporal," where they are "disorganized and wait for a reorganization."[49] Sacraments in this framework do not symbolize or portend eternal realities; they constitute them, since the medium ("corporeal elements" and "visible actions") itself is the stuff of the eternities.

Mormon sacramentalism is a logical extension of Augustine's belief that "the essence of grace is love and the essence of man's salvation that he should become loving."[50] Mormon sacraments (with their accompanying covenants) simply channel and concretize that love into durable relationality. Through baptism, we formally and publicly agree that we accept Christ's invitation to be our spiritual Father. We thus signal our desire to be adopted into His family. Through further covenantal gestures, we affirm our commitment to bind ourselves more closely to him and concretely establish a relationship of reciprocity, through progressively greater demonstrations of our love and fidelity. And in Mormon temple marriage, individuals enact their willingness to expand the intimate association with the Divine, both laterally through marriage and vertically through posterity. These examples illuminate Joseph Smith's cardinal insight and most fundamental theological claim: Elijah, he came to believe, "*shall reveal the covenants to seal the hearts of the fathers to the children and the children to the fathers.*"[51]

Sacred sacraments provide an unchanging framework for fashioning and sustaining an intimate, individualized relationship to other beings, human and divine. As Ryan Davis argues, the connection to this view of sacramentalism is implicit in Smith's designation of heaven as primarily characterized by the relationships of which it consists.[52] In a revelation to Smith so theologically significant that early Mormons referred to it as simply "The Vision" (section 76 of the Doctrine and Covenants), heaven is portrayed as a three-tiered realm. In this vision that Smith (together with Sidney Rigdon) experienced in 1832, the wicked of the earth are consigned to inhabit the telestial kingdom, the lowest of the kingdoms of glory. Here, as in Dante's Hell, we find those "who are liars, and . . . adulterers, and whoremongers." But in Smith's vision, their inheritance is no inferno but a kingdom of glory, which "surpasses all understanding."[53] The middle kingdom of heaven or second degree of glory is described as a more conventional heaven, consisting of "the honorable men of the earth," and those who accept Christ after being taught in the spirit world.[54] Theirs is a kingdom of salvation and of glory, and they "receive of the presence of the Son." And the terrestrial kingdom "excels in all things the glory of the telestial."[55] This heaven, it would appear, is the heaven of conventional Christian tradition. Good people, believers in Christ, who will live with him eternally.

But the highest Mormon heaven is not the heaven of conventional Christian soteriology. Smith wrote in a canonized revelation that "that same sociality which exists among us here will exist among us there, only it will be coupled with eternal glory, which glory we do not now enjoy."[56] "Divine families encircled by his fire and light are the very essence of life and eternal," in Truman Madsen's words.[57]

Many writers have noted that Mormonism's heaven is anthropocentric rather than Christo- or theocentric. In other words, heaven seems more about eternal families than about heavenly choirs adoring the ineffable Divine. Such a characterization perpetuates a false dichotomy. For in the Mormon conception, the ideal of all godly striving eventuates in eternal communion with spouse, family, friends— *and a Heavenly Father and Mother.* It is not either/or, but both/and. Considering themselves literal progeny of heavenly parents, Mormons aspire to fully realize a web of kinship in the next life that incorporates virtually everyone into the Heavenly Family. Another way of saying this is that for Mormons, heaven is relational, not situational. It is not where you are but in what kind of relationship you find yourself that determines the degree of blessedness or perdition.

Mormonism is in this regard a profoundly personalist theology. It is in full accord with Martin Buber's principle that "the longing for relation is primary, the cupped hand into which the being that confronts us nestles." Relationships can become the mechanism for effecting the salvific transformation of humans as objects into persons as subjects: "the individual *It* can become a *You* [only] by entering into the event of relation."[58] A heaven constituted of and by relationality to other beings, unlike the static condition of eternal contemplation, would be a dynamic mode of being. For as Emmanuel Levinas notes, loving relations, whether of kindred or friends, are marked by "something unfilled, a permanent desire. . . . The burning bush that feeds flames is not consumed."[59]

And so Mormonism, as Smith's vision of heaven portended, effects a distinction between simple moral goodness and the constituting of celestial relationships. The most perfect man or woman—the one who embodies the most perfect honesty, humility, purity, wisdom, kindness—is not necessarily or therefore in relationship with anyone or any God. Davis's insight, in other words, is that perfect compliance with moral law cannot of itself create the sociability of which heaven consists. Virtuous attributes acquired in a vacuum are not themselves constitutive of any relationship. Even sinlessness is itself not indicative of any bond with any other person, divine or human, since one may be honest, chaste, benevolent, and virtuous, in isolation or remoteness from any other human being—as generations of desert ascetics proved. Being a good person doesn't of itself put us into meaningful connection with anyone. That is why, according to Joseph Smith's vision of the heavenly kingdoms, the honorable men and women of the earth are saved in a kingdom of glory but are not in the Father's presence. Not because they do not "deserve" it or qualify for it but because, given the opportunity, they have not yet created the virtuous, love-filled relationships such a position entails. We forge relationships with individuals interpersonally in the world of action, not privately in the chambers of our own conscience or by habits of moral reflection.

This groundwork also explains how seemingly arbitrary performances can be indispensable in the process of divinization. Gospel ordinances become the very ground on which the particularism of a specific, personal relationship with the Divine becomes enacted. Ordinances make possible our response to God's invitation. Acquiescence to laws that are not grounded in or motivated by external moral considerations may be what makes compliance with these kinds of ritual performances particularly powerful in constituting relationship. Kenneth Kirk seems in implicit agreement here. As he writes, "A system of thought which is primarily moralistic, in so far as it sets before men a rule of conduct by which it is their first duty to measure themselves, is in essence egocentric."[60] Covenantal relationships may be seen, therefore, as Mormonism's response to the almost insoluble problem that Kirk laid at the feet of all religious systems: "If my aim in life is to attain a specified standard, or to live according to a defined code, I am bound continually to be considering myself, and measuring the distance between my actual attainment and the ideal. It is impossible by such a road to attain the self-forgetfulness which we believe to be the essence of sanctity."[61] Covenants reassert relationship rather than dutiful obedience at the summit of worship, turning our preoccupation outward rather than inward. This is the crucial sense in which Mormon sacramentalism guides Latter-day Saints in the direction of true worship that is other-directed.

In C. S. Lewis's masterful retelling of the Fall, an angel in human form explains to Eve's counterpart why some of God's directives seem random, capricious. "He made one law of that kind in order that there might be obedience. In all these other matters what you call obeying Him is but doing what seems good in your own eyes also. Is love content with that? Where can you taste the joy of obeying," he asks, "unless He bids you do something for which His bidding is the only reason?"[62] In the Mormon version of this kind of covenantal interaction, an angel asks a recently exiled Adam why he is offering sacrifice to God. "And Adam said unto him: I know not, save the Lord commanded me."[63] Martin Luther gestured in a similar direction when he reasoned that as "feasts [are] the test of temperance, pleasures the test of chastity, so ceremonies are the test of the righteousness of faith."[64] But it is not blind obedience that is the supposed virtue here demonstrated. What is revealed is rather a relationship of loving trust, and that relationship alone is the impetus behind Adam's compliance. It is what Reinhold Niebuhr refers to as the love that "transcends obedience."[65] It is submission to a father's request that has no apparent grounding, rational basis, or inherent moral worth—and the less the logical, rational, or moral motivation for obedience to that personal request, the more the subject's loving trust is foregrounded and developed. Its very arbitrariness is the precondition for its exemplary drawing forth of love and of the bonds that ensue. This is a truth experienced by any who have known the love that is forged in the fires of devotion to a beloved's desires rather than in the calculations of reasonableness and reciprocal benefit.

Sacramental performances constitute a living, dynamic relationship through a set of ritual performances. We willfully and bodily participate in the forging of that relationship as a response to a personal beckoning, rather than an impersonal moral imperative. Personal holiness is a *precondition* for living in the presence of a being who is compared to "devouring fire" and "everlasting flames."[66] But holiness does not itself constitute a relationship with that Being—and is in fact inconceivable apart from such relationship. Interpersonal relationships, with humans and with the Divine, are forged in the realm of interactions: promises, pledges, obligations, and freely rendered acts of love. In earthly domains, as in heavenly kingdoms, we create meaningful bonds and connections by what we specifically do with, for, and at the behest of the other. Ordinances make possible, through covenants and sacraments God established "before the world was,"[67] a personal response to his invitation. This is why Mormonism must reject a Protestant leader's eminently reasonable supposition that "the true believer, considered in the abstract, possesses all the *moral* qualifications necessary for salvation," and ordinances are therefore dispensable if God so determines.[68]

In the Mormon view, sacramental covenants are not a prerequisite to salvation—they are constitutive of salvation. This is the sense in which Mormons believe that "a covenant *is* a special relationship with the Lord into which a person or a group may enter" (my emphasis).[69] And this special relationship is one in which, from the beginning of time, Heavenly Parents envisioned as available to the entire human race—not a fortunate few.

RESCUE OF THE DEAD

"A self-understanding as a set-apart community of the saved . . . has been a hallmark of Christian communities since their earliest days, and the Christian imagination in the West has usually drawn a sharp boundary at death, following this general principle: If an individual did not join up with the saved community during this life, joining after death would be impossible."[70] Along with the doctrine of Original Sin, this damnation of the uncatechized and unbaptized is one of the most distressing—and ancient—problems in the history of Christian thought. As the author of the *Clementine Recognitions*, a fourth-century narrative, put the urgent question: "If those shall enjoy the kingdom of Christ, whom His coming shall find righteous, shall then those be wholly deprived of the kingdom who have died before his coming?"[71] The answer for the vast majority of Christian history has been an almost unqualified yes. With the exception of a few righteous patriarchs rescued by Christ's "harrowing of hell," there was emphatically no salvation outside the Mother Church.[72] Indeed, for Thomas Aquinas, the existence of a populous hell was a factor in the happiness of the saved. The psalmist foretells a perverse Schadenfreude in God's justice: "The righteous will rejoice when they see vengeance done; they will bathe their feet in the blood of the wicked."[73] Aquinas took this quite literally: "In order that the happiness of the saints may be more delightful to them and that they may render more copious thanks to God for it, they are allowed to see perfectly the sufferings of the damned."[74] Catholics had no monopoly on esteeming hell's place in the scheme of things. The Anglican William Dawes also felt eternal suffering of the wicked gave the saved "a motive to be 'still more sensible' of their own felicity."[75]

The Reformation made some (or all) sacraments expendable, but salvation was still a highly limited affair. Free or predestined, relying upon faith or relying upon works, most of humankind would find themselves outside of paradise, especially given the fact that the greater part of the earth's billions never had access to either church sacraments or knowledge of Christ. This takes us to a second and a third of Smith's major ruptures with Protestantism after his sacramental theology: the scope of salvation available through salvific sacraments, and the role of the living in the state and condition of the dead. Like Catholics, Mormons believe sacraments are requisite for salvation. Unlike Catholics (and Protestants), Mormons believe sacraments can be performed universally, on behalf of the dead as well as the living. This belief follows logically from the universalist impulse in Mormon theology, which sees the mortal experience as a stage through which—on their path toward the full *imitatio dei*—all eternally existing human spirits must pass, albeit the greater number under less than ideal conditions. Provisions were therefore instituted for a practice of sacramentalism that would be available to the entirety of the race. That is why the ordinances were "ordained and prepared before the foundation of the world, for the salvation of the dead who should die without a knowledge of the gospel."[76]

Clearly, many more humans have died without receiving Christian sacraments of any kind than with them. Even more minuscule is the number of earthly inhabitants who have complied with the New and Everlasting Covenant and the accompanying sacraments restored through Smith. To some (even within Mormonism) this imbalance suggests an elitist religion, a heaven narrowly confined to a few presumptuous Latter-day Saints elevated above teeming billions of humanity. But the expansive view of vicarious salvation proffered in Mormon theology suggests a very different state of affairs. As J. Reuben Clark described the salvational plan of the Divine Council, "God will save all of His children that he can; and while, if we live unrighteously here, we shall not go to the other side in the same status, so to speak, as those who lived righteously; nevertheless, the unrighteous will have their chance, and in the eons of the eternities that are to follow, they, too, may climb to the destinies to which they who are righteous and serve God, have climbed to those eternities that are to come."[77]

"Eternity," as James Talmage wrote, "is progressive."[78] That is because, Parley Pratt wrote, God creates those conditions most favorable for the endless advance of his progeny "through every form of life, birth, change, and resurrection, and every form of progress in knowledge and experience." This great work of the Father, like the universe itself, will be "endless or eternally progressive. . . . While eternal charity endures, or eternity itself rolls its successive ages, the heavens will multiply and new worlds and more people will be added to the kingdoms of the Fathers. Thus, in the progress of events, unnumbered millions of worlds and of systems of worlds will necessarily be called into requisition and be filled by man, beast, fowl, tree, and all the vast varieties of beings and things ever budded and blossomed in Eden."

While the Catholic Church had condemned Origen's hope of universal salvation in the sixth century,[79] the heresy had reappeared from time to time—notably in eighteenth-century universalism. Universalists like Charles Chauncy and John Murray hoped for a general salvation but were unsure how the dead could comply with the requirements of Christian discipleship. " 'Tis true," Chauncy conceded, God "will not, in this state, prevail upon all willingly to bow down before him as their Lord. . . . May he not, . . . use means with sinners in the next state, in order to make them good subjects in the moral kingdom of God?"[80] Sacraments could have no place in their scheme, since these Universalists lacked any concept of vicarious availability. As for the biblical edicts forecasting eternal damnation for some, Murray reasoned that the pain of a candle flame is brief, but the pain is still "of everlasting fire."[81] Smith's grandfather Asael Smith was a devoted Universalist, and Joseph Sr. was for a time.[82] In an 1829 revelation, before he had even organized the church, Joseph adopted the same rationalization as Murray in explaining away endless torment of the wicked ("eternal punishment is God's punishment"[83]), and a twentieth-century General Authority was still channeling the spirit of Murray and Chauncy with a Catholic sensibility; Hyrum M. Smith cited one Thomas Shackelton as arguing that

the definition of eternal punishment, or everlasting punishment, is much misunderstood, and that the ordinary thought that it means an unending punishment is not taught in the Holy Bible. The Holy Bible teaches that the Author and Father of all life is eternal; is everlasting; hence the punishment meted out to unrepentant souls is the punishment of the eternal or everlasting Father, and the words eternal punishment have no reference to time whatsoever, but simply refer to the punishment, as being God's punishment; hence is eternal punishment, or punishment by the Eternal One. As proof I refer to the Epistle of Peter in which he speaks of Christ whilst His body was in the tomb, preaching to the spirits of those who for some time during the days of Noah were unrepentant; showing there was a hope of final salvation for all through faith in Christ, and thus it's right to pray for our dead.[84]

Mormonism effects a unique theological synthesis between a Catholic-like necessity for sacraments and a Universalist-like refusal to make access to the gospel and its sacraments dependent upon birth in the right place, circumstance, and historical moment. The consequence of this synthesis is an ambitious program to perform on a massive scale those sacraments that enable and concretize the divinization of humanity and their incorporation into a celestial community, on behalf of the departed by the small numbers of believers. John Wesley had called the paradise of scripture "the porch of heaven," where "the spirits of just men are made perfect."[85] So do Latter-day Saints see paradise, or the spirit world, as a temporary abode (along with hell), where those receptive to the gospel continue to work out their salvation. In a reversal of the usual Christian perspective, Latter-day Saints see salvation as primarily a work of redeeming the dead, through the instrumentality of the living curators of the temples where such work is performed. Such priorities are not inconsistent with Mormon missiology. Like other Christian churches, Mormonism takes the Great Commission as a divine mandate regardless of the prospects of universal success. Believing in "the blessed and happy state of those that keep the commandments of God," that "this life is the [optimum] time for men to prepare to meet God," and that the laborers in the vineyard are "few," Mormonism aspires to enlist fellow workers and promulgate a gospel of peace and joy to the maximum benefit of the world's population.[86]

The Book of Mormon details a panoramic vision of the earth's future and the role of the restored church in the latter days. On a par with the Revelation of John, this vision of Nephi describes the great contest between the people of God and those who oppose his work. Whether Nephi's terminology refers to adherents of the Restored church or a more general invisible church that transcends institutional boundaries, he notes that "the church of the Lamb of God, and its numbers were few, . . . and their dominions upon the face of the earth were small."[87] Rodney Stark may have predicted, to the delight of many Mormons, a church on the threshold "of becoming the first major faith to appear on earth since the Prophet Mohammed rode out of the desert."[88] But Mormon scripture makes no such prognosis; nor, in light of over a hundred temples and a genealogical program that already involves billions of names, are such numbers essential to Mormonism's self-conceived mission.

The fact that the dead must rely upon the living for the execution of sacramental rituals, effecting a chain of influence between the two realms, was so starkly reminiscent of the Catholic perspective that critics were quick to see the parallel. "You are as bad as the papists," said some, as soon as Mormonism inaugurated vicarious sacramental work. Rather than deny the similarity, the Mormon editor Thomas Ward responded: "We believe, that fallen as the Roman church may be, she has traces of many glorious principles that were once in the church of Christ, of which . . . the protestant world knows nothing."[89] When Smith affirmed, in his last recorded sermon, that "the old Catholic Church is worth more than all" the other sects, he might well have had in mind its refusal to regard the barrier of death as limiting human works of mercy to the living.[90]

Of Luther's ninety-five theses, a high percentage expressed his dissent from orthodox teachings regarding the dead, and the ability of the living to affect their future condition (especially via indulgences). Penance can only be imposed on the living, he insisted (Thesis 8). Papal decrees cease to apply at death (9). "The dying are freed by death from all penalties" (13), and "Who knows whether all souls in purgatory wish to be redeemed?" (29).[91] Meanwhile in England, the second version of the Book of Common Prayer (1552) removed even burial prayers offered on behalf of the dead. "Graunte . . . that at the daye of judgement his soule and all the soules of thy electe, departed out of this lyfe, may with us and we with them, fully receive thy promises," read the first version.[92] But wishing to shun every vestige of Catholic reaching beyond the grave, Thomas Cranmer decided such prayers "smacked of the old religion in which the living could perform religious acts on behalf of the dead," in one scholar's words.[93] Calvin agreed that even "commending [the dead] to his grace" was unscriptural and inappropriate.[94] Three hundred years later, Protestants were still hostile to any gestures that suggested living Christians could influence the disposition of the departed. And all Protestants had been united in rejecting purgatory. As Calvin's biographer notes, "There is, for Protestants, only heaven and hell," and the disposition to one or the other was final.[95] But if, as apostle James Talmage pointed out crucially, the LDS faith envisions "the possibility of a universal salvation,"[96] then that universalism must find a way to include the vast billions of the uncatechized within its orbit. And so Mormonism developed a theology of the period between mortality and final judgment where evangelizing continues, in a process that encompasses the living and the dead with little regard for boundaries between the two. And the permeability of that membrane radically reshapes the nature of human interdependence.

Luther wrote that a Christian should "give [him]self as a Christ to [his] neighbor, just as Christ offered himself to me."[97] The imitation of Christ has generally been taken as a challenge to emulate the life and deeds of Jesus. Luther's analogy goes a bit further, suggesting that in ministering to a fellow pilgrim, we can function in a comparable role—serving as a conduit of relief or succor, sacrificing our time or means as "a Christ." Latter-day Saints take the analogy further still, by a robust reading of Obadiah, who referred to "saviours [who] shall come up on mount Zion."[98] Smith first invoked that scriptural expression in 1841, seeing in it a reference to the Abrahamic promise of a literal seed who would bless "all the families of the earth . . . with the blessings of the gospel."[99] He apparently had more than missionary work in mind. Less than a year earlier, he had introduced a doctrine of vicarious baptism for the dead, and he soon drew the expression and the practice together. That October he preached publicly that " 'Baptism for the Dead' was the only way that men can appear as saviors on mount Zion."[100]

The project of performing vicarious baptisms on behalf of the deceased soon grew to include the entire range of saving ordinance. Mormons see God's "work and glory" to be the "bring[ing] to pass the immortality and eternal life of man."[101] Christ's atonement is the seminal event that makes the grand project possible; the *imitatio Christi*, in this vision, entails a shared, cooperative engagement in the ministry of the gospel and the administration of its ordinances. "Administer salvation to your fellow beings," Young said more than once.[102] "I administer to others in the priesthood, and that make me a savior."[103] (Given the participation of women in administering temple ordinances and being ordained as missionaries, the prerogative is clearly not limited to males in LDS practice.) The effect of this joint endeavor in the Mormon mind is not the arrogation of divine authority or function but the burden and vision of a shared purpose, one that emphasizes human dependence on Christ and on each other. Or, as Young phrased the principle, "You need not expect salvation, except you can administer the same salvation to others, both in precept and example."[104] "We are all dependent on one another for our exaltation [and] our interests are inseparably connected," he said in another setting.[105] If the major challenge facing the institutionalization of religion is to counteract the self-directedness of a programmatic Christianity, then making salvation a communal enterprise in this way can be a powerful prophylactic, reversing the direction of religious concern from self to other.

Though there is no evidence of direct influence, Mormons have long cited the epistle of Peter as providing the biblical foundation for Mormonism's conception of vicarious ordinance work. Certainly one of the first questions that must have occurred to early Christians concerned the destiny of those good men and women who live and die before or outside the reach of the Christian message. As we saw, the

Pseudo-Clement put the question to Peter, "Shall then those be wholly deprived of the kingdom who have died before His coming?"[106] The New Testament says little on the subject, with a few critical exceptions. The first epistle of Peter made provocative reference to Christ having gone, in the spirit after his death, to "the spirits in prison" where he preached to those who were disbelievers "in the days of Noah" This was so that hearing the "gospel . . . proclaimed" to them, they could "live in the spirit as God does."[107] And when Jesus gave the keys of the kingdom to Peter, he did so with the promise that "the gates of hades will not prevail against" the church.[108]

If the gates of hades are taken to mean the barriers that keep the dead entombed, then the verse can suggest a power whereby "liberty is proclaimed to the captives" in spite of Satan's dominion. Such a reading of this postmortal event would suggest mere announcement of Christ's victory over death and a coming resurrection. An alternate reading would see in such passages the promise of an actual ministry among deceased pre-Christians. In the early church, many documents emphasized just such a postmortal reach of the gospel into the spirit world. In particular, Adolf von Harnack and Carl Schmidt noted that a major theme of the forty-day ministry of Jesus, in the extra-canonical sources, was salvation for the dead.[109] One popular text in the second century, the *Epistula Apostolorum*, described what Jesus was teaching following his resurrection. "Stand up and I will reveal to you what is on earth, and what is above the heaven," he said, *after* "the work that was accomplished in the flesh, that he was crucified, and his ascension."[110] Describing his descent into hell, Jesus indicated that in order to make possible their ascent "from the rest which is below into heaven," he brought the deceased both the gospel and "*the baptism of life and forgiveness* [emphasis added]," because "whoever believes in me and does not do my commandment receives . . . no benefit from it." And then he adds, "for what I have promised you I will also give to them, that they may come out of the prison."[111]

This theme is also present among the Church Fathers, who were acutely aware of the difficulties involved in models of limited redemption and envisioned a more expansive gospel. Clement of Alexandria wrote that "Christ is mighty to save, according to principles of justice and equality, those who turn to him, whether here or in the next world" (which is why "the Lord [and 'the apostles'] preached the Gospel to those in Hades") in order that "all who believe shall be saved, . . . on making profession there." Even the punishments of hell, therefore "are saving and disciplinary, leading to conversion."[112] Irenaeus was equally emphatic: "It was not merely for those who believed on Him in the time of Tiberius Caesar that Christ came, nor did the Father exercise his providence for the men only who are now alive, but for all men altogether, who from the beginning, according to their capacity, in their generation have both feared and loved God."[113] Although Christ's descent into

hell was inscribed in both the Apostles' Creed and the Athanasian Creed, it has seldom been taken by orthodox Christians to suggest an actual work of preaching and
conversion taking place among the dead.

Some early nineteenth-century Shakers claimed visions of the spirit world in
which they beheld some of the dead "receiving the gospel," with a consequent less-
ening of their torments.[114] Earlier, Ann Lee and her companion James Whittaker
claimed to see many spirits "which appeared to be attentive to hear and receive the
word."[115] Emanuel Swedenborg, too, saw in a vision that "the Lord called together
his twelve disciples, who are now angels, and sent them out to the entire spiritual
world with the command to preach the gospel there anew."[116] What Smith added to
this modern history of the idea was an entire range of sacramental work performed
here to the accompaniment of preaching the Word there. In other words, while
Catholic sacramentalism brought the blessings of eternity to the living, Mormon
sacramentalism extended those blessings to the already dead. Believing that the
work of evangelizing in the spirit world would open the hearts of myriad spirits to
Christ, Mormons perform the ordinances of salvation on their behalf. The efficacy
of such sacraments is contingent on the other-worldly acceptance of the gospel by
those departed souls. As to why those sacraments cannot be performed in the world
of spirits or how the principle of vicarious substitution works, Mormon theology
has little to say. Brigham Young stated the standard position, when he asked rhetorically, "Can [departed souls] have hands laid upon them for the gift of the Holy
Ghost? No. None of the outward ordinances that pertain to the flesh are administered there, but the light, glory, and power of the Holy Ghost are enjoyed just
as freely as upon this earth; and there are laws which govern and control the spirit
world, and to which they are subject."[117]

John Durham Peters has argued that Smith espoused a principle of substitutional
validity that ran parallel with a law of sacred recordkeeping, according to which an
agent can stand in for a departed soul, just as a properly attested document fills the
function of a live witness. As Peters quotes Smith, in regard to the recording of sacraments themselves,

> the Record shall be just as holy, and shall answer the ordinance just the same as
> if [the general recorder] had seen with his eyes and heard with his ears. . . . The
> recorder need not have been a direct witness; certificates from those who were
> present are just as binding. Here documents make experience transportable—
> or irrelevant. . . . Here he substitutes documents for people. We have almost
> arrived at Smith's vision of vicarious action. The operations of witnessing with
> a certificate and baptizing a living person for a dead one both invest great
> power in proxies.[118]

Smith affirmed, but did not fully explain, the power behind the principle. "It may seem to some, to be a very bold doctrine that we talk of; a power which records, or binds on earth, and binds in heaven. Nevertheless, . . . whatsoever those men did in authority, in the name of the Lord, and did it truly and faithfully, and kept a proper and faithful record of the same, it became a law on earth and in heaven; and could not be annulled according to the decree of the great Jehovah."[119]

Belief in a virtually universal salvation predicated on vicarious sacraments explains the Mormon church's colossal program of genealogical research. As Nathaniel Givens has remarked, "Mormons view physicality as so axiomatic that the entire problem [of universal vicarious baptism] became essentially logistical rather than theological."[120] In 1894, church president Wilford Woodruff framed the implications of Mormon theology of salvation as a simple if daunting imperative: "We want the Latter-day Saints from this time to trace their genealogies as far as they can, and to be sealed to their fathers and mothers . . . and run this chain as far as you can get it."[121] Smith had laid the foundations for this endeavor when he preached, "The greatest responsibility resting upon us is to look after our dead,"[122] later adding in a paraphrase of the letter to the Hebrews that "we cannot be made perfect without [each other]."[123] The reciprocity of the relationship suggests more is involved here than a requirement that the living act charitably to perform ordinances on behalf of the deceased. The active work of excavating one's family history and performing ordinance work on their behalf is not a gauge of unselfish service that *qualifies one* or is a *requirement* for salvation; the incorporation of the deceased into sacred relationship with the living is—like the binding of living families through ordinance work—*constitutive* of heaven. That is why it "is necessary . . . to meet the promises made by Jesus Christ before the foundation of the world for the salvation of man."[124]

Following Woodruff's announcement, the church sponsored the Genealogical Society of Utah to facilitate the task. Today, the renamed Family History Department, with its thousands of satellite libraries, provides access to over two billion names, found in sources "from 14th century English church records to African oral histories."[125] The locus for this ambitious project of universal salvation is a structure which Smith reintroduced in a Christian context: the temple. Long before Solomon's temple, writes one scholar, temples had served as representations of "the eternal existence of an ordered universe as opposed to the chaotic forces which . . . attempt . . . to destroy that order."[126] Of primary importance in that notion of eternal order, in Mormon thought, is the status and durability of human relations to each other and to the Divine. The temple is where those relations are most fully articulated and concretized.

TEMPLE IN ANTIQUITY

In its role as "the site of the revelation of the Divine Presence," the temple is inescapably charged in Jewish history and memory with the glory of God as "the place from which the Divine Presence reveals itself to the prophet."[127] In spite of what came to be its principal function as "a place of assembly for the entire people for purposes of sacrifice, prayer, and thanksgiving," its roots in the portable tabernacle point to a deep-seated identity as God's domicile.[128] "The dwelling of the Lord" is the translation of the phrase *Mishkan YHWH*; the " 'Tent of Meeting,' i.e., where the Lord meets with—reveals Himself to—man," is the meaning of the Tabernacle's other designation, *'Ohel Mo'ed*.[129]

Consistent with this motif, Kenneth Kirk, bishop of Oxford and theologian, quotes an ancient Jewish text that portrays a coming day when God and men freely mingle on companionable terms. "A king went into his garden to speak to his gardener, but the gardener hid himself from him. Then said the king, 'Why hidest thou from me? See I am even as thou.'—So too shall God walk with the righteous in the earthly Paradise after the resurrection; and they shall see Him and quake before Him. Then shall He say unto them, 'Fear not; for lo! I am even as ye.' "[130] Such Jewish motifs have much in common with a Platonic strain of theosis, which describes God as one who "being free of jealousy, . . . wanted everything to become as much like himself as was possible."[131] During canonical formation, however, Kirk notes that textual editors "developed the habit of substituting the phrase 'appear before Jahweh' or 'be seen by Jahweh' for the phrase 'see Jahweh. . . . When therefore the Old Testament canon closed, various influences combined to dim the hope of the individual Jew that he could see God."[132] Christians did not relinquish hope in a beatific vision. Indeed, as Kirk argues, the promise of Jesus that "the pure in heart . . . shall see God" is the aspiration around which the whole history of Christian ethics is plotted.[133] But temples were decidedly irrelevant to that purpose. As Gerald Smith notes, Daniel had prophesied the destruction of the Jerusalem sanctuary, and for Christians "the great spiritual body of believers had replaced any physical notions of modern temple architecture."[134]

Jon Levenson is correct that for prior generations the Hebrew Bible was often "essentially the only source of . . . knowledge" about the ancient Near East, while it "now provides only a small portion of our knowledge, one that becomes smaller with each new discovery."[135] Smith, however, relied heavily upon his reading of the Old Testament for what he knew about temples (and much else). In addition, given his own experience of an earthly encounter with the godhead and his recognition that God was not an ineffable, omnipresent spirit but an embodied being, Smith had no trouble seeing in temple tradition a literal, sacred interface of the eternal and the temporal realms. Christ was recorded in the New Testament as saying he had "nowhere to lay his head."[136] Upon laying the cornerstone of the Kirtland Temple and noting the absence of such a sanctuary in the long period before the era of Restoration, Smith declared that now "the Son of Man [has] where to lay his head."[137] And so he invoked God, in the dedicatory prayer to the temple, to "let thy house be filled, as with a rushing mighty wind, with thy glory."[138] In the days following the 1836 dedication, Smith claimed that Jesus Christ—the Jehovah of the Old Testament—did in fact physically appear within those temple walls, twice. On the second appearing, Smith saw him "standing upon the breast work of the pulpit. . . . His eyes were as a flame of fire; the hair of his head was white like the pure snow; his countenance shone above the brightness of the sun."[139]

A locus of sacred encounter between God and mortals is thus an enduring feature of temples and a motive for Mormon temple-building. Of greater significance, however, are the conditions temples supply for the enactment of those sacraments that constitute the celestialization and eternalization of relationships. If, as Geoffrey Wainwright notes, liturgy is "the symbolic focus of communion with God,"[140] then temple liturgy aspires to move beyond symbolism to the concrete rendering of relationship with the Divine. But why is a sacred edifice necessary? Christ was baptized in the river Jordan, and in many epochs old and modern, no more than an altar in the wilderness or portable tabernacle was available for holy rites. The answer, in Mormonism's reading of sacred history and biblical precedent, is that while stone altars and portable tabernacles would suffice in conditions of duress, a holy space representing a sacrificial offering of resources is more appropriate when circumstances permit. As Smith recorded the Lord's command to this effect, ad hoc performance of higher ordinances (like baptism for the dead) in wilderness rivers "cannot be acceptable to me, only in the days of your poverty." Therefore, as a people with growing stability and resources, the Lord indicated, "I command you, all ye my saints, to build a house unto me."[141] One can sense in this principle the words of King David, "I will not offer burnt offerings to the Lord my God that cost me nothing."[142]

These edifices, sanctified by sacrifice, are the designated place for the holiest of encounters between God and humans, in precincts visited by the divine presence, for sacred knowledge to be conveyed, instruction given, and the way back to a permanent divine presence fostered. Smith found a pattern for the full range of temple experience when he spoke of Moses having received saving, keys, signs, and words "on the Mountain top."[143]

In this literal visitation of Yahweh to Moses, described by Joseph Smith, the ancient prophet is tutored by means of a panoramic, cosmic vision that conveys the primordial origins, eternal destiny, and cosmic scope of God's plan for humankind.

"And it came to pass that Moses looked, and beheld the world upon which he was created; and Moses beheld the world and the ends thereof, and all the children of men which are, and which were created; and of the same he greatly marveled and wondered. And the presence of God withdrew from Moses."[144] Smith read in this episode the archetypal instance of that body of sacred instruction and sacramental covenants that constitute the temple ceremony. As Smith develops his temple theology, this heavenly endowment of knowledge and saving power came to constitute an "ancient order of things,"[145] that is, the entirety of an original everlasting covenant designed in primordial councils, one that affirms humanity's premortal origins, a sojourn into mortality that is a planned ascent rather than a calamitous fall, and an anticipated celestial destiny that the covenants and ordinances and communicated knowledge are designed to facilitate.

Smith believed that this crucial knowledge and its accompanying ordinances were taken away at the time of Israel's wilderness idolatry. As Smith revised the book of Exodus to read, after Moses destroys the tablets in wrathful response to the golden calf worship, Yahweh tells Moses he will reissue the stone tablets—but with a crucial caveat. He will deprive the Israelites of the fullness of the gospel that had accompanied them. "I will take away the [Melchizedek] priest-hood out of their midst; therefore my holy order; and the ordinances thereof, shall not go before them."[146] (Krister Stendahl refers to the idea of a revised, second set of tablets as a "common teaching in both Judaism and Christianity," and finds corroboration in Paul's words that the law "was added because of transgressions.")[147] This emended verse radically restructures Mormonism's understanding of the whole law/gospel and works/faith polarities that underlie so much of the Protestant theology of *sola gratia, sola fide*. In the light of Smith's corrections, the Mosaic law is powerless to save not because it is predicated on a doomed theology of works or a failed covenant of obedience, but because the Mosaic law is a New and Everlasting Covenant shorn of its saving power, that is, that higher priesthood and those sacramental ordinances "without [which] no one can behold the face of God."[148]

Christians by and large associate temples with Judaism, with an utterly pre-Christian history and purpose. However, Luke records matter-of-factly a time when "Peter and John were going up to the temple" to worship, and "there is an abundance of evidence," as S. G. F. Brandon writes, "that the Jerusalem Christians continued faithful in their reverence for the temple and in their observance of its cultus."[149] Marcus von Wellnitz notes the obvious fact that "the early Christians not only had their Sunday services, either in a Jewish synagogue or a member's domicile, but also that they still retained the periodic visit to the temple and saw no conflict in the dual nature of their worship."[150] As Margaret Barker has extensively shown, "the world view of the first Christians was expressed in, and derived from, the shape and the

liturgy of the temple in Jerusalem."[151] In particular, Barker sees incarnation, mediation, and atonement as key temple themes that are central to Christian thought.[152]
Though much of what transpired in the temple at Jerusalem involved sacrificial
offerings, the Temple Scroll discovered at Qumran envisions an eventual return to
the temple's ancient purpose: "renewal of the covenant made at Sinai, i.e., the temple
ordinances that were present before; from the beginning, the building was necessary
to accommodate them."[153] Barker's work illustrates the extent to which "the original
gospel message was about the temple, not the corrupted temple of Jesus' own time,
but the original temple which had been destroyed some six hundred years earlier."[154]
These views, however controversial, are consistent with Smith's understanding that
by recuperating the temple and the fullness of the priesthood he was restoring an
ancient order of things.

In early Israel, more than one temple was sacred to the Jewish people. Only with
Hezekiah and, more definitively, with Josiah, was the temple at Jerusalem "finally
established as the one and only sanctuary for the whole nation."[155] As with this earlier Israelite era, so did the Book of Mormon depict at least three temples among the
Nephite peoples, and Smith emulated that model of plurality.[156] More than 160 LDS
temples were planned or in operation by 2015. Greater access for the fifteen million
Mormons, however, has not made the temple more accessible to those outside the
pale of the church—and to even many within. This is because Mormons consider
temples to be holy sanctuaries, set apart from the quotidian, protected from the
curious and the inquisitive, and inaccessible even to many within the faith who do
not demonstrate the level of commitment and seriousness of purpose sufficient to
qualify for admission.

Temple Secrecy

The practice of restricted access to the Mormon temple has long provoked a range
of speculation. In 1870, Senator Aaron Cragin of New Hampshire went so far as to
repeat the rumor, on the Senate floor, that "an altar of sacrifice was actually built . . .
in the temple block, upon which human sacrifices were to be made."[157] By opening
temples to the public during an open house period, Mormons have precluded such
hysteria in the modern era; however, the hurt and resentment over exclusion has
often remained. Many of these sentiments signify a conflation and confusion in the
modern climate of the two concepts, secrecy and sanctity. As Spencer Fluhman notes,
"Just as sacred space can enclose secrets and mark membership in a Pueblo kiva or
for Muslims in Mecca, so it has been with Mormon temples' spatial restrictions."[158]

Moses was commanded to remove his shoes on the holy ground before the Lord's
presence signified by the burning bush. Only seventy elders were permitted to

assemble with him at the tabernacle to converse with the Lord.[159] The high priest alone could enter the Holy of Holies on the annual Day of Atonement. Christian architecture commemorated this practice in restricting the chancel, the area surrounding the altar of Eucharistic sacrifice, to the officiating clergy (and sometimes choir). Holy places, and holy knowledge, have traditionally depended upon being sequestered from the public gaze as a sign and guarantor of their sanctity. Jesus admonished his disciples to "not give what is holy to dogs; and . . . not throw your pearls before swine," and after the sacred encounter on the Mount of Transfiguration, he told Peter, James, and John to "tell no one about the vision" until a later time.[160] Paul wrote to the Corinthians that they might do well to consider the apostles as "servants of Christ and stewards of God's mysteries."[161] Mystery (μυστήριον) in its New Testament usage is generally taken to mean a truth that lies outside the province of normal ways of knowing, and is imparted by God to the spiritually minded. The Incarnation of Christ, or the Real Presence in the Eucharist, or the Atonement have all been referred to as such mysteries. However, examples appear in early Christianity of a conception of mysteries as certain practices kept hidden from the eyes of inquisitive outsiders. "Baptism, the Eucharist, and the oil of Chrism, were things that the uninitiated were not allowed to look upon," noted St. Basil (330–379). So, too, he said, with many particulars of church sacraments. They were all "guarded in a silence with which no prying curiosity might meddle, [our fathers] having been well taught to preserve the sanctity of the mysteries by silence."[162] As Spencer Fluhman writes, "Based on Jesus's instructions in Matthew 7:6, the 'discipline of the secret' guarded Christian practices and doctrines amid a skeptical pagan populace but also marked them as potentially subversive."[163]

Mormons resuscitated this conception of "silent sanctity," restricting the highest ordinances and their descriptions alike to those initiated into the temple and its ceremonies. The great irony is that Mormons practice a restrictive temple policy, and yet within those temple walls they aspire to initiate every human being who has ever lived into those same practices. And in his efforts to forge a "kingdom of priests,"[164] Smith opened the sacred space of the temple to all—including women, to the dismay of Masons from whom Smith adapted many of the temple rituals—who would prepare themselves to enter the Lord's presence. As Willard Richards remarked after his own endowment as one of the original handful: "there was nothing made known to us but [what] will be made known to all Saints, of the last days, so soon as they are prepared to receive [them]."[165] And for those not prepared in this life, Mormons profess the expectation that virtually all will eventually embrace the everlasting covenant in the worlds to come. As President Wilford Woodruff said in explaining why non-believers would henceforth be eligible for temple ordinances, "there will be very few, if any, who will not accept the Gospel" in the hereafter.[166]

Similarities between Mormon temple ritual and Masonic ritual have been noted from the beginning. Smith and most early Mormon leaders were Masons in the early 1840s, and in Nauvoo he borrowed extensively in creating the symbols, rituals, and oaths of secrecy that constituted Nauvoo Temple practice. Like many of his era, Smith believed the origins of masonry were in Solomon's temple, and so it seemed eminently reasonable to him, as he told Benjamin Jonson, that "Freemasonry, as at present, was the apostate endowments, as sectarian religion was the apostate religion."[167] Today the consensus is that Freemasonry was largely a development of the eighteenth century, with roots in medieval masonry guilds.

Michael Homer is correct that "Mormon historians in particular have neglected Masonic influences on their religion and rituals."[168] This is owing to a narrow view of prophetic inspiration that ignores Smith's explicit syncretism, and disregard of Smith's emphasis on cosmic narratives over forms and mechanics. Regarding the first, Smith was brazenly assimilationist in his restorationism, and Masonry was a prime example of his willingness to borrow freely. "The first and fundamental principle of our holy religion," he wrote to Isaac Galland, "is, that we believe we have a right to embrace all, and every item of truth, without limitation."[169] ("If you can find a truth in heaven or hell, it belongs to our doctrine," seconded Young. "We believe it; it is ours; we claim it.")[170] Here he was following in Augustine's steps, who wrote that there were "heathen" truths, which it was the right—even task—of Christians to retrieve, and put to "their proper use in preaching the gospel."[171]

Regarding narratives and mechanics, Smith employs Masonic elements promiscuously, but in the service, as we have seen, of a New and Everlasting Covenant that traces the human journey from premortal beginnings to an anticipated incorporation into a heavenly family. Richard Bushman's analysis is correct in plumbing the limits of parallelism. Unlike Masonry, he writes, "the spiritual core of the Nauvoo endowment was not male bonding. By 1843, women were sitting in the ordinance rooms and passing through the rituals. Adam and Eve, a male-female pair, were the representative figures rather than the Masonic hero Hiram Abiff. The aim . . . was not male fraternity but the exaltation of husbands and wives."[172] The elements of the temple ritual are of spiritual and symbolic significance and are prone to misapprehension for that reason, even among LDS faithful. The president of the church, David O. McKay, confessed that he was a "young man, out of college, anticipating great things when I went to the Temple. I was disappointed and grieved. . . . I have now found out why. There are two things in every Temple: mechanics, to set forth certain ideals, and symbolism, what those mechanics symbolize. . . . That great ordinance, the endowment, is simple in the mechanical part of it, but sublime and eternal in its significance."[173]

That earth is the estate and the temple the setting where the highest sacraments are performed means it is impossible to overstate the significance of the temple in Mormon sacramental life. If the New and Everlasting Covenant is the master plan for effecting salvation and eternal life, the binding to God and to each other, of the entire human family, then the temple is the locus where that covenant finds its highest sacramental expression. For many years, there was a tragic exception to this universalist impulse. While Smith ordained blacks to the priesthood, a ban initiated by Brigham Young in 1852 deprived black males of the priesthood ordination and, later, deprived black men and women of participation in temple ritual and thus full participation in the Abrahamic promises. Young's explanation was that "Cain cut off the lines of Abel to prevent him & his posterity getting the ascendancy over himself & his generations." Consequently, to repair the intended eternal family organization, the Lord "cursed Cain's seed with blackness & prohibited them the Priesthood [until] Abel & his progeny ... come forward & have their dominion place and Blessings in their proper relationship with Cain & his race in a world to come."[174] In other words, without the priesthood that gave access to temple ordinances, Cain and his posterity could not be constituted into the eternal human chain until Abel and his posterity were. The ban was removed in 1978, reasserting the universality of Smith's original vision. Because the vast majority of ordinances that are administered in the temple are performed on behalf of the deceased, Mormon temple work of necessity takes the form of that disinterested service that Kirk considered the essence of true worship.

4

Priesthood

AUTHORITY, POWER, AND THE MYSTERIES OF GODLINESS

IN RETURNING TO a profoundly sacramentalist view of religion, Mormonism reopened the question of authority, for if certain sacraments are indeed essential ingredients in our salvation, one cannot avoid the question of who can properly administer those sacraments. The role of authority in the functioning of the church is one of the most fundamental issues in ecclesiology and was at the heart of the Reformation's outbreak. By 1538, John Calvin's erstwhile colleague and friend Louis du Tillet decided the Reformation had been a catastrophic error. Central to his assessment was the problem of authority. His words to Calvin were to the point: "I doubt that you have had your vocation from God, having been called there only by men." Calvin could only insist that his call was "quite clear to my own satisfaction," even as he granted that his "office, which the Lord laid upon us when he made use of our services in collecting churches, is one that is altogether anomalous."[1] "Calvin's personal authority as a prophet of the Church loomed large," his biographer notes.[2] In fact, writes one Protestant theologian, "Luther, Calvin, Zwingli, Knox all arrogated to themselves a complete independence of authority. . . . They exercised the prophetic office in all its fullness."[3] Of course, Calvin already has a conception of authority in mind different from that of his Catholic peers. As Horton Davies observes of the Catholic/Reformation divide, "The difference between the respective understandings of the status and the function of the sacred ministry was great."[4] Rather than a sacerdotal, hierarchical priesthood derived from apostolic descent, many Protestants emphasized the ministerial, teaching authority bestowed by the

Holy Spirit. Each, of, course found ample basis in New Testament writings, and Mormonism would meld both views with important additions.

According to the Gospel of Matthew, one of Jesus Christ's most important actions before his Passion was the formal bestowal of his power and authority upon his apostles. "I will give you the keys of the kingdom of heaven," he said to Peter, "and whatever you bind on earth will be bound in heaven, and whatever you loose on earth will be loosed in heaven."[5] This was not universally taken to mean that Peter was himself the foundational stone of the church. Several Church Fathers, like Augustine's contemporary Theodore of Mopsuestia, for example, held that Jesus, "having said that [Peter's] confession is a rock . . . means he will build his church upon this same confession and faith."[6] (Some Shakers in the nineteenth century would likewise interpret the rock as "the revelation of the spirit of God.")[7] For the most part, however, the punning on Peter's name ("on this Petra") suggested to early Christians that with Peter and his successors resided the authority to preside in Christ's earthly kingdom.

If Iscariot's replacement by Matthias portended an attempt to sustain the original number of apostles, the practice was soon cut short. By the early second century, wrote a chronicler of that era, "none of the apostles was left."[8] At the same time, an important late first-century source claimed a clear intent to provide some kind of enduring authority. The writer of the so-called Epistle of Clement maintained that "our apostles also knew . . . there would be strife on account of the office of episcopate [or position of oversight]. For this reason, therefore, . . . they appointed those [ministers] already mentioned, and afterwards gave instructions, that when these should fall asleep, other approved men should succeed them."[9] For centuries, the necessity of a special class of men, ordained to officiate as God's intermediaries, administering his sacraments and holding the keys pertaining to salvation, was unquestioned in Christendom. As a third-century document laid down the principle, "how dare any man thrust himself into the priesthood who has not received that dignity from his superior."[10] More specifically, the principle of apostolic succession maintained that an unbroken chain of authorized men from the original apostles was a guarantee of continuing ecclesiastical authority.

A major impetus of Luther's Reformation was his conviction that such a priestly class, holding unique spiritual privileges and powers and existing in distinction from the Christian laity, was an abomination. As early as 1520, he considered this the "first wall of Jericho" in need of overthrow: "Let us begin by attacking the first wall. It is pure invention that pope, bishop, priests, and monks are called the 'spiritual estate'" as distinct from everyone else from princes to farmers. "This is indeed a fine bit of lying and hypocrisy. . . . All Christians are truly of the 'spiritual estate,' and there is no difference among them but that of office. . . . For whoever comes out of the water of baptism can boast that he is already a consecrated priest."[11] Elsewhere he affirmed,

"All Christians are priests, and all priests are Christians. Worthy of anathema is any assertion that a priest is anything else than a Christian."[12] Luther quoted by way of evidence not Matthew but 1 Peter: "You are a chosen race, a royal priesthood, a holy nation, God's own people, in order that you may proclaim the mighty acts of him who called you out of darkness into his marvelous light."[13]

Calvin invoked the same scripture ("Peter is speaking of the whole church"),[14] arguing that the priests' claim to special authority was not only unwarranted but an offense to God as well. For they are in effect attempting to set themselves up "as the vicars and successors of Christ. By this surrogation they not only rob Christ of his honor, and take from him the prerogative of an eternal priesthood, but attempt to remove him from the right hand of his Father."[15] Catholics responded that Church Fathers back to Ignatius taught it was the clergy alone who were "exercising the Priesthood of God ['the chief and sum of all man's good'] for the salvation of the world."[16] And so the battle was joined. William Allen wrote *A Treatise Made in Defence of the Lawful Power and Authoritie of the Priesthood to Remitte Sinnes* (Foulerus, 1567) a year after the Second Helvetic Confession rejoiced that "we have repudiated the papal priesthood" and replaced it with "the priesthood of all believers."[17]

Even those religious innovators disinclined to see themselves as dissenting from the principle of apostolic succession, like John Wesley, were forced to recognize in that principle a non-negotiable Rubicon. And so the question of Wesley's relationship—and the Methodists' generally—to apostolic authority was settled definitively when Wesley began to ordain his own ministers. He wished to retain his association with the established Church of England, but "Ordination is separation," declared the Lord Chief Justice of England, in response to Wesley's actions.[18] Wesley would insist near his life's end that "I am now as firmly attached to the Church of England as I ever was," but he revised the liturgy, revised the Thirty-Nine Articles of belief, and most radically, ordained men to preach and administer communion.[19] Like Calvin and the other Reformers, Wesley could not avoid claiming a special authority for his actions. "I, John Wesley, think myself to be providentially called to set apart some persons for the work of the ministry," he wrote.[20] By this time he had of necessity reinterpreted the high-church position on apostolic succession. Following Wesley, Methodists reinterpreted the principle to mean the transmission of the gospel message through a continuing ministry and body of disciples, not the literal and linear transmission of authority from individual to individual.

Wesley respected the tradition and established order enough, however, to invoke his own ordination as priest as giving him sufficient authority to ordain others. It was hardly a compelling case. Knowing that Anglican priests had no authority to ordain bishops, his own brother Charles captured the crisis of authority these developments represented in a wry verse:

> How easy now are bishops made
> At man or woman's whim.
> Wesley his hand on Coke hath laid,
> But who laid hands on him?[21]

From Wesley's practice a next logical step was to attribute the priesthood of all believers to, and ground ministerial authority in, the empowerment of the Holy Spirit (which "Holy Spirit hast appointed diverse orders of ministers in the church").[22] That was an interpretation with ample biblical precedent to satisfy the majority of Protestants. This view of an authority associated with the Holy Ghost rather than with Aaron or Melchizedek has roots in the New Testament, was explicated by Church Fathers, and was picked up by Protestants, for whom an effectual priesthood that was not conferred by apostolic succession was especially attractive. Richard Hooker, one of the earliest Anglican theologians, argued that no continuing apostolic office or authority was divinely commanded or intended by Christ.[23] But he found other scriptural bases for a ministerial authority. In addition to Peter's statement that "God anointed Jesus of Nazareth with the Holy Spirit,"[24] the gospel of John asserts a similar bestowal of authority. In John 20, the resurrected Christ appears to the assembled disciples, "And . . . he breathed on them, and said to them, 'Receive the Holy Spirit. If you forgive the sins of any, they are forgiven them; if you retain the sins of any, they are retained.' "[25]

Hooker read this passage as the fulfillment of Christ's earlier promise to Peter that he would "give his Apostles the keys of the kingdom of heaven," to bind on earth and in heaven.[26] Thus while Hooker acknowledged an Old Testament priesthood of Aaron signified by an anointing of oil, those contemporaries who were exercising a priesthood by claiming apostolic succession to officiate at altar and Eucharist were "sacrilegious wretches" and "profane persons."[27] What many call priesthood, he argued, was referred to by "the fathers of the church" as "the ministry of the gospel." Hooker agrees that "the ministry of things divine" requires "authority and power given unto them in a lawful manner" and it constitutes "a special *order*, . . . a distinct *order*" and "power" (his emphasis).[28] But he argues, based on John's words, that "the Holy Ghost is author" of "the very authority and power which is given men in the church to be ministers of holy things." In this Holy Ghost are the "well-springs of that power which ecclesiastical ordinations do bestow." The ordination conferred by the laying on of hands is important only insofar as it is a similitude of his breathing upon his disciples that power, described by John (regardless of the exact "effect their imposition of hands hath"). This is the basis of that ministerial authority others call priesthood. "The Holy Ghost which he then gave, was an holy . . . authority over the souls of men."[29]

Similarly, the seventeenth-century Anglican Robert South held that "in the ordination of priests . . . ministerial power" was conveyed with the words, "receive ye the Holy Ghost."[30] Joseph Smith's contemporary, the Quaker William Gibbons, was making the same point in 1822. "There is but one source from which ministerial power and authority ever was, is, or can be derived, and that is the Holy Spirit."[31] Presbyterians of the era agreed that this "holy unction" was "the origin of our priesthood."[32] The Methodist theologian Adam Clarke similarly held that "no mode of ordination, whether Popish, Episcopal, Protestant, or Presbyterian, can ever supply," that is, take the place of, "the Divine unction."[33]

Reforming figures like Alexander Campbell pushed the point even further. As one historian notes, "There was scarcely anything in the Westminster Confession of Faith from which he himself felt inclined to dissent, except it was the chapter which gave to the clergy a position and an authority which he thought unauthorized."[34] In fact, Campbell insisted there neither could nor should be any assertion of divine authority whatsoever. In his own words, Campbell neither claimed nor needed any: "And, as for authority, it can have no place in this business; for, surely, none can suppose themselves invested with a Divine right. . . . For our part, we entertain no such arrogant presumption; nor are we inclined to impute the thought to any of our brethren, that this good work should be let alone till such time as they may think proper to come forward and sanction the attempt, by their invitation and example. It is an open field, an extensive work, to which all are equally welcome, equally invited."[35] And he charged the leaders of his movement to "remove human opinions and the inventions of men out of the way, . . . casting out the assumed authority, that enacting and decreeing power by which those things have been imposed and established."[36]

Mormonism, in this regard, was a clear and—in the eyes of many—objectionable departure from Protestant views, for Smith was emphatic in claiming a literal and indispensable priesthood; he ordained priests by the dozens, and he made bishops high officials in the church. From most Protestant perspectives, this was clearly reverting to papist errors, and nineteenth-century writers frequently condemned Mormonism and Catholicism jointly. Orvilla Belisle published *The Arch Bishop; or, Romanism in the United States* followed the next year by *The Prophets; or Mormonism Unveiled*, for instance.[37] In 1842, the Reverend John Clark had lamented the "Mormon Jesuitism," and another author went so far as to allege "the bold design of introducing the whole Mormon community into the Romish fold."[38] In a significant departure from Catholic practice, however, Mormons did not relegate the priesthood to a special clerical class but opened its ranks to all worthy adult males. (As mentioned, a racial ban intruded on this practice from the 1850s until 1978.) The result was an unusual "priesthood of [virtually all male] believers" claiming apostolic authority.

Widespread access to the priesthood did not allay the criticism of those who found its high priestly pretensions offensive. A typical protest was Alexander Campbell's, who located the problem in pseudo-Jewish practice rather than Romish error. He acknowledged that "God . . . instituted a priesthood and a high priesthood," but it was with the Jews. He gave the priesthood "to the tribe of Levi, and the high priesthood to Aaron. . . . So irrevocable was the grant of the priesthood to Levi, and of the high priesthood to Aaron, that . . . Jesus himself was excluded from officiating as a priest on earth."[39] Charles Buck's highly influential *Theological Dictionary* (fifty editions before the Civil War) noted three biblical "orders" of the priesthood (high priest, priests, and Levites), but declared that "if the word *priest* be taken to denote a person commissioned by divine authority to offer up a real sacrifice to God, we may justly deny that there is a priest upon the earth." Catholics are the "erroneous" exception, whereas Protestants, by offering only a commemoration of an original sacrifice, are not priests "in the rigid sense of the word."[40]

In Smith's understanding, the church was instituted as the vehicle that would provide the framework of worship, community-building, and sacramental ordinances necessary to bring to fruition the New and Everlasting Covenant. In the words of Brigham Young, "the Gospel and the Priesthood are the means [God] employs to save and exalt his obedient children to the possession with him of the same glory and power, to be crowned with crowns of glory, immortality and eternal lives."[41] In Smith's early thought, priesthood is the divine authority to administer the church and its ordinances while maintaining its living connection to its source. At his hands, however, priesthood comes to far transcend its administrative functions and permeates an eternal order of things.

Ecclesiastical Authority

Joseph Smith taught unequivocally that "nothing will save a man but a legal Administrator."[42] Smith's conception of such administrative authority—and his own authority in the church he led—found precedent in the Book of Mormon's explicit conflation of the roles and functions of Hebrew prophets and church administrators. The transition from, or rather merging of, prophetic leadership over an Israelite tribe and administration of an organized church with ordained clergy happens in the days of Alma, in the second century BC. Alma the Elder converts several Nephites to the gospel, then leads them in a way clearly evocative of a New World Moses, receiving warnings "of the Lord," and conducting them through a wilderness sojourn as he "delivers them from bondage."[43] Subsequently, this prophet figure is given authority by the king to "establish churches throughout all the land," introducing a new era of organized churches as distinct from tribal religion.[44] From then on, Alma functions as "the high priest," having administrative "authority over the church."[45] His son Alma the Younger succeeds him as "high priest over the church"[46] and inherits the sacred records of his people, maintained by prophets from Lehi onward. The conflation of prophetic and administrative authority is now complete, a model Smith will replicate. Like his Old Testament predecessors, he finds that God appeared to him in a glorious theophany, "spake unto him from heaven," and commanded him to warn the earth of "the calamity which should come."[47] Supplementing this authority and calling, he will subsequently claim formal ordination by heavenly messengers, authorizing him to organize and administer an ecclesiastical organization, as its presiding high priest.[48]

Smith applied the title of legal administrator to Zachariah, John, and even Jesus Christ;[49] the prophet is whoever holds "keys," and the exact "Order and Ordinances of the Kingdom" were non-negotiable.[50] We "have got to be subject to certain rules & principles" established "before the world was," he taught.[51] In Oliver Cowdery's 1834 version of Mormonism's articles of faith, he wrote, "We believe that God is the same in all ages; and that it requires the same holiness, purity, and religion, to save a man now, as it did anciently."[52] In Smith's final version, that tenet drops out, and "a man must be ordained of God by one having authority" comes in.[53]

Mormons felt little need to belabor the question of authority. True enough, they were emphatic in their claim to literal transmission of an authentic apostleship. But as to the question of authority itself, there seemed little need to justify the principle as a foundation for a Christianity restored. The only question most Christians were asking, as we saw, concerned the form such authority would take: Apostolic succession? Formal ordination? Commission by the Spirit? Congregational appointment? Or a combination of the above? What defense Mormons did make of its indispensability almost always appealed to the self-evident value of order. "My house is a house of order," said Orson Pratt, borrowing from Paul. "What we mean by this is, that everything pertaining to the salvation of men, which is acceptable in the sight of heaven, must be in accordance with strict . . . laws that were ordained by [God]."[54] Rejecting creation ex nihilo, Mormons have always seen the essential creative power of God as residing in his majestic drive toward order, resolving randomness into purposiveness, chaos into system, anarchy and confusion into harmony and concord.

At times, Smith's soteriology seemed not focused on the change of heart or second birth as much as on the forms and authorized procedures of an inflexible sacramental theology. And it is true that Smith took seriously the designation of God's church as a "kingdom." Referring to John the Baptist's ministry and the imminent kingdom of God he preached, Smith said, "Here was a legal administrator, & those that were baptized were subjects for a King & also the laws & oracles of God were there therefore the Kingdom of God was there for no man Could have better authority to Administer than John & our Savior submitted to that authority himself by being Baptized by John."[55] Melchizedek, after whom the higher priesthood was named, was "a king & a priest" according to "a perfect law of Theocracy."[56]

From another angle, what at times could appear excessive legalism might in a broader context be seen as an alternative to the well-intentioned but disastrous illusion of an ungrounded human autonomy. The Holy Priesthood, in Benjamin Winchester's treatise on the subject, is but another term for "the economy of God"—a term already in use at that day.[57] Webster defined "economy" in 1828 as "the management, regulation, and government of a family or . . . household"—with God's family and household in the ecclesiastical case taking in its purview the entire universe.[58] It sounds especially appealing in the modern age of the supremely liberated self and atomistic individualism to see intent as the only measure of true spirituality. Warren Cowdery noted such a perspective in 1834 but found it illogical that God "looks at [believers'] sincerity only and that he has respect to any and every ordinance, even though they may not be of divine appointment." God having given commands and codes and ritual law through time, the only reasonable inference, he wrote, was that conformity to the original pattern unless modified by modern revelation setting forth a new one must be his intent.[59] Priesthood authority in this view functions as a failsafe to maintain the bounds of correct doctrine. According to the LDS church's *Times and Seasons*: "In the absence of laws and administration, the governments of men would become confused and crumble into ruin, so in the absence of the priesthood, the children of men" fall into "anarchy and confusion."[60] The priesthood is, wrote Lorenzo Snow, the "medium or channel through which our Heavenly Father has purposed to communicate light, intelligence, gifts, powers, and spiritual and temporal salvation."[61]

Smith built upon this foundation in his insistence upon an actual legal authorization behind sacramental activities: "All the ordinances Systems, & Administrations on the earth is of no use to the Children of men unless they are ordained & authorized of God for nothing will save a man but a legal Administrator for none others will be acknowledged either by God or Angels."[62] Priesthood authority is thus the guarantee of God's own authority, transmitted through the principle of delegation, that links sincere intent with divine recognition. As an influential early Mormon treatise frames the issue, priesthood is "a delegation from God, or a legation from heaven, which is an authority conferred upon individuals authorizing them to act in the name of the Lord, or to administer ordinances and transact business as appertains to the kingdom of God." It is, in other words, the "proxy" authority to act in God's stead, as "his agents."[63] Such authority is necessary to maintain the integrity and efficacy of a divinely inspired organization that has been committed to human, fallible hands. This is similar to the Catholic reliance on priesthood authority "to protect the doctrine of Christ by a living and authentic teaching authority and to propagate it complete and uncorrupted."[64]

This "living" quality of a divinely recognized authority that transcends any one individual and maintains a conduit to divine supervisory guidance is explicit in Smith's revelatory claim that his restoration represented the only "true and *living* church."[65] As Smith explained, priesthood "is the channel through which all knowledge, doctrine, the plan of salvation and every important matter is revealed from salvation and every important matter is revealed from heaven. . . . It is the channel through which the Almighty commenced revealing his glory at the beginning of the creation of this earth and through which he has continued to reveal himself to the children of men to the present time and through which he will make known his purposes to the end of time."[66] An authoritative, "living" tradition directs the affairs of church in an ongoing process, supplementing the pages of past scriptural writ with verbal scripture in the present.

So priesthood is in this regard a principle of authorized guardianship against fragmentation, schism, and error entering into the body of Christ and thwarting his purposes, and ensuring recognition on God's part for actions performed in his name. It is, then, not just a divine power of attorney but a mechanism "to regulate and perpetuate the kingdom of God"; in "the absence of the priesthood," the laws and government of God's kingdom "would become confused and stumble into ruin."[67]

In the modern LDS church, it is a commonplace for Mormons to define priesthood as "the authority to act in God's name."[68] This model of priesthood as a principle of ecclesiastical authority and order dominated in the church's founding period, when the need to convincingly assert divine sanction for the church's establishment and organization after a New Testament model was paramount. As Jonathan Stapley notes, the renewed emphasis in the contemporary Mormon church on priesthood as ecclesiastical authority is to some extent a shift away from more expansive views of a "cosmological priesthood" that dominates Smith's subsequent thinking about priesthood, especially in the context of his temple theology.[69] This may reasonably be seen as a natural consequence of a muted "disenchantment," a la Charles Taylor, that has to some extent infiltrated even Mormon culture, a general disengagement with Smith's more speculative and daring theology among church leadership generally, along with the bureaucratic demands of a church that now spans more than a hundred nations embracing millions in its fold. In the mid-twentieth century, the church moved to centralize and coordinate all church programs and curricula in a massive priesthood "correlation program," under the leadership of Harold B. Lee. A primary impetus was Paul H. Dunn's doctoral project, which established that "what the Brethren thought ought to be taught, and what was actually being taught, . . . were miles apart."[70]

The consequence of Lee's reform was to move beyond simple coordination of curricula and to centralize church authority in the Quorum of the Twelve to an unprecedented degree. Local initiative became relatively constrained, and most vestiges of autonomy and self-governance were erased. The women's Relief Society, especially, felt the shift. In the nineteenth and early twentieth centuries, women were "not part of the ecclesiastical priesthood structure of the church," and the Relief Society maintained its own grain storage programs, independent journal, and finances ("vast sums that have been gathered in various ways and disbursed to many benevolent purposes," noted one report).[71] All now fell under the direct supervision of priesthood leaders. The trade-off is a church that operates with uncommon efficiency, "mobilizing like a mighty army" when crisis strikes, wrote one journalist.[72] (Even the members' expressions have "something *organized* about them," jibed Harold Bloom.)[73] And respect for a hierarchically organized chain of priesthood authority believed to originate with God creates the conditions for a higher than average adherence to church standards and teachings.[74] Some faithful Mormons, in other words, would call discipleship what observers might see as unsettling conformity and deference to authority.

Priesthood has suffered recurrently bad press through the centuries—much of it deserved. For as long as humans have clothed themselves with authority of any sort—civil or religious—abuse has followed. Smith restated Lord Acton's famous maxim about corruptive power while suffering judicial abuse himself: "We have learned by sad experience," he wrote, "that it is the nature and disposition of almost all men, as soon as they get a little authority, as they suppose, they will immediately begin to exercise unrighteous dominion."[75] The Protestant Reformation drew a good deal of its energies from the legacy of papal and clerical abuses and began to redeploy a seldom used word with new and pejorative meaning to address the evil. In the fifteenth century, "priestcraft" signified the religious labors of the priest, as in his "priestcraft at the altar."[76] Less than two centuries later, the term had become a word of reproach that often targeted Catholic priesthood in particular but grew to encompass a general hostility toward the entire clerical class, and it became omnipresent in book titles, pamphlets, and popular preaching, such as Edmund Hinckeringill's *Priest-craft, Its Character and Consequences* (London, 1705); John Dennis's *Priestcraft Distinguish'd from Christianity* (London, 1715); and Richard Baron's *The Pillars of Priestcraft and Orthodoxy Shaken* (London, 1768). So extensive were the broadsides that by the century's end one concerned Christian, noting the age's "great outcry . . . against priestcraft," wrote that while he was "very willing that every thing which merits that opprobrious name may be treated with due severity," he was not sure that the efforts of *every* Christian minister "should be discredited and suspected on account of their office, nor that the whole business of supporting Christianity should be left in the hands of laymen."[77]

In instituting a formal priesthood, Mormonism was swimming against a massive cultural tide. Not only was the Protestant world hostile to such "Romish" practices; the Book of Mormon and a revelation to Smith had also presented red flags on the subject. The Lord's "vineyard has become corrupted every whit . . . because of priest-crafts," Smith pronounced mere months after the founding.[78] The Book of Mormon warned against "priestcrafts" and defined the offenders as men who "preach and set themselves up for a light unto the world," and who pervert the truth with both cunning words and violence.[79] Such abuses of clerical position were high on Smith's mind, and one hedge against misuse was to define priesthood as non-coercive power in its very essence. According to Smith's classic statement on this theme, "No power or influence can or ought to be maintained by virtue of the priesthood, only by persuasion, by long-suffering, by gentleness and meekness, and by love unfeigned; By kindness, and pure knowledge."[80] The striking claim in this passage is that employing the priesthood coercively does not just render it ineffective, but it also negates the power and alienates the man who so employed it from any further claim to that authority: "When we undertake to . . . exercise control or dominion or compulsion upon the souls of the children of men, in any degree of unrighteousness, behold, the heavens withdraw themselves; the Spirit of the Lord is grieved; and when it is withdrawn, Amen ['there is the end'] to the priesthood or the authority of that man."[81] In addition, as a safeguard against institutional coercion under the authority of priesthood, Smith initiated the Law of Common Consent—a practice that would make it impossible for leaders to implement policy or govern without the support of the members.

COMMON CONSENT

In the New Testament church, Luke records that the apostles "appointed elders for them in each church."[82] Adam Clarke noted that the verb χειροτονέω (cheirotoneo), often translated as ordain or appoint, actually signifies "to hold up the hand" in "approval." What is happening, in this reading, is that in each case, "the Church [is] agreeing in the election of the person."[83] The *Didache* suggests a congregational role in the process of appointment by actually directing Christians to "appoint, therefore, for yourselves, bishops and deacons worthy of the Lord."[84] Toward the end of the first Christian century, Clement effectively synthesized the appointment from a higher authority and the principle of self-governance by directing that the apostles or "other eminent men" should appoint local leaders "with the consent of the whole Church."[85]

The principle of governance by common consent was a staple of British political culture, especially in the aftermath of John Locke's *Second Treatise* (1689). Locke had made the rule of "common consent" absolutely foundational to his theory of government. In leaving a state of nature behind, he argued, the first principle of civil society is the replacement of a natural law, variably and imperfectly understood by the masses, for "an established, settled, known law, received and allowed by common consent."[86] The expression, not surprisingly, was already becoming a commonplace in religious discourse of the Reformation era and beyond. Catholics like Thomas Ward appealed to the principle of common consent in preferring their canon to the Protestant canon, while the Puritan divine Richard Baxter chastised the Catholic Church for its alleged disregard for the "common consent" of the church which declared councils higher than popes.[87] In the earliest days of his movement, Luther had insisted that "no one must push himself forward and take [priestly office] upon himself without our consent and election."[88] In the Reformed tradition, this rule or law became a standard practice: "The Deacons or Treasurers . . . must be chosen yearly in every Parish by the common consent of the Church," declared a seventeenth-century treatise on ecclesiology, making use of the expression almost a dozen times in reference to both civil and ecclesiastical appointments.[89]

The English Moravians (United Brethren) in the eighteenth century celebrated the fact that in all areas where their churches were planted, all members paid equal "Submission to the Statutes agreed on among themselves by common Consent."[90] "Common consent," notes one scholar, "was central to Elizabethan presbyterian arguments against episcopal appointment."[91] The Congregationalists of New England were especially adamant about resisting any imposition of ecclesiastical authority from outside the local, self-governing congregation. In defining the principle, John Cotton differentiated common consent from democratic governance, even as he recognized that requiring universal assent could be paralyzing to concerted action:

> When we say do this or that with *common consent*, our meaning is, we do not carry on matters either by the overruling power of the presbytery or by the consent of the major part of the church, but by the general and joint consent of all the members of the church. . . . But if it so fall out, that any difference do arise, . . . then such as do dissent from their brethren are required to propound the grounds of their dissent. . . . But if the grounds of such as do dissent do upon due consideration appear to have little or no weight in them, . . . "take further pains,"—"lovingly inform them,"—"patiently bear with them,"—till at

length they can either act with their brethren, or "for their part sit still," . . .
and the church doth proceed with common consent . . . and . . . leave them
under the censure of admonition.[92]

Smith's innovation was to combine the authoritative role of a prophet (or pope),
whose words the Saints were to receive "as if from [God's] own mouth,"[93] with the
democratic principle of consent by the governed entrenched in the Protestant tradition. Members would have had a fairly well-defined understanding of what was
meant when one of Smith's earliest revelations decreed that "all things shall be done
by common consent in the church," and two subsequent revelations reaffirmed the
principle.[94] Early meetings make frequent reference to conference business proceeding "by the unanimous voice of the assembly," or "by a unanimous vote."[95] Quorum
of the Twelve minutes note "the business of necessity was done by common consent";[96] in another special meeting, Smith was "by common consent & unanimous
voice chosen president of the quorum."[97] The principle applied to a range of actions
from endorsing new scripture to affirming position statements on marriage.[98]

Most frequently, however, the principle applied to the appointment of leaders.
In the Book of Mormon, the theocratic Nephites chose kings, judges, and religious
leaders "by the voice of the people,"[99] and the church's 1835 "Articles and Covenants"
repeated the principle in language reminiscent of the biblical precedent: "No person
is to be ordained to any office in this church, where there is a regularly organized
branch of the same, without the vote of that church."[100] In this case, the principle works much as Adam Clarke imagined the scene in Acts—with this difference: Clarke believed the ancient practice amounted to Christians choosing their
own pastors, whereas Latter-day Saints believe all leaders are chosen by revelation
through priesthood channels—with those leaders formally accepted by the voice of
the congregation (or church as a whole in the case of General Authorities).

Difficulties emerged in Mormon governance for at least two principal reasons.
First, because attributing church callings to revelation (or, to what amounts to the
same thing, a delegated authority), suggests less room to maneuver in accepting
or rejecting the appointment of such leaders. Even so, in the nineteenth century,
members were prone to occasionally voice dissent, often persuasively. Even Smith's
preferences for filling top leadership positions could be overruled. An October 1843
conference took up the question of Sidney Rigdon's disputed fitness for his office
as counselor in the First Presidency of the church. Smith said "he did not wish to
retain him in that station" and "signified his lack of confidence in his integrity and
steadfastness." But others urged forbearance, and the conference voted that "elder
Rigdon be permitted to retain his station."[101] And sometimes the principle moved
in the opposite direction. So in 1877, for instance, "a number of people objected" to

Young's appointment of a new stake president—so the move was postponed until an acceptable co-president was found and nominated. Similarly, in Salt Lake's Third Ward the same year, members rejected Elder George Q. Cannon's choice to replace a popular bishop.[102] That was apparently not uncommon.

A second problem with Smith's governance emerged when he very early on presumed to dictate on a wider range of issues than purely ecclesiastical ones. Conceiving of his mission as building Zion rather than a church, welding together a people not a congregation, and presiding over a kingdom rather than a denomination, Smith's revelations explicitly presumed to direct "the Church both in temporal as well as spiritual things."[103] These efforts to create a theocracy impinged on the fierce individualism of Jacksonian Americans. In the days before disestablishment, American Puritans had found no difficulty in wedding the political, the civic, and the spiritual. After the Revolution, however, church authoritarianism that blurred the lines between spiritual guidance and secular control, and intruded into the economic in particular, was bound to meet resistance. In 1838, Oliver Cowdery had sold some of his land holdings in Missouri, in defiance of a revelation by Smith. Chastised, he and several dissenters declared opposition to Smith for "endeavoring to unite ecclesiastical and civil authority."[104] The leadership initially hedged, but a few months later the high council in Far West, Missouri, charged him with "virtually denying the faith by declaring that he would not be governed by any ecclesiastical authority or revelations whatever in his temporal affairs." Cowdery readily admitted the offense: "I will not be influenced, governed, or controlled, in my temporal interests by any ecclesiastical authority or pretended revelation whatever, contrary to my own judgment."[105] In the newfound spirit of American republicanism, Cowdery invoked his "constitutional privileges," the rights adumbrated by Locke, and his Plymouth ancestors. The council agreed with Cowdery. He was convicted of various other offenses, but the court pointedly rejected the charge of "virtually denying the faith by declaring that he would not be governed by any ecclesiastical authority nor Revelation whatever in his temporal affairs."[106]

At about the same time, the Missouri stake presidency had engaged in questionable financial practices, and "the Church in general … had become dissatisfied with their conduct as Christians." Accordingly, other area leaders "called the whole church in Zion [Missouri] together, who almost unanimously voted them out of their presidential office."[107] Clearly, there was at this time in the LDS church a feeling that Smith's ecclesiastical authority was balanced by what Cowdery called "principles of English liberty"[108] and the voice of congregations in church governance. As Robert Quinn has written, Mormon leaders initially believed

that the membership should be directly involved in decision-making meetings, including making motions on policy issues, … and voting to finalize decisions. . . . The conduct of their meetings followed the congregational model that was familiar to them. However, before long early Latter-day Saints began to realize that having a prophet as their leader was a reality that must be recognized in decision making, and that they could not follow the traditional congregational model without denying the authority and revelations that God had bestowed on Joseph Smith.[109]

Smith referenced the principle only occasionally in the context of council meetings, Young is not known to have ever invoked or alluded to the principle in public sermons,[110] and no official policy statement on the principle of common consent, or its place in church governance, has emerged to explain or guide an evolving view, with the result that controversy and friction recurrently erupt around its exact meaning and application. In 1905 the apostle John W. Taylor resigned from the quorum over disagreement with polygamy's cessation. He gave as his rationale the fact that while the manifesto ending the practice had been subject to common consent, its application as a worldwide ban had not. The ban "was never presented for adoption by 'Common Consent' as was the Manifesto itself and I have disputed its authority as a law or rule of the Church."[111]

In the contemporary church, common consent is a seldom heard phrase. The reasons for this shift are both cultural and institutional. With policies now issuing from a leadership presiding over millions of members from a centralized hierarchy administering a well-oiled program of "correlation," common consent has infrequent application, other than in the sustaining of officers. At the same time, Mormons now tend to view "callings" as essentially a fait accompli at the time they are announced, with the sustaining vote an opportunity to formally declare support, not a referendum on the choice. Hence, the opportunity to "sustain" leaders or policies by vote, in conformity with this practice, can seem largely formal. At the same time, however, the raised hand of men and women alike has a sacramental quality to it, since it represents not mere assent to an ecclesiastical decision but a pledge of personal support in upholding the person or policy so validated. "We raise our hands in token of a covenant to uphold and sustain our leaders," according to Joseph F. Smith.[112] Church members, for instance, are specifically enjoined by scripture to "uphold him [who is appointed] before me by the prayer of faith."[113] And those who so sustain approved leadership "in all patience and faith" are promised that "the Lord God will disperse the powers of darkness from before you, and cause the heavens to shake for your good, and his name's glory."[114]

Recurrently, some in the church have publicly voiced dissent during the sustaining of church officers, to protest political positions (such as the ERA) or church policy (as a priesthood restricted to males). By way of general response, the church official handbook limits the grounds for dissent to private knowledge of personal unworthiness: "If a member in good standing gives a dissenting vote when someone is presented to be sustained, the presiding officer or another assigned priesthood officer . . . determines whether the dissenting vote was based on knowledge that the person who was presented is guilty of conduct that should disqualify him or her from serving in the position."[115]

A significant countercurrent to these historical developments of an increasingly centralized authority may be found in a recently renewed emphasis on the principle of family, congregational, and general councils, in every case moving to accord a greater role for women in particular in the governance process. Whereas church rhetoric traditionally assigned the man the role of "presiding" over the home, leaders now speak of parents as "co-equals" and "co-presidents" in family governance.[116] Locally, ward councils, which include women leaders, assumed new importance beginning in the 1900s, and globally, three powerful churchwide committees that were previously run exclusively by priesthood holders in 2015 added women to their ranks: the Priesthood Executive Council (renamed the Priesthood and Family Executive Council), the Missionary Executive Council, and the Temple and Family History Council.[117] All of these developments can be seen as reinforcing the principle of non-coercive employment of priesthood.

Salvific Power

If priesthood authority is the legal mandate from heaven to act in God's name, priesthood power we may consider as the effective agency by which such influence is exercised in non-coercive ways. Joseph Smith's understanding of priesthood would culminate in a vision of the power to create sealing bonds of belonging that would transcend death and hell, through sacramental temple rituals. This is not a priesthood distinct from the authority to administer the church as an organization, for that would create a false dichotomy between the church as an institution and the eternal order of relationality. They are not the same, but the aspiration to create a Zion society in the here and now, Enoch's vision of a time when the heavenly and earthly cities of Zion unite and "fall upon" one another's necks, and most significantly, the Lord's promise that his heavenly city "shall come forth out of all the creations which I have made" suggest continuity and overlap, if not identity, between the earthly church and the eternal ordering of God's people.[118]

Like the authority to administer the institutional church, which was predicated upon non-coercive principles of love and persuasion, priesthood power to save and redeem the human family is predicated on principles of non-coercive authority wedded to love's compelling power. The pattern for this salvific priesthood is the power by which the Great High Priest effects his atonement and models the power of non-coercive love as that which binds all humans in perfect at-one-ment. Scripture is emphatic that Christ's atoning sacrifice is efficacious by virtue of the draw, the pull, the attractive power it exerts upon our hearts. If "every knee shall bow to" Christ and "every tongue" confess him,[119] LDS scripture indicates it will be in consequence of the vulnerability of the Savior, a God given to weeping over the misery of his creation, and not in consequence of his active demand. His sovereignty is a non-coercive sovereignty: "he layeth down his own life that he may *draw* all men unto him. Wherefore, he commandeth none that they shall not partake of his salvation."[120] And he confirmed in his own voice, "I ha[ve] been lifted up upon the cross, that I might *draw* all men unto me."[121] The words seem deliberately chosen to emphasize salvation as an invited response rather than pressured choice or foregone conclusion. "Men are free according to the flesh . . . free to choose liberty and eternal life," the Book of Mormon emphasizes.[122] As Dietrich Bonhoeffer, in another context, put the same principle: "The God of the Bible . . . wins power and space in the world by his weakness."[123] For Smith, God's dominion over the souls of men, like that of exalted beings over each other, is one that "without compulsory means . . . shall flow unto thee forever and ever."[124]

At the same time, priesthood is indispensable as the power given humans to enter into full communion with God and participate in the divine nature. Smith was told in his first visionary experience that other Christian traditions had "a form of Godliness but they deny the power thereof"—words borrowed from the second epistle to Timothy.[125] These words were frequently invoked by Methodist preachers[126] and are easily taken to refer to a general habit of simple hypocrisy; in the context of Mormon theology they acquire more specific meaning. Believing as they do that participating in the divine nature refers to a robust theosis, Mormons take references to the power to become like God literally. The power of godliness, in this light, would mean the actual power to become as God is, essentially and not just figuratively. If the letter to Timothy saw the denial of the power of godliness as a sign of the "last days," and the divine personage quoted it to Smith as indicative of a general apostasy ("they have turned aside from the gospel"),[127] then we here find corroboration of the definition of apostasy we presented earlier: a tragic attenuation of the New and Everlasting Covenant, indicating a failure to understand its premortal origins and its universal invitation to become divine beings in an eternal heavenly family. A revelation to Joseph Smith in 1832 reinforces this reading, indicating the key role of priesthood in accessing that path to theosis. "And this greater priesthood administereth the gospel and holdeth the key of the mysteries of the kingdom, even the key of the knowledge of God. Therefore, in the ordinances thereof, the power of godliness is manifest. And without the ordinances thereof, and the authority of the priesthood, the power of godliness is not manifest unto men in the flesh."[128]

This twinning of temple ordinances with an underlying priesthood authority constitute the process by which men and women find access, through temple ordinances, to the fullest expression of human salvation and are enabled to come home "unto Mount Zion, and unto the city of the living God, the heavenly place, the holiest of all."[129] The priesthood, in this sense, *is* the power of godliness. "Now the great and grand secret of the whole matter, and the summum bonum of the whole subject that is lying before us, consists in obtaining the powers of the Holy Priesthood. . . . Herein is glory and honor, and immortality and eternal life."[130] This is the sense in which B. H. Roberts could say, "It is by the power of the priesthood that a person may attain celestial glory. Without the power of the Priesthood one cannot enter into the presence of God."[131] Priesthood is the only channel through which men, *jointly with women*, acquire the divine nature and co-participate fully in his eternal activity. Women, too, enter into "an order of priesthood" upon entering "the new and everlasting covenant of marriage."[132] The Melchizedek priesthood, in particular, Smith associated with this power. It was the power, he said, of "administering endless lives."[133] This reason alone is sufficient to explain Smith's practice of admitting all men (and through temple marriage, all women) to the priesthood. Priesthood was far more important for its power of godliness, the access to eternal lives it provided, than as a mere source of institutional administrative authority.

To similar effect, an 1832 revelation to Smith described the priesthood as a kind of schooling in sanctification and eventual theosis. As Smith taught, "I advise all to go on to perfection and search deeper and deeper into the mysteries of Godliness—a man can do nothing for himself unless God direct him in the right way, and the Priesthood is reserved for that purpose."[134] Those who prove themselves faithful in obtaining and "magnifying their calling" in the two orders of priesthood "are sanctified by the spirit unto the renewing of their body that they become the Sons of Moses and Aaron and the seed of Abraham and the church and kingdom and the elect of God." They are further promised that "all that [the] father hath shall be given unto" them, according to "this oath and covenant."[135] James Talmage took this to mean that "exaltation in the kingdom of God implies attainment to the graded orders of the Holy Priesthood."[136]

If there is one image that encompasses the range of Mormon teachings about priesthood, it may have been best expressed by Parley Pratt. He envisioned an endlessly expanding order that comprehended God's eternal, ongoing purposes into which humans are invited as collaborators. He wrote, "Men [and women] are the offspring or children of the Gods, and destined to advance by degrees, and to make their way by a progressive series of changes, till they become like their father in heaven (like "our Heavenly Parents," Orson Pratt corrected[137]). "Thus perfected, the whole family will . . . continue to organize, people, redeem, and perfect other systems which are now in the womb of Chaos." Ultimately, priesthood is the power to achieve this order, or in Smith's thought, the name for the overarching matrix itself, the template, that patterns and guides the whole. It is a power and system into which God invites human co-participation. As Richard Bushman suggested, "The priesthood goes back before the foundations of the earth and includes all the gods who have gone before. They are bound into one God whose combined force and intelligence is the source of glory. We may even add to the glory by joining them—like computers strung in parallel, generating power. . . . In this sense, the priesthood is God."[138]

Endless and Eternal

Orson Pratt, the church's foremost early theologian, believed that God's power was manifest in harmony with universal, natural laws. "To search out the laws of nature," he wrote, "is nothing less than searching out the laws by which the Spirit in nature operates."[139] But God's operations in the cosmos—as church government and the plan of salvation—are non-coercive, and Pratt believed that all elements in the universe were more than "blind, unintelligent, and unconscious matter." He believed, on the contrary, that the elements in their most fundamental aspect exhibit a degree of intelligence, or agency, and are therefore responsive to the Divine Will. Young taught that "there is life in all matter, throughout the vast extent of all the eternities; it is in the rock, the sand, the dust, in water, air, the gases, and in short, in every description and organization of matter, whether it be solid, liquid, or gaseous, particle operating with particle."[140]

Orson Pratt took this to mean that "an unintelligent particle is incapable of understanding or obeying a law, while an intelligent particle is capable of both understanding and obedience. It would be entirely useless for an Intelligent Cause to give laws to unintelligent matter."[141] In the *Seer*, Pratt argued further that the law of gravity made more sense if articulated in terms of self-propulsion rather than passive attraction: "by which every particle of matter in the universe has a tendency, not to *attract*, (for such a mode of action is, in all cases, impossible), but to *approach* every other particle with a force varying inversely as the square of its distance."[142] John Widtsoe echoed Pratt's language in 1908, writing that "Life is nothing more than matter in motion; that, therefore, all matter possesses a kind of life. . . . Matter . . . [is] intelligent . . . hence everything in the universe is alive."[143] Like Pratt, Widtsoe believed intelligence was a precondition of adherence to law.

It is difficult to resist comparing this variety of panpsychism with developments in quantum physics: "Even physicists will ask why a photon makes up its mind or 'chooses' to manifest in one location rather than another, careful to bracket the word chooses in quotation marks but lacking any better lingo than the language of choice and volition to describe what's going on."[144] Thomas Nagel, an atheist philosopher who finds Darwinist materialism incapable of accounting for consciousness, finds panpsychism a perfectly reasonable hypothesis: panpsychism "appears to follow from a few simple premises, each of which is more plausible than its denial."[145] Theologian Niels Gregersen moves in a similar direction when considering possible theistic accommodation to evolution. In one version, he writes that the realization of particular possibilities in the natural world may "depend on the actions of free agents, which may include fundamental particles and their associations."[146] LDS scientist/philosopher W. H. Chamberlin, developing Pratt's and Widtsoe's ideas in his own quest to reconcile contemporary science with Mormon theology, held that "Mind is inherent in all Nature in the form of innumerable spiritual agents or selves, which are free causes."[147] LDS biologist Steven Peck finds rich possibilities in this view that "the conditions in which God and a society of minds find themselves as individuals include both ourselves and all of matter that is spiritual."[148]

The scriptural basis for Pratt's and Widtsoe's interpretation of "the power of God" as a priesthood power that evoked a willed response in nature (and Chamberlin's natural universe of free agents) was perhaps found in the Abrahamic text Smith produced in 1835. In that version of the creation story, Smith added an intriguing phrase to the sequence of creative acts. The Gods (plural) "ordered the expanse," so that it divided the waters, then they "ordered, saying: let the waters under the heaven be gathered," and finally they "organized the earth to bring forth" its array of flora; in all three cases they "saw that they were obeyed"—by agents or by the natural elements themselves is not clear.[149] In the Book of Mormon, too, God "commandeth the earth" and it responds.[150] In the *Lectures on Faith*, whose writing and delivery at the School of the Prophets Smith oversaw, it is claimed that "faith . . . is the first great governing principle, which has power, dominion, and authority over all things." It is this "principle of power, which existed in the bosom of God, by which the worlds were framed," and "it is by reason of this principle of power, existing in the Deity, that all created things exist—so that all things in heaven, on earth, or under the earth, exist by reason of faith, as it existed in HIM."[151]

This idiosyncratic usage of faith, where a modern Latter-day Saint would expect to see priesthood, was soon emended in LDS teachings. (Priesthood not being a popular concept in Protestant America, the substitution of another term like faith in the church's earliest theological class was understandable.) The *Lectures* were dropped from the canon in 1921, and long before that, several authorities were restating the principle there described with the substitution hinted at in Abraham. In 1852, Young was teaching that the power of the priesthood is "the power of Gods" to make "worlds like this."[152] He elaborated that "there is no world made" that is not "governed and controlled by the law of the Eternal Priesthood." It is the system by which "planets and all creations are governed."[153] Elsewhere he called it "a code of laws perfectly calculated to govern and control eternal matter"[154]—"the power of the eternal worlds,"[155] "that system which brings worlds into existence and peoples them, gives them their revolutions, their days, weeks, months, years, their seasons and times and by which they . . . go into a higher state of existence."[156] These latter teachings are still official doctrine in the church. A current manual states simply that "Jesus Christ created this world and everything in it. He also created many other worlds. He did so through the power of the priesthood, under the direction of our Heavenly Father."[157]

Priesthood is then the principle of authority and power that undergirds the institutional church, enables our integration into most intimate communion with God, and organizes and governs the cosmos. And so, even as Smith found scriptural precedent for both institutional and prophetic authority, he eventually traced its origins to an order that extended beyond the patriarchs, through Adam, and into premortal realms. In the book of Hebrews, the author refers to Melchizedek as "Without father, without mother, without genealogy, having neither beginning of days nor end of life."[158] Smith reconstrued the passage as saying that "Melchizedek was ordained a priest after the order of the son of God, which *order* was without father, without mother, without descent, having neither beginning of days nor end of life" (my emphasis).[159] "Its institution," he taught elsewhere, "was prior to 'the foundation of this earth [before] the morning stars sang together or the Sons of God shouted for joy.' "[160]

One source of this idea, apparently, was Smith's translation of the Book of Mormon, wherein the priesthood was declared an order "from the foundation of the world, . . . prepared from eternity to all eternity."[161] Smith went on to preach that to Adam, "the Priesthood was first given. . . . He obtained the first Presidency & held the Keys of it, from generation to Generation; he obtained it in the creation before the world was formed."[162] For this reason, presumably, early Mormon leaders sometimes referred to the priesthood as the "order pertaining to the Ancient of Days."[163] To Adam were delegated "the keys of the Universe," a priesthood that "existed with God from Eternity & will to Eternity."[164] The patriarch Noah, in another example cited by Smith, was ordained by his grandfather Methuselah, with ancestors going back to Noah all ordained as high priests.[165]

As Smith taught, then, "the Priesthood is an everlasting principle & Existed with God from Eternity & will to Eternity, without beginning of days or end of years."[166] Neither does it end with the temporal existence of the church or the world. John Taylor, commenting on the passing of Brigham Young, said the priesthood by which he administered here on earth was "the same, if you please, in the eternal worlds, for the one is combined and united with the other. The Priesthood that has lived before, and that which lives now are eternal, and administer in time and in eternity; and the principles which God has revealed to us draw aside the curtains of the eternal worlds, giving us a glimpse within the veil."[167] More specifically, Orson Pratt added, "the Priesthood is not given for a few years and then to cease; but all the servants of God who have ministered here below by authority of the Priesthood will continue their work among immortal beings."[168] This work is not mere evangelizing of the dead, taught George Q. Cannon, but a more extensive ministry that parallels the earthly: "And that same Priesthood which has brought us here, and through the power of which we were inducted into this Church, and through the power of which we have been nourished and guided in the Church, that same Priesthood will continue to teach and direct us, until we shall be brought back into the presence of God our Father."[169]

Far more than a simple temporal authority for ecclesiastical performances, the priesthood "binds the hosts of heaven together, and authorizes the angels to act in the name of God throughout the boundless realms of light."[170] In Young's words, priesthood is "as broad as the heavens, deep as hell, and wide as eternity."[171] In this conception, possessing the priesthood initiates one into an order of heavenly governance without temporal limitations. Supreme power and authority reside in God, but "a person may have a portion of that priesthood, the same as governors or judges of England have power from the king to transact business."[172] As Young taught, "The priesthood is a perfect system of government, it is the principle of government that governs the Gods in eternity; it governs the Gods and holy angels, they were created and organized by it."[173] In sum, priesthood is the authority and power by which the universe, the church, and the web of relationality to God and the human family are governed and maintained according to celestial laws and principles.

PRIESTHOOD RESTORATION
Aaronic Restoration

In echoing Catholicism's emphasis on sacramentalism, Mormonism's commitment to an uncompromising foundation in priesthood authority presented a problem. Catholics could make a credible claim to a chain of succession, whereas Mormonism was emphatic that such a history of transmission had been abrogated by "an apostasy . . . from the Apostolic platform."[174] Alexander Campbell was a Primitivist, but he was not in search of some elusive holy grail of authority to guide his version of restoration. He insisted that "there lives not the man on earth that can assure himself, or anyone else, that there is one official in Christendom that could, by any possibility, believe, know, or rationally conjecture, that the hands laid on his head had any more connexion, lineal or direct, from Peter or any of the Apostles, than they have with Aaron or Melchisedek."[175] That was not a problem in his view, since, as we saw, Campbell thought priestly authority was a red herring.

The direct connection to Peter that Campbell so confidently dismissed was precisely what Smith claimed—as well as personal contact with Jesus Christ's forerunner, the Baptist. In May 1829, Smith was nearing the end of his Book of Mormon translation. That month he began dictating to Oliver Cowdery the Third Book of Nephi, which recounts the ministry of the resurrected Christ to a group of New World proto-Christians. Whatever Smith's and Cowdery's feelings might have been at this point on the subject of priesthood and authority, the words Cowdery transcribed on this occasion had Christ specifically saying to a disciple, "I give unto you power that ye shall baptize this people."[176] He then prescribed the particular mode of the sacrament: "On this wise shall ye baptize them—Behold ye shall go down and stand in the water, and in my name shall ye baptize them."[177]

Five years later, Cowdery recalled the events set in motion by those verses. He said the account convinced the two of them that "none had authority from God to administer the ordinances of the gospel."[178] This may well have been a decisive moment in the evolution of Smith's ideas about priesthood authority. The experience of producing the Book of Mormon was itself an emphatic repudiation of the Protestant *sola scriptura*. Having rejected the doctrine of the Bible as sole and sufficient arbiter of truth and doctrine, Smith likely found it natural also to reject the Bible as the sufficient ground of sacramental authority. The account in 3 Nephi made the case explicitly clear: one needed the personal authorization of Christ, conveyed by ordination, to administer saving ordinances. Accordingly, Cowdery remembered, "we only waited for the commandment to be given, 'Arise and be baptized.' "[179] Days later, after "fervent" prayer, "the veil was parted and the angel of God came down clothed with glory, and delivered the anxiously looked for message, and the keys of the gospel of repentance. . . . Then his voice, though mild, pierced to the center, and his words, 'I am thy fellow servant,' dispelled every fear."[180] Cowdery specified the date as May 15, 1829.[181]

Smith's 1842 account added the ensuing words of the messenger, whom they identified as a resurrected John the Baptist: "Upon you my fellow servants I confer the priesthood of Aaron, which holds the keys of the ministering of angels, and of the gospel of repentance, and of baptism by immersion for the remission of sins." Then the angel informed Smith and Cowdery that further authority to lay on hands "for the gift of the Holy Ghost" would be conferred thereafter.[182] The canonical account of this episode was written much later, and the phrase "Aaronic priesthood" does not appear in the first years of the church. However, the name and order are clearly indicated in an 1832 revelation, in which "two priesthoods" are discussed; the "lesser priesthood" is associated with "the house of Aaron," and distinguished from a "holy priesthood," the "high priesthood" or "greater priesthood" possessed by Moses.[183]

This episode was consistent with the undeviating model for priesthood transmission that Smith believed was given by the author of Hebrews: "And no man taketh this honour unto himself, but he that is called of God, as was Aaron."[184] Smith incorporated those words into an article of faith, asserting that "a man must be called of God, by prophecy and by the laying on of hands by those who are in authority, to . . . administer in the ordinances of the gospel."[185] The analogy with Aaron is not strictly accurate. The voice of God specifically singled out one individual, Aaron, to "serve me as priest."[186] But an 1830 revelation to Joseph Smith directed that "as many as shall come, . . . embracing this calling and commandment, shall be ordained and sent forth."[187] And so a general invitation, rather than a specific prophetic voice, calls all men to the priesthood in Smith's new church.[188] In an 1832 revelation, all are enjoined to "obtain" and "magnify" their priesthood calling.[189] Considering such scriptural basis to be the voice of God, the analogy is valid. Aaron was called to his position through the voice of the prophet Moses, and was "anointed" and "consecrated" by him.[190] When Moses calls Joshua as his successor, the laying on of hands is explicitly indicated as part of the ordination.[191] In fact, as the *Jewish Encyclopedia* notes, "The ceremony of ordination derives its name, 'semikah,' from the custom of the laying on of hands."[192] The practice of bestowing authority by the laying on of hands is in this way implied in the New Testament, where Jesus calls and appoints his twelve apostles and bestows upon them power and authority.[193] That Smith received his priesthood authority in that same manner would have more than sufficed to establish the Mormon pattern.

Aaron, a Jewish source declares, was "the founder of the priesthood in Israel."[194] He and his sons were consecrated priests in perpetuity by Moses to officiate over the rites of the tabernacle, and later the temple. Aaron was of the tribe of Levi, and to the Levites in general was given responsibility for the physical care of the tabernacle and its furnishings, by way of "assisting" "Aaron the priest," but to Aaron's particular line within Levi's lineage was given the right to "attend to the priesthood."[195] So says the author of Numbers; according to Deuteronomy, "the entire Levitical tribe is appointed to serve in the priesthood."[196] This confusion is why Christians like Charles Buck understood there to be three divisions of priesthood in the Old Testament: high priests, priests, and Levites.[197] In reality, as the *Encyclopedia Judaica* notes, "the classification of the priests is a fairly simple one into just two levels: the high priest and the ordinary priests." The only question is whether all must be descended from Levi or from Aaron to be eligible, on which point the P and D authors (assumed writers of different biblical sections) differ.[198]

It was generally understood by Christians, in the words of one contemporary writer, that the "priesthood of Aaron was to cease when the true High Priest had, by the offering of himself, . . . made an end of sin."[199] Another writer with similar views thought the Mormon restoration of the Aaronic order a step in the wrong direction. "The priesthood of Aaron ceased when the temple was destroyed," objected Samuel Haining. "To talk of their being of the order of Aaron would be to restore Judaism, and banish Christianity."[200] The objection about Judaic obsolescence was no impediment to Smith because he believed a cardinal Christian error was in seeing the New and Everlasting Covenant as displacing, rather than incorporating and therefore restoring, all its prior forms. Any genuine restoration, in this view, must include the priesthood associated with Aaron. In restoring this order, Smith followed Old Testament precedent by associating it with ritualistic activities—in this case, the sacraments of baptism and the Eucharist. In a gesture toward the hereditary nature of its Old Testament institution, Smith declared that lineal descendants of Aaron had a right to the Aaronic office of bishop, "descending from father to son."[201] How one would recognize such a candidate was never specified, and invoking this right is unknown in practice. But the very recognition of a continuing lineal right from Aaron shows how literally Smith interpreted his full restoration mandate.

The author of Hebrews writes that Christ's priesthood, "according to the order of Melchizedek," is one that "supersedes and replaces the inferior priesthood of Aaron."[202] And so Mormonism refers to the Aaronic order as the lesser priesthood, a preparatory priesthood on the way to conferral of the higher. Within the Aaronic priesthood, Mormonism recognizes three main offices: priest, teacher, and deacon. (A bishop is technically an Aaronic office but can only be occupied by a holder of the Melchizedek priesthood, unless he be a literal descendant of Aaron, as will be treated in a later section.) In the church's early years, adults were ordained to all three of these offices along with a few youths, but with no particular pattern. In general, Smith intended that the ranks of the higher priesthood preside, evangelize, and direct church affairs. Those in the Aaronic priesthood were "standing ministers of the church" and their job was to attend to congregational matters, both spiritual and practical. A telling analogy from the period held that elders "quarried the stone" that was sent on to Zion, where Aaronic priesthood holders "polished it."[203]

Priests

In the Old Testament, the word kohen (ἱερεὺς or hiereus in the Septuagint) is translated as priest, as it is in the New Testament. Little confusion or disagreement surrounds this term or its biblical translation. The primary meaning of priest implies one who is authorized to offer sacrifices, and priests in Israel were the men authorized "to engage in cultic ceremonies which they conducted mainly in the Temple."[204] As Aaron was the high priest in Israel responsible for sacrificial rites, so do Christians see him as a type of Christ. And as early Christians understood Old Testament offerings by priests as a shadow and type of Christ's sacrifice, so the man who presided over the Eucharist commemorating—or reenacting—that sacrifice is seen to officiate in a priestly office. As J. N. D. Kelly writes, "The rite itself was wrapped in the sacrificial atmosphere with which our Lord invested the Last Supper. The words of institution, 'Do this' (τοῦτο ποιεῖτε), must have been charged with sacrificial overtones for second-century ears; Justin at any rate understood them to mean, 'Offer this.'"[205]

Since Catholics have seen the Eucharist in sacrificial terms, as a continuation of the original sacrifice, that church has preserved the title "priest" for those whose principal task is to administer the Eucharist. As the Baltimore Catechism describes the ceremony, "The Mass is the same sacrifice as the sacrifice of the cross because in the Mass the victim is the same." An officiating priest is requisite, for he "offer[s] . . . the Holy Sacrifice."[206] This priestly role related to sacrificial rites is at the heart of the Catholic demarcation between laity and clergy. It is the latter, the priests, who alone are entitled to "take their place at the altar."[207] Innocent III affirmed in the twelfth century that "however honest, religious, holy, and prudent anyone may be, he cannot nor ought he . . . perform the sacrifice at the altar unless he be a priest."[208]

Much more vexed is the question of another term often translated as priest—which is zaqen, rendered πρεσβύτερος, or presbyter. Generally translated as "elder," the term refers to men mature in age and judgment who exercised leadership in Israel, some of whom by the New Testament era came to be constituted as a college or council. Christians followed suit: in Acts, for example, Paul and Barnabas bring collected relief money to the presbyters of the Jerusalem church.[209] Later, the pair appeals to the same council of presbyters to settle a dispute over circumcision.[210] Eventually in the early church the bishop appears to emerge as the effective president of the council, and soon the council drops out of church organization. Presbyters, however, remained—along with deacons and bishops—as one of the principal offices of the early church. In the third century, the Constitutions of the Apostles place the presbyter, translated as priest in the Catholic tradition, between the bishop and deacon in authority.[211]

Conflict enters the picture with the English translations of that title in a post-Reformation era: is elder or priest the more accurate rendering? Catholics hold that since the Eucharistic sacrifice is the central activity performed by ordained clergy, the word "priest" and not "elder" best conveys the function of the πρεσβύτερος. Hence, the priest is considered a "sacerdos" of the second degree, subordinate to the bishop, who is a sacerdos of the first degree—a high priest with "total and complete" priesthood.[212] In Protestant thought, since Christ was the culminating and final sacrifice, "there is room for no other sacrifice nor for any repetition of sacrifices. In Christ both priesthood and sacrifice have been brought to fulfillment and to finality."[213] Protestants, therefore, find the administrative, non-priestly connotations of the term πρεσβύτερος to be more accurately and fittingly translated as "elder."

Luther's position became typical: "I have my doubts," he wrote, as to whether New Testament authors like James "would have us understand 'priests' when he says 'presbyters,' that is, 'elders.' For one who is an elder is not necessarily a priest or a minister. We may suspect that the apostle desired the older, grave men of the church to visit the sick, to perform a work of mercy, and pray in faith and thus heal."[214] So from the beginnings of Protestantism, rendering πρεσβύτερος as "priest" was seen to be affirming the importance of sacerdotal office in a religious reformation that was deliberately challenging the exclusivity and centrality of a formal priesthood. And so we find among the many demands of 1,000 Protestant ministers in their "millenary petition" to King James I an insistence that "the word priest" should be corrected in church usage to elder.[215]

In the Mormon restoration, at least three sources inform Smith's understanding and restoration of the priestly office. First, of course, the Old Testament is replete with priests and high priests. Smith clearly strove to incorporate rather than transcend Old Testament forms, so not only would their presence in that record not be dissuasive, but it would also make their inclusion in the restored church entirely reasonable. And as temples became central to Mormonism's sacramental orientation, so would priests be utterly indispensable; second, the Book of Mormon had also affirmed the presence of a priesthood among the ancient Christians of the Western hemisphere. Nephi records that he ordained "priests and teachers over the land of my people," and Moroni mentions them as well a thousand years later, according to the record.[216] Given the directive to rely upon the Book of Mormon in restoring the church, those offices would have been among the first to appear in the organization Smith directed (along with elders, mentioned less frequently).[217] Finally, the book of Revelation holds out the promise of being "priests of God and of Christ" (elsewhere "kings and priests unto God" who "will reign").[218] A better rendering of those passages would indicate a future in which the righteous constitute "a kingdom, [as] priests."[219] Smith seemed clearly to have such a destiny in mind when he told the females of Nauvoo that he intended to make of them "a kingdom of priests as in Enoch's day."[220]

Smith's blatant reversion to a formal priesthood was bad enough in Protestant eyes—ordaining actual priests only accelerated the spilling over of anti-Catholicism into anti-Mormonism in the popular press of his day. Smith ordained priests a few weeks after the church's formal organization—on June 9, 1830. A revelation of the era defined their responsibilities: "to preach, teach, expound, exhort, and baptize, and administer the sacrament, And visit the house of each member, and exhort them to pray vocally and in secret and attend to all family duties."[221]

Initially, most men who were baptized into the new church were ordained priests or teachers, serving a kind of apprenticeship before being ordained an elder (which in a few years came to be associated with the higher, Melchizedek order of priesthood). So Wilford Woodruff was ordained a teacher days after baptism, ordained a priest ten months later, then an elder after a further six months.[222] Priests were in many cases the work horses of the early church, old enough to engage in the expansive missionary work but not yet mature enough in the gospel to preside over branches or assume weightier responsibilities. From early Mormon conference minutes we get an idea of the relative distribution of priests (and other offices) where convert rates were high. Missionary Willard Richards gave a report from England in 1840 of having baptized, with his companions, 112 and confirmed 200. Of those, one teacher was ordained, two elders, and "about 20 priests."[223] At a British conference of that same year, total numbers for priesthood offices in the United Kingdom were given as eight deacons, thirty-eight teachers, and thirty-four elders. Priests numbered fifty-two.[224] In other words, even with Aaronic office holders moving up to the higher priesthood, priests sometimes remained the most numerous of the priesthood offices.

The numerous priests gradually gave way to a greater number of Melchizedek priesthood holders. In the United Kingdom, site of most dramatic church growth and highest membership in the mid-nineteenth century, priests were already outnumbered by elders in 1853: 1,913 to 2,752. By 1878, there were more than three times as many elders as priests.[225] In Utah, the pattern was the same, with the ranks of the Aaronic priesthood offices particularly thin in this period. As Young remarked in 1852, "This vast concourse of persons are all Elders in Israel, with but a very few exceptions; for there are some Priests, Teachers, and Deacons present, but not a great many."[226]

Most priests were mature men, but as the century progressed, the ranks of adult priests began to be replaced by youths. Part of the shift was attributable to the growing practice of ordaining ever younger men to the Aaronic priesthood offices, and progressing them through the ranks, as apprentices to senior priesthood holders, so to speak. The reasons for these changes were to some extent cultural. In the church's infancy, establishing the church, spreading its stakes, survival, and settlement were the dominant concerns. Once Mormons were settled, prosperous, and comfortable in Utah, the same worldliness and distractions infiltrated the younger generation as anywhere else. In the half century following their establishment in Utah, attention shifted to the church's young, with an array of programs taking shape to guide their spiritual formation. Sunday Schools were launched in 1867, and the Young Men's (and Young Ladies') Mutual Improvement Associations the next decade. By fits and starts, bishops were ordaining younger men into the priesthood "that they may commence in the harness."[227]

In an 1877 circular, the First Presidency had made it clear that they expected mature men to fill the ranks of the Aaronic priesthood, with younger men serving as apprentices rather than mere replacements.[228] By 1908, in response to President Joseph F. Smith's call to give boys "something to do that will make them interested in the work of the Lord," the church began to ordain deacons at twelve, teachers at fifteen, priests at eighteen, and elders at twenty-one.[229] In 1934, the First Presidency instituted a schedule that modified the ages slightly: deacons were to serve from the age of twelve until fifteen, teachers until seventeen, and priests until nineteen.[230] That schedule was subsequently modified again to progression at fourteen, sixteen, and eighteen, respectively. In addition to serving as home teachers (along with a Melchizedek priesthood holder), priests in today's LDS church can baptize and administer the sacrament. Priests are as a result almost entirely young men, though newly baptized adult male converts of any age are ordained as priests in preparation for receiving the higher priesthood, much as they were in the LDS church's first generation.

Teachers

Teachers (διδάσκαλος or didaskolos) are mentioned in the New Testament as what appears to be one in a litany of callings. In one case they are named along with prophets, once with prophets and apostles, and once along with several offices.[231] As with the Hebrew rabbi, the term was often an acknowledgment of learnedness or competence in moral instruction. The teacher did not evolve into a particular clerical position in the early church, but it finds a place in the Mormon hierarchy of priesthood offices nonetheless. While clear clerical precedent was lacking for the office, Smith defined it in ways that did resonate with earlier and contemporary Christian practices.

In rejecting episcopacy, early Protestants frequently organized in small groups and congregations, with diminished lines of demarcation between clergy and laity. The stewardship over the flock was often more dispersed and intimate as a consequence. Given the Puritan emphasis on purifying the visible church, supervision could be as much a matter of oversight and discipline as of comfort and strengthening. Calvin organized pastors, elders, and *dizeniers* "to visit all of the households in their quarter each year before Easter 'to examine each person briefly regarding his faith' so that no one would come to the Lord's Table 'without an understanding of the grounds of his salvation.'"[232] English Protestants as well adopted the pattern. The Puritan John Dickson admonished fellow ministers to "Watch over the Church," and be "Watchm[e]n over Souls in a Special manner."[233] A century later, one of John Wesley's innovations was to organize worshippers into small, intimate units, or classes. Class leaders were specifically charged "to see each person in his class once a week. To enquire how their souls prosper. To advise, reprove, comfort, or exhort them."[234] The *Book of Discipline* added the charge "to receive what they are willing to give toward the relief of the preachers, church, and poor."[235]

All this language is echoed in the way Joseph Smith described the duties of what he denominated priests as well as the "teachers": "The priest's duty is to . . . visit the house of each member, and exhort them to pray vocally and in secret and attend to all family duties. . . . The teacher's duty is to watch over the church always, and be with and strengthen them; And see that there is no iniquity in the church, neither hardness with each other, neither lying, backbiting, nor evil speaking."[236] The Book of Mormon was again likely influential here. Teachers appear in those pages more than two dozen times, usually in a supporting capacity serving with the priests.[237]

A teachers quorum—Smith's name for an organized body of priesthood holders of the same office—with its own president was organized by the church's "Grand Council" at the same time as the first deacons quorum, in January 1836.[238] In the church's first years, men received specific assignments to serve in this capacity as watchmen over the flock, with the duty to visit "the house of each member" in their ministry.[239] A detailed narrative survives of such a visit made by a presumably nervous William Cahoon to the Joseph Smith family home in Kirtland. Cahoon related how he

> was called and ordained to act as a ward teacher to visit the families of the Saints. I got along very well until I was obliged to pay a visit to the Prophet. . . . I went to the door and knocked and in a minute the Prophet came to the door. I stood there trembling and said to him; "Brother Joseph, I have come to visit you in the capacity of a ward teacher, if it is convenient for you." He said, "Brother William, come right in. I am glad to see you. Sit down in that chair there and . . . ask all the questions you feel like." By this time my fears and trembling had ceased and I said, "Brother Joseph, are you trying to live your religion?" He answered, "Yes." I then said, "Do you pray in your family?" He answered "Yes." "Do you teach your family the principles of the gospel?" He replied, "Yes, I am trying to do it." "Do you ask a blessing on your food?" He said he did. "Are you trying to live in peace and harmony with all your family?" He said that he was.

William Cahoon then asked a series of questions of his wife Emma, before he "left my parting blessing upon him and his family, as a teacher, and departed."[240]

As the significant pastoral responsibility implies, such watching over and "teaching" was generally confined to adults in the early Mormon church. That is likely why a question arose in 1843 as to whether it wouldn't be advisable "for a priest [who was generally older and more experienced] to be appointed to accompany a teacher to the house of each member."[241] Rather than just supervise the younger teachers, at an 1847 meeting at the Council House in Winter Quarters, Nebraska, Willard Richards urged appointment of "the smartest & aged & kind men to act as teachers in the stakes," and Young agreed.[242] "When I get into the valley," he said, "I shall take some of the gray haired & aged High Priests and set them apart as teachers"—"acting teachers," they were called.[243]

Those men and mature youth who were ordained as teachers and priests in the Aaronic priesthood had primary responsibility as "local ministers presiding over branches, collecting and dispursing Church funds, dealing with membership discipline problems and making pastoral visits to the homes of members."[244] Accordingly, equal and sometimes greater importance was attached to these offices in the "Lesser Priesthood" than to those in the "Greater." As one bishop made the case, elders and high priests were like volunteer soldiers in a time of peace. Teachers, on the other hand, "are the Regulars. . . . The others meet together, truly, & preach around the Territory, . . . but we are 'The Laborers.' We are called to act."[245] For a time, high priests were called to serve as acting teachers, and they were intended as well to mentor younger priests with whom they served. "Let the young Priests go along with their old men that they may learn," counseled Young.[246]

During one particular time of crisis, when federal troops occupied Salt Lake City in 1862, teachers assumed extraordinary duties: in order that "the people might be kept from associating with the troops that have come into our city," Young directed that "the teachers of the several wards should be constituted policemen to look after the interests of the people, and that there be added to the present number of teachers in each ward sufficient to make the aggregate in each ward 36; that if these teachers became suspicious of any persons in their wards, they should watch them day and night until they learned what they were doing and who frequented their houses."[247]

In the best of times, the teachers were an effective tool to fill ministerial gaps in a church run locally by lay clergy. Their use by local leaders—and even apostles—to "exhort" slackers and "labor with" those who neglected tithes and offerings could be perceived at times as, and perhaps was, a bit heavy-handed—especially with the older "acting teachers" in the picture.[248] "We protest against the inquisitional practice of catechising the members of this Church through the Teachers, as to their private views respecting church measures," wrote two leaders of a dissident faction.[249] Even Brigham Young Jr. noted in 1890 that too many "insignificant items" were brought forward for a teachers to investigate,[250] and George Q. Cannon reprimanded teachers for overzealousness in monitoring plural marriage practices a decade later.[251]

About this time, President Lorenzo Snow directed that with regard to sensitive financial questions, leaders needed to "take up a private labor themselves," and "not leave such matters to the ward Teachers."[252] For the next few decades, teachers took literally their commission to watch over and exhort their assigned families, but soon age changes would effectively curtail their function. As noted, in the effort to involve the young men of the church in meaningful service and participation, local leaders began to ordain Aaronic officers at younger ages. It came as a development to celebrate when, in 1934, leaders realized that "in several stakes the greater part of the teaching is being done by young men of the Lesser Priesthood quorums."[253] That fall, the First Presidency officially directed that teachers be ordained at the age of fifteen.[254] The trend had long been under way. George Cannon had noted to the readership of the youth magazine in 1891 that "it is probable that many of the boy readers of the *Juvenile Instructor* have been ordained as deacons and teachers; at least, we hope this is the case."[255]

As a result, these younger teachers of necessity turned their efforts more in the direction of friendly home visitations and inspirational messages rather than assessing faithfulness and reproving backsliders. In subsequent years, leaders pointed out that the admonition to "watch over the church" was given by revelation to elders as well.[256] At the present day, home visits are done by an elder or high priest, accompanied by another elder or, ideally, a young teacher or priest. Since 1963, the practice has been called home teaching.[257] In theory, a companion visits every individual or family in a ward at least monthly, reporting on needs or concerns to his appropriate priesthood leader.

Home teaching, along with visiting teaching—a Relief Society counterpart involving women ministering to women—has become a major source of Mormon interconnectedness at the local level. In theory, if not always in practice, every adult man and woman is responsible for spiritually and emotionally sustaining three, four, or more other families (or women, in the visiting teaching program). Many Christians practice "the passing of the peace," where they embrace one another or shake hands during worship, as "a prominent sign of reconciliation and love,"[258] and church socials provide occasion for sociability and confraternity. Mormonism takes the symbolism of the former and the randomness of the latter and transforms them into a deliberate ordering of relations that builds a warp and woof of sociality throughout the ward. Home (and visiting) teaching is thus the most manifest operational template for a Zion community, operating at the ward level.

Deacons

The calling of deacon is mentioned in the New Testament, the term meaning one who serves or waits upon another. Appropriated by early Christians, the term apparently referred to those who ministered to the needs of others.[259] The role emerges when the early Christians were criticized "because their widows were neglected in the daily distribution of food." As a result, the apostles chose several men (a woman, Phoebe, is later mentioned) and "laid their hands on them," appointing them to "wait on tables" while they attended to evangelization.[260] Deacons were viewed in the early Christian centuries as serving at the behest of the bishop, to whom they should minister "as Christ does to His Father," or as Aaron did to Moses.[261] The appointment is often mentioned alongside bishops, suggesting it represents a formal office. Deacons were to be "the bishop's ear, and eye, and mouth, and heart, and soul, that the bishop may not be distracted with many cares."[262]

Third-century texts similarly direct the deacons to administer relief "to [persons] in distress," under the direction of the bishop.[263] In the Catholic tradition, deacons could function in other ways involving the liturgy and sacraments. Anglican deacons can baptize but more generally work among the disadvantaged. Baptist deacons can lead prayer services and assist in communion, as well as serve in outreach efforts. In Methodism, too, deacons help with the administration of sacraments and are also involved in their own ministries. In virtually every case, the role of a deacon is seen as a helper or assistant, subordinate to the priest or pastor, with at least some orientation toward physical welfare.

Occasionally in early Mormonism, deacons functioned in a capacity similar to the deacons of earliest Christianity, though Smith seems not to have said anything about the office. In those "Articles and Covenants" that laid out the responsibilities of the various offices, only deacons lacked a specific function (he is to "assist . . . [the teacher] in all his duties in the church").[264] Neither was the Book of Mormon helpful in this regard, since it mentions only elders, priests, and teachers—with accompanying responsibilities of those offices.[265] But as Brigham Young determined to assert leadership in the chaotic months between the death of Smith and the exodus westward, he noted, "When you have got your Bishop, he needs assistants, and he ordains Counsellors, Priests, Teachers, and Deacons, and calls them to help him."[266] Young seemed influenced by the New Testament, specifying elsewhere that "there are bishops and deacons plenty to help" with the challenges of maintaining order and attending to the poor.[267]

Brigham Young kept such duties in mind in his direction a few years later: "Some may want medicine and nourishment, and to be looked after, and it is not the business of boys to do this; but select a man who has got a family to be a Deacon, whose wife can go with him, and assist him in administering to the needy in the ward."[268] He relied upon the epistle to Timothy for his understanding that a deacon was a man of maturity whose principal task was to assist the bishop in taking care of the poor and needy in their midst.[269] A deacons quorum with a president had been organized on January 15, 1836[270]—but it faded into neglect. Young reorganized a deacons quorum in Nauvoo in 1845,[271] but in the decades following, the tendency was to ordain men to be elders and seventies, with the Aaronic offices neglected. One reason is that to participate in the ceremonies of the Nauvoo Temple, use of which had begun in 1845, and later to participate in missionary work, men needed to hold the Melchizedek priesthood. That left few non-Melchizedek priesthood holders.[272]

After a period of appointing Melchizedek priesthood holders to act in an Aaronic capacity, leaders came to see the wisdom of appointing younger men to those deacons quorums. By the 1870s, boys from eleven to seventeen began to be ordained as deacons.[273] Some bishops in that era were ordaining boys as young as ten, primarily to assist with housekeeping and custodial duties in the ward houses, cleaning, carrying fuel, and the like; in the early twentieth century, the age of twelve years had become the norm for deacon ordination.[274] Today, their principal task is in distributing the sacrament in church services and helping with custodial duties. This former, incidentally, is one of the tasks associated with deacons from the earliest Christian era. After praying over the Eucharist, noted Justin Martyr in the second century, "those whom we call deacons give to each of those present to partake a portion of the consecrated bread and wine mixed with water, over which the thanksgiving was pronounced."[275]

MELCHIZEDEK PRIESTHOOD

One of Smith's more novel innovations was not just to recuperate a formal priesthood evocative of Catholicism but to incorporate both Old and New Testament offices in doing so. The Aaronic or Levitical orders have clear precedent in the Mosaic law; the higher priesthood Smith instituted—or restored—a few years later finds little by way of biblical information. The New Testament provides only cryptic allusions with its reference to Jesus as "a high priest forever after the order of Melchizedek." The author of Hebrews then suggests a possible dichotomy of priesthood into two distinct orders: "If perfection had been attainable through the Levitical priesthood—for the people received the law under this priesthood—what further need would there have been to speak of another priest arising according to the order of Melchizedek, rather than one according to the order of Aaron?"[276]

A standard reading of these passages has been to see Melchizedek as an anomaly, a priest with "no successor," in the words of one biblical dictionary owned by Joseph Smith.[277] Commentators saw him as a foreshadowing and type of Christ, the ultimate and final high priest. Thus Origen, the first theologian of Christianity, held that "humans can be high priests according to the order of Aaron, but only the Christ of God according to the order of Melchizedek."[278] The problem is that Melchizedek was presumably himself of the order named after himself, but where do we find such an order? Adam Clarke avoids the dilemma by loosely—and inaccurately—translating "after the order" as "after the similitude" of Melchizedek, meaning inhabiting both priestly and kingly roles.[279] Other commentators went so far as to see Melchizedek as another name for Christ to avoid that difficulty—he and he alone was of that order. George Faber was one of many who asserted that "Christ and Melchizedek are one person."[280] Yet other clergy saw in Melchizedek a real person who, in contrast to those possessed of a hereditary, Levitical priesthood, was ordained "without regard to the family from which he sprung."[281] He was a priest who "did not descend from priests, or from the tribe of Levi," agreed another.[282] In other words, Melchizedek was a priest "by appointment" rather than descent, and priest of an order neither as "inferior" or "comparatively modern" as the Levitical.[283] Carl Moll argues that one cannot explain him away as a mythical type, as he is "one of the most extraordinary men of sacred history," possessed of "a peculiar Priesthood" that makes him "a higher priest than the Levitical,"[284]—a priest "of a much more ancient order of Priesthood than that of Aaron," wrote one of Smith's contemporaries.[285] As to why we should find here an order nowhere mentioned among the Hebrews, we have no explanation.

Joseph Smith would come to see Melchizedek as these last writers did, as representing a priesthood that encompassed and existed before the Levitical (which he will call Aaronic), albeit one with an obscured Old Testament history. In critical junctures, Smith provided biblical interpolations that supported such a view. One of the more significant of Smith's revisions to the Old Testament came in the story of Moses's destruction of the tablets of the testimony. In the canonical account, Moses returns from Mt. Sinai with the Ten Commandments to find the Israelites reveling in debauchery and worshipping a calf of gold. In his fury Moses destroys the tablets, but God subsequently writes upon new tablets of stone "the words that were on the former tablets."[286] Smith makes a dramatic corrective to this version, whereby God tells the prophet he will write upon them again, but "it shall not be according to the first, for I will take away the priest-hood out of their midst; therefore my holy order, and the ordinances thereof, shall not go before them."[287] Henceforth, through Old Testament history, the Melchizedek priesthood is absent "as a body." (The church newspaper in 1833 explained that even so, many high priests had authority between Adam and Moses, and a twentieth-century church publication makes the important caveat, quoting Smith, that "there were at various times, and perhaps at all times, holy men, prophets of the Lord . . . who received the Holy Priesthood as part of their special commissions.")[288]

In an 1832 revelation, Smith filled in more of the details. God took from the Israelites "the holy priesthood," but "the lesser priesthood continued which priesthood holdeth the keys of the ministering of Angels and the preparatory gospel."[289] That Aaronic priesthood, along with the Mosaic Law, remained with Israel as a lesser, preparatory order until such time as God's people were again prepared for a fullness of the gospel. Smith reinforced an understanding of two distinct priesthood orders in another biblical emendation. In the book of Numbers, Moses reproves a wicked Levite and his fellow tribesmen for seeking, in addition to their Levitical prerogatives, "the priesthood as well!"[290] This is of course a problematical exchange, since, as the Deuteronomic author makes clear, "the entire Levitical tribe is [already] appointed to serve in the priesthood."[291] Smith emends the text with one word: "seek ye the *High* priesthood also?"[292]

Smith found corroboration of the two-order priesthood structure in the Book of Mormon. Like the book of Hebrews, the book of Alma sketched the life of Melchizedek, a high priest and king of Salem.[293] However, Alma adds the crucial detail that a whole class of priests had been ordained in an indefinite past to this order of Melchizedek, "the holy order of God" or "order of the Son."[294] Elsewhere, the Book of Mormon refers to the "high priesthood of the holy order of God," suggesting a possible alternate name for the Melchizedek priesthood, in distinction from an implied lesser priesthood.[295] In his September 1832 revelation, Smith associated the Melchizedek priesthood with the line of Old Testament prophets and patriarchs, from Adam and Abel, through Enoch and Noah, down to Jethro and Moses. John the Baptist, by contrast, as the forerunner of Christ, operated with the authority of the Aaronic, or preparatory priesthood.[296]

Curiously, neither Joseph Smith nor his associates ever provided a date for the restoration of the high, or Melchizedek priesthood. (Smith never even used the term "priesthood" in reference to the church he organized before June 1831.)[297] Smith and Cowdery both said merely that it occurred sometime after the Aaronic priesthood was received. Smith made first reference to two distinct priesthood restoration events when he enumerated in 1832 the key episodes of "the rise of the church of Christ." Third in his list of key events was "the reception of the holy Priesthood by the ministering of Angels to administer the letter of the Gospel . . . and the ordinances"; fourth was "a confirmation and reception of the high Priesthood after the holy order of the son of the living God."[298] In spite of intimations that he would provide such details (perhaps in his 1832 history), he did not. In a revelation dated to about August 1835, he indicated that it was Peter, James, and John who conveyed that high priesthood, "the first documentary reference to angelic visitations" by those three.[299] Thus, the circumstances of Smith's receipt of the Melchizedek priesthood are the most poorly attested facts of any seminal event pertaining to the Restoration.

Even in an 1838 history, he would simply say that in response to "fervent prayer . . . the word of the Lord came to us commanding me to ordain Oliver Cowdery to be an Elder in the Church of Jesus Christ and that he should ordain me to the same office."[300]

Smith claimed visitation by numerous angels, restoring to him an array of "keys," powers, authority, and commissions, and the record clearly reveals that Smith needed some time to make sense of it all and to institute a coherent order and priesthood hierarchy. Smith's failure to refer to these angelic visitations earlier has caused some early dissenters and modern skeptics alike to find the delayed accounts troubling. He did publicly lament the "slothfulness" of early recordkeeping, noting that "here is a fountain of intelligence or knowledge of infinite importance which is lost. . . . In consequence of a neglect to write these things when God reveals them, not esteeming them of sufficient worth the Spirit may withdraw and God may be angry."[301] As a result, such poor recordkeeping meant he and others too often "cannot bear record to the Church nor unto the world of the great & glorious manifestation that have been made to us with that degree of power and authority which we otherwise Could."[302] He was reproving others, but may have had himself in mind as well. Upon commencing his first journal in 1832, Smith stated his intention "to keep a minute account of all things that come under my observation." After recording only nine more entries, his editors note, Smith "abandoned journal keeping for ten months."[303]

Latter-day Saint historians date the reception of the Melchizedek priesthood to anywhere between late May 1829 and July 1830.[304] A date *after* April 1830 is viewed as problematic by some LDS historians, since the apostolic keys have been thought a necessary precondition for the organization of the church. In a significant early departure from this view, Brigham Young claimed it was "the Aaronic priesthood upon which the church was first organized."[305] He may have spoken in response to the fact that if Smith did receive a higher priesthood before 1830, he did not mention it or ordain others to it during the church's first year. In any event, Smith and Cowdery had been ordaining elders, priests, and teachers, according to the pattern of the Book of Mormon and the Articles and Covenants—but none of those offices were explicitly associated with the Melchizedek or high priesthood until a conference of June 1831. At that time, twenty-three men, already elders, were first ordained to the "high priesthood," a designation fraught with confusion for a few reasons. As we have seen, the *higher priesthood* is now in the LDS church that order of the priesthood known as the Melchizedek priesthood. The *high priest* is an office *within* that priesthood. So was Smith ordaining men to the Melchizedek priesthood, to the office of high priest *within* that priesthood, or just to a higher office without putting it in any larger order? Because conferral of the higher priesthood is now seen as prerequisite to being ordained a high priest or an elder, and Smith had been ordaining elders for some time, the second option has been sometimes taken to be the case in modern accounts. At the time, however, elders were not seen as an office within a high priesthood. Elders were ordained to that office without reference to or prior conferral of any order of priesthood, high or low. Smith mentions ordaining men to offices from the date of the church's organization but does not ever record conferring priesthood. ("We proceeded to ordain several of the brethren to different offices of the priesthood," he writes in one typical entry.)[306] This was the pattern in the Book of Mormon, where prophets ordained priests and teachers, and where a resurrected Jesus instructed his disciples to lay hands on the head of a candidate, saying, "I ordain you to be a priest" (or teacher).[307] As Richard Bushman points out, Protestants ordained clergy all the time. Conferral of priesthood, on the other hand, had unpopular, papist associations in the Protestant mind.[308]

For a hundred years and more in the LDS tradition, no unanimous consensus existed as to the necessity for a conferral of priesthood prior to and separate from ordination to a specific office. In 1894, Woodruff's counselor George Q. Cannon noted the confusion. "We have been asked," he wrote in a church periodical, "whether it is right to confer the priesthood first and then ordain [the candidate] to the particular office to which he is called, or to directly ordain him to that office in the priesthood." His authoritative reply? "The Lord has revealed no particular form. . . . Both forms have been and are being used by those officiating.[309] Largely through the advocacy of Joseph F. Smith, the practice of conferring priesthood as a precondition for office eventually prevailed, although it was 1964 before an official handbook so specified the procedure.[310]

Apparently, at that June 1831 conference, Smith understood the moment to be right to call high priests for the first time, even as he now conceived of that office as entailing a higher order unto itself, associated with Melchizedek. (Ezra Booth said just months after the conference that the "high priesthood" was an "order of Melchizedek," and John Corrill and others also remembered the development in that light.)[311] Still, the picture was not fully resolved for several more months. After this conference, those ordained as high priests were still listed as elders on church records.[312] And a revelation at a November 1831 conference did little to clarify the status of elders and their relationship to the high priesthood. That revelation still lacked a clear dichotomy between what became two distinct orders of priesthood. It referred to most offices in one grouping: "Deacon to Teacher & from Teacher to Priest & from Priest to Elder"; and "then," the revelation continued, cometh the "high Priest hood," but the reference is to "the *office* of the High Priesthood," not the order, even though the bishop is designated, confusingly, as an office within the office of the high priesthood.[313] (Compounding the ambiguity, there is evidence that just as Smith in the beginning of organization thought of the higher priesthood as the order of high priests, so did he initially consider the lower priesthood the order of priests.)[314] If all this is confusing to modern historians, it was no clearer to contemporaries. In 1832, Levi Hancock and Lyman Wight "had some conversation of the priesthood and neither of us understood what it was." William McLellin remembered being "willing to do anything that was the will of God, but he did not understand the duties of the office" when he was ordained to the high priesthood. He was told "to take upon him the office," and the duties would be explained later.[315]

So neither the June nor the November 1831 conferences signaled simple, straightforward developments as much as a growing understanding or emerging configuration of priesthood and realignment of already existing offices. A high priesthood was now beginning to emerge as distinct from a lesser priesthood. Men ordained to the high priesthood were understood to be in receipt of the higher or greater priesthood. With time, offices already in use would be relegated to a standing within a lesser priesthood. This understanding would explain why Smith could in retrospect consistently believe that he had received a higher, apostolic authority from Peter, James, and John in 1829 (or 1830), but that he had not conferred that priesthood to others until 1831. Operating on the basis of his priesthood authority, he had simply ordained them to particular ecclesiastical offices.

Only some time after Smith's death did ordination become a two-step process of conferral of priesthood, and ordination to office within that priesthood order. The existence of two discrete orders of priesthood was decisively effected with Smith's recasting of the November 1831 revelation. In its canonical 1835 version, the scripture declared unambiguously that "two priesthoods, namely, the Melchizedek, and the Aaronic" constituted "two divisions or grand heads."[316] In the language that followed, Smith laid claim to at last putting in place an eternal ordering of priesthood, however laborious the process of reconstituting and articulating that order had been. The Melchizedek priesthood, the document continued, "holds the right of presidency, and has power and authority over all the offices in the church, in all ages of the world, to administer spiritual things." This meant it held the keys of the knowledge of God, and the keys to administer the gospel and its higher ordinances (baptism fell under the Aaronic).[317] The lesser priesthood, the revelation continued, was "preparatory" and related to the ministering of angels.[318] In sum, the view of priesthood that emerges from available documents suggests a process of inspired adaptation and incremental reconstitution rather than a linear unfolding. This is quite obviously the case as well with the shifting modes of church organization themselves, as we will see.

The significance of naming two divisions of priesthood in a Christian church after Jewish orders was not lost on contemporary observers. Freemasons had employed an anointing ritual, making adherents "High Priests after the Order of Melchizedek,"[319] but Christians found the revival in a Christian setting disturbing. A few exceptions existed, as among the eighteenth-century Pietists at the community in Ephrata, Pennsylvania. There, the few hundred followers of Conrad Beissel were considered "priests of Melchizedek"; this higher "priesthood of Melchizedek," founded with the "love fire," supplanted the "Aaronic priesthood," which was founded with the "wrath fire."[320] In general, however, Samuel Haining was typical of Christians in protesting "the continuance of the Melchizedek and Aaronic orders in the church as 'priestly assumption,'" and feared that "to talk of there being of the order of Aaron would be to restore Judaism and banish Christianity."[321] Alexander Campbell believed the presence of Levitical priests in the Book of Mormon had already served as evidence of Smith's fraud, since the Nephites were presumably of Joseph's tribe, not Levi's.[322] In the face of Campbellite objections, Mormon Joel Johnson told a crowd with several of their "priests" present (more likely ministers) that lacking the Aaronic or Melchizedek priesthoods, they must of necessity fall into the third biblical category of priests, those of Baal.[323]

While Mormons and their scriptures speak of a lesser and greater priesthood, Smith clarified: "Altho there are two Priesthoods, yet the Melchisadeck Priesthood comprehends the Aaronic or Levitical Priesthood and is the Grand head, for . . . all other Priesthoods are only parts, ramifications, powers and blessings belonging to the same and are held controlled and directed by it." Most important in this regard, the Melchizedek order represents "the highest authority which pertains to the Priesthood the keys of the Kingdom of God" and "the plan of salvation."[324] It was only with receipt of this priesthood that Smith could restore the temple and its ordinances, pertaining to the New and Everlasting Covenant. Like the Aaronic, this order has several offices within it: elders, seventies, high priests, patriarch, and apostle. Unlike the Aaronic, the Melchizedek offices are not progressive in nature; only ordination to the office of elder is required for access to the full range of temple ordinances. Hence, the vast majority of men are ordained to the office of elder within this order of priesthood.

Elders

Elders, as we saw above, were in the Old Testament men of maturity and judgment with overlapping civic and religious authority. In some settings, they were authorized to "conduct political negotiations" and in others to "perform sacred ceremonies."[325] It has long been assumed that the New Testament term is adopted from its Jewish use with regard to the synagogue, but the evidence is unclear; Hellenistic as well as Jewish contexts may have shaped its usage.[326] Neither is the function of elders clearly indicated in the New Testament. Titus is directed to "appoint elders in every town," the letter to Timothy makes reference to "the elders who rule well," as well as to his blessing at the hands of "the council of elders," and younger Christians are admonished in the letter of Peter to "accept the authority of the elders."[327] All this suggests some kind of leadership role assigned to mature and trustworthy members of a congregation.

Also as we saw above, the term πρεσβύτερος (presbyter) is generally translated as priest in the Catholic tradition and elder in the Protestant. Whereas elders and priests derive from the same New Testament term, churches generally employ one or the other office—most Protestants, employing the former with Catholics and Anglicans using the latter (Lutherans have both elders and priests). Smith established priests and elders as two adjacent offices, consistent with the Book of Mormon pattern; the priest is the highest office in the Aaronic priesthood, and the elder the first office in the Melchizedek. In fact, elder is the first office mentioned in association with the Restoration. After Smith and Cowdery baptized each other, Smith recorded that he was told by the angelic John the Baptist that "I should be called the first Elder of the Church and he the second."[328]

Elder is in many ways the foundational office in the priesthood. It is this office that comprises a sufficiency of the rights and privileges necessary for the full blessings of salvation. Smith described priesthood and the covenants associated with it as the key to exaltation (salvation in the highest degree of glory) in what is now called "the Oath and Covenant of the Priesthood." It stipulates that those who are faithful in obtaining the two priesthoods of which he has spoken (the "greater priesthood" and the "lesser priesthood") and "magnifying their calling," that is, faithfully executing their responsibilities therein, "become . . . the seed of Abraham," that is, are made lawful heirs of the fullness of the Abrahamic covenant and promises. He consequently "receiveth my Father's kingdom, therefore all that my Father hath shall be given him."[329]

As Bruce McConkie taught, an elder possesses that office "which enables a man to enter the new and everlasting covenant of marriage and to have his wife and children bound to him with an everlasting tie; . . . the office which prepares a man to be a natural patriarch to his posterity and to hold dominion in the house of Israel forever; . . . the office required for the receipt of the fulness of the blessings in the house of the Lord; . . . the office which opens the door to eternal exaltation in the highest heaven of the celestial world, where man becomes as God is."[330] For that reason, all Aaronic priesthood offices are seen as preparation for ordination to the office of elder, and with that ordination, no subsequent ordination represents any greater growth or powers. Other "keys," in the sense of ability to direct other men in their priesthood offices, may pertain to such offices as bishop or apostle, but an elder possesses the fullness of the priesthood necessary for the securing of eternal life.

The office of elder was not initially understood in such a light. Smith and Cowdery were called First and Second Elders of the church before any Melchizedek order was restored, and that November 1831 revelation had referred to the priesthood offices from "Deacon to Teacher & from Teacher to Priest & from Priest to Elder." And after them "cometh the high Priest hood."[331] With hindsight, it appears that Smith was relegating elders to the lesser priesthood, but it is not clear he had yet understood the high priesthood as an order encompassing other offices. At any rate, elders were not yet considered offices in the higher priesthood as they soon became. (The fact that elders and priests were specifically designated in 1830 to officiate in the Eucharist similarly implied that the two were still closely related offices with similar standing.)[332] In Smith's expansion of the 1831 directive on priesthood, and with the introduction of the "high priesthood," he took steps to disambiguate the standing of elders. The placement of other offices was apparently understood; only elder was singled out for special attention: "The office of an elder comes under the priesthood of Melchizedek," the revelation now definitively declared.[333]

Seventy

Luke records that after he had commissioned twelve apostles, and noting that "the harvest is plentiful but the laborers are few," Jesus "appointed seventy others and sent them on ahead of him."[334] Little consensus emerged in the early Christian centuries about the significance of that group. Eusebius (ca. 265–340) thought they were special disciples of some sort.[335] Bede (672–735) believed they were the future presbyterate, a "lesser rank of the priesthood" than bishops.[336] Protestants, predictably, were not likely to associate the calling with a particular office. Thus John Bradford saw Christ's apostles and the seventy as simple forerunners to modern "pastors and missionaries of the Christian church."[337] Adam Clarke added the insight that as Jesus chose twelve apostles as an echo of the "twelve patriarchs" of the "twelve tribes," so now did he choose seventy other disciples, "as Moses did the seventy elders," to be "ministers of righteousness."[338] While some were insistent that the seventy of New Testament times was not intended as a fixture of the church or part of "the permanent ministry," at least one contemporary of Joseph Smith, the Presbyterian minister Dirck Lansing, appointed "seventy disciples" in his congregation to serve as assistant ministers to the flock.[339]

From the LDS church's founding in 1830, the organization and function of the seventies followed the most convoluted history of any priesthood office. After Smith had reinstituted the office of apostles, it was natural that he would soon thereafter, following the New Testament pattern, appoint an assisting group of seventy. However, Smith took the step of deriving from the biblical example the office rather than (at least initially) the number. On February 28, 1835, just two weeks after appointing twelve apostles, and invoking not New Testament precedent but rather "the visions and revelations which I had received," Smith ordained several men to the office of the seventy. He selected forty-three individuals "from the number of those who went up to Zion with me." In the New Testament, Peter determined to fill the vacancy in the apostleship out of "the men who have accompanied us" until the day of Christ's death.[340] In a similar spirit, Smith seemed determined to choose the church leadership from those who had risked life and limb in the expedition to reclaim a Missouri Zion and succor the beleaguered Saints. It was, for him, the crucible and proving ground of latter-day discipleship, as joint suffering and persecution with Jesus had been for the church's first generation.

The day before calling men to the seventy, Smith had asked the apostles to consider the question of how their calling was "different from the other callings and offices of the church."[341] Initially, the role of the seventy was virtually identical to that of the apostles. Both were assigned in an early revelation "to build up the church, and regulate all the affairs of the same," with the seventy operating "under the direction of the twelve." The Twelve were to be "special witnesses of the name of Christ," while the seventies were called to be "especial witnesses unto the Gentiles."[342] The apostles had the additional responsibility of "opening the door by the proclamation of the gospel of Jesus Christ."[343] While both were responsible for proclaiming the message of the gospel restored, in other words, the apostles were tasked with leading the way in the Great Commission—which is why when the first mission abroad to England commenced, it fell to the apostles to inaugurate the work. Still, the callings were similar enough that months after the office was created, new members were ordained to the "apostleship of the first Seventy."[344]

At the time of initiating this office, Smith appointed seven men to be presidents within the First Quorum of Seventy (one would be appointed as president of this First Council of Seventy after Smith's death).[345] This was in accord with a subsequent revelation that portended substantial future growth in the numbers of seventies. The seven presidents were not only to preside over this quorum of seventy, eventually to have that many members, but "these seven presidents [were eventually] to choose other seventy" to constitute a new quorum, and "also other seventy, until seven times seventy, if the labor in the vineyard of necessity requires it."[346] So an organization was envisioned with a President of the First Council at the head, who presided over seven "presidents of the quorum" who in turn were to preside over a quorum of seventy (with up to seventy members), and eventually over several quorums of seventy. That vision would be more than a century in its fulfilment.

Of the first seven presidents called in 1835, five had been ordained high priests, and it was subsequently determined that the seventy and high priest were to be considered separate offices, and those five were replaced.[347] Smith organized second and third quorums in Kirtland in 1836.[348] In the Nauvoo era, leaders decided that all men under thirty-five should be ordained seventies, presumably because as relatively young men, they were best suited for the rigors and sacrifice of mission service soon to surge, and missionary work was their particular responsibility. As a result, the three quorums of Kirtland became thirty-five by 1846, with more than 3,000 members.[349] The seven presidents of the original quorum were now designated the First Council of Seventy and made General Authorities (leaders with churchwide jurisdiction).[350]

Reflecting the importance attached to this office, the seventies had their own Hall in Nauvoo, housing their offices and a library—the only priesthood quorum to have its own building in Nauvoo or any city. The purposes to which that building were dedicated reflect a liberal conception of the reciprocal influences a worldwide missionary labor could exert and absorb. Missionary seventies were charged with taking the gospel abroad—but they were also tasked by Smith with bringing cultural fruits of their labors back to Zion. A Nauvoo newspaper announced, "According to a Revelation, received not long since, it appears to be the duty of the members of the Church of Jesus Christ of Latter Day Saints to bring to Nauvoo their precious things, such as antiquities, . . . as well as inscriptions and hieroglyphics, for the purpose of establishing a Museum of the great things of God, and the inventions of men, at Nauvoo." The collection of "ancient records, manuscripts, paintings and hieroglyphics," like the city library, was to be housed in the Seventies Hall.[351] Designs for the library's museum were ambitious:

> Among the improvements going forward in this city, none merit higher praise, than the Seventies' Library. The concern has been commenced on a footing and scale, broad enough to embrace the arts and sciences, everywhere: so that the Seventies' while traveling over the face of the globe, as the Lord's "Regular Soldiers," can gather all the curious things, both natural and artificial, with all the knowledge, inventions, and wonderful specimens of genius that have been gracing the world for almost six thousand years. Ten years ago but one seventy, and now "fourteen seventies" and the foundation for the best library in the world! It looks like old times when they had "Kirjath Sapher [*sic*]," the city of books.[352]

Susan Easton Black notes other intellectual fruits of the calling particular to the seventies. In this newly stable climate, and "knowing that mission calls were forthcoming, the seventies sought opportunities to increase their knowledge of countries and peoples and to improve their speaking and writing skills. They invited James M. Monroe, one of their number, to teach English grammar and George D.

Watt, another seventy, to teach classes in shorthand."[353] The number of quorums had grown to dozens in Nauvoo, but after Utah settlement, geographical dispersion inhibited the functioning of seventies quorums, leading to years of "disarray and confusion." Their connection with mission work was still clear in 1894, when President Cannon discouraged the ordination of young men to the office "unless they were about to go on missions."[354] As a result, the proportion of seventies to elders decreased, at least in Utah.

In 1852, there were two seventies for every elder. By 1877, the proportion was almost exactly reversed.[355] In the British Isles, however, the decline in seventies took much longer. In an 1899 Liverpool conference, elders, priests, and teachers were equally represented at six each, to fourteen seventies.[356] In Birmingham, the pattern was similar: seventies outnumbered elders twenty-two to twenty, with only eight priests, eleven teachers, and five deacons. Other conferences recorded comparable distributions.[357] In 1904 President Joseph F. Smith reaffirmed that their calling was "to preach the gospel . . . to all the nations," but of course full-time missionaries were also filling this role.[358] Gradually, seventies were understood to be responsible for missionary work within their home units, and they were organized by stake in 1936 with that emphasis in mind.[359] Reflecting their missionary focus, beginning in 1974 the presidencies of those stake quorums also served as the mission presidency of the stake.[360] The era of locally called and serving seventies ended in 1986, when seventies quorums at the stake level, which once constituted the backbone of priesthood in the church, were disbanded, their members assimilated into elder or high priest quorums, and the office of seventy thereafter confined to authorities at the General or Area level.

High Priest

The office of high priest evoked two distinct associations in the nineteenth century. First, the office would be associated with the Jewish priesthood of Aaron and his descendants. Although priests were many, the high priest was apparently "an office of supremacy regarding certain functions within the Temple."[361] By the Second Temple period, priestly responsibilities had merged with political authority to make the high priest the de facto head of the Jewish people. So in the gospel narratives, we find the role of the high priest (Caiaphas) is in fact more political than spiritual, since under Roman rule, "the office of high priest became a political tool in the hands of the administration."[362] Political patronage, rather than Aaronic descent or holy anointing, had become the source of his authority.

The second way in which high priest would have resonance was in reference to Jesus Christ, whom the author of Hebrews called our "Great High Priest."[363] He was, in the words of one Reformation work, "the Alone High-Priest, Prophet, and King of Saints."[364] Although some commentators saw the reference to the priesthood "after the order of Melchizedek" as constituting an obscure ancient priesthood, it was more commonly read as referring to Christ in his unique role of the "Alone High-Priest." A third association could be mentioned, which is the Masonic order of high priesthood and high priests.

Smith would have been familiar with all these precedents as well as the Book of Mormon example where the high priest presided over the church of the Nephites.[365] As we saw, Smith began to ordain high priests from June 1831, at which time the high priesthood seemed in his conception to be the priesthood pertaining to high priests. With time, the high priesthood or Melchizedek priesthood was construed as an order of the priesthood within which different offices were possible, including but not limited to the high priest. High priests were generally charged with spiritual rather than temporal responsibilities (one exception was bishops, who had to be high priests). From their ranks were chosen men to serve on high councils (deliberative and advisory councils with authority over large areas of the church) as well as to serve as leaders of local congregations and far-flung branches of the church. Today higher offices in the ecclesiastical structure—members of most bishoprics, stake and mission presidencies, and Area and General Authorities—also require prior ordination to the office of high priest.

In the modern church, high priests also have primary responsibility over temple and family history work. Elders and the Aaronic priesthood offices are organized into quorums at the ward level, whereas high priests have a stake quorum but meet with their ward "group" on Sundays. Until recent decades, ordination to high priest was only done to qualify men for church callings where such ordination was a requirement. In practice this has meant that the elders quorum was populated by a mix of younger and older men, while the preponderance of high priests were typically in their mature years with a sprinkling of younger men who had served in bishoprics. Currently, the practice is to transition men from elders to the high priest quorum when they are in their fifties or sixties, regardless of their church calling or office, to create more age-based social groupings. Ordination to the office is at the recommendation of the stake president.

Patriarch

The term patriarch has varied usage in the Judeo-Christian tradition. Most commonly, the patriarchs are taken to be, in Charles Buck's simple language, "heads of families; a name applied chiefly to those who lived before Moses, who were both priests and princes."[366] The Catholic Church has a more specific group of referents in mind, holding that the term "properly refers to Abraham, Isaac, and Jacob, although two other exceptions are acknowledged": the twelve sons of Jacob, and the twenty men named from Adam through Noah and from Shem through Abram.[367] In the post-biblical world, the word came also to refer to bishops who had particularly wide jurisdiction, with "patriarchal rights." Initially these were the bishops of Rome, Alexandria, and Antioch; later Jerusalem and Constantinople were added. By the time of Christendom's Great Schism, several more bishops "claimed the title of patriarch," and eventually the title came to signify the leader of a non-Roman, national church.[368]

Most offices Smith restored found their clear precedent in the scriptures he relied upon: elders, priests, and teachers from the Book of Mormon, and bishop, deacon, apostle, and seventy from the New Testament; the office of patriarch he drew straight from the Old Testament and incorporated into the burgeoning priesthood organization. In this case, however, he defined the office not in terms of its place in an ecclesiastical hierarchy but principally in terms of a very limited function that he associated with the Old Testament patriarchs: the dispensing of a particular genre of blessing, which was a priesthood ordinance. As the apostle James Faust said, describing both past and present cases: "The office of patriarch is an office . . . of blessing, not of administration."[369] Making that position into a church office, like restoring prophets and high priests, was but one more indication of Smith's refusal to recognize a fundamental distinction between the old and the new. It was yet another version of his repudiation of Alexander Campbell's entirely reasonable and typical Christian insistence that the New Testament was a model "for the worship, discipline, and government of the New Testament Church . . . as the Old Testament was for the worship, discipline, and government of the Old Testament Church."[370]

Smith had noted, in an 1832 revelation, that the "Holy Priesthood" had been conveyed anciently through primarily patrilineal lines. It passed from Adam to Abel to Enoch and so on down to Noah and Abraham "through the lineage of their fathers."[371] Initially, Smith referred to this patriarchal priesthood in connection with the office of church patriarch, which was at first an office of tremendous prestige, though with little actual ecclesiastical authority. Then, in 1835, Smith preached on "the evangelical order."[372] He used the term evangelist interchangeably with patriarch and appears here to be speaking of a patriarchal order. Smith, we will see, comes to develop that order as it relates to temple sealing powers, though he seems to have something in mind more like a hereditary priesthood office than a distinct order. In a revelation received months earlier, Smith had referred to "evangelical ministers," or patriarchs, saying that "this order of the priesthood was confirmed to be handed down from father to son."[373] So Smith defined the patriarch as an office patterned on the Old Testament patriarchs, a patriarch in his understanding being "the oldest man of the Blood of Joseph or of the seed of Abraham."[374]

Smith may have said the patriarch should be "the oldest man of the blood of Joseph," but in fact he came to understand the patriarchal line to belong to his family in particular. The Old Testament figure Joseph of Egypt, great-grandson of Abraham, was plainly key in this regard, and a passage in the Book of Mormon doubtless played a role. The biblical Joseph received Isaac's longest and most effusive blessing of the twelve sons, being likened to a "fruitful bough, a fruitful bough by a spring; [whose] branches run over the wall." He was promised from the "Almighty . . . blessings of heaven above, blessings of the deep that lies beneath, blessings of the breasts and of the womb," and told "the blessings of your father are stronger than the blessings of the eternal mountains, the bounties of the everlasting hills."[375] Toward the end of the translation process, Smith found himself written into scriptural and providential history by that same Joseph. For the Book of Mormon recorded that patriarch as "saying: A seer shall the Lord my God raise up, who shall be a choice seer unto the fruit of my loins. Yea, Joseph truly said: Thus saith the Lord unto me: A choice seer will I raise up out of the fruit of thy loins; and he shall be esteemed highly among the fruit of thy loins. And unto him will I give commandment that he shall do a work for the fruit of thy loins, his brethren, which shall be of great worth unto them, even to the bringing of them to the knowledge of the covenants which I have made with thy fathers."[376] Given this attestation of his own direct descent from Joseph of Egypt, Smith apparently understood "the oldest man of the Blood of Joseph" to be his father and made the office hereditary. As Brigham Young was ready to acknowledge, "the right of patriarchal blessings belongs to Joseph's family."[377]

In December 1834, Smith ordained his father, Joseph Smith Sr., to the office of church patriarch, saying later that "wherever the Church of Christ is established in the earth, there should be a patriarch for the benefit of the posterity of the Saints as it was with Jacob."[378] As Jacob blessed his posterity in the concluding chapters of Genesis, so was the LDS patriarch directed to pronounce prophecies and words of blessing to those in the church. Originally, as Oliver Cowdery indicated, "a patriarch was expected to bless the fatherless and those whose fathers were either not church members or lived far from their children."[379] Within a short time, however, the patriarch's blessing was seen to be independent of, or in addition to, fathers' blessings and was administered accordingly to all who requested one. When Joseph Sr. died, the office passed to Hyrum, Smith's elder brother. Others in that line were ordained successively to the office, with two non-Smiths, Frank Woodbury and George Richards, functioning in that capacity in the 1930s.[380]

Two years after the appointment of Joseph Smith Sr., church growth was making it impractical for one man to cover the distances involved or volume of requests for blessings, and so an 1835 revelation directed the ordination of local patriarchs. "It is the duty of the Twelve," the revelation said, "in all large branches of the church, to ordain evangelical ministers, as they shall be designated unto them by revelation."[381] Subsequently, the church, or presiding, patriarch attended primarily to the needs of those who lived outside of organized stakes where such blessings were unavailable. In 1979, the church announced that the office of Patriarch to the Church was being eliminated "because of the large increase in the number of stake Patriarchs and the availability of patriarchal service throughout the world."[382]

Brigham Young indicated in an 1847 sermon on the patriarchal priesthood that Smith's early usage pertaining to church patriarchs and late usage of the term with reference to certain temple sacraments of endowing and marriage sealing (see chapter 6) had actually been consistent, because initially patriarchs both pronounced personal blessings and confirmed Abrahamic promises. "It is necessary to have Patriarchs to bless the people that they may have blessings by the spirit of prophecy and revelation sealed upon their heads and their posterity and know what awaits their posterity." And this same patriarchal authority, Young added, was the power "necessary in order to redeem our dead and save our children," that the Abrahamic promises may be ours, with seed "as numerous as the stars of heaven and the sands of the seashore."[383] It is with these latter promises in mind that Young and others frequently referred to plural marriage as a "patriarchal order."[384] Confirming or "sealing" the full extent of these covenantal promises was the special province of patriarchs as Smith defined the office. Invoking a patriarchal office on one occasion, Smith told James Ivins, "I seal thee up unto eternal life," and the patriarch Joseph Smith Sr. frequently sealed up to eternal life the Saints he blessed.[385] Young even complained in 1877 that elders were occasionally usurping the prerogative of the patriarch, to "seal all the blessings upon" new members that it was his province to seal.[386]

An official 1939 treatise on priesthood held, in words Young would have seconded, that "the Patriarchal order of Priesthood is the Melchizedek Priesthood under patriarchal organization, such as prevailed in the First Dispensation."[387] However, in distinction from the dynastic implications of past models of patriarchy, leaders of the modern era emphasize instead the eternally foundational status of companionate marriage as the essence of this order. James Talmage defined the patriarchal order as a condition wherein "woman shares with the man the blessings of the Priesthood, . . . seeing and understanding alike, and cooperating to the full in the government of their family kingdom."[388] It is, in sum, an order of priesthood that can only be entered into jointly, over the sealing altar of the temple.

The term, patriarchal priesthood, had faded from general use by the twentieth century. It has in the modern church been defined as a subset of, rather than distinct from, the Melchizedek priesthood—but in language consistent with Smith's 1843 sermon on the subject. "The patriarchal order is not a third, separate priesthood. Whatever relates to the patriarchal order is embraced in the Melchizedek Priesthood. 'All other authorities or offices in the church are appendages to [the Melchizedek] priesthood' [D&C 107:5]. The patriarchal order is a part of the Melchizedek Priesthood which enables endowed and worthy men and women to preside over their posterity in time and eternity."[389]

5

Ecclesiastical Structure

IT IS CONCEIVABLE that a body of believers could operate on a premise of authority and rituals without the imposition of formal structures and institutional forms. Even an assortment of offices like deacon and elder, based on New Testament precedent, says nothing about larger patterns of organization. Hugh Nibley surveyed the scholarly debates of a century ago over the extent to which early Christians saw themselves as an organized body. Ernst Renan, he notes, believed that the early Christians "knew little else than the law of love"; Karl Holl "argued that the Twelve were historical but that they had no office"; J. B. Lightfoot saw order gradually emerging from within the ranks; and Olof Linton argued that Christians only learned by experience that "the church can exist without any organization," but not "persist without organization."[1] Nibley referred to such positions as part of a "'spirit' controversy: the charisma as a free, formless principle versus the idea that the Spirit can and does bring order, law, and discipline."[2]

Those controversies have long since faded. The question today concerns the specifics of that process by which order, offices, and procedures were instituted in the very earliest years. Roman Catholicism predicates its claim to authority on Christ's commission to Peter, considering him to be personally delegated as the "vicar of Christ," "the foundation of the church," "from whom the episcopacy and all authority have emerged."[3] Accordingly, a literal apostolic succession is the guarantee of the church's enduring claim to that authority, even as it entails a church government that is hierarchical, centrally administered, and episcopal (since they see Peter as the first bishop of Rome). Critiques of the papacy by the early Reformers were direct attacks on this centralization of authority. Hence Luther argued that office was the result of egregious power grabs, not divine commission: "The Roman bishops have from the first sickened, ailed, wheezed, and gasped for sovereignty over all the bishops."[4] Calvin went further, denying any distinction to the office of bishop to begin with: "According to the usage of Scripture, bishops do not differ from presbyters [elders] in any way. But through vice and corruption it came about that those who held the leading place in individual cities, began to be called 'bishops.'"[5]

Alternatives to the Catholic model generally involved forms of government that were at first only slightly less hierarchical. Anglicans sustained the bishops as legitimate successors of the apostles but denied the Roman supremacy. "Our authority is built," John Henry Newman declared, on "our apostolic descent.... The Lord Jesus Christ gave His Spirit to His Apostles; they in turn laid their hands on those who would succeed them; and these again on others and so the sacred gift has been handed down to our present bishops."[6] Lutherans, too, denied the supremacy of any one bishop but maintained an essentially episcopal structure but replaced the pope with the monarch as the supreme head of the church. That model had to be revised under the cumulative blows of Charles I's execution and James II's embrace of Catholicism. Their Methodist descendants tended to opt for a loose episcopal hierarchy but with power emanating from the bottom and flowing upward. Calvin replaced the Catholic hierarchy with three different offices derived from the New Testament: ministers or pastors had authority to preach and administer sacraments, elders performed a pastoral and disciplinary ministry, and deacons supervised relief of the poor and needy. Governing authority resided in councils and the local and district levels, though even in his lifetime Reformed churches split on whether governing authority should be vested in the local congregation or should inhere in presbyteries, synods, and general assemblies.[7]

The process of Protestant denominational formation has often been gradual and difficult to delineate precisely. By contrast, the process of Mormonism's unfolding was marked by a few decisive events transpiring in relatively quick succession, largely because Smith's claim to divine authority was emphatic and dateable to specific moments. Smith himself dated his heavenly commission to September 1827, at which time an angel conveyed to him an ancient record.[8] As we saw above, the directive to establish a church came in spring 1829. That same May, Smith claimed to be ordained to the priesthood by an angel identified as John the Baptist and was designated "first Elder" of a church still yet to be established. With the publication of the Book of Mormon in March 1830, Smith began to extend his core of followers beyond an extended family circle. Then, days later on April 6, Smith formally organized the Church of Christ. On that occasion, he recorded a revelation known as the Articles and Covenants of the church.[9]

This was the first official pronouncement of Joseph Smith on the subject of church organization—and it gave only the barest of rudiments. As is true of LDS theology generally, official narratives have tended to consider restoration as an event rather than an ongoing process—and this is the case with the priesthood in particular. Though the establishment of the church occurred as a definitive step following specific determinative events—the receipt of the priesthood, the publication of the Book of Mormon, and formal incorporation—the ordering of that priesthood into offices and councils and hierarchies proceeded unevenly and only with years of experience, acquired understanding, and successive revelations. This should not be surprising. True, a church article of faith declares the church to be modeled on "the same organization that existed in the primitive church, that is, apostles, prophets, pastors, teachers, evangelists, and so forth."[10] However, it is also the case, as Kevin Giles has written but many Mormons forget, that in the New Testament, "we do not find a clearly defined and continuing pattern of leadership, nor a given definition of the functions of those who lead, nor agreed and uniform titles for leaders. The structure of the church evolved."[11]

Such was also the case with the Latter-day Saint organization. A quorum of apostles (initially "disciples") was anticipated in 1829 but would be six years in its establishment.[12] In the 1830 "Articles and Covenants," Smith was affirmed as an apostle and First Elder of the church. (As late as 1839, Smith was still being sustained as the "presiding Elder" over the church.)[13] The offices of priest, teacher, and deacon were also mentioned, in descending order of authority beneath elder, with some associated rights and duties (priests and elders could baptize and administer the sacrament).[14] Of special significance, the revelation was submitted to the church's first conference for their approbation, intimating a participatory model of church government.[15] Further emphasizing a horizontal power structure, directions were given for the elders of the church to convene in conference every three months to transact church business, along a model similar to the Methodists. The initial ordering of the hierarchy unfolded quickly at the same time. A revelation announced the same day, but—unlike the other—in the voice of God himself, declared Smith "a seer, a translator, a prophet, an apostle, and elder." The revelation then explained the special authority associated with Smith's calling: "the church . . . shalt give heed unto all his words and commandments which he shall give unto you as he receiveth them, walking in all holiness before me; For his word ye shall receive, as if from mine own mouth."[16]

In a church predicated upon the universal accessibility of personal revelation from God, the revelation was essentially declaring Smith to be first among equals. The

Book of Mormon's most substantial theological contribution had been to democratize revelation, making divine communication "the gift of God unto all."[17] "Man,
being created but little below the angels, only wants to know for himself," proclaimed the first issue of the church newspaper, which Smith oversaw.[18] The resultant problem, quick to emerge, was the possibility of conflicting revelations from
Smith and from those equals. Hiram Page was one of the eight men who saw and
handled the gold plates, and his name is appended to an affidavit prefacing the Book
of Mormon to that effect. Some five months after the Mormon church's organization he began to claim, through a seer stone, authoritative revelations for the nascent
church, prompting Smith to produce a revelation that established the principle of
the presiding spiritual authority in the church. The September 1830 revelation, by
declaring that "no one shall be appointed to receive revelations and commandments
[for] this church excepting my servant Joseph Smith, . . . until I shall appoint . . .
another in his stead," effectively transformed the role of a prophet into the virtual
office of Prophet. His sole authority to receive revelations as "the head of the church"
established his presiding primacy.[19]

In the first generation of Mormonism, members were organized into branches
of the church wherever sufficient baptisms occurred to justify them. A few such
centers existed in Mormonism's first months in New York and Pennsylvania. Not
more than a handful of believers lived in each area, presided over by a "branch president." Traveling through Ohio as part of a fall 1830 proselytizing mission to the
Native Americans on the Missouri frontier, Parley Pratt and his companions baptized over 100 converts near Kirtland—most of them followers of Sidney Rigdon, a
Campbellite preacher who embraced the new faith. Almost immediately thereafter
(December 1830), Smith pronounced that all Saints should "assemble together at
the Ohio."[20] The "gathering" of Mormons had begun.

By February, converts new and old were streaming into Kirtland, many of them
destitute. The needs of the congregation, significant in the best of times on the
frontier, grew particularly acute. In this context, Smith pronounced a revelation
that designated a new office, that of bishop, to function in the role as described
in the New Testament church. His associate and ex-Campellite Rigdon, himself
a bishop in his old movement, may have influenced Smith in restoring the office
of bishop and others not found in the Book of Mormon.[21] In this new dictate, the
Lord "called my servant Edward Partridge; and I give a commandment, that he
should be appointed by the voice of the church, and ordained a bishop unto the
church, . . . [t]o see to all things as it shall be appointed unto him in my laws in
the day that I shall give them."[22] Five days after Partridge's call, Smith instituted
by revelation an economic principle variously known as the Order of Enoch, or
the Law of Consecration, which explained the onerous burden the bishop was

about to assume. Aimed at replicating the Zion of Mormon belief, the law required members of the church to "consecrate all thy properties, that which thou hast unto me. . . . And they shall be laid before the bishop of my church." The bishop's unenviable task was then to "appoint every man a steward over his own property, or that which he has received, inasmuch as is sufficient for himself and family."[23] The residue was to be "kept in [a] storehouse, to administer to the poor and needy, as shall be appointed by the . . . bishop."[24] In other words, members were called upon to deed their possessions over to the church. The bishop and family would agree upon their needs, receive back accordingly, and use the balance to succor the poor and needy. The plan met such impediments—including legal challenges by disgruntled members suing to recover contributions—as have afflicted most communitarian ventures, and its implementation was suspended a few years later (the underlying principle of consecration remains in force and is affirmed in the temple). But for the practice's duration, the bishop's administrative obligations were immense, and his flock was the entire church, or the entire church in one of two areas of gathering. By the end of the year, the nucleus of gathering had shifted to Missouri, and Partridge was reassigned to that region, replaced by Newel K. Whitney as bishop of Ohio.

As the church grew in disparate locations, a centralized hierarchy developed in complexity and offices, beginning in 1832. Until then, Smith's authority rested largely on his apparent calling from God, manifest principally in his translation of the Book of Mormon. His authority was in part a matter of charismatic leadership. True, revelations like the 1831 pronouncement declared that he was "called upon by God," who "spake unto him from heaven, and gave him commandments." But the same revelation acknowledged that God "also gave commandments to others, that they should proclaim these things unto the world."[25] Other declarations had designated him "first Elder" and the man authorized to receive revelations for the church. It was in 1832, however, that Smith put in place a formal governing structure, with clearly differentiated and hierarchically ordered priesthood offices.

THE FIRST PRESIDENCY

A major step forward was the creation of a presiding council to govern the church. In November 1831, a revelation directed that "one be appointed of the high Priest hood to preside over the Priest hood & he shall be called President of the high Priest hood of the Church or in other words the Presiding high Priest." He was to "preside over the whole church, & to be like unto Moses."[26] The revelation did not specify who should be appointed, but it does not appear that there was any question in anyone's mind as to the obvious choice. On March 8 of the year following, Smith constituted a new leadership council when he "ordained brother Jesse Gause and Brother Sidney [Rigdon] to be my counselors of the ministry of the presidency," with time to be called the First Presidency of the Church.[27]

A week later, a revelation confirming Gause's appointment used language that conspicuously connected the creation of this presidency directly to the apostolic authority bestowed upon Peter in the New Testament (and given to Joseph Smith a few years before). The text declared that the Lord had "given the keys of the kingdom" to Smith, which keys "belong always unto the Presidency of the High Priesthood."[28] At about the same time, Smith received a revelation that he never promulgated but which detailed the purview of this presidency: it consisted of the "authority to preside . . . over all the Concerns of the church."[29] Smith's decision to share the presidency with two counselors was indicative of a trend that reached its climax over the next three years. As Richard Bushman has written, "There are signs that he intended the revelatory power to pass from himself to the councils of the church which were organized in 1834 and 1835."[30] The intention seems to have unfolded in accordance with a vision he left unrecorded, in which he saw "the order of councils in ancient days."[31] Apparently, this was the understanding which had led him to share his presidency with two counselors in 1832. For he now recorded his understanding that "the apostle Peter . . . held the keys of the kingdom of God on earth. . . . He had two men appointed as councilors with him."[32]

In February 1834, he instituted the next stage of church government modeled on this vision. "Jerusalem was the seat of the Church Council in ancient days."[33] Accordingly, Smith appointed twelve men "for the purpose of settling important difficulties which might arise in the church, which could not be settled by the church or the bishop's council to the satisfaction of the parties."[34] And, as "Peter was the president of the Council" anciently, so would Smith and his counselors serve as a presidency over this church council. They were "acknowledged presidents by the voice of the council."[35] And unlike previous ad hoc assemblages, this council was to be a standing council, called the high council, consisting of twelve high priests. A key emphasis in creating this council was Smith's dispersion of revelatory authority. In other words, Smith accorded this council not just the authority for independent action but also the right to personal revelation pertaining to their stewardship. "In cases of difficulty respecting doctrine or principle," he directed, "(if there is not a sufficiency written to make the case clear to the mind of the council) the President may inquire and obtain the mind of the Lord by revelation."[36]

The jurisdiction of this council was limited to diocese-like areas indicated in the first revelation to the church that created ecclesiastical units larger than branches, or individual congregations. Referring to the church in the environs of Kirtland,

Ohio, where converts had begun to gather a year earlier, the April 1832 revelation declared in God's voice that "I have consecrated the land of [Kirtland] . . . for the benefit of the Saints of the Most High, and for a stake to Zion."[37] For Latter-day Saints, the term "stake," taken from Isaiah, became the designation for a geographical area of church gathering, initially of fairly substantial scope.[38] At first, Smith and his counselors presided over the stake—since it composed the bulk of the church's membership. But missionary work was drawing in a steady stream of converts from places as distant as Canada, Maine, the Indian Territory, and the American South, and the canonized minutes of the first high council's organization anticipated there would be more high councils, and therefore more stakes, to come ("whenever a high council of the church of Christ is regularly organized . . . ," they noted).[39] The second stake was not far off. Beginning in the fall of 1830, a new area of gathering had been announced, together with plans for the city of Zion to be built in the land of Missouri. The border state quickly rivaled Kirtland as a center of convert population; by summer 1834 more than a thousand had migrated there—many having been expelled from Jackson County in 1833, relocating to the north in Clay County. And so that area was designated a stake of Zion, and in July 1834 Smith appointed David Whitmer to preside over the Missouri High Council, assisted by counselors William W. Phelps and John Whitmer. That made Whitmer the second ranking administrator after Smith.

With the formation of this second high council there was no longer one "high council of the church"; Smith and his counselors for the time being continued to preside over the Kirtland High Council, which was parallel to its counterpart in the West; at times, the presidency of the Missouri stake joined the presidency of the Kirtland stake to constitute an ad hoc super council of sorts. (It was referred to as the High Council of the Presidency on those occasions.)[40] Early the next year, with the inclusion of both high councils, the two bishoprics, and the Quorum of the Twelve Apostles, this Grand Council met to further solidify the growing leadership structure.[41]

Since Smith and Whitmer were both now presidents of high councils, a few months later the position of Joseph Smith was more sharply defined, consistent with his long-standing status as First Elder of the church. Minutes of a meeting in which Smith added three counselors to his presidency made clarifications "for the benefit of the reader, that he be instructed concerning the power and authority of the above named Priesthood. First. The office of the President is to preside over the whole Church; to be considered as at the head; to receive revelations for the Church; to be a Seer, Revelator, and Prophet having all the gifts of God:—taking Moses for an ensample. Which is the office and station of the above President Smith, according to the calling of God and the ordination which he has received."[42] And yet, even as Smith's position as unquestioned head of the church had been emphatically reaffirmed (in a description of the office that is virtually unchanged in the present church), he moved at the same time to further delegate his authority to additional councils. In part, this was a response to his inability to supervise church affairs in what were now two widely dispersed centers, in Ohio and Missouri. The most dramatic move in this regard was to call a dozen men to constitute a quorum of twelve apostles.

THE QUORUM OF THE TWELVE APOSTLES

Apostle (ἀπόστολος or apostolos) signifies emissary, messenger, or ambassador. Peter established the qualifications and principal duty pertaining to the office when he presided over the selection of a disciple who had "accompanied us during all the time that the Lord Jesus went in and out among us" and would "become a witness with us to his resurrection."[43] As traveling witnesses of Christ, the original twelve apostles had apparent authority over all geographic areas of the church they visited. Even so, the term "apostle" has always been fraught with an ambiguous tension between the special group of twelve so denominated by the evangelists on the one hand and a more general meaning of emissary or missionary on the other. Luke uses the term with reference to an original council of twelve, intimating that designation was to be applied to a perpetual council of that precise number (or, at the least, to the original council with one admissible replacement for Iscariot).[44] The author of Revelation also associates the term with a finite group of a dozen.[45]

Paul, by contrast, employs the term to refer to himself, separate and apart from any organized council or quorum. One authority even believes the relegation of the title to the original twelve "was apparently unknown" or even "resisted" by him.[46] However, the author of the later *Clementine Recognitions* was emphatic that the twelve held office of a very particular kind: "Do not look for any other prophet or apostle except us; there is one true prophet and twelve apostles."[47] Paul clearly believed that his vision of the risen Christ qualified him to be a witness ("Have I not seen Jesus," he affirmed), and that he was personally commissioned to "serve and to testify" to the nations by Jesus himself.[48] Whether the New Testament pattern is taken to be a quorum of twelve or a smattering of special emissaries, the general Christian consensus is that "in spite of the theory of 'apostolic succession' that developed in the church's doctrine of the ministry, the title and office of apostle were not transferable and died out with the passing of the original bearers of the name. . . . The church has never had apostles in the NT sense since the first century."[49] However, the same quest for New Testament forms and practices that characterized the Primitivist impulse among nineteenth-century seekers could at times prompt a reconsideration of that truism. "Where is our Peter and John? Our apostles?" asked the young John Taylor.[50] Some of his fellow dissenters from Methodism said, " 'Let us be agreed and ask for God to commission us by revelation.' Others said, 'it might be that the Lord had already commissioned apostles in some parts of the world; and if he had, it must come from them.' "[51]

One church in the 1830s that satisfied such longing was the Catholic Apostolic Church, also known as the Irvingites.[52] Edward Irving was a Scottish minister who disavowed the legitimacy of Catholicism, but, like many of his contemporary Anglo-Catholics, found himself drawn to many aspects of Catholic heritage and practices. In particular, he felt the Protestants' democratic government unbiblical, as well as their view that sacraments signified rather than channeled grace. At the same time, he became influenced by preachers like Alexander Scott, who held that "the early supernatural endowments of the Church were not intended to be restricted to the Apostolic age, but ought to be claimed by the Church of the present day as well."[53] Charismatic gifts began to appear in Irving's church, but it was the content as much as the nature of the prophecies in particular that defied convention; one member of Irving's congregation, Robert Baxter, prophesied and taught that the established churches were in a state of apostasy and apostolic succession had ceased, but God would send new emissaries commissioned by the spirit. This would constitute a "new order of 'apostles.' "[54] By 1832, the first apostle was called to the Catholic Apostolic Church, with a full complement of twelve in place by 1835. Walter Scott was another contemporary who preached "the restoration of the true, original apostolic order which would restore to the church the ancient gospel as preached by the apostles. The interest became an excitement; All tongues were set loose in investigation."[55]

In Mormonism's earliest years, the term "apostle" was used in a general sense, more reminiscent of Paul than Luke. And so, a March 1829 revelation spoke to Oliver Cowdery and David Whitmer "even as unto Paul mine apostle, for you are called even with that same calling with which he was called," and an 1830 revelation repeated the designation with Cowdery. A subsequent revelation noted that he, along with Joseph Smith, had been "ordained" and "confirmed . . . apostles, and especial witnesses," with no mention in any of those cases of a place in a quorum.[56] Smith and Cowdery had also been called First and Second Elder in the church, and as Michael MacKay and fellow editors note, "The way church members understood the relationship between the terms apostle and elder at this time is unclear. In the earliest years, the term apostle was often applied to elders involved in missionary activities." They cite as one example Jared Carter, who wrote in his journal after being ordained an elder, "I now commence to give some short sketches of a mission that I performed from Ohio to Vermont after I had been to Kirkland where I received the authority of an apostle [and] commenced a mission."[57]

Intimations of an apostolic office that would form part of a quorum as in the New Testament, however, had come in the months before the church was even organized. As Smith completed work on the Book of Mormon and about the time of his showing the gold plates to eleven witnesses, the two of them most closely connected with the final stages of its translation, David Whitmer and Oliver Cowdery, received a special commission. They were required to choose twelve men desirous of taking Christ's name upon themselves "with full purpose of heart," to go "into all the world to preach [his] gospel unto every creature," with his authority to baptize.[58] The title of apostle was not at that time indicated nor that they would function as a council with ecclesiastical authority. In 1831, the directive to choose "the twelve" had been repeated to Cowdery and Whitmer.[59] The New Testament pattern of that number had been repeated in the Book of Mormon, though that scripture referred to a group of twelve "disciples."[60]

Almost six full years later, with the church presidency, bishops, and two high councils in place, the time was set for the twelve disciples to be called. Smith and a band of followers had just returned from the failed expedition to restore Missouri Saints to their lands in Jackson County, from which old settlers had forcibly expelled them in late 1833. The paramilitary operation, called "Zion's Camp," commenced a 1,000-mile trek in May 1834 with more than a hundred volunteers, gathering more along the way, but the expedition turned out to be futile except for the spiritual winnowing and maturation it accomplished on the part of the volunteers who suffered weeks of hardship in the arduous attempt. In February 1835, Smith convened a Kirtland meeting "of those who journeyed to Zion for the purpose of assisting the foundation of its redemption last season with as many more of the brethren & sisters as felt disposed to attend."[61] He seated the Zion's Camp veterans in a special section, paid them homage, and then directed the Three Witnesses (Oliver Cowdery, David Whitmer, and Martin Harris) to make known the names of the Twelve.

As had been the case with the first men called as seventies, every name that followed was one of the veterans, except for three who were living in Missouri at the time, thus having occupied the role of besieged rather than rescuers.[62] After their selection (with the designation of "apostles" rather than "disciples"), Cowdery told the assembly that since the original commission to search out the twelve, "our minds have been on a constant stretch to find who these Twelve were." He then delivered their commission, which was to emulate the apostles of old in holding "the keys of this ministry" and bearing witness of the gospel at home and "to other nations."[63] Smith may have called some or all twelve men to office before the formal organization of the quorum, but if so, no ordinations took place.[64] A few days later, Smith counseled them to carefully record quorum decisions, as being on a par with "the great and glorious manifestations" made to Smith's presidency, with a view to publication as a matter of "covenant or doctrine."[65] As Bushman has noted, "The implication was that decisions in council were to be of equal authority with revelations to the prophet."[66]

Initially, the Quorum of the Twelve functioned largely as a "travelling high council," resolving doctrinal and disciplinary matters in areas outside the two organized stakes, engaging in missionary work and organizing new units, or branches. After controversy regarding their degree of authority relative to the standing high councils, Smith clarified in 1836 that they stood "next to the . . . presidency" of the church.[67] Still, confusion and contention emerged again in 1838, when the stake presidency in Missouri was charged with misconduct. Three overlapping authorities were present to try a fourth authoritative body; the Missouri bishopric, the Missouri High Council, and two apostles sent by Smith to oversee the crisis were putting the Missouri stake presidency on trial. W. W. Phelps and John Whitmer objected to the participation of the bishopric and apostles in the proceedings, and they had reasonable grounds for doing so. A revelation had declared that the standing high councils were "equal in authority in the affairs of the church, in all their decisions, to the . . . traveling high council," that is, the quorum of the twelve apostles.[68] But the revelation had also, ambiguously, designated the apostles as "a quorum equal in authority and power to the three presidents" (of the first presidency), and that ranking above high councils and near the top of the ecclesiastical hierarchy was becoming the norm.[69] Phelps and Whitmer were overruled, but the case demonstrated that lines of authority were still sorting themselves out.[70]

In the final year of his life, Smith was reported to have celebrated the fact that he had fully relinquished sole responsibility for the church by disseminating his authority upon the twelve apostles. Young later claimed that in spring of 1844 Smith said to a large council of leaders, "I roll the burthen and responsibility of leading this Church off from my shoulders on to yours. Now, round up your shoulders and stand under it like men; for the Lord is going to let me rest a while."[71] Referring to the fullness of priesthood keys associated with the temple, Wilford Woodruff added the detail that he "sealed upon your heads all the powers of the Aaronic and Melchizedek Priesthoods and Apostleship, with all the keys and powers thereof."[72]

Orson Hyde similarly recorded that Smith "gave the Quorum of the Twelve the final priesthood key in early 1844."[73] The conflation, in the apostles' eyes, of priesthood keys pertaining to the temple and of the authority requisite to "leading the church" again illustrate how the priesthood as ecclesiastical authority and as saving priestly power was merged in what that 1831 revelation had called the "President of the high Priest hood of the Church or in other words the Presiding high Priest."[74] With the dispersal of those principal keys to the quorum, Smith was continuing the decentralization of his authority he had been moving to accomplish for some time.

As Richard Bushman notes of his 1835 restructuring of the leadership, "Smith not only shifted the responsibility for revelation from himself to his councils, he moved the locus of revelation from the individual prophet to the church's administrative bureaucracy."[75]

At the present day, the quorum of the twelve apostles—who are appointed for life—are the principal administrators, along with the first presidency of the church, of a worldwide institution. At the same time, they are looked upon as having a commission that transcends any administrative function. In the words of the 1835 revelation on priesthood, they are "special witness of the name of Christ in all the world."[76] Joseph F. Smith explicated the significance of that designation: "These twelve disciples of Christ are supposed to be eye and ear witnesses of the divine mission of Jesus Christ. . . . They must *know*, they must get the knowledge for themselves, it must be with them as if they had seen with their eyes and heard with their ears, and they know the truth. That is their mission, to testify of Jesus Christ and him crucified and risen from the dead and clothed now with almighty power at the right hand of God, the Savior of the world. That is their mission, and their duty."[77] That was not far removed from the commission Oliver Cowdery delivered to the first twelve chosen: "Receive a testimony from Heaven for yourselves, so that you can bear testimony . . . that you have seen the face of God: that is more than the testimony of an Angel."[78]

THE QUORUM OF SEVENTY

As we saw above, the first seventies were called and organized in a way that closely resembled the office and authority of the apostles. The original plan envisioned a President of the First Council at the head, who presided over seven "presidents of the quorum" who in turn were to preside over a quorum of seventy (with up to seventy members), and eventually over several quorums of seventy. Dozens of seventies' quorums took shape over subsequent decades, then hundreds, but the plans for the First Quorum to constitute a body "equal in authority to that of the Twelve" did not come to fruition.[79] The seven presidents of that quorum, constituting the First Council of Seventy, persisted but with a low profile, functioning with varying responsibilities and degrees of authority. (In 1961, for instance, they were empowered to organize stake presidencies.)[80] The absence of a governing role for a presiding group of seventies changed in 1976, when President Spencer W. Kimball reminded the church that the First Quorum of Seventy was one of "three governing quorums of the church defined by the revelations."[81] At a time of rapid worldwide growth and expansion, Kimball proceeded to reorganize the First Quorum of Seventy, designating all its members General Authorities rather than just its seven presidents, as had been the case in Kirtland. Those seven presidents were no longer called the First Council; the members of that group, which had persisted in one form or another since Kirtland, were absorbed into the First Quorum of Seventy, along with several men who had been functioning as "Assistants to the Twelve." The First Quorum is now led by a presidency of seven rather than a council. To meet the demands of a church numbering millions, Kimball's successor Ezra Taft Benson created a Second Quorum of the Seventy in 1989, and others have followed since.

In the current church, members of the First Quorum of Seventy serve as General Authorities until age seventy, members of the Second Quorum are appointed to five-year terms, and several other quorums of seventy, also with five-year appointments, serve as Area rather than General Authorities. As with their 1835 organization and calling, modern seventies administer throughout the world, serving under the direction of the apostles.

Stake Presidents

In the church's first decades, the surge in converts required division into manageable units, and so stakes were formed. The first two stakes were in Kirtland, Ohio, presided over by Smith himself, and Clay County, Missouri, led by David Whitmer (who, like Smith, also presided over that stake's high council, a group of twelve subordinate leaders). Whitmer had been made the president of the "church in Zion" by his 1834 appointment, suggesting a stake president was highest in authority after the prophet. And indeed, for some time, the high council with the stake president at the head did function with great authority over most matters in their jurisdiction. Once established in Missouri, the pattern of semi-autonomous stakes was repeated, with a president and counselors presiding over a high council of twelve. After relocation in Utah, the pattern continued until by 1875 more than 100,000 Saints were divided into ten stakes.[82] (Where the church was less established, missions, conferences, and branches constituted organizational units.)

In 1877, sensing his imminent passing, Brigham Young embarked upon a massive reorganization of the church's governing structures. Principal among these actions was clarification of stake governance. Much as the bishop of Rome acquired precedence among other bishops in the ancient church, the stake of Salt Lake had acquired effective "center stake" authority over all the others. Young made all stakes "equal and autonomous" relative to each other, and freed six apostles from their positions as stake leaders.[83] Stake presidents, assisted by two counselors and a stake high council, administer stakes, usually with a dozen or so wards and branches in their domain, but occasionally as few as five and as many as nineteen or eight,[84] consisting of perhaps 2,000 to 7,000 members.

During most of the nineteenth and twentieth centuries, stake presidents reported directly to the First Presidency. Apostles and, later, Assistants to the Twelve gave periodic training and instruction at quarterly stake conferences. Expansion of the church since 1950 has required more layers in the reporting structure. In the late 1960s and '70s, stake presidents reported to Regional Representatives, who in turn answered to the Twelve. Since the 1980s, stake presidents report to an Area Presidency comprising Area Seventies, who answer to the First Quorum of the Seventy. If all politics is local, however, so is all religion. Stakes are the units with which the church hierarchy deals, empowering the stake presidents to administer their wards with a fair amount of autonomy. LDS members meet for semi-annual stake conferences, and many activities (and high priest quorums) are administered at the stake level, as multi-ward events. However, the local units that shape the religious life and worship experience of most Mormons is not the stake but the local congregation, which is generally a ward, presided over by a bishop.

Bishops

For some time it has been common to assert that presbyter or elder (πρεσβύτερος) and bishop (ἐπίσκοπος) were synonymous terms in the early church—and, as one typical website continues to argue, that they are merely different "descriptive terms that describe the ONE same office."[85] That is the position of the Catholic Church, which holds that in the New Testament church "no clear distinction was made between bishops and priests. . . . No distinction is made between the two terms." As one authority opines, the subsequent precedence of the former, or the "monarchical episcopate . . . must have been based on oral apostolic tradition."[86] This apparent shift was one reason that John Wesley, who endorsed the Book of Common Prayer for the most part, was uncomfortable with its assumption of "an essential difference between bishop and presbyter."[87] However, recent studies on the subject suggest that a clear demarcation between the two occurred quite early in the Christian church.[88]

In pre-Christian usage, the term ἐπίσκοπος (episcopos) meant one who oversees or watches over others. In Greece, for example, episcopoi were state officials who functioned in a supervisory capacity, and with some judicial powers, in assigned cities.[89] New Testament writers adopted the term with reference to a local community of Christians, referring to the "office of a bishop" or "ordained" bishops, often in conjunction with deacons.[90] The *Apostolic Constitutions*, with origins in the early third century, refers to the bishop as a "pastor who is to be ordained . . . in every parish."[91] His responsibilities were to shepherd his flock, keeping "firm in the faith who is already strong, feeding the people peaceably; strengthening the weak."[92] They were also to receive "your first-fruits, and your tithes, and your free-will offerings," that therefrom he might "supply the wants of those who really are in distress."[93] As Alistair Stewart recently argued, bishops were "the original officers in the church," with responsibility limited in the first centuries "to individual congregations."[94] A growing consensus agrees that as there were "multiple and independent communities within a single city," so were there "multiple *episkopoi* in a single city, each holding office in his congregation."[95]

Whereas Lutheran and Anglican reformers retained episcopal office, the Reformed tradition did not, instituting rule by presbyters instead. Methodists followed their Anglican forebears in continuing the office of bishop, Wesley's reservations notwithstanding. Given the clear references to that office in the New Testament, it was inevitable that at least some of the Primitivists—those committed to a return to New Testament forms—would reinstitute the office. And so we find that Alexander Campbell disparaged the proliferation of priestly offices, recognizing only "the divinely established order of bishops and deacons." Walter Scott seconded his point, noting that "it pleased the Head of the church to appoint bishops and deacons."[96] Doubtless Sidney Rigdon, who joined Mormonism in 1830—after rising to the rank of bishop in the Campbellite church[97]—was influential in bringing the office to Smith's attention; it was nowhere mentioned in the Book of Mormon, which in other cases so conspicuously served as a template for church organization.

The first Mormon bishops, we saw above, presided over vast geographical regions of the church. Smith specified by revelation that bishops were designated to administer "in all temporal things."[98] More a welfare coordinator than pastor, the first Mormon bishop was principally responsible for the temporal well-being of the entire Mormon community in Ohio. In addition, he was to preside over ecclesiastical courts as a "judge in Israel."[99] It was anticipated early on that once the church's "borders [were] enlarged," it would be "necessary to have other Bishops."[100] These two first bishops, Partridge and Whitney, presided over what became the stakes (like dioceses) of Kirtland and Missouri, respectively.

In the period of settlement in Nauvoo, Illinois, stakes were subdivided into more manageable units called wards (effectively parishes). Soon thereafter, a major transformation in the office occurred. Bishops were assigned to each of Nauvoo's thirteen wards in 1842 (organized after the model of political districts), where they continued to bear the primary responsibility of administering to the poor. Tithing, interpreted as a 10 percent donation of one's "interest," had become the law of the church in 1838, and donations in money or in kind became the public welfare fund over which the bishop presided. After Smith's death, as the Saints prepared for the exodus, the population, soon to be known as "the Camp of Israel," was organized "into streets, Blocks, and wards And a Bishop was appointed over each ward to see to the poor, widows, and to keep an account of what each man is doing."[101] With bishops now the effective pastors of each congregation, the office split into the local bishops and a general or "presiding Bishop" who served with churchwide jurisdiction. Assisted by two counselors, the Presiding Bishop is today the General Authority chiefly responsible for all temporal and financial interests of the church.

Once in Utah, Brigham Young chose a prime site for a new temple—high ground with a good water supply—that could not be the exact center of a mile-square city since there were steep hills immediately to the north and northeast. He divided the city into wards, as in Nauvoo, and with a bishop assigned to each ward, these divisions became the fundamental ecclesiastical and administrative units of the city and the church.

Mormons generally enforce a rigid adherence to the geographical boundaries that demarcate the units of church participation. They attend where they live; parish-shopping is not permitted. Because religious life for Mormons is an inescapable confrontation with the entirety of one's actual lived community, the project is indeed Zion-building rather than Zion-hunting. In a classic expression of this organizational genius, Eugene England wrote that

> the Church is as "true," as effective, as sure an instrument of salvation as the system of doctrines we call the gospel—and that is so in good part because of the very flaws, human exasperations, and historical problems that occasionally give us all some anguish. . . . Martin Luther, with prophetic perception, wrote, "Marriage is the school of love"—that is, marriage is not the home or the result of love so much as the school. I believe that any good church is a school of love and that the LDS church, for most people, perhaps all, is the best one, the "only true and living Church" (D&C 1:30)—not just because its doctrines teach and embody some of the great and central paradoxes but, more important, because the Church provides the best context for struggling with, working through, enduring, and being redeemed by those paradoxes and oppositions that give energy and meaning to the universe.[102]

WOMEN AND THE PRIESTHOOD

Jesus chose men and ordained them to positions of ecclesiastical authority: twelve male apostles, and "seventy others" as traveling preachers.[103] However, the "prophets," "evangelists," "pastors," and "teachers" called by Jesus and referred to in the epistle to the Ephesians are not all identified by gender.[104] Paul makes note of Priscilla, wife of Aquila, as a fellow laborer (συνεργός or synergos), though it's not clear she holds a particular office.[105] Similarly, Paul makes mention of Euodia and Syntyche as women who "have struggled beside me in the work of the gospel."[106] More strikingly, Paul refers to Junia as "prominent among the apostles," though as we saw above, he does not seem to use the term in the same special sense as Luke does in referring to an officiating group of twelve.[107] In the same epistle, he refers to Phoebe as a deacon (διάκονος or diakonos).[108] The New Testament record, in other words, is ambiguous and incomplete on the subject of women and authority. Some scholars, like N. T. Wright, have seen the events surrounding the resurrection as suggesting a new order of things in this regard, for according to the account in Mark, Jesus "appeared first to Mary Magdalene." The author of the gospel then chides the apostles for refusing to believe her witness to his resurrection.[109] The account in John adds the detail that Mary is specifically commissioned by the risen Christ to go and bear witness of his return from the grave.[110] In the new order Christ initiates, in other words, more boundaries than the temple's veil may be rent asunder.[111]

Joseph Smith did not appear to intend for women to be ordained to, and incorporated into, the offices of the Melchizedek or Aaronic priesthood. However, he did have in view to endow them with comparable power and prerogatives that have been variously interpreted. The exact meaning and extent of those possibilities, and whether they amounted to holding the priesthood (or a priesthood) or merely sharing in its blessings, have been debated since the 1970s. In July 1830, for instance, Smith declared in God's voice that his wife Emma was to be "ordained . . . to expound scriptures, and to exhort the church."[112] In the Methodism of the day, exhorters were lay preachers; however, they were *un*ordained in distinction from ministers. No record of a formal ordination performed for Emma is recorded, but Smith later said, "She was ordained at the time the Revelation was given," and that gesture clearly imputed some ecclesiastical authority to her.[113]

A dozen years later, Sarah Kimball moved to organize a women's benevolent association. She asked Eliza Snow to prepare a constitution, which Snow took to Smith for approval. At that time, he praised the document but indicated he had other plans in mind for the women, an organization "in the Order of the Priesthood after the pattern of the church."[114] What followed over subsequent weeks was a remarkable program of female empowerment. On March 17, 1842, accompanied by John Taylor and Willard Richards, Smith met with the assembled group of some twenty leading women of Nauvoo. After opening remarks, the men withdrew to allow the women to formally establish themselves as a new institution. Smith then suggested they should organize in a manner parallel to the male priesthood: "elect a presiding officer . . . and let that presiding officer choose two Counsellors to assist in the duties of her Office . . . and let them preside just as the Presidency, preside over the church."[115] Smith even suggested that "Officers . . . be appointed and set apart, as Deacons, Teachers &c are among us."[116] (Emma Smith declined to emulate the male priesthood ranks, but in 1868, a Relief Society document did in fact stipulate the duties of female "teachers" and "deaconesses.")[117]

In a further show of independence, the women rejected Taylor's suggestion for a name: the Nauvoo Female Benevolent Society, which mirrored the names of many contemporary women's clubs. Instead, they chose the Nauvoo Female Relief Society. "Relief" was an important idea in Masonic thought, and Smith had adopted core Masonic language and ritual into the priesthood and higher sacraments, believing Masonry to be a degenerate form of the true priesthood order. At the same time, of course, Masonry was an exclusively male organization, while Smith was opening the temple rituals to women. Some scholars have therefore seen the women's choice of name as a bold reflection of their self-understanding as an effectual female priesthood organization, commensurate with the male counterpart.[118] Just where Smith intended to take the women's organization was at least a little clearer by the third meeting. "The Society should move according to the ancient Priesthood," he told them, and promised "he was going to make of this Society a kingdom of priests as in Enoch's day."[119]

The Relief Society accumulated members and directed charitable efforts over the next few meetings. Then, the sixth meeting on April 28 saw further significant if contested developments. Smith again visited and discoursed on the subject of "different offices, and the necessity of every individual acting in the sphere allotted to him or her," and of "the disposition of man ... to look with jealous eyes upon the standing of others."[120] The rebuke, however, was not directed at the sisters for aspiring to higher calling. On the contrary, he was chastising those sisters showing jealousy of other women who were acting according to their enhanced female prerogatives. "He said the reason of these remarks being made, was, that some little thing was circulating in the Society," complaints that "some persons [women] were not going right in laying hands on the sick &c," instead of rejoicing that "the sick could be heal'd." The simple fact was, the women were now properly organized for works of righteousness, whereas "the time had not been before, that these things could be in their proper order."[121]

And so Smith vigorously encouraged the women to be more, not less, actively engaged in mirroring their priesthood-holding counterparts: "He ask'd the Society if they could not see by this sweeping stroke, that wherein they are ordained, it is the privilege of those set apart to administer in that authority which is confer'd on them—and if the sisters should have faith to heal the sick, let all hold their tongues, and let everything roll on."[122] True enough, these developments were according women roles and prerogatives not common in the Christianity of the day. Still, he said, "if God has appointed him, and chosen him as an instrument to lead the church, why not let him lead it through? Why stand in the way?"[123] And more was in store for the women—much more. With the completion of the Nauvoo Temple, he intimated, women's roles would be further expanded.

In the meantime, Smith "spoke of delivering the keys to this Society,"[124] and one key in particular pertained to discernment. He said, "The keys of the kingdom are about to be given to them, that they may be able to detect everything false—as well as to the Elders."[125] To speak of keys was, in Smith's parlance, generally to speak of priesthood powers, and in fact, Smith had earlier declared that no one could exercise the gift of discernment "without the Priesthood."[126] And then, moments later, Smith fulfilled his own promise. To Emma, president of the Relief Society, Smith then said, "I now turn the key to you in the name of God and this Society shall rejoice and knowledge and intelligence shall flow down from this time."[127] On the meaning of this language and this gesture hinges the status of the Relief Society and the women of the church with regard to the priesthood. Some Mormon feminists see in the language a bestowal of priesthood authority later denied, especially given twentieth-century Mormon connotations of "keys" as authoritative priesthood powers of administration.[128] James Talmage, in his influential book on the temple, held it to be "a precept of the church that women of the Church share the authority of the priesthood with their husbands," though they "are not ordained to specific rank in the priesthood."[129] Most recently, an official church statement on the topic clearly announces that "these statements indicate that Joseph Smith delegated priesthood authority to women in the Relief Society."[130]

However, that acknowledgment is muted by Elder Dallin Oaks's qualification (which is cited in the official essay): "All that is done under the direction of those [Melchizedek] priesthood keys is done with priesthood authority."[131] Indeed, in the early twentieth century (and perhaps much earlier), the leadership of the church redefined (or, in some views, clarified and affirmed) the Relief Society's status as an auxiliary functioning *under* the direction of the male priesthood. About this same time, the text of Smith's words to Emma was edited to modulate the reading of Smith's gesture as an actual bestowal of priesthood keys. By 1928, the church newspaper described Smith as saying, "I now *turn the key on your behalf* in the name of the Lord (emphasis in original)."[132] The more ambiguous formulation downplayed the bestowal of greater autonomy suggested in the original language. Smith's own account of that day's proceeding gives some clarity to his original designs: he "gave a lecture on the pries[t]hood shewing how the Sisters would come in possession of the privileges & blessings & gifts of the priesthood & that the signs should follow them, such as healing the sick casting out devils &c. & that they might attain unto these blessings."[133]

A traditional way to reconcile these apparent contraries and ambiguities is to finesse the problem by indicating, as Talmage did, that "it is not given to woman to exercise the authority of the Priesthood independently; . . . woman shares with man the blessings of the priesthood."[134] The source of this formulation is probably John Taylor, who in 1880 said that women who participated in the highest temple ordinances never had the priesthood "conferred" upon them but held "a portion of the priesthood in connection with their husbands."[135] Such formulations hint that women *possess* a priesthood, if Taylor's and Talmage's point is that it is "not given [them] to *exercise*" it, or that they "are not ordained to specific rank in the priesthood." One possible context for clarifying Smith's ambiguous pronouncements on the subject is to be found in Smith's several references to a particular order of priesthood associated with women, one with a long Christian past and one that is distinct from the Aaronic and Melchizedek orders.

Orson Spencer inferred from Smith's teachings that the priesthood incorporated different orders or "grades," "*extending from Jesus the High Priest, to the lowest grade of priesthood in conjunction with the Holy Ghost.*"[136] Indeed, as we saw was well established in Protestant thought, Smith indicated that the gift of the Holy Ghost was itself a precursor to, or source of, certain priesthood powers. In part, this may have meant they were two powers to be exercised in tandem. He admonished his apostles always to speak "by the power of the Holy Priesthood & the Holy Ghost."[137] But on another occasion, he indicated that "there is a priestHood with the Holy Ghost & Key,"[138] and on another, that the Holy Ghost brought with it prerogatives generally associated with priesthood. He taught that Cornelius, the New Testament convert, for instance, until he received "the gift of the Holy Ghost . . . could not have healed the sick or commanded an evil spirit to come out of a man."[139] That was a reasonable reading of Luke's account of Cornelius, in which Peter states that "God anointed Jesus of Nazareth with the Holy Ghost and with power."[140] This power and authority were such that evil spirits would recognize it, he said.[141] Additionally, the Book of Mormon indicated that according to the instructions of the resurrected Jesus, his New World disciples "ordained [priests and teachers] by the power of the Holy Ghost."[142]

Smith considered that women had some such authority that empowered them to bless the sick, cast out devils, and perform the other functions later associated with priesthood power. Smith may also have seen such a basis for authority in the Mosaic text that he himself produced. Describing Adam's reception of the Holy Ghost after his loss of Eden, the additions to Genesis suggest the Holy Ghost's link to priesthood authority: "And thus he was baptized, and the Spirit of God descended upon him, and thus he was born of the Spirit, and became quickened in the inner man. And he heard a voice out of heaven, saying: Thou art baptized with fire, *and with the Holy Ghost*. . . . And *thou art after the order of him* who was without beginning of days or end of years, from all eternity to all eternity" (emphasis added).[143]

The reference to an "order" of the priesthood, given the echoes of Hebrews 7, is unmistakable.

Whether Smith understood women to have certain priesthood prerogatives by virtue of their receipt of the gift of the Holy Ghost is difficult to determine. What is clear is that though Smith did not ordain women to office within the two priesthood orders of the church, he did "ordain them to preside" within the Relief Society, in a manner he said was parallel to or "just as the Presidency, preside[s] over the Church."[144] And after promising the sisters that "the keys of the kingdom [were] about to be given to them," in the temple rites he instituted days later, women would, within his lifetime, receive and administer the highest sacraments of salvation.[145] And as we saw, a canonized revelation emphatically states that in participating in the temple marriage ceremony ("the new and everlasting covenant of marriage"), women along with men "enter into [an] order of the priesthood."[146] Official statements from the LDS leadership have not foreclosed the possibility of a day when women are ordained to the priesthood and participate in all offices pertaining to it. For the present, however, the official line is that "women do not hold the priesthood because the Lord has put it that way."[147] Whether that is meant to ground LDS practice on a reading of New Testament precedent, on Smith's appointment of males only to positions of general church leadership, or on another source is not clear.

At the same time, there have been recent and dramatic shifts in official teaching about the place women have relative to priesthood. In language clearly reminiscent of Smith's vision for the Relief Society, Elder Dallin Oaks asserted that "Relief Society is not just a class for women but . . .—a divinely established appendage to the priesthood." He was implicitly recognizing here that the Relief Society was originally understood as an order put in place within a framework of temple theology, and Smith had in mind facilitating the participation of women in the highest and holiest priesthood ordinances; it was not a church auxiliary. In addition, Oaks stated that "priesthood authority pertain[s] to women as well as men."[148] Recognizing that this represented a clarification of doctrine if not a shift in understanding, he reasoned:

> We are not accustomed to speaking of women having the authority of the priesthood in their Church callings, but what other authority can it be? When a woman—young or old—is set apart to preach the gospel as a full-time missionary, she is given priesthood authority to perform a priesthood function. The same is true when a woman is set apart to function as an officer or teacher in a Church organization under the direction of one who holds the keys of the priesthood. Whoever functions in an office or calling received from one who holds priesthood keys exercises priesthood authority in performing her or his assigned duties.[149]

The point seems to be that priesthood power and authority are eternal, and all have access to that power and authority and the right to be integrated into the heavenly society it orders, according to the New and Everlasting Covenant. Within the domain of church ecclesiology, keys to administer and supervise that priesthood are delegated by office, and those offices at present are confined to men. However, as we saw above, priesthood was far more important in Smith's religious understanding as the power to officiate over and participate in the sacraments of the temple. And in that context, women become full participants in the priesthood.

6

Sacramental Ordinances—Salvific

⌒

IN JOSEPH SMITH'S experience, as we saw, the principle of priesthood arose in the context of baptism. He and Oliver Cowdery learned from their work producing the Book of Mormon that in the contemporary Christian world, "none had authority from God to administer the ordinances of the gospel."[1] And rather than reduce the number of those ordinances—or sacraments—as had been the pattern with the Reformation, Smith elaborated an expanded series of sacraments that together constituted the New and Everlasting Covenant. He believed that "the Order & Ordinances of the Kingdom were instituted by the Priesthood in the council of Heaven before the World was."[2] And God not only revealed all these ordinances of salvation to Adam, Smith taught, but intended them "to be the same forever."[3] Their unvarying employment was the token of a covenant that binds us to premortal conventions we participated in creating: they constitute "the most perfect order and harmony—and their limits and bounds were fixed irrevocably and voluntarily subscribed to."[4]

The sacraments Mormons perform on behalf of the dead, a seeming adjunct to the primary work of ordinances for the living, are the most dramatic indication of a salvational scheme that is universal—or almost universal—in its scope. But how many sacraments are there? In the medieval church, there were seven: baptism, confirmation, the Eucharist, penance, extreme unction, ordination, and marriage, as Peter Lombard defined them in the twelfth century and as affirmed by the Council of Lyons in 1274.[5] Luther quickly dismissed confirmation, extreme unction, ordination, and marriage as sacraments lacking scriptural support. Then he decided penance as well failed the definition.[6] In the decades following, the Anglicans followed suit, also recognizing only "two sacraments ordained of Christ our Lord in the Gospel, that is to say, baptism and the supper of the Lord." And for Anglicans, too, these sacraments were not means of grace but "signs of grace," serving to "strengthen and confirm, our faith."[7] Calvin followed Luther in recognizing "two sacraments of Baptism and the Lord's Supper . . . for use of the whole church."[8]

Wesley's position, and thus Methodism, were not always clear and evolved on the subject of the sacraments. Both Anglo-Catholic "high church sacramentalists" and "anti-sacerdotal evangelicals" find support in his writings.[9] Wesley himself said that early on he "was (fundamentally) a Papist," placing too much emphasis on the sacraments.[10] At the same time, even though he held in those same early years (in this case 1733) that regeneration was not to be found in baptism "or any other outward form," he apparently believed that one received God's grace through the sacraments.[11] As an Anglican, Wesley considered baptism and the Lord's Supper to have special status as sacraments "ordained of Christ," in the words of the Thirty-Nine Articles, or "sacraments properly so-called."[12] However, Methodists to some extent circumvented sacramental debates by avoiding the term "sacrament" altogether. (It is used only once in the first Book of Discipline [1784], as a synonym for the Lord's Supper.) They preferred rather to employ a more generic category they called "means of grace," of which five were considered divinely instituted: prayer, scripture study, the Lord's Supper, fasting, and "Christian Conference," by which they meant orderly conversation.[13]

Mormons, rather like early Methodists, do not have formal categories of sacraments, though some are clearly essential to salvation and others are not. Those requisite to (and constitutive of) salvation are baptism, confirmation and bestowal of the Holy Ghost, conferral of the priesthood (for men), the endowment, and marriage sealing. The first three are performed for the living outside the temple, most often in meetinghouse, but sufficient water is the only necessary condition for immersive baptism. The final two, endowment and sealing, are performed for the living only in the temple. All five, however, are performed in the temple on behalf of the departed, so that the dead as well as the living may be incorporated into the heavenly family. Because the greater sum of humanity has died without opportunity to know Christ, his gospel, or his ordinances, the vast proportion even of those sacraments that can be administered outside the temple will ultimately be performed within its walls. In this sense, then, all five essential sacraments are primarily temple sacraments and are best understood within the context of Joseph Smith's temple theology.

THE ENDOWMENT OF POWER (OF TEMPLE
ORDINANCES GENERALLY)

The word "endowment" has followed a peculiar path of development in religious usage. According to the gospel of Luke, the resurrected Christ directs his apostles to tarry in Jerusalem "until you have been clothed with power from on high."[14] The Greek word is ἐνδύω (enduo) and does indeed mean to clothe. Early English translations such as the 1611 King James Version of the Bible (KJV) use the expression "*endued* with power from on high," because "endue" was thought to derive from a Latin root meaning "to clothe" and so the word acquired that meaning. But by the seventeenth century, "endue" had also acquired the meaning of its near kin "endow," which originally had an entirely separate derivation. "Endow" comes from a root signifying "to enrich with privilege" or "to gift with an inheritance."[15] The spelling of the two words was so uncertain, notes one authority, that the two became confounded and interchangeable.[16] The fortuitous consequence is that "to endow" with power now carries a nicely compatible duality of meaning: to clothe (with spiritual power), and to bestow an inheritance or set of (spiritual) privileges.

The clothing with power that Jesus promised was fulfilled, in general Christian understanding, at the time of the Pentecostal outpouring. The same Luke who recorded the promise chronicled its fulfillment: "When the day of Pentecost was fully come, they were all with one accord in one place. And suddenly there came a sound from heaven as of a rushing mighty wind, and it filled all the house where they were sitting. And there appeared unto them cloven tongues like as of fire, and it sat upon each of them. And they were all filled with the Holy Ghost."[17] Peter saw the event as an unprecedented outpouring from heaven that had been foretold not just by Jesus days earlier but by Old Testament figures from Joel to David, to the end that "the entire house of Israel [might] know with certainty that God has made him both Lord and Messiah, this Jesus whom you crucified."[18] Clothed with such power and spirit, the apostles then, and only then, commenced to fulfill the Great Commission.

Mormonism in this regard, as in so many other ways, recapitulates Christian history in a recognizable but altered form. LDS history replicates the biblical events of communion with supernatural entities, prophetic utterance, canon formation, charismatic beginnings—even an exodus of God's covenant people to a new land of promise. Similarly, Mormonism recasts the spiritual endowment of power that prepares and qualifies the church—and its members individually—to enter a new stage of maturity and expansion. We saw a critical point of transition in Mormonism's self-understanding occur when the focus on physically recuperating the land of Zion became instead a focus on spiritual preparation by way of the temple and its ordinances. In 1831, a revelation had commanded the Saints to gather in Ohio, where they would receive the law of the Lord and "be endowed with power from on high."[19] But the promise was vague, its precise meaning unclear. After the tragic 1834 failure of Zion's Camp, the Lord renewed his promise that an endowment of power would be received—in the Kirtland Temple. Still, there was nothing to suggest to Smith that the endowment of power portended more than the erection of a holy sanctuary and perhaps visible signs of God's acceptance, a Pentecostal outpouring similar to its New Testament antecedents.

Two years later, the work on the Kirtland edifice was nearing completion. Smith told the quorum of twelve in November 1835 that "great blessings await us at this time, and will soon be poured out upon us."[20] Days after the temple's March dedication and a series of remarkable visions and spiritual manifestations, Smith suggested that he believed these developments signified the fulfillment of the Lord's promises and the completion of his own work. Smith triumphantly remarked at the time that he "had now completed the organization of the church and we had passed through all the necessary ceremonies, that I had given [the priesthood quorums] all the instruction they needed."[21] His assessment would turn out to be entirely premature. What changed Smith's mind, and portended a vastly greater mission yet to follow, was a visionary experience that followed that pronouncement four days later. If John the Baptist, and later Peter, James, and John, had indeed appeared to Smith and committed to him authority by means of which he had largely completed the organization of Mormonism's ecclesiology and implemented the proper forms of a few essential sacraments, then his April 3 visionary encounter complicated everything.

Just days after the temple's dedication, Oliver Cowdery joined Smith in prayer in a curtained section of the pulpit. At that time, "the veil was taken from their minds and the eyes of their understandings and . . . they saw the Lord standing upon the breast work of the pulpit."[22] His most significant words hinted at new beginnings rather than completion of Smith's project. Cowdery recorded the Savior as saying that "the hearts of thousands and tens of thousands shall greatly rejoice in consequence of . . . the endowment with which my servants have already been endowed, *and shall hereafter be endowed in this House*" (emphasis added).[23] Further hints of an altogether more comprehensive endowment of power to come were evident moments later, with the appearance of the prophet Elijah. This figure who "was taken to Heaven without tasting death," and thus personified a bridge between the living and the dead, on this occasion declared to the pair the fulfillment of Malachi's prophecy spoken to Smith more than a dozen years earlier. He had come, Elijah now declared, "to turn the hearts of the Fathers to the children, and the children to the fathers."[24]

This prophecy, which constituted the last words recorded in the Old Testament, has had no definitive interpretation in the Judeo-Christian tradition. For some commentators, the prophecy suggests to Jews that Elijah will be the "herald of the

Messiah."[25] Other readings are more imaginative. One Jewish tradition, full of antic-ipation and yearning, weaves this story: At the coming of the great judgment day, "the children of the wicked who had to die in infancy . . . will be found among the just, while their fathers will be ranged on the other side. The babes will implore their fathers to come to them, but God will not permit it. Then Elijah will go to the little ones, and teach them how to plead in behalf of their fathers. They will stand before God and say, 'Is not the measure of good, the mercy of God, larger than the mea-sure of chastisements? . . . [May they] be permitted to join us in Paradise?' God will give assent to their pleadings, and Elijah will have fulfilled the word of the prophet Malachi; he will have brought back the fathers to the children."[26]

Earliest Christian theologian Origen believed that John the Baptist, as Christ's forerunner, was that Elijah who was to come—as Jesus suggested.[27] Tertullian held to a dual fulfillment. He agreed that John was a prophet "in the spirit and power of Elijah," but he believed that the actual Elijah "will return . . . for the fulfilment of a prophecy. He will come back as Elijah, with the same name." He did not suggest when or why that future appearing of Elijah would come to pass, but a century later the churchman Victorinus opined it would be as a "precursor of the times of the antichrist," in the last days.[28]

Mormon reading of the prophecy is nearest to that of Tertullian and Victorinus, seeing Elijah's appearance to Smith on April 3, 1836, as the actual fulfillment of a literal promise. Mormons have long pointed out, in this connection, that during Passover Jews set a place for Elijah in symbolic anticipation of his return. "It is cus-tomary to have on the *seder* table a full cup of wine," notes the *Encyclopedia Judaica*, "known as 'Elijah's cup.' . . . Toward the end of the *seder*, the front door of the house is opened to demonstrate that this is a 'night of watching.' "[29] To Latter-day Saints, there is a divine typology evident in the fact that in 1836, Elijah did return, but not at the Passover meal, "when the cup was offered on the evening of Friday, April 1. Instead, he returned on Easter Sunday, the second day of Passover, the day of the presentation of the firstfruits of the harvest."[30]

Believing himself now in possession of Elijah's priesthood keys, Smith further developed expanded Kirtland Temple rituals. Until now, these had included foot-washing, other washings and anointings, and sealings. The latter, however, at this time was primarily a confirmation of anointing blessings, and a kind of Hosanna shout that "continued the [Protestant] theme of seals as declarations of divine own-ership."[31] Over the next few years, Smith's understanding of what constituted the "necessary ceremonies" and adequate "instruction" into the mysteries of godliness underwent substantial development—as he moved ever closer to fully developing the implications of Elijah's keys to mutually bind parents and children. The most imme-diate significant development was Smith's reinterpretation of Malachi's promise that

Elijah would "turn the hearts of the children to the fathers" and vice versa as a prom-ise to "seal or bind" their hearts together.[32] He comes to see the endowment of power associated with the temple as—in the most general sense—the power to fully access the gift of the atonement in such a way as to be fully and eternally integrated into the heavenly family. The first step in this process—whether living or dead—is the adoptive ordinance of baptism. Even this ordinance will take shape in his thought as a ritual to be understood as primarily a temple ordinance and only secondarily as an ordinance performed outside those holy precincts for the living.

Baptism

Ritual washings and sacral baths appear in many ancient religious traditions. Christian baptism finds its earliest scriptural version in John the Baptist, and the Baptist's influential precedents are almost certainly Jewish. Although an earlier school of scholarship argued for the originality of the Christian rite, many Jewish texts refer to proselyte baptism, which was itself linked to purification rituals.[33] John's practice seems to have combined both elements in a new way. He preached an imminent new order of things his baptism heralded, and his practice clearly raised questions among the Jews relative to their understanding of purification rituals.[34] It may have served as "an initiatory rite for the gathering Messianic community"; more certain is that it signified (according to all three synoptic writers) a commitment to moral improvement, or "repentance."[35] Mark in particular declares it a "baptism of repentance for the remission of sins."[36] Jesus's submission to, practice of, and call to baptism gave the sacrament its unimpeachable standing in Christian practice.[37] Many Christian writers saw substantial differences between John's practice and that of Jesus and his disciples. John, wrote the Catholic theologian Johann Eck, merely foreshadowed the sacrament of the new covenant; "John washed the body alone; he accomplished nothing in the soul."[38] Calvin, by contrast, denied any substantive difference, believing both the baptisms of John and of Jesus were valid forms of the ritual.[39]

The gospel of John seemed especially emphatic about the necessity of the sac-rament: "no one can enter the kingdom of God without being born of water and Spirit."[40] The principal scriptural basis for baptism in the gospel of John, however, is not as unambiguous as its pervasive employment suggests. Jesus's dialogue with Nicodemus is predicated on a series of dualisms, two kinds of birth: first birth and second birth, born once and born again, birth from "mother's womb" and birth "from above," "flesh" and "spirit," and "water" and "Spirit." So first birth, flesh, womb, and water are all one associated set of consistently parallel images, and second birth, spirit, and "from above" are a second set. If the second birth, rebirth, is the one from above—the birth of the spirit—then the first birth, the one associated with the birth of flesh (from the womb), would most reasonably be the literal birth of water. To read baptism into this exchange may be to introduce a third element unrelated to the dichotomies Jesus is drawing. Still, virtually all readers have taken the reference to water to mean baptismal water. The Catholic Church anathematized those who would "distort" the unambiguous formula "into some sort of metaphor."[41] Water and spirit, meaning baptism and the Holy Ghost, was the orthodox reading. LDS scripture rewrites the formula of Jesus's exchange with Nicodemus, sorting out the deficient parallelism by establishing three, rather than two, levels of symbolism. "As ye were born into the world by water [of the womb], and blood [of birth], and the spirit which I have made [ensoulment], . . . even so ye must be born again into the kingdom of heaven, of water [baptism], and the Spirit [the Holy Ghost], and be cleansed by . . . the blood of mine Only Begotten [atonement]."[42]

In any case, the New Testament scriptures elsewhere affirm baptism's essential role in the process of salvation. "The one who believes and is baptized will be saved," in the simple formula of Mark.[43] The supposed indispensability of baptism explains the urgency of child baptism through the early Christian centuries and the perceived hopelessness of the predicament of those who died without the ordinance, through early death or birth outside the Christian world and centuries. The pagan poet Virgil, Dante's virtuous but unbaptized guide through hell and purgatory, but barred forever from Paradise, is a stand-in for millions denied the joys of Heaven because of a birth on the wrong side of Christian history.

Luther not only retained baptism (along with the Eucharist) as a sacrament but he also defended its necessity. We must be baptized or we cannot be saved, Luther declared in his *Large Catechism.* For "through it perfect holiness and salvation become accessible to us, which are otherwise beyond [our] reach."[44] The Augsburg Confession affirmed his stance: baptism "is necessary to salvation" and "by baptism the grace of God is offered."[45] John Calvin wrote, "By water is meant . . . inward cleansing and quickening of the Holy Spirit," and therefore concluded that "so far as this passage is concerned, I cannot at all bring myself to believe that Christ is referring to baptism."[46] As for the necessity of baptism, Calvin sent ambiguous signals. In his commentary on John 3:5, written in the 1550s, he took an orthodox view: "It is true indeed that we are excluded from salvation if we neglect Baptism; and in this sense I confess it is necessary."[47] But the operative word here seems to be "neglect," meaning a willful refusal to signify our participation in the covenant of grace through an available sacrament. For as he wrote in his more authoritative *Institutes,* "We must not deem baptism so necessary as to suppose that everyone who has lost the opportunity of obtaining it has forthwith perished."[48] (Similarly, the Westminster Confession holds that "grace and salvation are not so inseparably annexed unto [baptism], as that no person can be regenerated or saved without it.")[49] At the same time, the Episcopal Church held that "none can enter into the kingdom of God" without being born anew, "of water."[50]

Trends in the modern Protestant church have decidedly moved against baptism's necessity. The independent minister Charles Buck typified this direction when he wrote in 1802 that baptism is an initiation into a visible church, but "it is not, however, essential to salvation. . . . To suppose it is essential," he reasoned, "is to put it in the place of *that* which it signifies."[51] Alexander Campbell tackled the question of necessity for baptism head-on in a series of articles and found it useful to endorse the position of Southern Baptist leader Thomas Meredith. "Is baptism essential for salvation?" the latter asked, and he returned an ambiguous reply. "Baptism is not, in the nature of things, indispensable to salvation." However, he was unwilling to say that "any can be saved, on strictly Christian principles, without it." It would seem, in other words, to be a general requirement, "a highly imperative duty devolving on every believer who possesses the power of compliance." At the same time, the requirement "may be set aside whenever it suits the divine clemency to do so."[52]

Calvin's belief that baptism was not absolutely essential for salvation was a logical corollary of the centrality of faith in the process—or event—of salvation. If it is indeed by faith that we are saved, then the ordinances or sacraments are the signs, tokens, or even seals of that salvation, but not the means. Wesley, too, clearly taught that faith was the means of salvation; and that faith produced justification, or "forgiveness of all our sins." Accompanying such justification, "in that very moment— sanctification begins." In that instant we are "born again" (as the first stage, but not the final stage or "full salvation").[53]

Since Abraham's circumcision was a seal of his faithfulness and assured place within God's covenant, it made sense that for Christians, baptism would serve the same function. And so the Westminster Confession declared baptism to be "a sign and seal of the covenant of grace."[54] Wesley made the equivalence explicit: "Circumcision was the seal of the covenant. . . . When the old seal of circumcision was taken off, this of baptism was added in its room."[55] Most Protestants followed suit, in seeing baptism as an important ordinance, but not one on which salvation depended.

Infant Baptism

Only adult baptisms are noted in the New Testament—when age is at all indicated—but no explicit guidelines exist. The pairing of baptism with repentance would seem to argue against its administration to infants, and the earliest church guidelines on the subject carry the same clear assumption: "Baptize into the name of the Father, and of the Son, and of the Holy Spirit in living water . . . but thou shalt order the baptized to fast one or two days before," commends the *Didache*, an early second-century manual for Christian communities.[56] The later *Apostolic Constitutions* reaffirms that counsel.[57]

Infant baptism soon became the norm, however, and it is likely that the doctrine of original sin was influential in guiding practice. Most Protestants followed Catholics in embracing the doctrine of original sin, a condition that extended to every soul. The universality of original sin was proof of the universal necessity for baptism. If sin is co-extensive with our very existence, then universal baptism at the earliest reasonable moment in order to lift that burden is a rational response to the problem of universal fallenness. In Augustine's formulation, "Everyone, even little children, have broken God's covenant, not indeed in virtue of any personal action but in virtue of mankind's common origin in that single ancestor in whom all have sinned. . . . Original sin is common to all men, regardless of the personal sins of each one."[58] And so we find in Augustine the first developed theory that unambiguously assigns actual guilt to, and justifies the infliction of eternal torments upon, creatures who may not even live long enough to make a choice or decision of any kind, who are damned even as they draw their first breath. So as early as 418, the church declared that "even infants, who in themselves thus far have not been able to commit any sin," need "the bath of regeneration" to have the "original sin [inherited] from Adam" expiated.[59]

When baptism is connected to a "new birth," with its implications of personal repentance and a conversion to Christ and his gospel, this baptism theology complicates the matter of infant baptism, since repentance and conversion are clearly criteria that can apply to adults only. Hence Luther opines that faith being indispensable to the sacrament, the infant must therefore be "aided by the faith of others, namely, those who bring them for baptism." Thus the infant is "changed, cleansed and renewed by inpoured faith."[60] Reformed theology took a similar path. If repentance is required for baptism, the Anglican Catechism asks, "why then are infants baptized, when by reason of their tender age they cannot [repent and forsake sin]?" "Because they promise [to do so] by their sureties," that is, by means of those who take responsibility for them, the catechism explains[61] (a vicarious dimension to sacramentalism, if there ever was one).

The Puritans struggled with a theology of baptism, in the wake of redefining the church as a voluntary association of the elect. What could the meaning of baptism be in the absence of an experience of saving grace and consequent membership in a church? Only if Puritans had "been willing to abandon infant baptism" could they have "avoided the embarrassment" of the consequent contradictions between practice and theology, noted Edmund Morgan.[62] They did not abandon the practice, but other Protestants soon would. Wesley confesses to uncertainty on this seeming contradiction. He believed that "infants are guilty of original sin, . . . [and] need to be washed from original sin; therefore they are proper subjects of baptism." At the same time, he confessed, "We cannot comprehend how this work [of new birth] can be wrought in infants," but says weakly that "neither can we comprehend how it is wrought in persons of riper years."[63]

Other Protestants found it more logical to withhold baptism altogether from persons until they were of an age to repent. Radical reformers like the Anabaptists emphasized free will and de-emphasized original sin as unscriptural. Connecting baptism with repentance rather than cleansing from an Adamic inheritance, infant baptism was therefore not merely unnecessary or inappropriate; it was "the greatest and first abomination of the pope," according to their first statement of faith.[64] Their first work of theology conveyed their essential doctrine in its simple title: *The Christian Baptism of Believers*.[65]

As original sin lost much of its purchase in the eighteenth and nineteenth centuries, Protestant theologies of baptism developed accordingly. Baptists saw baptism as an act of obedience and an outward demonstration of a cleansing that has already been effected on cognizant adults—with mixed views on the effects of Adam's sin on children. Nineteenth-century trends were clearly in the direction of further weakening the doctrine of original sin, or at least emphasizing inherited disposition rather than actual accountability (*vitium* or vice rather than *reatus* or guilt).[66] Consequently, Protestants increasingly associated baptism with a personal rather than inherited sinfulness.

Reformed Baptists like Thomas Campbell and Barton Stone went further than almost all others, rejecting altogether the original sin that had so long been the rationale behind baptism of child and adult alike. Unlike their more conservative namesakes, they practiced baptism for the remission of *personal* sins and therefore considered it essential to adult salvation. Only adults were capable of professing faith, so only adults could rightly be baptized. ("An infant cannot have faith; but it needs neither faith, nor regeneration, nor baptism," in Campbell's words.)[67] As children could not profess faith, neither could they be culpable for their sins until they are able to commit themselves to God; furthermore, humans are born innocent, not guilty and depraved. "We are not guilty of Adam's sin. . . . The guilt of sin attaches only to him who commits sin."[68] With this development, we arrive at a doctrinal position very close to that of Mormonism's founder, Joseph Smith.

Baptism and Regeneration

The exact role of baptism in the process of personal salvation became a point of controversy among many American Restorationists like the Campbells in the early nineteenth century. Reformers intent on returning Christianity to New Testament patterns aligned themselves with American Baptists beginning about 1815, but by 1830 they had formed their own union of "Disciples" or "Christians." A major reason for the rift was a fundamental difference regarding the theology of baptism. "The act of baptism, reasoned Baptists, was a sign that remission of sins and regeneration already had transformed the believer. But Reformed Baptists generally insisted that baptism was *for* the remission of sins."[69] This was, unavoidably, a return to a more sacramentalist posture, one that saw baptism as effecting something, rather than signifying something. Alexander Campbell had tried to skirt the theological minutia by insisting that faith, repentance, and baptism were a total package, "a system as a *whole*," and any who claim to know when remission of sins occurred in this "order of time . . . have taken for granted more than is proved."[70]

Sidney Rigdon, a disciple of Campbell, felt no doubt on this score. He was adamant that baptism of the repentant *effected* remission of sins and was therefore absolutely essential. This was why a young Parley Pratt fell under Campbellite influence. He had rejected Methodists and Presbyterians on account of their practice of infant baptism. With the Baptists, on the other hand, it was not their mode of baptism but their doctrine of baptism that troubled him. He complained to his father that the Baptists did not baptize "for *remission of sins*."[71] When he learned that Sidney Rigdon, a Campbellite minister, was emphatic that Christ's apostles "baptized penitential believers for the remission of sins,"[72] he found a spiritual mentor. Along with over a hundred other members of Rigdon's congregations, Pratt found a congenial home in Mormonism in part because of this shared understanding of baptism.

Mormon Baptism

Following New Testament and Campbellite precedent, Mormons practice baptism "for the remission of sins." Mormon scriptures are ambiguous as to the exact sequence of baptism and remission, presumably because repentance and remission of sins are associated with faith, a change of heart, and are both a process, rather than necessarily instantaneous events. The Book of Mormon teaches that candidates "shall receive a remission of their sins" (not original sin) *after* they "come down into the depths of humility and [are] baptized."[73] But a revelation to Joseph Smith indicates that candidates shall "manifest by their works that they have received the Spirit of Christ unto the remission of their sins," and *then* they "shall be received by baptism into his church."[74] Cowdery strongly objected to Smith's wording in the revelation, and its ordering of remission before baptism may have been the reason. But he protested to no effect.[75]

Mormonism is unusual in allowing no exceptions whatsoever for the salvational requirement of baptism as a sacrament. Orson Spencer's reading of John 3:5, in his popular letters on LDS doctrine, was typical in its agreement with the pre-Reformation position: "Jesus Christ has . . . explicitly said, in the most unequivocal language possible, that no man can 'enter the kingdom' without water baptism, or being 'born of the water.'"[76] Smith had taught emphatically and clearly that remission of sins was obtained by baptism, the decisive doctrinal point for Parley Pratt.[77] A Christian journal found it significant that Mormons were "laying great stress on baptism 'FOR' the remission of sins," and Young believed that the Latter-day Saints were virtually alone—and indeed they almost were among Protestants—in believing adult baptism to be absolutely "necessary or efficacious for the remission of sins, [not] simply as a profession of faith."[78] For Mormons, baptism was therefore not seen as a sign or symbol but as the divinely ordained means through which the atonement is to effect on the repentant sinner its first work of cleansing, subject to the candidate's genuine repentance.

In the larger cosmological scheme, however, the ordinance signifies a shift in eternal status that moves far beyond simple forgiveness of sin. Parley Pratt was not unusual in his emphasis on adoption theology as consisting of the "laws and ordinances"—especially baptism—that qualified one for membership in the kingdom of God. But consistent with New Testament usage, Pratt emphasized that this adoption also fully qualified one to be a "son" of God. He was here doubtless influenced by his mentor Alexander Campbell, who had described baptism as the means by which the adopted were "born into the Divine family, enrolled in Heaven."[79] Such had been the position of Anglican divine John Bradford, who called baptism "initiation . . . wherewith we be enrolled, as it were, into the household and family of God."[80] Mormons embraced this same logic but with radically literalized meaning. As we saw above, the constituting of the human race into a celestial family was a principal purpose of mortality itself, and the church was the instrument through which those relations were to be ordered and constituted. Baptism was therefore the sacrament by which an individual began the process of initiation, actually re-incorporation, into heirship with heavenly parents, with Christ as spiritual father. Taking upon oneself the name of Christ, in this context, meant a legally valid process of adoption—parallel to an earthly version of incorporation into a family with new parents. It represented the first step of one's inauguration into the New and Everlasting Covenant.

In the early twenty-first century, a number of major Christian traditions declared Mormon baptism invalid.[81] Though Mormons were hurt to be labeled outside "the bounds of the historic, apostolic tradition of Christian faith," Mormons have from the beginning failed to recognize other Christian baptisms (much to the dismay of Alexander Campbell, who protested that "re-baptizing believers is making void the law of Christ").[82] The rationale in Mormonism's case came in an early revelation on the subject and explained why all new converts, previously baptized or not, needed to submit to the ordinance at the hands of Mormon elders. The revelation declared that "all old covenants have I caused to be done away in this thing; and this is a new and an everlasting covenant, even that which was from the beginning." Here we find the most emphatic statement that baptism in Latter-day Saint theology is the first formal and effectual integration of the individual into the New and Everlasting Covenant, making one the seed of Abraham, and by extension, a literal child of heavenly parents in the celestial family order. Lacking that particular covenantal context and understanding, "although a man should be baptized an hundred times it availeth him nothing."[83] Baptism's covenantal significance—which transcends its status as a sign and vehicle of personal cleansing—is the defining meaning of the ordinance. Other criteria are necessary as well, including the personal readiness of the candidate, the mode of baptism, and the authority by which it is administered.

Accountability, Mode

In Mormonism, given a rejection of the concept of original sin, and believing forgiveness is contingent on repentance (and covenantal adoption contingent on personal choice), infant baptism is theologically incoherent. Mormon aversion to infant baptism at the same time finds emphatic scriptural basis—founded not on its absence in the New Testament but on its explicit condemnation in the Book of Mormon, which called it "solemn mockery before God." As the ancient prophet Moroni continued, rather harshly, "little children need no repentance, neither baptism. . . . But little children are alive in Christ, even from the foundation of the world; . . . he that supposeth that little children need baptism is in the gall of bitterness and in the bonds of iniquity."[84] The specific age at which persons were considered accountable was pronounced as Smith worked on his biblical revisions in 1831. As he came to Genesis 17, he revised the passage referring to circumcision of children to add these words: "that thou mayest know forever, that children are not accountable before me, until they are eight years old."[85]

The requirement of accountability emphasizes the intent of the candidate at the time of baptism. You "might as well baptize a bag of sand as a man if not done in view of the getting of the Holy Ghost.—baptism by water is but ½ a baptism—& is good for nothing with[out] the other, the Holy Ghost," taught Smith.[86] He was not talking about the ordinance of confirmation but the actual baptism of fire. "The baptism of water, without the baptism of fire and the Holy Ghost attending it, is of no use; they are necessarily and inseparably connected. He must be born of water and the spirit."[87]

The specific criteria for baptism are given in the Articles of the Church, which stipulate that "whosoever humbleth himself before God and desireth to be baptized, and comes forth with a broken heart and a contrite spirit, and witnesseth unto the church, that they have truly repented of all their sins and are willing to take upon them the name of Christ, having a determination to serve him unto the end, and truly manifest by their works that they have received the Spirit of Christ unto the remission of their sins, shall be received by baptism into his church."[88] The covenant of devotion to Christ, serving him to the end, finds another articulation in the Book of Mormon, this time expressed by the founder of "the Church of Christ" in the second century BC. Alma indicates that those who present themselves for baptism implicitly promise "to come into the fold of God, and to be called his people, and are willing to bear one another's burdens, that they may be light; Yea, and are willing to mourn with those that mourn; yea, and comfort those that stand in need of comfort, and to stand as witnesses of God at all times and in all things, and in all places."[89] The significance of this covenant for Mormon theology is that it reaffirms both the horizontal and vertical dimensions of the New and Everlasting Covenant; assuming one's place as a child of Christ is inseparable from assuming one's place as comforter and fellow-traveler in the community of his disciples.

What Mormons now universally understand as an implicit covenant undertaken at the water's edge was in earlier years of Mormonism a formal element of the ritual itself. As late as 1894, Wilford Woodruff's First Counselor, George Q. Cannon, addressed a question as to whether new members had to explicitly and verbally place themselves under a covenant. He responded that "the practice generally has been to ask candidates for baptism, before administering the ordinance to them, concerning their willingness to repent, . . . take upon themselves the name of Christ, and serve him."[90] Reciting the covenant at water's edge appears to have faded as a practice soon thereafter. That is lamentable, since Mormons now understand the sacrament as a renewal of (or occasion to remember) life-defining baptismal covenants, but those covenants were never explicitly made, depriving the candidate of some of their sacramental power.

As for mode, Mormons again found precedent in the Book of Mormon, which they had been told to rely upon as a pattern. In that record, a resurrected Christ visits the inhabitants of ancient America and instructs a core of disciples in the administration of the sacrament: "And then shall ye immerse them in the water, and come forth again out of the water."[91] No one disputes that the New Testament directs disciples to baptize (βαπτίζω or baptidzo), which means to immerse (though some have argued that it also functions metaphorically in the New Testament, as when persons are baptized by the Holy Spirit).[92] Even Luther said that "*baptismos* . . . means to plunge something entirely into the water, so that the water closes over it. And although in many places it is the custom no longer, . . . but only to pour the baptismal water upon them out of the font, nevertheless the former is what should be done." ("It would be well to give to a thing so perfect and complete a sign that is also complete and perfect," he said elsewhere.)[93] However, sprinkling (or pouring) developed as an alternative mode of baptism and was continued by most Protestants. (Reformed Baptists, from whom many Mormon converts came, were a stark exception.) The *Didache* had allowed for pouring when "living water" was not available.[94] Two additional, reasonable grounds could be invoked: it was more practical with both the young and the infirm (and was indispensable once infant baptism became the norm), and it seemed to effect the same symbolic purpose of cleansing.

By contrast, in addition to the Book of Mormon's model, and following Paul, Smith's description of baptism as in "the likeness of the resurrection of the dead in coming forth out of their graves" makes immersion the only appropriately symbolic mode.[95] Early Mormons baptized in streams and ponds, and though the first font was in the Nauvoo Temple, meetinghouse fonts are the principal venue today; the only requirement is sufficient water to make submersion possible. The words of the baptismal prayer also follow from Book of Mormon precedent: "these are the words which ye shall say, calling them by name, saying: Having authority given me of Jesus Christ, I baptize you in the name of the Father, and of the Son, and of the Holy Ghost."[96]

Rebaptism

Baptism as a sign of adoption into the fold was the norm and raison d'etre for the ordinance, but a few variations on the theme existed in Mormon practice. One indication that adoption was the principal but not only purpose behind the ordinance was that the expression, baptism "for the remission of sins," acquired a meaning in the church's early years that distinguished it from the normal practice of convert baptism. As a general rule, adoption was a one-time event. Remission of sins, however, was an event that should accompany every gesture of genuine repentance and recommitment. With such an idea in mind, early Mormons initiated a pattern of rebaptisms of those needing or wishing for a fresh start in their spiritual journey, and they referred to the practice as baptism "for remission of sins." A few instances were recorded as early as 1832, but the practice really gained currency in the Nauvoo years.[97] As Oliver Olney explained in an 1842 letter, "When they do wrong they get rebaptized they then stand fair in the sight of god altho they have done ever so bad this is the theme amongst those that are a wallowing in the mire."[98] The next year, the practice swept the community. John Scott recorded that "nearly all the church have been baptized again for the remission of their sins since they joined the church, I have also by the hands of br joseph as he himself has been."[99]

The practice persisted into the Utah years. William Clayton noted an occasion during the 1847 trek west when "many of the brethren went and were baptized on the dam by Elder Kimball for the remission of sins."[100] Under the rigors of expulsion, westward migration, and colonization and resettlement, Mormons experienced "a long separation from organized branches and wards of the Church: and consequently an interruption in the observance of regular Church duties." It was these circumstances, George Cannon related, that led Brigham Young to institute the practice of rebaptism after the exodus from Nauvoo.[101] Decades later, he noted that it still continued "as a custom for all members of the Church who come here as emigrants to go forth and be re-baptized."[102] It is apparent that on occasion, the slackness was not caused by distance alone, and rebaptism was more a consequence of simple spiritual lapses than excusable inattention. In an 1854 address, Young thundered that if any in his audience had done wrong and not repented, they should "leave in the intermission, and go home again . . . or get an Elder to immerse you in City Creek, and wash away your sins, that you may not hinder those that are pure."[103]

One pioneer recorded in his journal, a decade after settlement in Utah, "The sacrament was ordered to be withheld until the people humbled themselves and again renewed their covenants by baptism. The most of Union Ward was rebaptized on the 28th of Oct 1856. I was rebaptized with the rest, feeling a determination to keep the commandments of God more faithfully here after, the Lord being my helper."[104] That year marked the beginning of what has been called "the Mormon Reformation," a time of fervent evangelizing within the Mormon community, to recommit the willing and winnow out the lukewarm. "All that saved us this year was renewing our covenants," preached Young, and rebaptism was common in that two-year period.[105] During the Mormon Reformation, the ordinance of rebaptism was altered slightly, by the substitution of the words, "for the renewal of your covenants" for "remission of sins."[106]

Not only the backsliders or congregations in the throes of Mormonism's equivalent to revivals were typical candidates. "Nearly the whole" of a tabernacle full of the church leadership and "Priesthood in General . . . Covenanted to Renew their Covenants & be rebaptized" on July 13, 1875.[107] Four days later, five of the apostles entered the waters again, the other seven having been rebaptized several weeks earlier. For some of them, it was the fifth or sixth time.[108] Rebaptism could also signify recommitment prior to any new spiritual undertaking. First-time temple attenders were supposed to certify their rebaptism in an 1881 requirement.[109] Participation in one of the church's united orders, or communalistic enterprises, could also require rebaptism.[110]

Mormon rebaptism gradually faded, with George Cannon advising in 1892 that "it is not necessary for men and women who have transgressed to always be re-baptized."[111] The fading of the practice was paralleled by a cultural shift in the significance of the sacrament of the Lord's Supper. With no particular scriptural warrant, partaking of the bread and water was seen as a means of renewing the baptismal covenant. Regular services where the Lord's Supper was administered, preached apostle Francis Lyman in 1884, were "for the purpose of renewing our covenants," language that became standard.[112] The ordinance "amounts to a virtual renewal of the covenant of baptism," confirmed apostle Marion G. Romney in 1946 in a typical expression.[113]

Shifting the burden of spiritual recommitment from baptism to the Lord's Supper obviated the need for an actual rebaptism to signify recommitment, which was fading as a practice by the end of the century—so much so that in 1893, the church's semi-official theologian queried the church presidency about the practice. James Talmage recorded that "the authorities were unanimous in declaring that rebaptism is not recognized as a regularly constituted principle of the Church; and that the current practice of requiring rebaptism as a prerequisite for admission to the temples ... is unauthorized." At the same time, they ruled, "nothing should be put in the way of anyone receiving the covenants of rebaptism if he feels the necessity of so doing."[114] A few years later, a similar question arose concerning members wishing to commit after passing most of their lives outside the church. Woodruff's successor Lorenzo Snow again discouraged the practice "if they could be admitted without another baptism."[115] Noting a potential analogy with Catholic confessional (supposedly implying "a premium on sinning"),[116] leaders grew less inclined to support the practice, and it ceased completely soon thereafter.

Healing Baptisms

Mormons were also unusual in practicing rebaptism for reasons of health. In 1840, Smith had declared that "if the Saints are sick or have sickness in their families, and the Elders do not prevail every family should get power by fasting & prayer & anointing with oil & continue so to do their sick shall be healed."[117] The next year, however, he added another tool to the healing arsenal: baptisms for health. It seems significant that Smith associated such healing with temple powers and prerogatives. Normal convert and recommitment baptisms could be done in the river, he said, but "baptisms for the dead, and for the healing of the body must be in the font."[118] Jonathan Stapley and Kristine Wright suggest that the healing waters of the pool of Bethesda and Namaan's restoration from washing in Jordan provided biblical precedent for the Mormon practice.[119] And indeed, invoking the pool of Bethesda as type, the apostles wrote a joint letter urging the Saints to speed completion of the temple with healing baptisms in mind. "The time has come," they wrote, "when the great Jehovah would have a resting place on earth, a habitation for his chosen, . . . where the saints may enter the Baptismal Font for their dead relations . . . a place, over which the heavenly messengers may watch and trouble the waters as in days of old, so that when the sick are put therein they shall be made whole."[120]

The sacramental origins of baptism for health may also be in James 5:15, where the apostle indicates that after anointing the sick for healing purposes, "anyone who has committed sins will be forgiven," thus linking remission of sins and physical healing (a connection, we will see, that played out in Catholic sacramental developments). Since baptism was associated with such remission, it was a logical stand-in for anointing the sick. Smith taught in 1839 that "by our obedience to the ordinances . . . the sick may be healed."[121] Eliza Snow recalled that once the Kirtland Temple had been dedicated, the washings and anointings performed there were physically and well as spiritually therapeutic: "The sick and the lame came to be healed. . . . [They] would throw away their crutches and go home whole."[122] Baptismal healings, by contrast, were not always performed in the temple and sometimes required several iterations. Brigham Young mentioned in 1862, for instance, how one "Br. Taft had the mountain fever and could not live till morning; we dipped him seven times in the river, and the next day he was comparatively well."[123]

In the first decades of the twentieth century, with the general decline in charismatic gifts and experiences generally (and the rise of germ theory and scientific medicine), the practice lost the support of church leadership. In 1921, the First Presidency relegated such temple healings to the temple annex rather than the temple proper, and then the next year ended the practice altogether, considering anointing of the sick to be the appropriate and sufficient vehicle for ecclesiastical healing.[124]

Vicarious Baptism

As we saw, a recurrent theme in the protests of the first generation of Protestant reformers was impatience with the Catholic theology of postmortality. Denigrating the doctrine of purgatory and ceasing prayer and masses for the dead were two Protestant attempts to deny what Catholics had seen as a permeable membrane between the dead and the living. Scriptural statements on the subject were of doubtful canonicity or clouded meaning. In the seventeenth century, the Apocrypha was still part of the King James Bible, and its book of Maccabees had intimated both a duty and a capacity for the living to concern themselves with the disposition of the dead. In chapter 12, "The noble Judas . . . took up a collection, man by man, to the amount of two thousand drachmas of silver, and sent it to Jerusalem to provide for a sin offering. In doing this he acted very well and honorably, taking account of the resurrection. For if he were not expecting that those who had fallen would rise again, it would have been superfluous and foolish to pray for the dead."[125] Luther had demoted Maccabees and other books of the Apocrypha to its own category of dubious standing in 1534 and Protestants at first followed suit, then in the English-speaking world they removed this section altogether (in the nineteenth century).

A second source with bearing on the role of the living in the salvation of the dead comes from a canonical text with particularly high standing in Christianity: Paul's first letter to the Corinthians. There readers and churchmen have found a tantalizingly cryptic reference to a practice little understood. In defending the reality of the resurrection, Paul asks, "What will those people do who receive baptism on behalf of the dead? If the dead are not raised at all, why are people baptized on their behalf?"[126] The words seem to clearly point to a sacrament performed by proxy, and as even dissidents from such a reading acknowledge, "The majority of exegetes and commentators hold that 15:29 is a reference to some form of vicarious baptism."[127]

The second-century *Shepherd of Hermas*, which was considered scriptural by many of the earliest Christians and was even bound with the New Testament in some codices, appears to sanction baptism performed for the deceased. The Shepherd is told that the apostles and teachers, after dying, "preached the name of the Son of God" to others who were dead. Those dead were "obliged to ascend through water in order that they might be made alive."[128] In his own discussion of salvation for the dead, Clement of Alexandria cites the Shepherd's apparent reference to the practice: "They went down with them therefore into the water, and again ascended. But these descended alive, and again ascended alive. But those who had fallen asleep, descended dead but ascended alive."[129] Everett Ferguson notes several other ancient sources contending that "the righteous who died before the coming of Christ must receive baptism before entering the heavenly kingdom," including the *Apocalypse of Peter* (ca. 135) and the *Epistle of the Apostles* (ca. 150). The *Apocalypse of Paul* (third to fifth centuries) adds repentant sinners to the vicariously baptized and redeemed.[130]

Apologists associate other historical references to vicarious baptism with heretical practices. Tertullian urged readers of Paul's reference to "never mind that practice, (whatever it may have been)."[131] Church Father and bishop of Salamis Epiphanius (ca. 315–403), in his encyclopedia of heresies, associated vicarious baptism with a group called Cerinthians.[132] John Chrysostom (349–407), another Father and archbishop of Constantinople, wrote an entire homily on 1 Corinthians 15:29. In it, he describes the Marcionite practice of vicarious baptism. If a convert dies before the ordinance can be performed, a stand-in requests it on her behalf, and is so baptized. "Extreme ridiculousness . . . Madmen," he fumes.[133] Didymus the Blind (313–398) also alleged that "the Marcionites baptize the living on behalf of dead believers."[134] Some version or versions of the practice were apparently common enough that authorities moved against it at the Synod of Hippo held in 393, declaring, "The Eucharist shall not be given to dead bodies, nor baptism conferred upon them." Four years later, the sixth canon of the Third Council of Carthage affirmed the position.[135]

Little more is heard of the practice for a thousand years and more. Then, in the early 1700s, the German pietist Conrad Beissel imigrated to Pennsylvania and founded a religious community at Ephrata that reached some 300 residents by 1750.[136] In trying to recuperate a pure Christianity, these seventh-day Sabbatarians and mystics introduced celibacy, foot washing, the love feast, and, at some point, baptism for the dead. That practice lasted only a few years, and by 1820 the community had evaporated.[137] In years following, however, the idea with its mention in Paul's letter generated a good deal of Christian speculation. As Ryan Tobler chronicles, "Christian newspapers and exegetical journals in Bible-breathing America published a steady stream of analyses of this verse and the notion of 'baptism for the dead' throughout the nineteenth century."[138] In addition, the Marcionite practice of baptism for the dead mentioned above was discussed in Buck's *Theological Dictionary*, which description Smith clearly read. However, that practice was unlike anything Smith would institute:[139] "After a catechumen was dead, they hid a living man under the bed of the deceased; then, coming to the dead man, they asked him whether he would receive baptism; and he making no answer, the other answered for him, and said he would be baptized in his stead; and so they baptized the living for the dead."[140]

Joseph Smith was contemplating the possibilities of baptism for the dead as early as 1838. Writing in the church's *Elders Journal*, he addressed the puzzle of reconciling Mormon universalism with the necessity for baptism. "If Mormonism be true," he quoted an inquirer, "what of all those who died without baptism?" Smith's answer hinted at a solution: "All those who have not had an opportunity of hearing the Gospel, and being administered unto by an inspired man in the flesh," it said, "must have it hereafter, before they can be finally judged."[141] The essential but undefined role of those "administrators in the flesh" was further affirmed the next year, when in 1839 he quoted words from Hebrews that "they without us cannot be made perfect."[142]

The decisive moment arrived during a funeral service in 1840 for Seymour Brunson. Smith had been reading to the audience the greater portion of Paul's epistle on the resurrection (1 Corinthians 15) with its reference to baptism for the dead. Then, noticing a widow in the audience who had lost an unbaptized child, and invoking the words of Jesus that "except a man be born of water and of the spirit he cannot enter the kingdom of heaven," he "said that this widow should have glad tidings in that thing. He also said the apostle was talking to a people who understood baptism for the dead, for it was practiced among them. He went on to say that people could now act for their friends who had departed this life, and that the plan of salvation was calculated to save all who were willing to obey the requirements of the law of God."[143]

Regardless of where Smith first encountered the idea, and in spite of his gloss on Paul's letter to the Corinthians, Smith claimed that his understanding of this principle was based on knowledge "independent of the Bible."[144] In any case, one of the crucial keys in Smith's aspirations for a universally accessible salvation was coming into place. The revelation that families need no longer mourn as forever lost their unbaptized relatives who had died was enthusiastically received. "The day was joyful because of the light and glory that Joseph set forth. I can truly say my soul was lifted up," wrote Vilate Kimball to her husband.[145] One member spoke for multitudes when she wrote "What a glorious thing it is that we believe and receive the fulness of the gospel as it is preached now and can be baptized for all of our dead friends. . . . Oh, mother, if we are so happy as to have a part in the first resurrection, we shall have our children just as we laid them down in their graves."[146] From the start, those who found the practice peculiar or illogical were reminded that "where would we be but for the application of the principle of substitution?" Resistance to the idea "strikes at the very root of the scheme of redemption, for . . . 'he who knew no sin, was made sin for us.'"[147]

Over ensuing weeks, Smith worked out his understanding of the principle and, together with apostle Lyman Wight, sermonized on the topic at the next church conference, in October.[148] Meanwhile, Mormon elders immediately began baptizing members in the Mississippi River on behalf of their deceased ancestors, by dozens and then hundreds. As work on the Nauvoo Temple progressed, river baptisms were halted until they could be done in the proper setting of a completed temple. In October of the next year, J. H. Johnson published a poem on the subject, rejoicing that God had "prepar'd the way, Through which the dead may hear his word, And all its truths obey," and enjoined his fellow Saints to "rise without restraint, And act for those we love: For they are giving their consent, And wait for us to move."[149] Days later, they continued to move, this time in a proper setting. On November 21, 1841, Wilford Woodruff reported that "we repaired to the Baptismal Font in the Temple for the purpose of Baptizing for the dead, for the remission of Sins & for healing. It was truly an interesting scene. It was the first FONT erected for this glorious purpose in this last dispensation. It was dedicated By President Joseph Smith & The Twelve for Baptizing for the Dead &c & this was the first time the font had been prepared for the reception of candidates."[150]

The Mormon practice of baptism by immersion, based on the New Testament precedent, was no doubt aided by the ordinance's dual symbolic value to which the author of Romans alluded: both Christ and the carnal self descend into a tomb/watery grave, and emerge with new life.[151] But something of Smith's universalizing perspective is revealed in his new reading of its symbolism. "The ordinance of baptism by water," he wrote in 1842, "to be immersed therein in order to answer to the likeness of the dead, that one principle might accord with the other; to be immersed in the water and come forth out of the water *is in the likeness of the res-urrection of the dead in coming forth out of their graves*; hence, this ordinance was instituted to form a relationship with the ordinance of baptism for the dead, being in likeness of the dead" (emphasis added).[152]

This is an astounding assertion. The *primary* referent to which immersive baptism points, in other words, is not the tomb of the sinful self or of the crucified Christ, but the tombs of the millions and billions who passed through life with no exposure to the gospel or its saving sacraments. The placement of the temple font beneath ground level, unlike normal Mormon baptismal fonts of the modern era, further emphasizes the dead whom it serves. Since their numbers far outweigh the numbers of those who are baptized by authorized administrators while living, Smith suggests, the ordinance is primarily an ordinance for the dead, and secondarily for the living—not the other way around, and its symbolism conveys that priority.

Extending the rite of baptism to the dead was more than an ordinance performed on their behalf. A number of biblical promises and theological innovations began to coalesce around this first foray into vicarious sacramentalism—with the total picture suggesting a binding together rather than a crossing over between divergent realms. In other words, Smith was convinced that a principal function of vicarious baptism was to bring the dead into the orbit of salvation *with their kindred*. The problem posed by the uncatechized dead was not just their failure to comply with a saving ordinance, but their consequent separation from those who *had* complied. The revealed program of evangelizing and baptizing the dead erased the dominion of hell over all the earth's unbaptized dead and bridged a gulf that had separated millions of believing Christians from their unbaptized forebears.

Ryan Tobler has argued that the concept of adoption may have linked the two ideas together: "The widespread Christian doctrine of adoption into the kingdom of God, which many Latter-day Saints identified with baptism, may have enabled Joseph Smith to understand baptism for the dead as a way to seal people together."[153] Certainly the basis was there already. As Geoffrey Wainwright notes, "Baptism is the sacrament of entry into a new set of family relationships. Rebirth as sons and daughters of God implies the acquisition of new brothers and sisters in the persons of all the Father's children."[154] Smith just developed both relationships into a more robust conception of eternal family connectedness. As he elaborated in a canonized statement on the new practice of baptism for the dead,

> In all ages of the world, whenever the Lord has given a dispensation of the priesthood to any man by actual revelation, or any set of men, this power has

always been given. . . . For we without [the dead] cannot be made perfect; neither can they without us be made perfect. Neither can they nor we be made perfect without those who have died in the gospel also; for it is necessary in the ushering in of the dispensation of the fulness of times, which dispensation is now beginning to usher in, that a whole and complete and perfect union, and welding together of dispensations, and keys, and powers, and glories should take place, and be revealed from the days of Adam even to the present time.[155]

This language of binding, union, and welding would form the constant theme of the entire program of vicarious ordinances yet to unfold. Smith characterized the new world he had pointed toward with uncharacteristic understatement: baptism for the dead "presents the gospel of Christ in probably a more enlarged scale than some have viewed it."[156]

Gift of the Holy Ghost

In the Old Testament, notes one scholar of Christianity, the operations of the spirit are "intermittent." By contrast, "The spirit is given to all [Christians] at their Baptism," he writes in describing the New Testament perspective on the Holy Ghost.[157] In the Jewish Bible, figures often bestowed blessings by pronouncing prayerful or prophetic words while placing their hands on the subject's head. Ordination to special positions could also be performed this way, as when Moses "laid his hands on" Joshua in a bestowal of prophetic authority and wisdom.[158] In the New Testament, Paul "laid his hands" on recently baptized converts, and "the Holy Spirit came upon them."[159]

The Christian church imitated Paul's practice but called it confirmation as a result of a particular rationale that developed. The term originally referred to the laying on of hands performed by a bishop to validate or "confirm" an emergency baptism performed by a lay "person of the faith" in cases of impending death or peril.[160] By the laying on of hands, the efficacy of baptism was essentially verified or sealed, and the candidate was made eligible for the gifts of the spirit. As early as the year 300 or so, a church council convened to declare that every sacrament of baptism needed "the imposition of the hand" to make the ordinance "perfect."[161] Subsequent statements specified the use of oil and equated the sacrament with the "bestow[al of] the Spirit, the Paraclete."[162] "Be sealed with the gift of the Holy Spirit" are the words the priest speaks at the ordinance.

We saw that when Luther made his break with Rome, he wasted little time in stripping down the Catholic sacraments from seven to three, then two.[163] Confirmation or chrismation by the laying on of hands, though it had ample New Testament precedent, he did not believe had been commanded of God for Christians generally. In fact, he considered the idea "amazing," adding that "if everything the apostles did is a sacrament, why have they not rather made preaching a sacrament?"[164] In a similar vein, Calvin argued that Augustine himself called the laying on of hands "nothing but prayer." Calvin went much further, though, saying that those who claim that giving the "Holy Spirit by the laying on of hands" is a sacrament are claiming to bestow by a separate ceremony that which is already "truly given in baptism" (because "as many as have been baptized unto Christ, have put on Christ with his gifts," he writes, citing Galatians 3:27). Thus, that which "dissevers the proper promises of baptism from baptism" teaches a "doctrine of Satan."[165]

For Wesley, baptism is the "outward and visible sign" of "a new birth unto righteousness." This second birth, the baptism by fire, or gift of the Holy Ghost, he reminds us, is likened by the Savior to "the wind [that] bloweth where it listeth."[166] That seems to be why baptism can be ordained as an ordinance, but the bestowal of the Holy Ghost lies outside our "power or wisdom," beyond human control or reckoning.[167] Even as fervent a disciple of New Testament Christianity as the Restorationist Walter Scott believed that faith, repentance, and baptism were within the province of the believer, but the bestowal of the Holy Ghost, like forgiveness and eternal life, were God's gift. The only human exception allowed by his colleague Alexander Campbell occurred eighteen centuries earlier. "The pretension of imparting the Holy Spirit by imposition of hands," Campbell taught, "is an unscriptural intrusion on the exclusive prerogative of the primary apostles."[168] And so while the idea of the second birth and the role of the Holy Spirit in Christian regeneration remained vibrant, a particular sacrament associated with its bestowal largely disappeared from Protestantism.

Latter-day Saints are in agreement with other Christian faiths that "the gift of the Holy Ghost . . . cannot be received through the medium of any other principle, than the principle of Righteousness."[169] Nevertheless, Mormons, once again, revert to a Catholic (and Anglican) rather than a Protestant model in the manner of its bestowal. Like baptism, whose efficacy is likewise conditional on personal motive, intent, and sincerity, the gift is communicated by way of a formal sacrament, in this case, the laying on of hands by one in authority. Mormons believe biblical authority for the sacrament is clearly affirmed by the author of Hebrews, who refers to four "doctrines of Christ" as "repentance from dead works, . . . faith toward God, . . . baptisms and laying on of hands."[170] As an Anglican tract reasoned, the laying on of hands for the sick or for ordination is not required of "all Christians." But the laying on of hands, mentioned as a doctrine in proximity to baptism, faith, and repentance, apparently is. Hence, the expression "laying on of hands" must refer "to that rite which universally prevailed in the primitive Church," known today as confirmation.[171]

In Mormonism's original vision of a restoration of New Testament Christianity, Smith saw confirmation as the occasion for the actual bestowal of the Holy Spirit (or Holy Ghost in Mormon parlance). He believed Mormons were virtually an exception in the Protestant world in this regard, noting that "faith, repentance, and baptism . . . were believed by some of the religious societies of the day, but the doctrine of laying on of hands for the gift of the holy ghost, was discarded by them."[172] He doubtless felt assured by the fact that in the scriptures he restored, the gift of the Holy Ghost, in association with the sacrament of baptism, is in evidence in both an Adamic and an ancient American context.[173] And an 1830 revelation to him had specified the laying on of hands as the proper mode for the sacrament of bestowing the Holy Ghost.[174] In a further echo of Catholic (or primitive church) precedent, Mormons employ this sacrament both to confirm or "make perfect" the baptism and to bestow the gift of the spirit. Hence, the candidate is first "confirmed" a member of the church, thus rendering explicit and institutional what was implicit and personal—the member's adoption into the family and church of Christ through baptism. And then, in the same sacrament, the candidate is directed to "receive the Holy Ghost." The imperative form of the wording follows from John's gospel and echoes the Anglican ordination of a priest: "Receive ye the Holy Ghost," which Smith's contemporary the curate John Cawood aptly interpreted to mean, "Be ye ready to receive Him."[175]

In the New Testament, Luke records of a certain group of converts that the Holy Spirit "had not yet come upon any of them, although they had been baptized."[176] In a similar pattern, Smith recorded that at the time of his and Oliver Cowdery's reciprocal baptisms in the presence of a heavenly angel, by the authority of the Aaronic priesthood to which they had recently been ordained, he was told a higher authority was necessary to confer the gift of the Holy Ghost.[177] With these two incidents as precedent, Smith referred to baptism as "a holy ordinance preparatory to the reception of the Holy Ghost." The latter is a separate ordinance, received "by the laying on of hands [and it] cannot be received through the medium of any other principle."[178] A seeming contradiction to such a principle appears in Smith's own text, when he notes in the same account of his baptism that "no sooner had I baptized Oliver Cowdery than the Holy Ghost fell upon him."[179] The same quandary was apparent in the early Christian church. Peter asks the Saints at the day of Pentecost to qualify themselves to "receive the gift of the Holy Spirit" after they have already been so conspicuously and dramatically "filled with the Holy Spirit."[180]

Smith would later explain the apparent discrepancy with these words: "There is a difference between the Holy Ghost & the gift of the Holy Ghost," using Cornelius of the New Testament as an example: "Cornelius received the Holy Ghost before he was Baptized which was the convincing power of God unto him of the truth of the gospel but he could not receive the gift of the Holy Ghost until after he was Baptized."[181] What Smith had in mind was apparently not a simple distinction between a member of the godhead and a personal experience of that personage. Rather, he considered the gift of the Holy Ghost as itself the guarantee (provisional on righteousness) of an abiding presence of God's spirit, whereas the Holy Ghost could transiently manifest itself at any time in its role of Comforter, Teacher, or Testifier. In this capacity, the Holy Ghost can at times function in a way analogous to the role served by prevenient grace in other faiths. Before the work of conversion or regeneration is complete, or the sacrament performed, the Holy Ghost may lead to Christ through its preparatory ministrations.

For Smith, biblical precedent and revelatory command were sufficient to warrant the sacrament in its prescribed form, using physical imposition of hands. A few generations later, B. H. Roberts posited a naturalistic explanation for the emphasis on laying on of hands as the mechanism of transmission. With Jesus's observation that "virtue" was "gone out" of him to the woman with the issue of blood as illustration, he reasoned that "when a servant of God, who has the companionship of the Holy Ghost, is filled with that Spirit, . . . lays his hands upon one who has prepared himself, . . . some of the influence of the Holy Spirit passes from the one" to the other. "The transmission of the influence of the Holy Ghost from one person to another by an observation of the principles and ordinances of the Gospel . . . is as natural and philosophical in the spiritual things of the universe, as it is for electricity or steam to perform the wonder which these forces are now made to enact."[182] Such speculations, more common in an era when Mormonism was emphasizing its compatibility with modern science, never acquired official sanction.[183]

If sacraments serve the ends of worship, being the modes by which eternal relationships are strengthened and constituted, the conferral of the Holy Ghost can be seen as ancillary to this general purpose. Its principal calling, as Paraclete, Greek for advocate or counselor, is to testify of Jesus as the Messiah, and to "bring all things to your remembrance."[184] Given the Mormon view of life as an educative and formative sphere veiled from our premortal beginnings, in which context all humans sustained Christ's foreordination as earthly Savior, those words have special resonance. The paradigm role of the Holy Ghost, Mormons believe, was manifest in Peter's response to Jesus. "Who do you say that I am?" "You are the Messiah, the Son of the living God."[185] (Paul agreed, telling the Corinthians that only the Spirit can give humans such knowledge.)[186] The rock that Jesus then alludes to, Mormons believe, is the rock of revelation confirming the Savior's identity, that is, the form of knowledge that is the unique province of the Holy Spirit.[187] In this capacity, the Spirit restores to individuals the most important truth obscured from premortal beginnings: the foreordained role of Jesus as the Messiah.

In addition, the Holy Ghost is the instrumentality through which the divine makes its influence felt across the veil, enabling the process of improvement and sanctification and deification to proceed in spite of the countervailing influences of genetics, environments, and weakness of spirit and flesh. As Parley Pratt wrote, "the gift of the Holy Ghost adapts itself to all these organs or attributes. It quickens all the intellectual faculties [gives you 'sudden strokes of ideas' in Smith's description[188]], increases, enlarges, expands, and purifies all the natural passions and affections, and adapts them, by the gift of wisdom, to their lawful use. It inspires, develops, cultivates, and matures all the fine-toned sympathies, joys, tastes, kindred feelings, and affections of our nature."[189]

We also have seen that the gift of the Holy Ghost has been understood as a special dispensation of power and authority, related to or analogous in some ways to priesthood itself. Biblical texts, early Church Fathers, and Smith himself suggested this linkage. This understanding explains why, in the early days of the restoration, both women and men performed certain functions by invoking an authority that did not derive directly from priesthood ordination. Women healed, for example, without specific priesthood authorization, and men too healed by invoking the name of Christ, not priesthood power. The Book of Mormon's Jacob similarly mentions "command[ing] in the name of Jesus," not in the name of priesthood authority, "and the very trees obey us."[190]

The Holy Ghost is also a source of revelatory access to God. As a testator or teacher, the Holy Ghost is a conduit of spiritual knowledge. As Smith taught, "No man can receive the Holy Ghost without receiving revelations, The Holy Ghost is a revelator."[191] "This first comforter or Holy Ghost has no other effect than pure intelligence," said Smith.[192] "We believe we are entitled to the gift of the Holy Ghost in extent according to the discretion and wisdom of God and our faithfulness; which gift brings all things to our remembrance, past, present, and to come, that are necessary for us to know, and as far as our minds are prepared to receive the knowledge of God revealed by that all-wise Agent. The Holy Ghost is God's minister."[193]

And finally, as Brigham Young explained, true conversion occurs through the gift of the Holy Ghost, "which spirit broods over them continually for their good, heals their bodies, enlightens their minds, and makes them humble, meek, and harmless as little children. When a person receives the Holy Ghost by legal authority, he is like a child in its mother's lap."[194] For all these reasons, when Smith was asked by President Martin van Buren "wherein we differed in our religion from the other religions of the day. Bro. Joseph said we differed in mode of baptism and the gift of the Holy Ghost by the laying on of hands— We considered that all other considerations were contained in the gift of the Holy Ghost."[195]

Baptism, Smith had learned, was universally required. God intended for all, living and dead, to be adopted into the heavenly family. At the same time, and by the same logic, any sacrament necessary for human sanctification and salvation would be universally necessary. And so Smith reasoned: "On the Principle of entering in by Water and Spirit . . . you must not only be baptized for the [dead] but they must receive the Holy Ghost by Proxy."[196] Smith taught that "it will be a great while after the grave before you learn to understand the last, for it is a great thing to learn salvation beyond the grave and it is not all to be comprehended in this world."[197] Apparently, the guidance and capacity of that Spirit to teach and strengthen will be as indispensable in the worlds to come, where we will continue an endless process of learning and growth, as it is in this mortal domain. So the laying on of hands for the gift of the Holy Ghost, like immersive baptism, is performed outside the temple for the living and within for the dead.

Priesthood Ordination

In the normal course of a Mormon's religious life, baptism and confirmation mark the sacramental commencement of one's religious pilgrimage. The next step for males is conferring of the priesthood. Smith, we saw, did not understand priesthood as a simple delegation of power to men to act on God's behalf and with his authority. Since Mormons understand priesthood as an eternal order into which individuals are initiated and in which God himself both participates and presides, all men must be inducted into that order, here or hereafter. Indications, as we will see, suggest that their wives are introduced into that same priesthood order by virtue of their marriage and sealing—so no priesthood ordination is administered to them independently. Like baptism and confirmation, priesthood ordination takes place in temples for the dead, and any appropriate location for the living.

Washing and Anointing

Washing, clothing in special garments, and anointing with oil were important ritual forms that had both priestly and royal functions among the Israelites. Exodus records an early instance: "Then you shall bring Aaron and his sons to the entrance of the tent of meeting, and shall wash them with water, and put on Aaron the sacred vestments, and you shall anoint him and consecrate him, so that he may serve me as priest."[198] One authority notes that "anointment conferred upon the king the *ru'ah YHWH* ('the spirit of the Lord')," whereas "the anointment 'sanctifies' the high priest by removing him from the realm of the profane and empowering him to operate in the realm of the sacred."[199] Though this scholar calls the latter "an entirely different function" from the former, in the logic of Christian thought the two roles of king and priest are intimately related. The author of Revelation, for example, contemplates a heavenly choir praising Him who "hast made us unto our God kings and priests."[200] Other ancient texts like the *Testament of Levi* similarly link several ritual acts together in such a way as to conflate the kingly and priestly. In that text, "the first man anointed me with holy oil, and gave me a staff of judgment. The second washed me with pure water . . . and clad me with a holy and glorious robe. The sixth placed a crown on my head. The seventh placed on my head a priestly diadem . . . that I might serve as a priest to the Lord God."[201] In such a way, anointing could be seen as prefiguration of the disciple's receiving his heavenly "crown of glory that never fades away," "the crown of life that the Lord has promised to those who love him," "the crown of righteousness, which the Lord . . . will give . . . to all who have longed for his appearing"; in sum, the status of priest and king converge in the Christian anticipation of becoming "joint-heirs with Christ."[202]

Accordingly, early Christians saw Old Testament anointing as a pattern for a Christian sacrament that anointed catechumens with such a destiny in mind. Church Father Cyril of Jerusalem (313–386) cites the anointing of Aaron by Moses in the Old Testament as just such a type: "For what time Moses imparted to his brother the command of God, and made him High-priest, after bathing in water, he anointed him; and Aaron was called Christ or Anointed, evidently from the typical Chrism. To [Aaron] these things happened in a figure, but to you not in figure, but in truth."[203] The author of the *Clementine Recognitions* similarly mentions Aaron's anointing as typifying his status as prophet, priest, and king, in similitude of how the Father "anoints with similar oil every one of the pious when they come to his kingdom."[204] Several apocryphal sources detailing the forty-day post-resurrection ministry of Christ among his apostles include "numerous references to washings, anointings, and special garments," as Kent Brown and Wilfred Griggs have noted.[205] Hugh Nibley cites a large array of texts that explicitly address this ministry, many of which refer to "rites of washing and anointing" and clothing in "a symbolic but real and tangible garment" (recalling the Greek ἐνδύω or "endue" as a literal "clothing" in garments).[206]

In early Christian practice, baptism largely supplanted the ritual washing, but anointing and clothing in special garments after baptism followed the more ancient pattern. With time, anointing (also called chrism or unction) became subsumed within the Catholic sacrament of confirmation (with which it had a "supposed identity," notes one Catholic scholar[207]). Even so, chrism persists as a distinctive moment in Catholic confirmation (and is now done usually in teen years rather than immediately after baptism), when the candidate is anointed with consecrated oil. In the early Christian centuries, the individual was anointed on the forehead, ears, nose, and breast, that her "face . . . might reflect as a mirror the glory of the Lord," and that the candidate "might receive the ears which are quick to hear the divine mysteries," that she might be "to God a sweet savour," and that she might put on "the breast-plate of righteousness."[208]

Washing and chrism did not survive as a practice in Protestantism, but a related form of washing, with a different provenance, did. The writer of John's gospel records that hours before his crucifixion, Jesus "poured water into a basin and began to wash the disciples' feet and to wipe them with the towel that was tied around him."[209] Jesus was here engaging in a common practice, albeit one generally relegated to servants, in order to exemplify the humility and mutual servitude proper to discipleship. "You also ought to wash one another's feet. For I have set you an example," he said.[210] With such clear and distinguished precedent, foot washing persisted as a practice among Catholics and some Protestants alike, with varying frequency. Sometimes it occurs in conjunction with the Lord's Supper, and sometimes it is observed as part of Maundy Thursday of Holy Week.

Joseph Smith initiated the practice of foot washing, but saw it as a sacramental practice with roots deeper than the New Testament model, and therefore as one that went beyond the enactment of humble servitude. Smith first performed foot washing in the School of the Prophets, a small, intimate training school for the leadership that Smith launched in 1833 in Kirtland. A perfect instance of his determination to blend spiritual and intellectual pursuits (the class studied scriptures and theology but also German and Hebrew), the School's meetings commenced with a beautiful salutation: "Art thou a brother or brethren? I salute you in the name of the Lord Jesus Christ, in token or remembrance of the everlasting covenant, in which covenant I receive you to fellowship, in a determination that is fixed, immovable, and unchangeable, to be your friend and brother through the grace of God in the bonds of love, to walk in all the commandments of God blameless, in thanksgiving, forever and ever. Amen."[211] This was followed by the ritual of foot washing, which the minutes described. "After much speaking, singing, praying, and praising God, all done in tongues, . . . the President girded himself with a towel and . . . washed the feet of all the Elders. . . . The President said, after he had washed the feet of the Elders, as I have done, so do ye. Wash ye therefore one another's feet, pronouncing at the same time through the power of the Holy Ghost that the Elders were all clean from the blood of this generation."[212] That early experiment in sacred education, with its invocation of the everlasting covenant, the pledges of fidelity, and the ritual cleansing from sin, attests to a sacramental setting that foreshadowed the full range of temple sacraments that unfolded in the next few years—and that replicated in Smith's mind the intent and purpose of ancient washing and anointing rituals.

Oliver Cowdery recorded other occasions on which Joseph Smith and others of the leadership performed ritual washings in private ceremonies, as a renewal of covenants and to effect unity.[213] Gradually, these ordinances took fuller shape, consciously employing "the same kind of oil and in the manner" used by "Moses and Aaron and those who stood before the Lord in ancient days."[214] In January 1836, as the first Mormon temple in Kirtland neared completion, Smith recorded that his presidency had met "in the loft of the printing office, where we attended to the ordinance of washing." Next,

> I took the oil in my left hand, Father Smith being seated before me and the rest of the presidency encircled him round about,—we then stretched our right hands to heaven and blessed the oil and consecrated it in the name of Jesus Christ—we then laid our hands on our aged father Smith, and invoked the blessings of heaven—I then anointed his head with the consecrated oil, and sealed many blessings upon him, the presidency then in turn, laid their hands upon his head . . . and pronounced such blessings, upon his head as the Lord put into their hearts. . . . I then took the seat, and father anointed my head, and sealed upon me, the blessings, of Moses, to lead Israel in the latter days, even as Moses led him in days of old,—also the blessings of Abraham, Isaac and Jacob,—all of the presidency laid their hands upon me and pronounced upon my head many prophesies, and blessings.[215]

The procedure was then followed with some thirty other men. The reference to the biblical patriarchs is key here, indicating as it does the constant theme in Mormon sacramentalism of all ordinances converging on that Abrahamic covenant.

With the completion of the Kirtland Temple, Smith presided over the ceremony of foot washing; on March 29, the leaders assembled, "cleansed our faces and our feet, and then proceeded to wash each other's feet . . . after which we partook of the bread and wine."[216] The next day, more than 300 men joined in the solemn ceremony.[217] As Smith explained its purpose, "It is calculated to unite our hearts, that we may be one in feeling and sentiment and that our faith may be strong." More than a simple ritual of humility and brotherhood, Smith considered it an ordinance of purification—an ordinance as "necessary now as much as it was in the days of our Saviour," he said.[218] Five years later, the Saints had fled Kirtland and Missouri alike and were reestablished in Nauvoo, Illinois. In January 1841, a revelation directed that ad hoc sacred settings were insufficient for the fullness of temple sacraments already revealed and yet to come.

Like the transition from the portable tabernacle to Solomon's temple, early Saints were directed to finish their temple, which would be used for a fuller range of sacred purposes: "And again, verily I say unto you, how shall your washings be acceptable unto me, except ye perform them in a house which you have built to my name?"[219]

Three months later, they laid the cornerstones for the Nauvoo Temple. With time, washings and anointings more in line with Old Testament temple practice came to the fore in the Mormon ritual, and foot washing dropped out of the ceremony. (The ritual of foot washing survived among the Mormon leadership; President Wilford Woodruff noted in his journal half a century later, "This was a day of fasting and prayer with the leaders of the Church. I took a Bath and washed in the Morning and went to the Endowment House at 9 o'clock to receive the washing of feet as it was done in Kirtland 47 years ago by the Prophet Joseph Smith as an initiatory ordinance into the school of the Prophets.")[220]

In the present church, the washing and anointing in the temple, writes Boyd K. Packer, are "initiatory ordinances," symbolic cleansing for the greater ordinances to follow.[221] He sees the meaning of such symbolic rites in the words of Revelation, which refer to those "which came out of great tribulation, and have washed their robes, and made them white in the blood of the Lamb."[222] As baptism signifies adoption into the family of Christ, washing points toward the sanctification and preparation to reenter his presence, made possible by the atoning blood of Christ. "As the Saints come into the sacrosanct washing and anointing rooms and are washed, they will be spiritually cleansed," wrote James Faust. "As they are anointed, they will be renewed and regenerated in soul and spirit."[223]

Following the symbolism of ancient Israel, and consistent with the language of kings and priests that pervades the New Testament, the anointing rituals of the temple envision the day when "they into whose hands the Father has given all things . . . become priests and kings," priestesses and queens, unto God.[224]

New Garments

In the earliest Christian church, following one's washing and anointing the baptismal candidate was clothed in new garments. As we saw, this was influenced by Old Testament practice and is alluded to in many apocryphal Christian documents as well. The canonical clue to this practice is found in several places, including the epistle to the Colossians, in which the author refers to converts to Christ as those who "have stripped off the old self with its practices and have clothed yourselves with the new self."[225] As a commentary on the widely used Common Lectionary (Protestant manual of worship) notes of the Colossians passage, "It seems likely that when the apostle refers to taking off old clothing and putting on the new, he is not only metaphorical. He reflects the early Christian practice of baptism, where the candidate strips off the old clothes before entering the baptism waters, emerges, and is clothed anew."[226]

There may be more to the early Christian practice of new clothing than a mere enactment of a new identity. Jewish antecedents make reference to Adam's pre-Fall

clothing, and several texts likewise refer to glorious garments that clothed our premortal selves and will again clothe our glorified bodies. Jung Hoon Kim notes a variety of Jewish sources for the idea "that Adam had been adorned with another type
of clothing before the Fall, and out of this thought the rabbinic tradition of the garments of glory was derived."[227] In the Gnostic *Hymn of the Pearl* mentioned above,
the pilgrim spirit "took off [his] bright robe of glory" before descending to earth
in embodied form. At the end of his successful mortal sojourn, he remembers the
garment he "had left . . . in [his] father's house" and is again presented with the magnificent robe, adorned with "the image of the king of kings. . . . Therein I clothed
myself and ascended to the gate of salutation and adoration."[228] One tradition with
echoes of *Hymn of the Pearl* holds that Adam's original garment was a garment of
light. ("Like a torch," reads one source; "as beautiful as a jewel," adds another.)[229] For
some early Christians conversant with such traditions, the white robes received by
converts at the time of baptism represented "the garment worn by Adam before his
fall, a return to that pre-transgression state of glory and grace."[230]

But Genesis has God clothing Adam *after* eating the fruit, not before. This makes
good sense in Mormon theology, for Latter-day Saints deny the action was sinful.
And so, in Smith's reworking of Genesis, God both clothes Adam and Eve in special
garments and initiates Adam and Eve into the gospel plan *after* their eating of the
fruit, and their subsequent enlightenment. In this reading, and in dramatic contradistinction to Protestant covenant theology, Adam and Eve's transgression is what
puts them in a place to receive the everlasting covenant that was the only covenant
ever presented to them. "An angel of the Lord appeared unto Adam, saying: Why
dost thou offer sacrifices unto the Lord? And Adam said unto him: I know not, save
the Lord commanded me. And then the angel spake, saying: This thing is a similitude of the sacrifice of the Only Begotten of the Father, which is full of grace and
truth. Wherefore, thou shalt do all that thou doest in the name of the Son, and thou
shalt repent and call upon God in the name of the Son forevermore."[231]

As Carlos Asay, an LDS seventy explained, "Prior to their expulsion from the
Garden of Eden [but *after* partaking of the forbidden fruit], Adam and Eve were
clad in sacred clothing. . . . They received this clothing in a context of instruction
on the Atonement, sacrifice, repentance, and forgiveness. The temple garment given
to Latter-day Saints is provided in a similar context."[232] Most significantly from the
Mormon perspective, this garment is not a symbol of either a lost Eden or a past premortal glory; it is the sign of entrance into a covenant relationship under conditions
that were fully anticipated and divinely sanctioned, leading to the embodiment of
the human family as Adam and Eve's posterity. "They were born into the world by
the fall," in the words of LDS scripture.[233] In Adam's remarkable view that reverses
2,000 years of reading Genesis: "Blessed be the name of God for my transgression,

for in this life I shall have joy, and again in the flesh I shall see God."[234] In Smith's concise formulation, God "fore-ordained the fall of man."[235] As in Robert Frost's re-imagining of human premortality, Mormons see a noble couple who knowingly choose the loss of Eden, "the sacrifice of those who for some good discerned Will gladly give up paradise," in order to enter upon "The trial by existence named, The obscuration upon earth."[236] Hence, God's clothing of the first parents in sacred garments signifies a similarly anticipated step in their ascent toward his holy station. In the hierarchy of essential sacraments, washing, anointing, and the new garment are the first ordinances that are administered exclusively in the temple, for the living and for the dead.

Endowment

We saw that the concept of an "endowment of power" developed in Mormonism from a New Testament Pentecostal experience and into a panoply of temple ordinances. If Smith originally used the term in its early Christian sense of a fiery baptism of the spirit, sufficient to clothe with faith and power those elders who were preparing "to go forth and build up the kingdom of God,"[237] he eventually gave the word endowment a more particular meaning. By spring 1842, Smith was referring to the "endowment with power" as certain teachings "elders must know . . . to finish their work and prevent imposition."[238] The transitory outpourings at Kirtland were becoming transformed into a stable program of instruction, covenant, and ritual. (At the present day, rooms where the endowment is received are called "instruction rooms," thus conveying that a principal function of the endowment is an education in the divine perspective.)

Joseph at this time expanded on the washings and anointing administered in Kirtland and administered what came to be known simply as "the endowment" to select members, using the upper room of his brick store while waiting for the temple to be completed. (It was not until after the prophet's death that the first group of Saints participated in endowment ceremonies in the temple, on December 11, 1845.) Like "the sacrament," a term of general application originally that now references a specific Mormon sacrament (the Eucharist), "the endowment" now refers to a specific kind of bestowal of spiritual power, which takes place within the temple as one particular, essential sacrament Smith inaugurated in the spring of 1842. Smith was recorded as describing the endowment as consisting of "those plans and principles by which any one is enabled to secure the fullness of those blessings, which have been prepared for the Church of the first born, and come up and abide in the presence of the Elohim in the Eternal worlds."[239] Brigham Young, to whom Smith gave the work of committing the endowment to textual form, defined the endowment more specifically as "all those ordinances in the House of the Lord, which are necessary for you, after you have departed this life, to enable you to walk back to the presence of the Father, passing the angels who stand as sentinels, being enabled to give them the key words, the signs and tokens, pertaining to the Holy Priesthood, and gain your eternal exaltation in spite of earth and hell."[240]

In its underlying structure, this endowment ritual replicates much of what is known about Israelite temple practice. Louis Ginzberg, for instance, notes the tradition that the erection of the Tabernacle represents the "first day of creation," with its various elements corresponding to succeeding days of creation ("I shall put a division between the terrestrial waters and the heavenly waters; so will he hang up a veil," "I will make the luminaries; so will he make a golden candlestick," etc.).[241] Margaret Barker makes a persuasive case that the First Temple tradition was predicated on the possibility of ascent to the very presence of the Lord, which she names "temple mysticism," and that this is the "key to understanding Christian origins." (Isaiah's vision of the Lord upon his throne—in the holy of holies—she sees as an early type of this pattern.)[242] Mormon thought incorporates these precedents in its temple ritual. As James Talmage indicates, the actual endowment begins in what is called—or depicted as—"the creation room," where the story of the earth's creation is depicted.[243] Commencing from that point, in Andrew Ehat's words, the endowment is "a staged representation of the step-by-step ascent into the presence of the Eternal," from premortal beginnings, into the mortal sphere, and culminating in celestial glory.[244] Along the way, participants are instructed in a series of promises, or obligations, and blessings that give full shape to one's total commitment to a covenant relationship with heavenly parents.

The sacramental covenants of the endowment transcend mere contractual obligations in the way specified by Roger Scruton in describing sacred vows: "The world of vows is a world of sacred things, in which holy and indefeasible obligations stand athwart our lives and command us along certain paths. . . . They have an existential character, in that they tie their parties together in a shared destiny and what was once called a 'substantial unity.' "[245] If adoption inaugurates the promise of enfoldment in God's family, and the washings and anointings prepare for and presage full membership in God's heavenly community, then the endowment inaugurates the conditions of its full realization. Talmage described these covenants that constitute a new relationality to God within the Abrahamic covenant of eternal belonging:

The ordinances of the endowment embody certain obligations on the part of the individual, such as covenant and promise to observe the law of strict virtue and chastity, to be charitable, benevolent, tolerant and pure; to devote both talent and material means to the spread of truth and the uplifting of the race;

to maintain devotion to the cause of truth; and to seek in every way to contribute to the great preparation that the earth may be made ready to receive her King—the Lord Jesus Christ. With the taking of each covenant and the assuming of each obligation a promised blessing is pronounced, contingent upon the faithful observance of the conditions.[246]

Smith initially presided over the endowing of only a select group of trusted individuals in his inner circle. Those initiated into the endowment ceremonies before the completion of the Nauvoo Temple were called the "Anointed Quorum" or the "Holy Order." As Heber C. Kimball told Parley Pratt, Smith now felt "he has got a Small company that he feels safe in their hands."[247] Nevertheless, controversy over plural marriage put a halt to these temple rituals from 1842 to late May 1843, when activities again began, including the first sealing of couples for eternity. During fall 1843, women, beginning with Emma Smith, began to enter the Anointed Quorum. The circle of those permitted to participate in these higher temple ordinances expanded soon thereafter. By the next year, Young was urging all worthy members to "obey the proclamation of Joseph Smith concerning the Elders going forth into the vineyard to build up the Temple, get their endowments, and be prepared to go forth and preach the Gospel."[248]

The Nauvoo Temple had seen the first baptisms performed on behalf of the dead. With the next temple's opening in 1877 (in St. George, Utah), endowments joined baptisms as an ordinance available to those in the spirit world.[249] In the mid-twentieth century, the delivery of that endowment shifted from live enactment of the ritual to filmic presentation of large components, and language has been occasionally modified over the years since Smith's initial presentation above his store. The core elements, involving the covenants Talmage enumerated and the promises associated with them, and culminating in what David O. McKay called a "step by step ascent into the Eternal Presence," remain constant.[250]

Sealing

Among the functions that Babylonian seals performed, two stand out. Seals, such as those imprinted on damp clay by a seal cylinder, could mark an item as belonging to its owner; or seals imprinted by cylinder or signet ring could make a document legally valid.[251] The latter meaning especially is typical of the Old Testament use of the term, as when Jezebel forged letters "in Ahab's name and sealed them with his seal."[252] In the New Testament, the word sphragis (σφραγίς) generally blends both meanings, by suggesting that one is guaranteed, or legally entitled, to an affiliation with God. This is the case when the author of Romans refers to Abraham's circumcision as "a seal of the righteousness he had by faith" in God. Or when Paul declares that the Lord knows who are his by virtue of their having "this seal";[253] or the author of Revelation describes the redeemed as having "the seal of God in their foreheads."[254]

Catholics employed this powerful image in sacramental and theological contexts as well. The sacrament of baptism, for instance, was believed to "impress the sign" of one's belonging to God.[255] The Council of Trent affirmed that sacraments in general "imprint on the soul a sign, . . . a certain spiritual and indelible mark."[256] For Calvin, this denotation of "sealing" was maintained, but the sealing was "on our consciences" of "his promises of good-will toward us," not of any guarantee introduced by the sacrament itself.[257] In fact, as the Westminster Confession had stated, the other recognized sacraments in general were also seals, a mutually binding "pledge," and conferred the same promise to the faithful as "an infant heir[, who] has right to his estate."[258]

As we saw, upon dedication of the Kirtland Temple, Smith believed the church was fully organized and the necessary ceremonies and instruction fully delivered. The visitation of the prophet Elijah to Smith and Cowdery changed that appraisal. The development of the endowment was one consequence, but the priesthood keys associated with this prophet went beyond the endowment of spiritual power. Smith taught that "Elijah was the last [Old Testament] prophet that held the keys of this priesthood," and it was he whom God commissioned to "restore the authority and deliver the Keys of this priesthood in order that all the ordinances may be attended to in righteousness."[259] More specifically, the keys that Smith derived from this figure were "sealing" keys. We have invoked this term repeatedly in preceding sections, generally in reference to the Mormon understanding of relationships made durable, a meaning that is related to but distinct from these earlier Christian uses.

When Jesus referred to the establishment of his church in the gospel of Matthew, he promised an apostolic authority to "bind" and "loose" on earth with the guarantee of heavenly recognition for those actions. In the same pronouncement, he promised that "the gates of Hades [would] not prevail against" his church.[260] For Mormons, those assurances are interconnected, the crucial point here being twofold. First, gates do not in the normal course of events function in an active sense. It is rather curious to imagine gates "prevailing against"—or failing to prevail against—anything. Gates don't function actively, but what gates can do is keep inhabitants within or intruders without. Since no one is likely to attempt to infiltrate hell (Christ's "harrowing" aside), a reasonable reading of the Savior's words would be the promise that the gates of hell would fail to keep its inhabitants forever in bondage, remote from the saving church.

Second, Mormons find in this verse a warrant for the theological foundations to their sociable heaven: the sealing referred to, in other words, is for Latter-day Saints an eternal bond or connection to other human beings, within the kingdom of God. The power intimated is an apostolic authority to render human relationships eternal; "until death do you part" becomes "for time and all eternity."[261] Together, the two assertions (authority to bind and permeable gates) create the basis of Mormon temple theology. God has hereby vouchsafed to human representatives a power stronger than death or hell, to reunite in everlasting bonds of love and association all the living and the dead who comply with the sacraments of temple "sealing." Elijah was uniquely qualified for this bridging role since he was, according to scripture, taken into heaven without tasting death. As such a "translated" being,[262] he united both realms in his own person. Smith was familiar with the original sense of sealing in its conventional Christian meaning of a pledge or assurance of salvation. However, he also developed the term in a uniquely Mormon way as Elijah loomed larger and larger in his theological understanding.

In a July 1843 sermon, Smith employed a powerful metaphor to reflect his enduring preoccupation with unity and relationality. "If as a skillful mechanic in taking a welding heat I use a borax & allum &c. and succeed in welding you all together shall I not have attained a good object?"[263] At this point, Smith may have had a social unity primarily in mind. He had already forged a people and was endeavoring to forge a holy community, a city of Enoch, a Zion of "one heart and one mind." But a conception of more enduring, heavenly bonds had already taken shape in conjunction with temple rituals.

"Souls are not saved in bundles," Ralph Waldo Emerson would preach a few years hence.[264] On the contrary, Smith insisted, that is precisely how salvation occurs; individual salvation is really damnation by a different name. Salvation is not just *achieved* in community; eternal community is the form salvation takes. To be saved, he had already hinted in 1833, was to be made part of a "chosen family."[265] That this chosen family was to include wives and husbands bound together, Smith was apparently privately teaching soon thereafter. In 1835, just months after taking up temporary residence with Smith, W. W. Phelps made one of the first public references to the idea. "New light is occasionally bursting in to our minds," he wrote in the *Messenger and Advocate*. "We shall by and by learn that we were with God in another world ... that we came into this world and have our agency, in order that we may prepare ourselves for a kingdom of glory; become archangels, even the sons of God where the man is neither without the woman, nor the woman without the man in the Lord: A consummation of glory, and happiness, and perfection so greatly to be wished."[266] And Parley Pratt wrote that it was during their shared time in Philadelphia, in early 1840, that Smith taught him "the heavenly order of eternity.

It was at this time that I received from him the first idea of eternal family organization, and the eternal union of the sexes."[267]

In a second July 1843 sermon at the temple, Smith spoke publicly and specifically about the principle. Referring to the marriage question raised in Luke 20, he
preached, "No man can obtain an eternal Blessing unless the contract or covenant
be made in view of Eternity. . . . Those who keep no eternal Law in this life or make
no eternal contract are single & alone in the eternal world." As such, he continued,
they could not be "heirs of salvation never becoming Sons of God." Here he explicitly defined salvation in relational terms. Those who did not establish such connection through the priesthood power now available would be "angels to minister to
those" who had.[268] Weeks earlier, he had already put that principle into practice,
being sealed to his wife Emma for time and eternity in the upper rooms of his Red
Brick Store in Nauvoo, the temple not being completed.[269] Other sealings of couples
quickly followed.

That August, Smith confirmed this transposing of the Christian notion of sealing into a Mormon version of relational binding at a funeral sermon for Elias
Higbee. On that occasion, Smith indicated that being "sealed unto the throne" of
God was tied to the principle of being sealed to loved ones, "the father & children
together."[270] Initially, those connections were not necessarily along the lines of biological connectedness. The dominant model by which early Mormons understood
the order and society of heaven was the kingdom of God. And Mormons of that
era tended toward extreme literalism in their understanding of such models. So
while kinship ties were absolutely central to the family-centric nature of Mormon
society and Mormonism's heaven, those kinship networks constituted, in Parley
Pratt's language, a "great and *royal* family of heaven and earth" (emphasis added).[271]
Accordingly, though Mormons employed the language of family associations and
family connectedness, the sociality envisioned was more dynastic than familial.

As a consequence, in early Mormon practice, when sealing rituals took place in the
temple, chains of association were not always—or even usually—formed by simple
patrilineal or matrilineal lines. Rather, after Smith's death, organization was formed
by adoptions that frequently sealed individuals not to parents or children, but to
Mormon leaders considered the most prominent "kings and priests unto God." In
the weeks following the Nauvoo Temple dedication, for instance, ninety sealings
linked biological children to parents, whereas 211 adults were sealed, adoptively, to
non-related couples.[272] Fostering even more disruption of natural birth lines was the
requirement that sealings could only be effected with those who had been baptized
members of the church (strangely, the posthumous baptisms Mormons practiced as
early as 1843 were not sufficient grounds for posthumous sealings). "We have not
permitted wives to be sealed to their dead husbands unless such husbands were in

the Church, nor have we permitted children to be sealed to dead unbaptized parents," Woodruff had noted to his leadership.[273]

Orson Hyde explained the adoptive theology with a diagram that depicted a vertical line representing God's effective lineage. Radiating outward along its length were other lines representing his adopted posterity. "The eternal Father sits at the head, crowned King of kings and Lord of lords. Wherever the other lines meet, there sits a king and a priest unto God. . . . The most eminent and distinguished prophets . . . will be crowned at the head of the largest kingdoms under the Father."[274] Members (or the leaders themselves) therefore chose those "most eminent lines" into which they would be inserted. Joseph Smith was the most popular choice; records also indicate men and women alike "adopted to Patriarch Hyrum Smith and his wife Mary."[275] As one Saint noted, "President Young, Kimball, and many of the Twelve Apostles, and many others in the Church, have had hundreds adopted to them who were not their descendants, or even blood relations."[276]

Two untoward effects resulted from this decades-long practice. The first consequence, as soon became apparent, was to engender ambition and jealousy that undermined rather than strengthened family unity. As one member noted, the doctrine created "strife and anxiety of some to get men, women and children into their kingdom regardless of others' rights, to add to their power and glory. . . . Some men,—and even among those high in the Church,—Apostles, have felt that it would degrade them to be sealed to a common man such as their fathers may have been."[277] A second effect was to thwart the natural inclinations of families to be sealed together. As one Latter-day Saint lamented, "I wished to be adopted or sealed to my father, and he to his father and so on. But this could not be done, [for my] forefathers were not in the Church, and their descendants who received the gospel in the flesh could only be brought into the covenant by the branches being cut off from the natural tree, and being grafted into an unnatural one."[278]

As we saw, Smith's work of uniting heaven and earth, the living and the dead, was guided by his lodestar fixation on the prophecy of Malachi, that Elijah would turn the hearts of the children to the fathers and the fathers to the children. At least one member saw the tragic irony in the failure of nineteenth-century temple practice to comport with this vision: "Elijah was to turn the heart of the fathers to their children, and the children to their fathers, not to some other person's father."[279] Young, too, seemed to sense something was out of kilter with the Malachi pronouncement. "I will answer a question that has been repeatedly asked me, 'should I have a father who is dead that has never heard this gospel, would it be required of me to redeem him and then have him adopted into some man's family and I be adopted to my father?' (I answer no.) If we have to attend to the ordinances of redemption for our dead relatives, we then become their saviors and were we to wait to redeem our dead relatives before we could link the chains of the priesthood we would never accomplish it." As he admitted, "This Principle I am aware is not clearly understood by many of the Elders in this Church at the present time as it will Hereafter be: And I confess that I have had only a smattering of those things but when it is necessary I will attain to more knowledge on the subject."[280]

More knowledge came and the situation was remedied in 1894, with a change in policy that represented the most momentous shift in the history of Mormon temple practice. The timing was no coincidence. Federal anti-polygamy legislation had brought the church to its knees, and the cessation of plural marriage was a precondition for its continued viability as an institution. So in 1890, church president Wilford Woodruff declared the end to the practice of polygamy. With relief from the intense pressures brought to bear on Mormonism's unconventional family organization, and no longer expending enormous intellectual and political resources defending it, Mormon leaders were free to reconsider the theological meaning of the fifty-year-old practice of sealing—and they did.[281] More specifically, they could turn attention back to the simple principle at the heart of Smith's mission: the binding of children to parents and parents to children.

Now, with plural marriage a historical digression rather than a permanent institution in Mormon family life, Woodruff reconsidered the way in which Mormons should order their connections in the "eternal sociality" of heaven. And it almost immediately occurred to Woodruff and his counselors that plural marriage and the practice of adoption as ways of extending kinship lines and building dynastic associations did not follow naturally or logically from Smith's original vision as intimated by Malachi's prophecy and described by Young: "The human family . . . must be joined together, so that there would be a perfect chain from Father Adam to his latest posterity."[282] He told his counselors and the quorum that their adoption theology and the practice of disrupting the natural connections of children to their parents simply felt "wrong."[283] As prophet, he sought "more revelation concerning sealing under the law of adoption" and was answered by the Spirit of God, who told him, "Let every man be adopted to his father."[284] With an announcement he referred to as a revelation, Woodruff set new parameters for future practice: "When a man receives the endowments, adopt him to his father; not to Wilford Woodruff. . . . We want the Latter-day Saints from this time to trace their genealogies as far as they can, and to be sealed to their fathers and mothers. Have children sealed to their parents, and run this chain through as far as you can get it."[285]

In a theologically crucial aside, Woodruff made a remarkable confession about the nature of revelation as exercised by prophets. He suggested that in the case of baptism for the dead, Smith had "this revelation from heaven" that the practice was to be implemented, but rather than wait for "the fullness of the word of God to him concerning the baptism for the dead, . . . he went into the Mississippi River, and so did I, as well as others, and we each baptized a hundred for the dead, without a man to record a single act that we performed." In other words, they acted precipitously at worst, and tentatively and stumblingly at best. "Why did we do it? Because of the feeling of joy what we had," he explained.[286] Plural marriage reveals a similar pattern. Smith appeared to understand plural marriage as a practice countenanced in the Old Testament and mandated by a "restoration of all things." He limited the practice to an inner circle and had virtually ceased taking plural wives in the year before his death.

Young transformed a limited temple ritual into a general practice that he and others defended on social as well as pragmatic grounds. "The most effectual means of rapidly multiplying a righteous seed upon the earth," a church newspaper explained after the 1852 public announcement; a "divinely ordained species of eugenics," according to B. H. Roberts.[287] But in implementing plural marriage through various phases and forms, leaders acknowledged some missteps; as apostle Amasa Lyman said from the Tabernacle, "we obeyed the best we knew how, and, no doubt, made many crooked paths in our ignorance. We were only children."[288] And so it was too, Woodruff explained, with the law of sealing and adoption. Brigham Young "did not receive all the revelations that belong to this work; neither did President Taylor, nor has Wilford Woodruff." But he was now aware, along with his counselors, that the church had failed to fulfill "the revelations of God to us, in sealing the hearts of the fathers to the children and the children to the fathers."[289]

Woodruff's corrective was a simple and uncomplicated implementation of the words of Malachi. After a fifty-year meander through various experimental forms, Mormon temple rituals began thereafter to seal parents to children and children to parents, in ascending and descending lines. Family was to replace kingdom, the domestic sphere displaced the dynastic. Hearing of these developments, longtime Mormon Warren Foote noted wryly to a temple president, "There had been a great deal of work done that would have to be undone."[290] The stops and starts of theological developments, dead ends, and rerouting were taken more in stride in the nineteenth-century church than at present, where assumptions about infallibility and neatly packaged dialogic revelation are the norm. But as apostle Marriner Merrill noted sanguinely eighteen months after Woodruff's announcement, "Perhaps the Lord has not revealed everything to [the presidency of the church] yet, but He will reveal line upon line, as He did to the Prophet over a year ago the propriety of extending the sealing ordinance farther than we had previously done. . . . So other things may be revealed by and by. But suffice it to say, we have a great many things revealed that we have not done anything about yet."[291] Since 1894, an increasingly family-centered orientation to both LDS practice and rhetoric has firmly entrenched the traditional, nuclear family as the core image of both Mormon social life and heavenly aspirations. Still, the possibility of polygamous unions in heaven, clearly intimated by the continuing practice of having widowers sealed serially to subsequent wives, persists to the great concern (and distress) of present Latter-day Saint women (and not a few men).[292]

In current temple practice, the principal sealing that occurs is that of man and wife. In those countries (like the United States) where the state recognizes religious marriages, the temple sealing is at the same time a legal marriage ceremony. However, with this sealing ordinance, Mormonism turns the historical Christian position on marriage on its head. As Kathleen Flake points out, the wording of an early marriage ceremony directed by Smith "included two . . . blessings that also rejected the traditional limitation of marriage to its social function or 'as a remedy against sin.' The couple was blessed with no less than 'immortality and eternal life' and given 'part in the first resurrection.' In Mormonism, there was no other rite unrelated to marriage that conveyed these blessings, demonstrating the centrality of marriage to Latter-day Saint . . . soteriology."[293] In other words, Mormonism elevates marriage from a hedge against sin, a rite needed to sacramentalize a sexual urge necessary for human procreation, an institution of merely temporal duration and provisional purpose, into a union that is prerequisite to, even constitutive of, the highest form of human salvation.

Those whom Smith initiated into the highest temple sacraments, constituting a "quorum of the anointed," had received the ordinances of marriage for time and for eternity. And only in that sacramentalized union are man and wife fitted for companionship with the gods. The irony is striking. It was in rituals pertaining to an order of priesthood designated patriarchal, as we will see below, that women entered into eternal relationships with men, constituting them both as fitted for eternal life and eventual status as gods and goddesses.[294] The sealing together of a man and woman constitutes a unity that is the Mormon definition of theosis: for as Erastus Snow put the case succinctly, "Deity consists of man and woman," in a saved and exalted eternal relation.[295]

Husband-wife sealing is the principal instance of temple sealing, but not the only one. Those children born to temple-sealed couples are considered to be "born in the covenant," already imbricated in eternal relationship to their parents and siblings born to that union. If children are not born to temple-sealed parents, they may themselves be sealed after birth (or posthumously) to their parents. This vision of a family with eternal connectedness that is sanctified and made eternally durable is at the heart of Mormonism's family-centric orientation. The original meaning of seal as a legal affirmation merges completely with sealing as relational binding, when Smith reminded his listeners near the end of his life that "the seals are in our hands to seal our children and our dead."[296]

Though Mormon rhetoric is replete with allusions to the family as the indispens-able unit of social cohesion and cultural and individual well-being, the family's pri-macy is ultimately eternal, not sociological. Though in Mormon belief those two pillars of society and family should be mutually reinforcing, recent developments have questioned the harmony between religious teachings on family relations and shifting social values.

Theology of Gender, Natural Law, and Marriage

In the nineteenth and twentieth centuries, Mormonism tracked with most other Christian traditions in its language of affirmation regarding heterosexual norma-tivity and its rhetoric of unqualified condemnation of homosexuality. From Parley Pratt's reference to "lawless abominations" to Spencer W. Kimball's positing of homosexuality as a sin "equal to or greater than that of fornication or adultery,"[297] leaders condemned the category wholesale. In recent decades the church has virtu-ally eliminated such harsh rhetoric along with most others in the Christian world and has attempted to negotiate a critical demarcation between condition or identity on the one hand and behavior or choices on the other. In a seminal interview, apostle Dallin Oaks acknowledged that homosexuality may be related to a genetic predis-position to which no judgement should attach; "[homosexuals] may have certain inclinations," and their origin is a "scientific question." An individual who keeps such feelings of attraction "under control . . . is eligible to do anything in the Church that can be done by any member of the Church who is single." But Oaks was insistent that "we have the agency to choose which characteristics will define us; those choices are not thrust upon us."[298]

Even more recently, the church moved to make actions rather than inherent dis-position the decisive element in this area of sexual morality by supporting expanded civil rights for persons regardless of sexual orientation. As the *New York Times* reported in 2015, a Utah bill banning "discrimination against lesbian, gay, bisexual and transgender people in housing and employment" passed the legislature "with the backing of Mormon church leaders."[299] At the same time, in a move that sur-prised many who anticipated a further softening of the church's ecclesiastical and theological policies regarding homosexuality, the leadership announced a handbook change that now requires gay marriage to be treated as apostasy, requiring church discipline.[300] Complicating the church's attempt to negotiate a position that affirms individuals while decrying the institutionalization of gay marriage is not the nature/choice controversy alone. There is also the fact that the church has appealed to socio-logical rationales for its public opposition to gay marriage, while being committed to a deep theological system that renders gay marriage incompatible with church doctrine. In other words, it has invoked both sociology and theology to make its case. Confusion ensues when the public believes theology is being invoked to contaminate a political process and constrain personal liberty, and when Mormons assume that shifting cultural and political attitudes should or will shape theology.

For example, in supporting the Proposition 8 campaign (a California ballot initiative to recognize only marriage between a man and woman as valid), the Mormon church appealed to the same logic cited by the lone dissenter in the proposition's defeat on appeal: Judge N. Randy Smith argued that "the family structure of two committed biological parents—one man and one woman—is the optimal partnership for raising children."[301] So, too, an official church statement in support of Proposition 8 declared that *"Children are entitled to be born within this bond of marriage."* At the same time, the church intruded the theological alongside the sociological by holding that marriage is "ordained of God," and the "formation of families is central to the Creator's plan."[302]

Mainstream Protestants have found ways around apparent biblical prohibitions, but Mormonism presents its own additional difficulties. First and most vital is the conflict with a fundamental Mormon doctrine of a dual-gendered godhead, and the related doctrine of gender essentialism. As Erastus Snow put the case, " 'What,' says one, 'do you mean we should understand that Deity consists of man and woman?' Most certainly I do. If I believe anything that God has ever said about himself, and anything pertaining to the creation and organization of man upon the earth, I must believe that Deity consists of man and woman. . . . I have another description: There never was a God, and there never will be in all eternities, except they are made of these two component parts; a man and a woman; the male and the female."[303] What Snow is saying, plainly, and what has been reaffirmed repeatedly in official church pronouncements is that human beings are children of heavenly *parents*, and those parents comprise two exalted divinities called Heavenly Father and his exalted eternal companion, Heavenly Mother. (One such 1909 pronouncement declares that "all men and women are in the similitude of the universal Father and Mother, and are literally the sons and daughters of Deity.")[304] It is clear from long-standing church teachings, reaffirmed in a 1995 proclamation, that each individual "is a beloved spirit son or daughter of heavenly parents, and, as such, each has a divine nature and destiny."[305] That "nature and destiny" are presumably modeled on the parental template and involve a companionate marriage in the eternities and "a continuation of the seeds forever and ever," that is, a creating and nurturing of "the souls of men" eons into the future.[306] The teaching could not be more at odds with the traditional Christian position, taken for granted by such philosophers of religion as Richard Swinburne: "The theist, of course, claims that God is neither male nor female."[307]

Finally, Mormonism may be unique among Christian traditions in arguing not that sexual differentiation is the basis of marriage, but that gender differentiation is. Progressive Mormons may be correct that, as Tertullian and Pseudo-Justin held, sexual organs serve no reproductive purpose in the resurrection.[308] Origen, too, held that sexual differentiation "was a mere passing phase, . . . a dispensable adjunct of the personality that played no role in defining the essence of the human spirit,"[309] and C. S. Lewis preferred the term "trans-sexual" to "sexless" for the future he envisioned in our "heavenly life."[310] But such a condition would only render heterosexuality dispensable in the eternities if sexual biology is the essential locus of companionate marriage. However, sexual relations are more than a biological event. As Elder Jeffrey Holland states, "Sexual union is also, in its own profound way, a very real sacrament of the highest order, a union not only of a man and a woman but very much the union of that man and woman with God."[311] And Mormon understanding is that conjugal complementarity is more than sexual or biological.

Mormonism's rejection of gay marriage as a sacramental—if not a legal—possibility moves beyond biological arguments (which underlie Catholic natural law arguments) with a substitution of gender for sex. In one version of Catholic theological understanding, heterosexual marriage is alone sanctioned, in part, because in it biologically matched individuals engage in "reproductive type activity."[312] Such a procreative function and coupling consistent with natural law are also intrinsic to the Mormon conception. As a Mormon scripture notes, "It is lawful that he should have one wife, and they twain shall be one flesh, and all this that the earth might answer the end of its creation; And that it might be filled with the measure of man, according to his creation before the world was made."[313] However, the Mormon theological rationale is predicated upon a more deeply rooted anthropology than one that sees sexual differentiation as primarily oriented toward reproduction. In Mormonism, the essential element of eternal human identity is gender, not sexual orientation, and the place of gender as a constituent of eternal human identity suggests that the complementarity of eternally gendered agents is non-substitutable and provides the basis for the fullest human flourishing.

Old and New Testaments emphasize binaries and distinctness as the primary mode by which God engages in creation, makes covenants, establishes ritual, and articulates morality. Mormonism adds to this pervasive motif the emphatic reality of eternal human intelligences, who are differentiated from before the creation of the world by maleness and femaleness. One might object that such gender, taken by virtually all theorists to be a social construct, is given transcendent status without being theorized or defined or addressed with any theological refinement by Mormonism. That is true; Mormon teaching implicitly responds only that gender is an irreducible, just as "intelligence" itself is. Intelligence is the eternal, essential, irreducible component of human identity in Mormon thought. And that intelligence is posited as, forever and unalterably, gendered. Given the Mormon belief in a soul that exists long before birth, this statement entails a belief that one's gender has an eternal past as well; as Talmage wrote, "The body takes form as male or female according to the sex [gender] of the spirit whose appointment it is to tenant that body."[314] "Gender is eternal," reaffirms the 1995 "Proclamation on the Family," reiterating a position that has never varied in Mormon theology.[315] Gender is defined as co-eternal with core human identity, that is, intelligence.

Certainly, one does not experience one's own sexual orientation as a contingent rather than essential facet of one's identity. However, Mormon theology of the human soul implies that, notwithstanding the reality and validity of the affective and emotional bonds that may unite same-sex couples as deeply and powerfully as those that govern heterosexual unions, the sexual component of a same-sex bond (which the church acknowledges is not itself a willed factor) is an epiphenomenal aspect of identity, in contradistinction to a competing eternal constituent, that is, gender. Hormones and chemistry and conditioning all play indisputable roles in sexual attraction and sexual satisfaction, and Mormon theological anthropology implies that these may be aspects of a transitory mortal form peculiar to our temporal existence. And in the case of same-sex attraction, that epiphenomenal dimension threatens to usurp the primacy of a more essential gendered difference and re-directing two mortal beings from the only path that would in the eternities eventuate in the fullest measure of joy consistent with a particular eternal identity and destiny. Such, at least, appears to be the Mormon theology of gender and sexuality that drives the shape and limits the scope of temple sealing. At the same time, Mormon leaders have acknowledged that Mormon theology is not—or not yet—fully adequate to address a range of sex and gender issues that have become urgent in the contemporary environment. For instance, the apostle Dallin Oaks readily admitted that "the unique problems of a transgender situation is something we have not had so much experience with, and we have some unfinished business in teaching on that."[316] The same is doubtless true for other hard cases, like intersex births, which assertions of premortal gendered identity do not resolve.

Highest Ordinances

Near the end of his life, as we saw in chapter 4, Smith referred to the priesthood as consisting of three orders. Explicating Hebrews 7 to a congregation, he named them the "Aaronic, Patriarchal, & Melchisedec,"[317] complicating the picture of a simple bifurcation of Aaronic and Melchizedek orders. All priesthood, for Smith, found its most important expression in temple ordinances, and he related each of these three orders to aspects of temple theology. And so, the Aaronic was a preparatory priest-hood and largely concerned with what Smith designated "outward ordinances,"[318] but it also encompassed aspects of the temple endowment. Smith associated the Aaronic ordinances of the temple with the prophet Elias, who appeared to Smith in the Kirtland Temple in 1836 as a forerunner, bestowing the promise but not the authority of a numerous posterity.[319] With the institution of temple marriage, or sealing of man and woman for time and eternity, Smith moved a step closer to bring-ing the New and Everlasting Covenant to its fullest realization. For these rites, the higher or Melchizedek priesthood was necessary, and the "endowments of the ful-ness of the Melchizedek Priesthood" he associated with the prophet Elijah.[320] And here, as a subcategory pertaining to the ordinances of marital sealing in particular, Smith employed the term patriarchal, or "Abrahamic patriarchal" order.

The patriarchal priesthood, then, is not so much a separate order as a category that Smith associated with the higher ordinances of the temple and the sealing of family lineages in an eternal chain of belonging that would connect them to God through "the most eminent and distinguished prophets who have laid down their lives," according to Orson Hyde's rendering of Smith's vision. They will be "crowned at the heads of the largest kingdoms under the Father." And those kingdoms, con-sistent with Abraham's promises and the words of Daniel, will have an increase with "no end."[321] This Abrahamic or patriarchal priesthood, Kathleen Flake has argued, is therefore the order of priesthood that is effectively secured over the marriage altar. As the final ordinance necessary to qualify for salvation, the sealing rite joining a man and woman in eternal marriage constitutes ordination to this priesthood.[322] Smith actually made the connection explicit in a canonized revelation: "In order to obtain the highest [kingdom of glory], a man must enter into *this order of priest-hood, (meaning the new and everlasting covenant of marriage)*" (emphasis added).[323] Here we see an emphatic differentiation from Catholic conceptions of priesthood, in which priestly power is essential to *mediate* salvation and is delegated to a *special class* of men. In Smith's conception, priesthood is indeed the power to access the fullest measure of godliness, but it is an order into which each and *every saved indi-vidual must be initiated*, granting them *direct* access to God's presence and powers.

This patriarchal order did not, however, include those ordinances that conferred the very highest powers and prerogatives pertaining to the priesthood. As Brigham Young said, "If any in the Church had the fullness of the Melchizedek Priesthood, he did not know it. For any person to have fullness of that priesthood, he must be a king and priest."[324] He spoke these words on August 6, 1843; similarly, Joseph Smith, in a sermon three weeks later, called the patriarchal power, with its endowment and marital sealing ordinance, "the greatest *yet experienced* in the church."[325] But more vital than these powers, Smith said, was the power of "administering endless lives," and "kingly powers of anointing" in the temple.[326] As Brigham Young clarified, "Those who come in here and have received their washing & anointing will [later] be ordained Kings & Priests, and will *then* have received the fullness of the Priesthood" (emphasis added).[327]

This culminating ceremony was first performed in September 1843. On that occasion, according to Smith's official record, he and Emma were "anointed & ordained to the highest and holiest order of the priesthood."[328] As the modern editors of Smith's journal note, "Other members of this council—including all nine members of the Quorum of the Twelve who were living in the area and their wives—eventually received the same ordinance, which Wilford Woodruff, a member of the council, often referred to as a 'second anointing' in his journal."[329] The participation of wives was not incidental. Consistent with Mormonism's view of exaltation as a joint entry of a man and woman into the Heavenly Family, and of God himself as an exalted man and woman, the culminating ordinance of LDS temple theology is jointly received. As Young described the practice, "It is a [higher] ordinance, . . . and above all the endowments that can be given you. It is a final sealing, an eternal principle, and when once made, can never be broken."[330] Joseph F. Smith called it simply "the crowning blessing of and the highest gift to be conferred by the Melchesidek Priesthood."[331] Sam Brown calls this "the sacrament of certain election," and he notes that this rite represents for Latter-day Saints "the final attainment of salvation." As opposed to the extreme unction of Catholicism, the Mormon unction sealed a couple to heaven long before they lay on their deathbed.

Young's reference to the highest ordinance as a "final sealing" points to different meanings that have been attached to this ordinance over time.[332] Some have found here the final assurance and guarantee, the culmination of the search for a *certitudo salutis*, or assurance of salvation, that launched Joseph Smith's initial spiritual quest when he entered a grove to pray in 1820. (The theme of such assurance was never far from his theological endeavors.) His 1832 vision of the Celestial Kingdom had referred to those "sealed by the Holy Spirit of Promise . . . into whose hands the Father has given all things—They are they who are priests and kings, who have received of his fulness, and of his glory."[333] Certainly to receive a place as priest and king (or priestess and queen) unto God in his kingdom represents the culmination of all that draws us heavenward. The question is, what is the role of the "Holy Spirit of Promise," and when does it convey a knowledge of one's salvation?

Jonathan Stapley points out that for Smith, the Holy Spirit of Promise, the Calling and Election made sure, and the sealing powers of Elijah were apparently synonymous. This, he demonstrates, is suggested by an 1841 revelation to Joseph Smith, when he appoints his brother Hyrum to "hold the sealing blessings of my church, even the Holy Spirit of promise."[334] Two years later, Smith is preaching the same equivalence, when he says that Elijah's restoration of the power "to seal the hearts of the fathers to the children and the children to the fathers" itself encompassed a power of "anointing & sealing—called elected and made sure."[335] For this reason, Stapley argues, the "Holy Spirit of Promise . . . *is* the power of Elijah" (emphasis added).[336] And indeed, others of Smith's pronouncements on the subject can be read in this way. Smith was preaching on Peter's exhortation "to make our calling and election sure" in 1839.[337] The injunction, he said, was a reference to "that sealing power spoken of by Paul" in Ephesians. The writer of that epistle had referred to those who were "sealed with the holy spirit of promise."[338]

Even section 132, which Mormons today take to refer to a confirmatory function of the Holy Ghost applicable to all ordinances, can be read as referring to the sealing keys of Elijah as they relate to temple ordinances: "All covenants, contracts, bonds, obligations, oaths, vows, performances, connections, associations, or expectations, that are not made and entered into and sealed by the Holy Spirit of promise, of him who is anointed, both as well for time and for all eternity, and that too most holy, by revelation and commandment through the medium of mine anointed, whom I have appointed on the earth to hold this power . . . are of no efficacy, virtue, or force in and after the resurrection from the dead."[339]

Another strand of thought associates the Holy Spirit of Promise with a specific function of the Holy Ghost, that of guarantor of all priesthood ordinances, ratifying their efficacy. Parley Pratt, for instance, preached that those who receive the gospel and abide its precepts will be "filled with the Holy Spirit of Promise" as a pledge that "the promise contained in the Gospel was to hold good."[340] In the modern church, this is the standard interpretation of that term. Bruce R. McConkie, to take one of countless modern examples, defined the Holy Spirit of Promise as "the sealing and ratifying power of the Holy Ghost," and the *Encyclopedia of Mormonism* calls it "a specific function of the Holy Ghost . . . by which ordinances and other righteous acts performed on this earth, such as baptism and eternal marriage, are ratified, validated, and sealed."[341]

And indeed, Smith could send out different signals on the meaning of and requirements for one's personal assurance of salvation. What Christians had understood to be the seal of salvation, of which baptism was the visible sign or seal, Smith described as such an assurance, but personally confirmed by the Savior himself: "After a person hath faith in Christ, repents of his sins & is Baptized for the remission of his sins & received the Holy Ghost (by the laying on of hands) which is the first Comforter then let him continue to humble himself before God, hungering & thirsting after Righteousness. & living by every word of God & the Lord will soon say unto him Son thou shalt be exalted. &c When the Lord has thoroughly proved him & finds that the man is determined to serve him at all hazard, then the man will find his calling

& Election made sure then it will be his privilege to receive the other Comforter." Smith then interprets the promise of Jesus to "give you another comforter. . . . I will come to you."[342]

On that occasion, Smith believed, the Savior would personally "seal you up" to eternal life. Here again, Smith found precedent in the Book of Mormon. In response to the faithfulness of the priest Alma, he receives the personal assurance of the Lord, who says to him, "I covenant with thee that thou shalt have eternal life."[343] This version of the Spirit of Promise was consistent with a poem capturing Smith's ideas on the subject, published a few months earlier. The words—attributed to Smith but probably penned by W. W. Phelps—again relate the spirit of promise to a validation after personal triumph in life's trials.

> For these overcome, by their faith and their works,
> Being tried in their life-time, as purified gold,
> And seal'd by the spirit of promise, to life,
> By men called of God, as was Aaron of old.[344]

This sounds like Parley Pratt's use of the term, when he called "The Holy Spirit of promise . . . the seal of their adoption."[345] In light of these ambiguous signals, it seems most likely that the power of Elijah to seal with the power and authority necessary for assurance was, in Smith's view, ultimately to be blended with a personal conviction born of the spirit (or of Christ personally) that one's personal faithfulness had qualified one for the highest celestial glory. In 1843, after instituting the sealing rituals with the authority he received from Elijah, Smith continued to urge that disciples secure a personal attestation from heaven in support of one's calling and election made sure. Combining elements of his 1839 "second comforter" sermon with the power of temple sacraments, he said: "Though they might hear the voice of God & know that Jesus was the Son of God this would be no evidence that their election & Calling & election was made sure. . . . [T]hey then would want that more sure word of Prophecy that they were sealed in the heavens & had the promise of eternal life in the Kingdom of God. . . . Then Knowledge through our Lord & savior Jesus Christ is the grand Key that unlocks the glories & mysteries of the Kingdom of heaven."

This "key," he continues, referring to the knowledge associated with temple ordinances, is the "main key that unlocks the heavens & puts in our possession the glories of the Celestial world." And then, clearly indicating that ordinances are not sufficient, he urges his listeners "to go on & continue to call upon God until you make your Calling & election sure for yourselves by obtaining this more sure word of Prophesy & wait patiently for the promise until you obtain it."[346] Finally, a canonized statement by Smith similarly affirmed a blend of spiritual witness and priesthood power: "The more sure word of prophecy means a man's knowing that he is sealed up unto eternal life, by revelation and the spirit of prophecy, through the power of the Holy Priesthood."[347]

What is not in doubt is that, by his death, Joseph Smith had put into place what he considered to be the fullness of the priesthood, which was requisite to and the means by which salvation was to be secured, and which included sealing keys that offered assurance of eternal bonds of belonging, to God and to one's kin. These ordinances, beginning with baptism, progressing through priesthood ordination and "endowments" and culminating with eternal "sealings" or binding between man and woman (or women in his original version),[348] constituted at last the "fulness of the priesthood," which Smith defined with reference to Elijah, the most important figure in his temple theology: "Now for Elijah, the spirit power & Calling of Elijah is that ye have power to hold the keys of the revelations ordinances, oracles powers & endowments of the fulness of the Melchisedec Priesthood & of the kingdom of God on the Earth & to receive, obtain & perform all the ordinances belonging to the kingdom of God even unto the sealing of the hearts of the fathers unto the Children & the hearts of the Children unto the fathers even those who are in heaven."[349]

How that binding was to be effected became fully clear to him only as the Nauvoo Temple neared completion. Smith had thought his work done on a few occasions, perhaps nearing the completion of his Book of Mormon translation, before any mention of a church to be restored had come—probably again in 1836, when he announced he had "completed the organization of the church," restored "all the necessary ceremonies," and given "all the instruction [the priesthood quorums] needed."[350] Elijah's visit had imposed a greater work yet to unfold, as he recognized in its aftermath. In March 1839, in prison and facing possible execution for a treason charge, Smith expressed a telling lament: "Oh that I could be with [the Church.] . . . I would pour out my soul to God for their instruction. . . . I never had the opportunity to give them the plan that God has revealed to me."[351]

That had all changed in the two years before his 1844 death, with his restoration of the temple endowment and sealing ordinances. And so, in January of that year he sermonized to an audience of thousands, finally tracing the full implications of the cryptic prophecy of Malachi first spoken to him by the angel Moroni when Smith was a seventeen-year-old youth.

The Bible says, I will send you Elijah. . . . But what is the object of this important mission or how is it to be fulfilled, The keys are to be delivered the spirit of Elijah is to Come, The gospel to be established the Saints of God gathered Zion built up, & the Saints to Come up as Saviors on mount Zion but how are they to become Saviors on Mount Zion by building their temples erecting their Baptismal fonts & going forth & receiving all the ordinances, Baptisms, Confirmations, washings anointings ordinations & sealing powers upon our heads in behalf of all our Progenitors who are dead & redeem them that they may Come forth in the first resurrection & be exalted to thrones of glory with us, & here in is the chain that binds the hearts of the fathers to the Children, and the Children to the Fathers which fulfills the mission of Elijah.[352]

Thus, heaven is constituted piecemeal through the universal compliance with these sacred binding activities: In "the celestial glory," said Pratt, one is restored to an association with "his family, friends, and kindred," as part of "the chain which connects the great and royal family of heaven and earth, in one eternal bond of kindred affection, and association."[353]

7

Sacramental Ordinances—Non-Salvific

IN ADDITION TO those saving sacraments, the five temple ordinances surveyed above, an array of non-saving ordinances are also performed in Mormonism, more as a "help to faith" than as instrumental to salvation, administered "for our comfort, guidance, and encouragement."[1] Mormons consider them sacraments because they are performed by virtue of priesthood authority and are often (though not always) accompanied by covenantal obligations, though they are not requisite to salvation. First of these in importance is the Mormon version of the Eucharist.

"THE" SACRAMENT

Along with baptism, commemoration of the Lord's Last Supper has been a constant feature of Christian life and worship from the earliest days of the Christian tradition. The *Didache* gives the name of Eucharist, meaning "thanksgiving," to the ceremony,[2] and that term is used by Catholics and some Protestants. "Communion" is what Catholics call the partaking of the consecrated elements, and many low-church Protestants prefer the term "Lord's Supper" or "breaking of bread" for the ritual. It was the one feature of regular worship practiced by all Christians. All four gospel writers detail a final dinner Jesus shared with his apostles, set on the first night of Passover by the synoptic writers, the eve before by John. Matthew, Mark, and Luke all record the Savior as saying of the bread he broke and shared, "This is my body."[3] He then poured wine, and likened it to his "blood of the covenant."[4]

All Christians have seen in these words a proclamation that the ancient Passover was finding its fulfillment in a final sacrifice that would rescue all humanity through Christ's broken body and spilled blood. The injunction to engage in a ritual reenactment of the solemn occasion was inferred from the words recounted by Luke: "Do this in remembrance of me."[5] Paul, writing to the Corinthians, describes a repetitive ceremony, occurring "as often as you drink of [the wine]."[6] Indeed, he goes on to chastise Christians who ostensibly meet regularly to "eat the Lord's supper," but do so in a spirit of gluttony and drunkenness rather than in generosity and reverence. The writer of Acts subsequently referred to Sunday in particular as the day when disciples "met to break bread."[7]

These first church suppers were referred to in early documents by the term *agape* or "love feast." At some point in the first Christian decades, the *agape* came to be celebrated separately and apart from the commemorative partaking of bread and wine, then the love feast fell into disuse almost entirely—leaving the Eucharistic celebration as the worship focus of the primitive church. As early as the mid-second century, Justin Martyr describes a simple ceremony in which a presiding brother takes bread and wine, gives thanks "at considerable length for our being counted worthy to receive these things at His hands," and distributes the emblems "to each of those present to partake of the bread and wine mixed with water."[8] Only the person "who believes that the things which we teach are true, and who has been washed . . . for the remission of sins" was permitted to participate.[9] The prayer spoken over the emblems was beautifully evocative of Christian hopes for a unified, invisible church: "Even as this broken bread was scattered over the hills, and was gathered together and became one, so let Thy Church be gathered together from the ends of the earth into Thy kingdom."[10]

If defining the Trinity was the major point of contention among contending Christian factions of the fourth century, then interpreting the meaning of the Eucharist was perhaps the most disputed point of doctrine in early Reformation debates. Catholics asserted the "Real Presence," the fact of Christ's actual bodily presence in the elements of bread and wine. As early as the fourth century, Cyril of Jerusalem was urging his listeners that if Jesus could turn water into wine, he could turn wine into his blood ("Judge not the matter from the taste, but from faith," he urged).[11] The wine and wafer retain their original appearance, these proponents hold, but are "transubstantiated" by the priest into Christ's flesh and blood.

Protestants, at least initially, found no doctrine more divisive within their own ranks that the meaning and efficacy of the Eucharist. The Reformation splintered, and splintered again, on the sharp rock of Eucharistic theology. The fine distinctions over which they debated, anathematized, and warred are at times too minute for moderns to follow. Luther, for example, accepted the real presence of Christ in the Eucharist but denied transubstantiation, which he said was based on dubious Aristotelian categories. So Christ was miraculously present, but not in a way that differentiated substantial and accidental qualities ("Laymen have never become familiar with their fine-spun philosophy of substance and accidents, and could not grasp it if it were taught to them," he said).[12] Others broke more conspicuously with Catholic views, like Zwingli, who argued that when Christ said, "I am the vine," in John's gospel, he didn't mean he was literally the vine. So "this is my body" should be taken in the plain and simple sense of symbolism. The bread *signified* his body.[13]

Calvin found nothing plain and simple in the utterance. He disagreed with Zwingli that the Eucharist is a mere symbol. He agreed with Catholics and Lutherans that there was a real presence in the bread, but he disagreed that Christ was bodily present ("We are not to dream of such a presence"; he was bodily in heaven, but the Spirit effected a connection that accorded believers an effectual connection with Christ).[14] Even his sympathetic biographer, however, agrees that his complex views were "shifting and perhaps even contradictory."[15] In the mid-sixteenth century, disputes on the subject among the Reformers became increasingly bitter and tragically divisive. "We detest the dishonesty of those who invidiously disseminate among the people that we take away the presence of Christ from the Supper," wrote Calvin. "Troop after troop is on the attack; they are bearing arms; everyone is rising up against us," lamented Heinrich Bullinger of the contention over Eucharistic theology. Failure to reach accord or compromise among the Reformers on the meaning of the Eucharist in particular doomed efforts at church unity.[16]

Neither could the Puritans agree among themselves, holding "at least three distinct perspectives on the Lord's Supper," according to Brooks Holifield: an emphasis on "inward preparation" that overshadowed "the objective reality of the sacrament," "an efficacious rite capable of converting the unregenerate," and affirmation of "the mystical presence as the basis of efficacy in the sacrament."[17] And so it went. By the nineteenth century, the dominant understanding in American Protestantism was largely devoid of metaphysics: eating bread and partaking of wine was a commemorative ritual. Wesley captured a widespread attitude in one of his many hymns, which gently chided metaphysical expectations:

> We need not now go up to heaven
> To bring the long-sought Saviour down,
> Thou art to all already given.
> Thou does e'en now thy banquet crown;
> To every faithful soul appear;
> And shew thy real presence here.[18]

The importance of the Eucharist in Latter-day Saint thought is indicated by the fact that according to an 1830 revelation it is referred to by the voice of Christ himself as "*the* sacrament," and the usual worship service where the sacrament is administered is called "sacrament service."[19] This may be in recognition that (1) as a commemoration of the atoning death of Christ, it is the most fundamental instance of sacramental worship. Partaking the broken bread and water is to Mormons a perpetual reminder that the entirety of the covenant relationship for which they yearn and to which they aspire depends utterly on the one-time sacrifice of Christ's atoning death and on its continuing efficacy in a life of repentance and progressive sanctification, and (2) as the most regularly repeated sacrament, it is the center and mainstay of Christian worship, the central feature of Sabbath observance, and the only ordinance open to all members, from early childhood on. It is also possible that this usage was a Methodist borrowing. The word "sacrament" is used only once in the first *Book of Discipline* (1784), and it is as a synonym for the Lord's Supper.[20]

Although the emphasis in Mormon observance of the sacrament is on commemoration (forms of "remember" occur four times in the prayer of consecration), this ritual is, in Mormon practice, profoundly sacramental in precisely the mode of LDS sacramentalism. That is to say, Mormon participation in this ordinance is emphatically and explicitly constitutive of relationship to, or insinuation into, the divine Family. The Church Father Ignatius called this sacrament "the medicine of immortality," related, writes Roger Olson, to Catholic (and Orthodox) "belief in salvation as a sacramental process of *theosis*—'divinization' or 'deification.'"[21] In such a sacramentalist view, grace is progressively imparted to the communicant through all church sacraments, until one participates in the divine nature, but with no collapse of infinite ontological difference. In the Mormon sacramental prayer, those partaking are agreeing to "take upon them the name of thy Son."[22] They are, in other words, verbally reenacting the process of adoption initiated in baptism—but an adoption according to the New and Everlasting Covenant that envisions such a relationship—such theosis—in a robustly literal way.

In addition to a biblical template for the observance of the sacrament, Mormons find a pattern in a Book of Mormon text wherein a recently resurrected Christ institutes the ordinance in the New World. In that account, the Savior commands a multitude to regularly partake of bread and wine "in remembrance of [his] body," with the promise that if they "always remember" him, they will "have [his spirit] to be with [them]."[23] As Kathleen Flake has pointed out, the body to which the New World sacrament points is not a body facing imminent crucifixion but one that is recently resurrected, restored to life—an immortal body "which I have shown unto you," in the Savior's words to a Nephite multitude.[24] In this way, the commemoration is at least partially shifted from the tragic to the triumphant. Additionally, Flake notes, Smith revises the New Testament account of the Last Supper to have Jesus tell his disciples that the meal should be ritually re-dramatized to point partakers to "this hour that I was with you."[25] This de-emphasis on the cross as the focus of sacramental commemoration is consistent with a general unease in Mormonism with representations of the crucifixion. Since the mid-twentieth century this aversion has been pronounced, extending to a cultural taboo on wearing the cross (its exile from chapel architecture and accoutrements extends back even further).[26] As President Gordon B. Hinckley explained the (non)-practice, "For us, the cross is the symbol of the dying Christ, while our message is a declaration of the living Christ."[27]

Flake's observations are technically true. In actual practice, however, the meaning of the sacrament is essentially the same for Latter-day Saints as it is for other Christians. This is because the actual words of the sacramental prayer that consecrates the bread and water focus on Christ's expiation, not his resurrection. The *broken* bread is eaten in remembrance of the body of Christ, and the water is drunk in remembrance of "the *blood* of th[e] Son, *which was shed for* them" (emphasis added).[28] Like the New Testament authors, the Book of Mormon writers testify "boldly of [Christ's] death and sufferings," with the prophet Mormon praying that "his sufferings and death" may "rest in your mind forever."[29] Brigham Young also counseled his missionaries to keep their eyes "riveted on the cross of Christ."[30] In sum, as those same prophets proclaim from first to last portions of the Book of Mormon, it is the spectacle of Christ's willing death on the cross that is designed to "draw all men unto [him]," and the sacrament is designed to keep it ever before us.[31]

Joseph Smith intimated that a form of the Eucharist predated Christianity itself, in an anticipatory way, along with other forms of sacrifice. In his revision of the Bible, he turns Melchizedek into the first recorded observer of the sacrament. Genesis records how Melchizedek comes out to meet Abraham upon his return from successful battle. "And king Melchizedek of Salem brought out bread and wine; he was [the] priest of God most high."[32] Smith saw in this gesture more than refreshment. In his revision of the scene, Melchizedek "brake bread and blest it; and he blest the wine, he being the priest of the most high God."[33] If other commentators did not see the meal as an explicit Eucharist, as Smith seems to, they have seen it as a *type* of the Eucharistic meal. Thus the third-century Cyprian wrote that "our Lord Jesus Christ . . . offered the very same thing that Melchizedek had offered, bread and wine, that is, actually, his body and blood."[34] A sixth-century Christian mosaic in Ravenna similarly depicts Melchizedek's Eucharistic meal as analogous to the sacrificial offerings of Abel and Abraham.[35]

Along with debates over the Real Presence, differences over the frequency of the Eucharist divided Christian groups. Luther warned against any rule concerning frequency but believed anyone participating fewer than "three or four times a year despises the sacrament and is no Christian."[36] Calvin believed the sacrament was ordained "that all Christians might have it in frequent use. . . . Each week, at least, the table of the Lord ought to have been spread for the company of Christians, . . . that all, like persons famishing, should come to the feast."[37] In line with such a pattern, John Wesley observed weekly communion and the prayer book he edited assumed a weekly practice.[38] With the decreasing emphasis on sacramentalism, Protestants generally tended toward more infrequent practice of communion—often monthly or less as a general rule. Presbyterians observe the ritual monthly or quarterly. Modern Wesleyans are directed to take communion at least every three months. About two-thirds of Baptist churches similarly celebrate communion four or fewer times per year.[39]

From its founding, the LDS church has held it a commandment to "meet together oft to partake of bread and wine, in remembrance of the Lord Jesus."[40] The wording seems borrowed from a Book of Mormon scripture describing post-resurrection Christians in the New World, who "did meet together oft to partake of the bread and wine, in remembrance of the Lord Jesus," in response to a direct command to do just that.[41] Initially in Mormon practice, the sacrament was not confined to Sunday services. Its first observance was actually a Tuesday, on the day of the church's organization (April 6, 1830). Smith said he had been commanded on that occasion to gather with other new believers and "to bless bread and break it with them, and to take wine, bless it, and drink it with them."[42]

In Mormonism's first years, the sacrament was administered frequently but irregularly. Smith had it administered in leadership meetings, at the convening of the School of the Prophets, and at other times of his choosing. Sometimes, as in the New Testament church, the sacrament took the form of a meal, as when, at the Kirtland Temple dedication, bread and wine were provided and blessed in quantities "sufficient to make our hearts glad" after a day of fasting.[43] "A feast," Edward Partridge called it.[44] By 1845, the leadership of the church was meeting every Sunday to take the sacrament, and Young suggested the wisdom, on the trek west, of weekly observance for all members.[45] In the early Utah period, the practice reverted to more infrequent administration in the immense tabernacle. But in 1894, the decision was made to move the ritual to the ward chapels.[46] In outlying areas, most wards had been observing the sacrament weekly for a few decades, and that practice has continued to the present day.[47]

An 1829 Smith revelation directed Oliver Cowdery to "rely upon the things which are written" in building up the church.[48] Taking the Book of Mormon as his guide, he found therein the actual prayer used in an ancient American setting to consecrate the Eucharist—which became in his "Articles of the Church" and forever thereafter the only prescribed prayer used in LDS Sunday worship services.[49]

An early revelation directed that the priest was to "kneel with the Church" during the sacrament prayer, though only the officiator kneels in current practice.[50] The language of the Eucharistic prayers in the Book of Mormon was codified in a set of formal prayers instituted at the church's organization, to be regularly spoken at the celebration of the Eucharist or "sacrament."[51] Even so, they do not appear to have been regularly employed in the early decades, as Young complained in 1856, chiding a congregation over "how few in blessing the bread and water followed the form laid down in the Book of Doctrine and Covenants."[52] Two decades later, things hadn't changed, as Brigham Young complained that "the people have various ideas with regard to this prayer. They sometimes cannot hear six feet from the one who is praying, and in whose prayer, perhaps, there are not three words of the prayer that is in this book, that the Lord tells us that we should use."[53] The solemnity of the ritual and the status of the sacrament prayers as divinely revealed texts are today emphasized by the requirement to pronounce the blessings without error (as judged by the presiding priesthood authority).

In tension with the solemnity of the ritual was (and is) the disruption caused by including children in the ritual. Travelers to nineteenth-century Utah were scandalized by this practice: one wrote that he "had to withdraw, as they were beginning to distribute the bread and water of their sacrament, which seemed to have little or nothing of the solemn reverence of our Lord's Supper." A second went further, complaining that "the sacred ordinance of the Lord's Supper is profaned every Sabbath in all the Mormon places of meeting," largely because "the bread is distributed to all in the house, children and even infants eating the same."[54] Though all in the congregation are invited to participate, in 1946, the First Presidency directed that the sacrament be administered first to the bishop or presiding authority, so that "members of the Aaronic Priesthood officiating may have a lesson in Church government."[55]

In the church's early months, bread and wine were used. However, in August 1830, Smith recorded that while setting out to procure wine for a church meeting, a heavenly messenger appeared with the warning that he should not obtain "wine neither strong drink of [his] enemies."[56] The Saints were to prepare their own wine for ritual purposes. The frequent dislocations and hardships of the ensuing months and years made home production of wine difficult and irregular. Then, in 1833, the church's revealed health code, or "Word of Wisdom," pronounced the drinking of wine as well as "strong drink" "not good."[57] In the early Utah period, wine continued to be the rule, but in accordance with the warning against wine of unknown make. "When we administer the sacrament of the Lord's Supper, I wish as good wine as can be made in any country, and that too made by ourselves from grapes grown in our own mountain valleys," counseled Young in 1862.[58] Water increasingly came to be substituted for the wine, which was only formally banned from sacramental use in 1893, though the Quorum of the Twelve continued to use "good Dixie wine" for several more years.[59] Water has been the general practice ever since.

While the ordinance was performed in keeping with the scriptural injunction to commemorate Christ's passion, early Mormons also saw it—in Protestant terms—as a channel of grace. As Young explained the ordinance, it was a vehicle for the outpouring of the Holy Spirit to participants. "If bread and wine are blessed, dedicated, and sanctified, through the sincerity and faith of the people of God, then the Spirit of the Lord, through the promise, rests upon the individuals who thus keep His commandments, and are diligent in obeying the ordinances."[60] Over time, the emphasis of the sacrament shifted from worship (commemorating Christ's offering) to introspection (renewal of covenants and self-checking). By 1884, leaders were referring to the sacrament as a time for "renewing our covenants," including those of remembering the Savior, taking upon oneself his name, and keeping his commandments.[61] Those particular covenants are part of the sacrament prayer itself. However, with time the covenant being commemorated subtly shifted to the baptismal covenant. Only in the early twenty-first-century church have Mormon leaders questioned the gradual shift in the sacrament's meaning. Apostle Neal Anderson pointed out in a 2015 leadership meeting that the expression "'renewing our baptismal covenant' is not found in the scriptures. It is not inappropriate. Many of you have used it in talks; we have used it talks. But it is not something that it is used in the scriptures, and it can't be the keynote of what we say about the sacrament."[62]

Paul warned the Corinthians that anyone participating in the Lord's Supper "unworthily" was eating and drinking "damnation to himself, not discerning the Lord's body."[63] Puritans and others considered participation in the Lord's Supper not just a duty but a privilege, and prohibition from the "Lord's Table" was employed as a form of discipline or sanction. Latter-day Saints, too, have been persistently enjoined to be spiritually prepared. Young often reminded the congregation that they were forbidden from "partaking unworthily," but he urged that such judgment generally be left to individuals themselves. Even non-members were not to be prohibited from participating, though they would do so "at their own risk, no matter whether they belong to a religious society or not, or make any profession of religion or not."[64] In other words, although personal worthiness is urged for those participating in the sacrament, the ordinance generally is self-policing. At the same time, Smith taught that if "the church," apparently meaning a collective unit, is unworthy, "the servants of the Lord will be forbidden to administer it."[65] During the Mormon Reformation of 1856–57, suspension of the sacrament was churchwide. As late as 1894, an entire Utah ward was so disciplined "on account of derision and strife."[66] Otherwise, unless a member has been sanctioned by a church disciplinary council, access to the sacrament is unrestricted.

PATRIARCHAL BLESSINGS

Whereas the sacrament of the Lord's Supper is emphatically a covenant renewed in community, the most intensely private and personal sacrament may be one derived from the Old Testament. The last recorded act of the patriarch Jacob was to assemble his twelve sons and pronounce upon each one "a suitable blessing," involving words of reproof and counsel, and prophesies pertaining to their futures. Simeon and Levi were chastised for their "anger," Judah was promised a perpetual right to "the scepter" and "the ruler's staff," and Joseph was assured a particularly "fruitful" posterity.[67] With that precedent in mind, Joseph Smith instituted the office of patriarch in 1833 and bestowed it upon his father, Joseph Smith Sr.

As Jacob, by virtue of his patriarchal status, enjoyed the gift of prophecy relative to his posterity, so was Joseph Sr. implicitly given with his ordination the same gift to be employed for the benefit of the church members over whom he served as an effective patriarch. The new office functioned in a further way to validate in new terms the Abrahamic covenants and blessings that had been associated with the age of patriarchs. The senior Smith would be enabled to pronounce the recipient's particular lineage, connecting him to an Abrahamic ancestry and its attendant promises. In some cases, the patriarch affirmed a literal descent and in some an adoptive relationship. (The former was not surprising, since Young held that "the Church is mostly composed of the literal descendants of Abraham.")[68] Other cases were ambiguous. So in blessing Hyrum Smith, for instance, Joseph Smith Sr. pronounced him a "true descendant" through the house of Ephraim; another convert, Isa Ames, was "initiated into the family of Joseph"; others, like Orson Pratt, were simply assured that they were "entitled to . . . the blessings of Jacob, who was called Israel," or, like Sarah Harmon, were simply declared "the seed of Israel."[69] In every case, however, the point was to affirm the candidate's membership in the House of Israel, and heirship to the New and Everlasting Covenant. The blessing thus became a highly particularized confirmation of those covenantal promises as they pertained to the individual.

The church's first patriarchs, in addition to declaring lineage, often identified spiritual gifts to be developed ("thou shalt receive of the spirit of prophecy and become a mother in Israel"), prophesied of work to be accomplished ("many shall come to a knowledge of the truth through thy ministry"), warned of spiritual dangers ("thou hast conducted foolishly and . . . must repent"), and promised future blessings ("thou shalt see the Savior in peace").[70] The general pattern has changed little in the contemporary church. As John Widtsoe described the ordinance in 1943, after pronouncing lineage, "blessings are added as the spirit may indicate, to meet our special requirements in life for our comfort, success, and strength. Our special needs may be pointed out; special gifts may be promised us; we may be blessed to overcome our weaknesses, to resist temptation, or to develop our powers, so that we may the more surely achieve the promised blessings. Since all men differ, their blessings may differ; but a patriarchal blessing always confers promises upon us, becomes a warning against failure in life, and a means of guidance in attaining the blessings of the Lord."[71]

The blessing, which is generally administered once in a member's life (though it could be more often in the nineteenth century), is taken to be a highly personal, sacred compass to provide spiritual sustenance and direction. Because these blessings are given by revelation, leaders urge that they are best understood by revelation. Brigham Young referred to members who studied their blessings regularly,[72] and the practice is to treat them as personal scripture. There is no age requirement, but modern practice tends to encourage teens to receive their blessings while in their most vulnerable and decision-fraught years, and to prepare by fasting and prayer.

Under the church's first patriarch, Joseph Smith Sr., a few families—or up to several dozen members—would often gather on the occasion of the blessing for a "blessing feast." On this celebratory occasion, there were hymns, sermons, and both spiritual and literal feasting.[73] Today the event is generally observed in company of the family only.

BLESSING THE SICK

As we saw, miraculous healings pervade the ministry of Christ and his apostles and are named a spiritual gift and sign to those who believe. But blessing the sick also became an ordinance, both in Catholicism and in Mormonism. What Catholics call extreme unction began as a healing rite. Catholicism explicitly traces this sacrament's origin to the admonition of James to anoint the sick with oil.[74] In the early fifth century, St. Innocent I declared extreme unction "a kind of sacrament," and approved its administration to "the sick faithful."[75] However, at the Council of Trent it was emphatically declared that James never intended the sacrament to be a "healing grace" or "grace of curing" only, but one to "remit sins."[76] Certainly the linkage of curing and forgiveness are explicit in James's promise that "the prayer of faith will save the sick, and . . . anyone who has committed sins will be forgiven."[77] The connection is also implicit in Christ's encounter with the paralytic in Mark's gospel. Breaking through the roof of a house to gain access to the Savior, his expectation of physical relief was met with the unexpected pronouncement, "Son, your sins are forgiven."[78] As Clement of Alexander read the episode, "The Word of the Father . . . cares for the whole nature of his creature. The all-sufficient Physician of humanity, the Savior, heals both body and soul conjointly."[79]

More uncertain is what James intended by writing that the sacrament "will save the sick." Was the original practice primarily directed toward physical restoration or spiritual salvation? The pattern of the New Testament seemed predominantly one of physical restoration—of the blind, the lame, the infirm—by both Christ and later his apostles. And so Innocent I (who first described it as a sacrament) may have seen the anointing of the sick as primarily directed toward a temporal relief of the sick "in their own necessity."[80] Already by the ninth century, however, the focus had shifted. The sacrament is by then considered "a truly great mystery" through which the sins of the penitent "are forgiven." "It may even follow," St. Leo IV noted, but only as an added bonus, that health of the body is restored, "but such was not the principal concern or purpose."[81] A few centuries later the ordinance was named "extreme unction" and authorities were specifying that "this sacrament should only be given to the sick of whose death there is fear."[82] From that point on, descriptions refer to the sacrament as a defense of "our souls" against "spiritual injury."[83]

One of Luther's protests against this Catholic sacrament criticized the very transition here traced, from a ritual performed to heal the sick—a "general" anointing—to one that is "administered only to those who are at the point of death"—an "extreme" anointing or unction. "[James] says expressly, 'Is any one sick?' He does not say: 'Is any one dying?'" The whole point, as Luther reads James, is to heal the sick, not prepare a person for death. In any case, Luther adds, if James commended the sacrament, he had no "right on his own authority" to do so.[84] Calvin also dealt harshly with the practice. The anointing of the sick was "mere hypocritical stage-play, by which, without reason or result, [priests] would resemble the apostles."[85] Given the essentially anti-sacramental bent of Reformed religion, it is no wonder that the early American religious tradition saw virtually no place for formalized healing rituals.[86]

Among Joseph Smith's robust restoration of spiritual gifts, healing among early Mormons was conspicuous (see below). Healing as a faith-practice, associated with spiritual giftedness, overlapped for some time with healing as a distinct priesthood ordinance. In the Book of Mormon, Jesus heals the sick with no apparent unction—it appears as an example of a spiritual gift.[87] However, both forms—the gift and the ordinance—are indicated in the New Testament. Peter apparently heals by merely invoking "the name of Jesus Christ," for instance, while James directs that the sick receive an "anointing . . . with oil."[88] So we find during an 1838 epidemic that Joseph Smith "went through the midst of [the sick] taking them by the hand & in a loud voice Commanding them in the name of Jesus Christ to arise from their beds . . . and they leaped from their beds made whole by the power of God."[89] In those first decades, elders reported many episodes of healing "in the name of Jesus" with no reference to oil or sacramental forms.[90]

The practice resolved into a priesthood ordinance gradually. Jonathan Stapley and Kristine Wright have shown that the now-standard two-part healing ritual, of an anointing with consecrated oil followed by a prayer of "sealing," was adapted from early temple anointings. After the Kirtland Temple ceremonies, they write, anointing for healing "became the standard form."[91] Wilford Woodruff recorded the seamless continuity between the former and the latter practice in an 1838 journal entry. "I had some oil that was Consecrated for my anointing while in Kirtland. I again Consecrated it before God for anointing the sick." He then "laid my hands upon [his wife] in the name of JESUS CHRIST and rebuked the fever the destroyer the deadly malady that was preying upon her system."[92] Today, olive oil for the blessing of the sick is prayerfully consecrated by a short ordinance and used to anoint the head of the infirm (though in the past century, afflicted parts of the body were often anointed). Then a second priesthood holder (if one is available) "seals and confirms" the anointing and pronounces a blessing. Such anointing and blessing is one of the most frequently performed ordinances in the church, and one whose practice has altered little in the past century and more.

Olive oil was employed for sacred purposes going back to Hebrew tradition. The *Jewish Encyclopedia* explains the employment of oil for sacred purposes in terms of the connection between sacrifices and oil's "use in the preparation of food."[93] For Christians, the oil of the olive can be read typologically. The poet George Herbert, remembering Christ's "sweat [that] became like great drops of blood," wrote of "God himself being pressed for my sake."[94] Herbert had the winepress in mind, but Christ's great agony occurred in the garden of Gethsemane, which word in Hebrew means "olive press." Olive oil, then, has clear Christological resonance, especially for Mormons who believe that Christ's atonement was actually effected in an olive grove.[95]

As we will see below, women commonly participated in the gift of healing in the Mormon church's first few generations. However, as the exercise of healing shifted from a spiritual gift after the model of the gospels to the sacramental form administered by priesthood (following James), women—and the church—were deprived of that participation.

BLESSING OF CHILDREN

Matthew records the famous episode where "little children were being brought to [Jesus] in order that he might lay his hands on them and pray." As they desired, so did he take "them up in his arms, laid his hands on them, and blessed them."[96] The gesture was a familiar one in that era among the Jewish people. Abundant precedent for the blessing of children was found in the Hebrew Bible and it was—and remains—an important Jewish practice. Noah, Isaac, and Jacob laid hands and pronounced blessings upon their children, and Ben Sira stresses, in the book of Ecclesiasticus, that "a father's blessing strengthens the houses of the children."[97] In Jewish culture, fathers (and sometimes rabbis) bless their children "on Sabbath eve either in the synagogue or in the home; on the eves of holy days, on the Day of Atonement, and before leaving for a journey."[98]

A comparable Christian practice has not been the norm. "This consecration of children to God seems to have grown out of use," lamented the Methodist commentator and older contemporary of Joseph Smith, Adam Clarke.[99] For Smith, the custom seems to have been one more New Testament practice in need of restoration. As he put it simply, "Children have no sins.—He Jesus blessed them—do what you have seen me do."[100] And so, the week of the LDS church's organization, members having children were directed by a revelation "to bring them unto the Elders before the Church Who are to lay their hands upon them in the name of the Lord & bless them in the name of Christ."[101] Smith may have been doubly primed for such a practice by a Book of Mormon account. During the Savior's New World appearing, as in his Old World ministry, disciples brought children to him for blessing. But in the Book of Mormon, the consequence was one of the most supernal manifestations in all LDS scripture.

> And it came to pass that he commanded that their little children should be brought. So they brought their little children and set them down upon the ground round about him, and Jesus stood in the midst; and the multitude gave way till they had all been brought unto him. And it came to pass that when they had all been brought, and Jesus stood in the midst, he commanded the multitude that they should kneel down upon the ground . . . and he took their little children, one by one, and blessed them, and prayed unto the Father for them. And when he had done this he wept again; And he spake unto the multitude, and said unto them: Behold your little ones. And as they looked to behold they cast their eyes towards heaven, and they saw the heavens open, and they saw angels descending out of heaven as it were in the midst of fire; and they came down and encircled those little ones about, and they were encircled about with fire; and the angels did minister unto them.[102]

That children would be the recipients of the greatest Pentecostal outpouring in LDS scripture is not surprising. In a radical break with both Protestant and Catholic views, Mormonism imputes to children a status that was unprecedented until the advent of Romanticism a generation earlier. "Mighty prophet! Seer blest!" the poet

William Wordsworth had enviously addressed a six-year-old, "on whom those truths do rest which we are toiling all our days to find."[103] When the Book of Mormon prophet pronounces that "little children are alive in Christ, even from the foundation of the world,"[104] the premortal origins of children are intimated[105] and explain, as they did for Wordsworth, why a child's "exterior semblance doth belie [its] soul's immensity." In the context of this theology, the blessing of children is rather like the blessing described in the *Hymn of the Pearl*. The premortal spirit referred to there is sent to earth by his parents "on a mission," but not before "they made a covenant with me and wrote it in my heart so I would not forget."[106] So do LDS parents believe that in blessing their child, they equip her to fulfill a mission or purpose designed from before her birth.

One of the earliest documented baby blessings was Joseph Smith Sr.'s benediction on Hyrum Smith's child on "the 8th day" of its life, in September 1832.[107] The timing was evocative of the Abrahamic practice of circumcision on the eighth day, which would make sense as an even earlier induction of the child into Abrahamic covenant than baptism offered.[108] This reading is substantiated by wording in early baby blessings that invoked that very covenant. Smith frequently blessed children with "the blessings of the new and everlasting covenant," and more emphatically, when Wilford Woodruff gave his child its eighth-day blessing he declared its access to "the blessings of Abraham Isaac and Jacob" and "of the new & everlasting covenant," while promising him a "station in the celestial kingdom in the lineage of thy Fathers in the family organization of the celestial world."[109] In 1894, George Cannon was still approving the practice. "In the blessing of male infants, it is not inconsistent to pronounce upon them the blessings of Abraham, Isaac, and Jacob."[110] No clearer instance could be imagined of Mormon sacramentalism as arranging human beings into a heavenly order and preparing them for eternal life in that social heaven.

Early in church history, it became traditional to formally name the child at the time of its first blessing—roughly parallel to the naming of a child at christening. On one occasion, Joseph Smith passed Reynolds Cahoon, a new father, who asked him to do the honors. He did so, claiming that the name "Mahonri Moriancumer," a hitherto anonymous "brother of Jared" in the Book of Mormon, had been given him by revelation.[111] Soon, the blessing of children became a feature of regular church conferences. Days after the Kirtland Temple dedication, the church presidency performed "the confirmation & blessing of the children."[112] In 1838, at a meeting commemorating the church's anniversary, "95 infants were brought forward and blessed."[113] At an April 1845 session, "owing to the immense number it was found impossible to complete the whole."[114] Young explained in 1847 that "the father has a right to bless as a patriarch in his own family," and when he blesses his child, "the blessing has a hold on them till the years of accountability."[115] In other words, the father has the power to provide a spiritual protection and guidance that serves to fulfill the function of the Holy Ghost until that gift can be bestowed at the age of eight. Today, such blessings are typically performed by fathers for their newborn children—accompanied by other priesthood holders—as part of the monthly Fast and Testimony meeting in most cases.

PRIESTHOOD BLESSINGS AND DEDICATIONS

A range of other ordinances may be included under the heading of non-essential ordinances. Priesthood holders may pronounce blessings of comfort or guidance on others by the imposition of hands on any occasion of felt need. Fathers especially employ this ordinance to pronounce blessings on children at times throughout their lives. As John Taylor taught, every father functions as a patriarch to his own children, with prerogatives similar in kind but more limited in scope than the holder of that church office possesses. The office of patriarch was intended that "those who are orphans, or had no father to bless them, might receive [a blessing] through a patriarch who should act as proxy for their father."[116] But the right to bless children is by natural right the father's. Latter-day Saint fathers commonly exercise this right on any occasion that warrants a particular blessing of comfort or guidance.

Another blessing unique to an early period was "Zion Blessings," which Smith bestowed over a period of several months on Saints who had participated in the Zion's Camp expedition and thereby shown themselves "willing to lay down thy life for thy brethren."[117] The priesthood has also been used to pronounce a kind of anathema, when rejection of preaching turned particularly bitter or even violent. Thus Wilford Woodruff recorded that in accordance with "a solemn duty that is required of all the Elders of Israel whose testimony is rejected by this generation while they are preaching the gospel of Jesus Christ," he and his companions "Cleansed our Bodies with Pure water & also with strong drink or spirits . . . then according to Commandment cleansed our hands and feet and bore testimony unto God against the Benton County mob & also against Paris & many others who had rejected our testimony."[118] No warrant exists for such a practice in the modern church. More commonly and happily, apostles have frequently bestowed apostolic blessings upon congregations they address, as local leaders have pronounced blessings upon their congregations. "Inasmuch as I have the right and privilege," said Brigham Young in a typical expression, "through the Priesthood, I bless you in the name of the Lord."[119]

Another frequent use of priesthood is when priesthood leaders "set apart" persons who have been appointed to specific tasks or callings, blessing them with the capacities and inspiration appropriate to their responsibilities. Finally, graves, buildings, and fields of evangelization may be dedicated by the priesthood holder to the uses specific to those places.

ORDINANCES YET TO COME

In the church today, Mormon priesthood is primarily invoked as the authority to administer or govern in the church and to administer the ordinances or sacraments of blessing and of salvation. However, Mormonism, as we saw, attributes to the priesthood cosmic powers that transcend the institutional church. As a member of the Quorum of the Seventy recently declared, "Through its power, worlds—even universes—have, are, and will be created or organized."[120] Brigham Young had laid out the idea much earlier: "We are in possession of all the ordinances that can be administered in the flesh; but there are other ordinances and administrations that must be administered beyond this world. I know you would ask what they are. I will mention one. We have not, neither can we receive here, the ordinance and the keys of the resurrection. . . . We hold the authority to dispose of, alter and change the elements; but we have not received authority to organize native elements to even make a spear of grass grow. We have no such ordinance here."[121]

Joseph Smith mentioned other keys besides resurrection, not yet bestowed or not yet known to humans. "Now the doctrine of translation [of a person from mortality to immortality] is a power which belongs to this priesthood, there are many things which belong to the powers of the priesthood and the keys thereof that have been kept hid from before the foundation of the world. They are hid from the wise and prudent to be revealed in the last times."[122] Priesthood will yet have a vital role to play in the eternities, in the Mormon conception of things.

8

Spiritual Gifts

BRINGING TO FRUITION the New and Everlasting Covenant, organizing humanity into the kingdom and family of God, is the principal purpose of the (re)established church. The church is the conduit through which authority is channeled to perform the several ordinances and pronounce the covenants pertaining to that New and Everlasting Covenant. The church has stewardship over those temples, or sacred edifices, in which the full range of those saving ordinances is administered. And the church constitutes the collective of people, the community, which, by providing opportunities for fellowship, service, instruction, and edification, facilitates an ever-growing compliance with the terms and conditions of those covenants—which include the duty to evangelize the living and to redeem the dead.

Within this church, Paul taught, God apportioned a variety of spiritual gifts, for the mutual edification and harmonious constituting of what he called the body of Christ. In early Mormonism, those gifts were seen as having a relationship of interdependency with the priesthood. A particular order of priesthood connected with the Holy Ghost was never fully articulated by Smith or his successors. But we have seen that the view of the Holy Ghost as associated with—or enabling—a type of priesthood authority found powerful if occasional expression in early Mormonism as it did in Protestantism. The hugely influential Orson Pratt, for instance, wrote a chapter on the qualifications for officers in God's kingdom. He does not even mention priesthood, but he does assert that "the first qualification absolutely necessary for every officer in the kingdom is the gift of the Holy Spirit. This is the most important qualification of all others. . . . The unlearned youth, who had not the knowledge of the English alphabet, if he were called of God, and qualified by the gift of the Holy Spirit, would have more power and authority, and could do more towards saving men, than all the theologians and doctors of divinity that the world affords. . . . No other qualification whatsoever can be substituted in the stead of the Holy Spirit. The Holy Spirit is the great distinguishing characteristic between the officers of the kingdom of God and impostors."[1] The church paper declared in 1842 that the Holy Ghost was "necessary to make and to organize the priesthood."[2]

More frequently, however, Mormon authorities emphasized the inverse relationship. In other words, rather than claiming the Holy Ghost as a source of priesthood, it was more common for the priesthood to be seen as the precondition for the proper exercise or rightful possession of spiritual gifts. So whereas Smith had declared that "the gift of the Holy Ghost . . . is necessary to make and to organize the priesthood," Heber C. Kimball was one of several who held that "the operations of the Holy Ghost" unfolded "through the priesthood."[3] "Spiritual gifts . . . are properly exercised under the power of the Priesthood," agreed John Widtsoe.[4]

Benjamin Winchester, an influential early leader in the LDS church, published the first independent Mormon periodical, *Gospel Reflector*, and wrote an important *History of the Priesthood* in 1843. In his account, the "Holy Priesthood . . . is the channel through which all the spiritual gifts, such as miracles, revelations, visions, &c., flow or are obtained."[5] Subsequently, the church affirmed that "the spiritual gifts which always accompany the Church of Christ and are the signs of its verity, are properly exercised under the power of the Priesthood."[6] They were, wrote Cowdery, "the fruits of the priesthood."[7] Their absence, wrote Orson Hyde, was proof of a clergy "acting without authority from God."[8] That is why, Winchester argued, when priesthood "ceases to exist on earth, the church falls into darkness, and ultimately degenerates into apostasy." This "apostasy commenced," he added, in the days of the original apostles. Consequently, restoring this loss of priesthood authority, and of the proper forms of "true order" and "true worship," was the great project Saints understood as the purpose of Smith's ministry.[9] And the controversial evidence for this Restoration, according to Mormonism's first missionaries, resided first and foremost in the exercise of spiritual gifts.

For Mormonism, however, spiritual gifts are much more vital to the purposes of the church than as mere witness of its divine origins. Orson Pratt made the case most fully and eloquently for the centrality of the gifts to the carrying out of the church's role as the vehicle for God's purposes in saving and exalting the human family:

Any gospel destitute of supernatural power is destitute of God. It is barely on a level with other human Systems. But the gospel of Christ is the power of God unto salvation. Take away the power of the gospel and you take away the remission of sins and the healing of diseases and the spirit of prophecy; take away the power of the gospel and you take away the ministry of angels, and the illuminations of visions and dreams and the doctrines of miracles, &c. But when these things shall be taken from the New Testament what will there be left? What a feeble and contemptible relic of a system would the New Testament become without these things? . . . Look at a bible without . . . a Holy Ghost to derive intelligence and power from Christ. Without the gift of prophecy to acquaint men with things future or call to remembrance things past, without a healing ordinance for the blind, the lame, the deaf, the palsied, the sick,—without miraculous power to cast out devils—shut the mouths of lions—quench the violence of fire—seal up the heavens against rain—rebuke the angry elements, and feed the famishing; without any order of angels to communicate between the heavens and earth. . . . Take the principle of power from the ancient scriptures and where is the doctrine of the resurrection of countless millions of the human family from the dust of death? From whence comes the hope of harmonizing the adverse spirits of the animal and human race and of establishing familiar intercourse between the heavens and earth and of causing a perfect conformity to the divine will and celestial order on the face of the whole earth?[10]

In the first generations of the Mormon church, the principal role of spiritual gifts was serving as a witness to the restoration rather than providing individual edification. And given the indispensability of the church to God's saving purposes, that evidentiary function was critical as the church developed a foothold in a crowded religious landscape. At the time of his ascension into heaven, Jesus left his apostles with the promise that certain signs, such as healing, tongues, and power over demons, "will accompany those who believe."[11] Few Christians would dispute the exhibition of miracles and signs in the early Christian church. The question that has riven Christianity is, for how long would those signs accompany belief? Were they meant to be a feature of the apostolic age only or a perpetual sign of the true church? Biblical miracles were performed as evidence of God's power and, in the New Testament, of Christ's divinity and to strengthen believers in their faith. For a while, charismatic gifts like tongues and prophecy persisted in the church. In the era after Christ's death, miracles acquired the modified function of serving as "God's irrefutable proof of God's sponsorship" of the institutional church in which those manifestations occurred.[12] So Justin Martyr (AD 100–165), for instance, argued that since "among us until now there are prophetic charismata," Christianity was a living and true faith by contrast with Judaism, where such gifts had ceased.[13] And that is why, in Catholic thought, "God would not work a miracle under such circumstances that it could reasonably be interpreted as divine confirmation of another religion."[14] Even so, the dearth of miracles after the apostolic age was conspicuous enough to engender debate on exactly what this decline meant.

Jaroslav Pelikan finds that a seminal rupture in the history of miracles emerges in the context of the church's confrontation with the Montanists, a late second-century charismatic group of Christians. In suppressing their claims to prophecy inspired by the Holy Ghost, the official church opted to privilege apostolic authority over "the ecstasy and prophecy that the Paraclete granted" to seemingly random, self-selected members of the laity. And so the canon, the creed, and the episcopate supplanted "the Spirit's extraordinary gifts." The spiritual gifts promised in the New Testament were thereafter considered to refer "primarily to the Pentecostal event" itself.[15] But the subsequent decline of all gifts concerned the devout and skeptical alike, who saw in the dearth a failure of the New Testament promise.

Augustine explained the decline of spiritual gifts by arguing that once "the Catholic Church had been founded and diffused throughout the world, ... miracles were not allowed to continue till our time, lest the mind should always seek visible things." But Augustine and others were uneasy with such a complete concession to cessationism (the belief that miracles and gifts ceased with the death of the apostles) for they also wanted to affirm their continuing manifestations as evidence of the presence of the Spirit in the church. And so Augustine later reported several dozen contemporary instances of miracles and explained that such ongoing marvels "are relatively unknown not because they no longer occur, but because of bad communication" and disbelief generally.[16] In the sixth century, Pope Gregory the Great was reassuring those disturbed by their absence. "Is it," he asked, "because we do not have these signs that you do not believe? These were needed at the church's beginning," he explained. Young plants do not need solicitous care "when they have once taken root."[17]

Cessationist statements like those of Gregory and the early Augustine notwithstanding, signs and wonders constituted an important aspect of ecclesiastical history in the early Christian centuries. Wonder-working, apparitions and visions, and other manifestations of the miraculous continued to erupt; the result was a rhetoric of the miraculous that could appear inconsistent but in general accommodated only privileged exceptions to the rule of a general decline. Throughout the Middle Ages, exceptions became less exceptional. At the popular level, miracles grew increasingly to be associated with relics connected to Jesus, the apostles, or the saints. Belief in miracles as continuing signs of divine approbation and of personal sanctity continue to the present in the Roman church, especially crucial in the qualifying of individuals for beatification and canonization. Here, however, as with relics, the miracles (usually healings) are not generally evident as spiritual gifts exercised by the living but as postmortal "evidence of the intercessory power of the Venerable Servant of God and thus of his or her union after death with God."[18]

The first Protestants, by and large, admitted of no such exceptions to the cessation of gifts. Miracles in the contemporary church, they insisted, were largely a cynical imposition on the gullible, born of credulity, superstition, or popish machinations (like the talking crucifix in Boxley Abbey in Kent revealed to be operated with "certain engines and old wire," or in other cases, Mary's milk discovered to be a "peece of chalke" and Christ's blood revealed as that of a duck).[19] Protestants dismissed weeping icons, restorative powers of relics, and visionary apparitions wholesale, along with the exercise of New Testament charismatic gifts. As James I declared decisively: "All we that are Christians ought assuredly to know that since the comming of Christ in the flesh, and establishing of his Church by the Apostles, all miracles, visions, prophecies, and appearances of angels or good spirites are ceased. Which served only for the first sowing of faith."[20] On the other hand, goes the counterargument, if gifts persisted at all beyond the lifetime of the apostles, then there is no good reason why they would have gradually subsided altogether.[21] Ultimately, charismata severely declined in the Reformation because its movers well understood the logic of confirmatory miracles. As a Protestant critic of Catholicism wrote, they necessarily "rejected miracles . . . not because they were miraculous, but because they were *Romish*. They had no choice. If the miracles were real, the doctrines were true."[22]

Not surprisingly, then, when the first Reformers were challenged to support their own faith claims with miracles, they declined. As Keith Thomas notes, "In Protestant mythology the Middle Ages became notorious as the time of darkness, when spells and charms had masqueraded as religion and when the lead in magical activity had been taken by the clergy themselves."[23] Luther's crusade against relics and associated miracles was relentless, and Calvin reminded challengers that "we may also fitly remember that Satan has his miracles, which, though they are deceitful tricks rather than authentic acts, are of such sort as to mislead the simple-minded and untutored."[24] In America, Jonathan Edwards was extolling the superiority of charity and envisioning the day "when the church of God shall be in its most perfect state, and when the other gifts of the Spirit shall have vanished away."[25] Eventually, however, the Reformers' impulse to purify the church of non-biblical practices implied its twin: the desire to restore those biblical practices that were missing. And so by the eighteenth century it was not uncommon to hear the question, "Where have the spiritual gifts gone?" A scattering of religious groups and leaders emerged, claiming the restoration of those gifts.

The founder of the Shakers, her followers asserted, enjoyed a ministry abounding in the "power and operations of God" and "filled with visions and revelations of

God."[26] In a chapter of their collected *Testimonies* designated "Miraculous Gifts," they chronicle several healings, by Ann Lee and others, of the diseased, the crippled, and one girl possessed of a demon.[27] A period of particularly intense spiritual gifts was denominated by their historians as "the Era of Manifestations" and included "visions, dreams, voices, leadings, prophecies, healings, miracles," as well as speaking in tongues and angelic appearances.[28] Early Methodists also found visions, prophetic dreams, and even healings to be evidence of God's presence. The Methodist pursuit of such gifts led one scholar to refer to their "militant supernaturalism," though Wesley himself warned against enthusiasm, or supernatural manifestations from God.[29] "As to the nature of enthusiasm," he preached, "it is undoubtedly a disorder of the mind. . . . Every enthusiast, then, is properly a madman."[30] Especially alarming were "those who imagine they have such gifts from God as they have not. Thus some have imagined themselves to be endued with the power of working miracles, of healing the sick by a word or a touch, or restoring sight to the blind. . . . Others have undertaken to prophesy, to foretell things to come."[31] At the same time, Wesley was adamant that legitimate gifts of the spirit were historically rare by virtue of disbelief, not divine intention. As he wrote in "The More Excellent Way,"

> the cause of [their rarity] was not, (as has been vulgarly supposed), "because there was no more occasion for them," because all the world was become Christians. This is a miserable mistake; not a twentieth part of it was then nominally Christian. The real cause was, . . . the Christians had no more of the Spirit of Christ than the other Heathens. The Son of Man, when he came to examine his Church, could hardly "find faith upon earth." This was the real cause why the extraordinary gifts of the Holy Ghost were no longer to be found in the Christian Church; because the Christians were turned Heathens again, and had only a dead form left.[32]

Lacking Wesley's clear stand against spiritual gifts, Methodists gained a reputation for their exercise. Freeborn Garretson noted that many people "thought the Methodists could work miracles," and he had both seen and performed them himself.[33] Historian John Wigger goes so far as to claim that "this quest for the supernatural in everyday life was the most distinctive characteristic of early American Methodism."[34] Still, Wesley and others of the more prudent variety had good reason to fear the excesses of enthusiasm. Among the Methodists, camp meetings produced widespread physical displays of spiritual awakening and rapture. A visiting Anglican described a Carolina congregation as "a Gang of frantic Lunatics broke out of Bedlam," with singing, howling, ranting, dancing, and laughing.[35] Shaker spirituality could manifest as wallowing in the mud and pounding on furniture till the hands bled, or playing the role of a mop "being scrubbed across a dirty floor."[36] On other occasions, some "crowed like cocks, mewed like cats, and other again barked and made the noise of squirrels."[37]

Such disruptive practices caused alarm within congregations and to observers without. One nineteenth-century historian noted that "while these extraordinary meetings were exerting a hallowed influence upon the older states, . . . those in Kentucky ran into such wild excesses in some instances, as to bring them into disrepute in the estimation of the more sober part of the community." Even the normally staid Presbyterians could be divided over the phenomenon. In one southern communion, the old-stock Calvinists, unused to such "experimental religion," provoked the more spiritually adventuresome in their midst into leaving to form their own Springfield Presbytery in 1803. They lasted a year, before splintering apart. An observer explained, "Some . . . ran into the wildest freaks of fanaticism. Hence originated those unseemly exercises so humiliating to recount, of jumping, dancing, jerking, barking, and rolling on the ground, by which these schismatics were at last distinguished and disgraced."[38]

The Campbellites, otherwise thoroughly committed to New Testament primitivism, found it prudent to stop short of endorsing any charismatic gifts. "The *gifts of the Holy Spirit* is not a Scriptural phrase," wrote Campbell. "The Holy Spirit is himself a gift," and "by 'a manifestation of the Spirit' [Paul] meant such an *exhibition* of his *presence* and residence in the heart, as would convince the understanding of all that these spiritual men, who *professed to have received the Holy Spirit himself*, did in truth possess that divine agent."[39] (This position was one reason for Sidney Rigdon's break with that group.)

One way Christians found to reconcile New Testament Christianity with modern suspicion of charismata was to divide "the work of the Holy Ghost" into two categories, "extraordinary and ordinary," as Charles Buck did in his dictionary. The former category operated "by immediate inspiration, making men prophets, the latter by his regenerating and sanctifying influences making men saints. It is only the latter which is now to be expected."[40] Mormonism defined itself as a church of prophets and saints alike, and recognized no such distinctions.

MORMON CHARISMATA

Popular religion, not creedal statements, provided the context for the flourishing of early Mormonism. Into this religious landscape fractured by contending views about cessationism and exhibiting an entire spectrum of charismatic gifts, Mormonism arrived with its own predispositions. Key in this regard were the legacy and doctrine of the Book of Mormon itself, which was fundamental both in shaping early Mormon religious attitudes and attracting those inclined to the enchanted world it described and portended. Its very appearance in the world, heralded by theophanies and angels, and incorporating gold plates, Nephite interpreters, supernatural compasses—this whole entourage of other-worldly visitants and priestly articles was like the vibrant and extravagant uncials in an illuminated manuscript, drawing attention to a new chapter in God's conversation with humankind.

In its essential function of collapsing the old and the new into one, repudiating supersessionism of every form, the new scripture necessarily rejected cessationism as well. In Book of Mormon language, the absence of spiritual gifts was an irrefutable sign of apostasy needing remedy, not of post-apostolic developments in accord with providential intent. The Book of Mormon's self-identified editor, Mormon, laments that "the work of miracles and of healing did cease because of the iniquity of the people. And there were no gifts from the Lord."[41] Their restitution in the modern world was anticipated in Moroni's condemnation, to a future readership, of those skeptics who say "that there are no revelations, nor prophecies, nor gifts, nor healing, nor speaking with tongues and the interpretation of tongues; Behold, . . . he that denieth these things knoweth not the gospel of Christ."[42]

In spite of the examples we have surveyed, belief in charismatic gifts was still rare enough in the early nineteenth century, and their manifestations sufficiently infrequent, that suspicion and hostility were the standard reaction to claims of the miraculous. In one of the earliest LDS evangelizing missions, Parley Pratt announced to a group that he had himself witnessed spiritual manifestations, and he predicted the imminent display of "as great miracles wrought, as there was at the day of Pentecost." He had also testified of the Book of Mormon as additional scripture, but it was the former claim that aroused ridicule. This assertion of a new Pentecostal age, "and much more equally absurd, was advanced by these deluded mortals," remarked one witness.[43] "They can mutter Indian and traffic in new Bibles," scoffed Campbell himself.[44]

On the other hand, for those seekers after truth who believed the promise of charismatic gifts had never been revoked, healings and visions and the like were powerful evidence for God's renewed presence in the world. In Mormonism's early years in particular, its principal candidates for evangelizing and conversion were those already inclined to accept spiritual gifts as a sign of true Christianity. In a story that is paradigmatic of many in that generation who sought apostolic authority, Wandle Mace had been excommunicated from his own Presbyterian church and was working in New York City while spending time as an itinerant lay preacher. Along with Mace's acquaintance Elijah Fordham, Parley Pratt attended a Methodist meeting at which Mace lamented the lack of spiritual gifts in contemporary Christianity.

Though some in the audience "declared they [gifts] were not needed in this age," the "portly" Pratt "expressed his pleasure at my remarks in the meeting and said he would like a further conversation with me. . . . In the course of our conversation he learned from me this, that I was waiting and watching for the gifts of the gospel as they once existed." How singular, Mace remembered him as saying, "to find a man . . . waiting for Apostles and Prophets and the gifts of the spirit as enjoyed anciently. . . . Then he began telling me about a young man in New York who had been visited by an angel."[45]

As the editor of the LDS church newspaper declared, "How shall we know whether [claimants to be the true church] are built upon the rock or not? If there is no sign given, then one man's say so, is as good as another's. . . . Here is a sign given: 'These signs shall follow them that believe, They shall heal the sick, cast out devils,' &c. We ask for these signs. We look among the Presbyterians: no such signs there. We look among the Methodists, Episcopalians, Baptists, Universalists, &c. &c. &c.: but, we find none of these signs."[46] Apparently, the litmus test was reciprocally applied. Smith said one of the questions "which are daily and hourly asked by all classes of people whilst we are traveling" was "what signs does Jo Smith give to establish his divine mission?"[47]

Four years later, LDS church editors were continuing the theme. Responding to a pamphlet advocating Anglican theology, a Mormon writer replied in print, "Do they teach [believers] to believe in, and pray for the gifts of the Spirit, such as revelations, visions, prophesyings, miracles, tongues, interpretations, healings, ministering of angels, &c?"[48] Of course, for the most part signs were not to be found in the Protestant denominations for the simple reason that they did not seek them, nor believe them to be valid signs of a church's claim to divine origin or sanction. That is why many saw in Mormonism's charismatic manifestations prima facie evidence not of true foundations, but of "the most wild, frantic, and horrible fanaticism."[49] And initially, especially, grounds for such a view were not lacking.

Shortly after the Mormons established branches in Ohio in the fall of 1830, spiritual manifestations made their appearance. Enthusiasm was rife in the area, a blend of Methodist, Baptist, and African influences[50]—and sometimes it took a uniquely Mormon twist. Whitmer recorded that during meetings, "some would fancy to themselves that they had the sword of Laban, and would wield it as expert as a light dragoon, some would act like an Indian in the act of scalping, some would slide or scoot and [on] the floor, with the rapidity of a serpent, which the[y] termed sailing in the boat to the Lamanites."[51] Other Christians were quick to condemn these early Mormon exhibitions, which apparently included not just imitation of "Indian modes of warfare" but "speaking in all the Indian dialects."[52] True, Pratt had announced to the press that "when they [the missionaries] got among the scattered tribes, there would be as great miracles wrought, as there was at the day of Pentecost."[53] But the unseemly displays he witnessed in Ohio struck him as indecorous and improper, and he asked Smith for counsel on the subject. Smith inquired of the Lord, and in May 1831 he produced a revelation that established official Mormon policy on charismata. The extreme displays were condemned as "abominations" attributable to "false spirits" and demonic deception.[54] The revelation invoked the criterion of rationality (or cognates) six times for ascertaining the legitimacy of spiritual gifts. Smith would later give a question as the litmus test: "Is any intelligence communicated?"[55]

Rationality is of course a relative term, especially in the context of religion, and Pratt would continue to find a harmonious co-existence in his own ministry of intellectual disquisitions on the gospel alongside his exercise of spiritual gifts like healing and prophesying. But he declared in the semi-authoritative *Key to Science of Theology* that "all the strange ecstasies, swoonings, screamings, shoutings, dancings, jumpings, and a thousand other ridiculous and unseemly manifestations" were "fruits of these deceptive spirits."[56] Mormons were at times apparently hard-pressed to create their own variety of charismata. One Mormon referred to false manifestations in their meetings erupting from "a Shaker spirit." Other delusions of his fellow Saints he called "the Methodist and Presbyterian falling-down power."[57] Still, avoiding the sensationalistic appeal and employment of spiritual gifts was an ongoing challenge for Mormons devoted to their reality. On the 1834 expedition known as Zion's Camp, for instance, "Martin Harris having boasted to the brethren that he could handle snakes with perfect safety, while fooling with a black snake with his bare feet, he received a bite on his left foot. . . . I took occasion to reprove him," said Joseph Smith, "and exhort the brethren never to trifle with the promises of God."[58]

By the early twentieth century, "the emergence of Pentecostalism was a tangible challenge to a theological position maintained in the church for centuries: that the miraculous gifts of the Holy Spirit had ceased."[59] But their return never extended to a significant degree in mainstream Protestantism. Max Weber weighed in with his own theory of the "routinization of charisma," a now standard explanation from a secular standpoint for the decline of spiritual gifts. In this view, charisma is "a quality of things and persons . . . set apart from the ordinary." It serves as "a phase of moral authority," establishes "legitimacy," and finds its paradigm instance in the figure of the prophet. Once that authority is validated and effects its revolutionary purposes, the charisma becomes "routinized" by transfer of that charismatic authority to an "office" or "institutional structure."[60]

Mormonism has recapitulated in brief the millennia of Christian church history, with its own Pentecostal beginnings and the gradual diminution of its own spiritual manifestations. In the days immediately following Smith's dedication of the Kirtland Temple on March 27, 1836, spiritual manifestations paralleling Luke's description of the Jerusalem Pentecost were recorded by dozens of participants—all of whom considered the events to be patterned after the New Testament model. Smith had himself petitioned in the dedicatory prayer that spiritual manifestations would be present "as upon those on the day of Pentecost."[61] Over a thousand Saints were present, and many recorded the invocation's fulfillment. That evening, the scene was repeated, according to one diarist, who reported "angels of God came into the room, cloven tongues rested upon some of the servants of the Lord like unto fire, & they spake with tongues and prophesied."[62] After three days of spiritual outpouring, Smith pronounced it "a penticost and enduement indeed, long to be remembered . . . to all generations as the day of Pentecost."[63]

Strikingly, when the temple at Nauvoo was dedicated years later, amid even more spiritually wrought conditions and at greater sacrifice than the Kirtland precedent, nothing to equal the Pentecostal manifestations of Kirtland took place. Mormons are not cessationists, still affirming belief "in the gift of tongues, prophecy, revelation, visions, healing, interpretation of tongues, and so forth."[64] Even so, few would dispute the diminishment of charismatic gifts in the modern LDS faith community. It is possible, of course, that with the tilt toward secularism and scientism, supernatural gifts are not more infrequent, just more infrequently acknowledged or celebrated. It is possible, as well, that the reasoning of a historian contemporary with Smith is relevant to the Mormon case. Spiritual gifts diminished, John Kaye wrote, "at a time when Christianity, having obtained a footing in all the provinces of the Roman Empire, the miraculous gifts conferred upon the first teachers had performed their appropriate office—that of proving to the world that a new revelation had been given from heaven."[65] In Mormonism's case, the decline in gifts began with Smith's own ministry. As John Durham Peters summarizes, "Smith used and spoke of a variety of mysterious technologies such as seer stones, the Urim and Thummim, divining rods, and the Liahona (a kind of compass), but these exotic media soon gave way to more reliable religious media of text, community, temple, service, music, and the whisperings of the Holy Ghost in an almost conscious cooling of charisma."[66] Initially, however, the range of charismatic gifts was both anticipated and amply in evidence.

Revelation

Revelation—"the disclosure or communication of truth to men by God himself"[67]—may be the broadest in scope of charismatic gifts (though not specifically enumerated by Paul), is the most contested in meaning, and has been the most pervasive of all of them in Mormon discourse, both past and present. Avery Dulles considers "revelation as inner experience" the most common version of the term when it is used to describe a personal spiritual phenomenon, but he tempers its charismatic nature by emphasizing that most theologians have denied that revelation can have propositional content.[68] God may have "spoken" to Adam, Eve, Noah, Abraham, Rebekah, Moses, and myriad other biblical characters, but general consensus has consistently moved in the direction of reading such encounters as figurative at best. In an essay revealingly titled "The Scandal of Revelation," critic George Steiner writes, "Scriptural literalism or any peremptory attribution to God of 'speech acts' such as we know and use them . . . only offends reason and historical evidence."[69] Steiner's is not a merely secular example; much of Christianity has long been in agreement. This is in part because to attribute literal speech acts to the Divine is to defy modern Christianity's persistent hostility to the anthropomorphism that speech implies. And so, in the Western religious tradition, dialogic exchange between God and human beings generally becomes metaphorized into a more nebulous understanding of "revelation." As Nicholas Wolterstorff argues, rewriting "divine speech" as a vaguely conceived "divine revelation"

> was not just fortuitous error; an interesting reason was sometimes offered. Since God has no vocal cords with which to utter words, and no hands with which to write them down, God cannot literally speak, cannot literally be a participant in a linguistic communication. Accordingly, attributions of speech to God, if not judged bizarrely false, must be taken as metaphorical.[70]

And so, as Sandra M. Schneider writes, outside of an anthropomorphic model it is "evident" that "divine discourse cannot be taken literally. . . . Language, in other words, is a human phenomenon rooted in our corporeality as well as in our discursive mode of intellection and as such cannot be literally predicated of pure spirit."[71] In similar fashion, William Abraham concludes that Christianity's turn away from propositional revelation is a de facto rejection of the belief that God "reveals Himself by speaking to man." That step, in turn, "is to so whittle away the analogy on which the concept of divine revelation is built that it must be seriously asked whether the concept of divine revelation has enough content to license its continued use. Revelation in the fully personal sense characteristic of personal agents has been abandoned."[72]

Even evangelicals and Restorationists, otherwise keen on New Testament models, were wary of anything that seemed a return to personal revelation so conceived. The seventeenth-century Boston preacher John Cotton was advising his church "not to be afraid of the word *Revelation*," even as he warned them "not to look for any revelation out of the Word."[73] And the ever-cautious Wesley admonished, "Trust not in visions or dreams; in sudden impressions, or strong impulses of any kind. Remember, it is not by these you are to know what is the will of God, on any particular occasion, but by applying the plain Scripture rule, with the help of experience and reason, and the ordinary assistance of the Spirit of God."[74]

In the face of such widespread rejection of Old Testament literalism regarding God's interaction with human beings, Mormonism is an emphatic exception. Smith was inflexible in his insistence that his encounters with deity included literal speech acts between divine persons and himself (other forms of revelation than verbal are treated below). The Book of Mormon he produced emphasizes as one of its cardinal teachings that dialogic revelation is the birthright of righteous seekers in all ages. The particularity and specificity, the vividness, the concreteness, and the accessibility of revelatory experience—those realities both underlie and overshadow the narrated history and doctrine that constitute the record. The "knowability" of all truth, the openness of mystery, the reality of personal revelation find vivid illustration within the record and invite reenactment outside it.[75]

What then of the substance of revelation? The Book of Mormon may indeed grapple with the "exegesis of existence"[76] or matters of "ultimate concern,"[77] as others have defined the matter of revelation, but that doesn't seem to be the point of most of the revelatory process it describes. Questions can address one's personal standing before God or arise from pious curiosity.[78] But queries that prompt divine replies are also, in turn, theological, quotidian, or starkly pragmatic in their specificity. From "What is the state of the soul after death?" and "Who needs baptism?" to "Where will the enemy attack?" and "Where should I hunt?" all prompt divine response.[79] The insistence that God would speak to lay individuals with personal, dialogic, propositional revelation was a bedrock principle of Mormonism. As Parley Pratt imagined in a whimsical dialogue he published, Satan is "decidedly in favor of all creeds, systems, and forms of Christianity, of whatever name and nature," with one caveat. They must steer clear of the one abominable principle with the power to bring his whole kingdom to ruin: "direct communication with God, by new revelation."[80]

INSTITUTIONAL VERSUS PERSONAL REVELATION

Revelation in the LDS church takes place in two domains that can potentially conflict. As we saw with Hiram Page's claims of revelation, Smith's announcement that the heavens were again open and gifts like visions and prophecy were available to all was an invitation to holy bedlam. In response to competing claims to authoritative revelation, the dictum came that for the church as a whole, "no one shall be appointed to receive commandments and revelations . . . excepting my servant Joseph" and his successors.[81] Smith later taught that "it is also the privilege of any officer in this church to obtain revelations so far as relates *to his particular calling or duty* in the church" (emphasis added).[82] And so the injunction to obtain personal revelation for one's own life has never slackened, but it comes with the recognition that such revelation is constrained to personal stewardship.

Given the human proclivity, in Dostoevsky's words, to search out "someone to keep one's conscience,"[83] the real lurking danger in a church that emphasizes priesthood hierarchy and a presiding prophet is not for individuals to replicate the presumption of Hiram Page but rather for them to relinquish their own revelatory privileges in deference to higher authority. Hence Brigham Young tellingly preached that he was "more afraid that this people have so much confidence in their leaders that they will not inquire for themselves of God whether they are led by him. I am fearful they settle down in a state of blind self-security, trusting their eternal destiny in the hands of their leaders with a reckless confidence that in itself would thwart the purpose of God in their salvation."[84] In the twenty-first century, apostle Dallin Oaks urged complementary revelatory responsibility when he declared that as a General Authority of the church, "it is my responsibility to preach general principles. . . . I only teach the general rules. Whether an exception applies to you is your responsibility. You must work that out individually between you and the Lord."[85] More recently, apostle Todd Christofferson quoted Shakespeare to similar effect: "Every subject's duty is the king's, but every subject's soul is his own."[86]

In that sense, Mormonism maintains a tenuous balance between institutional and personal sources of revelation. On the one hand, the church continues to affirm, referring to the church president, counselors, and twelve apostles, that "the prophets, seers, and revelators have had and still have the responsibility and privilege of receiving and declaring the word of God for the world."[87] At the same time, the leadership insists, as Joseph Smith taught, that "the Holy Ghost is a revelator." Therefore, "no man can receive the Holy Ghost without receiving revelations."[88] Verbal interactions between God and humans, like Moses on Mt. Sinai, were infrequent in the biblical record, and Smith himself more often experienced revelation in terms he described in an 1829 pronouncement he attributed to God: "I will tell you in your mind and in your heart, by the Holy Ghost, which shall come upon you."[89] Still, examples of more dramatic communications were frequently cited in the LDS church as instances of spiritual gifts, such as visions and prophecies.

Visions

Visionary encounters might be considered a subset of revelatory experience, and ecstatic visions may be accounted one of the most frequent and enduring of the spiritual gifts mentioned throughout the Christian centuries. Visionary encounters fill the pages of the Old Testament and continue into the New. Prophets like Micaiah, Isaiah, and Ezekiel have visions of the Lord on his throne; Stephen sees "Jesus standing at the right hand of God" and is stoned for so claiming. The young Paul (still Saul at this point) witnesses the martyrdom and subsequently makes his own claim to be visited by Christ and called to his ministry.[90] Catholicism has a long history of heavenly personages seen in vision, such as Julian of Norwich's sixteen "showings" of Jesus Christ and Joan of Arc's visitations by the archangel Michael, St. Margaret, and St. Catherine. Claims of appearances of the Virgin Mary surpass 200 reported in the twentieth century alone.[91] The Roman church exercises some control over the spiritual gift of visions by officially acknowledging some of them (nine according to one source, seventeen by another count), condemning some, and indicating that others "have neither been approved or condemned by the Apostolic See."[92]

Protestantism, as we saw, recognized the power of spiritual gifts to confirm a church's truth-claims. Consequently, Protestants' hostility to Catholic claims of visions and gifts entailed a logical reluctance to countenance them in their own midst. Nevertheless, popular manifestations would continue to erupt from time to time. One burst of visions appears in the accounts of the French Prophets around the turn of the eighteenth century. In a typical instance, Elizabeth Gray, prominent in that group, announced to spectators a vision of angels.[93] A generation later, Shaker head Ann Lee described one of her visions that preceded her voyage to America: "I knew by the revelation of God that God has a chosen people in America; I saw some of them in vision; and when I met them in America I knew them. I saw a large tree, every leaf of which shone with such brightness as made it appear like a burning torch, representing the Church of Christ, which will yet be established in the land."[94]

By 1760, the Swedish mystic Emanuel Swedenborg was widely known to have experienced multiple visions; not only was he visited by entities from beyond the veil, but he was soon comfortable making repeated visits there himself, virtually at will. By the dawn of the nineteenth century, the Second Great Awakening gave new impetus to ecstatic religious experience. Jemima Wilkinson, while suffering a fever from typhus or some other malady, experienced the first of several visions: "The heavens were open'd," she later recorded, "And She saw two Archangels descending from the east, with golden crowns upon their heads, clothed in long white Robes, down to the feet; Bringing a sealed Pardon from the living God."[95]

Additional examples, as Donna Hill points out, include Lorenzo Dow, who had a dream-vision of God and Jesus in 1791; Charles Finney and Elias Smith had visions of Christ preceding their ministries; John Samuel Taylor, a Palmyra neighbor of the Smiths, heard Christ call him to a public ministry in a dream; and in the same year that Moroni appeared to Joseph Smith, Asa Wild received one of several revelations confirming Smith's announcement that all Christianity had gone astray.[96] Richard Bushman has found more than thirty-two pamphlets relating personal visions in the period 1783 to 1815—and those are just the published ones.[97] John Wigger notes that "a great many early Methodists believed in the efficacy of prophetic dreams, visions, and supernatural impressions. . . . Examples of this kind of supernaturalism abound in the journals and autobiographies of Methodist preachers and lay men and women."[98]

VISIONS IN MORMONISM

The veil between the living and the dead seemed as permeable with Joseph Smith as it had been for Emanuel Swedenborg. His most famous vision, called his "First Vision" since the early twentieth century, is viewed retrospectively as the dawn of the Restoration he would usher in, though he understood that 1820 experience in strictly personal terms for some time. The most famous vision in the early Mormon era, called "The Vision" by his followers, was his 1832 glimpse of the three kingdoms of glory, in which Sidney Rigdon also participated. Rigdon collapsed in spiritual exhaustion at the vision's conclusion, whereat Smith remarked wryly, "Well, Brother Sidney is not as used to it as I am."[99] Smith's sanguine assessment was borne out by a prodigious record of heavenly encounters: seventy-six documented visions, by one count.[100] He saw in vision the Father and the Son, figures from the Book of Mormon and both testaments, departed friends in glory, the location for Zion, and patterns of quorum organization and temple construction.

Smith was an unusual seer in that he endeavored to democratize his gift. As one scholar remarked, "Joseph Smith was the Henry Ford of revelation. He wanted every home to have one, and the revelation he had in mind was the revelation he'd had, which was seeing God."[101] In one typical example of that impulse, recorded John Murdock, "the Prophet told us if we could humble ourselves before God, and exercise strong faith, we should see the face of the Lord. And about midday [April 3, 1833] the visions of my mind were opened, and . . . I saw the form of a man, most lovely, the visage of his face was round and fair as the sun." As he struggled to take it all in, the vision disappeared, "but it left on my mind the impression of love, for months, that I never felt before to that degree."[102]

In January 1836, in the weeks leading up to the period Saints called the Kirtland Pentecost, many of the church leadership participated in a meeting where "some of them saw the face of the Saviour, and others were ministered to by holy angels." The next morning, Smith and others "spent the time in rehearsing to each other the glorious scenes that [had] transpired."[103] The promise Smith made to Murdock was actually canonized, so it remains a robust possibility in Mormon belief: according to words imputed to Christ himself, "It shall come to pass that every soul who forsaketh his sins and cometh unto me, and calleth on my name, and obeyeth my voice, and keepeth my commandments, shall see my face and know that I am."[104] From Brigham Young onward, LDS prophets have muted their claims to divine epiphanies. A rare instance of a theophany acknowledged by a modern Mormon prophet was Christ's appearing to fifth president Lorenzo Snow in the Salt Lake Temple in 1898, and that experience was shared privately.[105] George Q. Cannon asserted that he "saw and conversed with the Savior face to face,"[106] Joseph F. Smith's 1918 vision of Christ and the spirit world was canonized as scripture in 1976,[107] and the apostle David B. Haight recounted a detailed vision of the Savior in a 1989 address.[108]

Many other LDS prophets and apostles have made subtle allusions to private, sacred experiences of a visionary nature. Because visions are privately rather than publicly experienced, instances have been seldom publicized throughout LDS history. (This is probably why Heber J. Grant wrote in 1926 that he knew "of no instance where the Lord has appeared to an individual since his appearances to the Prophet Joseph Smith.")[109] All the same, numerous sources indicate that visionary experience was not unusual among the laity as well in the first, charismatic generation of Mormonism.

An English elder reported that after a patriarchal blessing promising him spiritual gifts, "I received the gift of discernment or vision, . . . which gift I still retain." He then added that "many have it in a greater degree than I have. Perhaps nearly half of the people in these churches have the gift of vision, . . . wherein the most marvelous things are made known unto them."[110] He may not have been exaggerating. In private journals and narratives, the early years of Mormonism registered numerous visionary experiences on a variety of themes. One convert described his vision of the three kingdoms of glory, the priesthood's restoration, and the lost Ten Tribes.[111] Another saw the premortal world, with innumerable spirits "arranged in classes" where "they were taught in the arts and sciences, and everything necessary to make the heart happy." He also "saw Joseph, Brigham, and many others engaged in this work of education."[112] Some visions were of a more local, personal nature. Philo Dibble had a recurring vision of his own death and took action to avert it.[113] A brother Sterrett lived to see his vision of his son's mission labors fulfilled,[114] while Benjamin Brown was visited by a deceased brother, in addition to seeing in vision "various scenes described in the revelations of the ancient prophets."[115] In Nauvoo, shortly before Smith's death, Stephen Farnsworth saw the westward exodus, under Young's guidance and the protection of angels.[116]

Some Mormons recounted visions in anticipation of or prior to their conversion. Thus Eliza Gibbs, in a state of religious anxiety in 1833, had "a beautiful vision opened up to her where she was able to glimpse the beauties of eternity."[117] LDS missionaries soon found and baptized her. A few years before his 1831 conversion, Lorenzo Young had a vision of the postmortal world, where spirits assembled before the judgment, as well as the city and abode of God. He also had dreams and visions of Christ and of angels.[118] Benjamin Brown recorded how an unnamed woman who hosted him foresaw in vision the coming of two Mormon missionaries,[119] and Vienna Jacques related that "a vision of the Book of Mormon was presented to her mind" while she was yet a seeker in Boston. She journeyed to Kirtland and was baptized.[120] Many early Methodists, more inclined to charismata than their successors, enjoyed visionary experiences—and a large percentage of early Latter-day Saints came from those backgrounds. Christopher Jones has chronicled a number of prominent Mormon converts, including Thomas Marsh, David Patten, Phineas Young, and many others, who as Methodists experienced "the spirit of prophecy" and "dreams and visions . . . of the Holy Spirit" or "saw the Heavens open," and they felt that these experiences prepared their entry into Mormonism.[121]

As the nineteenth century advanced, publicly shared visionary experience suffered the same general decline that other charismata did. One possible factor may have been the competing claims of spiritualists. Parley Pratt remarked in 1853 on the widespread "visions, trances, clairvoyance . . . by which the world of spirits is said to have found means to communicate with spirits in the flesh."[122] Young also alluded to "the revelations from the wicked through the spirit rappers."[123] This was the decade of the "spirit rapping" phenomenon, launched by the Fox sisters, Leah, Margaret, and Kate. By the 1860s, spiritualism had infiltrated Mormon circles, leading a splinter group to claim numerous visitations from deceased Mormon leaders, as well as from Peter, James, and John.[124] The faction, led by William Godbe, challenged Young's leadership, defected, and died out within a dozen or so years. In the twentieth century and beyond, visionary experiences become less and less a part of Mormonism's public record. In the twenty-first century, a few Mormons have spun private visionary experiences into best-selling works. The official church response, as with the Godbeites of Young's era, has been to warn members that such writings reflect—in this case—the author's "own personal experiences and . . . may distort church doctrine."[125]

At the same time, a vibrant tradition of private visionary encounters flourishes within Mormonism. A theology of pre-existence, a pervasive engagement in "searching out one's dead" for vicarious temple work, and historic roots in a hallowed visionary past all combine to make visitations by children yet unborn and relatives who have passed on a common part of folk tradition and personal experience.[126] Visions associated with the temple are particularly difficult to chronicle, especially given the counsel typified by apostle Boyd K. Packer: "There are some things just too sacred to discuss: not secret, but sacred; not to be discussed, but to be harbored and protected and regarded with the deepest of reverence." Discretion has largely replaced proclamation as the response to charismatic gifts.[127]

Prophecy

Like visions, prophecy could be considered another variety of revelation. The word "prophecy" (nebuah; προφητεία or propheteia) is imbued with various shades of meaning. Hebrew imported the term "prophet" (nabi), the probable loan word signifying a diviner. Related words in Hebrew suggest the role of visionary or seer.[128] The Greek root originally signified "one who speaks for a god and interprets his will."[129] This root is mirrored in the etymology of the English word, "forth speaker." Biblically, prophecy most often carries the meaning of a predictive statement, warning, or admonition, uttered by inspiration. "Prophecy was preeminently the privilege of the prophets,"[130] notes one authority. Though that is the general Old Testament pattern, in the New Testament all Christians are urged to seek the gift of prophecy. "Strive for the spiritual gifts," wrote Paul, "and especially that you may prophesy."[131] He also admonishes the Thessalonians not to "despise the words of the prophets,"[132] and to "test everything [and] hold fast that which is good," suggesting that discernment is called for in appraising expressions of the prophetic gift. The clear implication is that "prophesying was a normal congregational activity" among these first Saints.[133]

For the first Christian century and more, John Mosheim contended, in the absence of a literate class or trained leaders, instruction often fell to those "irradiated" with a "more than ordinary measure of his holy spirit," who were denominated prophets. Whatever the frequency or exact nature of prophetic utterances among early Christians, the trajectory of the spiritual gift was forever altered by the Montanist controversy of the second century.[134] At a time when charismata had begun to fade, Montanus, a Christian convert from Asia Minor—along with followers—claimed authoritative new visions and revelations. He trumpeted the imminent coming of Christ, urged the church to practice more rigorous discipline, and claimed to be the Spirit's authorized spokesman (or even embodiment, according to some sources).

It is significant, as Mosheim points out, that neither Montanus nor his disciples challenged "the principal dogmas of Christianity." Rather, the threat was in the power and authority of prophecy he and two female disciples invoked, claiming to speak "oracles dictated by the Holy Spirit for the benefit of the universal church."[135] This represented a challenge to institutional authority of a virtually unprecedented kind. With no general consensus on the continuation of spiritual gifts, only a few generations removed from the abundant charismata of the apostolic era, and with the authoritative creeds and councils still in the future, the appeal of a charismatic figure publicly speaking in tongues and propounding doctrines in the name of the Holy Spirit was widespread.[136] Even the Church Father Tertullian weighed in with the Montanist faction, and it spread throughout the Mediterranean world from Rome to North Africa and Asia Minor. Its core tenet was that "the Holy Spirit continued to speak through prophets."[137] The crisis effectively forced the Christian community to decide between charismatic leadership and institutional boundedness. The majority responded by choosing "to develop a tighter organization and to give added attention to the clarification and formulation of their beliefs."[138] Prophecy and other charismatic gifts were henceforth viewed with growing suspicion because of their capacity for institutional disruption and factionalism.

Almost two millennia later, in the decades preceding Mormonism, the question was reopened, with the split occasioned by Montanus in particular being reconsidered. In a journal entry for August 15, 1750, John Wesley noted a portentous discovery. After reading John Lacy's *General Delusion of Christians*, he recorded, "I was fully convinced of what I had long suspected, 1. That the Montanists, in the second and third centuries, were real, scriptural Christians; and, 2. That the grand reason why the miraculous gifts were so soon withdrawn, was not only that faith and holiness were well nigh lost; but that dry, formal, orthodox men began even then to ridicule whatever gifts they had not themselves, and to decry them all as either madness or imposture."[139]

Lacy's book had been, in part, a reexamination of the "French Prophets," a kind of neo-Montanist outbreak of the seventeenth century. A contemporary described these French Protestant refugees who fled to England, loudly proclaiming such events as the fall of Roman Catholicism, impending apocalyptic destructions, and the imminent return of Jesus Christ: "They spun round with great violence, like tops in fact; then they fell on to the floor. Next, their eyes rolled, their breasts heaved, their throats swelled, and they foamed and dribbled at the mouth. Then, all of a sudden, they started to their feet, shook their heads, hiccupped, clapped their hands, and moved their feet about oddly and shook their whole bodies as if in convulsions. Next, as the stage of speaking under the influence of the Spirit approached, they groaned, sighed, quaked, belched, sang and shrieked hideously. Finally, their mouths opened wide in a distorted fashion, and they spoke prophecies."[140]

An embarrassed French church (Calvinist in orientation) pronounced its stream of prophecies "childish Repetitions, unintelligible Stuff, gross Contradictions [and] manifest Lies," but the phenomenon soon spread to impressionable English observers, men and women alike.[141] The Lacy whom Wesley was reading found the group's behavior excessive but ventured to suggest that "God did vouchsafe to afford supernatural support of various kinds to several of His servants who were witnessing to His truth against the abominations of the Papacy."[142] Lacy and Wesley both illustrate how a window had opened again in the modern Christian era to the possibility of inspired, prophetic utterance. Some prophet figures, like the Swedish seer Emanuel Swedenborg, earned widespread respect (he was lauded by Immanuel Kant, cited and imitated by the young William Blake, and later quoted by Ralph Waldo Emerson). Others, like Matthias the Jewish Prophet (Robert Matthews), ended up discredited and shamed.[143] And even magnificent failures could prove surprisingly resilient. William Miller's predictions of Christ's return in October 1844 led to "the Great Disappointment." Though Miller died believing in the failure of his prophecies, the Seventh-day Adventists grew out of the soil he plowed.[144]

PROPHECY IN MORMONISM

The earliest exercise of the gift of prophecy in the Restored church occurred within moments of the first baptism: "No sooner had I [Joseph Smith] baptized Oliver Cowdery than the Holy Ghost fell upon him and he stood up and prophesied many things which should shortly come to pass."[145] Smith declared, "No man is a minister of Jesus Christ without being a Prophet. No man can be a minister of Jesus Christ except he has the testimony of Jesus & this is the Spirit of Prophecy."[146] At the same time, he clearly practiced and encouraged the *gift* of prophecy in its more conventional meaning. As a consequence, many besides Smith practiced the gift of prophecy in the church's formative years. As part of the Kirtland Temple Pentecost of 1836, prophesying was frequently in evidence. At this season, Smith and the leadership spent long hours into the night, noting on March 29 a burst of "prophesying and giving glory to God," followed the next day by Smith and others again "prophesying," with "the Spirit of prophecy" on this occasion being "poured out upon the congregation."[147] Meanwhile, in England, one convert reported in October 1841 that "prophecy is common in all our meetings."[148]

Often patriarchal blessings, ordinations, and other priesthood blessings included very specific predictions and promises pertaining to the future. Other times, prophecies were carefully recorded and preserved as proofs against claims of fraud, as when apostles Orson Hyde and Heber Kimball wrote and sealed up a prophecy about the defection of one Elder Webster, months before the event.[149] When Parley Pratt was ordained an apostle by Smith, Oliver Cowdery, and David Whitmer, they promised him he would "cross the mighty deep" and spend years laboring in distant countries in "great" and "incessant" toil. Finally, he would be "dragged before the authorities" for his religion and spend time in "strong dungeons and gloomy prisons."[150] (He went on to missions in Great Britain and Chile, was at one time sentenced to be shot by a military court-martial in Missouri, and languished seven months in various jails and prisons, some of it in heavy chains.)[151] Sometimes, Mormon elders would prophecy more spontaneously. Heber C. Kimball had visited a despondent Pratt and promised that his ailing, infertile wife would recover and bear a son, while he would evangelize in Toronto and England and have gold beyond counting. All came to pass as he foretold (though Pratt had to be content with interpreting the promise of gold beyond counting as figurative).[152]

Pratt could be the promulgator, as well as recipient, of the gift of prophecy. John Taylor recorded an occasion when "Br. Parley prophesied concerning me in a manner that almost made my hair stand on my head: much of that prophecy has since been fulfilled."[153] Others would similarly note Pratt's gift of prophecy. David Whitmer wrote that "Joseph Smith gave many true prophecies . . . but this was no more than many of the other brethren did," and among those "other brethren" he singled out Pratt in particular.[154] Pratt reported that on the point of departing the unfruitful mission field of New York, at a farewell meeting "the room was filled with the Holy Spirit, and so was each one present. We began to speak in tongues and prophesy. . . . The principal burthen of the prophesyings was concerning New York City, and our mission there. The Lord said that He had heard our prayers, beheld our labors, diligence, and long suffering toward that city; and that He had seen our tears." Pratt prophesied that "the Lord had many people in that city, and He had now come by the power of His Holy Spirit to gather them into His fold."[155] Pratt stayed, and within a month, he recorded, "we had fifteen preaching places in the city, all of which were filled to overflowing. We preached about eleven times a week, besides visiting from house to house. We soon commenced baptizing, and continued doing so almost daily during the winter and spring."[156]

As with healings, prophecies of Mormon elders and even prophets did not always come to pass. After the Saints' expulsion from Jackson County, Missouri, in 1833, Pratt declared that "if he ever spoke by the spirit of God he then did," and he prophesied that "we shall be enabled to return to our houses" by January 1 to "enjoy the fruit of our labor & none to molest or make afraid."[157] A few years later, the Mormons had been expelled from the county *and* the state of Missouri. Dozens of LDS faithful of the church's first generation were promised they would live to see Christ's return.[158] On the other hand, several of Smith's more dramatic prophecies were fulfilled in ways that became virtually mythic, strengthening conviction in his prophetic role to the present day. He successfully predicted that the outbreak of the Civil War would occur in South Carolina decades before the event, foresaw the settling of Mormons in the Rocky Mountains years ahead of the Mormon exodus, foretold the return of the Jews to the Holy Land, and told Stephen A. Douglas that he would "aspire to the Presidency of the United States," ominously adding that "if ever you turn your hand against me or the Latter day Saints you will feel the weight of the hand of the Almighty upon you; and you will live to see and know that I have testified the truth to you."[159] (Douglas, the professed friend of the Mormons, lost to Lincoln three years after recommending the government excise the "loathsome, disgusting ulcer" that was the Mormon church.)[160]

However, Smith failed at other times to accurately gauge the future. His revelation that the temple of the Missouri "New Jerusalem" would be built "in this generation" went unfulfilled.[161] In 1830, he wrote while in Salem, Massachusetts, that "its wealth pertaining to gold and silver shall be yours," but no fulfillment unfolded.[162] Earlier, he had promised in the name of the Lord that Oliver Cowdery, Joseph Knight, Hyrum Page, and Josiah Stowell would succeed "even in securing the [Canadian] copyright" to the Book of Mormon. The enterprise failed. Defenders explained that the men had not proceeded "with an eye single to [God's] glory," as the revelation stipulated.[163] Smith was more philosophical: "Some revelations are of God: some revelations are of man: and some revelations are of the devil," David Whitmer reported him as saying.[164]

Some prophetic failures could be humorous, though presumably not for those involved. A presiding high priest in Missouri, Aaron Lyon, told Sarah Jackson the Lord had revealed to him the death of her husband—who was in another state at the time. (The revelation was seconded by another who claimed visionary confirmation.) Shortly thereafter, Lyon claimed a prophetic vision in which the widowed Sarah became his wife. She was on the point of marrying him, when "to the astonishment" of Lyon, her husband showed up hale and hearty and "disannulled the proceedings." After the resulting church trial, Lyon lost his office, though not his membership, for using priestcraft and subterfuge to win a wife.[165]

In their own meetings, both formal and informal, women also exhibited the gift of prophecy, often in conjunction with the gift of tongues. In an early Relief Society meeting, Sarah Cleveland spoke in tongues, and Martha Sessions interpreted her words to be a prediction: "God was well pleased with this Society, that if we would be humble and faithful the Lord would pour out upon the members generally the gift of prophecy." A prophecy immediately followed, proclaiming a long and honored life for Lucy Mack Smith, mother of Joseph. In a subsequent meeting, a Mrs. Chase rose and prophesied.[166]

During the trek west, women "clustered informally to pray, sing, testify, prophesy, and bless."[167] In 1861, Young preached that the duty of the Holy Ghost was "to make prophets and prophetesses and revelators of men and women."[168] A few years later, Fillmore stake president Thomas Callister told the Relief Society women: "This society reminds me of the school of the Prophets and we might almost call you a school of Prophetesses."[169] The next year, Eliza R. Snow, herself renowned among her contemporaries as a prophetess, enjoined the sisters of the church generally to imitate the "devout and steadfast Miriam," "the prophetess, sister of Aaron."[170] Forthsaying more than foretelling may have been implicit in that title; still, the term affirmed at least a limited equivalence in the spiritual powers available to men and women alike.

In public forums, men continued to dominate the gift of prophecy. Heber C. Kimball famously prophesied during Utah's early days of deprivation that one day soon "clothing would be sold in Great Salt Lake City cheaper than it could be bought in St. Louis." Next year the gold rush led waves of passers through to unload spare belongings at bargain prices.[171] At a fast meeting in late July 1854, at which Parley Pratt presided, there was an outpouring of spiritual manifestations. Caroline Crosby recorded, "The good spirit was with us, and rejoiced our hearts exceedingly. Sister Jones spoke in tongues, br Curtis prophesied to Sister McLean, that her husband would yet come into the church, but that she would first have great troubles with him, but her prayers would eventually prevail."[172]

Young pronounced prophecy after prophecy from the pulpit. In 1849 he prophesied "that we would have an abundant crop this year."[173] ("The harvest of 1849 was abundant," reported the *History of Utah*.)[174] In 1851, he "prophesied that the time is near when all the emigration of the Saints from Europe and the East will come by way of . . . California instead of by . . . the Mississippi."[175] (Some, though not much, future European emigration was by sea to Utah via California ports.) At one gathering he cheerily noted that "nearly every man who had spoken during the conference had prophesied, and so it would be if a hundred others were to speak, and he would be glad if all the Lord's people were prophets."[176] Heber C. Kimball was so renowned for his gift in these years that Young called him "my Prophet, and he prophesies for me."[177]

Much prophecy heard in nineteenth-century sermons was of a fairly general nature. John Taylor prophesied "in the name of Jesus Christ" that the kingdom of God would "roll on." "I prophesy that this is only just the beginning, as it were of the great work of the gathering," said Orson Pratt. "I prophesy that any man who will be humble before the Lord . . . shall receive a knowledge from the Almighty that his kingdom has been established in these latter days," proclaimed Lorenzo Snow.[178] Even such generic pronouncements were fading with the dawn of the twentieth century. In the contemporary church, the language of prophesy has been transmuted into the language of testimony. "I testify" rather than "I prophecy" is the standard idiom by which faith is affirmed and doctrine taught from today's pulpits.

Healing

"Great crowds came to him," Matthew records of the Christ, "bringing with them the lame, the maimed, the blind, the mute, and many others. They put them at his feet, and he cured them."[179] At the time of the Great Commission, Jesus prophesied that those who believe would "lay their hands on the sick, and they [would] recover."[180] After Christ's ascension, Peter healed the cripple at the temple gate,[181] Paul raised an invalid to his feet,[182] and Philip cured the possessed, the paralyzed, and the lame.[183] Indeed, in the years to follow, one of the more common spiritual gifts in Christian history was miraculous healing. The history of healing is complicated, as the act has been considered both a spiritual gift and a sacrament. If healing was a gift, it became a gift with prescribed means of employing that gift, unlike the others. And so we find that the medieval church "venerate[d] the anointing of the sick with holy oil."[184] Based on its reading of the epistle of James, with its injunction to anoint the sick "with oil in the name of the Lord," the church made the anointing one of seven sacraments. Assigning healing to an officially circumscribed place in ecclesiastical sacraments performed at the time of imminent death was one way of routinizing a charismatic gift and limiting any miraculous displays—limiting but not eliminating entirely, since the miraculous can never be entirely suppressed.

Because supernatural healing was so often associated with relics and the cult of saints, it came under special suspicion and general condemnation in the Reformation. Even as non-sacramental practice, Luther denies the appropriateness of anointing the sick. "It was a rite of the early church, by which they worked miracles on the sick," he acknowledges, but such a spiritual gift "has long since ceased," along with picking up poisonous serpents without harm.[185] Calvin, too, held that "the gift of healing disappeared with the other miraculous powers which the Lord was pleased to give for a time, that it might render the new preaching of the gospel forever wonderful."[186] The rising tides of anti-Catholicism swept most healing claims and practices away. St. Anne's Well in Buxton, Derbyshire, was renowned for its healing properties. Hardly had the English Reformation commenced before, under Thomas Cromwell's orders, access to the well was barred. Mementos of the miraculous, "the crutches and sticks, and the offerings of the chapel were angrily dismissed as manifestations of 'papist idolatry.'"[187]

Many dissenters freely broke with such cessationism. George Fox, founder of the Quakers, filled his journal with accounts of miraculous healings. After being stoned and beaten near Mansfield-Woodhouse in 1649, he recorded, "The Lord's power soon healed me."[188] His colleague William Dewsbury was similarly beaten to the point of death but was also healed by "the Lord's power."[189] Such episodes could be dismissed as physical resilience, but Fox recorded more dramatic instances as well. On one occasion he encountered a violent, deranged woman being constrained. "In the name of the Lord . . . [he] bid her be quiet and still; and she was so." On another, he spoke words of healing to Richard Myer, who had a crippled arm, which was instantaneously restored to health.[190]

A generation later, the English baronet Richard Bulkeley claimed relief from fevers, kidney stones, and a hernia at the hand of an English follower of the Camisards, John Lacy. Lacy was also reputed to have cured the blindness of one James Jackson.[191] The early eighteenth-century French Prophets were more famous for their flamboyant bodily agitations and pronouncements than for other spiritual gifts—but several were believed to heal. The Camisards influenced the Shakers, who also practiced the gift of healing. Mother Ann Lee was reputed by her followers to miraculously heal by the same "authority and power [as] did Peter and John."[192] But in addition, in early Shakerism, the society espoused a more general access to "mighty works" like miraculous healings, and some converts came to the faith as a consequence of such episodes.[193] One member of that sect claimed to be a former "cripple" who had "been instantly healed through the power of God, through the instrumentality of one of his brethren."[194] Even before the Shaker "Era of Manifestations" (1837–1850s) mentioned above, miraculous healings were frequently reported of Shakers.[195]

As for Wesley, we have seen that he lamented the absence of spiritual gifts and the dangers of "enthusiasm" with equal vigor. Of healing in particular, he was typically circumspect. While acknowledging that "we are not sure there were ever any [miraculous healings] in the world," he also insisted to a correspondent that "this I assuredly know, that if a man born blind is restored to sight by a word, this is not nature, but miracle."[196] Faith healing would be more common in the later Holiness Movement and other late nineteenth-century faith healing currents than in Wesley's era, but numerous contemporary reports appeared in his day. His own experiences included abrupt improvement and strengthening of his health in response to prayer, which he counted a spiritual gift. In one such instance, overcome with fever and pain, he remembered the promise that "signs shall follow them that believe." Calling upon Jesus, his "pain vanished away, the fever left me; my bodily strength returned; and for many weeks I felt neither weakness nor pain."[197] Indeed, he was open enough to these spiritual interventions that he reserved space "in his journals and the *Arminian Magazine* for faith healing and reports of miraculous cures."[198]

Among Primitive Methodists who broke off from Wesleyanism in England, miraculous healing was a commonplace. James Crawfoot preached "the significance of dreams, and the importance of healing, together with the descending presence of God." His associate Hugh Bourne reported a rather nondescript 1810 healing of an ailing woman but also some of the "power encounters" of Crawfoot, like his "astonishing" healing of a woman severely injured in a horse- and cart-accident.[199] In the first decades of the nineteenth century, evangelicals in Scotland also recorded various instances of miraculous healing. (One preacher possessed of "supernatural power" commanded a Scottish invalid by letter "to rise and walk," whereupon by "a mighty power" she was "made to stand upon my feet, leap and walk, sing and rejoice.")[200] In America, marginalization, distrust of white doctors, and the syncretic blend of Christianity "with African religious and magical systems" led to an African American tradition of spiritual healing as well, though it has been little excavated.[201]

HEALING IN MORMONISM

In the LDS faith, healing emerged very quickly as a spiritual gift, heralded by missionaries especially as evidence of divine authority undergirding the restored church. The contemporary practice was explicitly approved by a revelation to Joseph Smith in the church's first year, which indicated that under limited circumstances, God could command disciples to perform miracles, including "healing the sick."[202] Less dramatically, the Saints were commanded months later to minister to the sick by the prayer of faith, but in a manner more reminiscent of Catholic extreme unction of the dying than the New Testament gift of healing. "And whosoever among you are sick," the revelation read, "*and have not faith to be healed*, but believe, shall be nourished with all tenderness, with herbs and mild food.... And the elders of the church, two or more, shall be called, and shall pray for and lay their hands upon them in my name; and if they die they shall die unto me, and if they live they shall live unto me."[203]

The next month, a pronouncement reaffirmed the Pauline gifts of First Corinthians, indicating that they should be sought and would be given "for the benefit of those who love me & keep all my commandments," and "not for a sign that he may consume it upon his lusts."[204] Both healing and the faith to be healed were included in the catalogue of gifts to expect. A few weeks later, Parley Pratt recorded that Chloe Smith, a Kirtland convert, had long lingered with fever, apparently "on the point of death." He and Smith "kneeled down and prayed vocally all around, each in turn; after which President Smith arose, went to the bedside, took her by the hand, and said with a loud voice, 'in the name of Jesus Christ arise and walk!' She immediately arose and ... from that minute was perfectly restored to health."[205] Pratt later ministered to a young widow suffering from "inflammation in the eyes," which had left her "totally blind." "She threw off her bandages," he related, "with eyes as well and as bright as any other person's."[206] A Disciple of Christ historian related how Ezra Booth, a Methodist preacher, visited Smith at his house in Kirtland in 1831, accompanied by an invalid friend, Mrs. Johnson. "Someone said: 'Here is Mrs. Johnson with a lame arm; has God given any power to men on the earth to cure her?' A few moments later, ... Smith rose, and walking across the room, taking Mrs. Johnson by the hand, said in the most solemn and impressive manner: 'Woman, in the name of Jesus Christ, I command thee to be whole'; and immediately left the room. . . . Mrs. Johnson at once lifted [her rheumatic arm] with ease."[207]

Parley Pratt later claimed he had "seen some hundreds of sick healed in the name of Jesus, in almost every country where the Saints have planted the truth."[208] In the mid-nineteenth century, the church newspaper regularly published a column reporting on recent healings. "Several Cases of Miraculous Healing by the Power of God" was the heading of one such article.[209] The report included some twenty recent cases, ranging from dislocated bones and tumors to stroke, consumption, and cholera. Fifty years later, the church still felt that public sharing of spiritual gifts was a boon to the faith, and another series of miraculous healings appeared in response to a readership ready to share their stories. In the *Juvenile Instructor*, a magazine for LDS children, a special column "For Our Little Folks" heralded hundreds of accounts over a fifteen-year period.[210]

Some accounts rivaled New Testament miracle stories. In 1844, a Mormon elder wrote how, following his daughter's fatal accident, he "placed [his] hands upon her" and called out, "Lord, heal my child!" whereupon "in one moment she shewed signs of life."[211] Sometimes, such miraculous healings could be too much even for the Mormon faithful to believe. Alfred Young and his brother evangelized in Tennessee in the early 1840s. They administered to a man whose death earlier that day was being mourned by his family. Commanding him three times to breathe, Young records that "immediately the lungs of the man began to inhale the air. He opened his eyes and again lived." Arriving soon thereafter in Nauvoo, the Young brothers were surprised to find that John D. Lee had accused them of working works "of the devil." Called before the high council, they were disfellowshipped for "acting under evil influence," the leaders disbelieving that "two ordinary elders like us could have such great power from God as to raise the dead." Hearing their story, Hyrum Smith published an exoneration of the two and restored them to fellowship, saying their labors were "of God."[212]

Healing is both the most difficult spiritual gift to deny, since it is so clearly enjoined in the New Testament (and Old) and bears such undeniable value in a suffering world, and the easiest to challenge, since it is the most susceptible to disproof. Accordingly, healing was both frequently claimed in early Mormonism and frequently derided. So on the one hand, as Christopher Jones has written, it was "the quest for spiritual gifts, especially the gift of healing, and a belief in visions, miracles, and prophecy that led many unsatisfied Methodists to embrace Mormonism."[213] On the other, we find an Ohio critic who responded to the many reports of Mormon miracles by claiming that "whenever any [healing] miracle fails, they have a convenient salve at hand to account for the failure; that is the want of faith."[214] "The greatest misfortune of those gentlemen of healing notoriety," chimed in another anti-Mormon pamphlet, "is that they do their work in such a bungling manner: we first hear that their patients are a little better; then that they get worse again; after awhile that they are able to be about."[215]

After the introduction of anointing in Kirtland Temple ceremonies, the practice of anointing the sick with oil, in Jamesian fashion, emerged. Still, sacramentalism did not preclude miraculous manifestations, and some healings persisted independent of any priesthood ordinance. For example, Smith's most famous episode of healing, during a wave of killing infection in July 1839, was described by Wilford Woodruff: "Joseph was in Montrose & it was a day of Gods power. There was many Sick among the Saints on both sides of the river & Joseph went through the midst of them taking them by the hand & in a loud voice Commanding them in the name of Jesus Christ to arise from their beds & be made whole & they leaped from their beds made whole by the power of God.' "[216] Women frequently employed the gift of healing as well—using oil in the same way as their male counterparts—and with full approbation of the leadership.

From the beginning, women had been as conspicuous as men in exhibiting the spiritual gifts like speaking and singing in tongues, so healing would be no exception. As we saw, early Mormons saw a strong connection between the priesthood and the exercise of spiritual gifts, so Smith's injunction to the Relief Society women—"these signs, such as healing the sick, casting out devils &c. should follow all that believe whether male or female"[217]—further implied a nebulous line between male priesthood and female prerogatives. To the Relief Society, Smith said, "Respecting the female laying on hands . . . there could be no devils in it if God gave his sanction by healing—that there could be no more sin in any female laying hands on the sick than in wetting the face with water."[218] Elizabeth Ann Whitney, a counselor to Emma Smith, recalled that she was thereafter "ordained and set apart under the hand of Joseph Smith the Prophet to administer to the sick. . . . Several other sisters were also ordained and set apart to administer in these holy ordinances."[219] One form such healing rituals took was the blessing of women prior to childbirth—but ministrations to sick and infirm of all ages and both genders were common. Instances of women blessing each other, children, and even men proliferate in the early Mormon church.[220]

Men saw women's ritual healing as a natural extension of their long-standing role as midwives and caregivers. Brigham Young himself had preached that he desired a wife "that can take care of my children when I am away, who can pray, lay on hands, anoint with oil, and baffle the enemy; and this is a spiritual wife."[221] Once in their western refuge, Young reaffirmed the right of women to act as healers, though within a circumscribed stewardship. "It is the privilege of a mother to have faith and administer to her child; this she can do herself, as well as sending for the Elders to have the benefit of their faith."[222] Women continued to perform washings and anointings of other women "preparatory to their confinement" into the twentieth century. The First Presidency of the church in 1914 approved such actions, adding that sisters "have the same right to administer to sick children as to adults, and may anoint and lay hands upon them in faith." By this time, however, the Presidency was noting that elders have the authority to "seal" the blessing, while sisters should only "confirm" it.[223] Still, women performed healings into the 1940s, ministering principally to their own families. At that point, Joseph Fielding Smith directed the president of the women's church organization that "it is far better for us to . . . send for the Elders of the Church to come and administer to the sick and afflicted."[224]

Throughout LDS history, members continued to find miraculous healings a strength to believers and a sign to doubters. Women no longer participate in healings, and with the demise of publicized charismatic manifestations in general, healing has almost entirely assumed the status of a priesthood ordinance rather than a spiritual gift.

Tongues

Two types of tongues find warrant in the New Testament: one is described in the book of Acts, and one in Paul's writings. They could be read as different reports of the same phenomenon, or, as one authority writes, "as witnesses to a diversity of practice as well as understanding."[225] Luke's account suggests that the experience of suddenly speaking a new language, as the apostles did on the day of Pentecost, has a pragmatic application insofar as foreigners can hear the gospel in their own language: "Divided tongues, as of fire, appeared among them, and a tongue rested on each of them. All of them were filled with the Holy Spirit and began to speak in other languages, as the Spirit gave them ability. Now there were devout Jews from every nation under heaven living in Jerusalem. And at this sound the crowd gathered and was bewildered, because each one heard them speaking in the native language of each. Amazed and astonished, they asked, 'Are not all these who are speaking Galileans? And how is it that we hear, each of us, in our own native language?' "[226] Complicating this picture are a few details: the experience is clearly ecstatic or supernatural ("divided tongues, as of fire"); and some in the audience hear what seems to them a drunken cacophony ("they are filled with new wine").[227] Nevertheless, the fact that meaningful communication is achieved across linguistic divides leads some to classify this particular spiritual gift as *xenoglossia* (from "foreign language" or "strange tongue" in Greek).

By contrast, Paul, in his letters, emphasizes a mode of speaking in tongues that is without inherent meaning but is a conspicuous sign of the Spirit. What is produced in this instance is not any known language. Accordingly, Paul writes, persons employing this gift of *glossolalia* (literally "talking tongues," but meaning speech that has no known speakers) "do not speak to other people but to God"; as a consequence, "how will anyone know what is being said?"[228] And indeed, many studies of glossolalia have confirmed that what is uttered in this ecstatic manifestation is not part of any recognizable language system.[229] In the New Testament, new converts in particular "speak in tongues," as with Gentile converts in Acts 10:46, and again with disciples whom Paul baptizes in Acts 19:6. At the same time, another spiritual gift Paul relates to this variety of speaking in tongues is the gift of interpretation. Those who speak in tongues should pray for the power to interpret their utterances, he admonishes, or keep silent unless another is present to do the interpreting.[230]

With the Reformation, resistance to charismatic gifts could be emphatic in the case of tongues. Anglicans declared in their Thirty-Nine Articles that speaking in tongues in a worship service was "plainly repugnant to the word of God and the custom of the primitive church."[231] Luther was only slightly muted in his opposition. He wrote a contemporary that "whoever comes forward, and wants to read, teach, or preach, and yet speaks with tongues, that is, speaks Latin instead of German, or some unknown language, he is to be silent and preach to himself alone. For no one can hear it or understand it, and no one can get any benefit from it." He did, however, allow some leeway: "Or if he should speak with tongues, he ought, in addition, to put what he says into German, or interpret it in one way or another, so that the congregation may understand it."[232]

In the early eighteenth century, John Lacy, a follower of the French Prophets, frequently lapsed into Latin pronouncements. Latin may have been a tongue of choice, since even the unlettered European populace of the age heard it spoken every mass and had some familiarity with its sound and rhythms. His "prophecy in a pompous Latin stile" failed to impress a visiting Earl of Shaftesbury; however, even knowing Lacy had had a smattering of Latin as a schoolboy, two visiting scholars interrogated him following an ecstatic outburst, and they pronounced it a credible example of the gift of tongues.[233] The Shakers, whose origins some scholars have traced to the French Prophets,[234] also exercised the gift of tongues. The uneducated Mother Ann Lee was reputed to speak a dozen languages (other reports put the number at seventy-two), some known and some unknown.[235] Convert Thomas Brown witnessed one Shaker demonstration when an inhabitant of the Mt. Lebanon village spoke in an unknown tongue "with much earnestness," though no one translated.[236] Shaker Mary Hocknell also reported "many operations by the power of God, and wonderful gifts [such as] speaking unknown tongues."[237] Primitive Methodists, an offshoot of the Wesleyan church, taught that "speaking with tongues was the first sign that [early Christians] were filled with the Holy Ghost." Accordingly, "the church ought to be able now to speak with tongues."²³⁸ And indeed, the church gave such emphasis to "the holy possession of the spirit through speaking in tongues" that the members soon became known as "Ranters."²³⁹

Scottish and English evangelicals also reported many instances of speaking in tongues in these same years of the early nineteenth century. The Irvingites were practicing the gift, preaching that "tongues are still in the Church and ought properly to belong to it."²⁴⁰ A Scottish girl, Mary Campbell, spoke in unknown tongues for two days following a miraculous 1830 healing, bringing "several of the good people from Edinburgh . . . to investigate." Days later, at Port-Glasgow, a "young James Macdonald stared suddenly up and spoke the unknown tongue." Another letter writer describes other meetings where "strange words . . . were given."²⁴¹ Prophesying was added to healing and tongues, and soon "the whole religious world of Scotland was stirred by those extraordinary happenings," notes one historian.²⁴²

TONGUES IN MORMONISM

Brigham Young recorded in his history that, a few weeks after his April 1832 baptism, during a simple family prayer in Heber Kimball's home, one "Alpheus Gifford commenced speaking in tongues. Soon," he added, "the Spirit came on me, and I spoke in tongues." That November, Young journeyed to Kirtland, Ohio, to meet Smith. In the evening of his introduction, a small group convened, and Smith asked Young to pray. "In my prayer," he recorded, "I spoke in tongues." In response to questions about what the group had witnessed, Smith asserted that what they heard "was the pure Adamic language," and that "it is of God."²⁴³

As for Smith, he later reported that, on the same occasion, he "received the gift myself."²⁴⁴ It may have been Smith's first exposure to speaking in tongues, but other Mormons—in addition to Young—had already reported experiencing the gift. B. H. Roberts reported that "the gift of tongues . . . was first exercised in one of the Pennsylvania branches; next at Mendon . . . ; then in the branches between Mendon and Kirtland. . . . Shortly afterwards it was a gift quite generally exercised by the Saints in Ohio."²⁴⁵ "In spring 1831," Alpheus Gifford noted of his labors in Pennsylvania, that "the gifts of the Gospel were enjoyed by many; signs following those that believed, devils were cast out; the sick were healed; many prophesied; some spake with new tongues; while others interpreted the same."²⁴⁶ "And it came to pass," wrote John Whitmer in his history of the early Mormon church, "that in the fall of 1832, the disciples in Ohio received the gift of tongues, and in June, 1833, we received the gift of tongues in Zion [Missouri]."²⁴⁷

A sense of the overall prevalence of glossolalia in these early years of Mormonism is evident in missionary Moses Nickerson's report from Canada at the end of 1833: "There are thirty four members attached to the Church at Mount Pleasant, all of whom appear to live up to their profession, five of whom have spoken in tongues, and three sing in tongues."[248] Striking a balance between edifying manifestations and indecorous excess was not easy, and the church struggled for a middle ground. Also in 1833, one local leader urged Salmon Gee to "remember the exhortation which I gave you while I was yet present with you, to beware of delusive spirits. I rejoice that our Heavenly Father hath blessed you greatly, as He also has me, in enabling me to speak the praises of God and the mysteries of the kingdom in other tongues according to promise; and this without throwing me down or wallowing me on the ground, or anything unbecoming. . . . Therefore . . . I command Brother Thomas King, (as though I were present), to cease from your diabolical acts of enthusiasm."[249] In another case, the high council dealt with a whole branch of the church that "believed that they received the word of the Lord by the gift of tongues" and considered the glossolalia of Sylvester Hulet and Sally Crandall more reliable than Smith's teachings. "The devil deceived them," declared the council. "The gift of tongues is so often made use of by Satan to deceive the Saints," noted the chronicler.[250]

By 1834, Smith was urging caution with regard to tongues. "Brother Joseph then proceeded to give an explanation of the gift of tongues: that it was particularly instituted for the preaching of the Gospel to other nations and languages, but it was not given for the government of the Church."[251] With those cautions expressed, the gift continued. Young spoke in tongues three times at the dedication of the Kirtland Temple in 1836—on at least one of those occasions delivering a whole sermon.[252] In early July, Mary Fielding described a church service full of reconciliation and spiritual outpouring; "the Spirit & power of God rested down upon us in a remarkable manner many spake in tongues & others prophesied & interpreted. It has been said by many who have lived in Kirtland a great while, that such a time of love & refreshing has never been known." Descriptions of bright lights, angels, and tongue-speaking recalled the temple dedication earlier that year.[253] Often, new converts experienced the gift subsequent to baptism or ordination. This was the case with Brigham Young, noted above, and with Alfred Young, who recorded that in 1841, "in the evening after my ordination there was a meeting of the branch at my brother's house. For the first time I was called upon to preach and spoke for some time in tongues and my brother gave the interpretation."[254]

Smith repeated his caution in 1839, distinguishing the useful xenoglossia from the more sensationalistic glossolalia: "Tongues were given for the purpose of preaching among those whose language is not understood. . . . Any man that has the Holy Ghost, can speak of the things of God in his own tongue."[255] Apparently, Smith's caution did not cross the Atlantic. From England Pratt claimed, doubtless with some hyperbole, that "I have seen and heard thousands of men and women speak in tongues and interpret them."[256] In 1840, Elizabeth Brotherton read a Latter-day Saint pamphlet "which told of a Prophet being raised up and of angels appearing that the true gospel was restored in the fullness with all its gifts and blessings." Brigham Young baptized her on September 4, 1840. Heber Kimball blessed her that she "should receive the gift of tongues which I did that night."[257]

That same year, William Clayton recorded five occasions of speaking in tongues (and one who "almost got the gift of tongues") within a span of a few weeks in the north of England.[258] A few months later, Thomas Taylor "of the Mason Street Sawmills" made hay out of a catastrophic public relations ploy that gave the Mormons substantial notoriety. In October 1840, Taylor challenged a young English convert, James Mahon, to demonstrate the gift of tongues before a panel of judges at a public meeting. Foolishly agreeing, Mahon was unable to interpret Hebrew when read to him. According to the *Annals of Manchester*, Mahon "then spoke what he declared to be Hebrew, but the teacher of languages, who was the referee, declared that there was not a word of Hebrew in his jargon."[259] Taylor gleefully wrote up the fiasco.

In the years after the Taylor pamphlet, Smith continued his cautionary note. To the women's Relief Society, he said in April 1842, "If you have a matter to reveal, let it be in your own tongue; do not indulge too much in the exercise of the gift of tongues, or the devil will take advantage of the innocent and unwary. You may speak in tongues for your own comfort, but I lay this down for a rule, that if anything is taught by the gift of tongues, it is not to be received for doctrine."[260] He repeated the counsel in print weeks later: "The gift of tongues is the smallest gift perhaps of the whole, and yet it is one that is the most sought after. . . . Be not so curious about tongues, do not speak in tongues except there be an interpreter present; the ultimate design of tongues is to speak to foreigners, and if persons are very anxious to display their intelligence, let them speak to such in their own tongues. The gifts of God are all useful in their place, but when they are applied to that which God does not intend, they prove an injury, a snare and a curse instead of a blessing."[261] Perhaps his warning was directed only at the women who were employing the gift, for minutes of the Kirtland Temple dedication mention in passing that "Elder B. Young, one of the Twelve, gave a short address in tongues; Elder D. W. Patten interpreted and gave a short exhortation in tongues himself."[262]

Dubious claims to glossolalia arose in Utah as well, where the task of sifting the legitimate from the merely enthusiastic challenged church leadership. John Gunnison reported the case of a woman who sprang up and spoke "in tongues" as follows—"Melai, Meli, Melee," which was immediately translated into the vernacular by a waggish young man, who first observed that he felt "the gift of interpretation of tongues" sorely pressing upon him, and that she said in unknown words to herself, "my leg, my thigh, my knee," For this he was called before the council, but he stoutly persisted in his "interpretation" being according to "the spirit," and they let him off with an admonition.[263]

Young persisted in his gift for years. (In 1846, Young recorded that he "conversed with Elder Kimball in an unknown tongue.")[264] So did Mormon women, as Young recognized from the pulpit. In an 1855 sermon, he spoke approvingly of "women present who have spoken in tongues."[265] A few years later, Heber C. Kimball noted their practice of "having your little circles of women come together," to bless and prophecy. Often, he continued, "one of you can talk in tongues and pour out your souls to God, and then one interpret; that is the course you take, and it is all right: go ahead, and God bless you and multiply blessings on you."[266] Yet even as he spoke, Young was noting that a charismatic age had all but passed. "Years ago," he reminisced, "in this Church . . . when quite young boys or girls would get up and speak in tongues, and others interpret." Even when such gifts were now manifest, he lamented, they were used with lesser intent and to lesser purpose.[267] Near the end of his life, he consoled an audience feeling the distance from Pentecost: "Now, to our experience again. Suppose you obey the ordinances of the Gospel, and do not speak in tongues to-day, never mind that. . . . On the Day of Pentecost there was special need for it."[268]

The new direction was not just a decline in spiritual gifts but a redirection in the understanding of tongues in particular. Smith, who had spoken more by way of warning than encouragement of glossolalia, had been unqualified in his approval of xenoglossia. As editor of the *Times and Seasons*, he wrote that the "ultimate design" of tongues was "to speak to foreigners."[269] One unique form of Mormon tongue-speaking had foreshadowed such a use. Other than the Adamic tongue ("Eve's tongue," insisted Eliza Snow),[270] Indian languages were the most commonly claimed variety of the gift. Given the paramount importance the Book of Mormon assigned to Native Americans in its version of providential history, the Mormons anticipated a great missionary work was to be conducted among the various tribes.

As late as mid-century, Young was still seeing the connection: he put women on notice that those who had spoken in tongues were likely candidates for such mission work "among the Lamanites."[271] Of the men, he said, he had heard them "speak in tongues and prophecy and say I have got to go and teach the Lamanites."[272] Yet again, he reminded a congregation, "How many times have you heard it spoken in tongues and prophesied of in days past and said that you should yet go and teach the Lamanites?"[273] By the 1870s, the dream of converting the Lamanites had taken a back seat to a growing, international missionary effort. And Young announced a more or less formal reorientation of the spiritual gift of tongues to coincide with that: "Let me say here, to the Latter-day Saints, it is frequently asked by our brethren,

'Why do not the people speak with tongues?' We do, and we speak with tongues that you can understand."[274]

An early example of tongues understood as xenoglossia in the nineteenth-century church comes from Joseph F. Smith. Called to a Hawaiian mission in 1854, he recorded, "I sought earnestly the gift of tongues, and by this gift and by study, in a hundred days after landing upon those islands I could talk to the people in their language as I now talk to you in my native tongue."[275] With the coming of the new century, a more concerted effort from the leadership effectively put the brakes on glossolalia and cast xenoglossia as a practical aid to missionaries. A church periodical in 1901 declared the gift "most benefi-cial when exercised by humble Elders in the missionary fields," and President Joseph F. Smith confirmed that principle in 1906.[276] Heber J. Grant and David O. McKay both affirmed or personally experienced the ministerial benefits of sudden competence in a foreign tongue, and by mid-century, the gift of speak-ing in tongues had essentially been delimited to the Holy Ghost's special aid to those in the mission field. "Every missionary who goes forth to teach the gospel in a foreign language," wrote Joseph Fielding Smith in 1957, "if he is prayerful and faithful, received this gift."[277]

Singing in Tongues

Speaking in tongues could be disconcerting and highly suspicious to the doubt-ing observer. Melody makes all things more palatable. And so, writes Melvin Butler, "churchgoers who deemed tongue-speaking to be strange and unortho-dox were more willing to embrace tongue-singing."[278] Marginally more willing, perhaps, since until the advent of modern Pentecostalism it has been limited almost entirely to small outliers of orthodoxy. The Albigenses practiced the gift in twelfth-century France, and it appeared occasionally among later Irvingites and Shakers.[279]

Thomas Brown, a Shaker convert, records an episode in 1800 when in an informal setting, an elderly Shaker closed his eyes and began to sing in an unknown tongue, which some present said was Hebrew. After thirty minutes of singing, he concluded with the announcement that he had sung "one of the songs of Zion."[280] It is not clear if this practice is what a Shaker intimated to a visitor when he said, "Though we sing vocally, we seldom sing words, or a composition of words. Our singing is that which St John heard, that no man could understand but those who were redeemed."[281]

Perhaps the first Mormon to sing in tongues was Lyman Wight, who abruptly burst into song "in another tongue" in an 1831 Kirtland meeting over which he was presiding.[282] In one 1833 meeting of the Missouri High Council, "a hymn [was] sung by Br W W Phelps in tongues and interpreted by Lyman [Wight] . . . concerning the travelling of the Nephites their toils troubles & tribulations &c."[283] Brigham Young himself could sing as well as speak in tongues when he felt so moved. At a Kirtland High Council meeting in 1835, "Elder Brigham Young arose and in the Spirit of God sung a song of Zion in a foreign tongue."[284] Benjamin Brown recorded an occasion in which a brother in a New York meeting sang in tongues, "a low, mournful strain," which upon being interpreted apprised those present of the state of their persecuted co-religionists in Missouri.[285] One episode of tongue singing was initially approved as a revelation and recorded as such. Elaborating an Enochian text Smith had recently produced, David Patten sang a text on the subject in tongues. In this revelation (entered into the "Revelation Book" but never canonized), which was interpreted by Sidney Rigdon and recorded in the hand of Frederick G. Williams,[286] Enoch "saw the beginning the ending of man he saw the time when Adam his father was made and he saw that he was in eternity before a grain of dust in the balance was weighed he saw that he emanated and came down from God."[287]

More commonly, perhaps, it was women who did the tongue-singing. Smith had even blessed one sister, Elizabeth Ann Whitney, with that particular gift.[288] Lucy Smith rendered one such tongue-singing as "Moroni's Lament," based on the Book of Mormon prophet's grief at his people's apocalyptic destruction:

> I have no home, where shall I go?
> While here I'm left to weep below
> My heart is pained, my friends are gone,
> And here I'm left on earth to mourn.[289]

A number of such tongue-singing episodes resulted in early Mormon hymns. Not surprisingly, Book of Mormon themes dominated the charismatic genre.

William Clayton noted of one English sister that she "began in her sleep to sing in tongues. She spake and sung in about 7 languages occupying about 2 hours."[290] Shortly after Smith's death, Elizabeth Ann Whitney, attending a meeting in the Nauvoo Temple, "sang a beautiful song of Zion in tongues. The interpretation was given by her husband, Bishop Whitney, and me, it related to our efforts to build this house."[291] Louisa Barnes Pratt recorded that at one prayer meeting, "the sisters laid their hands up on my head and blessed me in a strange language. It was a prophetic song. Mrs. E. B. Whitney was interpreter. She said that I should have health, and go to the valleys of the mountains, and there meet my companion and be joyful."[292] On June 16, 1847, Eliza Snow visited the Pratt family and "sang a song of Zion" in tongues, which another woman interpreted.[293] Sadly, lacking any apparent evangelizing usefulness, tongue-singing did not survive the transition in the LDS church from a charismatic gift to enhanced language-learning.

Discernment

Among the spiritual gifts enumerated by Paul, the discernment of spirits is perhaps the most enigmatic. Healing and tongues and prophesying are fairly self-explanatory, but discernment of spirits is less clear of meaning. Origen may have been the first to gloss the reference to discernment in Paul's catalogue of spiritual gifts, reading it in the light of John's admonition to "test the spirits, if they are from God."[294] Paul elsewhere notes that Satan can appear as an "angel of light."[295] Mindful of the story of Abraham entertaining angels who appear as simple guests,[296] the author of Hebrews notes that one might at any time be entertaining "angels without knowing it."[297] In this context of duplicitous devils and veiled angels, the ability to discern the origin of visiting spirits makes great sense. Paul also provided grounds for a more prosaic reading of the gift, when he warned early Christians about "wolves" who would enter the flock, including "wicked people" and "imposters" who would "deceive" others, leading disciples astray.[298] In a post-apostolic age, it became natural, therefore, to read the discernment of spirits as pertaining, in the words of one cleric, to the need to protect the church from "persons from whom great mischiefs should arise to it."[299]

The founder of the Jesuits read yet another meaning into the gift. Thoughts, he wrote, are of three kinds: one is "my own, . . . one from the good spirit and the other from the evil one." Discernment, aided by practical rules he provided, were essential for "perceiving and understanding to some degree the different movements that are produced in the soul—the good, that they may be accepted; the bad, that they may be rejected."[300] John Wesley believed in the literal existence of myriad demons as well as angels, and he sermonized on the wiles of the former and the subtlety of the latter, and the difficulty of detecting their respective operations. He warned, "We must not expect" them to appear "in visible shape," or to operate "in such a manner that we may clearly distinguish their working from the workings of our own minds"—something "exceeding difficult."[301] And he cautioned against the danger of imputing their influence to the wrong sources, given their respective powers to bless, preserve, deceive, and destroy. Hence, discernment and knowledge of "what God has revealed concerning them" can prevent the demons from gaining "advantage over us."[302]

Given not just Mormonism's Pentecostal beginnings but its thoroughgoing re-enchantment of the cosmos, its conflation of spirit and matter, angels and humans, heavenly and earthly, it is no surprise that Mormon reading of the gift of discernment encompassed a range of readings. And so we find an early revelation to Smith that details, in precise terms, how to distinguish angels, the spirits of just men made perfect, and the devil or his minions masquerading as the former.[303] Not their influence, but their actual identification as angels, spirits, or devils appearing in vision seems to be the point of this gift in this case. That revelation was not generally disseminated, however, and it was considered by Smith to be an esoteric teaching associated with temple ritual as it was unfolding in Nauvoo.[304]

More general application of the gift of discernment was quick in coming. In a universe where Satan is literal and is, with his myriad followers, active in "turning hearts from truth," inciting persecutors' "hearts to anger," "seeking to destroy souls," laying "cunning plan[s]," and placing devious thoughts "into [human] hearts," the difference between literal appearings of evil spirits and subtle machinations of those spirits fades to insignificance; discernment is equally vital in both cases.[305] And so Smith considered it "an imperative duty devolving upon me to say something in relation to the spirits by which men are actuated"—literal spirits as he believed. Many false spirits had "gone forth into the world," and it required "intelligence which God alone could impart to detect false spirits."[306] Mormons especially needed the gift of discernment to detect the "false spirits that so frequently are made manifest among the Latter-Day Saints." As Smith said of his own gift rather matter-of-factly, "The way he knew in whom to confide, [was] God told him in whom he might place confidence."[307]

For Young, too, discernment was a spiritual gift for identifying the source of the agencies and powers operating in the world. The Saints "must have the spirit by which the dead are raised, by which the sick are healed, and the eyes of the blind opened, or they cannot tell whether [works are] done by the power of God or the power of the devil, or whether there is a mist over their own eyes."[308] He later elaborated, "We know that there are many delusive spirits, and unless the Latter-day Saints live to their privileges, and enjoy the spirit of the holy Gospel, they cannot discern between those who serve God and those who serve Him not."[309] Among all gifts of the spirit, discernment is the least liable to enthusiastic excess. As such, teachings on the subject have varied little down to the present day. If tongues are the gift least to be sought, Joseph F. Smith counseled the Saints in 1904, that given the modern need for "peculiar wisdom and understanding," all saints should "seek the gift of discernment."[310]

Discernment is a gift with particular relevance to priesthood leaders, especially bishops and stake presidents who must serve as judges in Israel, extend myriad callings, and be shepherds to their people. Orson Hyde said that "it is given to the presiding officer to discern all things, and tell a man whether he is on the track or not."[311] More recently, Russell M. Nelson taught that bishops are "entitled to that gift as they face the task of seeking out the poor and caring for the needy" and traces such a focus back to President John Taylor.[312] Orson Pratt explained that the leadership needed the capacity to discern other spiritual gifts, in order to function effectively in administering the kingdom. For these reasons, Smith taught that "the gift of discerning spirits will be given to the Presiding Elder."[313] Joshua Mattson finds that the same principle has been taught by Harold B. Lee, Spencer Kimball, and Boyd Packer in the modern church.[314]

Exorcism

If discernment is the most subtle gift in its operation, exorcism may be the most dramatic. It would appear to be central to the purposes of the evangelist known as Mark that the first named miracle Christ performs is to exorcise a demon.[315] His lordship over all creation and his power over Satan and his minions in particular could find no better representation than in formal confrontations where Jesus triumphs and the forces of darkness are expelled. And so, too, the bestowal of just such power and authority upon the church was evident in his commissioning of the twelve and then the seventy to "cast out" devils and "unclean spirits."[316] Not surprisingly, then, the early Christian church made the exorcist into an office and filled its ranks abundantly. Two centuries after Christ's death, one report put the number of "exorcists and lectors" at fifty-two in the church at Rome alone.[317] At the Council of Chalcedon in 451, exorcists were reminded to "receive and commit to memory" the rites prescribed for exorcism in "the little book" they were provided.[318]

One historian notes that "despite Luther's use of them, the Protestant churches soon decided that exorcisms were superstitious, like consecrations, blessings, and holy water." Accordingly, "the Anglican church abolished the office of exorcist in 1550."[319] Actually, by then (in 1536), Luther had also decided that though the devil was real enough, in the case of possession he "must in turn be ridiculed and derided, but he must not be attacked with any exorcisms . . . for he laughs at all these things with diabolical scorn."[320] Calvin agreed that exorcism was a fraudulent practice, with demons more likely to possess the exorcist than the alleged victim.[321] Anglican Archbishop Tillotson was willing to acknowledge that the power to cast out demons "remained after the other miraculous Gifts ceased," but with the Christianizing of the world, it too "ceased, there being no further occasion for it." At least, "we have long been without any [cases] of undoubted Evidence."[322]

Because of the close association of demonic possession with witchcraft, the decline in Salem-type scenarios after 1700 meant the decline of allegations of possession.[323] In the post-Enlightenment world, writers not only shunned the idea of literal possession but increasingly read such biblical accounts through a skeptical lens. Hugh Farmer argued—rather implausibly in light of Jesus's pronouncements—that "the doctrine of possession" did not "ever receive the sanction of any of the prophets either of the Old or New Testament."[324] William Ashdowne believed that any biblical accounts of demonic expulsion "must be attributed to the mistaken opinion [New Testament] writers had concerning such a being, and his power over men."[325] He was responding to William Worthington's *Impartial Enquiry into the case of the Gospel Demoniacks*, written to "determine the controversy concerning them with precision."[326]

Worthington was one of several Christian writers fighting a rearguard action on the subject, trying to hold the line against encroaching skepticism. He found the biblical precedent unambiguous: the eyewitness "facts, thus attested, circumstanced, guarded, and safely conveyed down, . . . have all the requisite marks of historical credibility."[327] But he stops short of condoning present-day exorcism, arguing that the power of evil spirits is "checked, and overruled, by the supreme power of . . . our Almighty Creator," though they continue in the world, "incessantly employed in projecting and working the destruction of mankind."[328]

Thomas Church joined the fray in 1737, "vindicating," as his title put it, "the literal sense of the Demoniacks in the New Testament." The problem, as he acknowledged, was in vindicating their activities in Roman Palestine while explaining their absence in eighteenth-century England. Perhaps, he ventured, they are absent in the present era much as smallpox passed over the Grecian empire. Alternately, he suggested, invoking one Dr. Henry's argument, "there may be many such [possessions] at this Day," lurking under the guise of "many of those Diseases, which afflict Mankind."[329] In Germany, Pietists were conducting "a large number of exorcisms,"[330] and in spite of modern hesitancy to embrace the starkest supernaturalism of evil entities at work in the cosmos, both the scriptural record and persistent reports of demonic possession kept the issue alive in the Atlantic world of the nineteenth century.

John Wesley maintained a careful neutrality on the subject, though he confessed to a physician his suspicion that "some lunatics are really demoniacs." "Millions of spiritual creatures walk the earth unseen," he quoted Hesiod approvingly, while suggesting that the fallen angels, like their heavenly counterparts, have had 6,000 years to sharpen their infernal skills.[331] Here he was apparently accepting the details surrounding the celebrated case of one "George Lukins of Bristol," allegedly possessed of seven devils. Since he was apparently a dissenter, "the ceremony of exorcising him was conducted by five Ministers, who were not of the Established Church" (they were actually Methodist), noted the *Gentleman's Magazine*, one of many to report the case.[332]

Reverend Joseph Easterbrook, who conducted the 1788 exorcism, published an account "under J. Wesley's patronage" in the *Methodist Magazine*, concluding that his narrative "will by many be doubted; for this is the day of skepticism." However, he warned, "he who is altogether a skeptic upon this subject, is not far from sitting in judgment upon the Bible itself."[333] In the aftermath of the Lukins episode, in places such as Bristol, "Methodists conducted many exorcisms during their revival meet-ings,"[334] and disciples of their offshoot, the Primitive Methodists, "practiced exor-cism energetically and without a blush," reports one historian.[335]

While some affirmed demonic possession and others persisted in interpreting biblical devils and evil spirits as symbols of "the spirit of opposition to Jesus,"[336] some tried to remain above the fray. The influential Charles Buck gave the reader "the argument on both sides" so "that the reader may form [an independent] judg-ment."[337] He concluded, however, that "not the caution of philosophy, but the pride of reason" was the source of opposition to belief in demons.[338] Just the same, he relegates the ritual of exorcism to "the superstition of the church of Rome."[339] In the face of Protestant protests and the contempt of modern worldviews, the Catholic Church has steadfastly resisted any allegorizing or modernizing or relegation to antiquity of demonic possession. As recently as 2010, American bishops sponsored a conference on "how to conduct exorcisms," and more than a hundred bishops and priests attended.[340]

MORMON EXORCISM

The Mormon stance on possession derived from an explicit theology of demons and fallen angels. Mormons are literalists when it comes to cosmic mythologies that have largely faded from Christian consciousness. Few Catholics, for example, are aware that Michaelmas (September 29) commemorates the victory of the archan-gel Michael over Satan's fallen angels in the war in heaven, fleetingly alluded to in Revelation 12. For Latter-day Saints, such premortal contention and exiled angels are foundational elements of its doctrine. And any doubt about the reality of demonic entities was laid to rest when Smith produced revelations that affirmed Satan's exis-tence as a fallen angel "who rebelled against God and saught to take the kingdom of our God and his Christ; wherefore he maketh war with the saints of God and encompasseth them round about."[341] That background was important enough for Smith to elaborate in three separate scriptural texts.[342]

The New and Everlasting Covenant, propounded in premortal councils, antici-pated the embodiment of our eternal spirits, and life in this crucible of learning as the second stage of a human journey toward theosis. This explains both why the fall was necessary ("they were born into the world by the fall")[343] and why exile from this "second estate"[344] was a damning penalty for the rebellious souls. "The great principle of happiness consists in having a body," Smith taught, repeatedly empha-sizing that the bodily depravation of Satan and his followers was the price paid for rebellion: "The Devil has no body, and herein is his punishment. He is pleased when he can obtain the tabernacle of man."[345] Later he elaborated, "Any person that he can find that will yield to him he will bind him & take possession of the body & reign there glorying in it mightily not thinking that he had got a stolen tabernacle & by & by some one of Authority will come along & cast him out."[346] (Hence, in Mormon understanding, even the Gadarene swine were preferable to no corporeal home at all.)[347] At the same time, Smith taught of strict limits to diabolical power: "The devil has no power over us only as we permit him."[348] He added, "Wicked spirits have their bounds, limits, and laws by which they are governed."[349]

In the very month of the church's organization, Joseph Smith exercised a spiritual gift that members took as heralding the new dispensation in a display like those recounted in Mark that would not have been lost on his followers. Visiting the Knight family, a severely distressed Newel asked him to cast out an afflicting devil. Smith recorded that "I rebuked the devil, and commanded him in the name of Jesus Christ to depart from him and Newel immediately spoke and said that he saw the devil vanish from his sight. This was the first miracle performed in this Church."[350] At a conference in 1831, Smith cast another devil out of Harvey Whitlock.[351]

The same 1830 revelation that authorized healing the sick also authorized "casting out devils" ("if required by them that desire it").[352] No wonder, then, that missionaries reported similar episodes. In 1842, Alfred Young was preaching in the South, when they encountered a young man,

> 18 or 19 years of age who was afflicted with an evil spirit. He was continually making a noise and was very unpleasant company. . . . The mother of the lad wished me to lay hands on him for his recovery. When we attempted to do so, being strong, he contended with us and I simply rebuked the evil spirit. He came out of the lad and the latter lay at our feet a natural, pleasant looking boy. But when the evil spirit went out of the boy he entered into my oldest son, John William, who was standing near. He was at once seized with terrible contortions of body. This caused considerable excitement in camp. . . . We then laid hands on him, rebuked the evil spirit in the name of the Lord Jesus and bid it depart and trouble us no more. It departed and left us in peace.[353]

Side by side with such dramatic encounters, Smith noted more subtle varieties of Satan's "violent attack[s]," as when "his influence cast a gloomy shade over the minds of my brothers and sisters, which prevents them from seeing things as they really are" and caused "a division in the family, . . . among the 12, also among the 70."[354] Throughout the nineteenth century, scattered reports of Mormon elders casting out demons appeared. Three elders signed an affidavit that they had expelled several devils from a "sister in the Clackmanan Branch," Scotland, though it required "anointing and laying on of hands several times," as well as hymn singing (since "the devil is not over fond of music"). Two months later, they repeated the procedure with another woman in Edinburgh.[355] Into the early twentieth century, LDS writers continued to affirm the phenomenon. "The reality of demoniacal possession cannot be doubted," according to a 1909 editorial in the church-owned *Deseret News*, though its author, in claiming "numerous instances of possession by evil spirits," made no reference to contemporary examples in the church.[356]

Later in the century, Bruce McConkie, disinclined to associate Mormonism with Catholic practice, wrote that exorcism was a practice of "false priests," whereas the priesthood represents "the true order whereby devils are cast out of people."[357] Though the topic is virtually absent from contemporary publications or pronouncements, as recently as 1974 the seventy James Cullimore attested in a General Conference talk that "in the Church today," as in times past, "devils are cast out."[358]

9

Scripture

⌒

SPIRITUAL GIFTS ARE, as Orson Pratt taught, the forms through which Christ infuses "intelligence and power" into the church, "establishing familiar intercourse between the heavens and earth" to move us toward "conformity to the divine will and celestial order."[1] While the spirit moves where it lists and is variable in its gifts and operations, scripture represents a (semi-)fixed template, a repository of all essential information pertaining to what the Book of Mormon calls the "great plan of happiness."[2] If the apostasy consists of the loss of the essential terms, conditions, and promises of the New and Everlasting Covenant (and the powers and authority to bring that covenant to fruition), then a major task of the Restoration would be to provide a more complete and coherent account of God's covenantal purposes, beginning with premortal councils, extending to various covenant peoples with whom the Lord has dealt in this world, detailing his active engagement in human affairs down to the present dispensation, and previewing the conditions for progression through the worlds to come. Scripture, in this view, would need to be an ampler, more dynamic, and expansive (and expanding) record than the one Christians of Joseph Smith's generation inherited.

In 1817, the English radical William Hone endured three high-profile trials for his impious attacks on the Christian religion. Surprisingly, perhaps, his greatest offense against the orthodoxy of the day—and the only one of which he subsequently repented—was not any of his several published parodies. It was his publication of a scholarly work: *The Apocryphal New Testament*—a collection of various non-canonical writings from the early Church.[3] The offense that Christians read into his publication was twofold. First, the very existence of such documents, brought to the fore, could suggest that "the selection of the books contained in the New Testament [was] quite an arbitrary one, conducted according to the fancy or the caprice of the prelates assembled."[4] As another critic protested, the Christian canon was constituted "by progressive additions of genuine and authorized books, not by *selections* of what appeared to be best."[5] Second, Hone compounded that offense by presenting his documents in a typeface and two-column verse format that imitated the King James Version of the Bible. The visual impact of the volume was to blur crucial lines of demarcation between sacred and secular writ, and to usurp the emblems of scriptural utterance. In other words, Hone's work was viewed as an assault on what Thomas Rennell called the radical and unassailable "ground of distinction" between scripture and non-scripture. No middle ground was possible, in that view.[6]

Today the picture of early canon formation looks rather different, and it is more in line with the view that Hone himself came to deplore as "justly offensive to pious minds, and so . . . detestable to my own."[7] In other words, the history of the Bible, it is now clear, was neither neat nor linear nor inevitable. As one evangelical scholar writes, early Church Fathers had "a broader understanding of what constitutes 'Scripture' than the documents we know as canonical." (He goes on to show a "small sampling"—dozens—of the Fathers' citations of revered works that are today non-canonical.)[8] Such frequent and promiscuous citations of "scripture" suggest that Christian authorities had no conception of a "closed canon," he adds, noting that "this distinction between Scripture and canon may seem nitpicky to some."[9] Another historian is more emphatic: "One of the most original and tenacious ideas of the first Christian society was that nothing, in the religious state of the word, was yet definitive; that revelation had by no means said its last word."[10]

We have seen how the Montanist crisis in the middle of the second century shaped the history of spiritual gifts—but some historians see the idea of a closed canon emerging in the aftermath of that episode as well. With his claims of ongoing inspiration and prophetic authority responsive to the immediate present, Montanus threw all settled verities into doubt. If new revelations could irrupt into the church at any moment, then the past was no guide to the future. One scholar characterized this movement as a threat to "everything by which conditions in the church were to acquire a permanent form."[11] Montanus and his disciples were condemned and excommunicated, but the crisis had revealed the instability of any institution reliant upon a Spirit "that blows where it chooses."[12] The institutional reaction, therefore, was deeper and longer lasting than personal sanctions—it entailed the exile of "a continuing prophecy" in principle. The church "pushed the time of the second coming into the future . . . [and] the time of prophecy into the past."[13] The consequence followed ineluctably: "the gradual solidification of the church's message," and "fixed forms of dogma and creed," in other words, "the composition of the apostolic canon."[14] In the Christian world, the scriptural canon had been settled by the fifth century, and questions of biblical canonicity went relatively unchallenged in succeeding centuries. In the space of a few decades, Mormonism quadrupled the number of canonical volumes, with the promise of more to come.

THE BIBLE

In distilling the essential divide between the Roman and Protestant churches of the Reformation era, the nineteenth-century scholar Philip Schaff pointed to one "objective" or "formal" principle at stake: Protestants maintain "the absolute sovereignty of the Bible, as the only infallible rule of the Christian life and faith, in opposition to the Roman doctrine of the Bible and tradition."[15] But if there was one doctrine on which the Christian church found continuing general agreement both before and after the Reformation, it was on the doctrine of canonicity itself, which comprised two propositions. First, the canon was complete. Athanasius described the modern canon in 367, and a 382 synod confirmed it.[16] Only relatively minor quibbles would arise as to the exact status of certain deuterocanonical (or apocryphal) books that the Protestants challenged, even though they persisted in publishing them as part of the canon into the twentieth century. If it was complete, the canon was by definition closed. As early as the year 400, at the Council of Toledo, the church declared that if anyone "believes that any scriptures, except those which the Catholic Church has received, ought to be held in authority or venerates them, let him be anathema."[17]

The second proposition on which the canonicity of scripture rested is that the canon originated with God, not man. Catholics consistently affirmed the Bible as "having been dictated either by Christ's own word of mouth, or by the Holy Spirit" (in the Council of Trent);[18] Protestants, in a similar and typical formulation, regard the Bible as "given by the inspiration of God," carrying "the authority of God himself speaking therein."[19] On interpretation, Christian churches could be poles apart. But on the question of the Bible's inspiration and reliability, general agreement was the rule. Then, two centuries after the Reformation's beginnings, under an onslaught of unprecedented challenges, Christians were reassessing the meaning of "God's word."

The first cracks in a strict view of the canon and the inspiration behind it had begun to appear in the seventeenth century. Hugo Grotius, the influential Dutch jurist (1583–1645), "rejected significant textual corruption" of the Bible, but he also rejected "an inspirational origin for the historical books and moral wisdom of the Old Testament." In a bold challenge to Catholic and Protestant tradition alike, he argued that the Bible's "reliability had to be judged by the credibility of the biblical authors and their informants."[20] A few years later (1670), the philosopher from Rotterdam, Baruch Spinoza, produced an important *Theological-Political Treatise* wherein he argued that "knowledge of science and of matters spiritual should by no means be expected of [the prophets]. So we conclude that we must believe the prophets only with regard to the purpose and substance of the revelation."[21]

Then, in 1748, David Hume published a landmark essay in modern skepticism. His work "On Miracles" was a powerful critique of "the truth of the Christian religion," based largely on his carefully argued indictment of the plausibility of biblical supernaturalism.[22] His publication provoked a flood of responses, lending tremendous momentum to the religious skepticism already growing in the Age of Reason. Some Christians found the safest reply to his powerful critique was to renegotiate the question of the Bible's accuracy rather than its underlying salvational reliability. And so some writers showed a willingness to compromise on the principle of biblical inerrancy (though the expression was not invoked until centuries later) rather than refute Hume's argument in toto.

In 1776, Soame Jenyns published his *View of the Internal Evidence for the Christian Religion*. Agreeing that the Bible contains "errors and inconsistencies, fabulous stories, false facts, and false philosophy," he found refuge in a view of the scriptures "not [as] revelations from God, but the history of them; The revelation itself is derived from God; but the history of it is the production of men."[23] Even misattributions of authorship, he granted, would only "prove no more than this, that God, for reasons to us unknown, had thought proper to permit a revelation by him communicated to mankind, to be mixed with their ignorance, and corrupted by their frauds."[24]

A similar response was provoked by Thomas Paine's *Age of Reason* (first part, 1794), his best-selling "Investigation of True and Fabulous Theology." One reviewer felt Paine's critique of Christian scriptures had a salutary effect: a too rigid credence in biblical reliability had fed the ranks of the Deists, he opined. Paine's examination "may assist in separating divine truth from human error. This, among rational Christians, has long been a *desideratum*."[25] Then, in 1823, John Milton's *De Doctrina Christiana* was discovered and quickly popularized in William Channing's 1826 *Remarks on the Character and Writings of John Milton*. In that widely read work, the literary giant is quoted as boldly asserting that the Bible "has been liable to frequent corruption, and in some instances has been corrupted, through the number, and occasionally the bad faith of those by whom it has been handed down."[26] By the nineteenth century, the rise of both geology and of historical or higher criticism were feeding these flames of skepticism. Charles Lyell's *Principles of Geology* (1830–33) was persuasive in opposing gradualism over vast stretches of time to the miraculous and instantaneous events of Genesis. And Julius Wellhausen built the

Documentary Hypothesis on the work of scholars going back a century or more who, instead of attempting to reconcile biblical discrepancies, simply admitted them and attributed them to competing authorship in the Torah.

Counter-reactions were already under way. John Wesley responded to Jenyns's work by questioning his Christian credentials. "If he is a Christian," he noted in his journal, "he betrays his own cause by averring, that 'all Scripture is not given by inspiration of God; but the writers of it were sometimes left to themselves, and consequently made some mistakes.' Nay, if there be any mistakes in the Bible, there may as well be a thousand. If there be one falsehood in that book, it did not come from the God of truth."[27] Meanwhile, in the Catholic/Protestant debates of the era, a focus of contention was the church's claim to inerrancy. And so in 1825 the vicar Richard Grier borrowed the term from those debates, and laid down an enduring precept: "Scripture declares her absolute inerrancy," he wrote, in contrast to such certainties about "popish" religion.[28]

LDS Views

On the subject of biblical inerrancy, the LDS church initially found itself with a liberal, progressive wing of Christianity. True, Smith rooted Mormonism so deeply in biblical precedent that he could sincerely believe, as he said to inquirers, that "we differ from other christian denominations [in that] we believe the bible, and they do not."[29] At the same time, in 1833, the church's newspaper published an article titled, "Errors of the Bible." It minced no words, declaring bluntly that "any man possessing common understanding, knows, that both the old and new testaments are filled with errors, obscurities, italics and contradictions, which must be the work of man . . . including a ton of gross errors."[30] Though in principle—and in their official "Articles of Faith"—Mormons accepted the Bible "as the word of God," a crucial caveat loomed larger than at first appeared. "So far as it is translated correctly," Smith hedged. By translation, he seems to have meant "transmitted,"[31] and Smith leveled vigorous criticisms at the Bible's transmission history.

This critique Smith first introduced with the publication of the Book of Mormon, which described a corruption of the original holy writ. Most dramatically, that 1830 scripture claimed, in the voice of ancient American prophets, that enemies of the truth ("the great and abominable church") deliberately took "away from the gospel of the Lamb many parts which are plain and most precious; and also many covenants of the Lord have they taken away."[32] For unmistakable emphasis, Nephi repeated the allegation a further half dozen times in his record.[33]

Smith trusted more in his revelatory authority as a prophet of the Restoration than in the particulars of the biblical text. As he said rather audaciously, "Many things in the bible . . . do not, as they now stand, accord with the revelation of the holy Ghost to me."[34] Parley Pratt provided a logical rationale for such a position, comparing streams and fountains. "All revealed knowledge was obtained without books and independent of them. It is therefore a self-evident fact, that ... revealed knowledge is not originally produced from books. Hence a book cannot be the fountain or source of knowledge."[35] Smith agreed: "Some will say, the scriptures say so & so," he told a large congregation with some impatience. But "I have the oldest Book in the world [the Bible] & the Holy Ghost[.] I thank God for the old Book but more for the Holy Ghost. . . . If ye are not led by revelation how can ye escape the damnation of Hell."[36]

Other than asserting the need for caution in taking the Bible as God's word, Smith said little about how to read it. Before Christians even had a canon, some readers were interpreting the creation narrative of Genesis as a series of allegories and figurative meanings. The first-century Philo of Alexandria held that God's clothing of Adam and Eve in coats of skin was a reference to the process by which their premortal souls acquired mortal bodies.[37] Paul faulted Jewish readings of Judaism's own scriptures, believing the Christological meaning of the "old covenant" was veiled from their "hardened" minds.[38] Church Father Augustine found Genesis 1 to be replete with other meanings than the literal ("heaven does not mean the sky but the HEAVEN OF HEAVEN"; "Be light made" refers to the creation of spiritual illumination, that which is "capable of receiving light from You").[39] Anticipating the interpretive controversies that would fracture Christianity for centuries to come, he queried, "among so many meanings . . . can any of us find one of which he would dare to affirm that Moses meant this, or wished that to be understood from what he wrote?"[40]

If Smith laid down a foundation for caution in taking all biblical texts as inspired, Pratt emphasized a literal reading of those that were. In his case, it was not the interpretive practice that guided the theology as much as his theology that guided the interpretive practice. More specifically, Mormon conceptions of scriptural interpretation derived in great measure from their millennialism, which their scriptures repeatedly emphasized. "I come quickly," the voice of Christ affirmed almost a dozen times in Smith's revelations.[41] Belief in the Second Coming of the Messiah to rescue the righteous from the evils of the world (*pre*millennialism) goes back to the generation of Christ's apostles. But that belief alternated with spiritualized readings of God's coming kingdom on earth, and it also varied as to the process by which a literal kingdom would be inaugurated. Third-century Father Origen and later Augustine both taught that the church Christ had founded was his kingdom; its endurance through the centuries obviated any need for a more literal kingdom. Others, contemporary with Pratt, believed that it was Christian or civic duty to establish those millennial conditions themselves, prior to Christ's return (*post*millennialists). In this way, these writers "spiritualized" the millennial prophecies, seeing the reign of utopian peace as a figurative rather than historical event, largely a product of human moral progress. This interpretation survived alongside beliefs that God would return in dramatic, triumphal glory to usher in a thousand years of peace.

Pratt and other Mormons found the "spiritualizing" mode of interpretation—especially when invoked to avoid premillennialist commitments—to be a dangerous narcotic in a time of genuinely mortal peril. ("None of those ancient men knew anything of the modern system of spiritualizing," he declared in the most influential nineteenth-century book in Mormonism.)[42] To teach, as the postmillennialists did, that the words of prophecy do not mean what they say literally, although the scriptures "declare these things plainly," was a form of priestcraft he felt compelled to refute. Pratt, Smith, and the influential Sidney Rigdon were aided in their advocacy of literalism by both commonsense rationalism and an interpretive approach conformable to the populism of the era. As one historian explains, such commonsense rendering of scripture was the "common person's counterpart to the Enlightenment confidence displayed by intellectual elites."[43] Articles in the church newspaper frequently mirrored Pratt's views on spiritualizing. The *Evening and Morning Star* repeatedly affirmed literal scriptural exegesis and described "spiritualized" readings as a strategy by which doubters could reject the prophesied restoration of the "order of things" while still pretending "that they are great *sticklers* for the bible."[44]

Pratt's arguments, which resonated with all his Mormon contemporaries, were reprinted by Benjamin Winchester in his influential *Gospel Reflector*. From there, they were reprinted in the church newspaper, *Times and Seasons*, where they established a quasi-official doctrine of Mormon scriptural exegesis. "It is necessary to establish some definite rule for interpretation," one article ran. "The idea of spiritualizing the writings of the prophets and apostles" so that "none but the learned can understand them, is certainly repugnant to the word of God." Winchester called it an "evil practice" and argued that a "literal" reading, especially as regards prophecies of the millennium, was the proper and necessary rule.[45]

And so Mormonism's approach to biblical inerrancy mixed liberal views of human error with dogged but limited literalism. Smith clearly demonstrated by word and action that the biblical account was unreliable, incomplete, and often in error. "Selective literalism" was his general practice, notes Philip Barlow, the foremost authority on Mormons and the Bible.[46] Young, too, was no advocate of all-embracing literalism. Regarding the creation narrative, for instance, he declared, "I do not believe that portion of the Bible as the Christian world do," dismissing it as one of "the baby stories my mother taught me when I was a child." Only the Spirit can help us sort out its contradictions, he said elsewhere.[47]

In the twentieth- and twenty-first-century church, a few progressives like Lowell Bennion espoused a more liberal approach to scripture than the "fundamentalistic" Bruce R. McConkie, as Barlow has tracked the tradition. However, lacking any official statement on biblical interpretation other than the vague Article of Faith alluded to, church members have by and large been swayed by the writings and sermons of the more highly placed, conservative authorities like the apostle McConkie (and his equally influential father-in-law, President Joseph Fielding Smith), not by the lay members like Bennion and scholars in the church more open to contemporary developments in biblical scholarship. Even so, it is virtually unimaginable that any Mormons or any of their leaders would assent to the 1978 Chicago Statement on scriptural inerrancy.[48] Its denial "that any normative revelation has been given since the completion of the New Testament writings" is undermined by three entire additional volumes of Mormon scripture; the Chicago Statement's dismissal of the human element in revelation ("We further deny that the corruption of human culture and language through sin has thwarted God's work of inspiration" or "introduced distortion") is undone by Nephi's insistence that Christians are in an "awful state of woundedness, . . . because of the plain and most precious parts of the gospel of the Lamb which have been" removed from the record.[49] The Chicago Statement's denial that any alterations or imperfections have at any time intruded upon the text ("the whole of Scripture and all its parts, down to the very words of the original, were given by divine inspiration") is contradicted by the Book of Mormon editor's frank admission that his record may contain "the mistakes of men,"[50] and its insistence that biblical authority is not limited to salvific matters ("it is true and reliable in all the matters it addresses")[51] is contradicted by the First Presidency refusal to embrace creationism as a substitute for scientific accounts of evolution.[52]

The absence of a clear pronouncement from the Mormon leadership on matters of scriptural interpretation means that members have a good deal of latitude in how they interpret subjects from the manner of human creation to the scope of Noah's flood to the meaning of the beasts in John's Revelation. When a man was brought to a church court for his interpretations in the latter case, Smith protested: "I never thought it was right to call up a man and try him because he erred in doctrine, it looks too much like Methodism and not like Latter day Saintism. . . . It feels so good not to be trammeled."[53] Smith's statement that the Book of Mormon was "the most correct of any Book on Earth"[54] gives Mormons clear warrant to consider the Bible to be an inspired but fallible guide. Even so, developments like the Documentary Hypothesis that can balance reverence for the text with historical understanding are making only gradual inroads.[55]

The Joseph Smith Translation

The Reformation passion for a religion founded on "sola scriptura" found vibrant expression in a widespread, fervent biblicism in antebellum America. Bibles were being distributed in unprecedented numbers, read and explicated by thousands of lay preachers and myriad seekers, and retranslated into several new English-language editions. As early as 1755, John Wesley had retranslated the archaic King James New Testament into a version "for Plain, Unlettered Men who know only their Mother Tongue." Quakers followed suit with their translation in 1764. Prominent figures this side of the Atlantic were soon doing the same for an American audience; scholar and patriot (Secretary of the Continental Congress) Charles Thomson published an acclaimed English translation of the Septuagint in 1808. Restorationist Alexander Campbell published his version of the New Testament, *Living Oracles*, in 1826. A few years later, lexicographer Noah Webster added his contribution, a lightly revised King James Version (1833).[56]

At the same time, in virtually the same years that Joseph Smith was moving to affront orthodoxy with substantial additions to the scriptural corpus, Protestants were acting to subtract. In 1804, the British and Foreign Bible Society ceased publication of the Apocrypha in its English-language Bibles, while a campaign to eliminate those dubious books from all Bibles fractured the Society in the 1820s. It was against this backdrop that Smith, in 1833, inquired of the Lord about the Apocrypha's value. While "many things contained therein" were true, he was told, "many things" were the "interpolations by the hands of men."[57] As a result, Smith did not include the Apocrypha in the version of the Bible he would revise.

While Smith's verdict on the Apocrypha was itself not extraordinary, he had already pushed the question of scriptural reliability much further than his contemporaries. Any doubts Catholics or Protestants had about scriptural inspiration have been largely tamed by the strategy of varying the interpretive methods to which the Bible is subjected. In other words, from the earliest Christian centuries, the Bible has been viewed through the lenses not only of literal meaning but also of allegorical, analogical, or figurative meaning. More modern schools have historicized, demythologized, form criticized, and source criticized the Bible. But the question of what books constitute the Bible is not itself, to most Christian interpreters, up for negotiation. The Bible and the canon are largely equivalent terms, and they are both definitively established, with the Apocrypha controversy of the 1820s (and continuing disagreements on the Apocryphal books) a rare disturbance on a calm sea of consensus.[58]

Smith was ready not only to add extra-biblical scripture but to revise freely the Bible accepted by Christian accord. True enough, one important self-described task the Book of Mormon fulfilled in an age of growing skepticism was to "establish the truth of" the Bible.[59] But given its references to "the most plain and precious parts of the gospel" being "taken away from the book" over the course of its history,[60] Smith saw the scriptures as in need of inspired revision. And he believed he had the keys to do just that. On February 2, 1833, a simple entry in Smith's minute book reads, "This day completed the translation and the reviewing of the New Testament,"[61] but little is known about the genesis of his project. It commenced in the months after he published the Book of Mormon, as he turned his attention to a task so important he referred to it as one of three signs that the work of the last days had commenced. All three pertained to his role as revelator and creator of new scripture. The first, he said, was the publication of the Book of Mormon. "The covenants given to the Latter-day Saints"—published as the Doctrine and Covenants—was the second. Third, and so vital that he referred to it as "a branch of [his] calling,"[62] was what he called "the translation of the Bible."[63] Translation is a bit of a misnomer here since Smith did not actually use original manuscripts or languages in his work of revision. Guided by inspiration and his own judgment, Smith worked his way through both testaments, for the most part emending or editing lightly, but with occasional lengthy interpolations. In publishing the Book of Mormon, with the claim that it represented the word of God on a par with the Bible, he had shattered the Christian canon. In publishing the Doctrine and Covenants, he would indicate that the canon is perpetually open to additions, now and in the future. And with his project to redact the Bible, freely removing, editing, and interpolating, he impugned its accuracy and reliability in a way that exceeded most of his believing contemporaries.

Smith's version of the Bible never become the church's official text, the official explanation being that "apparently the Prophet Joseph never finally finished his revision."[64] Another relevant factor was that the translation manuscripts were passed on by Smith's widow to the Reorganized Church of Jesus Christ of Latter Day Saints, which first published a Bible based on Smith's revisions in 1867. With some significant exceptions (especially those noted below; see "Pearl of Great Price" section), most changes were relatively minor, and in any case, as an evangelizing church, Mormonism found it preferable to employ a version that could serve as a biblical lingua franca with the Protestant world. The Bible of Smith's nineteenth-century America was the King James Version. Smith used it personally, transmitted its diction and syntax into the Book of Mormon he produced, and now relied upon it as the basis of his revision. No serious consideration has ever been given to replacing this standard text with a more accurate or accessible version, probably because of the pronounced intertextuality that binds the Bible to the Book of Mormon in particular. In addition to a King James style, the Book of Mormon includes about a third of the book of Isaiah, most passages mirroring verbatim the King James Isaiah.

When the church published its own edition of the King James Version in 1979, this effectively shut the door to any potential change in the foreseeable future for the English-speaking membership in the church.

THE BOOK OF MORMON

Protestant reformers relied upon the Bible to ground their authority and their doctrines, but the lack of uniform interpretation of that standard doomed the church to factionalism and strife. The early dream of Calvin and like-minded reformers was to remake the Christian world into a unified body of believers, but the breach with the Catholic Church inaugurated by Luther soon multiplied into further irreconcilable divisions. Debates erupted over what the Bible said—or did not say—about the Eucharist, the mode of baptism, principles of church government, the order of worship, and a hundred other concerns.

The Book of Mormon shaped Mormon attitudes toward scripture both by the fact of its appearance and by its particular engagement with the topic of canonicity. By its mere appearance, it *enacted* the novelty of an expanded canon and the ongoing reality of scripture formation. As Smith claimed in a revelation, the "means" and "inspiration" of its translation as well as the "ministering angels" that attend its appearance in the world, "prove to the world that . . . God does inspire men and call them to his holy work in this age and generation, as well as in generations of old."[65] In addition, the record justified its own appearance when it *pronounced* a pluralistic view of scripture. "For behold, I shall speak unto the Jews and they shall write it; and I shall also speak unto the Nephites and they shall write it,"[66] maintained one of the Nephite prophets, thus putting the new scripture on a par with the old one. Smith even announced plans to bind the two records together in order to lend concrete form to their alleged equivalence.[67] "We shall print the Book of Mormon and the Testament, and bind them in one volume," announced the church paper.[68] The Book of Mormon even deserved a kind of priority over the Bible, noted one editor, since "it has not been tinctured by the wisdom of man, with here and there an Italic word to supply deficiencies."[69] It was, declared Smith, "the most correct of any book on earth."[70]

An astonishing fact about the Book of Mormon is that it was the most conspicuous and controversial emblem of the new church—while its content was being largely ignored. Members and detractors alike found the fact of its abrupt eruption on the religious landscape far more significant than any doctrinal innovations it presented. This fact was borne out to a comic degree. An editor of the *Baptist Religious Herald*, when asked for information on the Mormons, wrote a reader in 1840, "We have never seen a copy of the book of Mormon, nor any abstract of their creed upon which we could fully rely, as a fair exposition of their opinions." Nevertheless, he confidently adjudges without any sense of irony, "The book of Mormon is a bungling and stupid production. . . . It contains some trite, moral maxims, but the phraseology . . . frequently violates every principle and rule of grammar. We have no hesitation in saying the whole system is erroneous."[71] As historian/sociologist Thomas O'Dea humorously—but accurately—summarizes: "The Book of Mormon has not been universally considered by its critics as one of those books that must be read in order to have an opinion of it."[72]

But the same was true to some degree of its proponents. On the one hand, the Book of Mormon set the stage for the entire revitalized program of covenant theology that Smith would lay out. And as Gerald Smith has chronicled, the Book of Mormon was employed by Smith and Cowdery as a resource for early priesthood church organization and ordinances and both congregational and temple worship.[73] At the same time, Smith is not known to have given a single discourse on the scripture or any of its passages, and in writing an outline of church doctrine he quoted at great length from Luke, Acts, Revelation, Matthew, Isaiah, and Hebrews to teach the fundamentals of repentance, baptism, and the Gift of the Holy Ghost. The Book of Mormon received not a mention.[74] The overwhelming opinion of converts was that the Book of Mormon mirrored rather than supplemented biblical teachings.[75] In spite of its unparalleled influence on Smith's re-conceiving of covenant theology, an abundance of evidence concerning its early dissemination and reception confirms that for many, the Book of Mormon's miraculous origins overshadowed its doctrinal and devotional value.[76] An 1832 revelation even condemned the church for its neglect of the Book of Mormon.[77]

The relative disregard for the Book of Mormon within the church came to an end in 1986 with the presidency of Ezra Taft Benson. At that time, he warned that the 1832 condemnation was still in force, and as a hallmark of his tenure, he shifted the Book of Mormon's place in Mormon consciousness and culture. In 1988, he issued a stirring summons for a "massive flooding of the earth with the Book of Mormon," reaffirmed its role as "the instrument that God designed . . . to gather out [His] elect," and emphatically designated it as of more immediate spiritual relevance and value than the other scriptures. Noting the current churchwide curriculum that apportioned one year of study to every volume of scripture in a four-year sequence, he said: "This four-year pattern, however, must not be followed by Church members in their personal and family study. We need to read daily from the pages of the book that will get a man 'nearer to God by abiding by its precepts, than by any other book.'" By this call for Mormons to "read daily from its pages," it would not be unfair to say that the cultural momentum was building to make the Book of Mormon the principal scriptural focus, not just in missionary efforts but in the Mormon faith tradition generally.

Even in 1972, it was an exaggeration to say, as did Sydney Ahlstrom, "A few isolated individuals can still read [the Book of Mormon] as a religious testimony, . . . but not even loyal Mormons can be nourished by it as they were a century ago." Today, it is simply dead wrong. The Book of Mormon is now the focus of vigorous, scholarly research by Mormon academics that is unprecedented in scope, professionalism, and church support. The church's Brigham Young University now has a research center for Book of Mormon studies and publishes a journal devoted to Book of Mormon scholarship.[78] Meanwhile, an army of some 84,000 missionaries continues to use the Book of Mormon as the centerpiece of a proselytizing effort that was bringing in more than a third of a million converts a year by the new century.[79] In LDS worship services, Sunday Schools, and family devotionals, the Book of Mormon is fully central rather than peripheral.

THE DOCTRINE AND COVENANTS

Most language theory since Saussure has recognized that, in fundamental ways, a written text is a sign of absence.[80] Speech is the proof of presence. A text is what remains in the void left by the passing of a living voice. In a similar way, scripture, conceived as God's revelation, is a sign of absence. Luke records the Savior's remark that "the prophets were in effect until John came."[81] Christians have generally taken this to mean that the words of the prophets prevailed as witness of Christ until the Messiah's predecessor, the Baptist. The written records of their words, the traces of their living witness, now fill the silence even as they testify to those prophets' absence. After Christ's coming, scripture and living prophets co-existing in the same realm in the same historic moment, in the prevalent Christian paradigm at least, seem to most an impossibility, or at best a redundancy.

Mormonism had to iron out this paradox, for it was not without wrinkles in the early years of Smith's ministry. Replacing one canonical volume (the Bible) with two (the Bible and the Book of Mormon) could never repair the defect Mormons discerned in Christianity: a closed canon, of any shape or size. (Though a closed canon was undoubtedly the Christian norm, David Holland has demonstrated far more dissenters than Mormons to the status quo; from Shakers to Transcendentalists, "some people threatened to breach the canonical border and others worked to secure it.")[82] However, enlarging the canon is not the same thing as exposing it to never-ending expansion, making it a scripture "with the back cover torn off."[83] Given the biblical attestation of sacred texts not now extant (like the Acts of Solomon, or the Book of

Jasher),[84] the existence (if not the miraculous transmission) of an additional ancient witness to Christ such as the Book of Mormon is at least in principle reasonable. To argue for an ongoing expansion to be endlessly enlarged by contemporary prophets is another proposition entirely. Parley Pratt argued this point in "The Fountain of Knowledge," his 1844 pamphlet. Scriptures resulted from revelatory process and are thus the product of revealed truth, not the other way around. As a consequence, and not a source, of revelation, scriptures should not be assigned foundational status. People would do well to look to a stream for nourishing water but do better to secure the fountain. That fountain, Pratt proclaimed, is "the gift of revelation," which "the restoration of all things" heralds.[85]

The ossification of church doctrine was to early Mormons a sure sign of apostasy, and this ossification was most evident in closed canons and authoritative creedal statements. This is precisely why even as Smith was accepted by thousands as a prophet and revelator, misgivings arose among some of his followers over the plans to publish those revelations, to commit them to printed, fixed form. Even one of the three witnesses to the gold plates, David Whitmer, felt Smith's commission was to add ancient scripture, not his own. "We were strictly commanded in the beginning to rely upon that which was written," meaning the Book of Mormon, he later wrote in protest.[86] Most Mormons, however, felt as Parley Pratt did, that the foundation of revelation was again flowing, and that it merited ongoing publication and dissemination. Simultaneously with translating the Book of Mormon, and into the first months of the organized church's existence, Smith had received revelations on numerous topics. On the day of the church's organization, command had been given to keep a church record—and Smith's revelations (or "commandments" as they were often called) were generally transcribed and preserved. Several addressed the particular situation or needs of converts, but often and increasingly he pronounced on topics of more lasting importance.

Martin Harris was promised the role of witness to the gold plates, and Oliver Cowdery was reaffirmed in his role as translator.[87] But other early revelations shed light on the nature of Christ's atonement and his suffering in Gethsemane, gave detailed instructions on church sacraments and organization, affirmed spiritual gifts, and commanded the gathering of converts to select locations.[88] The need to disseminate such principles and commandments among a burgeoning membership was obvious, and by late 1831 Smith and his associates discussed publication. A conference convened in November to plan a volume, and the ambitious print run of 10,000 was approved (later downsized to 3,000).[89] The signal development at this time was the solicitation of support for the very step Whitmer would oppose: going "beyond" the Book of Mormon, and using Smith's revelations to "establish ... doctrine."[90] Smith asked the assembled elders "what testimony they were willing to attach to these commandments which should shortly be sent to the world. A number of the brethren arose," a scribe recorded, "and said that they were willing to testify to the world that they knew they were of the Lord."[91]

Days later, Smith pronounced a revelation naming himself and five others as "stewards over the revelations and commandments."[92] A subsequent directive ordered the "organization of the literary . . . establishment of the church," which took the form of the church's "Literary Firm," meeting in the following months to plan and prepare the publication of Smith's collected revelations.[93] As with early Christian winnowing of sacred writings, not all of Joseph's revelations were incorporated into LDS scriptures. (At least forty known revelations given to him have never been included.)[94] Those deemed inspired and essential were collected and sent to the press in 1833. In the original manuscript of the Book of Commandments, a testimony of eighteen elders was appended, affirming that the revelations therein contained were "given by inspiration of God . . . and are verily true."[95] The gesture was clearly intended to parallel the testimonies of eleven witnesses, similarly placed at the end of the Book of Mormon. In both cases, the testimonies were drawing attention to something more important than the particulars of the scripture within the covers: that this was a *living* church in a particular sense. If the Book of Mormon had attested to a God who presided over two covenant peoples a hemisphere apart, this collection of modern revelations brought God's interactions with his people into a vibrant present.

A mob assault on the printing press in July 1833 was followed by a partial rescue of the gatherings, which were bound and distributed. Sixty-five, of an intended seventy-seven, revelations were included.[96] A year later, sufficient developments had unfolded to warrant renewal of the aborted project. A committee was appointed to "arrange the items of the doctrine of Jesus Christ for the government of the church of Latter-Day Saints." And the decision was made to take these items "from the bible, book of Mormon, and the revelations which have been given to the church up to this date." "Or shall be [given], until such arrangement is made," the motion added, emphasizing a process of revelatory exposition with no end in sight.[97]

The new collection, renamed the Doctrine and Covenants, was published two years later. The number of revelations—now considered "covenants and commandments," grew to 102. A section titled "Theology," consisting of seven "Lectures on Faith," a catechism written by Sidney Rigdon, constituted the first seventy pages and accounted for the "Doctrine" of the new volume's title. In a preface, Smith and his counselors acknowledged the concerns some members had expressed about codifying doctrine, given Smith's—and others'—emphatic hostility to creedalism. "There may be aversion in the minds of some against receiving any thing purporting to be articles of faith," he wrote. "It does not make a principle untrue to print it," he insisted.[98] And so, upon publication, Smith recorded that a general assembly convened so the new compilation "may, if approved, become a law unto the church, and a rule of faith and practice."[99] Additional revelations were again incorporated into a new edition of the Doctrine and Covenants in 1876, one section was removed, and a "Manifesto" of Wilford Woodruff was included from 1908 on; in 1921, the "Lectures on Faith" that had been included since 1835 were removed. In 1976, two revelations received in 1836 and 1918 were added to another collection of scripture, the Pearl of Great Price. In 1981, they were transferred to the Doctrine and Covenants, along with a 1978 "Official Declaration" on the Priesthood, which overturned a long-standing priesthood prohibition based on race.

By contrast with the flood of revelation Smith produced in the 1830s and early '40s, Mormonism's open canon now sees infrequent expansion. The Doctrine and Covenants, where the anthology-type format would permit easy additions, has seen only the three mentioned above since 1908. The promise vouchsafed readers of the Book of Mormon, that the greater portion of the original plates, the "sealed portion," would one day be revealed, has all but faded in the modern church.[100] (Its tantalizing position at the threshold of disclosure is now more "a barometer of unworthiness rather than a source of hope for revelatory abundance," wrote one scholar.)[101] Still, occasional changes to the canon and continuing invocations by late twentieth-century leaders of those scriptures yet to be revealed persist as a reminder that, like Montanus, Mormons resist "chasing the Holy Spirit into a book."[102]

THE PEARL OF GREAT PRICE

We have seen that Mormonism constituted, in its most essential dimension, the recuperation of the New and Everlasting Covenant. This project required incorporating and amplifying its fragmentary Old Testament precedents along with New Testament doctrines into a comprehensive vision of human origins and destinies. This meant that Mormons gave more attention and consideration to the Old Testament as inspired if imperfect scripture than most Christians. An early church editorial decried the "Neglect of the Old Testament,"[103] which it saw as a "prevailing doctrine" in the current age of Christianity, one that Mormons resisted. A powerful catalyst in Smith's case was his reported visit by Moroni, in which the angelic messenger quoted and commented upon thirty-two scriptures; *all* of them were Old Testament passages, except for one New Testament quotation of the Old Testament figure Moses.[104] This experience would have anticipated by way of emphasis the Book of Mormon's haunting mantra about the Bible's missing "plain and precious parts" that caused Smith to look at the Old Testament with renewed scrutiny immediately after the work of translation and church organization was complete.

Weeks later, in June 1830, Smith recorded a "precious morsel" that he had received by revelation.[105] But this revelation was unlike others that he had received up to this time, consisting as they mostly had of timely directives, general admonitions, or doctrinal correctives.[106] On this occasion, which was either catalyst to or first fruit of the new translation of the Bible he was just embarking upon, he produced effectively ex nihilo a substantial ancient text purporting to be "the words of God, which he spake unto Moses at a time when Moses was caught up into an exceedingly high mountain."[107] In the twelfth chapter of Numbers, the Lord promises that he will speak face to face with his prophet, not in "visions" or "dreams," but "face to face," so that Moses will actually see "the form of the Lord."[108] The Bible, however, contains no account of this promised visitation. On this June day, Smith was revealing details of that lost event, which act of restoring he now depicted Moses as foreseeing. "And in a day when the children of men shall esteem my words as naught," Smith has Moses declaring, "and take many of them from the book which thou shalt write, behold, I will raise up another like unto thee; and they shall be had again."[109] And so Smith unfolded several chapters that began with an encounter of Moses with Satan and grew to include a creation narrative, an explanation of Lucifer's fall, and a description of Adam's introduction to the plan of salvation while still in the Garden of Eden. These were the texts that explicitly pushed back the New and Everlasting Covenant to the foundations of the human race. Then, sometime in December 1830, a further revelatory bonanza came.

One of the books owned by Joseph Smith was, coincidentally, a copy of the *Apocryphal New Testament*, published by that same William Hone who had suffered trial thirteen years earlier for exciting "impiety and irreligion in the minds of his Majesty's liege subjects."[110] It was likely this book, in addition to his work of revising the Bible, that strengthened Smith's interest in recuperating not just missing biblical passages but entire texts alluded to but absent from the canon. Ironically, in other words, the volume opened up precisely those possibilities to Smith's mind of which Hone himself repented: quasi-porous lines demarcating the sacred canon. "Much conjecture and conversation frequently occurred among the saints," the *Times and Seasons* reported, "concerning the books mentioned, and referred to in various places in the Old and New Testaments, which were now nowhere to be found." One missing scripture in particular seems to have caught Smith's interest: "The apostolic church had some of these writings," he continued, "as Jude mentions or quotes the prophecy of Enoch, the seventh from Adam."[111] The apparent provocation bore fruit, because sometime in December 1830, the church paper reported, "To the joy of the little flock . . . which numbered about seventy members" (he could not yet have known of the Missouri mission's success) "did the Lord reveal . . . the prophecy of Enoch."[112]

The pages that Smith produced in relation to the ancient figure Enoch became foundational to everything that he would hereafter accomplish—equaling or surpassing in doctrinal significance the entire Book of Mormon. Smith was excited enough by this prophecy that he rushed portions of it into publication almost as soon as the church had a newspaper to serve as a vehicle.[113] He skipped right over the other six chapters of Genesis he had revised and published Enoch's prophecy without introduction or explanation. In these passages, we find an impact far out of proportion to its modest textual length. The Enoch text sowed the seeds of Mormonism's most distinctive and vibrant doctrines: it produced the most emphatic version of a passible deity the Christian world then knew—a God of passions and emotions—the Weeping God of Mormonism. This was in contradistinction from the God of the Christian creeds, almost universally worshipped as a being "without body, parts, or *passions* [incorporeus, impartibilis, *impassibilis*]" (emphasis added).[114]

John may have had Christ declaring that "God is spirit,"[115] but for Smith, that meant an embodied spirit; Smith had personally experienced a God who defied all three criteria of the creedal God and had no scruples denying any scriptural passages that were interpreted otherwise. He could in this regard be compared to John Wesley, who once declared, "There are many scriptures the true sense of which neither you nor I shall know till death is swallowed up in victory. But this I know, better it were to say it had no senses at all, than to say it had such a sense as this."[116] Smith's depiction of Enoch's fully empathic and suffering God the Father was thus more than a supplement to an incomplete canon—it was a powerful corrective to creedal conceptions derived from that canon. This text, as we saw earlier, narrated Enoch's stunned response to a Heavenly Father who thrice sheds tears over the misery of his progeny.

This same Enoch text also provided an astoundingly compact recuperation of the entire cosmic narrative undergirding the New and Everlasting Covenant. He learned that God had told Adam, "I am God; I made the world, and men before they were in the flesh." Here we learn that the gospel fullness as well as the priesthood went back even further than Eden. The fullness of the gospel "was in the beginning." Enoch explains in this text that the fall was not a catastrophe, though it was a sojourn into a painful, educative mortality. In this account, humans become "partakers of misery and woe" in order to learn "to prize the good." The process is necessary and providentially designed, with Eve coming to the stunning realization that "were it not for our transgression we never should have known . . . redemption and . . . eternal life."[117] Enoch even confirms that the everlasting covenant, together with the priesthood, have been confirmed to him (as they were to Adam and would yet be to Abraham).[118]

In words that anticipate a yet-to-be developed doctrine of theosis, Enoch marvels that through this everlasting covenant which God has "sworn unto me" he has been given "a right to thy throne" ("not of myself, but through thine own grace").[119] Finally, the Lord assures Enoch that in a distant future, he will "gather out mine elect from the four quarters of the earth, unto a place which I shall prepare, an Holy City . . . and it shall be called Zion."[120] That was the Zion Joseph Smith set out to build. Premortal humans, a foreordained fall, an eternal gospel, a weeping God of passions, theosis, the promise—even preview—of participation in the divine nature ("Enoch knew, and looked upon . . . their misery, and wept and stretched forth his arms, and his heart swelled wide as eternity; and his bowels yearned; and all eternity shook"),[121] as well as the model and template of an earthly Zion: this avalanche of foundational Mormon doctrines all appeared within the compass of this relatively short but potent text. Never appearing in an LDS-produced version of the Bible, these interpolations into the biblical narrative have had a complicated textual history. Smith published extensive excerpts from the Enoch prophecy in August 1832 and in March 1833, and from the Moses vision that April.[122] A decade later, more portions appeared in the church's *Times and Seasons*,[123] and in 1851 portions appeared in the church's English periodical, the *Millennial Star*.[124]

Meanwhile, another body of texts had appeared under Smith's hand. In 1835, an entrepreneur from Pennsylvania, one Michael H. Chandler, passed through Kirtland with four Egyptian mummies and various scrolls of papyri. Given his immersion in ancient sacred texts, and the Book of Mormon's connection with things Egyptian in particular (that record purported to be written in "reformed Egyptian" characters, and quoted previously unknown prophecy from Joseph of Egypt),[125] Smith's interest in the collection led him to purchase the mummies and the papyri for $2,400. He immediately began a "translation" of the texts, to some extent working with an improvised Egyptian grammar. Smith proceeded as an amateur if inspired scholar with the papyri. (By contrast, he insisted he was called to translate the Book of Mormon and did so "by the gift and power of God"; his work retranslating Genesis he called another "branch of my calling," and "the Lord reveal[ed]" the prophecy of Enoch, according to the church newspaper, as we saw above.)[126]

What emerged from his work with the papyri was a remarkable first-person account of Abraham fleeing an attempt on his life in Chaldea by Egyptian priests practicing human sacrifice. Rescued by an angel, he immigrates to Haran, then moves on to Canaan where God renews his covenant with him. It was from this text that Smith received his fullest understanding to date of an Abrahamic covenant, one that did not foreshadow but itself embodied promises to Abraham and his posterity of the gospel fullness, an eternal priesthood, and innumerable seed, all of which elements would flower into essential Mormon theological principles and bridge the Everlasting Covenant of premortal worlds with its recuperation in the restored church.

In this re-rendering of the biblical account of the covenant with Abraham, God promises that

> I will make of thee a great nation, and . . . thou shalt be a blessing unto thy seed after thee, that in their hands they shall bear this ministry and Priesthood unto all nations; And I will bless them through thy name; for as many as receive this Gospel shall be called after thy name, and shall be accounted thy seed, and shall rise up and bless thee, as their father; . . . and in thy seed after thee (that is to say, the literal seed, or the seed of the body) shall all the families of the earth be blessed, even with the blessings of the Gospel, which are the blessings of salvation, even of life eternal.[127]

According to this restored Abrahamic narrative, when famine comes to Canaan, the patriarch departs for Egypt, where he recounts being taught celestial cosmology. He later describes a vision in which he sees the premortal souls of many "noble and great ones" and a pre-earth council where the plan of salvation is outlined and a Redeemer of the world chosen. This becomes another foundation for Mormon belief in the premortal existence of the human family, with the added element of their co-participation in the terms of the New and Everlasting Covenant established there, in the moment of its original articulation. Finally, the record narrates the creation story essentially as it reads in Genesis but emphasizing the process as one of shaping and ordering by the Gods (a challenge to trinitarianism that Smith would elaborate later), rather than a creation ex nihilo (out of nothing) as in conventional Christian understanding.

After Smith's death, the papyri changed hands several times. Scholars believe that most of the papyri were burned up in the Great Chicago Fire of 1871. Ten small fragments surfaced in 1967, and subsequent examination by Egyptologists revealed no apparent correspondence between the text and the published translation. Smith's revelatory practices ranged from the employment of seer stones to Nephite "interpreters" to visions to direct channeling of inspired texts, and if the Abrahamic material he produced was inspired, he seems not to have correctly located its origins in the papyrus scrolls. Some scholars emphasize that the surviving fragments represent a very small portion of the papyri in Joseph Smith's possession. They believe that the papyri containing the Abrahamic translations have not been found. An alternative view currently gaining ascendancy is that the ancient materials "catalyzed a process whereby God gave to Joseph Smith a revelation about the life of Abraham, even if that revelation did not directly correlate to the characters on the papyri."[128]

Like the expanded Genesis material, Smith did not initially publish the Abrahamic material, but much of it appeared in the church newspaper in 1842.[129] In 1851, Franklin D. Richards, president of the European mission, recognized the unheralded doctrinal significance of Smith's translated ancient texts. He took the initiative to assemble and publish them in pamphlet form as the Pearl of Great Price. (It was common for mission leaders and their elders to publish pamphlets for their own use in evangelizing as well as for instruction of new converts.)

Richards included, along with the Abrahamic and interpolated Genesis material, several other items: (1) Smith's retranslation of Matthew 24, a key apocalyptic text that reaffirmed Mormonism's commitment to fervent millennialist expectations; (2) a revelation from Smith on "the revelations of St. John," similarly themed; (3) an 1832 prophecy of Smith declaring South Carolina, the place where a civil war over slavery would erupt; (4) Smith's narrative of key events in his ministry, from his first theophany through his production of the Book of Mormon and his receipt of the priesthood; (5) an assortment of sections from the Doctrine and Covenants, which described the two sacraments of baptism and the Lord's Supper, and outlined priesthood offices and their duties; (6) an enumeration of LDS tenets, to be known thereafter as the Thirteen Articles of Faith; and (7) a poem titled, "O Say, What Is Truth."

Orson Pratt prepared an American edition of the collection in 1878, shortly after Brigham Young's death. Young had apparently been reluctant to elevate the volume's status, and so on the day John Taylor was sustained as church president in October 1880, it was he who presided over the canonization of the collection as Mormonism's fourth book of scripture. His role was telling: Taylor had penned the concluding words of the 1844 edition of the Doctrine and Covenants "to seal the testimony of [that] book" with an account of Smith's murder.[130] Several of Smith's revelations had been added in an 1876 edition, but they had not been presented to the church for a vote.[131] Now Taylor was confirming an expanded Doctrine and Covenants even as he added an entire new volume of scripture—even if the expansion consisted almost entirely of additional writings of Smith rather than revelatory output received in the years since his death. Shorn of its duplications with the Doctrine and Covenants (in 1902) as well as its concluding poem, the Pearl of Great Price today largely mirrors Richards's 1851 work.

Status of LDS Scripture

Wilford Woodruff recorded that on one occasion in the 1830s, "Brother Brigham took the stand, and he took the Bible, and laid it down; he took the Book of Mormon, and laid it down; and he took the Book of Doctrine and Covenants, and laid it down before him, and he said: 'There is the written word of God to us, concerning the work of God from the beginning of the world, almost, to our day.' 'And now,' said he, 'when compared with the living oracles those books are nothing to me; those books do not convey the word of God direct to us now, as do the words of a Prophet or a man bearing the Holy Priesthood in our day and generation. I would rather have the living oracles than all the writing in the books.' "[132] Apostle Mariner Merrill repeated the principle in 1897: "Here are the living oracles of God, and they are worth more to the Latter-day Saints than all the Bibles, all the Books of Mormon and all the Books of Doctrine and Covenants that are written."[133]

Though this authority is seldom expressed in such stark terms, Latter-day Saints persist in seeing the prophet's authority as superseding scripture, though the LDS canon serves in general to constrain the authority of its leadership. Joseph Fielding Smith taught that members need not accept his teachings or "the teachings of any other member of the Church, high or low, if they do not square with the . . . four standard works . . . by which we measure every man's doctrine."[134] However, church president Harold B. Lee noted that leaders may not write or speak "something that goes beyond anything you can find in the standard works, *unless that one be the prophet, seer, and revelation*" (emphasis added).[135] As the *Encyclopedia of Mormonism* summarizes, "above the authority of the written record stands the authority of the living prophet."[136]

In practice, Smith's pronouncements clearly if rarely trumped canonical texts (as when he pronounced God to be embodied, contra John's pronouncement that "God is spirit"; or when Smith claimed by his own experience an exception to John's rule that "No man hath seen God").[137] In such cases, his re-working of the texts in question was consistent with Mormonism's belief in a Bible not always translated (or transmitted) correctly. Additionally, the crucial caveat behind such prophetic prerogatives is the core principle that "in the last analysis, the burden of proof for scriptural status is placed upon the reader and hearer."[138] As Young counseled, "Let every man and woman know, by the whispering of the Spirit of God to themselves, whether their leaders are walking in the path the Lord dictates, or not."[139]

10

Worship

MORMON SCRIPTURE PROVIDES the expansive cosmic narrative in light of which the church acquires its purpose—to give structure and support to human efforts to abide by those principles that prepare Latter-day Saints to live in a celestial Zion community. The institutional church does this by providing a conduit for reliable, inspired guidance, channeling a divine will and wisdom responsive to the changing circumstances and needs of the human family. It provides the saving sacraments, performed by authorized administrators, instituted before the world was created, uniquely designed to forge eternal bonds of belonging. The church also exists as the assemblage of disciples united in their desire to celebrate and pay reverence to their God and Savior whose grace underlies the plan from beginning to end.

Mormons—like early Christians but unlike their contemporary peers—observe a twofold life of worship. Temples, we have seen, are where the highest sacraments of the Mormon faith are performed, with no regard for particular seasons or days of worship. Devout Mormons participate in each temple sacrament only once on their own behalf. They return as often as they desire or need in order to perform those rituals on behalf of deceased individuals (often kin) and to be reminded of the covenants that are part of the temple ordinances. The vast proportion of temple worship, then, is performed in the name and interest of another, deceased individual. This form of worship, noted one Mormon writer, is evocative of Kierkegaard's meditations on "The Work of Love in Remembering the Dead": "This loving the dead through recollection [a deliberate re-collecting rather than spontaneous remembering] is, in fact, the freest form of love because it is pure gift, a gift given with the knowledge that no repayment is forthcoming."[1] These acts of devotion performed across a veil of silence, a reaching after one's dead in the hope of uniting with them, are thus a kind of acme of Mormon worship, outward-looking service that honors God's intentions as it opens portals of salvation to myriad others.

THE CALENDAR

Temple worship, however, is more infrequent than the weekly congregational worship typical of Mormon religious life. Such weekly worship follows a general Christian pattern, though with marked peculiarities. "The calendar is the foundation of most Christian worship," writes James White.[2] Already in Paul we see his adaptation of the Jewish religious calendar to Christianity: with reference to Passover, he urged that believers "celebrate the festival, not with the old yeast, but with the unleavened bread of sincerity and truth."[3] By the fourth century, Easter, Pentecost, and Epiphany were all occasions of particular Christian commemoration. The calendar grew in complexity and detail over ensuing centuries, and if most Protestants simplified it (removing feasts and saints' days, for instance), they did not altogether abandon it. In its lack of a liturgical calendar, Mormon worship diverges sharply from these many Christian traditions. Unless motivated to do so individually, Mormons do not observe Advent or Lent or Holy Week or feast days (or holy days peculiar to themselves),[4] and the order of worship is unchanged even for Easter and Christmas—though they recognize those holy days with themed sermons or "talks." (Recently, perhaps in recognition of such ecclesiastical neglect, the church publishing house has begun to offer resources for families who wish to practice such religious observance in solidarity with other Christians.)[5] Mormons compensate for such liturgical neglect with an emphasis on Sabbath observance uncommon in modern Christianity.

Nine of the ten commandments given on Mt. Sinai maintain their moral force in the Christian world today. Only the fourth commandment (third for Catholics, who order them differently) has undergone substantial transformation. "Remember the Sabbath day, and keep it holy," commands the Decalogue. And then we find the principal mode of observance: "You shall not do any work."[6] In its very inception, which Jews trace to the double portion of manna granted the Israelites on the sixth day so that the seventh could be a day of respite, the Sabbath is defined by "rest and abstention from work."[7] The word, Sabbath (*Shabbat*), derives from *shavat*—which means "cease, desist, rest."[8] Sabbath keeping, therefore, in its etymology and practice, was a day commemorated by subtraction rather than addition. Abstinence from work is what set it apart and demarcated it as a holy day. At the same time, the space freed up was understood to be properly filled with acts of consecration and worship.

A casual reading of ecclesiastical history suggests that Christians simply changed the Sabbath from the seventh to the first day of the week, in commemoration of Christ's resurrection. However, the Christian Sabbath is more of a reinvention than a simple shift. Nothing in the New Testament indicates any continuity of what Christians recognized as "the Lord's Day" with the Jewish Sabbath. "On the first day of the week, . . . we met to break bread," Luke records.[9] Together with John of Patmos's reference to "the Lord's day," the implication is that Christians have begun to worship the risen Lord on the day of his rising.[10] Neither these references nor early Christian descriptions of their first worship services indicate any self-conscious continuity with or replacement of Jewish practice.

> On the day called Sunday, all who live in cities or in the country gather together to one place, and the memoirs of the apostles or the writings of the prophets are read, as long as time permits; then . . . the president verbally instructs, and exhorts to the imitation of these good things. Then we all rise together and pray, and, . . . when our prayer is ended, bread and wine and water are brought, and the president in like manner offers prayers and thanksgivings . . . and there is a distribution to each. . . . [Finally] they who are well to do, and willing, give what each thinks fit; and what is collected is deposited with the president, who succours the orphans and widows.[11]

So did Justin Martyr, a second-century Christian, describe a typical worship service. "Every Lord's day," directs the *Didache*, "do gather yourselves together, and break bread, and give thanksgiving."[12]

Church Fathers saw Sabbath observance according to the Jewish model as part of a Mosaic code fulfilled in Christ and no longer in need of observance. The Council of Laodicea "pronounced the anathema against the observance of the true Sabbath of Jehovah," writes one unsympathetic historian.[13] A church council in 538 decried any "Jewish superstition" in regulating Sunday activities.[14] But the pendulum had been swinging the other way since Constantine declared the "day of the Sun" a day of rest in 321.[15] A "moderated Sabbath law" became "the basis for Christian Sunday observance," and Sunday increasingly evoked the Jewish past. The laity was commanded to attend "the whole mass" on Sundays, along with bishops. Then, a Council of Orleans pointed out that these were indeed new expectations and that activities (like common labor) that had "heretofore been lawful" were no longer permitted.[16]

This was a development of enormous significance, since abstinence from labor has no biblical foundation whatsoever except as it relates to the Jewish Sabbath. What this step makes apparent is the process by which, fears of Judaizing notwithstanding, observance of the Christian Lord's Day does indeed assimilate Jewish practice in the process of constituting a Christian Sabbath. And following that first step, the Christian Sabbath became enmeshed in as many prohibitions as its Jewish predecessor. So much so that Pope Gregory IX had to "bring order into this chaos" with his authoritative *Decretals* in 1234.[17] At the same time, but in a futile gesture, Catholic authorities moved to reaffirm the early Christian position, that the new day of worship was not to be understood as continuous with its Jewish predecessor. In the fifteenth century, according to an edict, those who "observe circumcision and the Sabbath and the other requirements of the law, [the church] declares alien to the Christian faith."[18] Of course, a new holy day signified a new law with its own ground of authority. The Catholic apologist Johann Eck acknowledged the implications with no hedging: lacking explicit scriptural warrant for the change, "the church has transferred the observance from Saturday to Sunday by virtue of her own power, without scripture."[19]

Inevitably, then, in dissenting from papal sacramental innovations, Luther would similarly object to papal Sabbath institutions. The church had no authority to inaugurate a new Sabbath, he held. And as for the biblical injunction, in his *Small Catechism* the fourth commandment is completely stripped of any directive for weekly worship; it means simply "we should not despise his word and the preaching of the same."[20] Others in the Reformation, however, were moving to reinstitute a weekly Sabbath, causing dissension in their ranks. The Westminster Confession affirms God's intent to designate "one day in seven, for a Sabbath," declaring that the particular day "from the resurrection of Christ, was changed into the first day of the week," constituting the new "Christian Sabbath."[21] But not all were agreed. "Restless spirits are now making an outcry about the observance of the Lord's day," Calvin noted in his *Institutes*, and he argued for a middle-ground solution. On the one hand, he found the law of the Sabbath fulfilled in the perfect rest ushered in by the Resurrection. The Sabbath requirement was now "abrogated," and he warned against the "carnal superstition of sabbatism." Nevertheless, he insisted that a designated day of worship is "a necessary remedy for preserving order in the church," though the day didn't matter. He freely condoned those churches that were observing Sunday as a Christian Sabbath or even "holding their meetings on other solemn days."[22]

Sabbatarianism, a strict observance of the Christian Sabbath that parallels a fastidious Jewish observance, was effectively launched in the generation after Calvin with the publication of Nicholas Bownd's *True Doctrine of the Sabbath* (1595). His contribution was to insist on an absolute continuity between the Jewish and Christian obligations. "The Church of God did keep the Sabbath from the beginning," he asserted, and therefore "the Sabbath ought to be continued with us."[23] The

Puritans of the decades following were by and large united in their strict observance, which extended the Jewish prohibition against labor to include most forms of leisure as well. (Their heritage was long felt, especially in the "blue laws" that persist in many localities to this day in the form of ordinances against commerce, in whole or in part.)

Jonathan Edwards devoted a sermon to the contested topic of Sabbath observance in the early 1700s. He insisted that "it is the mind and will of God, that the first day of the week should be especially set apart among Christians, for religious exercises and duties." It makes no difference that "some deny it," some "refuse to take notice of the day, as different from other days."[24] A hundred years later, the Awakening of the early nineteenth century rekindled concern for a stricter observance of the Sabbath on the part of many Protestants. That was the world of Joseph Smith's religious formation.

MORMON SABBATH DAY

Mormons initially held prayer, fast, confirmation, and worship services on weekdays in addition to Sundays. Midweek prayer meetings, in which men as well as women participated, were especially common in the era of Brigham Young.[25] These other meetings notwithstanding, they never questioned the long-standing Christian recognition of Sunday as the new Sabbath, and a revelation received on a Sunday in August 1831 confirmed that "this [was] the Lord's day."[26] (On one occasion, however, Young dismissed temple construction workers on a Saturday in deference to "all the Saints who felt to keep today sacred" in recognition of the Jewish Sabbath; the important thing was attendance at meetings, and a modicum of Sabbath rest, "no matter what day we observe or rest upon.")[27] But determining the day for Sabbath observance does not resolve the question of how the day is to be observed. In this regard, Mormon Sabbath observance followed in microcosm the larger Christian developments of the first centuries.

Initially, Mormons defined the Sabbath in terms of worship. Revelation declared this day to be for offering "oblations and thy sacraments unto the Most High," with the additional proviso that members on this day "do none other thing, only let thy food be prepared with singleness of heart that thy fasting may be perfect, or, in other words, that thy joy may be full."[28] The vague "do none other thing" was not terribly helpful; as Young noted wryly, in order to truly "keep the Sabbath we must lie in bed all day and scarcely breathe."[29] Still, it was clear to him that not enough was being done to set the day apart. In 1845, he was complaining that "there is not a Sabbath that passes over your heads without breaking it."[30] As the Saints embarked upon their westward exodus, he imposed a stricter discipline like the Orleans council, adding a list of negative prohibitions to the positive command to worship. "We must give more attention to keeping the Sabbath, and quit shooting and trading, and not pass it off carelessly, for I know it is wrong."[31] Sabbath observance soon settled into a simple blending of the twin imperatives pertaining to Old and New Testament observance: "It is wisdom to rest on the Sabbath and partake of the Sacrament."[32]

In the early Utah settlement, an emphasis on strict Sabbath observance grew, with a recognition that it was not a universal Christian practice, at least, not what Young called "a Saint's Sabbath: there is not a nation nor a people that keep the Sabbath, not a Christian, from the Pope to the latest reformer; there is not one who keeps it."[33] Soon more prohibitions than work came into play: "no fishing, hunting, &tc. on the Sabbath day";[34] "cease your visiting on the Sabbath day";[35] do "not visit the "farm [or the] bath house on Sunday";[36] cook food "if it is necessary," but "if that could be dispensed with, it would be better."[37] If the regimen sounded Puritan, it was, but this was the case among many believing Christians of the nineteenth century. As Young noted, "They keep the Sabbath pretty tolerably well, and so do we."[38] Two meetings a day on Sunday were typical in the nineteenth century, but small, inadequately heated ward buildings, poor acoustics in the larger tabernacles, bad roads, and the demands of a struggling agrarian people meant attendance was often poor.[39]

Blue laws have mostly faded from the books, and Sunday has become synonymous with sports and entertainment. Pope John Paul II may have lamented Sunday's surrender to sport, but few religious voices resist the trend today; as Norman Vincent Peale remarked without complaint, "If Jesus Christ were alive today, he would be at the Super Bowl," which of course is always on Sunday.[40] Mormons depart from these modern developments, continuing to define Sabbath observance as an essential gospel principle, one that requires worship and devotion as well as abstinence from labor, commerce, and recreation. In 2015, the church even created a committee of apostles and seventies "to help Church members focus on better observing the Sabbath day at church and at home."[41]

MORMON WORSHIP SERVICE

Justin Martyr, in his second-century description of Christian worship, referred vaguely to "the place where those who are called brethren are assembled."[42] At his trial before execution, he was more specific. "Where do you assemble?" the Roman prefect Rusticus inquired. "Where each one chooses and can," he responded. "I live above one Martinus, at the Timiothinian Bath; and . . . am unaware of any other meeting than his."[43] In the Protestant Reformation, too, meetings were at first often secretive and intimate. Calvin declared it a duty for Protestants to open their homes for services, though that was largely in a setting of persecution and secrecy.[44] Early Latter-day Saints at first met in homes since their numbers warranted little space in the early years. Later, settled in Kirtland and with converts pouring in, larger build-ings like the Kirtland Temple could accommodate mass meetings. Joseph Smith preached outdoors to audiences as large as 8,000 in Nauvoo, but he also made use of other buildings. In 1840, apostle Wilford Woodruff converted a substantial group of Methodist defectors "who put into [his] hands one chapel," known as the Gadfield Elm chapel.[45] English Latter-day Saints thus had their own meetinghouse before Saints in America did.

Along the trek westward, bishops were counseled to "hold meeting wher[ever] the Saints might assemble."[46] Once in Utah, as in Nauvoo, meetings were generally large affairs held outdoors. The first large structure built to accommodate the masses was the quickly erected Bowery, a simple roofed area of logs and branches built by Mormon Battalion veterans mere days after arrival in the valley. It was replaced by the old Tabernacle five years later, then the one still standing in 1867. Other settle-ments built tabernacles for the same purpose, some of them the most beautiful struc-tures in Mormondom. Gradually, communities began to hold smaller, ward-sized meetings in schoolhouses or purpose-built ward halls in the afternoons to supple-ment the morning tabernacle meetings. By the end of the century, these smaller ward meetings had largely replaced the communal tabernacle meetings, except at time of conference.[47]

In the document known as the Articles and Covenants, put into final form at the time of the church's formal founding and later canonized as scripture, directions were given to the priesthood holders "to conduct the meetings as they are led by the Holy Ghost."[48] The directive was repeated a year later. Apparently, the guide-lines were insufficient, or insufficiently followed, for eighteen months after formally incorporating the church, Smith held a conference in Hiram, Ohio, "so that the members might understand the ancient manner of conducting meetings as they were led by the Holy Ghost." "This," he added, "was not perfectly known by many of the Elders of this Church."[49] The vagueness of the original directive was acknowl-edged by the addition, in editions of 1835 and later, of the words, "according to the commandments and revelations of God."[50]

The closest parallel to Mormon meetings were probably Methodist, as the Methodists "avoid[ed] formalism in worship" because it could "potentially stifle the spirit."[51] Mormon meetings were fairly typical low-church affairs, with hymns, prayers, the sacrament, and sermons—but no vestments or iconography. Often, the prayers took the form of communal orisons after the pattern of both early Christian and Protestant practice. Sometimes this appears to have been a prayer repeated by the assembly, as when the first two church conferences included "prayer by all."[52] Other times, a smaller group would unite in a circle and offer petitions, repeating aloud the prayer of the voice. So at an early meeting of the School of the Prophets, "a number joined in the circle, and prayed."[53] Or on another occasion, Smith and some of his close associates recorded in 1835 that they "assembled and united in prayer, with one voice before the Lord."[54] Hymn-singing was influenced by Methodist precedent—that denomination being the most enthusiastic about congregational singing. The Methodists had by this time published eight editions of hymns, some hopefully intended, as the subtitle indicated, "for the pious of all denominations." Emma Smith, herself a former Methodist, accepted the invitation to compile the first LDS hymnbook and relied upon her own copy of one such hymnal for many of her selections.[55] To this day, the Mormon hymnal is a blend of works authored by Mormons, Protestants, and Catholics.

In weekly LDS home meeting worship services today, in contradistinction to the highly formalized rituals of Mormon temple worship, the order of worship has very little ritual or ceremony. The general pattern (other than Fast Sunday, see below) is for opening and closing prayers, "talks" (which by their very name resist even the formalism of sermonizing), and the administration of the Lord's Supper, with three or four hymns (opening, sacrament, rest, and closing hymns). James White identifies nine Protestant liturgical traditions that encompass "almost all" Christians.[56] Mormon practice fits none of them, since by comparison even the Methodists, otherwise influential in Mormon worship, have a liturgical richness Mormonism lacked.[57] In its anti-formalism, Mormon worship may be closest to Quakerism.

"Virtually all worship makes use of the Bible," White goes on to say. In addition, "service books" or lectionaries "are regarded as necessities for worship in most Christian traditions."[58] Here again, we see a striking difference in Mormon worship. Scriptures are often employed in the talks, but there is no formal requirement to do so, no readings or recitations. And topics may include grace, or resurrection, or the beatitudes, but may also focus on practical matters of self-reliance or thrift. Wilford Woodruff once made a comment that may shed light on the general anti-formalism of most Mormon worship patterns (the temple being a crucial exception). "Strangers and the Christian world marvel," he said, at the Mormon emphasis on "temporal work," and he responded that "we can't build up Zion sitting on a hemlock slab singing ourselves away to everlasting bliss; we have to cultivate the earth, to take the rocks and elements out of the mountains and rear Temples to the Most High God."[59]

From the beginnings, this incongruous conflation of the sacred and the banal had been noticed. As persecution heated up in Nauvoo in the summer of 1842, the *New York Herald* editor James Gordon Bennett reported with amusement, "Jo goes on prophesying, preaching, and building the temple, and regulating his empire, as if nothing had happened. They are busy all the time establishing factories to make saints and crockery ware, also prophets and white paint."[60] Catholic theologian Stephen Webb noted of the Mormon propensity to sacralize the quotidian, with particular reference to liturgy: "Both Mormons and Catholics believe in transubstantiation. They just locate [it] in different theological places. . . . For Catholics, transubstantiation is dramatized in a quite literal way in the Eucharist, where the bread and wine become the first fruits of the eschatological economy of Christ's abundantly capacious body. That drama for Mormons is not localized in such a specific way. . . . The Saints actually locate transubstantiation in the potential for every event, no matter how mundane."[61]

Mormons have no paid or trained clergy at the local level—but that itself does not explain the practice of rotating the speaking duty among all adult members of the congregation. The custom might be better understood in light of White's definition of liturgy, Woodruff's comment, and its bearing on the Mormon understanding of worship. "To call a service 'liturgical,'" White writes, "is to indicate that it was conceived so that all worshippers take an active part in offering their worship together."[62] Particularly gifted Mormon congregants might be selected as lay preachers, but that does not happen, and the results are legendary in Mormon culture (Mormons feel particular empathy for Paul, the first recorded preacher to bore a congregant to his death).[63] Not only does such rotating participation engage all adult congregants in the worship service; it demonstrably privileges community forbearance and reinforcement over personal, self-directed edification. Women give talks about as frequently as men, though they apparently rarely spoke in the nineteenth century.[64] The labor of preparing and delivering a "talk" outweighs in devotional value, in the Mormon conception, the refinement of a more polished and qualified sermonizer. Like the early Methodists from whom they drew so many converts, Mormons have consistently valued exhortation and the low style of preaching over rhetorically elegant homiletics.

A second, little regarded way in which a Mormon worship service has a liturgical quality of the kind noted by White is in the observance of the Lord's Supper (which gives to the weekly worship service its name of "sacrament meeting"). The sacrament prayers, pronounced by youths holding the office of priest or mature men holding the Melchizedek priesthood, are the only formal prayers a Mormon will hear in the weekly public worship service. And although they pronounce the prayer, the administration of the sacrament is effected by all the members, who pass the bread and water to each other. Matthew Bowman has written about the subtle but profound sacramental implications of this mode of distribution: "The wonderful thing about . . . the institution narrative in Mark—and, more, in the way that we

Mormons administer the rite is that it is Christ's disciples who pass and gather the bread. We bear Christ's grace to each other; we serve it as we pass it down the rows; as the memory of that upper room makes us the spiritual children of the first apostles, so in serving the bread of life to each other do we make each other our brothers and sisters."[65]

Originally, people gave sermons or read scriptures during the administration of the sacrament. On one occasion, a scribe noted Young saying, "While we are administering the sacrament I will read the 16th verse of the 10th chapter of Corinthians."[66] On another, he indicated that "the sacrament is being administered, and we would like to talk about the spiritual welfare of the people."[67] Yet elsewhere, he anticipated the modern custom of reverential silence during the ordinance, even as he recognized it was a novel idea. "While partaking of the sacrament to meet my own feelings, I would not often speak.... I am pleased to hear the saints testify but it is not the design of the sacrament to preach a sermon but to make a few remarks, ask forgiveness and refrain from evil. I am always ready and willing to give way to brothers and sisters, my own feelings would be to meditate upon the principles of the Holy Ghost and if any think it a Quaker meeting they can go out."[68] In the first half of the twentieth century, music during the sacrament was the norm, offered by the congregation, ward choirs, organists, violinists, or even cellists.[69] In 1946, the First Presidency decreed "absolute quiet during the passing of the sacrament" as "the ideal condition."[70]

Another characteristic of early Mormon worship services, now largely absent, was the confessing of sins. James had encouraged the early saints to "confess your sins to one another," and the earliest document of Christian practice, the *Didache*, similarly admonished early Christians to "gather yourselves together, and ... confess ... your transgressions, that your sacrifice may be pure."[71] And so in this tradition, Smith's 1831 revelation on Sabbath observance had indicated a responsibility to offer up their sacraments on the appointed day, "confessing thy sins unto thy brethren, and before the Lord."[72] Early Mormons took the directive literally. "I opened the meeting by singing and prayer And addressed the people. I confessed my own sins And in some respects the sins of the 14th ward in which I dwell," noted Wilford Woodruff in his diary.[73]

Numerous accounts of early church councils and leadership meetings also include reference to frank confessions, expressions of contrition and forgiveness, and an ensuing unity and harmony. William Clayton described one 1841 meeting where the presiding elder "called upon all who had hardness and who had transgressed to confess and repent.... After many had confessed he called upon myself and Brother Nickerson to break bread and administer."[74] The practice was regularized in Sunday worship, with Young confirming that "confessions should be made before the sacrament is administered."[75] There was a fitting logic to the practice. The sacrament commemorated the atonement, vehicle of Christ's supernal mercy. Young reasoned that it made sense to "draw in our hearts to worship Him in truth, acknowledge Him in sincerity and believe on him with all our hearts, so that we may have the spirit of charity in our bosoms, which will lead us to forgive one another our trespasses that we may be forgiven."[76]

An early revelation had suggested that private confession was preferable to public and stipulated that "if thy brother or sister offend thee, thou shalt take him or her *between him or her and thee alone*. . . . And if he or she confess not thou shalt deliver him or her up unto the church, not to the members, but to the elders. And it shall be done in a meeting" (emphasis added).[77] And so in the decades after Young especially, a trend of privatization of confession took place. Only those major sins that touched on the church as a whole (such as adultery) required public airing. As a stake president explained in 1905, "When the offence becomes public a public confession is necessary."[78] A usual practice was for the guilty party to make confession to either the priesthood quorums or the full congregation, after which a vote to accept the confession was taken.[79] In 1976, the practice of public confession was dropped entirely.[80]

In early Mormonism, baptism was often followed up immediately by the laying on of hands for the gift of the Holy Ghost, or what was called "confirmation" ("Confirmed them at the water's edge," in one typical journal entry).[81] But it was also common to hold special meetings called "confirmation meetings" where the recently baptized were confirmed, sometimes to the accompaniment of spiritual manifestations.[82] "The spirit was given to some in great power," noted Smith of one such meeting.[83] A visitor to another noted that it "lasted all night. . . . I heard them prophecy and speak in tongues unknown to me."[84] Like some of the early Christian services, the occasion was solemn enough that members were unclear about public access to the proceedings. A curious John Murdock wanted to witness one but learned the Mormons "did not want those in that had not been baptized."[85] Even so, an 1831 revelation admonished members to admit strangers even to confirmation meetings, if they "are earnestly seeking after the kingdom."[86] In the modern church, confirmations are generally performed on the Sunday following baptism, as part of the sacrament meeting.

Puritan sermons were notoriously long-winded, and nineteenth-century Saints— as well as many Protestants—were true to that heritage. Pratt describes a sermon by then Campbellite Sidney Rigdon, who convened his congregation for a special meeting where he "addressed them very affectionately, for nearly two hours, during most of which time, both himself and nearly all the congregation were melted to tears."[87] He was just as prolix; a missionary companion noted a typical occasion where "Mr. Parley arose and addressed [a congregation] about 2 hours," by which time "some of them began to get very uneasy before he closed."[88] His brother Orson bested that marathon, recording a day he spent "preaching in the forenoon about 3 hours in the meeting house near Deacon True's."[89] This pattern seems to have been carried over into early Mormon services, for within a year of Joseph's death, Young proposed "having two meetings rather than to continue the practice of 'lengthy' morning meetings."[90] In 1852, the new order was instituted: "Pres. Young then gave notice that from henceforth we should hold meetings regularly each Sabbath at 10 a.m., and 2 p.m., and in the evening, the several quorums of the priesthood would assemble to receive instruction."[91] By the late twentieth century, Mormon holders of the priesthood were convening early Sunday for quorum meetings, bringing their families for Sunday School a little later, then reconvening in the evening for the sacrament service. Those meetings were combined in 1980, into Mormonism's notorious "consolidated block" of a three-hour series of meetings.

In the founding years of Mormonism, the principal mode of worship was in large gatherings, marked by quarterly conferences. "In virtually every respect these early LDS conferences were identical to those of the Methodists," notes Kathleen Flake, comprising sermons, instruction, and financial business.[92] Division into stakes and wards with local patterns of worship came later, as we have seen. Today, Mormons assemble twice yearly for stake conferences and twice yearly in the Salt Lake Conference Center (or via the airwaves) to replicate the pattern of "Methodist meetings with Moses in their midst."[93] The significance of these semi-annual General Conferences serves many functions. Profoundly invested in the doctrine of continuing revelation, Mormons expect to hear not just inspired sermons of uplift but any revealed developments in official policy or teachings coming through the instrument of a living prophet (cessation of polygamy, new temples, and changes to the scriptural canon have all been announced at General Conferences, as are the calling of new apostles). In addition, conferences are occasion to participate in the semi-sacramental ritual of sustaining the leaders of the church. Finally, and perhaps most meaningfully, General Conference represents a compelling instance of the entire, worldwide community of Latter-day Saints jointly assembled for purposes of worship. John Taylor commented on this aspect in 1859:

> What makes us so buoyant and joyful on occasions like this? Why is it that the Spirit and power of God is more visibly manifested at the time of our General conference, when the authorities of the Church from all parts are assembled together to talk on the things of God, regulate the affairs of his kingdom, to put in order anything that may be wrong, and counsel together pertaining to the interests of Zion and the building up of Israel? It is because there is a

union of good feelings, good desires and aspirations; and one spirit inspires the whole, forming a phalanx of power, of faith, and of the Spirit of the Lord. . . . With us it is a time of union, of light, of life, of intelligence, of the Spirit of the living God. Our feelings are one—our faith is one; and a great multitude possessing this oneness forms an array of power that no power on this side of earth or hell is able to cope with or overcome.[94]

Law of the Fast

In 1852, Brigham Young indicated that "on Thursday the brethren and sisters would come together at 2 p.m., for prayer and supplication; and on the first Thursday in each month, at 10 a.m., for the purpose of fasting and prayer, calling on the Saints to observe that day."[95] Fasting has been a part of most religious traditions, often an essential constituent of their ascetic strand. Depriving the body of necessary sustenance and natural cravings—whether for food, sleep, or pleasure—has been construed as an effective means of disciplining and subordinating the recalcitrant flesh to the nobler aspirations and preoccupations of the spirit. In addition, fasting can have a penitential function. Self-deprivation or willing subjection to self-inflicted pain has been practiced as a demonstration of contrition. One strand of Jewish thought considers the principal religious function of fasting to be that of eliciting God's compassion, in response to this ritual act "of remorse, submission, and supplication."[96] Because of its frequent association with other ritualistic forms of self-denial (from bathing to comfortable beds to sexual intercourse),[97] the fast might most profitably be seen as the sacrificial offering of selfhood. That provides the most reasonable rationale for the practice, a worshipful sacrifice that prepares the soul for greater communion with God.

The Israelites fasted to incur God's favor and allay his wrath as well as to demonstrate sorrow. David fasted to add power and efficacy to his prayers, as when he petitioned God for the healing of his child,[98] and Ezra fasted to obtain spiritual guidance on the return to Jerusalem.[99] The similar use of fasting to acquire and invoke greater spiritual power is enjoined by Jesus in the New Testament, and this becomes a principal motive in Christian fasting, though the ascetic purposes lurk frequently in the background. Thus Christ admonishes his disciples to fast for greater influence over demonic forces, and Paul urges the practice for resilience against Satan's temptations.[100]

Jewish practice is to observe six biblical fasts and some three dozen fast days decreed by the rabbis, in addition to several private fasts,[101] and the disciples of Jesus were criticized for not observing the regular fast days.[102] As we saw, however, Jesus did recommend fasting, and the *Didache* advocated regular fasts on Wednesdays and Fridays (in distinction to some of the Jewish fasts that occurred on Mondays and Thursdays).[103] In the Christian calendar soon to emerge, several particular days were designated for fasts (which as in Judaism often were dawn-to-dusk fasts), including Lent, Advent, and feasts of Peter and Paul. An early Methodist Book of Discipline admonishes preachers to ensure that "a fast be held in every society in his circuit, on the Friday preceding every quarterly meeting."[104] On the whole, however, fasting is no longer "a prominent feature of modern western Christianity," notes one standard reference.[105]

The Christian practice of fasting before feast days suggests an intention to heighten the joy of abundance by the experience of paucity. Such a logic appears in the first Mormon reference to fasting, an 1831 revelation that enjoins the preparation of food in such a frame of mind "that thy fasting may be perfect, or in other words, that thy joy may be full."[106] The Book of Mormon mentions fasting several times, always in conjunction with prayer.[107] Early in Mormonism, fasting acquired an additional function it maintains to this day. As Brigham Young expressed the principle in the Nauvoo years, "We have kept the poor by having fast meeting and giving to the poor—if we can sustain our poor by fasting one day in four weeks—it is a cheap tax—it makes them glad and we are all as one mind."[108] Like the Jewish prohibition against gleaning one's own fields, fasting became a communal form of social welfare. Thus, the experience of deprivation was to elicit solidarity with the needy, and the resources saved by that self-deprivation could be redirected to alleviate the hunger of the needy. Spiritual and pragmatic benefits were merged.

The practice of combining fasting with offerings began at Smith's instigation in Kirtland, when "at the monthly fast day . . . the brethren donated of their substance to help the poor."[109] As Young explained in more detail, "As to how much people should administer on a fast day for the sustenance of the poor, I will say, . . . reckon up how much you consume in your families of flour, meat, vegetables, groceries, etc., and carry two thirds of that day's rations to the Bishop of your ward. If you feel as though you could give a little more, give all the three meals. . . . I wish to remind every Bishop, that it is expected of him not to let a single family escape the performance of this important duty, that the poor may be fed and properly cared for."[110] (After some hardship apparently. Against a general background of scarcity and want, Young considered that five days of hunger warranted intervention.)[111]

Special services were also designated as fast meetings. In July 1845, Young announced matter-of-factly that "next Thursday will be a fast meeting," expecting the brethren to fast and donate proceeds to the poor, while the next Sunday was the regular day to "have the sacrament."[112] After Young's designation of the first Thursday of every month as a day of fasting, attendance at that meeting became one more mandatory meeting, with Young urging "upon the Elders of Israel the necessity of going to fast meeting regularly."[113] The day was moved to the first Sunday of every month in 1896, which remains the current practice. In addition, as Young frequently urged the Saints to individually "fast and pray until they get the spirit of God," so is fasting encouraged today as an aspect of private devotion and discipleship.[114]

FAST AND TESTIMONY MEETING

The first Sunday of the month follows a different format than normal Sunday worship services. In 1829, Oliver Cowdery had prepared the "Articles of the Church of Christ" at Smith's behest (later supplanted by Smith's own version). In those Articles, it was stipulated that "the church shall meet together oft for prayer & supplication casting out none from your places of worship but rather invite them to come And each member shall speak & tell the church of their progress in the way to Eternal life."[115] The opportunity for this format of spiritual intimacy and vulnerability occurs at fast meetings. Those were the times, as Young explained, when "the Saints meet to express their feelings and to strengthen each other in their faith of the holy Gospel. We will, so far as the time will permit, give all the Saints who may wish the privilege to freely express their views and reflections to this congregation."[116]

This practice of "testimony bearing" was practiced by Puritan churches, which required candidates for membership to narrate a conversion experience attesting to God's saving grace.[117] Mormon testimonies are more a distinctive version of Quaker spontaneity and informality infused with a rhetoric of propositional certainty. In other words, Mormons bear testimony as they feel moved by the spirit, and share what are at times deeply moving personal accounts of God's tender mercies. But the unscripted expressions can range from miraculous healings to professions of love for one's spouse (or roommate) to summer travelogues. At the same time, a virtually universal feature is the formulation "I know" in reference to core Mormon claims—which affirmations Bruce R. McConkie attempted to standardize in his magisterial *Mormon Doctrine*: "1. That Jesus Christ is the Son of God and the Savior of the world; 2. That Joseph Smith is the Prophet of God through whom the gospel was restored in this dispensation; and 3. That the Church of Jesus Christ of Latter-day Saints is the only true and living church upon the face of the whole earth."[118] The roots of such expressions of propositional certainty are in the Book of Mormon ("ye may know the truth of all things"), in Smith's personal predilections ("I know for a certainty of eternal things";[119] "the first principle of truth [is] to know for a certainty the character of God"),[120] and his published revelations ("you may know of a surety my doctrine"; "assuredly as the Lord liveth, . . . shall you receive a knowledge of whatsoever things you shall ask in faith").[121]

Visitors to LDS meetings—and Mormons themselves—often find such personal expressions of conviction and conversion by the laity to be lacking both polish and concision. Thomas Shepard, writing in the seventeenth century, felt the same frustrations: "There are many odd confessions by those who are received, and extravagant enlarged discourses of the set time of their conversion, and their Revelation, and ill Application of Scripture which makes such long doings, and are wearisome and uncomely."[122] Nevertheless, it is likely that such public, spontaneous professions of personal belief, which generally involve the most intimate of spiritual experiences and feelings, constitute another practice that forges those powerful communal bonds for which Latter-day Saints are known, and which tend toward the kind of Zion community to which Joseph Smith aspired.

11

Boundary Maintenance and Discipline

THE NEW AND Everlasting Covenant is a plan for human happiness that takes the entirety of the human family within its purview. And yet, ironically, the institutional church has from the beginning established boundaries. Like most of the Christian world, Mormonism envisions both an invisible or spiritual congregation of the elect as well as a visible body of believers belonging to its temporal version. And while God knows his own, Mormonism is among those institutional churches that have followed New Testament precedent in determining the parameters of its particular membership. Organizational identity presupposes boundaries, lines of demarcation, and criteria by which membership is achieved or maintained. As William Temple declared, "There must always be a tension between the right of the individual to freedom and the right of the institution to have a determinate character."[1] More recently, Timothy Keller has noted that "any community that did not hold its members accountable for specific beliefs and practices would have not corporate identity and would really not be a community at all."[2] Boundary maintenance, therefore, constitutes a virtually inescapable dimension of ecclesiology.

CUTTING OFF THE UNREPENTANT

Already in Paul's epistles we find a directive to cut persistent sinners off from the congregation. "You are to hand this man over to Satan for the destruction of the flesh," he says of the man consorting with his stepmother, for Christians are "not to associate with sexually immoral persons."[3] The meaning of this handing over is unmistakable: "Drive out the wicked person from among you," Paul says plainly, setting a pattern for subsequent Christian discipline. As one scholar notes, "Of the exercise of excommunication in the New Testament period there are ample instances. Constant references occur to 'rejecting,' 'withdrawing from,' 'convicting,' or 'not receiving' dissidents."[4] Third-century sources refer to the bishop's responsibility to maintain church discipline and purity, admonishing that if anyone "hardens himself, . . . receive him no longer into the Church."[5]

The motive in this practice goes beyond the mere maintenance of a "corporate identity" that Keller suggested. The concern is clearly for the well-being of disciples vulnerable to the ungodly influence of those who would seduce intellectually or morally. Such persons might "entice the disciples to follow them," like "savage wolves" coming in "among you, not sparing the flock" in Paul's analogy.[6] Even without intending, suggests Jude, persons of corrupt practices have a dangerous propensity to "contaminate" or "defile" by their proximity.[7]

Standards once introduced are easily abused, and so, notes a historian of Christian worship, increasingly into the medieval period and beyond, "excommunication was brought into effective and tyrannical use" by the church.[8] Two categories of the sanction developed: the "lesser" barred the person from officeholding and from access to the saving sacraments. The "greater" excommunication barred the person not only from the sacraments but even from any participation in the community of the faithful.[9] In no case, however, did the excommunicant "cease to be a Christian, since his baptism can never be effaced."[10]

At the Council of Trent, bishops and prelates were admonished to use this supreme censure with more restraint.[11] At the same time, as Edmund Morgan writes, some reformers were turning increasing attention to the task of purifying "not only corrupt forms of worship and organization but corrupt membership."[12] The Church of England has maintained the practice of censure in theory, though it fell into increasing disfavor with the Reformation. As for Lutherans, the catechism says simply, "The Christian congregation must exclude openly unrepentant sinners (excommunication)."[13] Calvin devoted a whole chapter in his *Institutes* to church discipline, the disregard of which was creating "a fearful devastation in the church."[14] He outlines three purposes of expulsion: protecting Christ from insult, protecting the innocent from corruption, and fostering the repentance of the sinner. With an eye to the first in particular, Calvinists see excommunication as principally a prohibition against participation in the Lord's Supper.[15] The Westminster Confession declared formal censures "necessary" for the reasons Calvin had listed, as well as for averting "the wrath of God, which might justly fall upon the church" if they did not expel the profane. The three ascending degrees of censure the Confession indicated were admonition, prohibition from the Lord's Supper, and excommunication.[16]

Puritans in particular felt the visible church was in need of pruning and cleansing, but to their frustration, the centralized church government of the Anglicans meant individual congregations "were unable to rid themselves of unworthy members."[17] Minor divisions aside, they all agreed "that every church should exclude and expel the wicked."[18] This was because the very definition of a church with which the Puritans operated was of "a company or congregatione of the faythfull called and gathered out of the worlde."[19] So non-negotiable was this definition of a church as a body of the faithful that the Separatists justified their rupture with Anglicanism accordingly. In its "rebellious refusal" to winnow its membership through strict discipline, the Anglican establishment had relinquished "the power to rid itself of unworthy members" and had therefore "cease[d] to be the Church of God."[20] So, too, Separatists believed, Calvin had erred in thinking the sacraments and true preaching were enough to constitute a church. Boundary maintenance was the essential third leg of the stool.

Some Puritan ministers simply debarred those they considered non-elect from the sacraments, while others barred them from participation in the Christian community generally.[21] Within a few decades, however, church membership declined enough that it was decided to include in church membership even those baptized as infants and never converted, as long as they were "not scandalous in life."[22] The Methodists who emerged out of the English church claimed to reject orthodoxy tests for the membership, but early manuals of discipline did include provisions for expulsion for "ministers and preachers, who hold and disseminate publicly or privately, doctrines which are contrary to our articles of religion." Members as well could be "cut off" and "expelled from the church" for "inveighing against either our doctrines or our discipline."[23] Expulsion generally took the form of ejection from a Methodist class; to remain in good standing, members were expected to "continue to evidence their desire for salvation."[24] Some Presbyterians argued in the 1830s that "every slaveholder ought to be excommunicated" from their church, but their General Assembly rejected the motion.[25]

As religious conflict heated up in nineteenth-century America, excommunication was common. Several early Mormons found their way to the church after being disbarred from their own. Smith complained with only some exaggeration that "Methodists have creeds which a man must believe or be kicked out of their church."[26] One convert to Mormonism agreed that "should you absent yourselves three weeks, without being able to render a satisfactory reason, according to the rules of the society, you must be cut off."[27] Alfred Young recorded that "for a season I continued a member of the Baptist Church but contended with the people, day by day, for the principles of the gospel until I was brought before the Church and cut off from their fellowship."[28] Shakers of the day could "cut off" members for failure to share their wealth, as Josiah Talcott learned to his dismay.[29]

Like virtually all other Christian traditions, Mormonism addresses in its founding documents the matter of boundaries and discipline. Cowdery's 1829 "Articles of the Church of Christ" followed Puritan precedent in barring access to certain sacraments as a form of sanction. With the Puritans, for example, the "Lord's Table" was reserved for the fully committed and proven visible saints. As Edmund Morgan explains, "The drive toward exclusive membership had always aimed primarily at excluding the unworthy from the Lord's supper."[30] So, too, Cowdery's rule, following the Book of Mormon, mandated, "If ye know that a man is unworthy to eat & drink my flesh & blood ye shall forbid him." Twice, however, the Articles stipulated that even the unworthy should not be "cast out . . . from among you" or from "your places of worship."[31] In actual practice, the principle of worthy participation in the Lord's Supper relies to a large extent on self-policing; in the modern church, only formal "disfellowshipment" or "excommunication" bars one from participating in ordinances (but not from joining in worship).

Subsequent revelations allowed for more drastic measures than withholding the Eucharist. "If they are not faithful they shall not have fellowship in the church," an 1832 revelation states plainly but rather vaguely.[32] A few years later, a church statement of belief affirmed that "all religious societies have a right to deal with their members for disorderly conduct, according to the rules and regulations of such societies," and have the right to "excommunicate them from their society, and withdraw from them their fellowship."[33] Noteworthy, however, is the caveat that membership can be withdrawn for *conduct*.

In general, church courts limited themselves to the same issues most commonly the province of ecclesiastical discipline: moral behavior. Of course, in the early years of the church the definition of moral conduct was especially broad and often hard to separate in practice from faithfulness to the church. Thus, a frequent charge was some variant—especially for priesthood holders—of disloyalty and disrespect for the leadership. In 1835, William McLellin did no more than relate to his wife Orson Hyde's low opinion of the Kirtland School of the Prophets, a small theological seminar under Smith's administration. In response, the high council voted "to inform Elders M'Lellin and Hyde that we withdraw our fellowship from them until they return and make satisfaction."[34]

Others in the first decade were disfellowshipped or excommunicated for such offenses as murmuring,[35] "want of benevolence to the poor,"[36] maintaining "tippling shops" (a drinking establishment), or, in the case of twenty-two brethren and sisters, for "uniting with the world in a dance."[37] (Dancing was not itself prohibited;

seeming disloyalty at a time of intense persecution and factionalism may have been the real issue.) Willful neglect of destructive livestock was also singled out as an offense worthy of disfellowshipment.[38] "Not observing the words of wisdom" was a charge leveled at David Whitmer in 1838, but that seems an inconsequential add-on in light of the more serious accompanying charges of writing against the church and "separating himself from the Church while he has a name among us."[39] Only flagrant violations of the Word of Wisdom, the health code proscribing certain substances, were usually actionable, falling under the offense of "intemperance." The vague "unchristian like conduct" also encompassed a multitude of unspecified sins.[40] In one instance, James Newberry was charged with "speaking reproachfully of youngsters."[41] Not surprisingly, he was a schoolmaster.

No mention was made in the LDS Articles of the Church regarding the acceptable limits of orthodoxy. Mormonism was emphatically opposed to fixed creeds, in fact. Smith declared that "I want to come up into the presence of God & learn all things but the creeds set up stakes, & say hitherto shalt thou come, & no further.—which I cannot subscribe to."[42] Excommunication for heresy has been more common, or perhaps more publicized, in the modern Christian world than excommunication for moral turpitude. Lyman Beecher was tried for heresy by his Presbyterian church. (His son Henry Ward was tried twice by church courts for adultery. Though apparently guilty, his accuser was excommunicated by the Congregationalist Plymouth Church; Beecher was exonerated.) In another high-profile case, Charles Briggs was suspended by the Presbyterian General Assembly for his resistance to biblical inerrancy in 1893. The twentieth century saw a number of prominent disciplinary actions for heresy: the Reformed, Presbyterian, Episcopalian, Lutheran, Baptist, and Catholic Churches have all held church courts or imposed discipline in the twentieth century and beyond.[43]

Smith, from Mormonism's very inception, practiced a tolerance for heterodoxy unusual for such an authoritarian institution. In 1843, a church court had summoned Elder Pelatiah Brown to answer for his views on the book of Revelation. He protested to Joseph Smith, who noted, "I never thought it was right to call up a man and try him because he erred in doctrine, it looks too much like the Methodism and not Latter day Saintism. . . . I want the liberty of believing as I please, it feels so good not to be trammeled."[44] Smith may have protested calling men up "for erring in doctrine,"[45] but high councils drew the line at "teaching doctrine injurious to the church" and sanctioned David Rogers accordingly.[46] So also Almon Babbit was disfellowshipped for teaching "doctrine contrary to the revelations of God, and detrimental to the interests of the Church."[47] In 1837, thirteen members lost their standing for "giving heed to revelations said to be translated" by one Collins Brewster.[48] Five years later, Gladden Bishop was similarly cut off for promulgating "revelations" he claimed to receive, which were "not consistent with the Doctrine and Covenants of the Church."[49] Sometimes discipline was employed for too firm an embrace of heresy or rejection of orthodoxy—but context suggests this was when private positions tilted toward public advocacy. Warren Foote noted in his journal that "[Ezra] Landon and others had been cut off for rejecting the vision concerning the three glories" (D&C 76).[50]

Some church leaders understood the principle of disfellowshipment very much in the tradition of Puritanism—as a way to purify a godly institution and, in so doing, shrink the distance between the visible and invisible churches. Presiding over a period of tremendous church growth in Great Britain, Parley Pratt reported in 1842 that "we numbered at our conference two weeks ago, near sixteen hundred members, and between one and two hundred officers. . . . There has been a general time of pruning, we have cut off upwards of 100 members from this Conference in a few months; this causes the young and tender Branches to grow with double vigour."[51] In the states as well, the decision was taken from time to time "to commence the work of reform" and "commence pruning the vine of God."[52] Pruning is a word that appears frequently in LDS scripture. In a Book of Mormon allegory, much emphasis is placed on a final "nourishing and pruning" of the Lord's vineyard, immediately preceding his return.[53] Latter-day Saint leaders apparently saw the gathering of converts and the winnowing of the Saints to be twin imperatives.

Mormon Excommunication Today

Judicial proceedings were outlined in early LDS revelations and could be conducted by various groups or councils. Bishops holding an Aaronic priesthood office can preside only over courts trying non-Melchizedek priesthood holders. Elders were tried before an "elders' meeting," as was Aaron Lyon in 1838,[54] or by high councils, as is now the practice. In early Mormon practice, "cutting off" or "disfellowshipment" were the normal terms for expelling a member from the church community; excommunication was an interchangeable term but seldom used.[55] The language of scripture made no fine distinctions, referring only to those who "have been expelled from the church" having their names "blotted out of the general church records."[56]

By 1879, the church was treating disfellowshipment and excommunication as two separate actions, and apostles differed on the question of whether bishops or stake leaders alone had the authority to impose the latter sanction on Melchizedek priesthood holders (both officers could "suspend" or "disfellowship" such members). President John Taylor ruled that bishops could only impose the lesser sanction on holders of the "higher priesthood."[57] The distinction was not clear, as both were forms of "cutting off," and in both cases "a repetition of the baptism is required" according to an 1893 source.[58] In 1910, George F. Richards added some clarity, noting that "disfellowshipped . . . is construed to mean a deprivation of all positions," a probationary state (in this case, of one month) to be followed by excommunication unless the person can subsequently "show cause if any why he should not be cut off."[59]

Soon, the sequence of those two events, disfellowshipment and excommunication apportioned to the ward and stake leadership, respectively, was made standard. This same year, the apostle Francis Lyman instructed that a member should be "handled by his Bishopric and if disfellowshipped then he should be handled by the [Stake] Presidency and High Council." He then related the example of a brother "disfellowshipped by his bishop[ric] & later excommunicated by the High Council." This, he said, was "a pattern of how to deal with such cases."[60]

In Mormonism's founding decades, especially after the 1837 Kirtland bank failure, the introduction of polygamy, and the aftermath of Smith's death, disaffection and excommunication reached all the way into the Quorum of the Twelve, with five apostles excommunicated in 1838 alone.[61] In the late nineteenth and early twentieth centuries, actions against high-profile Mormons were rare. The apostle Amasa Lyman was cut off for heretical teachings in 1870 (he denied the atonement, among other reasons).[62] Apostles John W. Taylor and Matthias F. Cowley were disciplined in 1911 for resisting the cessation of polygamy.[63]

The late twentieth and early twenty-first centuries saw a handful of Mormon excommunications of vocal critics and dissenters from orthodoxy. Following one such highly publicized episode involving "the September Six," a group of feminists and scholars disciplined by church councils in 1993, the church affirmed that the relevant criterion for church discipline was promulgating, not holding, heretical beliefs. As they clarified in an official statement,

> We have the responsibility to preserve the doctrinal purity of the Church. . . . Faithful members of the Church can distinguish between mere differences of opinion and those activities formally defined as apostasy. Apostasy refers to Church members who "(1) repeatedly act in clear, open, and deliberate public opposition to the Church or its leaders; or (2) persist in teaching as Church doctrine information that is not Church doctrine after being corrected by their bishops or higher authority; or (3) continue to follow the teachings of apostate cults (such as those that advocate plural marriage) after being corrected by their bishops or higher authority."[64]

Such public challenging of church doctrine has been the relevant factor in other publicized excommunications, from ERA activists who urged the public to oppose

LDS evangelizing, to women who have marched on the Tabernacle over exclusion from the priesthood and "aggressively recruited" others to their position.[65] In at least one case, the distinction between public and private views made all the difference. Sterling McMurrin was a prominent Mormon (later the US Commissioner of Education under John F. Kennedy) and known skeptic. When Joseph Fielding Smith wanted him disciplined, President David O. McKay told McMurrin, "All I will say is that if they put you on trial for excommunication, I will be there as the first witness in your behalf. . . . You just think and believe as you please."[66] Repaying irony with irony, the church not only tolerated McMurrin but its officials asked him to represent the church in giving a presentation on Mormonism at Ohio State University as well as at a Utah lecture series in 1955 and 1957.[67]

Early Christian documents urge restraint in "casting out" offenders, and one of the responsibilities of bishops, harking back to at least the early third century, was to "bring again that which is driven away, that is, do not permit that which is . . . cast out by way of punishment, to continue excluded."[68] Perhaps marking a shift from sanctions to nurture, the LDS church has changed the name of church *courts* to "disciplinary *councils*" (emphasis added). Reinstatement is the objective rather than punishment. As Bruce Hafen writes, "Because the fundamental purpose of Church discipline has always been to save souls rather than only to punish, formal disciplinary councils are considered 'courts of love,' marking the first step back to full harmony with the Lord and his Church, rather than the last step on the way out of the Church."[69]

Temple Recommend

Not all boundary maintenance involves the radical demarcation of the church from the outside world. The angel may have told John of Patmos that the Lord preferred his disciples either cold or hot rather than lukewarm,[70] but the visible church has most often found a way to accommodate those still in the valley of decision. New England Puritans devised a system to explicitly accommodate different classes of believers. By the terms of the halfway covenant, the church admitted into fellowship those children of record who had never attained full membership but were not guilty of egregious sin. Such persons were to be considered members, but not full members. Cotton Mather, in wishing to expand access to baptism to all professing Christians, argued that "persons may be Disciples, while not yet Risen to the more Experienced state of Brethren; and there may be Subjects in the Kingdom, which have not yet all the Privileges that the [full] Members . . . lay claim unto."[71] We saw participation at the Lord's Table as one privilege subject to suspension.

The Puritan system, then, could erect meaningful boundaries to maintain a separation from the worldly and to categorize members themselves as either "brethren" in full fellowship or the less committed "disciples," or those worthy and those unworthy to participate in the holy sacrament of the Eucharist. A closely analogous dichotomy obtains in the case of Mormonism. So are there two categories, two varieties or tiers of membership that pertain to Mormonism. This is because, again as with the Puritans, some sacraments are available to all professed Latter-day Saints, and some to those with a higher level of demonstrated commitment. This difference is evident not by effecting distinctions within the normal worship service but by making access to meeting house worship and its sacraments open to all and limiting access to temples and their higher sacraments to fully committed Latter-day Saints. Those who comply with a prescribed set of beliefs and conduct are considered "temple-worthy" and have access to the full range of church sacraments, several of which unfold only within the precincts of LDS temples. The rationale for this barrier to more general admission is twofold.

First, Mormons, like the Israelites before them, consider the temple a site of especial sanctity. The possibility is suggested in Mormonism that a temple should be viewed, not as just a place where worshippers come to find refuge from, and transcendence of, the blood and sins of their generation, but where Jehovah himself comes to find refuge from his pain and from the sorrow inflicted by the evils of his creation.[72] The Old Testament Jehovah had, after all, commanded his people to "build a house for *me*."[73] In recognition of the temple as a literal "house of the Lord," Smith enjoined in the same prayer that "no unclean thing shall be permitted to come into thy house to pollute it."[74] Malachi protested evil priests who "polluted" the temple and its altar, and in the intertestamental period especially, Jewish texts emphasized warnings against "defiling the sanctuary."[75] Manifesting comparable concern for Mormonism's holiest places, qualifications for temple admission constitute a higher standard of personal conduct than mere participation in weekly worship services, in order to maintain the sanctity of the temple precincts.

Second, Mormons consider that the temple ordinances entail much greater demands upon discipleship than a casual Christianity. So does any Christian church worthy of the name, one might point out. True, but temple worship involves not just an admonition or invitation to a full measure of devotion; it entails very specific injunctions and commitments that are explicitly accepted by sacred oaths and covenants. Potential Christians seeking baptism were commanded to first "bear fruit worthy of repentance."[76] So are modern LDS disciples seeking subsequent saving ordinances required to demonstrate evidence of a greater spiritual maturity and commitment.

To this end, ecclesiastical leaders interview prospective temple goers in order to confirm their readiness to commit to the highest obligations of discipleship pertaining to the New and Everlasting Covenant. When Smith first invited men and their wives to receive temple ordinances, the process was informal—and appears to have continued so for some time. In the church's first years, elders were issued formal licenses to certify their good standing and fitness to preach. Only in Utah did bishops come to issue adults a formal license, or "recommend," for purposes of participation in temple ordinances, subject to First Presidency review. They were asked to do so for members seeking to use the Endowment House (which operated in lieu of a temple) in 1856, approval being contingent on their paying of tithes, praying in their families, attending meetings, taking care of the poor, and avoiding immoral conduct such as criticizing the leadership, thieving, lying, and busibodiness. Over the next decades, similar counsel was given to bishops screening candidates, and in 1891 they were delegated authority to make the final decisions about admission.[77]

Lack of a uniform template made for unevenness in standards, and an 1886 general epistle of the First Presidency decried the laxity in issuing these recommends, calling their issuance to "unworthy persons" a "grave error." In addition to general worthiness, payment of "tithes and offerings" and observance of the Word of Wisdom were specifically enjoined.[78] "[It is] inconsistent to carry the smell of whiskey and tobacco into the sacred precincts of the Lord's House," explained President John Taylor and his counselors.[79] A few years later, however, bishops were warned against a too-strict uniformity in requirements. "We have an objection to laying down rules which may be construed so rigidly as to do at times great injustice to worthy people," the First Presidency wrote to a bishopric in 1889. In general, they continued, failure to heed the Word of Wisdom seemed to them a sign of insufficient faith to attend the temple.[80] However, almost a decade later President Woodruff continued to counsel that such adherence not be a hard-and-fast requirement.[81]

In 1899, the leadership took an important step toward standardization of several administrative policies with the publication of a fourteen-page booklet titled "Instructions to Presidents of Stakes, Bishops, and Clerks."[82] Local leaders were counseled on how to deal with tithing paid in-kind, and they were directed to keep records of tithe payers, but the practice was not explicitly tied to temple worthiness. Then, in 1918, the Presidency reiterated to bishops that "recommends should be issued only to those who are worthy and faithful," but the Presidency did not stipulate specifics.[83] Finally, the church published a standard recommend book in 1922, which has been modified several times up to the present.[84] Today, the temple recommend interview addresses both orthodoxy and orthopraxis. The temple-worthy must affirm a commitment to the core teachings of Mormonism's social trinity, the redemptive role of Christ, and the status of the church leadership as possessing the keys to administer Christ's earthly kingdom. The principal demonstrations of a committed life of discipleship—in addition to general standards of Christian morality—are adherence to the laws of tithing, the Word of Wisdom, and chastity.

Tithing

The practice of giving one-tenth of one's property for sacred purposes is found as long ago as the fourteenth century BCE in Ugaritic texts.[85] In Genesis, a triumphant Abram, returning from his battle against the four kings, gives "one-tenth of everything" he took as spoils to Melchizedek, priest of God.[86] A few chapters later, Jacob vows that "of all that you give me I will surely give one-tenth to you."[87] Generally, tithing proceeds were employed to maintain the temple and its priests. (It is the temple storehouse referred to in the specific injunction of Malachi to "bring the full tithe into the storehouse, so that there may be food in my house.")[88] The Deuteronomic code expands the use of tithes to include relief for "the resident aliens, the orphans, and the widows in your towns."[89]

As with many Jewish practices (like Sabbath observance), Christianity at first ceased the practice because "the tithes of the Old Testament were regarded as abrogated by the law of Christ."[90] Then in the Middle Ages, the Councils of Macon (585) and of Trent (1545–63) ordered the payment of tithes under penalty of excommunication. The advent of the secular state saw an end to most such mandates and enforcements, and as the Catholic Church holds, "in the present law of the Church there remains no commonly applicable provision for tithes."[91]

Obviously this is not to say charitable giving has no place in Christendom. In his efforts to sort out what Jewish practices deserved incorporation into Christian practice and which didn't, Luther followed a simple rule: "I keep the commandments which Moses has given, not because Moses gave commandments, but because they have been implanted in me by nature. . . . But the other commandments of Moses, which are not [implanted in all men] by nature, the Gentiles do not hold. Nor do these pertain to the Gentiles." The first rule he named in this regard was tithing— though he found it a fine practice, along with "others equally fine which I wish we had, too."[92] At the same time, he was emphatic that "I am under obligation to everyone; in return everyone owes . . . assistance to me when I am in need of help. We are not zealous enough, however, in seeking out the people who need us."[93]

Calvin admonished believers to follow this "rule for benignity and beneficence— that whatever God has conferred on us which enables us to assist our neighbor, we are the stewards of it, and . . . the only right dispensation of what has been committed to us, is that which is regulated by the law of love." In sum, alms and offerings spurred by charity correspond to those Jewish "offerings under the law."[94] John Wesley apparently thought there was no such parallel between the old and new forms of benevolence. He agreed that giving to the poor was "rendering unto God the things that are God's," providing we had first made provision for ourselves, our household, and "the household of faith." But giving in a strict proportion he associated with a stinting legalism. "Do not stint yourself, like a Jew rather than a Christian, to this or that proportion. 'Render unto God,' not a tenth, not a third, not half, but all that is God's, be it more or less."[95]

Tithing is easily construed as a measure of financial commitment to an institutional church. Its LDS origins, however, lie in an attempt to re-create the Christian communalism of the early Christian church and, more apropos to the Mormon mindset, the Zion community of Enoch the prophet. Smith's account of Enoch and his city records that Enoch's people were "of one heart and one mind, and dwelt in righteousness; and there was no poor among them."[96] Almost immediately after organizing the Mormon church, Smith laid out a plan for a literal Zion that would have as its first task the elimination of poverty and inequality. "It is not given that one man should possess that which is above another," a March 1831 revelation affirmed. "Wherefore the world lieth in sin."[97]

About the same time, he encouraged the family of convert Isaac Morley to abandon their own communal experiment for a more perfect version, captured in the Law of Consecration (which was, Orson Pratt informs us, originally called the Law of Enoch).[98] In May 1831 in Kirtland, Smith revealed the "Laws of the Church." Included, along with injunctions to preach the gospel and avoid murder, theft, and adultery, was the command to "consecrate all thy properties that which thou hast unto me with a covenant and Deed which cannot be broken & they Shall be laid before the Bishop of my church."[99] The heart of this law was the dedication of all one's assets to the church and the return by way of stewardship of that which one needed; in other words, the law effectively amounted to the disposition of one's surplus to satisfy the needs of the poor.

Human frailty being what it is, and the poverty of the Saints being especially extreme during their early years of hardship, relocation, and dispossession, insufficient funds were garnered to meet the church's financial needs or succor the destitute. The law was also instituted in Missouri, but the Mormons' expulsion from Jackson County in 1833 put an end to the experiment there. The Mormons made recurrent efforts over the next few years to abide by consecration but with little success. As financial needs of a temple-building people mounted, some leaders considered a program of additional offerings to relieve the burden. In December 1837, the bishop in Missouri, Edward Partridge, along with two associates proposed a "tithe" of 2 percent, which they hoped would "be in some degree fulfilling the law of consecration."[100]

Meanwhile, the apostle Thomas Marsh told Smith he believed the Saints were ready and willing to live the "whole law," if the "leaders shall say the word or show them how to do it."[101] Months later, spurred on by massive, crippling church debts, Smith petitioned the Lord for specific guidance that would supplement the unworkably vague requirement of the church law to donate "surplus." The consequent pronouncement transitioned the church into a new principle. A revelation directed the people to convey "all their surplus property" to the bishop, with an obligation to tithe one-tenth of their income thereafter. (Smith would subsequently appoint a committee to assist in the disposition and handling of properties.) Tithing became "a standing law unto them forever."[102]

Months after this announcement, the Mormons were again expelled—this time from the state, following burnings, beatings, a massacre of seventeen men and boys at Haun's Mill, and the imprisonment of Smith and other leaders. Any plans for living economic Zion principles collapsed, and attention shifted to survival, resettlement, and then, redress. From jail, Smith urged that there be in the new Illinois settlements "no organizations of large bodies upon common stock principals in property,"[103] and months later, he formally halted the great enterprise of the "consecration law," the blueprint for a Zion society: "It was the will of the Lord we should desist from trying to keep it" for the present, he told church leaders.[104] Smith was focused on the more pressing matter of petitioning the government for justice, stating that "the affairs now before Congress was [sic] the only thing that ought to interest the Saints at present."[105] Tithing, however, continued as church law and practice. Thereafter, a form of the law of consecration—the United Order—would be implemented in isolated communities during the Utah years, but never again as a churchwide endeavor. (The principle does survive as a personal commitment affirmed in the temple endowment to consecrate one's life and resources to God's kingdom.)

So tithing emerged out of an effort, among a communitarian Latter-day Saint body, to abide the cardinal Christian injunction to provide for the poor while attending to the material needs of a growing church- and temple-building people. Recognizing tithing as a law to the church, in 1873 Brigham Young directed that only those who were certified as being tithe payers receive temple recommends.[106] The law of tithing itself allows some latitude for interpretation. The revelation specified the payment of "one tenth of all their interest annually."[107] Bishop Partridge interpreted this to mean a payment of one tenth of the prevailing interest rate—generally agreed to be 6 percent—on one's net worth. A man worth $1,000 would therefore be expected to pay one-tenth of $60, or $6 per annum.[108] In the modern church, the rate is generally understood as 10 percent of one's annual income or profit. Whether that refers to net or gross income is left to the individual and depends on whether the person wants blessings in the net or gross form, according to often-heard wry counsel.

Word of Wisdom

The Word of Wisdom was a health law embedded in an 1833 revelation to Joseph Smith. It encouraged the use of grains and herbs and fruits "in the season thereof."

Meat was to be eaten sparingly, preferably "in times of winter, or of cold, or famine." And some substances were proscribed: alcohol ("wine" and "strong drinks"),
tobacco, and "hot drinks."[109] The immediate precipitating catalyst to the revelation was the dismay of Emma, Smith's wife, in the face of the unsavory remains
of tobacco use that she regularly confronted in cleaning a hall used by the elders.
Contemporary temperance movements and health reforms clearly provided a context in which Smith would have been aware of progressive standards of diet and
stimulant use. Even the conventional practice of medicine, writes one scholar, would
have provided "considerable 'medical' support" for the prohibitions on liquor.[110] In
the 1830s, Sylvester Graham famously advocated a regimen devoid of coffee, tea, and
meat (along with other alleged stimulants) in this same era. Tobacco, long valued
for its medicinal properties, was by this period "beginning to fall into disfavor."[111]
Nevertheless, the Word of Wisdom's status as a revelation, and its canonization in
1835, gave the health code a divine imprimatur for the faithful.

Even so, the Word of Wisdom has had an uneven history as a church law and measure of LDS faithfulness (and temple worthiness). To some extent, this is because
the revelation pronounced its own limited legalistic force; it was given "not by commandment or constraint, but by revelation and the word of wisdom."[112] As late as
1891, George Q. Cannon noted that members were using its status as counsel rather
than commandment to avoid compliance. "What difference is there?" he asked in
frustration.[113] Six years later, he again complained that "those who do not use these
articles in some form or other . . . may almost be called exceptions."[114] Also, some of
the prohibitions were vague enough to invite diversity of interpretation. The "sparing" consumption of meat, and especially its limitation to times of cold, has been
taken by some in the modern church (mostly all, judging by practice) to imply that
nineteenth-century problems of storage and spoilage must have been the reasons for
caution, and the warnings are taken to be less relevant in the modern age of refrigera-
tion. In any event, the fact that Mormons are selective in their adherence has been
noted since founding days. Young remarked that Smith's brother "Hyrum would
eat about 3 lb. of fat pork in a day; and yet be so severe upon a tobacco chewer."[115]
"Don't pile the table full of roast meat, boiled meat and baked meat, fat mutton, beef
and pork," Young admonished on another occasion, and urged mothers to "keep the
children from eating meat; and let them eat vegetables."[116] Young noted that he had
been a vegetarian himself for a while.[117]

If health was one rationale for the prohibition, as early leaders understood the
doctrine, a due respect for animals, which Smith said were possessed of spirits, also
entered the conversation. "The spirit of man [is] in the likeness of his person, as also
the spirit of the beast," he pronounced as revelation.[118] Orson Hyde, too, taught
that "every creature, beast and bird, man and woman, has a spirit peculiar to its

organization."[119] That may have been Lorenzo Snow's expressed reason for concern, since "he was convinced that the killing of animals when unnecessary was wrong and sinful."[120]

Orson Pratt pointed out that humans were necessarily vegetarians before the fall, and they would be again.[121] Snow agreed, saying the Word of Wisdom "was violated as much or more in the improper use of meat as in other things, and thought the time was near at hand when the Latter-day Saints should be taught to refrain from meat eating and the shedding of animal blood."[122] Heber C. Kimball reminded his audience that taking animal life was only justified "when we have need of meat, and are driven to it by necessity."[123] His contemporary apostle George Q. Cannon warned from the pulpit against "eating meats to excess."[124] And he invoked scripture to lend urgency: "Am I or my family hungry? If so, of course man is justified in killing animals or birds to satisfy his or his family's hunger. But if he has not any want of meat he 'sheddeth blood,' and he exposes himself to this woe which the Lord has pronounced."[125] The reference was to an earlier revelation of Smith's that pronounced a curse upon "man that sheddeth blood or that wasteth flesh and hath no need."[126] (Smith also revised a Genesis verse to warn, more direly, that "the blood of every beast will I require at your hands.")[127] Still, such views were not forcefully or frequently expressed from the pulpit, and tobacco and alcohol use quickly supplanted meat consumption as the ecclesiastical focus.

"Hot drinks" was equally ambiguous as an expression—however, Smith's brother Hyrum, patriarch of the church at the time, interpreted the expression to mean coffee and tea, and with little dissent, that has been the interpretation ever since.[128] Inferring that caffeine is the culprit behind the prohibition, some Saints find decaffeinated hot drinks acceptable.[129] Because a common thread in the prohibitions seems to be addiction, the church for a time discouraged the drinking of caffeinated beverages as well, though no such taboo currently exists.[130]

In spite of the revelation's "not by way of commandment" caveat, Smith had in 1834 encouraged compliance as a prerequisite for any member "to hold an office, after having the Word of Wisdom properly taught to him," and the same high council that approved his recommendation disciplined several members who failed to comply.[131] The Missouri High Council followed suit, resolving "that we will not fellowship any ordained member who will not or does not observe the Word of Wisdom."[132] They further moved in 1838 to "put a stop to the selling of Liquor" in the area.[133] Still, few heeded the directive—and even Smith himself was irregular in observation.

In 1873, Young indicated that temple recommends should be predicated on an individual's worthiness with respect to honesty, industriousness, and abstinence from alcohol.[134] But old habits were not soon to change. Another generation passed, and in 1908, church president Joseph F. Smith opened the General Conference with the lament that he was "sorry to say that I do not believe there is another . . . commandment given of the Lord that is less observed or honored that this 'Word of Wisdom,' and that, too, by members and officers of the Church."[135] His counselor Anthon Lund followed up with the suggestion that "obedience to the word of wisdom should be regarded as a requisite of church fellowship," noting that it was becoming a requirement for "those who accept positions in the Church that they will obey the Word of Wisdom."[136] Then, with the advent of America's Prohibition movement, the church directed renewed focus on alcohol consumption, and the Word of Wisdom received powerful new attention. By the 1920s, adherence to the Word of Wisdom became more generally enforced as a requirement for temple admission—the ultimate measure of good standing in the church. In 1942, the First Presidency asked "every officer in every Church organization, strictly to keep the Word of Wisdom . . . [or] step aside for someone who is willing and able to do so."[137]

Today, adherence to the Word of Wisdom has become an uncompromising sign of commitment to the church. In light of the commandment's checkered past, its original standing as counsel only, and its preoccupation with what is ingested rather than what is enacted by the disciple, the supreme importance attached to the health law by way of requirement for baptism and temple alike is hard to explain. Jewish precedent may be helpful here. "After the destruction of Jerusalem in 70 CE, the emerging rabbinic leadership emphasized external signs of piety, not because they were hypocrites interested in externals, but as distinctive markers of the holy people of God in a pluralistic society."[138]

Chastity

One of the distinctive moral tenets of the Judeo-Christian tradition has been the sanctity of human sexuality. The Old Testament condemned as sins whoredom, bestiality, homosexuality, and adultery. In the New Testament, Jesus condemned adultery and sexual lust, while Paul denounced "sexual immorality" in general, as well as homosexual acts in particular.[139] Marriage was made a church sacrament in the medieval period, and Christians saw little variation in sexual standards until the twentieth century. By the commencement of the twenty-first century, however, "Christian thought has found itself required to respond to theological, social, and intellectual upheavals in the understanding of sex," notes a standard reference work on Christian thought.[140] That rather vague observation belies seismic shifts in Christian teaching and practice. Though most churches still officially forbid premarital sex, nearly 80 percent of Christians report having sex before marriage.[141] An even more dramatic realignment of religious standards is in the area of same-sex relations. As of early 2015, the Presbyterian Church (USA), the Evangelical Lutheran Church of America, the Episcopal Church, and the United Church of Christ support same-sex marriage.[142] Momentum is building in other denominations for similar endorsement.

Mormonism, along with more conservative strains of Christianity, has been more resistant than other traditions to these cultural developments.[143] This is attributable in large measure to the role that sexual relations have in Mormonism's saga of eternal families. As we saw above, Mormonism espouses belief in "a continuation of the seeds forever and ever," that is, a creating and nurturing of "the souls of men" eons into the future.[144] C. S. Lewis wrote that "if Christianity is true, the mere fact of sexual intercourse sets up between human beings a relation which has, so to speak, transcendental repercussions—some *eternal* relation is established whether they like it or not."[145] His words are more self-evidently true in a framework like Mormonism where marital relations are envisioned in the context of eternal powers of increase rather than as an ad hoc expedient for the earth's peopling, and where an eternally bonded Heavenly Father and Mother constitute the Mormon idea of God.

Chastity is defined by the LDS church as the exercise of sexual relations solely within the bonds of heterosexual marriage. Related aspects of the principle include purity of thought, prohibitions against pornography, and any extramarital form of sexual intimacy. While tithing and adherence to the Word of Wisdom are generally requisite in the modern LDS church for baptism, disobedience to those laws is not grounds for church discipline. Chastity, however, ranks higher in the hierarchy of church law, being required for admission to the church and for continuing status therein. The paramount importance of chastity, or sexual continence, in Mormonism's moral code is apparent in the designation of sexual sin as near murder in the hierarchy of evil, and by the Book of Mormon's assertion that all other sins notwithstanding, because of the sexual virtue of the Lamanites their survival was assured by God.[146] The vital importance of this principle is reaffirmed by its explicit mention as requisite for temple attendance in the modern interview process.

Testimony

As we have seen, Mormons, on fast Sunday, express their "testimonies," or feelings of spiritual conviction regarding core doctrines of LDS belief. Because participation is voluntary and random, and only informal custom guides the content of such testimonies, they aren't reliable indicators of member accord with core doctrines. The Mormon temple recommend interview, therefore, functions in a manner analogous to the Puritan examination for membership. The Puritan practice, and the evangelical pattern today, is to base one's claim to legitimate discipleship on a transformative encounter with Jesus. The temple recommend interview allows for a Mormon version of this assessment of personal discipleship—though it has only in recent years been made explicitly Christocentric.

Members of the Church of Jesus Christ of Latter-day Saints find themselves in the ironic position of having to defend their inclusion in the Christian fold, given primarily their non-traditional view of a social trinity composed of three distinct individual deities and their acceptance of extra-biblical scripture. The legitimacy of their claim has been defended elsewhere.[147] A crucial point in this regard is that Mormons do not just profess the Christian label in facing a sometimes skeptical Christendom. The faith imposes on its own members who desire the fullest participation in Mormonism's sacramental rites an explicit assent to Jesus as the Christ, and a profession of personal faith in his atoning sacrifice as both personally redemptive and universally efficacious.

When asked about the fundamentals of the Latter-day Saint faith, Smith replied, "The fundamental principles of our religion are the testimony of the Apostles and Prophets, concerning Jesus Christ, that He died, was buried, and rose again the third day, and ascended into heaven; and all other things which pertain to our religion are only appendages to it."[148] However, fighting for a toehold on a crowded religious landscape, and identifying itself as a restoration of authentic Christianity in the midst of an apostate Christendom, early Mormonism tended to emphasize those teachings and tenets that were distinct from rather than shared with the larger Christian tradition. One observer of a Joseph Smith sermon, for instance, noted his "unbelief of what is called Original Sin," that God "fore-ordained the fall of man," that unbaptized young children "assuredly go to Heaven," that the human spirit "had existed from eternity in the bosom of Divinity," that "the punishment of man . . . must, according to his logic and belief have an end," and "the Mormon Bible [Book of Mormon] was communicated to him, direct from Heaven."[149] Jesus Christ elicited one passing mention.

This pattern of assuming rather than expounding the central role of the Savior in Mormon faith and practice was even observed—and lamented—by a modern apostle. "For a time and until recently our public talks and our literature were deficient in the frequency and depth with which they explained and rejoiced in those doctrinal subjects most closely related to the atonement of the Savior."[150] Three years later, the church crystallized the foundational role of faith in Christ by placing it at the beginning of the temple interview. After asking if the candidate has faith in and a testimony of the godhead, the ecclesiastical leader asks whether the person has a "testimony of the atonement of Christ" and of his role as Savior and Redeemer.[151] Affirmation of those truths, always implicit but only now requiring explicit assent, is a sine qua non of temple worthiness—and a reminder of the focus of the temple experience itself, which has Christ's atonement at its center. Smith made that centrality visually and palpably evident—and in doing so effected one of his most remarkable conflations of ancient typology with Christological fulfillment.

Mormons believe the New and Everlasting Covenant incorporates the entirety of God's provisions for humanity's sojourn from premortal realms into the heavenly community of divine beings, and the covenant makes its first biblical, attenuated appearance in the fifteenth chapter of Genesis. Believing that "all things which have been given of God from the beginning of the world, unto man, are the typifying of [Christ],"[152] accordingly Mormons expect the Abrahamic covenant—the New and Everlasting Covenant—to not only foreshadow but encompass the later, new covenant marked by Christ's atonement. All commanded sacrifice would be read, in this light, as pointing to that pivotal moment of the universe's history. The first Old Testament sacrifice described in detail accompanies the covenant's exposition in Genesis 15. Abraham is commanded to sacrifice a heifer, a goat, and a ram (along with two birds). He then splits each carcass in twain. Subsequently, like Moses on the verge of his theophany and Smith facing his, Abraham experiences "a horror of great darkness," following which the Lord personally affirms his covenant with Abraham. And it is at this point that "a smoking fire pot and a flaming torch passed between these pieces."[153] This intriguing sacrificial ritual, accompanied by covenantal affirmation, finds its fullest explanation and fulfillment in LDS temple practice.

Smith's great act of synthesis, wherein he drew Old Testament typology and New Testament teaching into harmony, was evident in the way he depicted temple architecture and designed temple ritual so as to bring all things together in Christ. The key to his final effort may have been his reading of Hebrews and the light it shed on Abraham's unusual rite. Explicating Old Testament sacrifices in light of the new covenant, the author of Hebrews invites the Christian to complete the pilgrim's journey by entering into the presence of God himself—"to enter into the holiest." And the meaning of all prior sacrificial victims now becomes clear, as the author explains that entry into God's very presence can only be "by the blood of Christ."

Christians all believe that the sacrificial animal is a type and foreshadowing of the Savior's death. But the writer of the letter to the Hebrews pushes the analogy further. We "enter into the holiest by the blood of Christ." We must pass *through* Christ's shattered body, as the lamp of the Lord did through the severed creatures, to find entry back into God's presence. The atonement is the pain-drenched portal through which alone access is to be found. And in the author's final invocation of symbolism, he directs our minds to the image of the temple veil, which becomes the physical counterpart to the body of Christ, through which we pass into the holiest place. The author of Hebrews says this explicitly: "The new and living way, which he hath consecrated for us," is "through the veil, that is to say, his flesh."[154]

In Mormon temples, as in Jewish, the veil of the temple represents the portal into the divine presence. The temple veil ("his flesh") was torn at the crucifixion, suggesting that only through the shattered body of the atoning Savior was access into God's presence possible for all. This startling image, replicated in the temples of the Latter-day Saints, captures the quintessence of the temple's purpose. It signifies the eternal human saga by which men and women progressively constitute fuller and richer relationship to divine parents, in their pilgrimage from incarnate spirits, through adoption into Christ's family, assuming greater levels of commitment and higher standards of holiness, entering into binding covenants that reify and extend human and divine connectedness, until cleansed and sanctified by the sacrificial offering of Christ's own flesh, they enter into the divine presence, part of an eternal sociality with those they love. The rituals of the temple are thus where the church's most concentrated liturgical forms are found, and they crescendo at the veil, that symbolic, porous membrane joining heaven and earth. It is through the atonement, through the severed flesh of Christ, typified in sacrifices that hark back to Adam himself, that all men and women may find full incorporation into the heavenly family, in accordance with the New and Everlasting Covenant that was propounded before the world was formed.

SOURCE ABBREVIATIONS

꒲ ──

ANF   *The Ante-Nicene Fathers*, ed. Alexander Roberts and James Donaldson. Grand Rapids, MI: Eerdmans, 1977.

BC   Book of Commandments for the Government of the Church of Jesus Christ of Latter-day Saints Christ. Independence, MO: W. W. Phelps, 1833.

C&C   *Creeds and Confessions of Faith in the Christian Tradition*, ed. Jaroslav Pelikan and Valerie Hotchkiss. New Haven, CT: Yale University Press, 2003.

CDBY   *The Complete Discourses of Brigham Young*, ed. Richard S. Van Wagoner. Salt Lake City, UT: Smith-Petit Foundation, 2009.

CDWW   *Collected Discourses Delivered by President Wilford Woodruff, His Two Counselors, the Twelve Apostles, and Others*, ed. Brian H. Stuy. n.p.: BHS Publishing, 1999.

CHL   Church History Library, The Church of Jesus Christ of Latter-day Saints, Salt Lake City, Utah.

CR   *Annual and Semi-Annual Conference Reports of the Church of Jesus Christ of Latter-day Saints.* Accessed at https://archive.org/details/conferencereport.

D&C   Doctrine and Covenants of the Church of Jesus Christ of Latter-day Saints. Revelations now in this scripture will generally be cited according to the edition in which they were first published or in the church newspaper where they first appeared, since those published forms and not the MS copy would usually be the most disseminated and influential version. The early editions subsequent to the Book of Commandments (1833) were the 1835 Doctrine and Covenants (Kirtland, OH: F. G. Williams), the 1844 edition (Nauvoo, IL: John Taylor), and the 1876 edition (Salt Lake City, UT: Deseret News). The current 1981 LDS version, also known as the Doctrine and Covenants, will always be indicated parenthetically, unless the 1876 version is cited, whose numbering is the same as in the 1981.

EJ   *Encyclopedia Judaica.* Jerusalem: Keter Publishing House, [1996].

EM   *Encyclopedia of Mormonism*, 4 vols., ed. Daniel Ludlow. New York: Macmillan, 1992.

EMS   *Evening and Morning Star.*

FFY   *The First Fifty Years of Relief Society: Key Documents in Latter-day Saint Women's History*, ed. Jill Mulvay Derr, Carol Cornwall Madsen, Kate Holbrook, and Matthew J. Grow. Salt Lake City, UT: Church Historian's Press, 2016.

HBLL   Harold B. Lee Library, Brigham Young University, Provo, Utah.

ICR   John Calvin. *Institutes of the Christian Religion*, trans. Henry Beveridge. Peabody. MA: Hendrickson, 2008.

IE   *Improvement Era.*

JD   *Journal of Discourses*, 26 vols., reported by G. D. Watt et al. Liverpool: F. D. and S. W. Richards et al., 1851–1886 (Reprint Salt Lake City, UT: n.p., 1974).

JI   *Juvenile Instructor.*

JSP-A   *Joseph Smith Papers: Administrative Records: Council of Fifty Minutes, March 1844–January 1846*, ed. Matthew J. Grow, Ronald K. Esplin, Mark Ashurst-McGee, Gerrit J. Dirkmaat, and Jeffrey D. Mahas. Salt Lake City, UT: Church Historian's Press, 2017.

JSP-D1   *Joseph Smith Papers: Documents Volume 1: July 1828–June 1831*, ed. Michael Hubbard MacKay, Michael Hubbard MacKay, Gerrit J. Dirkmaat, Grant Underwood, Robert J. Woodford, and William G. Hartley. Salt Lake City, UT: Church Historian's Press, 2013.

JSP-D2   *Joseph Smith Papers: Documents Volume 2: July 1831–January 1833*, ed. Matthew C. Godfrey, Mark Ashurst-McGee, Grant Underwood, Robert J. Woodford, and William G. Hartley. Salt Lake City, UT: Church Historian's Press, 2013.

JSP-D3   *Joseph Smith Papers: Documents Volume 3: February 1833–March 1834*, ed. Gerrit J. Dirkmaat, Brent M. Rogers, Grant Underwood, Robert J. Woodford, and William G. Hartley. Salt Lake City, UT: Church Historian's Press, 2014.

JSP-D4   *Joseph Smith Papers: Documents Volume 4: April 1834–September 1835*, ed. Matthew C. Godfrey, Brenden W. Rensink, Alex D. Smith, Max H. Parkin, and Alexander L. Baugh. Salt Lake City, UT: Church Historian's Press, 2016.

JSP-D5   *Joseph Smith Papers: Documents Volume 5: October 1835–January 1838*, ed. Brent M. Rogers, Elizabeth A. Kuehn, Christian K. Heimburger, Max H. Parkin, Alexander L. Baugh, and Steven C. Harper. Salt Lake City, UT: Church Historian's Press, 2017.

JSP-D6   *Joseph Smith Papers: Documents Volume 6*, ed. Mark Ashurst-McGee, David W. Grua, Elizabeth A. Kuehn, Alexander L. Baugh, and Brenden W. Rensink. Salt Lake City, UT: Church Historian's Press, 2017.

JSP-D7   *Joseph Smith Papers: Documents Volume 7*, ed. Matthew C. Godfrey, Spencer W. McBride, Alex D. Smith, and Christopher James Blythe. Salt Lake City, UT: Church Historian's Press, forthcoming.

JSP-H1   *Joseph Smith Papers: Histories Volume 1: Joseph Smith Histories, 1832–1844*, ed. Karen Lynn Davidson, David J. Whittaker, Mark Ashurst-McGee, and Richard L. Jensen. Salt Lake City, UT: Church Historian's Press, 2012.

JSP-H2	*Joseph Smith Papers: Histories Volume 2: Assigned Histories, 1831–1847,* ed. Karen Lynn Davidson, Richard L. Jensen, and David J. Whittaker. Salt Lake City, UT: Church Historian's Press, 2012.
JSP-J1	*Joseph Smith Papers: Journals Volume 1: 1832–1839,* ed. Dean C. Jessee, Mark Ashurst-McGee, and Richard L. Jensen. Salt Lake City, UT: Church Historian's Press, 2008.
JSP-J2	*Joseph Smith Papers: Journals Volume 2: December 1841–April 1843,* ed. Andrew H. Hedges, Alex D. Smith, and Richard Lloyd Anderson. Salt Lake City, UT: Church Historian's Press, 2011.
JSP-J3	*Joseph Smith Papers: Journals Volume 3: May 1843–June 1844,* ed. Andrew H. Hedges, Alex D. Smith, and Brent M. Rogers. Salt Lake City, UT: Church Historian's Press, 2015.
JSP-R&T	*Joseph Smith Papers: Revelations and Translations:Manuscript Revelation Books,* ed. Robin Scott Jensen, Robert J. Woodford, and Steven C. Harper. Salt Lake City, UT: Church Historian's Press, 2009.
JST	*Joseph Smith's New Translation of the Bible,* ed. Scott H. Faulring, Kent P. Jackson, and Robert J. Matthews. Provo, UT: Religious Studies Center, Brigham Young University, 2004.
KCMB	*Kirtland Council Minute Book,* ed. Fred C. Collier and William S. Harwell. Salt Lake City, UT: Collier's Publishing, 1996.
Key	Parley P. Pratt. *Key to the Science of Theology.* Liverpool: F. D. Richards, 1855.
KJV	King James Version of the Bible.
M&A	*The Messenger and Advocate.*
MHC	*Manuscript History of the Church,* Church History Library, Salt Lake City, Utah.
	Minutes Minutes of the Apostles of the Church of Jesus Christ of Latter-day Saints. In *The Prospect of Ready Access: Annals of the Apostles, 1835–1951.* CD-ROM. Salt Lake City: Privately published, 2015. (No pagination; citations are given by date.)
MS	*The Latter-day Saints Millennial Star.*
NCE	*New Catholic Encyclopedia,* 2nd ed. Detroit: Gale, 2003.
NPNF1	*Nicene and Post-Nicene Fathers of the Christian Church,* First series. Ed. Philip Schaff. Edinburgh: T&T Clark, 1993.
NPNF2	*Nicene and Post-Nicene Fathers of the Christian Church,* Second series. Ed. Philip Schaff. Peabody, MA: Hendrickson, 1999.
NRSV	New Revised Standard Version of the Bible.
PGP	*The Pearl of Great Price.* Salt Lake City, UT: Deseret, 1981. Earlier editions noted by date.
PWJS	*Personal Writings of Joseph Smith,* ed. Dean C. Jessee. Revised ed. Salt Lake City, UT: Deseret, 2003.
SCD	Henry Denzinger. *Sources of Catholic Dogma,* 30th ed., trans. Roy J. Deferrari. Fitzwilliam, NH: Loreto, 2007.
SJW	John Wesley. *Sermons on Several Occasions,* ed. Thomas Summers. Nashville: Stevenson & Owen, 1855.
SWML	Martin Luther. *Selected Writings of Martin Luther,* ed. Theodore G. Tappert. 4 volumes. Minneapolis: Fortress Press, 2007.

TD	Charles Buck. *A Theological Dictionary*. Philadelphia: Woodward, 1830.
T&S	*Times and Seasons*.
Voice	Parley P. Pratt. *The Voice of Warning and Instruction to All People*. New York: Sandford, 1837.
WJS	*The Words of Joseph Smith*, ed. Andrew F. Ehat and Lyndon W. Cook. Orem, UT: Grandin Book Company, 1991.
WWJ	*Wilford Woodruff's Journal*, ed. Scott G. Kenney. Midvale, UT: Signature Books, 1983.

Biblical quotations are from the New Revised Standard Version (NRSV), unless otherwise indicated. When the King James Version (KJV) is cited, it is generally because Smith and subsequent Mormons relied upon that edition with reference to a particular passage. Some citations, indicated as such, will be from Joseph Smith's translation of the Bible (JST). For citations from forthcoming volumes of the Joseph Smith Papers, I have added alternate citations from the website, www.josephsmithpapers.org, where available.

NOTES

PREFACE

1. John 21:15–17.

CHAPTER 1

1. At a time in the mid to late nineteenth century, when Mormons viewed plural marriage as the order of heaven, nineteenth-century leaders like Orson Pratt made the logical inference that "God the Father had a plurality of wives, one or more being in eternity, by whom He begat our spirits"—suggesting the existence of multiple heavenly mothers. By 1912, the leadership clearly differentiated "celestial marriage" from "plural marriage," and declared that for "a fullness of glory in the world to come . . . plural marriage is [not] essential." Consequently, conceiving of heavenly mother in the plural faded. Orson Pratt, *The Seer* 1.11 (November 1853): 172; Charles Penrose, "Editor's Table," *IE* 15.11 (September 1912): 1042.

2. 2 Nephi 2:25.

3. Thomas Watson, "Man's Chief End Is to Glorify God," in *A Body of Practical Divinity* (Philadelphia: T. Wardle, 1833), 8.

4. Roger E. Olson, *The Story of Christian Theology* (Downers Grove, IL: InterVarsity Press, 1999), 506.

5. *The Catechism of Christian Doctrine, Prepared and Enjoined by Order of the Third Council of Baltimore* became the standard catechism in American Catholic schools (Philadelphia: Cunningham and Son, 1885).

6. http://rickwarren.org/devotional/english/you-were-made-for-god-s-glory.

7. *T&S* 4.5 (16 January 1843): 73 (Moses 1:39, PGP).

8. Olson, *Christian Theology*, 277.

9. Stan Larson, "The King Follett Discourse: A Newly Amalgamated Text," *BYU Studies* 18.2 (Winter 1978): 204.

10. Ephesians 4:12–13.

11. Mrs. Humphry Ward, *Robert Elsmere* (New York: Macmillan, 1888), 572.

12. Matthew 26:41.

13. Matthew 18:20.

14. Kenneth E. Kirk, *The Vision of God* (New York: Harper & Row, 1966), 132–33.

15. Kirk, *Vision*, 133.

16. Kirk, *Vision*, xxi.

17. James F. White, *An Introduction to Christian Worship*, 3rd ed. (Nashville: Abingdon Press, 2001), 17.

18. White, *Worship*, 22–24.

19. Kirk, *Vision*, 66.

20. White, *Worship*, 23–24.

21. Geoffrey Wainwright, *Doxology: The Praise of God in Worship, Doctrine, and Life* (New York: Oxford University Press, 1980), 16.

22. The expression is Soren Kierkegaard's, *Fear and Trembling and the Sickness unto Death* (Princeton, NJ: Princeton University Press, 2013), 459.

23. Kirk, *Vision*, 442.

24. White, *Worship*, 23.

25. He writes, for instance, that "worship is seen as the proper mode of attaining and expressing agreement in the Church's . . . community life." *Doxology*, 7. See also 118ff.

26. 1876 D&C 130:2.

27. Charles Taylor, *A Secular Age* (Cambridge, MA: Harvard University Press, 2007), 222ff.

28. Acts 13:1; 1 Cor. 16:19; Matt. 16:18; Eph. 5:25.

29. Jon D. Levenson, *Sinai and Zion: An Entry into the Jewish Bible* (New York: HarperOne, 1985), 41.

30. Mensasseh ben Israel, *De Creatione Problemata* 30, cited in Johannes van der Berg, "Mennaseh ben Israel, Henry More, and Johannes Hoornbeeck on the Pre-Existence of the Soul," in *Religious Currents and Cross-Currents: Essays on Early Modern Protestantism and the Protestant Enlightenment*, ed. Jan de Bruijn, Pieter Holtrop, and Ernestine van der Wall (Leiden: Brill, 1999), 66. For his reliance upon the verse in Deuteronomy, see Howard Schwartz, *The Tree of Souls: The Mythology of Judaism* (Oxford: Oxford University Press, 2004), 164.

31. *EJ* 5:1018.

32. *SCD* #39, p. 15.

33. Peter Marshall, *The Reformation: A Very Short Introduction* (New York: Oxford University Press, 2009), 51.

34. "Canons on the Sacrament in General," Council of Trent, 1545–1563, in *SCD* #848–49, 262.

35. Bruce Gordon, *Calvin* (New Haven, CT: Yale University Press, 2009), 97.

36. Horton Davies, *Worship and Theology in England: From Cranmer to Baxter and Fox* (Grand Rapids, MI: Eerdmans, 1975), 17.

37. "Westminster Confession of Faith" XXVII.i, *C&C* 2:640; Philip Melanchthon, *Loci Communes* (Eugene, OR: Wipf and Stock, 2007), 243.

38. *ICR*, IV. I. 1, p. 672.

39. "Means of Grace," *TD*, 947.

40. *Constitutions of the Holy Apostles* II.iv.26, *ANF* 7:410. *Constitutions* is a late fourth-century text; however, the sections on bishops, priests, and deacons derive from the early third century *Didascalia Apostolorum; SCD* #2274, p. 608.

41. Luther, "A Brief Explanation of the Ten Commandments, the Creed, and the Lord's Prayer," in Hugh Thomson Kerr, ed., *A Compendium of Luther's Theology* (Philadelphia: Westminster Press, 1943), 123. The analogy with the human soul comes from his "Papacy at Rome."

42. Gordon, *Calvin*, 98.

43. *ICR*, IV.i.1, 4, pp. 672, 674.

44. Quoted in Roy Hattersley, *The Life of John Wesley: A Brand from the Burning* (New York: Doubleday, 2003), 385.

45. "Of the Church," *SJW* 3:236, 238.

46. "Of the Church," *SJW* 3:240.

47. "On Schism," *SJW* 3:254.

48. E. Brooks Holifield, *The Covenant Sealed: The Development of Puritan Sacramental Theology in Old and New England, 1570–1720* (Eugene, OR: Wipf and Stock, 2002), 1.

49. A. K. Walker, *William Law: His Life and Work* (London: SPCK, 1973), 21.

50. Nathan O. Hatch, "Sola Scriptura and Novus Ordo Seclorum," in *The Bible in America: Essays in Cultural History*, ed. Hatch and Mark A. Noll (New York: Oxford University Press, 1982), 59. Lincoln's words are cited by Hatch.

51. 1 Nephi 17:40; BC 9:13–17 (D&C 10:52–56).

52. "All people are under sin," one revelation declared, "except them which I have reserved unto myself, holy men that ye know not of." BC 52:9 (D&C 49:8).

53. Adolf von Harnack, *History of Dogma*, trans. William M'Gilchrist (London: Williams & Norgate, 1899), 6:133.

54. Martin Luther, quoted in Roland Bainton, *Here I Stand: A Life of Martin Luther* (New York: Abingdon, 1950), 65.

55. Arthur Masson, ed., *A Collection of English Prose and Verse for the Use of Schools*, 7th ed. (Edinburgh, 1773), 196.

56. Bainton, *Here I Stand*, 65.

57. Westminster Confession XVIII.1, 2, in *C&C* 2:627–28.

58. Westminster Confession, XVIII.3, in *C&C*, 2:628. The NT reference to calling and election is 2 Peter 1:10 (*KJV*; "call and election" in *NRSV*).

59. Kirk, *Vision*, 414.

60. John von Rohr, *The Covenant of Grace in Puritan Thought* (Eugene, OR: Wipf and Stock, 1986), 2.

61. Buck had seen the Mosaic laws and rituals as "exhibiting" the covenant of grace. Ebenezer Henderson freely rewrote Buck's entry in 1833, opting for the Mosaic covenant as recapitulating the Adamic. "Covenant," *TD*, 120; Charles Buck and Dr. Henderson, *Theological Dictionary* (London: James Duncan, 1833), 259.

62. Matthew 26:28; Mark 14:24. "New covenant" in Young's literal translation. "Covenant" in the *NRSV*, and "new testament" in *KJV*.

63. Hebrews 12:24; 10:1.

64. Roger E. Olson, *Arminian Theology: Myths and Realities* (Chicago: InterVarsity Press, 2009), 53.

65. "A Call to Backsliders," *SJW* 3:396–97, 394, 387.

66. John Wesley, "Predestination Calmly Considered," in *The Works of Reverend John Wesley* (London: John Mason, 1830), 10:240.

67. "[Even] twelve years after the event, the First Vision's personal significance for him still overshadowed its place in the divine plan for restoring a church." Richard Bushman, *Rough Stone Rolling: A Cultural Biography of Mormonism's Founder* (New York: Knopf, 2005), 39.

68. John Wesley, 24 May 1738, in *The Heart of Wesley's Journal* (New Canaan, CT: Keats, 1979), 43.

69. *JSP-H1*, 12; *WJS*, 183.

70. *M&A* 1.1 (October 1834): 13; *M&A* 1.3 (December 1834): 43.

71. *JSP-H1*, 11–13.

72. *JSP-H1*, 221.

73. For a discussion of Smith's vision within the context of Methodist conversion narratives and the "experience of assurance" especially, see Christopher C. Jones, "The Power and Form of Godliness: Methodist Conversion Narratives and Joseph Smith's First Vision," *Journal of Mormon History* 37.2 (Spring 2011): 88–114.

74. *JSP-H1*, 220 (JS-History 1:29, PGP); *JSP-J2*, 336.

75. *WJS*, 204.

76. "Free Grace," *SJW* 4:385.

77. *WJS*, 74.

78. "I have been laboring in this cause for eight years," he wrote in a letter published in *M&A* 1.12 (September 1835): 179.

CHAPTER 2

1. Levi Richards Journal, cited in Dean C. Jessee, "The Earliest Documented Accounts of Joseph Smith's First Vision," in *Opening the Heavens: Accounts of Divine Manifestations, 1820–1844*, ed. John W. Welch (Provo and Salt Lake City, UT: Brigham Young University Press and Deseret, 2005), 24.

2. 1 Nephi 13:26.

3. 1835 D&C 4:8 (D&C 84:57).

4. Thomas Campbell, *Declaration and Address of the Christian Association* (Washington, PA: Brown & Sample, 1809; reprint, Coraopolis, PA: Record Publishing, 1908), 9.

5. Alexander Campbell, "Sermon on the Law," *The Writings of Alexander Campbell: Selections Chiefly from the Millennial Harbinger*, ed. W. A. Morris (Austin: Eugene Von Boeckmann, 1896), 44–45.

6. It might be noted as an exception that Margaret Barker, a Methodist biblical scholar, agrees that "underlying the 'historic' covenants recorded in the Old Testament" by the Deuteronomists with their historicizing agenda "was the everlasting covenant," one "covenant of the priesthood of eternity. *Temple Theology: An Introduction* (London: SPCK, 2004), 35.

7. "He might redeem the promise made to the fathers, . . . while preparing the new people for Himself. . . . Jacob saw in the Spirit a symbol of the people to come." *Epistle of Barnabas* 5:7; 13:5, in *The Apostolic Fathers*, 2nd ed., trans. J. B. Lightfoot and J. R. Harmer, ed. and rev. Michael W. Holmes (Leicester: Apollos, 1989), 167, 180.

8. Ambrose Serle, *The Church of God* (London: M. Trapp, 1793), 91.

9. He connects the two concepts in Matthew Henry, *An Exposition of the Old and New Testaments* (London: Joseph Ogle Robinson, 1828), 186–87, 316–17.

10. Isaac Pennington, *The Works of the Long-Mournful and Sorely Distressed Isaac Pennington* (London: J. and T. Kendall, 1761), 2:276.

11. Amos 5:15; Ezekiel 37.

12. Smith and his contemporaries equated Lamanites with the Native Americans of North and South America as a whole. In more recent years, LDS scholars have argued that the Book of Mormon itself makes no such sweeping claims, and a revised introduction (2007) declares the Lamanites to be "among the ancestors" of the American Indians.

13. Alma 10:3.

14. This is a recurrent theme with Nephi. See, for instance, 1 Nephi 19:23–24.

15. 1 Nephi 13:30.

16. 1 Nephi 22:6–9.

17. "The Indians," *EMS* 1.7 (December 1832): 107.

18. "Indian Treaties," *EMS* 1.8 (January 1833): 126; 1 Nephi 22:12.

19. 1 Nephi 22:9.

20. 1 Nephi 1:4.

21. 1 Nephi 7:14.

22. Nephi notes that he writes "six hundred years" before the Messiah comes, while Samuel later announces the people are living "five years" before the event. 1 Nephi 10:4; Helaman 14:2.

23. Zenock foretells his crucifixion, and Zenos the three days of darkness at his death. 1 Nephi 19:10.

24. Alma 39:19.

25. Helaman 8:22.

26. 2 Nephi 29:10–11.

27. Jon D. Levenson, *Sinai and Zion: An Entry into the Jewish Bible* (New York: HarperOne, 1985), 44.

28. "Covenant," *EJ* 5:1014, 1022.

29. Philippians 2:12.

30. James D. G. Dunn, for instance, seeks to demonstrate that "the dimension of peoples and not just individuals is bound up in Paul's key slogan—'to Jew first but also Gentile.'" *The New Perspective on Paul* (Grand Rapids: Eerdmans, 2007), 19.

31. Peter Bulkeley, *Gospel-Covenant* (London, 1651), in John von Rohr, *The Covenant of Grace in Puritan Thought* (Eugene, OR: Wipf and Stock, 1986), 55.

32. Grant Hardy, "The Book of Mormon and the Bible," in *Americanist Approaches to the Book of Mormon*, ed. Elizabeth Fenton and Jared Hickman (New York: Oxford University Press, forthcoming).

33. Mosiah 5:5; 6:1; 18:10.

34. Enos 1:4–17.

35. 2 Nephi 25:24.

36. Alma 25:16.

37. Jacob 4:4; Alma 25:15; 2 Nephi 25:24.

38. 2 Nephi 31.

39. Mosiah 5:6–7.

40. *JST* Exodus 34:1, p. 701.

41. Galatians 3:24. "Schoolmaster" is the *KJV* translation of *paidagogos*.

42. BC 23:1 (D&C 22:1).

43. "The Church of Christ," *EMS* 1:10 (March 1833): 145; "The Gospel," 1.11 (April 1833): 161.

44. "The Gospel," 1.11 (April 1833): 161 (Moses 5, 6, PGP).

45. Parley P. Pratt, Miscellaneous Minutes from 25 April 1847 Meeting; cited in Terryl L. Givens and Matthew J. Grow, *Parley P. Pratt: The Apostle Paul of Mormonism* (New York: Oxford University Press, 2010), 242.

46. Roger E. Olson, *The Story of Christian Theology* (Downers Grove, IL: InterVarsity Press, 1999), 52.

47. 1 Nephi 10:17.

48. Alexander Campbell admonished his readers "who believe [Joseph Smith] to be a prophet, hear the question which Moses put into the mouth of the Jews, and his answer to it—'And if thou say in thine heart, *How shall we know the word which the Lord hath not spoken?*'—Does he answer, '*Ask the Lord and he will tell you?*' . . . Nay, indeed." In 1997, an evangelical protested that "without some external checks and balances, it is simply too easy to misinterpret God's answer when we try to apply a test like that of Moroni 10:4–5 and ask him to reveal through his Spirit the truth or falsity of the Book of Mormon." Alexander Campbell, *Delusions: An Analysis of the Book of Mormon* (Boston: Greene, 1832), 15; Craig L. Blomberg and Stephen E. Robinson, *How Wide the Divide: A Mormon and an Evangelical in Conversation* (Downers Grove, IL: InterVarsity Press, 1997), 40.

49. Moroni 10:4–5.

50. Von Rohr, *Covenant of Grace*, 26.

51. 2 Nephi 29:5.

52. Smith had received a cryptic promise in his First Vision that "the fulness of the gospel should at some future time be made known unto me," but even that assurance portended no leadership role in a formal church. *T&S* 3.9 (1 March 1842): 707.

53. BC 4:5. A subsequent version (D&C 5:14) referred to "the rising up and coming forth" of the church out of the wilderness.

54. BC 9:14 (D&C 10:53).

55. BC 15:4 (D&C 18:3).

56. "Articles of the Church of Christ," *JSP-D1*, 368–74.

57. David Whitmer, *An Address to All Believers in Christ* (Richmond, MO: David Whitmer, 1887), 33.

58. Whitmer, *Address*, 32. Cited in Larry C. Porter, "'The Field Is White Already to Harvest': Earliest Missionary Labors and the Book of Mormon," in *The Prophet Joseph: Essays on the Life and Mission of Joseph Smith*, ed. Larry C. Porter and Susan Easton Black (Salt Lake City, UT: Deseret, 1988), 74. Porter gives several other examples of individuals taking signatures of the Book of Mormon on evangelizing journeys.

59. "History of Joseph Smith," *T&S* 3.24 (15 October 1842): 944.

60. "History of Joseph Smith," *T&S* 3.24 (15 October 1842): 944.

61. Levi Richards Journal, cited in Dean C. Jessee, "The Earliest Documented Accounts of Joseph Smith's First Vision," in *Opening the Heavens: Accounts of Divine Manifestations, 1820–1844*, ed. John W. Welch (Provo and Salt Lake City, UT: Brigham Young University Press and Deseret, 2005), 24.

62. BC 1:4.

63. BC 23.1 (D&C 22:1).

64. *T&S* 3.10 (15 March 1842): 720 (Abraham 3:22–26, PGP).

65. *The Song of the Pearl*, trans. Han J. W. Drijvers, Robert M. Grant, Bentley Layton, and Willis Barnstone. In Barnstone and Marvin Meyer, eds., *The Gnostic Bible* (Boston: Shambhala, 2003), 388–89.

66. JSH, 1:223–25.

67. Malachi 4:5–6; 1876 D&C 110:14–15 (and 27:9); 3 Nephi 25:5–6; JSH 1:38–39.

68. *JSP-H1*, 225.

69. *Key*, 33.

70. *JSP-H1*, 241; "To Noah Saxton," 4 January 1833, in *JSP-D2*, 352.

71. "Millennium," *EMS* 2.17 (February 1834): 353.

72. "To Saxton," *JSP-D2*, 352.

73. *Writings of Alexander Campbell*, 480. Mormons also adopted Campbell's preference for "Godhead" over "Trinity."

74. "Ordinances of the Gospel," *TD*, 418.

75. Ryan G. Tobler, "The Only Way to Be Saved: Early Mormonism and the Sacrament of Baptism," unpublished MS, copy in author's possession.

76. John 8.

77. Luke 3:8.

78. John 11:52. The prophecy was delivered by Caiaphas, whom commentators have seen as an unwitting vessel of truth.

79. *T&S* 3.9 (1 March 1842): 706 (Abraham 2:9–11, PGP).

80. Brothers believed himself to be a prophet to "the Hebrews [hidden among the] people of London," called to "bring them out from the people, and gather them from the countries." Richard Brothers, *A Revealed Knowledge of the Prophecies and Times* (London: 1794), 19–20.

81. *JSP-D4*, 17.

82. BC 41:10 (D&C 39:11); see also BC 12:5 (D&C 14:10); BC 15:5 (D&C 18:6); *EMS* 1.2 (July 1832): 1 (D&C 42:39), etc.

83. *CDBY* 1:66.

84. E. Brooks Holifield, *Theology in America* (New Haven, CT: Yale University Press, 2003), 68.

85. He is quoting 2 Samuel 7:10. John Cotton, *God's Promise to His Plantations* (London: William Jones, 1630).

86. *WJS*, 67.

87. *WJS*, 4.

88. BC 52:16–17 (D&C 49:16–17).

89. Levenson, *Sinai and Zion*, 41.

90. Thomas Aquinas gave a number of reasons against the Donatist heresy; among them, priesthood power is grounded in Christ, not the agent, and faith must never be made dependent on the virtue of the administrator. Or as Aquinas writes, "a defect of the secondary agents" does not ruin the effect of "things made and governed by God." In part this is because there will always be "inferior agents as executors of divine providence." See his *Summa Contra Gentiles*, Book Three: Providence Part I, III.lxxi and lxxvii, trans. Vernon J, Bourke (Notre Dame, IN: University of Notre Dame Press, 1975), 238, 259.

91. "Lex orandi" is taken as a truism in liturgical studies, since liturgy precedes the Christian creed. I thank Kathleen Flake for this point.

92. Peter J. Leithard, *Defending Constantine* (Downers Grove, IL: IVP Academic, 2010), 29.

93. Joseph F. Smith, *Gospel Doctrine* (1949), 191; B. H. Roberts, *Rational Theology* (1937). Both in John A. Widtsoe, *Priesthood and Church Government* (Salt Lake City, UT: Deseret, 1954), 25. The title page indicates the volume was "compiled under the direction of the Council of the Twelve."

94. "Responses to Some Questions Regarding Certain Aspects of the Doctrine of the Church," http://www.vatican.va/roman_curia/congregations/cfaith/documents/rc_con_cfaith_doc_20070629_responsa-quaestiones_en.html.

95. BC 1:5 (D&C 1:30).

96. *WJS*, 34.

97. Revelation 12. See a longer discussion of this scripture, so pivotal to Smith's understanding of apostasy and restoration, in Terryl L. Givens, *Wrestling the Angel: The Foundations of Mormon Thought—Cosmos, God, Humanity* (New York: Oxford University Press, 2015), 34–41.

98. Henry B. Eyring, "The True and Living Church, *Ensign* 38.5 (May 2008): 20, 22.

99. The ordinances of baptism, gift of the Holy Ghost, and priesthood confirmation require no sacred precincts for their administration. Some ordinances of salvation, however, can only be performed in the temple for the dead and the living.

100. *WJS*, 256.

101. Bede's view is typical in seeing baptism in these terms: "Through the grace of baptism men can by receiving the holy spirit be changed . . . into sons of God." *Homilies on the Gospel* 1.12, cited in Gerald Bray, ed., *Ancient Christian Commentary on Scripture, Romans* (Downers Grove, IL: InterVarsity Press, 2005), NT VI:211. The author of the letter to the Colossians had taught that baptism corresponded to an inner "spiritual circumcision" (2:11).

102. Romans 8:15.

103. *ICR*, IV.xvi.4, p. 874.

104. Genesis 17:7.

105. Augustine, *Sermon on the Mount* 23.78, in *Ancient Christian, Romans*, VI:212.

106. Origin, *Commentary on the Epistle to the Romans*, in *Ancient Christian, Romans*, VI:211.

107. Chrysostom, *Homilies on Romans* 14, in *Ancient Christian, Romans*, VI:212.

108. *ICR* IV.xiv.13, p. 849.

109. Wesley, "The Spirit of Bondage and of Adoption," *SJW*, 1:133–34.

110. Jacob 5; Moses 7, PGP.

111. Abraham J. Heschel, *The Prophets* (New York: Harper & Row, 1962), 57. Heschel is here citing Exodus 3:7.

112. Heschel, *Prophets*, 50.

113. Heschel, *Prophets*, 50.

114. *EMS* 1.3 (August 1832): 46 (Moses 7:29–41, PGP). The text clearly identifies the speaker as the Father, "Man of holiness" (1.3.45; Moses 7:35).

115. *T&S* 2.1 (1 November 1840): 199–200.

116. "Paracletes" [W. W. Phelps], "Joseph's Speckled Bird", *T&S* 6.8 (1 May 1845): 892.

117. For Smith's initial conception of spirit adoption, see Givens, *Wrestling*, 213ff. For origins of the Heavenly Mother idea, see 108–110.

118. Meister Eckhart, "The Book of Divine Comfort," in *Meister Eckhart*, ed. and trans. Raymond B. Blakney (New York: Harper Torchbooks, 1941), xx, 44–45; *Key*, 33.

119. *WJS*, 299.

120. *EMS* 2.17 (February 1834): 284.

121. "Law of Adoption," *MS* 4.2 (June 1843): 31.

122. The term appears at least as early as Parley Pratt's 1845 "Materiality," *The Prophet* (24 May 1845); repr. *MS* 6.2 (1 July 1845): 19–22.

123. Law of Adoption," *MS* 4.2 (June 1843): 17, and "Editorial" *MS* 4.2 (June 1843): 31.

124. "Of Future Punishments," *MS* 3.2 (March 1843): 181.

125. "Law of Adoption," 18.

126. Orson Spencer, *Letters Exhibiting the Most Prominent Doctrines of the Church of Jesus Christ of Latter-day Saints* (Liverpool: Orson Spencer, 1848), 56.

127. B. H. Roberts, *The Mormon Doctrine of Deity* (Salt Lake City, UT: Deseret News, 1903), 165.

128. Kathleen Flake, "Translating Time: The Nature and Function of Joseph Smith's Narrative Canon," *Journal of Religion* 87.4 (October 2007): 518; *JST* Genesis 7:40, p. 618, cited in Flake, "Translating Time."

129. *Voice*, 99.

130. See Givens, *Wrestling*, chapter 20: "Salvation." "The seal of adoption" is Pratt's expression. *Voice*, 104.

131. C. S. Lewis, *Mere Christianity* (New York: HarperCollins, 2001), 199.

132. 2 Samuel 5.

133. Chrysostom, *Proof of the Gospel* 6.24, in *Ancient Christian Commentary on Scripture, Hebrews*, ed. Erik M. Heen and Philip D. W. Krey (Downers Grove, IL: InterVarsity Press, 2005), NT 10:223.

134. See Colleen McDannel and Bernhard Lang, *Heaven: A History* (New Haven, CT: Yale University Press, 2001), 209–75; and Barton Levi St. Armand, "Paradise Deferred: The Image of Heaven in the Work of Emily Dickinson and Elizabeth Stuart Phelps," *American Quarterly* 29 (Spring 1977): 55–78.

135. Recorded by Benjamin Johnson, quoted in Benjamin E. Park, "Early Mormon Patriarchy and the Paradoxes of Democratic Religiosity in Jacksonian America," *American Nineteenth-Century History* (2013): 7.

136. Adolph Jellinek, ed., *Bet Ha-Midrasch* (Jerusalem: Wahrmann Books, 1967), 4:129–31. Cited in Hugh Nibley, *Enoch the Prophet*, The Collected Works of Hugh Nibley (Salt Lake City/Provo, UT: Deseret/Farms, 1987), 252–53.

137. *EMS* 1.3 (August 1832): 45 (Moses 7:19–21), PGP. See other examples in David Larsen, "Enoch and the City of Zion: Can an Entire Community Ascend to Heaven?" *BYU Studies* 53:1 (2014): 25–37.

138. Hebrews 11:5, 10.

139. Hebrews 12:22–23.

140. *EMS* 1.3 (August 1832): 47 (Moses 7:62–64, PGP).

141. 1835 D&C 75:2; 96:heading; 98:heading, etc. (D&C 78:9; 96:heading; 104:heading).

142. *T&S* 3.13 (2 May 1842): 776.

143. BC 29:8 (D&C 29:7).

144. *WJS*, 210.

145. *JSP-R&T*, 53 (D&C 28:9).

146. "In the Name of the Prophet—Smith!" *Household Words* 8 (19 July 1851): 340.

147. "Brother Joseph & Sidney expect to start soon to appoint 11 or 12 new Stakes of Zion," wrote John Smith and Marcellus Cowdery to George A. Smith. Letter dated 26 September 1837, in *JSP-D5*, 445.

148. *T&S* 4.1 (15 November 1842): 24.

149. *EJ* 1.4 (July 1838): 54.

150. "Chronology of Church History," Appendix 2, in *EM* 4:1653.

151. *WJS*, 212.

152. *JSP-D3*, xxiii.

153. *JSP-D5*, 9.

154. *JSP-D5*, 10.

155. The document was reported in "The Mormonites," *Religious Intelligencer* (7 September 1833): 233.

156. B. H. Roberts, *A Comprehensive History of the Church of Jesus Christ of Latter-day Saints* (Provo, UT: Brigham Young University Press, 1965), 1:496–97.

157. George Q. Cannon, *JD* 20:2.

158. James E. Talmage, "The Story of Mormonism," *IE* 4.9 (July 1901): 692–98.

159. Editors Table, *IE* 6.2 (December 1902): 150.

160. *IE* 10.7 (May 1907): 483.

161. First Presidency, "Christmas Greeting to Saints in the Netherlands," *Der Stern* (1907). Cited in Terryl L. Givens and Reid L. Neilson, ed., *The Columbia Sourcebook of Mormonism in the United States* (New York: Columbia University Press, 2014), 150.

162. BC 35:16; 36:8; 37:31, etc. (D&C 33:18; 34:12; 35:27).

163. *JSP-A*, 113. Ahman Christ is a title appearing in some of Smith's revelations.

164. Parley P. Pratt to Joseph Smith, 19 April 1844, Joseph Smith Collection, CHL.

165. W. W. Phelps to Dear Brethren, 15 December 1833, *EMS* 2.16 (January 1834): 256.

166. A thorough treatment of the episode in its larger context is Roger D. Launius, *Zion's Camp: Expedition to Missouri* (Independence, MO: Herald House, 1984).

167. 1844 D&C 102:3 (D&C 105:10).

168. BC 40:28 (D&C 38:32).

169. 1835 D&C 81:5 (D&C 97:21).

170. *CDBY* 1:492.

171. "Counsel to Youth," *Ensign* 41.11 (November 2011): 19.

172. Terryl L. Givens and Matthew J. Grow, *Parley P. Pratt: The Apostle Paul of Mormonism* (New York: Oxford University Press, 2010), 65.

173. Bruce R. McConkie, "Come, Let Us Build Zion," *Ensign* 7.5 (May 1977): 117–18. President Spencer Kimball requested that McConkie's remarks on this subject be distributed churchwide.

174. Hugh W. Nibley, *Approaching Zion*, ed. Don E. Norton (Salt Lake City and Provo, UT: Deseret and Foundation for Ancient Research and Mormon Studies, 1989), 4.

175. Geoffrey Wainwright, *Doxology: The Praise of God in Worship, Doctrine, and Life* (New York: Oxford University Press, 1980), 118.

176. McConkie, "Come, Let Us Build Zion," 116.

177. Isaiah 33:20; 54:2 *KJV*.

178. Those numbers are 2013 statistics. See http://www.deseretnews.com/article/865578896/LDS-seminary-enrollment-reaches-all-time-high.html?pg=all.

179. FAQs, http://institute.lds.org/faq?lang=eng.

180. *JD* 3:372.

181. Bruce R. McConkie, *The Millennial Messiah: The Second Coming of the Son of Man* (Salt Lake City, UT: Deseret, 1982), 277.

182. *CDBY* 1:162.

183. https://www.lds.org/ensign/1983/05/statistical-report-1982?lang=eng.

184. https://rsc.byu.edu/archived/colonia-ju-rez-temple-prophet-s-inspiration/president-hinckleys-revelation-and- recent.

185. http://www.ldschurchnewsarchive.com/articles/62587/Worth-every-sacrifice.html.

CHAPTER 3

1. Revelation 12:6, 14.

2. Alexander Fraser, *Key to the Prophecies of the Old and New Testaments, which are not yet accomplished* (Philadelphia: John Bioren, 1802 [1795]), 157, 159.

3. Thomas Campbell, *Declaration and Address of the Christian Association* (Washington, PA: Brown & Sample, 1809; reprint, Coraopolis, PA: Record Publishing, 1908), 7, 10. See also Ryan Tobler, "The Only Way to Be Saved: Early Mormonism and the Sacrament of Baptism," unpublished MS, copy in author's possession.

4. *WJS*, 107–8.

5. 1835 D&C 4:3 (D&C 84:21–22).

6. Ryan G. Tobler, "'Saviors on Mount Zion': Mormon Sacramentalism, Mortality, and the Baptism for the Dead," *Journal of Mormon History* 39.4 (2013): 208ff. especially. Tobler gives examples from the journal of Warren Foote, the *Millennial Star, Times and Seasons*, and pamphlets by church leaders. See also his "The Only Way to Be Saved": Early Mormonism and the Sacrament of Baptism," unpublished MS, where he makes the case that "the baptismal practice and theology of early Mormonism were more distinctive than we have realized."

7. *Times and Seasons* 3.12 (15 April 1842): 751.

8. BC 1:3 (D&C 1:15).

9. 1844 D&C 103:13 (D&C 124:40).

10. Orson Pratt, *An Interesting Account of Several Remarkable Visions* (Edinburgh: Ballantyne and Hughes, 1840), 29.

11. Charles Taylor, http://blogs.ssrc.org/tif/2008/09/02/buffered-and-porous-selves/.

12. *SCD* #411, p. 161.

13. *SCD* #851, p. 263.

14. *SCD* #324, p. 130.

15. "Exultate Deo," *SCD* #695, p. 220.

16. *ICR* IV.xiv.26, p. 857. Calvin decried the idea of any "inherent efficacy" or "secret virtue" in the sacraments. IV.xiv.9, 14, pp. 847, 850.

17. Charles Taylor, *A Secular Age* (Cambridge, MA: Harvard University Press, 2007), 73, 75.

18. Taylor, http://blogs.ssrc.org/tif/2008/09/02/buffered-and-porous-selves/.

19. Niehbuhr believed that "it is not unfair to regard all Christian thinkers before Augustine as more or less Pelagian." Reinhold Niebuhr, *The Nature and Destiny of Man* (New York: Scribners, 1955), 245.

20. Sean Salai, S.J., "Catholic and Mormon: Author Q&A with Professor Stephen H. Webb," *America: The National Catholic Review*, http://americamagazine.org/content/all-things/catholic-and-mormon-author-qa-professor-stephen-h-webb.

21. *WJS*, 9.

22. *WJS*, 39.

23. *ICR* IV.xiv.1, p. 843.

24. "Sacrament," *TD*, 538.

25. Philip Melanchthon, *Loci Communes* (Eugene, OR: Wipf and Stock, 2007), 243.

26. *ICR* IV.xiv.3, 5, pp. 844, 845.

27. Writings of Moses 13, 1878 PGP (Moses 5:59, PGP).

28. Mosiah 5:12.

29. D&C 20:77, 79.

30. *CDBY* 1:484, 2:1015.

31. Romans 8:38–39.

32. Alma 45:16.

33. *WJS*, 4, 246, 254, 331, etc.

34. *WJS*, 41, 109.

35. BC 37:10 (D&C 35:9). As we will see, exorcism and healing are not exclusively prerogatives of priesthood holders.

36. *WJS*, 247.

37. Joseph Smith, "Letter to the Church at Quincy, 20 March 1839", in *PWJS*, 440 (D&C 121:36).

38. *WJS*, 247.

39. *WJS*, 331.

40. Catherine Bell, *Ritual: Perspectives and Dimensions*, rev. ed. (New York: Oxford University Press, 2009), x.

41. Geoffrey Wainwright, *Doxology: The Praise of God in Worship, Doctrine, and Life* (New York: Oxford University Press, 1980), 28.

42. Tal Asad, *Genealogies of Religion: Discipline and Reasons of Power in Christianity and Islam* (Baltimore: Johns Hopkins University Press, 1993), 78. Asad is citing G. S. Worgul, *From Magic to Metaphor* (New York: Paulist, 1989) for the symbolic view quoted.

43. See J. L. Austin, *How to Do Things with Words* (Oxford: Clarendon Press, 1962).

44. Dietrich von Hildebrand, *The Heart* (South Bend, IN: St. Augustine's Press, 2007), 7.

45. Jonathan A. Stapley, *The Power of Godliness: Mormon Liturgy and Cosmology* (New York: Oxford, forthcoming).

46. E. Brooks Holifield, *The Covenant Sealed: The Development of Puritan Sacramental Theology in Old and New England, 1570–1720* (Eugene, OR: Wipf and Stock, 2002), 2.

47. *WJS*, 232.

48. Smith quotes Paul (1 Cor. 15:46–48) to this effect, in 1876 D&C 128:13; 1876 D&C 77:2.

49. *CDBY* 1:350.

50. Kenneth E. Kirk, *The Vision of God* (New York: Harper & Row, 1966), 343.

51. *WJS*, 244.

52. See Ryan Davis's "Divine Authority and the Conditions of Salvation," http://publications .mi.byu.edu/fullscreen/?pub=3409&index=7. This discussion owes much to Davis's paper.

53. 1835 D&C 91:7 (D&C 76:89).

54. 1835 D&C 91:6 (D&C 76:74–75).

55. 1835 D&C 91:7 (D&C 76:91).

56. *WJS*, 169 (D&C 130:2).

57. Truman G. Madsen, "Are Christians Mormon?" *BYU Studies* 15.1 (Autumn 1974): 89.

58. Martin Buber, *I and Thou*, trans. Walter Kaufmann (New York: Simon and Schuster, 1996), 78, 84.

59. Emmanuel Levinas, *Existence and Existents*, trans. Alphonso Lingis (Pittsburgh: Duquesne University Press, 1988), 35.

60. Kirk, *Vision*, 449.

61. Kirk, *Vision*, 133.

62. C. S. Lewis, *Perelandra* (New York: Scribner, 1972), 101.

63. *EMS* 1.11 (April 1833): 161 (Moses 5:6, PGP).

64. Martin Luther, "The Freedom of a Christian," in *SWML*, 2:51.

65. Niebuhr explains, "There is an inner contradiction even in acts of obedience toward God. The fact the act is one of obedience rather than love means that it is not done with 'all thy heart and all thy soul and all thy might.'" Niebuhr, *Nature and Destiny of Man* (Louisville, KY: Westminster John Knox Press, 1996), 293.

66. Isaiah 33:14.

67. *WJS*, 254.

68. Restorationist Alexander Campbell quotes Baptist leader Thomas Meredith to this effect in "Immersion for Remission of Sins, Advocated by Elder Meredith," June 1843. *The Writings of Alexander Campbell: Selections Chiefly from the Millennial Harbinger*, ed. W. A. Morris (Austin, TX: Eugene Von Boeckmann, 1896), 90–91.

69. "Covenant," *EM*, 1333.

70. Jeffrey A. Trumbower, *Rescue for the Dead: The Posthumous Salvation of Non-Christians in Early Christianity* (New York: Oxford University Press, 2001), 3.

71. Clementine, *Recognitions* 1.lii, *ANF* 8:91.

72. Catholicism has since expressed recurrently a softening of this position, notably in John Paul II's *Redemptoris Missio*: "The universality of salvation means that it is granted not only to those who explicitly believe in Christ and have entered the Church. Since salvation is offered to all, it must be made concretely available to all," http://w2.vatican.va/content/john-paul-ii/en/encyclicals/documents/hf_jp-ii_enc_07121990_redemptoris-missio.html. Jesuit theologian Karl Rahner, with his notion of the "anonymous Christian," holds that "a person lives in the grace of God and attains salvation outside of explicitly constituted Christianity . . . because he follows his conscience." *Karl Rahner in Dialogue: Conversations and Interviews, 1965–82*, ed. Paul Imhof and Hubert Biallowons (New York: Crossroad, 1986), 207.

73. Psalm 58:10.

74. Thomas Aquinas, *Summa Theologica* (New York: Benziger Brothers, 1948), Suppl. Tertia Partis, Q 94 Art 1, 3:2972.

75. William Dawes, *Eternity of Hell Torments* (London, 1707), 11. Cited in John Casey, *After Lives: A Guide to Heaven, Hell, and Purgatory* (New York: Oxford University Press, 2009), 216.

76. 1844 D&C 106:5 (D&C 128:5).

77. J. Reuben Clarke, *Church News* (23 April 1960): 3.

78. James E. Talmage, *The Articles of Faith* (Salt Lake City, UT: Deseret Press, 1899), 421.

79. Justinian's ninth condemnation fell on those who say or think "that the punishment of demons and of impious men is only temporary, and will one day have an end, and that a restoration [apokatastasis] will take place." Henry P. Percival, *The Seven Ecumenical Councils of the Undivided Church* (New York: Scribner's, 1900), 320.

80. Charles Chauncy, *The Mystery Hid from Ages and Generations Made Manifest . . . , or, the Salvation of All Men* (Bedford, MA: Applewood, 2009), 191. (Reprint of London: Charles Dilly, 1784.)

81. John Murray, *Letters and Sketches of Sermons* (Boston: Joshua Belcher, 1812), 2:253.

82. Richard L. Bushman, *Joseph Smith and the Beginnings of Mormonism* (Urbana: University of Illinois Press, 1984), 27–28, 36.

83. BC 16:12 (D&C 19:11).

84. Hyrum M. Smith, *CR* (April 1909): 87.

85. John Wesley, "Of Hell," *SJW*, 3:223.

86. Mosiah 2:41; Alma 34:32; Jacob 5:70.

87. 1 Nephi 14:12.

88. According to sociologist Rodney Stark, some now living [in 1984] may see Mormonism grow from its eleven million in the year 2000 to the neighborhood of 267 million by the year 2080. See his Rodney Stark, "The Rise of a New World Faith," *Review of Religious Research* 26.1 (September 1984): 19, 22–23. Though this number has been criticized as extravagant by some sociologists, in 1999 Stark argued that his estimate might have been too conservative. As of 1999, "membership is substantially higher than my most optimistic projection." "Extracting Social Scientific Models from Mormon History," *Journal of Mormon History* 25.1 (Spring 1999): 176. The rate of growth has since declined.

89. *MS* 3.11 (March 1843): 177.

90. *WJS*, 381–82. Smith was certainly correct, from a Mormon perspective. Contrary to a popular Mormon narrative that sees the Reformation as paving the way for the LDS Restoration, Luther, Calvin, and others in fact shaped Reformation theology in a direction much further removed from the teachings Smith would propound than Catholicism ever was. They did this by emphasizing a God "without body, parts, or passions," human depravity, the Bible as the only source of authority, salvation by faith alone, and the incapacity of the living to aid in the salvation of the dead, and by de-emphasizing human freedom and the role of sacramentalism.

91. Martin Luther, "Ninety-five Theses," in *SWML* 1:51–59.

92. The Book of Common Prayer, 1549 edition, http://justus.anglican.org/resources/BCp/1549/Burial_1549.htm.

93. Mark Chapman, *Anglicanism: A Very Short Introduction* (New York: Oxford, 2006), 26.

94. Bruce Gordon, *Calvin* (New Haven, CT: Yale University Press, 2009), 255.

95. Gordon, *Calvin*, 336.

96. James E. Talmage, *The House of the Lord* (Salt Lake City, UT: Deseret, 1971), 54.

97. Martin Luther, "The Freedom of a Christian," in *SWML*, 2:43.

98. Obadiah 1:21 *KJV*.

99. Smith, *TS* 2.14 (15 May 1841): 430. Smith's revision of the Genesis account of the Abrahamic covenant first appeared in print in *T&S* 3.9 (1 March 1842): 706 (Abraham 2:11, PGP).

100. *T&S* 2.24 (15 October 1841): 577.

101. *T&S* 4.5 (16 January 1843): 73 (Moses 1:39, PGP).

102. *CDBY* 1:272.

103. *CDBY* 1:184.

104. *CDBY* 2:696.

105. *CDBY* 1:184.

106. *Recognitions of Clement* I:lii (*ANF* 8:91).

107. 1 Peter 3:19–20; 4:6.

108. Matthew 16:18.

109. Carl Schmidt, *Gespräche Jesu mit seinen Jüngen* . . . (Leipzig: Hinrich, 1908), 304–6. Cited in Hugh W. Nibley, *Mormonism and Early Christianity*, ed. Todd M. Compton and Stephen D. Ricks (Salt Lake City and Provo, UT: Deseret and Foundation for Ancient Research and Mormon Studies, 1987), 100, 114.

110. "The Epistle to the Apostles" 12, 18, in J. K. Elliott, *The Apocryphal New Testament* (Oxford: Oxford University Press, 2009), 563, 567.

111. *Epistle to the Apostles* 27–28, p. 573.

112. Clement of Alexandria, *Stromata* VI:vi (*ANF* 2:490–91). Nibley cites Pseudo-Clement, Clement, and Irenaeus in his survey, "Baptism for the Dead in Ancient Times," *Mormonism and Early Christianity*, 4:100–167.

113. Irenaeus, *Against Heresies* IV.22.2 (*ANF* 1:494).

114. John Symonds, *Thomas Brown and the Angels* (London: Hutchinson, 1961), 105.

115. Symonds, *Thomas Brown*, 105, 134.

116. Emanuel Swedenborg, *True Christianity, Containing a Comprehensive Theology of the New Church* (West Chester, PA: Swedenborg Foundation, 2006), 118.

117. *CDBY* 2:889.

118. John Durham Peters, "Recording beyond the Grave: Joseph Smith's Celestial Bookkeeping," *Critical Inquiry* 42.4 (Summer 2016): 852.

119. 1844 D&C 106:9 (D&C 128:9).

120. Nathaniel Givens, *Difficult by Design*, unpublished MS, copy in author's possession.

121. Wilford Woodruff, "The Law of Adoption," *CDWW* 4:73.

122. *WJS* 342.

123. *WJS* 346.

124. *WJS* 346.

125. https://www.mormon.org/values/family-history.

126. "Temples and Sanctuaries," *Anchor Bible Dictionary*, ed. David Noel Freedman (New York: Doubleday, 1992), 6:369.

127. "Temple," *EJ* 15: 954–55.

128. "Temple," *EJ* 15: 951.

129. "Tabernacle," *EJ* 15:679. The terms are found, respectively, in Leviticus 17:4 and Exodus 28:43, for instance.

130. Quoting Siphra on Leviticus 26:12, in Kirk, *Vision*, 22.

131. Plato, *Timaeus* 29e, trans. Donald J. Zeyl, in *Plato: Complete Works*, ed. John M. Cooper (Indianapolis: Hackett, 1997), 1236.

132. Kirk, *Vision*, 13–14.

133. Kirk, *Vision*, 2.

134. Gerald E. Smith, *Schooling the Prophet: How the Book of Mormon Influenced Joseph Smith and the Early Restoration* (Provo, UT: Neal A. Maxwell Institute, 2015), 6.

135. Jon D. Levenson, *Sinai and Zion: An Entry into the Jewish Bible* (New York: HarperOne, 1985), 9.

136. Luke 9:58.

137. Andrew Jenson, *The Historical Record* (Salt Lake City, UT, 1888), 7:859.

138. Prayer of Dedication, 27 March 1836, http://josephsmithpapers.org/paperSummary/prayer-of-dedication-27-march-1836-dc-109? (D&C 109:37).

139. *JSP-J1*, 219 (1876 D&C 110:2–3). Alexander L. Baugh notes this and an earlier appearance in "Parting the Veil: Joseph Smith's Seventy-Six Documented Visionary Experiences," in *Opening the Heavens: Accounts of Divine Manifestations, 1820–1844*, ed. John W. Welch (Provo and Salt Lake City, UT: Brigham Young University Press and Deseret, 2005), 284–85.

140. Wainwright, *Doxology*, 23.

141. 1844 D&C 103:10 (D&C 124:30–31).

142. 2 Samuel 24:24.

143. *JSP-J2*, 53.

144. *T&S* 4.5 (16 January 1843): 71–72 (Moses 1:8–9, PGP).

145. *MHC* C-1, 507.

146. *JST* Exodus 34:1, p. 701.

147. "The law received on Sinai was actually a second and revised edition because of what had happened when the tablets were first brought down—they were smashed by Moses in anger because of the golden calf. So Moses went up again to the mountain top to receive a second edition of the law which, say the exegetes, was actually a law which took into account the transgressions of the faithless and disobedient people." Krister Stendahl, *Paul among Jews and Gentiles* (Philadelphia: Fortress Press, 1979), 19–20; Galatians 3:19.

148. 1835 D&C 4:4 (D&C 84:21–23).

149. Luke 3:1; S. G. F. Brandon, *The Fall of Jerusalem and the Christian Church* (London: SPCK, 1951), 120–21. Cited in Hugh Nibley, *Temple and Cosmos*, ed. Don E. Norton (Provo and Salt Lake City, UT: Foundation for Ancient Research and Mormon Studies and Deseret, 1992), 46.

150. Marcus von Wellnitz, "The Catholic Liturgy and the Mormon Temple," *BYU Studies* 21.1 (1981): 5. Cited in Smith, *Schooling*, 243–44.

151. Margaret Barker, *Christmas: The Original Story* (London: SPCK, 2008), 2. She expounds her "temple theology" in several books, including *Temple Theology* (London: SPCK, 2004), *The Great High Priest: The Temple Roots of Christian Liturgy* (London: T&T Clark, 2003), and *Temple Themes in Christian Worship* (London: T&T Clark, 2008).

152. Margaret Barker, *The Gate of Heaven* (Sheffield: Sheffield Phoenix, 2008), 2, 104–32.

153. Hugh Nibley is here paraphrasing Yigael Yadin's discussion of the Temple Scroll, 112–15. Nibley, *Temple and Cosmos*, 52.

154. Barker, *Temple Theology*, 1.

155. "Temple," *EJ* 15:944–45.

156. Temples are mentioned in the Land of Nephi, Zarahemla, and Bountiful. 2 Nephi 5:16; Mosiah 1:18; 3 Nephi 11:1.

157. Senator Aaron Harrison Cragin (NH), debate on the Cummins Bill, *Congressional Globe*, 41st Congress, 2nd Session (18 May 1870), 3576–77.

158. Spencer J. Fluhman, "Secrets and the Making of Mormon Moments," in *Faith in the New Millennium: The Future of Religion and American Politics*, ed. Matthew Avery Sutton and Darren Dochuk (New York: Oxford University Press, 2016), 218–19.

159. Numbers 11:16–17.

160. Matthew 7:6; 17:9.

161. 1 Corinthians 4:1.

162. Cited by Edwin Gifford, "Introduction," Saint Cyril, Catechetical Lectures, *NPNF2* 7:xxxv.

163. Fluhman, "Secrets," 219, citing Guy G. Stroumsa, *Hidden Wisdom: Esoteric Traditions and the Roots of Christian Mysticism*, 2nd ed., rev. and enl. (Leiden: Brill, 2005), 29–32.

164. "A Record of the Organization, and Proceedings of the Female Relief Society of Nauvoo," in *FFY*, 43.

165. *MHC*, 4 May 1842, cited by Andrew F. Ehat, "Who Shall Ascend into the Hill of the Lord," in *Temples of the Ancient World*, ed. Donald W. Parry (Salt Lake City, UT: Deseret, 1994), 51.

166. *CDWW* 4:74.

167. Benjamin F. Johnson, *My Life's Review* (n.d.: Johnson Family Organization, 1997), 85.

168. Michael W. Homer, *Joseph's Temple: The Dynamic Relationship between Freemasonry and Mormonism* (Salt Lake City, UT: University of Utah Press, 2014), 1. Homer's is the definitive treatment of the role of Masonry in Mormonism's creation.

169. Joseph Smith to Isaac Galland, 22 March 1839, *JSP-D6*, forthcoming; http://www .josephsmithpapers.org/paper-summary/letter-to-isaac-galland-22-march-1839/4.

170. *CDBY* 5:2719.

171. Augustine, *On Christian Doctrine* II.xl.60, trans. J. F. Shaw, in *Nicene and Post-Nicene Fathers of the Christian Church*, First series, ed. Philip Schaff (Edinburgh: T&T Clark, 1993), 2:554.

172. Richard Bushman, *Rough Stone Rolling: A Cultural Biography of Mormonism's Founder* (New York: Knopf, 2005), 451.

173. Gregory A. Prince and William Robert Wright, *David O. McKay and the Rise of Modern Mormonism* (Salt Lake City: University of Utah Press, 2005), 277.

174. 13 February 1849, *Minutes*. For the most comprehensive treatment of this tragic policy, see W. Paul Reeve, *Religion of a Different Color: Race and the Mormon Struggle for Whiteness* (New York: Oxford University Press, 2015), esp. chapter 7.

CHAPTER 4

1. Cited in Bruce Gordon, *Calvin* (New Haven, CT: Yale University Press, 2009), 93–94, 268.

2. Gordon, *Calvin*, 303. "Exile" was "the foundation of his prophetic authority," he wrote elsewhere (318).

3. Kenneth E. Kirk, *The Vision of God* (New York: Harper & Row, 1966), 416.

4. Horton Davies, *Worship and Theology in England. From Cranmer to Baxter and Fox, 1534– 1690* (Grand Rapids, MI: Eerdmans, 1996), 31.

5. Matthew 16:19.

6. Theodore of Mopsuestia, Fragment 92, in *Ancient Christian Commentary on Scripture, Matthew 14–28*, ed. Manlio Simonetti (Downers Grove, IL: InterVarsity Press, 2002), NT 1b:45.

7. John Symonds, *Thomas Brown and the Angels* (London: Hutchinson, 1961), 92.

8. Eusebius quotes Hebesippus (c. AD 110–180), in *History of the Church* 3.32.8, trans. G. A. Williamson (Hammondsworth, UK: Dorset, 1983), 143.

9. "The First Epistle of Clement" XLIV, *ANF* 1:17.

10. *Constitutions of the Holy Apostles* II.iv.27, *ANF* 7:410.

11. "To the Christian Nobility," *SWML* 1:263, 265.

12. Martin Luther, *Concerning the Ministry*, cited in Bryan P. Stone, *A Reader in Ecclesiology* (Farnham, UK: Ashgate, 2003), 85.

13. *Right and Power of a Christian Church*, in *SWML* 2:329. He is citing 1 Peter 2:9.

14. *ICR* IV.xix.25, p. 961.

15. *ICR* IV.xviii.2, p. 935.

16. William Allen, *A True Sincere and Modest Defence of English Catholiques that Suffer for their Faith* (St. Louis: B. Herder, 1914 [1584]), 132–33.

17. Second Helvetic Confession, 18.10, *C&C* 2:500.

18. Roy Hattersley, *The Life of John Wesley: A Brand from the Burning* (New York: Doubleday, 2003), 377.

19. Hattersley, *John Wesley*, 372.

20. Hattersley, *John Wesley*, 375.

21. Hattersley, *John Wesley*, 376. Wesley had been ordained a priest, but Anglican priests had no authority to ordain a bishop, which was the title Coke assumed with Wesley's acquiescence.

22. *Doctrines and Discipline of the Methodist Episcopal Church* (New York: B. Waugh and T. Mason, 1832), 144.

23. Stanley Archer, "Hooker on Apostolic Succession: The Two Voices," *Sixteenth-Century Journal* 24.2 (1993): 67–74.

24. Acts 10:38.

25. John 20:22–23.

26. Richard Hooker, *Of the Laws of Ecclesiastical Polity* (London: John Walthoe et al., 1723), 277.

27. Hooker, *Of the Laws*, 136, 58.

28. Hooker, *Of the Laws*, 281, 275.

29. Hooker, *Of the Laws*, 236, 276–77.

30. Robert South, *Sermons Preached upon Several Occasions* (Oxford: Clarendon Press, 1823), 5:32–33. I thank Benjamin Keogh for this reference.

31. William Gibbons, *Truth Advocated in Letters Addressed to the Presbyterians* (Philadelphia: Joseph Rakenstraw, 1822), 95. Cited in the excellent study of Benjamin Keogh, "The Holy Priesthood, the Holy Ghost and the Holy Community," *Dialogue*, forthcoming.

32. "Hours with the Holy Scripture," *Reformed Presbyterian Magazine* (Edinburgh: Johnstone, Hunter, 1866), 46. Cited in Keogh, "The Holy Priesthood, the Holy Ghost and the Holy Community."

33. Adam Clarke, *Commentary with Critical Notes on the Holy Bible* (Nashville: Abingdon, n.d. [first published 1810–26]), 3:651.

34. Robert Richardson, *Memoirs of Alexander Campbell* (Cincinnati: Carroll & Co., 1872), 1:232.

35. Thomas Campbell, *Declaration and Address of the Christian Association* (Washington, PA: Brown & Sample, 1809; reprint, Coraopolis, PA: Record Publishing, 1908), 9.

36. Campbell, *Declaration and Address*, 13.

37. Orvilla S. Belisle, *The Arch Bishop; or, Romanism in the United States* (Philadelphia: William White Smith, 1854); *The Prophets; or Mormonism Unveiled* (Philadelphia: William White Smith, 1855).

38. John A. Clark, *Gleanings by the Way* (Philadelphia: W. J. & J. K. Simon; New York: Robert Carter, 1842), 259; Robert Richards [pseud.], *The Californian Crusoe; or, the Lost Treasure Found; a Tale of Mormonism* (London: Parker, 1854), 82. For an ampler discussion of this pattern, See Terryl L. Givens, *The Viper on the Hearth: Mormons, Myths, and the Construction of Heresy* (New York: Oxford University Press, 1997).

39. Alexander Campbell, *Delusions: An Analysis of the Book of Mormon* (Boston: Greene, 1832), 11.

40. *TD*, 491–92.

41. *CDBY* 4:2044.

42. *WJS*, 158.

43. Mosiah 23; Mosiah 24 heading.

44. Mosiah 25:19.

45. Mosiah 26:7–8.

46. Mosiah 29 heading.

47. BC 1:4 (D&C 1:17).

48. 1835 D&C 3:31 (107:65).

49. *WJS*, 234–35.

50. *WJS*, 215.

51. *WJS*, 254.

52. "Address," *M&A* 1.1 (October 1834): 2.

53. Article of Faith 5, PGP.

54. "God is not the author of confusion. . . . Let all things be done . . . in order." 1 Corinthians 14:33, 40 *KJV*; Orson Pratt, *JD* 14:271.

55. *WJS*, 157.

56. *WJS*, 244.

57. Benjamin Winchester, *The History of the Priesthood from the Beginning of the World to the Present Time* (Philadelphia: Brown, Bicking & Guilpert, 1843), 6.

58. "Economy," Noah Webster, *American Dictionary of the English Language*. Reprint of 1828 first edition (Chesapeake: Foundation for American Christian Education, 1995), n.p.

59. *M&A* 1.2 (November 1834): 21.

60. *T&S* 4.1 (15 November 1842): 24.

61. *MS* 2:39, in John A. Widtsoe, *Priesthood and Church Government* (Salt Lake City, UT: Deseret, 1954), 35.

62. *WJS*, 158.

63. Winchester, *History of the Priesthood*, 7.

64. *SCD*, SI 2a, p. 12.

65. BC 1:5 (D&C 1:30).

66. *WJS*, 38.

67. "Melchisedec Priesthood," *T&S* 4.2 (1 December 1842): 24.

68. This is from an official LDS website, and is one of dozens of examples, https://www.mormon.org/faq/purpose-of-priesthood.

69. Jonathan A. Stapley, *The Power of Godliness: Mormon Liturgy and Cosmology* (New York: Oxford, forthcoming).

70. Gregory A. Prince and William Robert Wright, *David O. McKay and the Rise of Modern Mormonism* (Salt Lake City: University of Utah Press, 2005), 144.

71. *FFY*, 184, 421.

72. "Religious Groups Joined Forces to Help Andrew's Victims," *Sun-Sentinel*, 24 August 2002.

73. Harold Bloom, *The American Religion: The Emergence of the Post-Christian Nation* (New York: Simon and Schuster, 1992), 116.

74. "Mormon youth," a comprehensive study finds, "showed a greater willingness to adhere to the requirement of their faith" than youth of any other religious group in America. (Results of the National Study of Youth and Religion were summarized in "Study Finds Mormon Teens Fare Best," www.news14.com, 12 March 2005). For other statistical examples, see Givens, *People of Paradox: A History of Mormon Culture* (New York: Oxford University Press, 2012), 14–15.

75. *PWJS*, 441 (D&C 121:39).

76. "Priestcraft," *OED*, 1971 edition.

77. Clericus "Outcry against Priestcraft," *Evangelical Magazine* 5 (London, 1797): 202.

78. BC 35:3 (D&C 33:4).

79. 2 Nephi 26:29; Alma 1:12–16.

80. *PWJS*, 441 (D&C 121:41–42).

81. *PWJS*, 440 (D&C 121:37).

82. Luke 14:23.

83. Clarke, *Commentary*, 3:797.

84. Teaching of the Twelve Apostles XV, *ANF* 7:381.

85. 1 Clement XLIV, in *ANF* 1:17.

86. John Locke, *Two Treatises of Government* (London: Whitmore and Fenn, 1821), 295.

87. Speaking of the Apocrypha, Ward writes, "For though they were, as we do not deny, doubted of by some of the ancient fathers, and not accepted as canonical, 'yet in the end,' to use Mr. Rogers's words, 'they were wholly taken and received by the common consent of the Church.'" Thomas Ward, *Errata of the Protestant Bible* (Dublin: James Duffy, 1841), 17; Richard Baxter, *A Key for Catholics to Open the Juggling of the Jesuits* (London: Hamilton, Adams & Co., 1839), 273.

88. "To the Christian Nobility," *SWML* 1:265.

89. John Spottswood, *History of the Church of Scotland* (London: R. Norton, 1668), 165.

90. *The Representation of the Committee of the English Congregations in Union with the Moravian Church* (London, 1754), 8.

91. Polly Ha, "Ecclesiastical Independence and the Freedom of Consent," in *Freedom and the Construction of Europe: Volume 1, Religious Freedom*, ed. Quentin Skinner and Martin van Gelderen (Cambridge: Cambridge University Press, 2013), 64.

92. John Cotton, "Way of the Churches," 94–96, in *A Historical Sketch of the Congregational Churches in Massachusetts*, ed. Joseph Sylvester Clark (Boston: Congregational Board, 1858), 284–85.

93. BC 22:5 (D&C 21:5).

94. BC 27:3 (D&C 26:2). BC 30:13 (D&C 28:13) repeated the point almost verbatim two months later, and common consent was made an underlying principle of Mormonism's cooperative venture, the United Order, in 1834 (1835 D&C 98:11–12; D&C 104:71–85).

95. See as a typical example "Conference minutes," 28 June 1838, in *JSP-D6*, forthcoming; http://www.josephsmithpapers.org/paper-summary/history-1838-1856-volume-b-1-1-september-1834-2-november-1838/253.

96. 29 June 1835, Record of the Twelve, 14 February–28 August 1835, http://josephsmithpapers.org/paperSummary/record-of-the-twelve-14-february-28-august-1835.

97. *JSP-J3*, 104. The quorum referred to was called "the quorum of the anointed," consisting of members who had received the higher temple ordinances.

98. A church conference in 1835 adopted a "Statement on Marriage". 1835 D&C 101.

99. Mosiah 22:21; 29:25. Nephihah is appointed chief judge from "among the elders of the church" and given "power according to the voice of the people" (Alma 4:16). That latter phrase occurs more than a dozen times in the Book of Mormon.

100. 1835 D&C 2:16 (D&C 20:65). Though this revelation was received for the most part in 1829, the relevant passage was not included in the 1833 Book of Commandments.

101. "Minutes of a Special Conference," *T&S* 4.21 (15 September 1843): 330.

102. William G. Hartley, *My Fellow Servants: Essays on the History of the Priesthood* (Provo, UT: BYU Studies, 2010), 242.

103. *JSP-D5*, 363.

104. Oliver Cowdery to Warren Cowdery and Lyman Cowdery, 4 February 1838, in *JSP-D6*, forthcoming; http://www.josephsmithpapers.org/paper-summary/journal-march-september-1838/39.

105. The nine formal charges against Cowdery and his letter of response are in *JSP-D6*, forthcoming; http://www.josephsmithpapers.org/paper-summary/minute-book-2/123.

106. *JSP-D6*, forthcoming; http://www.josephsmithpapers.org/paper-summary/minute-book-2/129.

107. Thomas B. Marsh to Wilford Woodruff, circa 18 June 1838, in *JSP-D6*, forthcoming; http://www.josephsmithpapers.org/paper-summary/letter-thomas-b-marsh-at-request-of-js-to-wilford-woodruff-circa-18-june-1838/3.

108. *JSP-D6*, forthcoming; http://www.josephsmithpapers.org/paper-summary/minute-book-2/124.

109. Robert E. Quinn, "Common Consent," *EM* 1:297. For a thorough treatment of this subject, where "authority flowed upward from the congregation," see Richard L. Bushman, "The Theology of Councils," in *Revelation, Reason and Faith: Essays in Honor of Truman G. Madsen*, ed. Donald W. Parry et al. (Provo, UT: Neal A. Maxwell Institute for Religious Scholarship, 2002), 433–46.

110. In addition to council meetings, Smith also used the term idiosyncratically in a letter in which he admonished elders to baptize minors only "with common consent" (Letter to the Elders, *M&A* 2.14 [November 1835]: 210. A word search of Smith's sermons and Young's *Collected Discourses* reveals no instances of its use.

111. John W. Taylor, 28 October 1905, in *Minutes*.

112. The phrase is a paraphrase in *Teachings of Joseph F. Smith* (Salt Lake City, UT: Church of Jesus Christ of Latter-day Saints, 2011), chapter 24, https://www.lds.org/manual/teachings-joseph-f-smith/chapter-24?lang=eng.

113. BC 45:11 (D&C 43:12).

114. BC 22:5 (D&C 21:5–6).

115. https://www.lds.org/handbook/handbook-2-administering-the-church/callings-in-the-church/19.3?lang=eng&_r=1#193.

116. Apostle James E. Faust taught that "every father is to his family a patriarch and every mother a matriarch as coequals in their distinctive parental roles." Apostle L. Tom Perry emphasized that "there is not a president and vice-president in a family" but "co-presidents working together eternally for the good of their family. . . . They are on equal footing." "Stick with the Brethren," *Deseret News* (7 April 1996); "Fathers' Role in Anchoring Families," *LDS Church News* (10 April 2004): 15.

117. "Women to Join Key, Leading LDS Church Councils," *Deseret News*, 18 August 2015, http://www.deseretnews.com/article/865634860/In-a-significant-move-women-to-join-key-leading-LDS-Church-councils.html?pg=all.

118. *EMS* 1.3 (August 1832): 47 (Moses 7:62–64, PGP).

119. Romans 14:11.

120. 2 Nephi 26:24.

121. 3 Nephi 27:14.

122. 2 Nephi 2:27.

123. Dietrich Bonhoeffer to Eberhard Bethge, 16 July 1944. In Larry L. Rasmussen, *Dietrich Bonhoeffer: Reality and Resistance* (Louisville, KY: Westminster John Knox Press, 2005), 17.

124. *PWJS*, 441 (D&C 121:46).

125. *JSP-H1*, 214; 2 Timothy 3:5.

126. "The local Anglican parish and its priest often reminded Methodists of 2 Timothy 3:5." Lester Ruth, "The Sources and the Tensions in the Methodist Worship Ethos," in *Oxford Handbook of Methodist Studies*, ed. William J. Abraham and James E. Kirby (New York: Oxford University Press, 2009), 324.

127. *JSP-H1*, 13.

128. 1835 D&C 4:3 (D&C 84:19–20).

129. 1835 D&C 91:5 (D&C 76:66).

130. 1844 D&C 106:11 (D&C 128:11–12).

131. Widtsoe, *Priesthood*, 42.

132. 1876 D&C 131:2.

133. *WJS*, 244.

134. *WJS*, 366.

135. 1835 D&C 4:6 (D&C 84:39–40).

136. James Talmage, *House of the Lord* (Salt Lake City, UT: Deseret, 1971), 83.

137. Orson Pratt, *JD*, 18:292.

138. Richard L. Bushman, *On the Road with Joseph Smith: An Author's Diary* (Salt Lake City, UT: Kofford, 2007), 60–61. In Philip L. Barlow, "To Mend a Fractured Reality," in *Journal of Mormon History* 38.3 (Summer 2012): 47.

139. Orson Pratt, "Powers of Nature," *The Seer* 2.3 (March 1854): 227.

140. *CDBY* 2:1075.

141. Orson Pratt, *Great First Cause, or the Self-Moving Forces of the Universe*, 10. In *A Series of Pamphlets* (Liverpool: R. James, 1851).

142. "Powers of Nature," *The Seer* 2.3 (March 1854): 226.

143. John A. Widtsoe, *Joseph Smith as Scientist* (Salt Lake City, UT: Young Men's Mutual Improvement Associations, 1908), 62–65.

144. Gary Kowalski, *Science and the Search for God* (New York: Lantern Books, 2003), 73.

145. Thomas Nagel, "Panpsychism," in *Mortal Questions* (Cambridge: Cambridge University Press, 1991), 181.

146. For Niels Henrik Gregersen's "temporal theism" (and four other theistic responses to evolution), see "Emergence: What Is at Stake for Religious Reflection?" in *The Re-Emergence of Emergence: The Emergentist Hypothesis from Science to Religion*, ed. Philip Clayton and Paul Davies (Oxford: Oxford University Press, 2006), 279–322. The paraphrase is from Steven L. Peck, *Evolving Faith: Wanderings of a Mormon Biologist* (Provo, UT: Neal A. Maxwell Institute, 2015), 53.

147. Ralph V. Chamberlin, *Life and Philosophy of W. H. Chamberlin* (Salt Lake City, UT: Deseret, 1925), 320, in Peck, *Evolving*, 61–62.

148. Peck, *Evolving*, 62.

149. *T&S* 3.10 (15 March 1842): 721 (Abraham 4:7–12, PGP).

150. Jacob 4:9.

151. 1835 D&C, Theology Lecture First, 7, 11.

152. *CDBY* 1:483.

153. *CDBY* 2:885.

154. *CDBY* 2:1114.

155. *CDBY* 1:289.

156. *CDBY* 5:2911.

157. *Gospel Principles Manual*, https://www.lds.org/manual/gospel-principles/chapter-5-the-creation?lang=eng.

158. Hebrews 7:3.

159. *JST* Hebrews 7:3, p. 539.

160. *WJS*, 38–39. The allusion is to Job 38:7.

161. Alma 13:7.

162. *WJS*, 8.

163. *CDBY* 1:20.

164. *WJS*, 8.

165. 1835 D&C 3:27–28 (D&C 107:50–53).

166. *WJS*, 8.

167. John Taylor, *JD* 19:127.

168. Orson Pratt, *JD* 19:176.

169. George Q. Cannon, *JD* 22:126.

170. Benjamin Winchester, *The History of the Priesthood from the Beginning of the World to the Present Time* (Philadelphia: Brown, Bicking & Guilpert, 1843), 7.

171. *CDBY* 1:35.

172. *CDBY* 1:26.

173. *CDBY* 2:915.

174. "To Noah Saxton," 4 January 1833, in *JSP-D2*, 352.

175. Alexander Campbell, "Importance of a Pure Version of the Christian Scriptures," *Millennial Harbinger*, Fourth Series, 2.1 (January 1852): 32.

176. 3 Nephi 11:21.

177. 3 Nephi 11:23.

178. *M&A* 1.1 (October 1834): 15.

179. *M&A* 1.1 (October 1834): 15.

180. *M&A* 1.1 (October 1834): 15.

181. Cowdery's statement is reproduced in Lyndon W. Cook, *The Revelations of the Prophet Joseph Smith* (Salt Lake City, UT: Deseret, 1985), 22–23.

182. *T&S* 3.19 (1 August 1842): 865–66.

183. This language appears in the 1832 revelation, 1835 D&C 4:2–4 (D&C 84:6–30). Current Aaronic and Melchizedek terminology appears in the 1835 edition of the D&C 3:1 (D&C 107:1).

184. Hebrews 5:4 *KJV*.

185. *T&S* 3.9 (1 March 1842): 709 (AF 5, PGP).

186. Exodus 28:1.

187. BC 38:3 (D&C 36:5).

188. As noted above, members of African descent were initially included in this invitation but banned a few years after settlement in Utah.

189. 1835 D&C 4:6 (D&C 84:33).

190. Exodus 28:41; Leviticus 8 also relates the calling and consecration of Aaron in the priestly office at Moses's hands.

191. Numbers 27:23.

192. Tosef., Sanh. i. 1; Ket. 112a, cited in Wilhelm Bacher, Jacob Zallel Lauterbach, "Ordination," *Jewish Encyclopedia*, 1906 edition, http://www.jewishencyclopedia.com/articles/11756-ordination.

193. Mark 3:14; John 15:16.

194. *EJ* 1:3.

195. Numbers 3:6–17.

196. "Priests and Priesthood," *EJ* 13:1070. See Deuteronomy 10:8–9 and 33:8–10.

197. *TD*, 491.

198. *EJ* 13:1074.

199. Robert Hamilton Bishop et al., *Western Peace-Maker and Monthly Religious Journal* (Oxford: W. W. Bishop, 1839), 101.

200. Samuel Haining, *Mormonism Weighed in the Balances of the Sanctuary and Found Wanting* (Douglas: Robert Fargher, 1840), 61.

201. 1835 D&C 22:2 (D&C 68:21).

202. Hebrews 5:6; "Aaron," *EJ* 1:8.

203. Hartley, *My Fellow Servants*, 43.

204. "Priests and Priesthood," *EJ* 13:1070.

205. J. N. D. Kelly, *Early Christian Doctrines*, rev. ed. (New York: HarperCollins, 1978), 196.

206. The Baltimore Catechism, Lesson 27, http://www.catholicity.com/baltimore-catechism/lesson27.html.

207. *NCE* 11:698.

208. *SCD* #424, p. 167.

209. Acts 11:30.

210. Acts 15.

211. *Constitutions* II.vii.57, *ANF* 7:421.

212. "Priest," *Catholic Encyclopedia* (New York: Appleton, 1911), 12:406.

213. Walter A. Elwell, ed., *Evangelical Dictionary of Theology*, 2nd ed. (Grand Rapids, MI: Baker Academic, 2001), 953.

214. Martin Luther, "Babylonian Captivity," in *SWML* 1:472.

215. Peter Ackroyd, *Rebellion: The History of England from James I to the Glorious Revolution* (New York: St. Martins, 2014), 8.

216. 2 Nephi 5:6; Moroni 3, 4.

217. Alma 4:7, Moroni 3:1, etc.

218. Revelation 20:6; also 1:6 and 5:10 *KJV*.

219. Thus the *NRSV* and the Douay-Rheims both render Rev. 5:10: "You have made them to be a kingdom and priests."

220. "A Record of the Organization, and Proceedings of the Female Relief Society of Nauvoo," in *FFY*, 43.

221. BC 24:35 (D&C 20:46–47).

222. "Chronology," *WWJ* 1:preface.

223. "To the Editor," *MS* 1.1 (May 1840): 23.

224. *MS* 1.1 (May 1840): 20.

225. *MS* 15.5 (29 January 1853): 78; *MS* 41.7 (17 February 1879): 110.

226. *CDBY* 1:496.

227. Hartley, *My Fellow Servants*, 50.

228. Hartley, *My Fellow Servants*, 55.

229. Hartley, *My Fellow Servants*, 58–60.

230. First Presidency to Rudger Clawson, 29 November 1934, *Minutes.*

231. Acts 13:1; 1 Corinthians 12:28–29; Ephesians 4:11.

232. Scott Manetsch, *Calvin's Company of Pastors: Pastoral Care and the Emerging Reformed Church* (New York: Oxford University Press, 2013), 190. I thank David Heap for this reference.

233. John Dickson, *A Sermon Preached in the Church of Air* . . . (n.p.: n.p., 1713), 22.

234. John Wesley, *Works* (London: Thomas Cordeux, 1810), 5:17.

235. This injunction of the *Discipline*, not present in the first version, had appeared by 1832. See *Doctrines and Discipline of the Methodist Episcopal Church* (New York: B. Waugh and T. Mason, 1832), 76–77.

236. BC 24:36–38 (D&C 20:46–54).

237. See the discussion in Gerald Smith, *Schooling the Prophet: How the Book of Mormon Influenced Joseph Smith and the Early Restoration* (Provo, UT: Neal A. Maxwell Institute, 2015), 186ff.

238. *JSP-D5*, 139.

239. The phrase appears as spoken by Brigham Young in an 1843 meeting. *CDBY* 1:27.

240. *JI* 27.16 (15 August 1892): 492–93.

241. *CDBY* 1:27.

242. Willard Richards, 30 November 1847, *Minutes.*

243. Brigham Young, 30 November 1847, *Minutes.* Young confirmed the practice of appointing "the best Old Hi[gh] P[riests] that can be found" over a year later, in Utah. 16 February 1849, *Minutes.*

244. Hartley, *My Fellow Servants*, 89.

245. Hartley, *My Fellow Servants*, 97–98.

246. 16 February 1849, *Minutes.*

247. 26 October 1862, *Minutes.*

248. George Q. Cannon reported an instance of two men accompanying Elders Orson Pratt and Wilford Woodruff "as teachers" to work with Elias Harrison and William Godbe, who were "giving way to a spirit of apostacy." *Minutes,* 25 October 1869.

249. Statement signed by Elias L. T. Harrison and William S. Godbe, 25 October 1869, *Minutes.*

250. Brigham Young Jr. Diary, 20 April 1890, *Minutes.*

251. "He told Brother Roberts that it should be made clear to such teachers that when the Manifesto was issued we did not pledge ourselves to abandon our plural wives." Journal History, 16 August 1900, *Minutes.*

252. Journal History, 22 March 1900, *Minutes.*

253. Hartley, *My Fellow Servants*, 108.

254. First Presidency Letter to Rudger Clawson, 29 November 1934, *Minutes.*

255. George Q. Cannon, "Editorial Thoughts," *JI* 26.4 (15 February 1891): 22.

256. BC 24:33 (D&C 20:42).

257. *EM* 2:655.

258. James F. White, *An Introduction to Christian Worsh*ip, 3rd ed. (Nashville: Abingdon Press, 2001), 85.

259. In 1 Timothy 3:8 and Philippians 1:1 we find the Greek word διάκονος. It also appears in Romans 16:1, where it is attached to a woman, Phebe.

260. Acts 6:2, 6.

261. *Constitutions of the Holy Apostles* II.iv.26, *ANF* 7:410–11.

262. *Constitutions* II.iv.44, *ANF* 7:416.

263. *Constitutions* II.iv.31, *ANF* 7:411.

264. BC 23:40 (D&C 20:57).

265. I thank Gerald Smith for this observation.

266. *CDBY* 2:843.

267. *CDBY* 1:75.

268. *CDBY* 2:861.

269. *CDBY* 2:842.

270. *JSP-D5*, 147.

271. *CDBY* 1:102.

272. Harley, *My Fellow Servants*, 90.

273. Hartley, *My Fellow Servants*, 349.

274. Hartley, *My Fellow Servants*, 53, 101.

275. Justin Martyr, *The First Apology, ANF* 1:185.

276. Hebrews 6:20; 7:11.

277. John Brown, *Dictionary of the Holy Bible* (London: William Baynes, 1818), 2:163.

278. Origen, *Commentary on the Gospel of John, Ancient Scripture Commentary, Hebrews*, ed. Erik M. Heen and Philip D. W. Krey (Downers Grove, IL: InterVarsity Press, 2005), NT 10:115.

279. Clarke, *Commentary*, 6:734.

280. George Faber, *Horae Mosaicae* (London: Rivington 1818), 2:73. Henry Kollock cites "Cunaeus, du Moulin, Gaillard, Alling, Asurrin, &c" as having this same opinion. See his "Life of Melchizedek," *Sermons on Various Subjects* (Savannah: S. C. and I. Schenk, 1822), 89.

281. Kollock, "Life of Melchizedek," 90.

282. Elias Smith, *The Herald of Life and Immortality* (Boston: n.p., 1819), 1:273.

283. Augustin Calmet, *Calmet's Dictionary of the Holy Bible* (London: Holdsworth and Ball, 1830), 4:352.

284. Carl Bernhard Moll, *Epistle to the Hebrews*, in *Commentary on the Holy Scriptures*, ed. John Peter Lange (Grand Rapids, MI: Zondervan, 1976), 11:126.

285. Granville Sharp, *Melchisedec, or an Answer to a Question Respecting the Reality of Melchisedec's Existence* (London: Richard Edwards, 1810), 40.

286. Exodus 32; 34:1.

287. *JST* Exodus 34:1, p. 701.

288. *EMS* 1.11 (April 1833): 161; Widtsoe, *Priesthood*, 18.

289. 1835 D&C 4:4 (D&C 84:25–26).

290. Numbers 16:10.

291. *EJ*, citing Deuteronomy 10:8–9 and 33:8–10. At the same time, as the *Encyclopedia* authors note, the P author limits such rights to the descendants of Aaron. 13:1070.

292. *JST*, Numbers 16:10, 707.

293. Alma 13:14–17.

294. Alma 13:6–10.

295. Alma 4:20; 13:6. In the *Times and Seasons*, Smith assigns some planned temples to the presidency of "the High and Most Holy priesthood, after the order of Melchisedec," and others to "the high priesthood of the holy order of God." As with the Book of Mormon, it seems likely that the expressions refer to the same "order" of priesthood. *T&S* 6.2 (1 February 1845): 785.

296. 1835 D&C 4:2, 4 (D&C 84:6–16, 27).

297. *JSP-D2*, 290.

298. *JSP-H1*, 10.

299. *JSP-D4*, 408. The revelation merely alludes to "Peter, James, and John, . . . by whom I have ordained you and confirmed you to be apostles and especial witnesses of my name." 1835 D&C 50:3 (D&C 27:12).

300. *JSP-H1*, 327.

301. *JSP-D4*, 251.

302. *WWJ* 5:35.

303. *JSP-J1*, 4.

304. Bushman finds an 1830 date plausible. See *Rough Stone Rolling: A Cultural Biography of Mormonism's Founder* (New York: Knopf, 2005), 118. D. Michael Quinn also also argues for the later date in his *The Mormon Hierarchy: Origins of Power* (Salt Lake City, UT: Signature, 1994), 20–26.

305. *CDBY* 4:2191.

306. *JSP-H1*, 371. This entry, made after 1838, refers to the day of the church's organization.

307. Mosiah 18:18; 25:19; Moroni 3:3.

308. Bushman, *Rough Stone*, 157.

309. George Q. Cannon, "Ordaining to the Priesthood," *JI* 29.4 (15 February 1894): 114.

310. Jonathan Stapley traces the question and its resolution in *The Power of Godliness: Mormon Liturgy and Cosmology* (New York: Oxford, forthcoming).

311. See *JSP-D1*, 320.

312. See *JSP-D1*, 320.

313. Revelation, 11 November 1831-B (D&C 107 partial), in *JSP-D2*, 134.

314. William V. Smith makes this point in "Early Mormon Priesthood Revelations: Text, Impact, and Evolution," *Dialogue* 46.4 (Winter 2013): 13.

315. Autobiography of Levi Ward Hancock, holograph, 43, CHL; W. E. McLellan, M.D., to Davis H. Bays, 24 May 1870, in *The William E. McLellin Papers, 1854–1880*, ed. Stan Larson and Samuel J. Passey (Salt Lake City, UT: Signature Books, 2007), 458. I thank Michael MacKay for these references.

316. 1835 D&C 3:1 (D&C 107:1).

317. 1835 D&C 3:3 (D&C 107:8).

318. 1835 D&C 3:10 (D&C 107:20), 12–13.

319. In one typical example, "Thirty candidates . . . were elected, introduced, and consecrated High Priests after the Order of Melchizedek." *Proceedings of the Grand Royal Arch Chapter of the State of Georgia* (Macon, GA: Smith & Watson, 1903), 197.

320. Jeff Bach, *Voices of the Turtledoves: The Sacred World of Ephrata* (University Park: Pennsylvania State University Press, 2003), 42, 53.

321. Samuel Haining, *Mormonism Weighed in the Balances of the Sanctuary* (Douglas, Isle of Man: Robert Fargher, 1840), 39, 61.

322. Campbell, *Delusions*, 11. One Mormon scholar suggests that Lehi may have been returning conceptually to the earlier Israelite sanctity of the firstborn to accommodate this Levite-less society. Jacob Rennaker, personal correspondence.

323. Joel Hills Johnson, *Journal*, 6 September 1835, http://www.boap.org/LDS/Early-Saints/Joel_Johnson_vol-1.html.

324. *WJS*, 38.

325. *EJ* 6:579.

326. See the chapter on "Presbyters in Early Christian Communities," in Alistair C. Stewart, *The Original Bishops* (Grand Rapids, MI: BakerAcademic, 2014), 121–85.

327. Titus 1:5; 1 Timothy 5:17; 1 Timothy 4:14; 1 Peter 5:5.

328. *JSP-H1*, 294.

329. 1835 D&C 4:6 (D&C 84:33–38). The original draft referred to its audience in the Oath and Covenant portion of the revelation as "eleven high Priests save one," a reference to ten high priests present, upon whom God, in an ambiguous formulation, "confirms" the priesthood just spoken of. *JSP-R&T*, 461.

330. Bruce R. McConkie, "Only an Elder," *Ensign* (June 1975): 66.

331. Revelation, 11 November 1831-B (D&C 107 partial), in *JSP-D2*, 134.

332. "The Elder or Priest shall minister it," say the Articles and Covenants. *JSP-D1*, 371.

333. 1835 D&C 3:3 (D&C 107:7).

334. Luke 10:1–2.

335. Eusebius, *Ecclesiastical History* 1.12.1–3, in *Ancient Christian Commentary on Scripture, Luke*, ed. Arthur A. Just Jr. (Downers Grove, IL: InterVarsity Press, 2003), 3:171.

336. Bede, *On the Tabernacle*, 3, in *Ancient Christian*, 3:171.

337. John M. Bradford, *The Schools of the Prophets* (New York: Green, 1813), in Rick Grunder, *Mormon Parallels: A Bibliographic Source* (LaFayette, NY: Rick Grunder Books, 2008), 278.

338. Clarke, *Commentary*, 1:430.

339. Matthew C. Godfrey et al. cite two early nineteenth-century commentators, Gamaliel Olds and Samuel Miller, who opposed the office's continuation. For Dirck Lansing's appointments, see "Queries," *Evangelical Magazine and Gospel Advocate*, 1 January 1831. All cited in *JSP-D4*, 257.

340. Luke 1:21–22.

341. *JSP-D4*, 251.

342. 1835 D&C 3:11–13 (D&C 107:23, 25, 34).

343. 1835 D&C 3:12–13 (D&C 107:33–34).

344. *JSP-D4*, 349.

345. *JSP-D4*, 256–57. BC 3:43 (D&C 107:94) had directed appointment of a president of the seven presidents, soon to be called the President of the First Council of Seventy.

346. BC 3:43 (D&C 107:94–96).

347. Richard C. Roberts, "First Council of the Seventy," *EM* 3:1303.

348. Susan Easton Black, "Early Quorums of the Seventies," in *A Firm Foundation: Church Organization and Administration*, ed. David J. Whittaker and Arnold K. Garr (Provo, UT: Religious Studies Center, Brigham Young University; Salt Lake City, UT: Deseret, 2011), 139–60.

349. Black, "Early Quorums," 153.

350. Alan K. Parrish, "Seventy," *EM* 3:1301.

351. *T&S* 4.13 (15 May 1843): 201. Little progress in the collection occurred during Smith's lifetime.

352. "Seventies' Library," *T&S* 5.24 (1 January 1844): 762. Kirjath Sepher, mentioned in Joshua 15:15, was a city in the hill country of Judah. The name "seems to indicate that it was the 'city of the roll,' i.e., for enrollment or enlisting purposes; but the second element, 'sepher,' may possibly be the name of a deity. To explain it as 'Library-city' appears to be assuming too much." Isidore Singer et al., ed., *The Jewish Encyclopedia*, 12 vols. (New York: Funk and Wagnalls, 1916), 7:509.

353. Black, "Early Quorums," 153.

354. 4 January 1894, *Minutes*.

355. William G. Hartley, "Common People: Church Activity during the Brigham Young Era," in *Nearly Everything Imaginable: The Everyday Life of Utah's Mormon Pioneers*, ed. Ronald W. Walker and Doris R. Dant (Provo, UT: Brigham Young University Press, 1999), 261.

356. *MS* 62.2 (11 January 1900): 27.

357. *MS* 62.3 (18 January 1900): 43.

358. Parish, "Seventy," 1302.

359. *EM* 3:1303.

360. First Presidency letter, 11 October 1974. Cited in Earl C. Tingey, "The Saga of Revelation: The Unfolding Role of the Seventy," *Ensign* 39.9 (September 2009): 58.

361. *EJ* 8:474.

362. *EJ* 8:474.

363. Hebrews 4:14.

364. Thomas Collier, *The Exaltation of Christ in the Dayes of the Gospel: As the Alone High-Priest, Prophet, and King, of Saints* (London: R. L. for Giles Calvert, 1646).

365. Alma 4:18; 8:11, etc.

366. "Patriarchs," *TD*, 431.

367. "Patriarchs, Biblical," *NCE* 10:948.

368. "Patriarchate," *NCE* 10:944–45.

369. James P. Bell, ed., *In the Strength of the Lord: Life and Teachings of James E. Faust* (Salt Lake City, UT: Deseret, 1999), 383.

370. Campbell, *Declaration and Address*, 16.

371. 1835 D&C 4:2 (D&C 84:6–16).

372. *MHC* B-1, 595.

373. 1835 D&C 3:18 (D&C 107:40).

374. *WJS*, 6.

375. Genesis 49:22–26.

376. 2 Nephi 3:6–7.

377. *CDBY* 1:42.

378. *WJS*, 6. Many accounts give 1833 as the date but are likely in error. See *JSP-D4*, 200–202.

379. *JSP-D7*, forthcoming; Oliver Cowdery, *M&A* 1.10 (July 1835): 147.

380. Irene M. Bates and E. Gary Smith, *Lost Legacy: The Mormon Office of Presiding Patriarch* (Urbana: University of Illinois Press, 1996), 198.

381. 1835 D&C 3:17 (D&C 107:39).

382. *CR* (October 1979): 25.

383. *CDBY* 1:242.

384. See *CDBY* 2:992 for one of many instances.

385. *JSP-D7*, forthcoming; http://www.josephsmithpapers.org/paper-summary/blessing-for-james-ivins-7-january-1840/2.

386. *CDBY* 5:3131.

387. Widtsoe, *Priesthood*, 3.

388. Talmage, "Eternity of Sex," *The Essential Talmage* (Salt Lake City, UT: Signature Books, 1997), 132.

389. Boyd K. Packer (February 1993), "What Every Elder Should Know—and Every Sister as Well: A Primer on Principles of Priesthood Government," *Ensign* 23.2 (February 1993): 7.

CHAPTER 5

1. Ernst Renan, *L'Antechrist* (Paris: Michel Lévy Frères, 1873), i; Karl Holl, "Der Kirchenbegriff des Paulus," in *Sitzungsberichte der preussischen Akademie der Wissenschaften* (Berlin, 1921), 928; J. B. Lightfoot, *Dissertations on the Apostolic Age* (London: Macmillan, 1892), 155; Olof Linton, *Das Problem der Urkirche in der neueren Forschung* (Uppsala: Almquist and Wiksells, 1932), 4–5. All cited in Hugh Nibley, "The Office of Bishop in the Early Christian Church," in *Apostles and Bishops in Early Christianity*, ed. John F. Hall and John W. Welch (Salt Lake City and Provo, UT: Foundation for Ancient Research and Mormon Studies), 1–4.

2. Nibley, "Office of Bishop," 4.

3. Denzinger cites many sources for these claims. See "Systematic Index," IIIa *SCD*, 15.

4. Martin Luther, "On the Councils and the Church," *SWML* 4:216.

5. John Calvin, *The Acts of the Apostles 14–28*, trans. John W. Fraser (Grand Rapids, MI: Eerdmans, 1966), 183.

6. John Henry Newman, "Tract One on Ministerial Authority," cited in Mark Chapman, *Anglicanism: A Very Short Introduction* (New York: Oxford University Press, 2006), 79.

7. Reformed writer Jean Morély argued against Calvin's hierarchical organization in 1562. Bruce Gordon, *Calvin* (New Haven, CT: Yale University Press, 2009), 326.

8. "I have been laboring in this cause for eight years," he wrote in a letter published in *M&A* 1.12 (September 1835): 179.

9. The revelation has an unusually complicated and confusing textual history. Portions were believed to have been received by Smith as early as summer 1829. See the discussion of dating problems at http://josephsmithpapers.org/paperSummary/articles-and-covenants-circa-april-1830-dc-20.

10. Article of Faith, 6, PGP.

11. Kevin Giles, *Patterns of Ministry among the First Christians* (Melbourne: Collins Dove, 1989), 7.

12. BC 15 (D&C 18).

13. *JSP-D7*, forthcoming; http://www.josephsmithpapers.org/paper-summary/note-circa-24-may-1839/1.

14. Presidents of the high priesthood, high councilors, high priests, high councils, and bishops are mentioned in the current version of this section, but they were added at the time of the 1835 publication of the *D&C*.

15. *JSP-D1*, 368.

16. BC 22:4–5 (D&C 21:4–5).

17. 1 Nephi 10:17; see also Terryl Givens, *By the Hand of Mormon* (New York: Oxford University Press, 2002), 209–39.

18. *EMS* 1.1 (June 1832): 7.

19. BC 30:2, 6 (D&C 28:2, 7).

20. BC 39:4 (D&C 37:3).

21. Gerald Smith makes this point in *Schooling the Prophet: How the Book of Mormon Influenced Joseph Smith and the Early Restoration* (Provo, UT: Neal A. Maxwell Institute, 2015). He also notes that David Whitmer complained of Smith's moving beyond Book of Mormon precedents, including his ordaining of apostles, when the Book of Mormon specified twelve "disciples" (183–84).

22. BC 43:11 (D&C 41:9–10).

23. BC 44:26–28 (D&C 42:30–33).

24. BC 44:29 (D&C 42:34).

25. BC 1:4 (D&C 1:17).

26. 1835 D&C 3:31, 42 (107:65, 91).

27. Note dated 8 March 1832, in *JSP-D2*, 134.

28. 1835 D&C 79 (D&C 81:1–2). The appointment was transferred to Frederick G. Williams a year later.

29. "Revelation, between circa 8 and circa 24 March 1832," in *JSP-D2*, 221.

30. Richard Bushman, "Joseph Smith and His Visions," *Oxford Handbook of Mormonism*, ed. Terryl Givens and Philip Barlow (New York: Oxford University Press, 215), 117.

31. *JSP-D3*, 437.

32. *KCMB*, 24.

33. *KCMB*, 24.

34. 1835 D&C 5:1 (D&C 102:2).

35. 1835 D&C 5:2 (D&C 102:3).

36. 1835 D&C 5:10 (D&C 102:23).

37. 1835 D&C 86:4 (D&C 82:13).

38. Isaiah 33:20; 54:2. A few Baptists had invoked the term to refer to far-flung Christian churches, but no systematic usage is evident before the LDS appropriated the term. See, for example, *Baptist Magazine for 1810* (London: J. Burditt and W. Button, 1810), 2:271, 527.

39. 1835 D&C 5:7 (D&C 102:12); see preceding note 38.

40. 14 September 1835, Minutes, in *MHC* B1, 612.

41. *JSP-D6*, forthcoming; http://www.josephsmithpapers.org/paper-summary/minute-book-1/204.

42. "Account of Meetings, Revelation, and Blessing, 5–6 December 1834," *JSP-D4*, 194.

43. Acts 1:23.

44. Luke describes the need for a new witness to replace Judas in Acts 1:15–26. Matthias is selected by lot to "take his position of overseer," and so is "added to the eleven apostles."

45. Revelation 21:14.

46. "Apostle," in F. L. Cross and E. A. Livingstone, ed., *Oxford Dictionary of the Christian Church* (Oxford: Oxford University Press, 1997), 88. The author notes, for instance, that in 1 Corinthians 15, Paul alludes to "the twelve" as a body distinct from "all the apostles" (5, 7).

47. *Clementine Recognitions*, IV.35, cited in Nibley, "Office of Bishop," 8.

48. 1 Corinthians 9:1; Acts 26:16–17.

49. M. H. Shepherd Jr., "Apostle," in *The Interpreter's Dictionary of the Bible*, ed. George Arthur Buttrick (New York: Abingdon, 1962), 1:172.

50. Parley P. Pratt, *Autobiography*, ed. Scot Facer Proctor and Maurine Jensen Proctor (Salt Lake City, UT: Deseret, 2000), 178.

51. Parley P. Pratt to John Whitmer, 9 May 1836, in *M&A* 2.20 (May 1836): 318.

52. P. E. Shaw, *The Catholic Apostolic Church; Sometimes Called Irvingite* (Morningside Heights, NY: King's Crown Press, 1946).

53. Shaw, *Catholic Apostolic*, 29.

54. Shaw, *Catholic Apostolic*, 42–43. Baxter himself did not approve of the church's subsequent direction; Irving ceded his preeminence to the first apostle, John Cardale, and died soon thereafter.

55. A. S. Hayden, *Early History of the Disciples in the Western Reserve, Ohio* (Cincinnati: Chase and Hall, 1875), 121.

56. BC 15:11 (D&C 18:9); BC 22:13 (D&C 21:10); 1835 D&C 50:3 (D&C 27:12–13).

57. *JSP-D1*, 123, citing Jared Carter Journal, 35.

58. BC 15:30–31 (D&C 18:28–29).

59. *Far West Record*, ed. Donald Q. Cannon and Lyndon W. Cook (Salt Lake City, UT: Deseret, 1983), 26.

60. Moroni 2:1 and elsewhere.

61. 14 February 1835, *KCMB*, 70.

62. The twelve were Lyman Johnson, Brigham Young, Heber C. Kimball, Orson Hyde, David Patten, Luke Johnson, William McLellin, John Boynton, Orson Pratt, William Smith, Thomas B. Marsh, and Parley P. Pratt. McLellin, Boynton, and Marsh were not veterans of the expedition.

63. 21 February 1835, *KCMB*, 80, 83.

64. Greg Prince provides contemporary evidence for an early calling of the twelve before formal organization in *Power from on High: The Development of Mormon Priesthood* (Salt Lake City, UT: Signature Books, 1995), 13.

65. 27 February 1835, *KCMB*, 85.

66. Bushman, "Joseph Smith and His Visions," 117.

67. *JSP-D5*, 152. This position was reaffirmed in "Conference Minutes," *T&S* 2.21 (1 September 1841): 521–22, and has been the order ever since.

68. 1835 D&C 3:14 (D&C 107:36).

69. 1835 D&C 3:11 (D&C 107:24).

70. *JSP-D6*, forthcoming; http://www.josephsmithpapers.org/paper-summary/letter-from-thomas-b-marsh-15-february-1838/1. The main charge involved the stake presidency's handling of land purchases and alleged profiteering.

71. Undated statement, Brigham Young Papers, in Leonard J. Arrington, *Brigham Young: American Moses* (New York: Knopf, 1985), 110. Some accounts say the words were spoken to a recently organized Council of Fifty that included the Quorum of the Twelve. Several apostles, however, affirm in any case that the words were directed at them (see Brigham Young and Orson Hyde, below). This Council of Fifty, while comprising many important leaders and exerting an advisory role in Smith's last years, had no formal function in the ecclesiastical structure of the church. It consisted of non-Mormons as well as Latter-day Saints and was millennialist in its purpose. That is, it was a skeletal government *in potentia*, created in anticipation of an imminent millennial era.

72. James R. Clark, comp., *Messages of the First Presidency of the Church of Jesus Christ of Latter-day Saints* (Salt Lake City, UT: Bookcraft, 1966), 3:134.

73. "Trial of Elder Rigdon," *T&S* 5.17 (15 September 1844): 651.

74. 1835 D&C 3:31, 42 (107:65, 91).

75. Bushman, "Joseph Smith and His Visions," 117.

76. 1835 D&C 3:11 (D&C 107:23).

77. "Joseph F. Smith, In the Presence of the Divine," in Clark, *Messages*, 5:10–11.

78. *JSP-D4*, 243–44.

79. 1835 D&C 3:11 (D&C 107:26).

80. https://www.lds.org/prophets-and-apostles/the-unfolding-role-of-the-seventy-time-line?lang=eng.

81. Spencer W. Kimball, "The Reconstitution of the First Quorum of the Seventy," *Ensign* 6.10 (October 1976): 9.

82. *Deseret News 2013 Church Almanac* (Salt Lake City, UT: Deseret News, 2013), 211.

83. William G. Hartley, *My Fellow Servants: Essays on the History of the Priesthood* (Provo, UT: Brigham Young University Studies, 2010), 229.

84. http://www.ldschurchtemples.com/statistics/units/size/.

85. http://www.bible.ca/ntx-elders-pastors-bishops.htm.

86. "Bishop, in the Bible," *NCE* 2:410.

87. Roy Hattersley, *The Life of John Wesley: A Brand from the Burning* (New York: Doubleday, 2003), 371.

88. This independent meaning and development of the offices of presbyter and bishop are the main subjects of Alistair C. Stewart's *The Original Bishops* (Grand Rapids: Baker Academic, 2014).

89. Gehard Kittel, ed., *Theological Dictionary of the New Testament* (Grand Rapids, MI: Eerdmans, 1991), 2:611.

90. 1 Timothy 3:1; Titus 3:15; Philippians 1:1; and 1 Timothy 3.

91. *Constitutions of the Holy Apostles* II.i.1, *ANF* 7:396.

92. *Constitutions* II.ii.20, *ANF* 7:404.

93. *Constitutions*, II.iv.27, *ANF* 7:410–11.

94. Stewart, *Bishops*, 2.

95. Stewart, *Bishops*, 4. Stewart cites the work of Peter Lampe and others as examples.

96. Alexander Campbell, "The Christian Religion," *Christian Baptist*, 3 August 1823; Walter Scott, "Primitive and Modern Christianity," *Christian Baptist*, 6 September 1824. Both sources cited in Gregory A. Prince, *Power from on High: The Development of Mormon Priesthood* (Salt Lake City, UT: Signature Books, 1995), 63.

97. See *Christian Baptist*, 2 June 1828, cited in Prince, *Power from on High*, 63.

98. 1835 D&C 3:32 (D&C 107:68).

99. BC 59:21 (D&C 58:17).

100. 1835 D&C 3:33 (D&C 107:74).

101. *WWJ*, 15 December 1846, 3:99.

102. Eugene England, *Why the Church Is as True as the Gospel* (Salt Lake City, UT: Bookcraft, 1986), 2–4.

103. Luke 10:1.

104. Ephesians 4:11.

105. Romans 16:3.

106. Philippians 4:2–3.

107. Romans 16:7.

108. Romans 16:1.

109. Mark 16:4, 9.

110. John 20:17.

111. See N. T. Wright's "The Biblical Case for Ordaining Women," in *Surprised by Scripture* (New York: HarperCollins, 2014), 64–82. Wright also rebuts traditional readings of Paul's strictures on women in authority.

112. BC 26:6 (D&C 25:7).

113. "A Record of the Organization, and Proceedings of the Female Relief Society of Nauvoo," in *FFY*, 32.

114. Sarah M. Kimball, "Reminiscence," in *FFY*, 495.

115. "Proceedings," *FFY*, 31.

116. "Proceedings," *FFY*, 31.

117. "Duties of Officers of F R Society," in *FFY*, 288.

118. See Fiona Givens, "The Perfect Union of Man and Woman: Reclamation and Collaboration in Joseph Smith's Theology Making," *Dialogue* 49.1 (Spring 2016): 1–26.

119. "Proceedings," *FFY*, 43.

120. "Proceedings," *FFY*, 54.

121. "Proceedings," *FFY*, 54.

122. "Proceedings," *FFY*, 55.

123. "Proceedings," *FFY*, 55.

124. "Proceedings," *FFY*, 56.

125. "Proceedings," *FFY*, 56–57.

126. "Try the Spirits," *T&S* 3.11 (1 April 1842): 744.

127. "Proceedings," *FFY*, 59.

128. For example, Bruce McConkie quotes Joseph F. Smith as saying, "What is a key? It is the right or privilege which belongs to and comes with the priesthood to have communication with God. . . . The key is in the priesthood." *Mormon Doctrine* (Salt Lake City, UT: Deseret, 1966), 410. However, Smith used "key" in various ways and contexts.

129. James Talmage, *House of the Lord* (Salt Lake City, UT: Deseret, 1971), 79.

130. "Joseph Smith's Teachings about Priesthood, Temple, and Women," https://www.lds.org/ topics/joseph-smiths-teachings-about-priesthood-temple-and-women?lang=eng.

131. Dallin H. Oaks, "The Keys and the Authority of the Priesthood," *Ensign* 44.5 (May 2014): 50.

132. See, for instance, *MS* 90.11 (15 March 1928): 170.

133. *JSP-J2*, 52.

134. James E. Talmage, "The Eternity of Sex," *Young Woman's Journal* 25 (October 1914): 602–3.

135. "R.S. Reports," *Woman's Exponent* 9.7 (1 September 1880): 55. Cited in "Joseph Smith's Teachings on Priesthood, Temple, and Women," https://www.lds.org/topics/joseph-smiths-teachings-about-priesthood-temple-and-women?lang=eng.

136. Orson Spencer, "On Priesthood," Letter IX, *Letters Exhibiting the Most Prominent Doctrines of the Church of Jesus Christ of Latter-day Saints* (Liverpool: Orson Spencer, 1848), 111.

137. *WJS*, 7.

138. *WJS*, 64.

139. *WJS*, 108.

140. Acts 10:38.

141. *WJS*, 108.

142. Moroni 3:4.

143. *EMS* 1.11 (April 1833): 161 (Moses 6:65–67, PGP). Keogh notes the implications of this linkage in "The Holy Priesthood, the Holy Ghost and the Holy Community," *Dialogue*, forthcoming.

144. "Proceedings," *FFY*, 31.

145. He gave these remarks on 28 April 1842; the first endowments were performed 4 May. *WJS*, 116–17.

146. 1876 D&C 131:2.

147. Gordon B. Hinckley, https://www.mormon.org/faq/women-in-the-church.

148. Dallin H. Oaks, "The Keys and Authority of the Priesthood," *Ensign* 44.5 (May 2014): 49–51.

149. Oaks, "Keys," 51.

CHAPTER 6

1. *M&A* 1.1 (October 1834): 15.

2. *WJS*, 215.

3. *WJS*, 39.

4. *WJS*, 253.

5. Lombard identified the seven in the *Sententiarum libri quatuor* IV.i.4; for the Council of Lyons II, see *SCD* #465, p. 184.

6. He lists "baptism, penance, and the bread" in his *Babylonian Captivity* of 1520. *SWML* 1:370. But before he has even finished his 100-page treatise, he decides that "there are, strictly speaking, but two sacraments in the church of God—baptism and the bread." 1:476.

7. Thirty-Nine Articles, XXV, in *C&C* 2:534.

8. *ICR* IV.xiv.20, p. 854.

9. Ole E. Borgen, *John Wesley on the Sacraments* (Nashville: Abingdon, 1972). See especially 16–17, 272–73.

10. John Wesley, *Journal*, ed. Nehemiah Curnock, 2:262, cited in Borgen, *Wesley*, 272.

11. See his sermon, "Circumcision of the Heart," cited and discussed in Borgen, *Wesley*, 273.

12. Thirty-Nine Articles," *C&C* 2:534. As the *Catholic Encyclopedia* notes, "After the ninth century, writers began to draw a distinction between sacraments in a general sense and sacraments properly so called." Even most Protestants recognized the two categories, even if they differed on the contents. "Sacraments," http://www.newadvent.org/cathen/13295a.htm.

13. *A Form of Discipline for the Ministers, Preachers, and Members of the Methodist Episcopal Church* (Eternity Ebooks, 2014 [Baltimore, 1784]), 119, 161–68.

14. Luke 24:49.

15. See the *OED* entry for "endue." Also, see the discussion of how endue/endow assimilated two distinct meanings into one in James Hastings et al., *Dictionary of the Bible* (New York: Scribner's Sons, 1901), 1:702.

16. Hastings, *Dictionary*, 702.

17. Acts 2:1–3 *KJV*.

18. Acts 2:36.

19. BC 40:31 (D&C 38:32).

20. *MHC* B-1, 640.

21. *JSP-D5*, 195.

22. The account was recorded in the hand of Warren Cowdery, as related to him by either his brother Oliver or by Smith. See *JSP-J1*, 219.

23. *JSP-J1*, 219. This revelation became part of the Doctrine and Covenants in 1876 (110:9).

24. *JSP-J1*, 219–22.

25. "Passover," *EJ* 13:167.

26. Louis Ginzberg, *Legends of the Jews*, trans. Henrietta Szold and Paul Radin (Philadelphia: Jewish Publication Society, 2003), 2:1021.

27. Matthew 11:14. Christ's identification of John with the prophet named by Malachi is lost in the *KJV*, which renders the name as "Elias." The *NRSV* translates it as "Elijah." Smith held that both Elias and Elijah were ancient persons, and both appeared to him at the time of the Kirtland Temple dedication. See *JSP-J1*, 222 (1876 D&C 110:12,13).

28. Origen, *Commentary on the Gospel of John*, 6.62; Tertullian, *On the Soul*, 36.6; Victorinus, *Commentary on the Apocalypse*, 11. All citations from *Ancient Christian Commentary on Scripture, The Twelve Prophets*, ed. Alberto Ferreiro (Downers Grove, IL: InterVarsity Press, 2003), OT 14:313.

29. "Passover," *EJ* 13:167.

30. John P. Pratt, "The Restoration of Priesthood Keys on Easter, 1836, Part 2: Symbolism of Passover and of Elijah's Return," *Ensign* (July 1985): 59.

31. Samuel Morris Brown, *In Heaven as It Is on Earth: Joseph Smith and the Early Mormon Conquest of Death* (New York: Oxford University Press, 2012), 161.

32. *WJS* 318, cited in Brown, *In Heaven*, 166.

33. Albrecht Oepke, βάπτω, βαπτίζω, *Theological Dictionary of the New Testament*, ed. Gerhard Kittel (Grand Rapids, MI: Eerdmans, 1991), 1:535–36.

34. John 1:31; 3:25.

35. Oepke, *Dictionary*, 537. Matthew 3:11; Mark 1:4; Luke 3:3.

36. Mark 1:4.

37. Acts 19 recounts a difference between John's baptism of repentance, and subsequent baptism "in the name of the Lord Jesus."

38. Johann Eck, *Christenliche Predigen*, in *Reformation Commentary on Scripture, Acts*, ed. Esther Chung-Kim and Todd R. Hains (Downers Grove, IL: InterVarsity Press, 2014), NT 6:264.

39. John Calvin, *Commentary on Acts*, in *Reformation Commentary*, NT 6:264.

40. John 3:5.

41. Canons on the Sacrament of Baptism, Council of Trent, 1545–1563, in *SCD* #858, p. 263.

42. *EMS* 1.11 (April 1833): 166 (Moses 6:59, PGP).

43. Mark 16:16.

44. Martin Luther, *Large Catechism*, in *A Compend of Luther's Theology*, ed. Hugh Thomson Kerr (Philadelphia;Westminster Press, 1943), 170.

45. Augsburg Confession Article IX, in Philip Schaff, *The Creeds of Christendom* (Grand Rapids, MI: Baker, 1990), 3:13.

46. John Calvin, *Commentary on John 3:5*. In Craig S. Farmer, ed., *Reformation Commentary on Scripture, John* (Downers Grove, IL: InterVarsity Press, 2014), NT 4:92.

47. John Calvin, *The Gospel According to John 1–10*, trans. T. H. L. Parker, ed. David W. Torrance and Thomas F. Torrance (Grand Rapids, MI: Eerdmans Publishing, 1995), 64.

48. *ICR* IV.xvi.26, p. 886.

49. *C&C* 2:642.

50. "The Ministration of Baptism," *Book of Common Prayer . . . according to the Protestant Episcopal Church* (Baltimore: E. J. Coale, 1822), 167.

51. "Baptism," *TD*, 40.

52. Campbell is here reprinting one of Meredith's essays, "Immersion for Remission of Sins, Advocated by Elder Meredith," June 1843. *The Writings of Alexander Campbell: Selections Chiefly from the Millennial Harbinger*, ed. W. A. Morris (Austin, TX: Eugene Von Boeckmann, 1896), 90–91.

53. *SJW* 2:236–37.

54. Westminster Confession XXVIII, *C&C* 2:641.

55. John Wesley, "Treatise on Baptism," *Works* (London: Wesleyan-Methodist Book Room, 1872), 10:194.

56. *Teaching of the Twelve Apostles* VII, *ANF* 7:379.

57. *Constitutions of the Holy Apostles* VII.ii.27, *ANF* 7:469.

58. *City of God*, 16.27; *Against Julian* 6.7.21. Both citations from Gerald Bray, ed., *Ancient Christian Commentary on Scripture, Romans* (Downers Grove, IL: InterVarsity Press, 1998), NT 6:132.

59. "Council of Carthage," in *SCD* #102, p. 45.

60. Luther, "Babylonian Captivity of the Church," in *SWML* 1:425.

61. "Anglican Catechism," *C&C* 2:370.

62. Edmund S. Morgan, *Visible Saints: The History of a Puritan Idea* (Mansfield Centre, CT: Martino, 2013), 128–29.

63. Wesley, "The New Birth," *SJW*, 2:273.

64. Article I, "The Schleitheim Confession, 1527," in *C&C* 2:697.

65. Balthasar Hubmaier, *On the Christian Baptism of Believers* (1525).

66. Thus in Adam Harwood's *Born Guilty? A Southern Baptist View of Original Sin*, Harwood writes to clarify the difference between "imputed sinful guilt" and "inherited sinful nature" in that religious tradition's history. (Carrollton, GA: Free Church Press, 2013).

67. *Writings of Alexander Campbell*, 133.

68. Charles Ready Nichol and R. L. Whiteside, *Sound Doctrine: A Series of Bible Studies* (Clifton, TX: Nichol, 1920), 1:35.

69. William E. Tucker and Lester G. McAllister, *Journey in Faith: A History of the Christian Church (Disciples of Christ)* (St. Louis: Bethany Press, 1975), 140.

70. Reprint of "Immersion for Remission of Sins, Advocated by Elder Meredith," June 1843, in *Writings of Alexander Campbell*, 92.

71. Parley P. Pratt, *Autobiography*, ed. Scot Facer Proctor and Maurine Jensen Proctor (Salt Lake City, UT: Deseret, 2000), 11.

72. A. S. Hayden, *Early History of the Disciples in the Western Reserve, Ohio* (Cincinnati: Chase and Hall, 1875), 211.

73. 3 Nephi 12:2.

74. BC 24:30 (D&C 20:37).

75. Richard L. Bushman, *Rough Stone Rolling: A Cultural Biography of Mormonism's Founder* (New York: Knopf, 2005), 120.

76. Orson Spencer, *Letters Exhibiting the Most Prominent Doctrines of the Church of Jesus Christ of Latter-day Saints* (Liverpool: Orson Spencer, 1848), 57.

77. Joseph Smith, "To the Elders of the Church of Latter Day Saints," *JSP-D5*, 11.

78. *Christian Advocate and Journal* (6 March 1840), quoted in *WJS*, 35; *CDBY* 4:2703.

79. Alexander Campbell, *Christian Baptism: With the Antecedents and Consequences* (Bethany, VA: Alexander Campbell, 1852). Cited in Samuel Brown, "Early Mormon Adoption Theology and the Mechanics of Salvation," *Journal of Mormon History* 37.3 (Summer 2011): 11. Brown indicates that Campbell had expressed this view in print as early as 1829.

80. John Bradford, *Works*, 2 vols, 1:82, cited in Horton Davies, *Worship and Theology in England: From Cranmer to Baxter and Fox, 1534–1690* (Grand Rapids, MI: Eerdmans, 1996), 34.

81. In May 2000 the United Methodist Church passed a resolution asserting that the Church of Jesus Christ of Latter-day Saints "does not fit within the bounds of the historic, apostolic tradition of Christian faith." The Presbyterian Church (USA) and the Southern Baptist Convention passed similar resolutions followed by the Vatican, which declared Mormon baptisms invalid in 2001. "United Methodists Claim LDS Not Really Christian," *Idaho Statesman*, 11 May 2000, p. A2; "Striving for Acceptance," *Washington Post*, 9 February 9, 2002, p. B9.

82. Hayden, *Early History*, 219.

83. BC 23:2 (D&C 22:1).

84. Moroni 8:11–14.

85. *JST* 17:11, p. 646.

86. *WJS* 230.

87. *T&S* 5.15 (15 August 1844): 617.

88. BC 24:30 (D&C 20:37).

89. Mosiah 18:8–9.

90. George Q. Cannon, "Editorial Thoughts," *JI* 29.15 (1 August 1894): 466–67.

91. 3 Nephi 11:26.

92. See for instance the Catholic apologetic website, http://www.catholic.com/tracts/baptism-immersion-only, which holds that Acts 1:4–5 and 11:15–17 "demonstrate that the meaning of *baptizo* is broad enough to include 'pouring.'"

93. Martin Luther, *Treatise on Baptism*, in Kerr, ed., *A Compend of Luther's Theology*, 167; *Babylonian Captivity*, *SWML* 1:420.

94. *Teachings of the Twelve* VII, in *ANF* 7:379.

95. "Buried with him by baptism into death," and "buried with him in baptism, you were also raised with him through faith." Romans 6:4; Colossians 2:12.

96. 3 Nephi 11:24–25. The phrasing is now slightly altered, to "having been commissioned of Jesus Christ . . ."

97. D. Michael Quinn cites David Johnson's 1832 rebaptism because he "had lived unworthy," and John Murdock's 1833 rebaptism of Benjamin Bragg. In D. Michael Quinn, "The Practice of Rebaptism at Nauvoo," *BYU Studies* 18.2 (1978): 228.

98. Olney Papers, 1 May 1842, cited in Quinn, "Rebaptism," 228.

99. Jacob Scott to Mary Scott Warnock, cited in Quinn, "Rebaptism," 229.

100. William Clayton, *An Intimate Chronicle: The Journals of William Clayton*, ed. George D. Smith (Salt Lake City, UT: Signature, 1995), 380.

101. James E. Talmage, journal entry, 29 November 1893, in *The Essential Talmage* (Salt Lake City, UT: Signature Books, 1997), 49–50.

102. George Q. Cannon, "Editorial Thoughts," *JI* 27.1 (1 January 1892): 27.

103. *CDBY* 2:768–69.

104. *Autobiography of Warren Foote* (Mesa, AZ: Dale Arnold Foote, 1997), 139.

105. *CDBY* 3:1281.

106. George Q. Cannon, "Editorial Thoughts," *JI* 26.7 (1 April 1891): 218.

107. *WWJ*, 13 July 1875, 7:233.

108. *WWJ*, 17 July 1875, 7:233. One scholar counts seven times for Woodruff, but she conflates at least two baptisms, misdating his 1875 baptism to 1874 and counting it twice. Jennifer Ann Mackley, *Wilford Woodruff's Witness of the Development of Temple Doctrine* (Seattle: High Desert Publishing, 2014), 144.

109. Edward L. Kimball, "The History of the LDS Temple Admission Standards," *Journal of Mormon History* 24.1 (1998): 140.

110. *EM* 3:1194.

111. George Q. Cannon, "Editorial Thoughts," *JI* 27.1 (1 January 1892): 27.

112. Francis M. Lyman, *JD* 25:60–61.

113. Marion G. Romney, *CR* (April 1946): 39–40.

114. Talmage, Journal, 29 November 1893, *Essential Talmage*, 49.

115. Journal History, 14 March 1899, *Minutes*.

116. Talmage, Journal, 29 November 1893, *Essential Talmage*, 50.

117. *WJS*, 37.

118. *WJS*, 111.

119. Jonathan Stapley and Kristine Wright, "'They Shall Be Made Whole': A History of Baptism for Health," *Journal of Mormon History* 34.4 (Fall 2008): 70–71.

120. Brigham Young et al., "An Epistle of the Twelve, Nauvoo, October 12, 1841," *T&S* 2 (15 October 1841): 569. Cited in Stapley and Wright, "They Shall," 76.

121. *JSP-D6*, forthcoming; http://www.josephsmithpapers.org/paper-summary/history-1838-1856-volume-c-1-2-november-1838-31-july-1842/146.

122. *Ogden Daily Herald*, 11 June 1881, 2. Quoted in Stapley and Wright, "They Shall," 75.

123. *CDBY* 4:2028.

124. See Stapley and Wright, "They Shall," 108–9.

125. 2 Maccabees 12:42–44.

126. 1 Corinthians 15:29.

127. Michael F. Hull, *Baptism on Account of the Dead (1 Cor 15:29)* (Atlanta: Society for Biblical Literature, 2005), 10–11. Hull argues, rather tortuously, that Paul is simply asking why are Christians baptized "on account of the fact that the dead are destined for life."

128. Shepherd of Hermas, III.9.16, *ANF* 2:49.

129. Clement of Alexandria, *Stromata* VI:vi (*ANF* 2:491), citing *Hermas III*:xvi, *ANF* 2:49.

130. Everett Ferguson, *Baptism in the Early Church: History, Theology, and Liturgy in the First Five Centuries* (Grand Rapids, MI: Eerdmans, 2013), 225–29.

131. Tertullian, *Against Marcion* 5.10, *ANF* 3:449.

132. Hull, *Baptism*, 40.

133. Chrysostom, *Homilies on First Corinthians*, XL (*NPNF1* 12:244).

134. *Pauline Commentary from the Greek Church*, cited in Gerald Bray, ed., *Ancient Christian Commentary on Scripture, 1–2 Corinthians* (Downers Grove, IL: InterVarsity Press, 1999), NT 7:163.

135. For the canons and details, see M. l'Abbè (Jacques Paul) Migne, *Dictionnaire Universel et Complet des Conciles* (Paris: Ateliers Catholiques du Petit, 1847), Vol. I, Col. 477, and Rt. Rev. Charles Joseph Hefele, DD, *History of the Councils of the Church* (Edinburgh: T & T Clark, 1896), Vol. 2, 397ff. Cited in John A. Tvedtnes, "Baptism for the Dead: The Coptic Rationale," Special Papers of the Society for Early Historic Archaeology, No. 2 (September 1989).

136. Jeff Bach, *Voices of the Turtledoves: The Sacred World of Ephrata* (University Park: Pennsylvania State University Press, 2003), 21.

137. Bach, *Voices*, 94.

138. He cites, for instance, "Baptism for the Dead," *Gospel Herald* (28 January 1823); "Baptism for the Dead," *Christian Intelligencer and Eastern Chronicle* (26 June 1829): 102; "Baptism for the Dead," *Episcopal Watchman* (9 January 1830), and several from subsequent years. See Ryan G. Tobler, "'Saviors on Mount Zion': Mormon Sacramentalism, Mortality, and the Baptism for the Dead," *Journal of Mormon History* 39.4 (2013): 187.

139. Smith quotes Charles Buck, without attribution, in "Baptism for the Dead," *T&S* 3.12 (15 April 1842): 761.

140. *TD*, 44.

141. *Elders Journal* 1.3 (July 1838): 43.

142. Hebrews 11:40 *KJV*; *WJS*, 10.

143. *WJS*, 49.

144. "Joseph Smith to the Traveling High Council and Elders of the Church of Jesus Christ of Latter-day Saints in Great Britain," 19 October 1840. In James R. Clark, comp., *Messages of the First Presidency of the Church of Jesus Christ of Latter-day Saints* (Salt Lake City, UT: Bookcraft, 1966), 1:124.

145. Vilate Kimball, Letter to Heber C. Kimball, September 6, 1840. Cited in Tobler, "Saviors," 190.

146. Sally Carlisle Randall to Betty Carlisle, Nauvoo, 21 April 1844, in Richard O. Cowan, "Joseph Smith and the Restoration of Temple Service," in *Joseph Smith and the Doctrinal Restoration* (Provo, UT: Brigham Young University, Religious Studies Center, 2005), 116.

147. "On Future Punishments," *MS* 3.11 (March 1843): 181.

148. *T&S* 1.12 (October 1840): 186–87.

149. "Baptism for the Dead," *T&S* 2.23 (1 October 1841): 565.

150. *WWJ* 2:138.

151. Romans 6:4–6.

152. Letter from Joseph Smith, *T&S* 3.23 (1 October 1842): 935 (D&C 128:12).

153. Tobler, "Saviors," 200. Tobler also makes the important point that "in Smith's later sermons 'the baptism for the dead,' may have been synecdochic for all ordinances performed for the dead." Tobler, "Saviors," 200.

154. Geoffrey Wainwright, *Doxology: The Praise of God in Worship, Doctrine, and Life* (New York: Oxford University Press, 1980), 29.

155. Wainwright, *Doxology*, 935–36 (D&C 128:9–18).

156. Joseph Smith to the Twelve, 15 December 1840, in *PWJS*, 521.

157. F. L. Cross and E. A. Livingstone, ed., *Oxford Dictionary of the Christian Church* (Oxford: Oxford University Press, 1997), 784.

158. Deuteronomy 34:9.

159. Acts 19:6.

160. See the statement of the Council of Illiberi, ca. AD 300. *SCD* 52e, p. 25.

161. "Council of Illiberi 300/306," in *SCD* 52d, p. 25.

162. "St. Innocent I 401-417," *SCD* #98, p. 43.

163. Luther, "Babylonian Captivity of the Church," in *SWML* 1:370.

164. Luther, "Babylonian Captivity," 1:443.

165. *ICR* IV.xix.8–9, p. 952.

166. Wesley, "The New Birth," *SJW* 2:267–73.

167. Wesley, "The New Birth," *SJW* 2:267.

168. Hayden, *Early History*, 219.

169. *WJS*, 3.

170. Hebrews 6:1–2 *KJV*.

171. John Henry Hobart, *The Candidate for Confirmation Instructed* (New York: Protestant Episcopal Tract Society, 1819), 5.

172. *WJS*, 72.

173. The gift of the Holy Ghost, though not its bestowal by the laying on of hands, is mentioned in Smith's retelling of Adam's gospel instruction (*EMS* 1.11 [April 1833]: 161 (Moses 6:51–68) and in Nephi's account of the Doctrine of Christ (2 Nephi 31).

174. BC 24:34 (D&C 20:41). The instruction is repeated in other revelations as well, i.e., D&C 33:15; 35:6; 49:14, etc.

175. John Cawood, *The Church of England and Dissent* (London: L. B. Seeley and Sons, 1831), 9; John 20:22.

176. Acts 8:16.

177. *JSP-H1*, 293.

178. *WJS*, 3.

179. *JSP-H1*, 295.

180. Acts 2:38.

181. *WJS*, 108.

182. B. H. Roberts, "The Holy Ghost," in *The Gospel and Man's Relationship to Deity* (Salt Lake City, UT: Deseret, 1901), 191.

183. In this same generation, the apostle John Widtsoe, a scientist and leading church intellectual, was charged with writing church manuals. He strove to show that Smith's teachings "were in full harmony with the most advanced scientific thought, and that he anticipated the world of science in the statement of fundamental facts and theories of physics, chemistry, astronomy and biology." John A. Widtsoe, *Joseph Smith as Scientist* (Salt Lake City, UT: Young Men's Mutual Improvement Associations, 1908), 9.

184. John 14:26 *KJV*.

185. Matthew 16:15–16.

186. 1 Corinthians 12:3.

187. *WJS*, 158.

188. *WJS*, 5.

189. *Key*, 98–99.

190. Jacob 4:6.

191. *WJS*, 256.

192. *WJS*, 4.

193. *CDBY* 4:1978.

194. *CDBY* 2:692.

195. *JSP-D7*, forthcoming; http://www.josephsmithpapers.org/paper-summary/letterbook-2/93.

196. *WJS*, 371.

197. Stan Larson, "The King Follett Discourse: A Newly Amalgamated Text," *BYU Studies* 18.2 (Winter 1978): 202.

198. Exodus 40:12–13.

199. "Anointing," *EJ* 3:27.

200. Revelation 5:10 *KJV*.

201. *Testament of Levi* 8.6–12. Quoted in *Temples of the Ancient World*, ed. Donald W. Parry (Salt Lake City, UT: Deseret, 1994), 715.

202. 1 Peter 5:4; James 1:12; 2 Timothy 4:8; Romans 8:17.

203. Cyril of Jerusalem, "On Chrism," *Catechetical Lectures on the Mysteries*, III.6, *NPNF2* 7:150.

204. Clement, *Recognitions* I.xlv–xlvi, *ANF* 8:89.

205. S. Kent Brown and C. Wilfred Griggs survey several relevant texts, especially the *Gospel of Thomas* in "The 40-Day Ministry," *Ensign* 5.8 (August 1975): 6–11.

206. Hugh W. Nibley, "The Forty-Day Mission of Christ—The Forgotten Heritage," *Mormonism and Early Christianity*, ed. Todd M. Compton and Stephen D. Ricks (Salt Lake City and Provo, UT: Deseret and Foundation for Ancient Research and Mormon Studies, 1987), 17. He cites, among many works, *The Testament in Galilee* 1, 45; *Apocryphon of James* 8:1–4; *Acts of Thomas* 1; *Gospel of the Twelve Apostles* 14; and the *Gospel of Bartholomew*.

207. Edwin Gifford, "Introduction," Saint Cyril, Catechetical Lectures, *NPNF2* 7:xxxiv.

208. Cyril, III.4, *NPNF2* 7:150.

209. John 13:5.

210. John 13:14–15.

211. 1835 D&C 7:41 (D&C 88:133). This language of solidarity in "the everlasting covenant" became common as a valediction in letter writing. Thus Joseph Smith's "Your friend And Brother in the New and everlasting Covenant" and Heber C. Kimball's "your friend . . . in the new and everlasting covenant," two of countless instances. *JSP-D7*, forthcoming; http://www.josephsmithpapers.org/paper-summary/history-1838-1856-volume-e-1-1-july-1843-30-april-1844/112, http://www.josephsmithpapers.org/paper-summary/letter-from-heber-c-kimball-9-july-1840/5.

212. *KCMB*, 6–7.

213. Oliver Cowdery, Diary, 16 January 1836, in *JSP-D5*, 154.

214. *JSP-D5*, 157.

215. *JSP-J1*, 167.

216. *JSP-J1*, 211–13.

217. *JSP-D6*, forthcoming; http://www.josephsmithpapers.org/paper-summary/journal-1835-1836/190.

218. *JSP-D5*, 49.

219. 1844 D&C 103:12 (D&C 124:37).

220. *WWJ*, 12 October 1883, 8:201.

221. Boyd K. Packer, *The Holy Temple* (Salt Lake City, UT: Bookcraft, 1980), 155.

222. Revelation 7:14 *KJV*.

223. James E. Faust, First Presidency Message, *Ensign* 31.8 (August 2001): 4.

224. 1835 D&C 91:5 (D&C 76:55–56).

225. Colossians 3:9–10; see also Romans 13:14; Ephesians 4:22–24; and Galatians 3:27.

226. David L. Bartlett and Barbara Brown Taylor, *Feasting on the Word: Preaching the Revised Common Lectionary* (Louisville, KY: Westminster John Knox Press, 2009), 159.

227. Jung Hoon Kim, *The Significance of Clothing Imagery in the Pauline Corpus* (London: A&C Black, 2004), 142.

228. *The Song of the Pearl*, trans. Han J. W. Drijvers, Robert M. Grant, Bentley Layton, and Willis Barnstone. In Barnstone and Marvin Meyer, ed., *The Gnostic Bible* (Boston: Shambhala, 2003), 392–93.

229. See Stephen D. Ricks, "The Garment of Adam," in Parry, *Temples*, 706.

230. Erik Peterson, *Pour une théologie du vêtement*, trans. M.-J. Congar (Lyon: Edition de l'Abeille, 1943), 6–13. Cited in Ricks, "Garment," 708.

231. Moses 5:6–8, PGP.

232. Carlos E. Asay, "The Temple Garment: 'An Outward Expression of an Inward Commitment,'" *Ensign* 27.8 (August 1997): 21.

233. Compare the 1851 edition of Moses 6:59: "inasmuch as they were born into the world by the fall which bringeth death," with the 1878 version: "By reason of transgression cometh the fall, which fall bringeth death." Robert J. Matthews, "How We Got the Book of Moses," *Ensign* 26.1 (January 1986): 46.

234. *EMS* 1.11 (April 1833): 161 (Moses 5:10–11, PGP [1851]). In 1878, the wording was changed slightly to "Blessed be the name of God, for because of my transgression my eyes are opened, and in this life I shall have joy."

235. *JSP-D7*, forthcoming; http://www.josephsmithpapers.org/paper-summary/history-1838-1856-volume-c-1-2-november-1838-31-july-1842/186.

236. Robert Frost, "Trial by Existence," *A Boy's Will* (New York: Henry Holt, 1913), 14.

237. *JSP-D5*, 221.

238. *WJS*, 120.

239. *MHC* C-1, 507.

240. *CDBY* 2:646.

241. Louis Ginzberg, *Legends of the Jews*, trans. Henrietta Szold and Paul Radin (Philadelphia: Jewish Publication Society, 2003), 1:48. Ginzberg's examples are noted in Margaret Barker, *King of the Jews: Temple Theology in John's Gospel* (London: SPCK, 2014), 65.

242. Margaret Barker, *Temple Mysticism* (London: SPCK, 2011), 1–2. The Isaiah passage is in chapter 6.

243. James Talmage, *House of the Lord* (Salt Lake City, UT: Deseret, 1971), 204.

244. Andrew F. Ehat, "Who Shall Ascend into the Hill of the Lord," in *Temples of the Ancient World*, ed. Donald W. Parry (Salt Lake City, UT: Deseret, 1994), 54.

245. Roger Scruton, *The Soul of the World* (Princeton, NJ: Princeton University Press, 2014), 90–91.

246. Talmage, *House*, 84.

247. Heber C. Kimball to Parley P. Pratt, 17 June 1842. In Terryl L. Givens and Matthew J. Grow, *Parley P. Pratt: The Apostle Paul of Mormonism* (New York: Oxford University Press, 2010), 208.

248. *CDBY* 1:35.

249. William G. Hartley, *My Fellow Servants: Essays on the History of the Priesthood* (Provo, UT: BYU Studies, 2010), 199.

250. Quoted in Ehat, "Who Shall Ascend," 58–59.

251. "σφραγίς," *Theological Dictionary of the New Testament*, ed. Gerhard Friedrich (Grand Rapids, MI: Eerdmans, 1988), 7:939–41.

252. 1 Kings 21:8.

253. Romans 4:11; see also 2 Timothy 2:19 *KJV*. The *NRSV* has "inscription," but the Greek is σφραγίς.

254. Revelation 9:4.

255. *SCD* #411, p. 161.

256. Council of Trent, Canon 9. In *SCD* #852, p. 263.

257. *ICR* IV.xiv.1, p. 843.

258. Wesley, "Baptism," 188, 194.

259. *WJS*, 43.

260. Matthew 16:18–19.

261. 1876 D&C 132:7.

262. "Elijah ascended in a whirlwind into heaven" (2 Kings 2:11).

263. *WJS*, 229.

264. Ralph Waldo Emerson, "Worship," in *Essays and English Tracts* (New York: Collier 1909), 290.

265. "To Noah Saxton," 4 January 1833, in *JSP-D2*, 352.

266. W. W. Phelps, "Letter no. 8," *M&A* 1.9 (June 1835): 130.

267. Parley P. Pratt, *Autobiography*, ed. Scot Facer Proctor and Maurine Jensen Proctor (Salt Lake City, UT: Deseret, 2000), 361.

268. *WJS*, 232.

269. The date was 28 May 1843, http://www.josephsmithpapers.org/reference/events#1843.

270. *WJS*, 239.

271. Parley P. Pratt, "Celestial Family Organization," *The Prophet* 1 (1844): 1.

272. Lisle G. Brown, Nauvoo Sealings, *Adoptions, and Anointings: A Comprehensive Register of Persons Receiving LDS Temple Ordinances, 1841–1846* (Salt Lake City, UT: Signature Books, 2006), 36, and Jonathan Stapley, "Adoptive Sealing Ritual," 66. Both cited in Jonathan A. Stapley, *The Power of Godliness: Mormon Liturgy and Cosmology* (New York: Oxford, forthcoming).

273. *CDWW* 4:67n.

274. Orson Hyde, "A Diagram of the Kingdom of God," *MS* 9.2 (15 January 1847): 23.

275. Howard Coray, Journal, typescript in HBLL.

276. Foote, *Autobiography*, 3:43.

277. Darius L. Clement to Warren Foote, in Foote, *Autobiography*, 3:13.

278. Clement to Foote, *Autobiography*, 3:13.

279. Foote, *Autobiography*, 3:43.

280. *CDBY* 1:184.

281. New directions in polygamy theology were soon evident. When a member queried the First Presidency in 1912, "Is plural or celestial marriage essential to a fulness of glory in the world to come?" he was answered that "celestial marriage is essential to a fulness of glory in the world to come, as explained in the revelation concerning it; but it is not stated that plural marriage is thus essential." This was a significant reversal of Young's teachings to the contrary. Charles Penrose, "Editor's Table," *IE* 15.11 (September 1912): 1042.

282. *CDBY* 1:188.

283. His words were recorded by Abraham Cannon, an apostle at the time. See *CDWW*, 4:67n.

284. *CDWW* 4:72–73.

285. *CDWW* 4:72–73.

286. *CDWW* 4:71.

287. *MS* 19.27 (4 July 1857): 432; B. H. Roberts, *Comprehensive History of the Church of Jesus Christ of Latter-day Saints* (Provo, UT: Brigham Young University Press, 1965), 5:297. (First published in 1912.)

288. *JD* 11:207.

289. *CDWW*, 4:72.

290. Foote, *Autobiography*, 3:13.

291. Marriner W. Merrill, "Temple Work," *CDWW*, 4:361.

292. See Carol Lynn Pearson, *The Ghost of Eternal Polygamy: Haunting the Hearts and Heaven of Mormon Women and Men* (Walnut Creek, CA: Pivot Point Books, 2016).

293. Kathleen Flake, "The Development of Early Latter-day Saint Marriage Rites, 1831–53," *Journal of Mormon History* 41.1 (Winter 2015): 88.

294. Jonathan Stapley finds it useful to demarcate this the "cosmological priesthood," an order that is independent of ecclesiastical priesthood. See his *The Power of Godliness: Mormon Liturgy and Cosmology* (New York: Oxford, forthcoming).

295. Erastus Snow, *JD*, 19:270.

296. *WJS*, 346.

297. Parley P. Pratt, *JD* 1:259; Spencer W. Kimball, *The Miracle of Forgiveness* (Salt Lake City, UT: Deseret, 1971), 82.

298. http://www.mormonnewsroom.org/article/interview-oaks-wickman-same-gender-attraction.

299. Laurie Goodstein, "Utah Passes Antidiscrimination Bill Backed by Mormon Leaders," 12 March 2015, http://www.nytimes.com/2015/03/12/us/politics/utah-passes-antidiscrimination-bill-backed-by-mormon-leaders.html.

300. Equally controversial was the new mandate that children of a person living in a gay relationship not be eligible for church sacraments until he or she reaches majority age, ostensibly "to protect children . . . in their minority years" from being caught in parent/church conflicts, https://www.lds.org/church/news/elder-christofferson-says-handbook-changes-regarding-same-sex-marriages-help-protect-children?lang=eng.

301. http://latimesblogs.latimes.com/lanow/2012/02/gay-marriage-divide-evident-even-among-judges-in-proposition-8-case.html.

302. First Presidency (Thomas S. Monson, Henry B. Eyring, and Dieter F. Uchtdorf), "Preserving Traditional Marriage and Strengthening Families," 29 June 2008, circular distributed by the Church of Jesus Christ of Latter-day Saints.

303. Erastus Snow, *JD*, 19:270.

304. "The Origin of Man," *IE* 13.1 (November 1909): 78.

305. "The Family: A Proclamation to the World," https://www.lds.org/topics/family-proclamation?lang=eng&_r=1.

306. *MHC* E-1, 1669, 1673; 1876 D&C 132:19, 63.

307. Richard Swinburne, *Is There a God?* (Oxford: Oxford University Press, 2010), 7.

308. See Outi Lehtipuu, *Debates over the Resurrection of the Dead: Constructing Early Christian Identity* (New York: Oxford University Press, 2015), 133–36. Joseph Smith emphasized spirit adoption rather than spirit procreation, and though "eternal seed" is a constant in Mormon projections of the afterlife, the nature of procreation has never been authoritatively declared to be sexual in nature.

309. For Peter Brown's reference to Origen (and others), see his *Body and Society: Men, Women, and Sexual Renunciation in Early Christianity* (New York: Columbia University Press, 1988), 168, 373.

310. C. S. Lewis, *Miracles* (New York: HarperCollins, 1996), 261.

311. Jeffrey R. Holland, "Of Souls, Symbols, and Sacraments," devotional address, 12 January 1988, Brigham Young University, Utah, http://www.familylifeeducation.org/gilliland/procgroup/ Souls.htm.

312. Robert P. George, "What's Sex Got to Do With It? Marriage, Morality, and Rationality," *American Journal of Jurisprudence* 49.1 (2004).

313. BC 52:17 (D&C 49:16–17).

314. Talmage, "The Eternity of Sex," *Essential Talmage*, 128.

315. "Proclamation on the Family." Orson Pratt declared spirits "male and female" in 1853. *The Seer* 1.3 (March 1853): 37; for other LDS statements on the subject, see Terryl L. Givens, *Wrestling the Angel: The Foundations of Mormon Thought—Cosmos, God, Humanity* (New York: Oxford University Press, 2015), 223–24.

316. Oaks's response came in a live interview, January 2015, reported in Taylor Petrey, "A Mormon Leader Signals New Openness on Transgender Issues," *Slate*, http://www.slate.com/ blogs/outward/2015/02/13/mormons_and_transgender_elder_dallin_h_oaks_says_the_lds_ church_is_open.html.

317. *WJS*, 247.

318. 1835 D&C 3:8, 10 (D&C 107:14, 20).

319. *WJS*, 334; 1876 D&C 110:12.

320. *WJS*, 329.

321. Cited in *WJS*, 298–99.

322. See Kathleen Flake, "The Development of Early Latter-day Saint Marriage Rites, 1831–53," *Journal of Mormon History* 41.1 (January 2015): 77–102.

323. 1876 D&C 131:2. The parenthetical phrase was later added in the canonized version of section 131 by Orson Pratt, though bracketed there.

324. *CDBY* 1:26.

325. *WJS*, 245.

326. *WJS*, 244.

327. Heber C. Kimball Journal, kept by William Clayton, 26 December 1845, Church Archives, italics added. Cited in *WJS*, 286.

328. *JSP-J3*, 104.

329. *JSP-J3*, xxi.

330. *CDBY* 2:1037.

331. Anthony W. Ivins, Diary, 8 April 1901, *Minutes*.

332. Samuel Morris Brown, *In Heaven as It Is on Earth* (New York: Oxford University Press, 2012), 197.

333. 1835 D&C 91:5 (D&C 76:53–58).

334. 1844 D&C 103:38 (D&C 124:124).

335. *WJS*, 244.

336. Stapley, *Power of Godliness* (forthcoming).

337. *WJS*, 4. Smith is quoting the *KJV* of 2 Peter 1:10; "confirm your calling and election," according to the *NRSV*.

338. Ephesians 1:13 *KJV*; marked with the seal of the promised Holy Spirit," *NRSV*.

339. 1876 D&C 132:7.

340. Parley P. Pratt, *JD* 3:183.

341. Bruce R. McConkie, *Mormon Doctrine* (Salt Lake City, UT: Deseret, 1966), 361; *EM* 2:651.

342. *WJS*, 5; he is quoting John 14:16, 18 *KJV*.

343. Mosiah 26:20.

344. *T&S* 4.6 (1 February 1843): 84. Cited in *WJS*, 26.

345. *Voice*, 105.

346. *WJS*, 201–2.

347. 1876 D&C 131:5.

348. For a discussion of polygamy in Mormon theology and practice, see Givens, *Wrestling*, 279–90.

349. *WWJ* 2:361.

350. *JSP-D5*, 220–21.

351. Joseph Smith to Presendia Huntington Buell, 15 March 1839, in *JSP-D6*, forthcoming; http://www.josephsmithpapers.org/paper-summary/letter-to-presendia-huntington-buell-15-march-1839/1.

352. *WJS*, 318.

353. Parley P. Pratt, "Celestial Family Organization," *The Prophet*, 1 March 1845, 1.

CHAPTER 7

1. https://www.lds.org/topics/ordinances?lang=eng.

2. "Teaching of the Twelve," VII:ix.4, *ANF* 7:380.

3. Matthew 26:26; Mark 14:22; Luke 22:19.

4. Matthew 26:28; Mark 14:24; Luke refers to "the new covenant in my blood" (22:20).

5. Luke 22:19.

6. 1 Cor. 11:25.

7. Acts 20:7.

8. Justin Martyr, "First Apology," LXV, *ANF* 1:185.

9. Justin Martyr, "First Apology," LXVI, *ANF* 1:185.

10. "Teaching of the Twelve," VII:ix.4, *ANF* 7:380.

11. Cyril of Jerusalem, Lecture XXII.6, *NPNF2* 7:152.

12. Luther, "Babylonian," in *SWML* 1:383.

13. Ulrich Zwingli, *Commentary on True and False Religion*, cited in Thomas J. Davis, *This Is My Body: The Presence of Christ in Reformation Thought* (Grand Rapids, MI: Baker Academic, 2008), 157.

14. *ICR* IV.xvii.12, 902.

15. Bruce Gordon, *Calvin* (New Haven, CT: Yale University Press, 2009), 249.

16. Gordon chronicles the disputes in great detail in *Calvin*, 243–49 especially.

17. E. Brooks Holifield, *The Covenant Sealed: The Development of Puritan Sacramental Theology in Old and New England, 1570–1720* (Eugene, OR: Wipf and Stock, 2002), 109.

18. "Hymns on the Lord's Supper," 116, quoted in Alistair E. McGrath, *The Christian Theology Reader* (Oxford: Blackwell, 1997), 317.

19. BC 28.2 (D&C 27:2).

20. *A Form of Discipline for the Ministers, Preachers, and Members of the Methodist Episcopal Church* (Eternity Ebooks, 2014 [Baltimore, 1784]), 119, 161–68.

21. Ignatius, *To the Ephesians*, 20, in Roger E. Olson, *The Story of Christian Theology* (Downers Grove, IL: InterVarsity Press, 1999), 48.

22. BC 23:57 (D&C 20:77).

23. 3 Nephi 18:7.

24. 3 Nephi 18:7.

25. Kathleen Flake, "Supping with the Lord: A Liturgical Theology of the LDS Sacrament," *Sunstone* (July 1993): 19. She is quoting from the *JST* Mark 14:22–24, p. 352.

26. Joseph Fielding Smith denounced cross-wearing at least as early as 1963. See Joseph Fielding Smith, *Answers to Gospel Questions* (Salt Lake City, UT: Deseret, 1963), 4:17–18. For a fine history of the subject, see Michael G. Reed, *Banishing the Cross: The Emergence of a Mormon Taboo* (Salt Lake City, UT: John Whitmer Books, 2012).

27. Gordon B. Hinckley, "The Symbol of Our Faith," *Ensign* 35.4 (April 2005): 3.

28. Moroni 4:3; 5:2.

29. 3 Nephi 6:20, also Alma 16:19; Moroni 9:25.

30. Young, *CDBY* 4:2431.

31. 2 Nephi 26:24; 3 Nephi 27:15.

32. Genesis 14:18.

33. *JST* Genesis 14:17, p. 640.

34. Cyprian, *Letters* 63.4, in *Ancient Christian Commentary on Scripture, Genesis 12–50*, ed. Mark Sheridan (Downers Grove, IL: InterVarsity Press, 2002), OT 2:26.

35. The Byzantine mosaic is in the lunette of the Basilica of San Vitale, Ravenna.

36. *The Small Catechism*, 22, in *C&C* 2:33.

37. *ICR* IV.xvii.44, 46, pp. 929–30.

38. http://wesleyanleadership.com/2013/10/15/a-wesleyan-practice-of-holy-communion/.

39. According to a 2012 Lifeway Research Survey, http://people.opposingviews.com/baptist-churches-practice-communion-8301.html.

40. BC 24:55 (D&C 20:75).

41. Moroni 6:6; 3 Nephi 18:22.

42. *T&S* 3.22 (15 September 1842): 915.

43. *JSP-D5*, 218.

44. Edward Partridge Journal, 29 March 1836, in *JSP-J1*, 213.

45. *CDBY* 1:110; 1:160.

46. Brigham Young Jr., Diary, 12 January 1894, *Minutes*.

47. William G. Hartley, *My Fellow Servants: Essays on the History of the Priesthood* (Provo, UT: BYU Studies, 2010), 348.

48. BC 15:3 (D&C 18:3).

49. *JSP-D1*, 371–72.

50. BC 23:56 (D&C 20:76).

51. BC 24:57, 59 (D&C 20:77, 79).

52. *CDBY* 4:2276.

53. *CDBY* 5:2990.

54. Henry Addison Nelson, *The Church at Home and Abroad*, Vol. 5 (Philadelphia: Presbyterian Board, 1889), 432; John Coyner, *Letters on Mormonism* (Salt Lake City, UT: Tribune, 1879), 14–15. I thank Jed Woodworth for these references.

55. James R. Clark, comp., *Messages of the First Presidency of the Church of Jesus Christ of Latter-day Saints* (Salt Lake City, UT: Bookcraft, 1966), 6:253.

56. BC 28:4 (D&C 27:3).

57. 1835 D&C 80:1 (D&C 89:5).

58. *CDBY* 4:1934.

59. Gerald Smith cites several sources for this date in *Schooling the Prophet: How the Book of Mormon Influenced Joseph Smith and the Early Restoration* (Provo, UT: Neal A. Maxwell Institute, 2015), 234n8; Brigham Young Jr. Diary, 4 April 1895, J. Golden Kimball Diary, 13 July 1899, etc. *Minutes*.

60. *CDBY* 2:729.

61. Francis Lyman, *JD* 25:60.

62. Neil L. Andersen, April 2015 General Conference Leadership Training Meeting, http://saskatoonstake.org/portal/training/sabbathday/Video/Seg_1-cut-04.mp4. (Thanks to Ugo Perego for this reference.)

63. 1 Corinthians 11:27–29 *KJV*.

64. *CDBY* 3:1251, 4:2078.

65. *KCMB*, 90.

66. Jean Bickmore White, ed., *Church, State, and Politics: The Diaries of John Henry Smith* (Salt Lake City, UT: Signature, 1990), 310 (entry for 17 June 1894). I thank Kirk Caudle for the reference.

67. Genesis 49.

68. *CDBY* 3:1813.

69. *Early Patriarchal Blessings of the Church of Jesus Christ of Latter-day Saints*, comp. H. Michael Marquardt (Salt Lake City, UT: Smith-Pettit Foundation, 2007), 12, 23, 26, 65.

70. *Early Patriarchal*, 84, 41, 13, 85.

71. John A. Widtsoe, *Evidences and Reconciliations*, ed. G. Homer Durham (Salt Lake City, UT: Bookcraft, 1976), 322.

72. *CDBY* 2:1015.

73. Christopher C. Jones, " 'We Latter-day Saints Are Methodists': The Influence of Methodism on Early Mormon Religiosity," MA thesis, Brigham Young University, 2009, 96–97.

74. James 5:14. The connection is made as anciently as the fifth century, and Pius X reaffirmed James's directive to be an intentional basis for the sacrament in his 1907 "Errors of the Modernists." *SCD* #99, p. 43; #2048, p. 511.

75. St. Innocent I, "The Minister of Extreme Unction," *SCD* #99, 43.

76. *SCD* #927, 285; *SCD*, "Systematic Index," 43.

77. James 5:15.

78. Mark 2:5.

79. Clement of Alexandria, *Christ the Educator* 1.4, in *Ancient Christian Commentary on Scripture, Mark*, ed. Thomas C. Oden and Christopher A. Hall (Downers Grove, IL: InterVarsity Press, 1998), NT 2:27.

80. St. Innocent I, "Consuelenti tibi," *SCD* #95, p. 41; "Si instituta ecclesiastica," #99, p. 43.

81. St. Leo IV, Council of Ticinus, *SCD* #315, p. 126.

82. Innocent IV, "Ecumenical XIII," in *SCD* #451, 179; Eugenius IV, "Council of Florence," in *SCD* #700, 224.

83. Council of Trent, in *SCD* #908, p. 280.

84. Martin Luther, "The Babylonian Captivity," in *SWML* 1:469–70.

85. *ICR* IV.xix.18, p. 957.

86. For some exceptions, including Welsh Baptists of the Delaware Valley and the Separate Baptist movement, see Jonathan A. Stapley and Kristine Wright, "The Forms and the Power: The Development of Mormon Ritual Healing to 1847," *Journal of Mormon History* 35.3 (Summer 2009): 50–51.

87. 3 Nephi 17:7–9.

88. Acts 3:6; James 5:14.

89. *WWJ*, 22 July 1839, 1:348.

90. See Alfred Young, "Autobiography," HBLL, and Benjamin F. Johnson, *My Life's Review* (n.p.: Johnson Family Organization, 1997), 11 (describing an incident with Jared Carter); Parley P. Pratt chronicles several examples in his *Autobiography*, ed. Scot Facer Proctor and Maurine Jensen Proctor (Salt Lake City, UT: Deseret, 2000), 80, 95, 193, etc.

91. Jonathan Stapley and Kristine Wright, "'They Shall Be Made Whole': A History of Baptism for Health," *Journal of Mormon History* 34.4 (Fall 2008): 62.

92. *WWJ* 1:306.

93. *EJ* 12:1347.

94. Luke 22:44; George Herbert, "The Bunch of Grapes," in *The Complete English Poetry* (New York: Penguin, 2004), 120.

95. BC 16:18 (D&C 19:17–19).

96. Matthew 19:13; Mark 10:16.

97. Ecclesiasticus 3:9.

98. "Blessing of Children," *EJ* 4:1087. The scriptural references cited above are mentioned in this article.

99. Adam Clarke, *Commentary with Critical Notes on the Holy Bible* (Nashville: Abingdon, n.d. [first published 1810–26]), 5:191.

100. *WJS*, 230.

101. *JSP-R&T*, 83–85 (D&C 20:70). The revelation was first published in 1835 D&C 2:20.

102. 3 Nephi 17:11–24.

103. William Wordsworth, "Ode: Intimations of Immortality," in *Poetical Works*, ed. Thomas Hutchinson (New York: Oxford University Press, 1989), 461.

104. Moroni 8:12.

105. This reading, in any case, is compatible with Smith's comments on another scriptural reference to children, which he cited as specific evidence of human premortality: "Our Savior speaks of Children & Says their angels always stand before my father." *WJS*, 9; citing Matthew 18:10.

106. *The Song of the Pearl*, trans. Han J. W. Drijvers, Robert M. Grant, Bentley Layton, and Willis Barnstone, in *Gnostic Bible* (Boston: Shambhala, 2003), 389.

107. Hyrum Smith diary, 45–46, cited in Jonathan Stapley, "Baby Blessing," *The Power of Godliness: Mormon Liturgy and Cosmology* (New York: Oxford, forthcoming).

108. Stapley notes the connection with Abrahamic circumcision, substantiated in later church publications in "Baby Blessing."

109. For Smith, see *JSP-J1*, 72–73, 81; for Woodruff, see *WWJ* 2:584–86. Both examples and several others cited in Stapley, "Baby Blessing."

110. George Q. Cannon, "Editorial Thoughts," *JI* 29.6 (15 March 1894): 195.

111. George Reynolds, "The Jaredites, Part II," *JI* 27.9 (1 May 1892): 282.

112. *JSP-D5*, 225.

113. *JSP-D6*, forthcoming; http://www.josephsmithpapers.org/paper-summary/minutes-6-april-1838/2.

114. *CDBY* 1:80.

115. *CDBY* 1:201.

116. "Patriarchal," *T&S* 6.9 (15 May 1845): 921–22.

117. *JSP-D4*, 379. See Benjamin E. Park, "'Thou Wast Willing to Lay Down Thy Life for Thy Friends': Zion's Blessings in the Early Church," *John Whitmer Historical Association Journal* 29 (2009): 27–37.

118. *WWJ* 1:100–101.

119. *JD* 2:10.

120. John H. Groberg, "Priesthood Power," *CR* (April 2001): 56.

121. *CDBY* 5:2917.

122. *WJS*, 41.

CHAPTER 8

1. Orson Pratt, "The Kingdom of God," *MS* 10.21 (1 November 1848): 322.

2. "Gift of the Holy Ghost," *T&S* 3.16 (15 June 1842): 823.

3. Joseph Smith, "Gift of the Holy Ghost," *T&S* 3.16 (15 June 1842): 823; Heber C. Kimball, *JD* 6:101.

4. John A. Widtsoe, *The Program of the Church of Jesus Christ of Latter-day Saints* (Salt Lake City, UT: Department of Education of the Church of Jesus Christ of Latter-day Saints, 1938), 129.

5. Benjamin Winchester, *The History of the Priesthood from the Beginning of the World to the Present Time* (Philadelphia: Brown, Bicking & Guilpert, 1843), iii.

6. John A. Widtsoe, *Priesthood and Church Government* (Salt Lake City, UT: Deseret, 1954), 38.

7. *M&A* 1.2 (November 1834): 27.

8. Orson Hyde, "A Prophetic Warning" (Toronto, 1836), http://olivercowdery.com/texts/Hyde1836.htm.

9. Winchester, *History of the Priesthood*, iv, 17, 74.

10. Orson Pratt, "The Gospel Witness," *Millennial Star* 10.11 (1 June 1848): 164.

11. Mark 16:17.

12. David Renaker, "A Miracle of Engineering: The Conversion of Bensalem in Francis Bacon's *New Atlantis*," *Studies in Philology* 87.2 (April 1990): 183.

13. Justin Martyr, *Dialogue with Trypho*, cited in Jaroslav Pelikan, *The Emergence of the Catholic Tradition (100–600)* (Chicago: University of Chicago Press, 1971), 99.

14. T. G. Pater, "Miracles (Theology of)," *NCE*, 9:670.

15. Pelikan, *Emergence*, 106–8.

16. Augustine, *City of God* 22, cited in Jon Ruthven, *On the Cessation of the Charismata: The Protestant Polemic on Postbiblical Miracles* (Sheffield: Sheffield Academic Press, 1997), 18.

17. Gregory the Great, *Homilies on the Gospels* 29, in Thomas C. Oden and Christopher A. Hall, *Ancient Commentary on Scripture, Genesis 12–50*, ed. Mark Sheridan (Downers Grove, IL: InterVarsity Press, 2005), NT 2:239.

18. Fr. Robert Victoria, "The Process of Beatification and Canonization," http://faithofthechurch .com/articles.html.

19. Tracy Borman, *Thomas Cromwell: The Untold Story of Henry VIII's Most Faithful Servant* (New York: Atlantic Monthly Press, 2014), 297–302.

20. James I, *Daemonologie* (1597), in Renaker, "Miracle," 184.

21. So reasons B. B. Warfield, *Counterfeit Miracles* (Edinburgh: Banner of Truth Trust, 1995), 29.

22. James Kent Stone, *The Invitation Heeded: Reasons for a Return to Catholic Unity* (New York: Catholic Publication Society, 1870), 76.

23. Keith Thomas, *Religion and the Decline of Magic* (New York: Penguin, 1991), 78.

24. From Calvin's 1536 *Institutes*, cited in Bruce Gordon, *Calvin* (New Haven, CT: Yale University Press, 2009), 59.

25. Jonathan Edwards, *Christian Love and Its Fruits* (Lafayette, IN: Sovereign Grace, 2000), 147.

26. *Testimonies of the Life, Character, Revelations and Doctrines of Mother Ann Lee* (Albany: Weed, Parsons & Co., 1888), 4–5.

27. *Testimonies*, 200–206.

28. Stephen J. Stein, *The Shaker Experience in America* (New Haven, CT: Yale University Press, 1992), 165ff.

29. John H. Wigger, *Taking Heaven by Storm: Methodism and the Rise of Popular Christianity in America* (New York: Oxford University Press, 1998), 115. See 106ff. for several examples; Wesley's definition appears in "Nature of Enthusiasm," *SJW*, 2:142.

30. *SJW*, 2:142.

31. *SJW*, 2:145.

32. "More Excellent Way," *SJW*, 3:431–32.

33. Freeborn Garrettson, *American Methodist Pioneer* (Rutland, VT: Academy Books, 1984), 41, 92, 84; in Wigger, *Taking Heaven*, 107.

34. Wigger, *Taking Heaven*, 110.

35. Charles Woodmason, *Carolina Backcountry on the Eve of the Revolution* (Chapel Hill: University of North Carolina Press, 1953), 101, in Wigger, *Taking Heaven*, 111.

36. Stein, *Shaker*, 166, 173.

37. John Symonds, *Thomas Brown and the Angels* (London: Hutchinson, 1961), 81.

38. Nathan Bangs, *A History of the Methodist Episcopal Church*, 2 vols. (New York: Carlton & Phillips, 1853), 2:161.

39. Alexander Campbell, "Reply," *Millennial Harbinger* 5 (Bethany, VA: A. Campbell, 1834), 170–71; "The Gift of the Holy Spirit," *Millennial Harbinger* 5 (Bethany, VA: A. Campbell, 1834), 217, 219.

40. "Holy Ghost," *TD*, 219.

41. Mormon 1:13–14.

42. Mormon 9:7–8.

43. "Beware of Imposters," *Painesville Telegraph* 2.26 (14 December 1830), http://www .sidneyrigdon.com/dbroadhu/oh/painetel.htm.

44. Alexander Campbell, *Delusions: An Analysis of the Book of Mormon* (Boston: Greene, 1832), 15.

45. Wandle Mace, "Autobiography," ca. 1890, 11–12, CHL.

46. "Beware of Delusion," *M&A* 2.4 (January 1836): 250–51.

47. *JSP-D5*, 483.

48. "Church of England," *MS* 1.1 (May 1840): 16.

49. E. D. Howe, *Mormonism Unveiled*, 104–5, in A. S. Hayden, *Early History of the Disciples in the Western Reserve, Ohio* (Cincinnati: Chase and Hall, 1875), 213.

50. See Mark L. Staker's excellent treatment of the Ohio context behind nineteenth-century Mormonism, *Hearken, O Ye People: The Historical Setting of Joseph Smith's Ohio Revelations* (Salt Lake City, UT: Kofford, 2009), especially chapters 2 and 8.

51. *JSP-H2*, 38.

52. *Mormonism Unveiled*, 105, in Hayden, *Early History*, 213.

53. "Beware of Imposters," *Painesville Telegraph* 2.26 (14 December 1830), http://www.sidneyrigdon.com/dbroadhu/oh/painetel.htm#121430.

54. BC 53:2, 4 (D&C 50:2, 4).

55. "Try the Spirits," *T&S* 3.11 (1 April 1842): 744.

56. *Key*, 117.

57. "Try the Spirits," *T&S* 3.11 (1 April 1842): 747.

58. *MHC* A-1, Addenda note 14, pp. 13–14.

59. Jon Ruthven, *On the Cessation of the Charismata: The Protestant Polemic on Postbiblical Miracles* (Sheffield: Sheffield Academic Press, 1997), 14.

60. Cited language is from Talcott Parsons, *The Structure of Social Action* (New York: Free Press, 1967), 662–65. Parson's is an authoritative treatment of Weber's thesis, spread across many original sources.

61. *JSP-D5*, 203.

62. Stephen Post, Journal, 27 March 1836. In *JSP-D5*, 190.

63. *JSP-J1*, 215–16.

64. Article of Faith 7, PGP.

65. John Kaye, *The Ecclesiastical History of the Second and Third Centuries* (Cambridge: Deighton, 1826), 98–99.

66. John Durham Peters, "Recording beyond the Grave: Joseph Smith's Celestial Bookkeeping," *Critical Inquiry* 42.4 (Summer 2016): 862.

67. "Revelation," Noah Webster, *American Dictionary of the English Language*. Reprint of 1828 First Edition (Chesapeake: Foundation for American Christian Education, 1995).

68. Avery Dulles, *Models of Revelation* (New York: Doubleday, 1983).

69. Keith E. Yandell, ed., *Myth and Narrative* (New York: Oxford University Press, 2001), 85.

70. Nicholas Wolterstorff, *Divine Discourse: Philosophical Reflections on the Claim that God Speaks* (Cambridge: Cambridge University Press, 1995), 10.

71. Sandra M. Schneider, *The Revelatory Text* (San Francisco: Harper, 1991), 27–29, cited in Wolterstorff, *Divine Discourse*, 10. Wolterstorff does cite a contrary view of Karl Barth that "we have no reason not to take the concept of God's word primarily in its literal sense" (*Church Dogmatics* I/I [London: T&T Clark, 2010], 130). Some contemporaries of Joseph Smith saw the body-speech problem in similar terms but from the other side of orthodoxy. In addition to criticizing Mormons, Hiram Mattison cites the heretical view of William Kinkade (1783–1832) that

"ears, hands, and eyes, are part of an intelligent ruler, and if God has none of these he cannot hear, handle, nor see us." *A Scriptural Defence of the Doctrine of the Trinity, or a Check to Modern Arianism as Taught by Campbellites, Hicksites, etc.* (New York: 1846), 44.

72. William J. Abraham, *Divine Revelation and the Limits of Historical Criticism* (New York: Oxford University Press, 1982), 24.

73. John Cotton, *A Treatise of the Covenant of Grace* (1636), cited in Michael G. Ditmore, "A Prophetess in Her Own Country: An Exegesis of Anne Hutchinson's 'Immediate Revelation,'" *William and Mary Quarterly* 57.2 (April 2000): 353.

74. "The Nature of Enthusiasm," *SJW*, 2:152.

75. See especially 1 Nephi 10–11, and Moroni 10.

76. Abraham Heschel's characterization of revelatory communication from God. *The Prophets* (New York: Harper & Row, 1962), xviii.

77. John Baillie considers divine revelation to address this sphere rather than matters of particular interest. *The Idea of Revelation* (New York: Columbia University Press, 1956), 148.

78. Hungering for "eternal life and the joy of the saints," Enos spends a night and a day in prayer, after which "there came a voice unto me, saying: Enos, thy sins are forgiven thee, and thou shalt be blessed." A further exchange then ensues (Enos 1:3–17); pondering the fate of three disciples, Mormon is given an explanation of translation (Moroni 8:7–9).

79. Alma 40:9; Moroni 8:7–9; Alma 16:5–6; 1 Nephi 16:24–31.

80. *New York Herald*, 25 August 1844.

81. BC 30:2 (D&C 28:2).

82. *JSP-D5*, 355.

83. Fyodor Dostoevsky, *The Brothers Karamazov* (New York: Penguin, 1978), 1:271.

84. *CDBY* 4:1941.

85. Dallin H. Oaks, "Dating versus Hanging Out," *Ensign* 36.6 (June 2006): 16.

86. D. Todd Christofferson, "Free Forever, to Act for Themselves," *Ensign* 44.11 (November 2014): 16.

87. James E. Faust, "First Presidency Message," *Ensign* 26.8 (August 1996): 5.

88. *WJS*, 256.

89. BC 7:1 (D&C 8:2).

90. 1 Kings 22:19; Isaiah 6:1; Ezekiel 1:28; Acts 7:55, 9.

91. Michael Carroll, "Apparitions," in *Theotokos, a Theological Encyclopedia of the Blessed Virgin Mary* (Collegeville, MN: Liturgical Press, 1992), 47.

92. Encyclical *Pascendi* of Pope Pius X, cited in Carroll, "Apparitions," in Theotokos, 47. "Nine Major Approved Apparitions" are tallied at http://www.theotokos.org.uk/pages/appdisce/nineapps.html; the number nineteen is given at https://carm.org/what-are-the-approved-mary-apparitions-of-the-roman-catholic-church.

93. Symonds, *Brown*, 29.

94. Symonds, *Brown*, 47.

95. Herbert A. Wiseby Jr., *Pioneer Prophet: Jemima Wilkinson, the Publick Universal Friend* (Ithaca, NY: Cornell University Press, 1964), 12.

96. Donna Hill, *Joseph Smith: The First Mormon* (Salt Lake City, UT: Signature Books, 1977), 53.

97. Bushman's tally does not include visionary experience embedded in longer narratives. "The Visionary World of Joseph Smith," *BYU Studies* 37.1 (1997/98): 183–204. For several examples

of revelations and visions in the Puritan era, see Michael G. Ditmore's "A Prophetess in Her Own Country: An Exegesis of Anne Hutchinson's 'Immediate Revelation,'" *William and Mary Quarterly* 57.2 (April 2000): 352n5, 354. In assessing the intensely private experience of Joseph Smith against the context of so much prior visionary experience, Leigh Eric Schmidt's observation about the abundance of "extraordinary revelations" in the seventeenth, eighteenth, and nineteenth centuries is pertinent: "From Shotts to Cambuslang to Booth Bay to Gaspar River, ecstatic religious experience was part of the communion occasion" associated with "festival events." *Holy Fairs: Scottish Communions and American Revivals in the Early Modern Period* (Princeton, NJ: Princeton University Press, 1989), 145.

98. Wigger, *Taking Heaven*, 106.

99. Philo Dibble, "Recollections of the Prophet," cited in Bushman, *Rough Stone Rolling*, 197.

100. They are treated in Alexander L. Baugh, "Parting the Veil: Joseph Smith's Seventy-Six Documented Visionary Experiences," in *Opening the Heavens: Accounts of Divine Manifestations, 1820–1844*, ed. John W. Welch and Erick B. Carlson (Provo and Salt Lake City, UT: Brigham Young University and Deseret, 2005), 265–326.

101. Kathleen Flake, PBS Frontline/American Experience, *The Mormons*, http://www.pbs.org/mormons/interviews/flake.html.

102. John Murdock, "Abridged Record of the Life of John Murdock," HBLL.

103. *JSP-J1*, 170–71.

104. 1835 D&C 82:1 (D&C 93:1).

105. The account was apparently first shared with Snow's granddaughter, Allie Young Pond, and was published in *IE* (September 1933): 677.

106. *CDWW*, 3:285, citing Francis Asbury Hammond Journal, 20 April 1893.

107. Provisionally added to the Pearl of Great Price, the vision is now section 138 of the D&C. See Robert L. Millet, "The Vision of the Redemption of the Dead (D&C 138)," in Craig K. Manscill, ed., *Sperry Symposium Classics: The Doctrine and Covenants* (Provo, UT: Religious Studies Center, Brigham Young University, 2004), 314–331.

108. David B. Haight, "The Sacrament and the Sacrifice," *Ensign* 19.11 (November 1989): 59–60.

109. Heber J. Grant to Mrs. Claud Peery, 13 April 1926, *Minutes*. It is also possible that Grant made a distinction between a personal appearance of God, and a vision.

110. "Letter from A. Gardner, late a 'Mormonite' Elder," *MS* 2.10 (February 1842): 159.

111. Alfred D. Young, "Autobiography," 4–12. Typescript in HBLL. He relates that he recorded this vision, experienced in the 1830s, years later, at the behest of the apostle George A. Smith (13).

112. "A Vision Given to Mosiah Hancock," *Levi and Mosiah Hanock Journals* (Genola, UT: Pioneer, 2006), 188.

113. "Philo Dibble's Narrative," in *Early Scenes in Church History* (Salt Lake City, UT: Juvenile Instructor Office, 1882), 75–93.

114. George Laub, "Autobiography," 2. Typescript, HBLL.

115. Benjamin Brown, *Testimonies for the Truth: A Record of Manifestations of the Power of God* (Liverpool: S. W. Richards, 1853), 2, 5.

116. Stephen M. Farnsworth, "'A Vision,' Nauvoo 1844 and biographical sketch." Typescript, HBLL. Also related by Orson Hyde in *JD* 5:142–43.

117. Autobiography of Eliza Dana Gibbs, 1813–1900. Typescript, HBLL.

118. James Amasa Little, "Biography of Lorenzo Dow Young," *Utah Historical Quarterly* 14 (1946): 26–31.

119. Brown, *Testimonies*, 14.

120. "In Memoriam" [Obituary of Vienna Jaques], *Woman's Exponent* 12 (1883–1884): 152.

121. Christopher C. Jones, "'We Latter-day Saints Are Methodists': The Influence of Methodism on Early Mormon Religiosity," MA thesis, Brigham Young University, 2009, 31–32.

122. Parley P. Pratt, "Spiritual Communication," *JD* 1:6–7.

123. *CDBY* 2:1024.

124. Orson Pratt, *JD* 13: 72–73. See also Ronald W. Walker, *Wayward Saints: The Godbeites and Brigham Young* (Urbana: University of Illinois Press, 1998).

125. http://kutv.com/news/local/lds-church-flags-members-book-about-latter-day-calamities-as-potential-misleading. The reference is to Julie Rowe's book, *A Greater Tomorrow: My Journey Beyond the Veil*. A second similar work, by John Pontius, is criticized in mainstream but non-official venues, e.g. http://ldsmag.com/article-1-13817/.

126. A whole literature of encounters with spirits of unborn children has sprung up, with LDS accounts a major factor. See, for instance, Elizabeth M. Carman and Neil J. Carman, *Cosmic Cradle: Souls Waiting in the Wings for Birth* (Fairfield, IA: Sunstar, 1999) and Sarah Hinze, *Coming from the Light: Spiritual Accounts of Life before Life* (New York: Pocket Books, 1997), among many others.

127. Boyd K. Packer, *Teach Ye Diligently* (Salt Lake City, UT: Deseret, 1975), 85.

128. "Prophecy (Preexilic Hebrew)," *Anchor Bible Dictionary*, ed. David Noel Freedman (New York: Doubleday, 1992), 5:482.

129. "Prophecy (Early Christian)," *Anchor Bible Dictionary*, 5:496.

130. "Prophecy," in F. L. Cross and E. A. Livingstone, ed., *Oxford Dictionary of the Christian Church* (Oxford: Oxford University Press, 1997), 1336.

131. 1 Corinthians 14:1.

132. 1 Thessalonians 5:20.

133. David Aune, *Prophecy in Early Christianity* (Grand Rapid, MI: Eerdmans, 1983), cited in Thomas W. Gillespie, *The First Theologians: A Study in Early Christian Prophecy* (Grand Rapids, MI: Eerdmans, 1994), 38.

134. John L. von Mosheim, *Historical Commentary on the State of Christianity during the First Three Hundred and Twenty-Five Years* (New York: S. Converse, 1854), 1:165–66.

135. Mosheim, *Historical Commentary*, 1:502.

136. Kenneth Scott Latourette, *A History of Christianity* (New York: HarperCollins, 1975), 1:128.

137. Latourette, *History*, 1:129.

138. Latourette, *History*, 1:129.

139. *The Journal of the Reverend John Wesley* (New York: T. Mason and G. Lane, 1837), 1:496.

140. The passage quoted is a paraphrase of an original report by Richard Kingston in Symonds, *Brown*, 13.

141. Symonds, *Brown*, 17.

142. John Lacy, *The General Delusion of the Christians: Touching the Ways of God's Revealing Himself to and by the Prophets* (London: R. B. Seeley and W. Burside, 1832 [1713]), ix.

143. See Paul E. Johnson and Sean Wilentz, *The Kingdom of Matthias* (New York: Oxford University Press, 1994).

144. See Ronald L. Numbers and Jonathan M. Butler, eds., *The Disappointed: Millerism and Millenarianism in the Nineteenth Century* (Knoxville: University of Tennessee Press, 1997).

145. *JSP-H1*, 295.

146. *WJS*, 10.

147. *JSP-D5*, 218.

148. "Letter from A. Gardner," *MS* 2.10 (February 1842): 159.

149. "Remarkable Prophecy Fulfilled," *MS* 2.1 (May 1841): 8. The prophecy was dated 13 April 1838 and was fulfilled that September.

150. *KCMB*, 77–79.

151. See Terryl L. Givens and Matthew J. Grow, *Parley P. Pratt: The Apostle Paul of Mormonism* (New York: Oxford University Press, 2010), 129ff.

152. Givens and Grow, *Pratt*, 82–83.

153. John Taylor, "History of John Taylor by Himself," 12, in "Histories of the Twelve," 1856–1868, CHL.

154. David Whitmer, *Address to All Believers in Christ* (Richmond, MO, 1887), 32.

155. Parley P. Pratt, *Autobiography*, ed. Scot Facer Proctor and Maurine Jensen Proctor (Salt Lake City, UT: Deseret, 2000), 213.

156. Pratt, *Autobiography*, 214.

157. Edward Partridge to Joseph Smith, November 1833, Joseph Smith Collection, CHL.

158. See several examples in *Early Patriarchal Blessings of the Church of Jesus Christ of Latter-day Saints*, comp. H. Michael Marquardt (Salt Lake City, UT: Smith-Pettit Foundation, 2007).

159. 1876 D&C 87; the earliest written record of the Rocky Mountain prophecy postdates Smith's death, but for evidence that he spoke it in the hearing of many, see Ronald K. Esplin, "A 'Place Prepared' in the Rockies," *Ensign* 18.7 (July 1988): 7–13, and *CDBY* 2:1069; Smith commissioned Orson Hyde to dedicate Palestine for the return of Judah, which he did 24 October 1841; Smith's blessing of Hyde anticipating the Jewish return and dating to 1832 or 1833 is in *T&S* 2:23 (1 October 1841): 553; Clayton, Journal, 18 May 1843, in *MHC* D-1, 1552–53.

160. The Springfield, Illinois, speech was reported in the *Daily Missouri Republican*, 18 June 1857, http://www.sidneyrigdon.com/dbroadhu/MO/Misr1850.htm.

161. 1835 D&C 4:2 (D&C 84:4).

162. 1876 D&C 111:4.

163. *JSP-D1*, 110–12.

164. David Whitmer, *Address to All Believers in Christ*, 31. Cited in *JSP-D1*, 110.

165. *JSP-D6*, forthcoming; http://www.josephsmithpapers.org/paper-summary/history-1838-1856-volume-b-1-1-september-1834-2-november-1838/247.

166. *FFY*, 51–52.

167. *FFY*, 178.

168. *CDBY* 3:1807.

169. *FFY*, 239.

170. Exodus 15:20 *KJV*; *FFY*, 325.

171. *CDBY* 4:2070.

172. Cited in Givens and Grow, *Pratt*, 362–63.

173. *CDBY* 1:331.

174. Orson F. Whitney, *History of Utah* (Salt Lake City, UT: G. Q. Cannon 1892), 412.

175. *CDBY* 1:421.

176. *CDBY* 4:2229. The allusion is to Numbers 11:29.

177. *CDBY* 2:1325.

178. *JD* 19:80–81; 21:135; 14:307.

179. Matthew 15:30.

180. Mark 16:18.

181. Acts 3:2–7.

182. Acts 14:9–10.

183. Acts 8:5–7.

184. "Profession of Faith . . . ," in *SCD* #423, p. 167.

185. Martin Luther, "Babylonian Captivity," in *SWML*, 1:472–73.

186. *ICR* IV.xix.18, p. 958.

187. Antonia Fraser, *Mary Queen of Scots* (New York: Delacorte, 1970), 437.

188. *Journal of George Fox*, ed. Wilson Armistead (London: W. and F. G. Cash, 1852), 1:77.

189. *Journal of Fox*, 1:166.

190. *Journal of Fox*, 1:77, 1:152–53.

191. Symonds, *Brown*, 25.

192. *Testimonies Concerning the Character and Ministry of Mother Ann Lee* (Albany, NY: Packard & Van Benthuysen, 1827), 13.

193. Sources from 1782 and 1783 affirm healings as a key practice, and an 1805 conversion of Richard McNemar followed a miraculous healing. Stephen J. Stein, *The Shaker Experience in America* (New Haven, CT: Yale University Press, 1992), 29, 59.

194. Symonds, *Brown*, 65. See also reports of healing, p. 100.

195. Stein, *Shaker Experience*, 166–67.

196. John Wesley, *Works*, 10:22. Cited in Robert G. Tuttle Jr., "John Wesley and the Gifts of the Holy Spirit," http://ucmpage.org/articles/rtuttle1.html.

197. John Wesley, *The Heart of Wesley's Journal*, ed. Percy Livingstone Parker (New Canaan, CT: Keats, 1979), 75 (8 May 1741).

198. James Robinson, *Divine Healing: The Formative Years, 1830–1890—Theological Roots in the Transatlantic World* (Eugene: Wipf and Stock, 2011), 115.

199. Robinson, *Divine Healing*, 119.

200. P. E. Shaw, *The Catholic Apostolic Church; Sometimes Called Irvingite* (Morningside Heights, NY: King's Crown Press, 1946), 30–31.

201. The African American synthesis "remains a largely unrecognized component" in historical surveys, notes Laurie A. Wilkie, "Secret and Sacred: Contextualizing the Artifacts of African-American Magic and Religion," *Historical Archaeology* 31.4 (1997): 93–94.

202. BC 25:23 (D&C 24:13).

203. BC 44:35 (D&C 42:43–44).

204. Circa 8 March 1831, BC 49:11 (D&C 46:9).

205. Pratt, *Autobiography*, 79–80.

206. Pratt, *Autobiography*, 175.

207. A. S. Hayden, *Early History of the Disciples in the Western Reserve, Ohio* (Cincinnati: Chase & Hall, 1875), 250.

208. "Reply to Mr. J. B. Rollo's 'Mormonism Exposed,'" *MS* 2.3 (July 1841): 44–45.

209. *MS* 11.13 (1 July 1849): 202–8. Similar compilations appear in 11.12 and other issues.

210. Gregory A. Prince and William Robert Wright, *David O. McKay and the Rise of Modern Mormonism* (Salt Lake City: University of Utah Press, 2005), 31.

211. *MS* 4.10 (February 1844): 160.

212. Alfred D. Young, "Autobiography," HBLL; the vindication was published in *T&S* 4.5 (16 January 1843): 80.

213. Jones, "We Latter-day Saints," 36.

214. Truman Coe, "Mormonism," *Ohio Observer*, 11 August 1836.

215. R. Clarke, *Mormonism Unmasked, or, The Latter-day Saints in a Fix* (London, 1850), 1.

216. *WWJ* 1:348–49.

217. "Proceedings," *FFY*, 55.

218. "Proceedings," *FFY*, 55.

219. Elizabeth Ann Whitney, "A Leaf from an Autobiography," *Woman's Exponent* 7.12 (15 November 1878): 91.

220. See extensive instances documented in Jonathan Stapley and Kristine Wright, "Female Ritual Healing in Mormonism," *Journal of Mormon History* 37 (Winter 2011): 1–85.

221. *CDBY* 1:35.

222. *CDBY* 5:2690.

223. First Presidency, "To the Presidents of Stakes and Bishops of Wards," 3 October 1914. In James R. Clark, comp., *Messages of the First Presidency of the Church of Jesus Christ of Latter-day Saints* (Salt Lake City, UT: Bookcraft, 1966), 4:312–13.

224. Elder Joseph Fielding Smith to General Relief Society Presidency, 29 July 1946. In Clark, *Messages*, 4:314.

225. Luke Timothy Johnson, "Tongues, Gift of," *Anchor Bible Dictionary*, 6:596.

226. Acts 2: 3–8.

227. Acts 2:3, 13.

228. 1 Corinthians 14:2, 9.

229. See Watson E. Mills, *Speaking in Tongues: A Guide to Research on Glossolalia* (Grand Rapids, MI: Eerdmans, 1986).

230. 1 Corinthians 14:13, 28.

231. Thirty-Nine Articles, XXIV, *C&C* 2:534.

232. Martin Luther, *Against the Heavenly Prophets*, ed. Conrad Bergendorff, *Works* XL, 142. Cited in George H. Williams and Edith Waldvogel, "A History of Speaking in Tongues and Related Gifts," in *The Charismatic Movement*, ed. Michael P. Hamilton (Grand Rapids, MI: W. B. Eerdmans, 1975), 72.

233. John Symonds, *Thomas Brown and the Angels* (London: Hutchinson, 1961), 25.

234. The French Prophets fade from history in the early 1700s. "Thirty years later they reappear, and in one of the same spots, Manchester, where they were known to have a cell." In their new incarnation they are Quakers who soon become followers of Ann Lee. See Symonds, *Brown*, 43–44.

235. Symonds, *Brown*, 68, 51, 76.

236. Symonds, *Brown*, 76–77.

237. Symonds, *Brown*, 69.

238. Nicholas Armstrong, *A Sermon Preached at the Primitive Methodist Chapel, Cambridge* (London: W. Harding, 1832), 7, 11.

239. James Allen Jaffe, *The Struggle for Market Power: Industrial Relations in the British Coal Industry, 1800–1840* (Cambridge: Cambridge University Press, 2003), 132.

240. Shaw, *Catholic Apostolic*, 159.

241. Shaw, *Catholic Apostolic*, 30–31.

242. Shaw, *Catholic Apostolic*, 32.

243. *MS* 25.28 (11 July 1863): 439.

244. *MHC* A-1, Note A Addenda p. 2.

245. Joseph Smith Jr., *History of the Church of Jesus Christ of Latter-day Saints*, 7 vols., ed. James Mulholland et al. (Salt Lake City, UT: Deseret, 1951), 1:297.

246. *MHC* C-1, p. 1267.

247. John Whitmer, *From Historian to Dissident: The Book of John Whitmer*, ed. Bruce N. Westergren (Salt Lake City, UT: Signature Books, 1995), 103.

248. *EMS* 2.17 (February 1834): 269.

249. *MHC* A-1, 272.

250. *MHC* A-1, 529.

251. *JSP-D4*,165. He added that he would not allow anything said in tongues as testimony in a church court.

252. *JSP-D5*, 190.

253. Mary Fielding to Mercy Fielding Thompson, 8 July 1837, Mary Fielding Papers, CHL.

254. Alfred Young, "Autobiography," HBLL.

255. *WJS*, 3–4.

256. "Reply to Rollo's," *MS* 2.3 (July 1841): 44–45.

257. Elizabeth B. Pratt, "Autobiography," 94–95. In Givens and Grow, *Pratt*, 206.

258. William Clayton, *An Intimate Chronicle: The Journals of William Clayton*, ed. George D. Smith (Salt Lake City, UT: Signature, 1995).

259. William E. A. Axon, *The Annals of Manchester: A Chronological Record from the Earliest Times to the End of 1885* (Manchester: Heywood, 1886), 211.

260. "Proceedings," *FFY*, 59.

261. *T&S* 3.16 (15 June 1842): 825–26.

262. *M&A* 2.6 (March 1836): 281.

263. John W. Gunnison, *The Mormons, or, Latter-day Saints in the Valley of the Great Salt Lake* (Philadelphia: Lippincott, Grambo, 1852), 74.

264. *CDBY* 1:168.

265. *CDBY* 2:802.

266. Heber C. Kimball, *JD* 5:176–77.

267. *CDBY* 2:1127.

268. *CDBY* 5:2834.

269. "Gift of the Holy Ghost," *T&S* 3:16 (15 June 1842): 825.

270. Maureen Ursenbach Beecher, "The Eliza Enigma," *Dialogue* 11.1 (Spring 1978): 38.

271. *CDBY* 2:802.

272. *CDBY* 2:793.

273. *CDBY* 2:996.

274. *CDBY* 5:2908.

275. *CR* (April 1900): 41.

276. Lee Copeland, "Speaking in Tongues in the Restoration Churches," *Dialogue* 24.1 (Spring 1991): 24.

277. *IE* 60 (September 1957): 622–23. Cited in Copeland, "Speaking in Tongues," 26. Modern Methodism has taken the same tack: "People with this gift 'pick up' the ability to communicate

across barriers of language," notes a United Methodist website, http://www.umc.org/what-we-believe/spiritual-gifts-tongues.

278. Melvin L. Butler, "Singing in Tongues," in *Encyclopedia of American Gospel Music*, ed. W. K. McNeil (London: Routledge, 2013), 344.

279. Butler, "Singing," 344.

280. Symonds, *Brown*, 77.

281. Symonds, *Brown*, 54.

282. Josiah Jones, "History of the Mormonites," cited in Michael Hicks, *Mormonism and Music* (Urbana: University of Illinois Press, 1989), 35.

283. *Far West Record*, ed. Donald Q. Cannon and Lyndon W Cook (Salt Lake City, UT: Deseret, 1983), 6 (11 September 1833).

284. "Minutes and Blessings," *JSP-D4*, 271.

285. Brown, *Testimonies*, 12.

286. "Mysteries of God," Broadside, Special Collections, HBLL.

287. "Sang by the Gift of Tongues and Translated," *Kirtland Revelation Book 2* (27 February 1833), in *JSP-R&T*, 509.

288. Hicks, *Mormonism and Music*, 39.

289. *EMS* 2.16 (January 1834): 272. Hicks gives this and other examples of tongue-singing in *Mormonism and Music*, 35–37.

290. Clayton, *Intimate Chronicle*, 55.

291. Clayton, *Intimate Chronicle*, 244.

292. Cited in Copeland, "Speaking in Tongues," 22.

293. Maureen Ursenbach Beecher, ed., *The Personal Writings of Eliza Roxcy Snow* (Logan: Utah State University Press, 2000), 178–79.

294. Origen, *Homilies on Exodus* 3, in *Ancient Christian Commentary on Scripture, 1–2 Corinthians*, ed. Gerald Bray (Downers Grove, IL: InterVarsity Press, 1999), NT 7:119. Origen is citing 1 John 4:1.

295. 2 Corinthians 11:14 *KJV*.

296. Genesis 18:1–15.

297. Hebrews 13:2; the Abraham story is in Genesis 18.

298. Acts 20:29; 2 Timothy 3:13.

299. Richard Watson, *Collection of Theological Tracts* (London: J. Nichols, 1785), 4:375.

300. Ignatius of Loyola, "Rules for the Discernment of Spirits," in *Spiritual Exercises of St. Ignatius*, trans. Anthony Mottola (New York: Doubleday, 1989), 50, 129.

301. Wesley, "Of Good Angels," *SJW*, 3:202; "Of Evil Angels," *SJW*, 3:214.

302. Wesley, "Of Evil Angels," *SJW*, 3:208.

303. 1876 D&C 129.

304. As Joshua Mattson points out, the revelation was not published until after Smith's death, being limited purposely "to a worthy and called few" and originally part of the temple endowment. See "For Their Benefit in Their Experience and Travels in the Flesh: The Dissemination of the Gift of Discerning Spirits in Mormon Theology," Mormon Scholars Foundation Summer Seminar, http://publications.mi.byu.edu/fullscreen/?pub=3526&index=2; Alonzo Gaskill, "Doctrine and Covenants 129:8 and the Reality of Satan's Physicality," *Religious Educator* 8.1 (2007): 44. Cited in Mattson, "For Their Benefit," 9.

305. 1835 D&C 75:2 (D&C 78.10); BC 64:28 (D&C 63.28); BC 65:21 (D&C 64.17); BC 9:2 (D&C 10:32); BC 9:3 (D&C 10:63).

306. "Try the Spirits," *T&S* 3.11 (1 April 1842): 743.

307. Clayton, *Intimate Chronicle*, 102.

308. *CDBY* 2:940.

309. *CDBY* 2:1007.

310. *CR* (April 1904): 74.

311. Orson Hyde, April 5, 1860, *Minutes*.

312. Russel M. Nelson, "Ask, Seek, Knock," *Ensign* 39.11 (November 2009): 83.

313. *WJS*, 12.

314. Mattson, "For Their Benefit," 16.

315. Mark 1:23–26.

316. Matthew 10:1; Luke 10:17.

317. Letter to Fabius, bishop of Antioch, 251, in *SCD* #45, p. 22.

318. "Ancient Statutes of the Church," in *SCD* #155, p. 63.

319. Jeffrey Burton Russell, *Mephistopheles: The Devil in the Modern World* (Ithaca, NY: Cornell University Press, 1986), 91.

320. "Martin Luther to Andrew Ebert," 5 August 1536, in *Luther: Letters of Spiritual Counsel*, ed. Theodore G. Tappert (Louisville, KY: Westminster John Knox Press, 2006), 44.

321. *ICR* IV.xix.24, p. 961.

322. Tillotson's *Sermons*, 1735, cited in Thomas Church, *An Essay toward Vindicating the Literal Sense of the Demoniacks, in the New Testament* (London: J. Bettenham, 1737), 116–17.

323. See Brian H. Levack, *The Devil Within: Possession and Exorcism in the Christian West* (New Haven, CT: Yale University Press, 2013), 215ff.

324. Hugh Farmer, *An Essay on the Demoniacs of the New Testament* (London: G. Robinson, 1775), 173.

325. William Ashdowne, *An Attempt to Prove that the Opinion Concerning the Devil, or Satan, as a Fallen Angel . . . Hath No Real Foundation in Scripture* (Canterbury: W. Bristow, 1794), 62–63.

326. William Worthington, *An Impartial Enquiry into the Case of the Gospel Demoniacks* (London: J. F. & C. Rivington, 1778), 1.

327. Worthington, *Enquiry*, 5.

328. Worthington, *Enquiry*, 307, 327.

329. Church, *Vindicating*, 118–21.

330. Levack, *The Devil*, 224–26.

331. John Wesley, "Of Evil Angels," *SJW* 3:217; "Of Good Angels," *SJW*, 3:199.

332. "Instructions for Exorcising Evil Spirits," *Gentleman's Magazine*, vol. 115 (1814): 219.

333. "A Man Possessed of the Devil," in Josiah Priest, *The Wonders of Nature and Providence, Displayed* (Albany, NY: Josiah Priest, 1826), 458–65. (Originally published in *English Methodist Magazine* 12: 155.)

334. Levack, *The Devil*, 224–26.

335. W. R. Ward, *Religion and Society in England, 1790–1850* (London: Batsford, 1972), 79. Cited in Robinson, *Divine Healing*, 119.

336. Walter Balfour, *An Inquiry into the Scriptural Doctrine Concerning the Devil and Satan* (Charlestown: Davidson, 1827), 106–7.

337. "Daemoniacks," *TD*, 133.

338. "Daemoniacks," *TD*, 135.

339. "Exorcism," *TD*, 178.

340. Rachel Zoll, "Catholic Bishops: More Exorcists Needed," *Deseret News*, 12 November 2010, http://www.deseretnews.com/article/700081096/Catholic-bishops-More-exorcists-needed.html?pg=all.

341. 1835 D&C 91:3 (D&C 76:29).

342. Abraham 3:22–28; Moses 4:1–4; PGP, 1835 D&C 91:3 (D&C 76:28–29).

343. The 1851 edition of Moses 6:59. The 1878 edition has "By reason of transgression cometh the fall, which fall bringeth death." Robert J. Matthews, "How We Got the Book of Moses," *Ensign* 26.1 (January 1986): 46.

344. *T&S* 3.10 (15 March 1842): 720 (Abraham 3:26, PGP).

345. *WJS*, 60.

346. *WJS*, 201.

347. Matthew 8.

348. *WJS*, 60.

349. *T&S* 3.11 (1 April 1842): 745.

350. *JSP-H1*, 385.

351. Levi Hancock, *Levi and Mosiah Hancock Journals Excerpts* (Genola, UT: Pioneer, 2006), 48.

352. BC 25:23–24 (D&C 24:13–14).

353. Alfred D. Young, "Autobiography," HBLL.

354. *JSP-J1*, 140–41.

355. *MS* 11.13 (1 July 1849): 207, 205.

356. "Spirit Possession," *Deseret Evening News*, July 3, 1909, 4.

357. Bruce R. McConkie, *Mormon Doctrine* (Salt Lake City, UT: Deseret, 1966), 259.

358. James A. Cullimore, "Gifts of the Spirit," *Ensign* 24.11 (November 1974): 27.

CHAPTER 9

1. Orson Pratt, "The Gospel Witness," *Millennial Star* 10.11 (1 June 1848): 164.

2. Alma 42:8.

3. William Hone, *The Apocryphal New Testament* (London: William Hone, 1820).

4. Thomas Rennell, *Proofs of Inspiration, or the Ground of Distinction* . . . (London: F. C. & J. Rivington, 1822), vi–vii. Cited in Timothy Larsen, *Crisis of Doubt: Honest Faith in Nineteenth-Century England* (New York: Oxford University Press, 2006), 37.

5. Samuel Butler, *The Genuine and Apocryphal Gospels Compared* . . . (Shrewsbury: Wm. Eddowes, 1822), 15. In Larsen, *Crisis*, 37.

6. Rennell, *Proofs of Inspiration*, in Larsen, *Crisis*, 35.

7. Larsen, *Crisis*, 36.

8. Craig D. Allert, *A High View of Scripture?* (Grand Rapids, MI: Baker, 2007), 73. The examples are in his Appendix.

9. Allert, *High View*, 74.

10. E. Gephart, *Mystics and Heretics in Italy*, 71, cited in Kenneth E. Kirk, *The Vision of God* (New York: Harper & Row, 1966), 220.

11. Nathanael Bonwetsch, cited in Jaroslav Pelikan, *The Emergence of the Catholic Tradition (100–600)* (Chicago: University of Chicago Press, 1971), 98.

12. John 3:8.

13. This move was first articulated by Hippolytus of Rome. Pelikan, *Emergence*, 106.

14. The creeds and episcopate also followed, by this line of reasoning. Pelikan, *Emergence*, 107.

15. Philip Schaff, *The Creeds of Christendom*, 6th ed. (Grand Rapids, MI: Baker Book House, 1990), 3:206.

16. Jaroslav Pelikan, *Whose Bible Is It?* (New York: Penguin, 2005), 117.

17. "Creed of Council of Toledo," article 12, in *SCD #32*, p. 14.

18. *SCD* #783, p. 244.

19. Irish Articles of Religion, II; Westminster Confession XIV.2, in Schaff, *Creeds of Christendom*, 3:527, 630.

20. H. J. M. Nellen, "Growing Tension between Church Doctrines and Critical Exegesis of the Old Testament," in *Hebrew Bible, Old Testament: From the Renaissance to the Enlightenment*, ed. Magne Saebo (Göttingen: Vandenhoeck & Ruprecht, 2008), 810, 814–15.

21. Benedictus de Spinoza, *Theological-Political Treatise*, trans. Samuel Shirley (Indianapolis, IN: Hackett, 2001), 32–33.

22. David Hume, "On Miracles," *An Enquiry Concerning Human Understanding*, in *Essays and Treatises* (London: A. Millar, 1768), 2:127–53.

23. Soame Jenyns published his *View of the Internal Evidence for the Christian Religion* (London: J. Dodsley, 1776), 123.

24. Jenyns, *View*, 132.

25. "Paine's Age of Reason," *Monthly Review* XIV (London: R. Griffiths, 1794), 391.

26. [William Ellery Channing], *Remarks on the Character and Writing of John Milton* (Boston: Benjamin Perkins, 1828 [Repr. New York: AMS, 1975], 97.

27. John Wesley, *The Journal of John Wesley*, 8 vols., ed. Nehemiah Curnock (London: Epworth Press, 1938), 6:117.

28. Richard Grier, *A Defence of the Reply to the "End of Religious Controversy"* (London: T. Cadell, 1825), 76.

29. *JSP-J1*, 166.

30. "Errors of the Bible," *EMS* 2.14 (July 1833): 106.

31. The 1828 Webster's defines translate as "interpret" as well as "render into another language." Noah Webster, *American Dictionary of the English Language*. Reprint of 1828 First Edition (Chesapeake: Foundation for American Christian Education, 1995), n.p. Smith clearly believed more than linguistic error was at the root of biblical fallibility.

32. 1 Nephi 13:26.

33. 1 Nephi 13:28; 13:29; 13:32; 13:34; 13:40; 14:23.

34. *WJS*, 211.

35. Parley P. Pratt, "The Fountain of Knowledge," in *An Appeal to the Inhabitants of the State of New York* (Nauvoo: John Taylor, 1844), 15.

36. *WJS*, 345.

37. Philo, *Quaestiones* I (53), in C. D. Yonge, trans., *The Works of Philo* (Peabody, MA: Hendrickson, 1993), 802.

38. 2 Corinthians 3:14.

39. Augustine, *Confessions*, XII.1; XIII.3. Trans. F. J. Sheed (Indianapolis, IN: Hackett, 1993), 233, 260.

40. *Confessions*, XII.24, 250.

41. BC 35:16 (D&C 33:18); BC 36:8 (D&C 34:12); BC 37:31 (D&C 35:27), etc.

42. *Voice*, 20.

43. Mark Noll, *America's God* (New York: Oxford University Press, 2002), 381.

44. *EMS* 2.19 (April 1834): 289–90; 2.15 (December 1833): 234; 2.20 (May 1834): 306.

45. "Spiritualizing the Scriptures" (from the *Gospel Reflector*), *T&S* 3.5 (1 January 1842): 644–46.

46. Philip L. Barlow, *Mormons and the Bible* (New York: Oxford University Press, 2013), 33–36, 70.

47. *CDBY* 2:731; "We are commanded in this Bible not to love the world and the things of the world; and then you read a little further in the same book, and you are commanded to love the world and the things of the world. How shall we understand these things? With the divinity that is within us" (3:1897).

48. I note one exception: inexplicably, LDS scholar Stephen Robinson claims in an exchange with evangelicals that "Latter-day Saints would agree with the five qualifications of the Chicago Statement on Biblical Inerrancy." See Robinson and Craig L. Blomberg, *How Wide the Divide: A Mormon and an Evangelical in Conversation* (Downers Grove, IL: InterVarsity Press, 2009), 57. Thanks to Matthew Bowman for this reference.

49. 1 Nephi, *Book of Mormon* (Palmyra: E. B. Grandin, 1830), 31 (1 Nephi 13:32). Subsequent editions changed "woundedness" to "blindness."

50. Title page, Book of Mormon.

51. The Chicago Statement on Biblical Inerrancy, http://www.bible-researcher.com/chicago1 .html.

52. See the treatment of evolution in Terryl L. Givens, *Wrestling the Angel: The Foundations of Mormon Thought—Cosmos, God, Humanity* (New York: Oxford University Press, 2015), 217–19.

53. *WJS*, 183–84.

54. *WWJ* 2:139.

55. LDS biblical scholar David Bokovoy gives the Documentary Hypothesis a powerful endorsement in his excellent *Understanding the Old Testament* (Salt Lake City, UT: Kofford, 2014), but it is unlikely it could have been published by the church-owned press.

56. John Wesley, *The New Testament with Notes for Plain, Unlettered Men Who Know Only Their Mother Tongue* (London: Boyer, 1755); Anthony Purver, *A New and Literal Translation of All the Books of the Old and New Testament; with Notes Critical and Explanatory* (London: W. Richardson and S. Clark, 1764); Charles Thomson, *Holy Bible, Containing the Old and New Covenant, Commonly Called the Old and New Testament. Translated from the Greek* (Philadelphia: Jane Aitkin, 1808); Alexander Campbell, *Living Oracles* (Buffaloe, VA: A. Campbell, 1826); Noah Webster, ed., *The Holy Bible, Containing the Old and New Testaments, in the Common Version* (New Haven, CT: Durrie and Peck, 1833).

57. 1835 D&C 92:1 (D&C 91).

58. Some notable countercurrents have emerged since; the Jesus Seminar, for example, has published *The Five Gospels*, adding the Gospel of Thomas in a self-advertising challenge to the canonical four (New York: HarperOne, 1993).

59. 1 Nephi 13:40.

60. 1 Nephi 13:34, 28.

61. Minute Book 1, 2 February 1833, http://josephsmithpapers.org/paperSummary/minute-book-1?p=12.

62. T&S 5.9 (1 May 1844): 513.

63. "To the Elders of the Church," M&A 2.3 (December 1835): 229. The third sign was "the covenants given to the Latter-day Saints."

64. J. Reuben Clark, Why the King James Bible? (Salt Lake City, UT: Deseret, 1956), 228.

65. BC 24:9–10 (D&C 20:11).

66. 2 Nephi 29:12.

67. MHC A-1, 289. Smith never saw his plans realized; however, today Mormons commonly use a "quadruple combination," a single volume incorporating all four LDS standard works.

68. "The Book of Mormon," EMS 2.14 (July 1833): 109.

69. EMS 1.8 (January 1833): 116.

70. MHC C-1, 1255.

71. "The Mormons," Religious Herald 59:1 (9 April 1840).

72. Thomas O'Dea, The Mormons (Chicago: University of Chicago Press, 1957), 26.

73. Gerald Smith, Schooling the Prophet: How the Book of Mormon Influenced Joseph Smith and the Early Restoration (Provo, UT: Neal A. Maxwell Institute, 2015). See also John W. Welch, "The Book of Mormon as the Keystone of Church Administration," in A Firm Foundation: Church Organization and Administration, ed. David J. Whittaker and Arnold K. Garr (Provo, UT: Religious Studies Center, Brigham Young University; Salt Lake City, UT: Deseret, 2011), 15–57.

74. M&A 1.12 (September 1835): 179–82.

75. See several examples in Terryl L. Givens, By the Hand of Mormon: The American Scripture that Launched a New World Religion (New York: Oxford University Press, 2003), 185–87.

76. See Givens, By the Hand, 62–88.

77. 1835 D&C 4:8 (D&C 84:57).

78. The Laura F. Willes Center for Book of Mormon Studies is part of the Neal A. Maxwell Institute for Religious Scholarship; it published the Journal of Book of Mormon Studies.

79. In recent years church growth has shown some decline. Convert baptisms for 2014 were just under 300,000. The number of missionaries was 85,000, http://ldschurchgrowth.com/current-lds-church-growth-statistics/.

80. This was true until Jacque Derrida's critique of logocentrism complicated the picture, at any rate.

81. Luke 16:16.

82. David Holland employs this term in his groundbreaking study, Sacred Borders: Continuing Revelation and Canonical Restraint in Early America (New York: Oxford University Press, 2011), 17.

83. Holland, Sacred Borders, 6, 209.

84. Mentioned in 1 Kings 11:41; Joshua 10:13.

85. Parley P. Pratt, An Appeal to the Inhabitants of the State of New York; Letter to Queen Victoria; The Fountain of Knowledge; Immortality of the Body; and Intelligence and Affection (Nauvoo, IL: John Taylor, [1844]), 17.

86. David Whitmer, Address to All Believers in Christ (Richmond, MO, 1887), 46.

87. BC 4, 8 (D&C 5, 9).

88. BC 16, 24, 37, 39 (D&C 19, 20, 35, 37).

89. http://www.josephsmithpapers.org/paperSummary/book-of-commandments-1833.

90. Whitmer, *Address*, 46.

91. *Far West Record*, ed. Donald Q. Cannon and Lyndon W. Cook (Salt Lake City, UT: Deseret, 1983), 27.

92. 1835 D&C 26:1 (D&C 70:3).

93. Revelation, 1 March 1832. *JSP-R&T*, 267. The phrasing dropped out of the published 1835 Doctrine and Covenants.

94. John W. Welch and David Whittaker, "Mormonism's Open Canon: Some Historical Perspectives on Its Religious Limits and Potentials" (Provo, UT: FARMS, 1986), 10. The Joseph Smith Papers publication of Smith's revelations includes nine that went unpublished (*JSP-R&T*, xxvi).

95. *JSP-D2*, 113–14.

96. For a reconstruction of the unpublished sixth gathering of the Book of Commandments, see *JSP-R&T*, 173–93.

97. *JSP-D4*, 175. Portions of the Bible and Book of Mormon were not, however, included in the new collection.

98. 1835 D&C preface.

99. *JSP-D4*, 386.

100. Many Book of Mormon passages refer to a sealed portion of the plates or scriptures yet to be revealed, e.g., 3 Nephi 26:8–10; Ether 4:16, etc. Many contemporaries noted that a substantial portion of the plates Smith possessed were sealed. See Rachael Givens, "Lost 'Wagonloads of Plates': The Disappearance and Deliteralization of Sealed Records," *Dialogue* 45.3 (Fall 2012): 118–19.

101. Givens, "Lost 'Wagonloads of Plates,' " 100.

102. Roger E. Olson, *The Story of Christian Theology* (Downers Grove, IL: InterVarsity Press, 1999), 31. For the twentieth-century leaders, see Rachael Givens's citations of Spencer W. Kimball and Bruce R. McConkie in "Lost 'Wagonloads of Plates,' " 124.

103. "Neglect of the Old Testament," *MS* 2.1 (June 1840): 28–30.

104. Acts 3:22; See Gerald Smith, *Schooling the Prophet: How the Book of Mormon Influenced Joseph Smith and the Early Restoration* (Provo, UT: Neal A. Maxwell Institute, 2015), 137. Many of these scriptures are recounted in *JSP-H1*, 223–25.

105. Though Smith recorded the text in June 1830, he did not publish it until more than a decade later. "History of Joseph Smith," *T&S* 4.5 (16 January 1843): 71. Other portions of his Genesis additions had first been published in August 1832.

106. One exception, a fragment of an ancient text which anticipates the recovered Genesis material, was BC 6 (D&C 7), a revelation "translated from parchment, written and hid up by John" the beloved. As with the Moses material, Smith made no claim to actually have the original parchment.

107. *T&S* 4.5 (16 January 1843): 71 (Moses 1:1, PGP).

108. Numbers 12:6, 8.

109. *T&S* 4.5 (16 January 1843): 73 (Moses 1:41, PGP).

110. Kenneth W. Godfrey, "A Note on the Nauvoo Library and Literary Institute," *BYU Studies* 14.3 (Spring 1974): 386–89; Larsen, *Crisis*, 18.

111. *T&S* 4.22 (1 Oct. 1843): 336.

112. *T&S* 4.22 (1 Oct. 1843): 336.

113. *EMS* 1.3 (August 1832): 44–47.

114. Philip Schaff, *The Creeds of Christendom: The Evangelical Protestant Creeds* (New York: Harper & Brothers, 1877), 487.

115. John 4:24.

116. *SJW* 4:384–85.

117. "The Church of Christ," *EMS* 1:10 (March 1833): 73 (Moses 5:11; 6:7–55, PGP).

118. "And thus all things were confirmed unto Adam, by an holy ordinance" (Moses 5:59, PGP). That verse does not appear in the *EMS* or the 1851 PGP. "Adam . . . was ordained unto the high priesthood of the holy order of God." *EMS* 1.11 (April 1833): 161. And Enoch was "ordained a high Priest after the order of the covenant" (*JST* Genesis 14:27, 127).

119. *EMS* 1.4 (September 1832): 58 (Moses 7:59, PGP).

120. *EMS* 1.4 (September 1832): 58 (Moses 7:59, PGP).

121. *EMS* 1.3 (August 1832): 46 (Moses 7:29–41, PGP).

122. *EMS* 1.3 (August 1832): 44–47; 1.10 (March 1833): 145–47; 1:11 (April 1833): 161–63.

123. *T&S* 4.5 (16 January 1843): 71–73; 4.22 (1 October 1843): 336–39.

124. *MS* 13.6 (15 March 1851): 90–93.

125. Mormon 9:32; 2 Nephi 4.

126. Preface, *Book of Mormon* (Palmyra: E. B. Grandin, 1830); *T&S* 5.9 (1 May 1844): 513; *T&S* 4.22 (1 October 1843): 336.

127. *T&S* 3.9 (1 March 1842): 706 (Abraham 2:9–11, PGP).

128. https://www.lds.org/topics/translation-and-historicity-of-the-book-of-abraham?lang=eng.

129. *T&S* 3.9 (1 March 1842): 703–6; 3.10 (15 March 1842): 719–22; 3.14 (16 May 1842): 783–84.

130. 1844 D&C 111:1 (D&C 136:1).

131. "Elder Canon then said I hold in my hand the revised edition of the Doctrine and Covenants . . . ; also the Pearl of Great Price. . . . As some additions have been made of revelations since the first publication [of the former] it was deemed advisable to submit it now for the acceptance of the members of the church. . . . Joseph F. Smith then moved the adoption of the books, and the motion being put was carried unanimously." *Salt Lake Herald*, 10 October 1880.

132. *CR* (October 1897): 22–23.

133. *CR* (October 1897): 6.

134. Cited in Kent P. Jackson, "Scripture, Authority of," *EM* 3:1281.

135. Harold B. Lee, "The Place of the Living Prophet, Seer, and Revelator," Address to Seminary and Institute of Religion Faculty, Brigham Young University, 8 July 1964. Cited in "Section 68—Scripture Is the Will, Mind, Word, Voice, and Power of God unto Salvation," *Doctrine and Covenants Institute Student Manual: Religion 324 and 325* (Salt Lake City, UT: Church Educational System, 2001).

136. W. D. Davies and Truman Madsen, "Scripture, Scriptures," in *EM* 3:1278.

137. "God is a spirit" (John 4:24 *KJV*). Smith emends this verse to read, "for unto such hath God promised his spirit." To John's other words (John 1:18 *KJV*) he adds the qualifier "except he hath borne record of the son." Scott H. Faulring et al., ed., *Joseph Smith's New Translation of the Bible* (Provo, UT: Religious Studies Center, Brigham Young University, 2004), 450, 443.

138. Davies and Madsen, "Scripture," *EM* 3:1278.

139. *CDBY* 4:1941.

CHAPTER 10

1. Jacob [Baker], "Generational Translation and Work for the Dead," https://bycommonconsent.com/2012/03/07/generational-translation-and-work-for-the-dead/.

2. James F. White, *An Introduction to Christian Worship*, 3rd ed. (Nashville: Abingdon Press, 2001), 47.

3. 1 Corinthians 5:8; cited in White, *Worship*, 54.

4. Mormons, especially in Utah, do celebrate with great fanfare Pioneer Day, the day the Mormon pioneer company entered the Salt Lake Valley on 24 July 1847. Though the day has profound religious significance, it is celebrated with parades rather than religious ritual.

5. See, for instance, Eric D. Huntsman, *Good Tidings of Great Joy: An Advent Celebration of the Savior's Birth* (Salt Lake City, UT: Deseret, 2011), and Wendee Wilcox Rosborough, *The Holy Week for Latter-day Saint Families* (Salt Lake City, UT: Deseret, 2016).

6. Exodus 20:8, 10.

7. "Sabbath," *EJ* 14:558.

8. "Sabbath," *EJ* 14:558.

9. Acts 20:7.

10. Revelation 1:10.

11. Justin Martyr, "First Apology" LXVII, *ANF* 1:185.

12. "Teaching of the Twelve Apostles" XV, *ANF* 7:381.

13. John Nevins Andrews and Louis Richard Conradi, *History of the Sabbath and the First Day of the Week* (Washington, DC: Review and Herald, 1912), 523.

14. Andrews and Conradi, *History*, 483.

15. White, *Worship*, 51.

16. Andrews and Conradi, *History*, 484–85.

17. Andrews and Conradi, *History*, 29.

18. "Council of Florence," *SCD* #712, p. 229.

19. Johann Eck, *Enchiridion* (1533), 78–79; cited in Andrews and Conradi, *History*, 587.

20. "Small Catechism," in *C&C* 2:34.

21. Westminster Confession XXI.vii, *C&C* 2:633–34.

22. *ICR* II.viii.32–34, pp. 252–53.

23. Nicholas Bownd, *Sabbathum Veteris Et Novi Testamenti: or The True Doctrine of the Sabbath*, ed. Chris Coldwell (Dallas: Naphtali Press, 2015), 42, 40.

24. Jonathan Edwards, *Works*, ed. Edward Hickman (Edinburgh: Banner of Truth Trust, 1992), 2:93–94.

25. William G. Hartley, "Common People: Church Activity during the Brigham Young Era," in *Nearly Everything Imaginable: The Everyday Life of Utah's Mormon Pioneers*, ed. Ronald W. Walker and Doris R. Dant (Provo, UT: Brigham Young University Press, 1999), 257.

26. BC 60:21 (D&C 59:12).

27. *CDBY* 1:92.

28. BC 60:21–22 (D&C 59:12–13).

29. *CDBY* 1:92.

30. *CDBY* 1:82.

31. *CDBY* 1:130.

32. *CDBY* 1:160.

33. *CDBY* 1:370.

34. *CDBY* 1:231.

35. *CDBY* 1:397.

36. *CDBY* 1:80.

37. *CDBY* 1:579.

38. *CDBY* 1:580.

39. Hartley, "Common People," 251–56.

40. Both figures are cited in Craig Harline, *Sunday* (New York: Doubleday, 2007), 379–80.

41. http://www.mormonnewsroom.org/article/church-leaders-call-for-better-observance-of-sabbath-day.

42. Justin Martyr, *First Apology, ANF* 1:185.

43. "The Martyrdom of the Holy Martyrs," *ANF* 1:305.

44. Bruce Gordon, *Calvin* (New Haven, CT: Yale University Press, 2009), 306.

45. *WWJ* 1:426.

46. *CDBY* 1:167.

47. William Hartley details these developments in "Mormon Sundays," *My Fellow Servants: Essays on the History of the Priesthood* (Provo, UT: BYU Studies, 2010), 343–54.

48. BC 24:35 (D&C 20:45).

49. *Far West Record*, ed. Donald Q. Cannon and Lyndon W. Cook (Salt Lake City, UT: Deseret, 1983), 17.

50. 1835 D&C 2:9 (D&C 20:45).

51. Karen Westerfield Tucker, *American Methodist Worship* (New York: Oxford University Press, 2001), 11. Cited in Christopher C. Jones, " 'We Latter-day Saints Are Methodists': The Influence of Methodism on Early Mormon Religiosity," MA thesis, Brigham Young University, 2009, 90.

52. *JSP-D5*, 24.

53. *JSP-D5*, 24.

54. *JSP-D5*, 24.

55. Jay Leon Slaughter, "The Role of Music in the Mormon Church, School, and Life," PhD diss., Indiana University, 1964, 49; *Collection of Sacred Hymns for the Church of the Latter Day Saints*, selected by Emma Smith (Kirtland: F. G. Williams, 1835).

56. White, *Worship*, 37.

57. Jones shows how recent scholarship dispels the "early treatments that portrayed [Methodist] worship as liturgically impoverished." "We Latter-day Saints," 88.

58. White, *Worship*, 41.

59. *JD* 16:268.

60. *New York Herald* (4 August 1842).

61. Stephen H. Webb, *Mormon Christianity: What Other Christians Can Learn from the Latter-day Saints* (New York: Oxford University Press, 2013), 74–75.

62. White, *Worship*, 26.

63. Acts 20:9.

64. Hartley, "Common People," 255.

65. Matthew Bowman, "This Is My Body: A Mormon Sacrament," *Dialogue* 44.3 (Fall 2011): 211.

66. *CDBY* 5:2644.

67. *CDBY* 3:1794.

68. *CDBY* 2:819.

69. LeGrand Ward, Liberty Stake, General Minutes, 1913–29, LR 4804 11, v. 9; Holladay Ward, General Minutes, Cottonwood Stake, 1923–41, LR 721 11, v. 4; University Ward, Ensign Stake, General Minutes, LR 9602 11, v. 8, 1935–41.

70. The First Presidency letter is cited in Lowell M. Durham, "On Mormon Music and Musicians," *Dialogue* 3.2 (Summer 1968): 36.

71. James 5:16; "Teaching of the Twelve Apostles" XIV, *ANF* 7:381.

72. BC 60:212 (D&C 59:12).

73. *WWJ* 3:100.

74. George D. Smith, ed., *An Intimate Chronicle: The Journals of William Clayton* (Salt Lake City, UT: Signature, 1995), 83–84.

75. *CDBY* 2:819.

76. *CDBY* 4:2078; also 5:2679.

77. BC 47:13-15 (D&C 42:88–89).

78. Malad Stake, General Minutes, LR 5190/11 v. 1. An official church statement confirmed that principle in 1913: "It is not necessary in all cases that those whose offenses are not generally known shall be required to confess in public." Lester Bush, "Excommunication and Church Courts: A Note from the *General Handbook of Instructions*," *Dialogue* 14.2 (Summer 1981): 79.

79. One couple was given the choice of rebaptism, confession to the Priesthood meeting, or in Fast and Testimony meeting. A few years later a woman confessed to her ward, and in 1916 records describe a man confessing to the priesthood. In all three cases, a vote to accept the confession was unanimous. Logan 7th Ward, Cache Stake, Historical Record 1904–07, LR 496911, v. 17; Logan 1st Ward, Historical Record, 1906–14, LR 4963 11, v.11, p. 238; Provo 5th Ward, General Minutes, LR 7225 11, v. 12.

80. Bush, "Excommunication," 80.

81. *JSP-J1*, 16.

82. Such meetings are mentioned in BC 49:8 (D&C 46:6).

83. *JSP-J1*, 16.

84. John Corrill, *Brief History of the Church of Christ of Latter Day Saints* (St. Louis, MO: John Corrill, 1839), 9, http://www.olivercowdery.com/smithhome/1830s/1839Corl.htm#pg007a.

85. John Murdock, "Journal and Autobiography," 8. HBLL.

86. BC 49:8 (D&C 46:6).

87. Parley P. Pratt, *Mormonism Unveiled: Zion's Watchman Unmasked* (New York: Pratt & Fordham, 1838), 41.

88. John W. Welch, "Acts of the Apostle William E. McLellin," in *The Journals of William McLellin, 1831–1836*, ed. Jan Shipps and John W. Welch (Provo, UT: BYU Studies and Brigham Young University; Urbana: University of Illinois Press, 1994), 93.

89. Elden Watson, ed., *Orson Pratt Journals* (Salt Lake City, UT: Elden Jay Watson, 1975), 70.

90. *CDBY* 1:81.

91. *CDBY* 1:523.

92. Kathleen Flake, "From Conferences to Councils: The Development of LDS Church Organization, 1830–1835," in *Archive of Restoration Culture Summer Fellows' Papers, 1997–1999* (Provo, UT: Joseph Fielding Smith Institute for Church History, 2000), 1. Cited in Jones, 'We Latter-day Saints,' 86.

93. Flake, "From Conferences to Councils," 86.

94. *JD* 7:318.

95. *CDBY* 1:523.

96. "Fasting and Fast Days," *EJ*, 6:1190.

97. See, for example, David's abstinence from washing and anointing and a bed for sleep in 2 Samuel 12. On sexual continence, see Jewish sources in "Fasting and Fast Days," 1190.

98. 2 Samuel 12.

99. Ezra 8:23.

100. Matthew 17:21; 1 Corinthians 7:5.

101. "Fasting and Fast Days," 1195.

102. Matthew 9:14.

103. Teachings of the Twelve Apostles VIIII, *ANF* 7:379.

104. *Doctrines and Discipline of the Methodist Episcopal Church* (New York: B. Waugh and T. Mason, 1832), 44.

105. Adrian Hastings et al., eds., *The Oxford Companion to Christian Thought* (New York: Oxford University Press, 2000), 236.

106. BC 60:22 (D&C 59:13).

107. Alma 6:6; 17:3; 28:6, etc.

108. *CDBY* 1:88.

109. *CDBY* 4:2511.

110. *CDBY* 4:2517.

111. "When you have gone [more than five days without eating] make your wants known to your neighbors and tell them that you need something to eat, and if you come to me I will feed you." *CDBY* 2:1070.

112. *CDBY* 1:88.

113. *CDBY* 4:2517.

114. *CDBY* 1:480.

115. *JSP-D1*, 372–73.

116. *CDBY* 3:1502.

117. Morgan, *Visible*, 88–89.

118. Bruce R. McConkie, *Mormon Doctrine* (Salt Lake City, UT: Deseret, 1966), 786.

119. *The Personal Writings of Joseph Smith*, ed. Dean C. Jessee (Salt Lake City, UT: Deseret, 1984), 408.

120. *WJS*, 350.

121. BC 10:8 (D&C 11:16); BC 7:1 (D&C 8:1).

122. Thomas Shepard, *The Parable of the Ten Virgins*, cited in Edmund S. Morgan, *Visible Saints: The History of a Puritan Idea* (Mansfield Centre, CT: Martino, 2013), 92.

CHAPTER 11

1. Quoted in G. T. Eddy, *Dr Taylor of Norwich: Wesley's Arch-heretic* (London: Epworth Press, 2003), 39.

2. Timonty Keller, *The Reason for God* (London: Hodder, 2008), 40.

3. 1 Corinthians 5:5, 9.

4. Kenneth E. Kirk, *The Vision of God* (New York: Harper & Row, 1966), 153.

5. *Constitutions of the Holy Apostles* II.v.38, *ANF* 7:414.

6. Acts 20:29–30.

7. Jude 22–23. New Living Translation renders the *NRSV* "defiled" as "contaminated."

8. Kirk, *Vision*, 172.

9. "Excommunication," F. L. Cross and E. A. Livingstone, ed., *Oxford Dictionary of the Christian Church* (Oxford: Oxford University Press, 1997), 584–85.

10. "Excommunication," http://www.newadvent.org/cathen/05678a.htm.

11. "Excommunication," http://www.newadvent.org/cathen/05678a.htm.

12. Edmund S. Morgan, *Visible Saints: The History of a Puritan Idea* (Mansfield Centre, CT: Martino, 2013), 2.

13. *Luther's Small Catechism, with Explanation* (St. Louis, MO: Concordia, 2005), #280, 229.

14. *ICR* IV.xii.1, p. 813.

15. *ICR* IV.xii.5, pp. 814–15.

16. Westminster Confession XXX.4, *C&C* 2:644.

17. Morgan, *Visible*, 11.

18. Morgan, *Visible*, 12.

19. John Field, *Seconde Parte of a Register* I, 86. In Morgan, *Visible*, 14.

20. Morgan, *Visible*, 21–23.

21. Morgan, *Visible*, 19.

22. This was part of the "half-way covenant," cited in Morgan, *Visible*, 130.

23. *Doctrines and Discipline of the Methodist Episcopal Church* (New York: B. Waugh and T. Mason, 1832), 64, 90.

24. *Doctrines and Discipline*, 77.

25. George Bourne, *Man-Stealing and Slavery Denounced by the Presbyterian and Methodist Churches* (Boston: Garrison and Knapp, 1834), 10.

26. *WJS*, 183–84.

27. "G[eorge] Mitchelson's Reasons for Renouncing Sectarianism," *MS* 1.3 (May 1842): 13.

28. Alfred D. Young, "Autobiography," ca. 1808–1842. Typescript, HBLL.

29. Stephen J. Stein, *The Shaker Experience in America* (New Haven, CT: Yale University Press, 1992), 33–34.

30. Morgan, *Visible*, 133.

31. "Articles of the Church of Christ," *JSP-D1*, 372; see 3 Nephi 18 which prohibits partaking "of my flesh and blood unworthily."

32. 1835 D&C 88:1 (D&C 83:3).

33. 1835 D&C 102:10 (D&C 134:10).

34. *MHC* B-1, 598.

35. Journal of the Camp of the Seventies during their Journey from Kirtland to Far West, *MS* 4952, CHL.

36. Preserved Harris and Isaac McWithy were charged with this offense in June 1836. See *JSP-D5*, 247.

37. *MHC* B-1, 774.

38. *MHC* C-1, 970.

39. *JSP-J1*, 256.

40. Jenkins Salisbury was excommunicated for intemperance sometime prior to 1834, and Charles Kellogg apparently for "unchristian" behavior in 1836. See *JSP-D5*, 244.

41. *JSP-D6*, forthcoming; http://www.josephsmithpapers.org/paper-summary/minute-book-2/113. Newberry apparently didn't like the way "some of the boys had hugged a girl in meeting."

42. *WJS*, 256.

43. An extensive list of dozens of modern excommunicants is provided at https://en.wikipedia.org/wiki/Christian_heresy_in_the_modern_era. Some prominent names include John Dietrich (Reformed Church), John Tietjen (Lutheran) J. Gresham Machen (Presbyterian), Frank Stagg (Southern Baptist), Walter Gill (Methodist), and William Brown (Episcopalian).

44. *WJS*, 183–84.

45. *WJS*, 187.

46. *MHC* C-1, 970.

47. *MHC* C-1, 1227–32.

48. *MHC* B-1, 777–78.

49. *MHC* C-1, 1287.

50. *Autobiography of Warren Foote* (Mesa, AZ: Dale Arnold Foote, 1997), 1:5.

51. Parley P. Pratt to Joseph Smith, 24 October 1841, *T&S* 3.7 (1 February 1842): 682–83.

52. *MHC* B-1, 774.

53. Jacob 5.

54. *JSP-D6*, forthcoming; http://www.josephsmithpapers.org/paper-summary/minute-book-2/140.

55. In one letter from Thomas Marsh, all three terms are used as synonyms. Letter to Wilford Woodruff, ca. 18 June 1838, *JSP-D6*, forthcoming; http://www.josephsmithpapers.org/paper-summary/letter-thomas-b-marsh-at-request-of-js-to-wilford-woodruff-circa-18-june-1838/1. In Brigham Young's collected discourses, forms of "disfellowshipment" appear thirty-four times, of excommunication twice. *CDBY*.

56. BC 24:63 (D&C 20:83).

57. Joseph F. Smith Diary, 6 and 7 September 1879, *Minutes*.

58. James E. Talmage Diary, 29 November 1893, *Minutes*.

59. George F. Richards Diary, 7 January 1920, *Minutes*.

60. George F. Richards Diary, 6 April 1920, *Minutes*.

61. "Half of the top leadership" was lost before 1839, noted Roger D. Launius and John E. Hallwas in *Kingdom on the Mississippi Revisited: Nauvoo in Mormon History* (Urbana: University of Illinois Press, 1996), 131.

62. Loretta L. Hefner, "From Apostle to Apostate: The Personal Struggle of Amasa Mason Lyman," *Dialogue* 16.1 (Spring 1983): 90–104.

63. Victor W. Jorgensen and B. Carmon Hardy, "The Taylor-Cowley Affair and the Watershed of Mormon History," *Utah Historical Quarterly* 48.4 (Winter 1980): 4–36. Apostle Richard R. Lyman was excommunicated in 1943 but for adultery rather than any heretical offense. Gary James Bergera, "Transgressions in the Latter-day Saint Community: The Cases of Albert Carrington, Richard R. Lyman, and Joseph F. Smith—Part 2: Richard R. Lyman," *Journal of Mormon History* 37.4 (Fall 2011): 173–207.

64. Statement by the First Presidency and the Quorum of the Twelve, 17 October 1993. https://www.lds.org/ensign/1994/01/news-of-the-church/statement-released-by-first-presidency-and-quorum-of-the-twelve?lang=eng. The definition of apostasy is from *General Handbook of Instructions* (Salt Lake City, UT: Church of Jesus Christ of Latter-day Saints, 1989), 10–13.

65. Sonia Johnson was excommunicated in 1979 for encouraging the public to "oppose church ... missionary programs" among other charges, https://www.washingtonpost.com/archive/politics/1979/12/06/mormon-bishop-excommunicates-woman-who-is-supporting-era/2194cbc1-806e-4014-8884-d1a527620a3f/; for the case of women protesting priesthood exclusion, see http://www.deseretnews.com/article/865605646/LDS-bishop-excommunicates-Ordain-Women-founder.html?pg=all.

66. Sterling M. McMurrin and L. Jackson Newell, *Matters of Conscience: Conversations with Sterling McMurrin on Philosophy, Education, and Religion* (Salt Lake City, UT: Signature, 1996), 199–200.

67. The lectures were published as *The Philosophical Foundations of Mormon Theology* (Salt Lake City: University of Utah Press, 1959).

68. *Constitutions of the Holy Apostles* II.iii.21; II.iii.20, *ANF* 7:396.

69. Bruce C. Hafen, "Disciplinary Procedures," *EM* 1:387.

70. Revelation 3:15–16.

71. Cotton Mather, *Blessed Unions*, quoted in Morgan, *Visible*, 144.

72. Pisqa 29, cited by Michael Fishbane, *The Exegetical Imagination: On Jewish Thought and Theology* (Cambridge, MA: Harvard University Press, 1998), 78; Isaiah 40:1 *KJV*.

73. 1 Chronicles 17:12.

74. 1876 D&C 109:20.

75. Malachi 1; see also Judith 9:8; 1 Maccabees 1:46; 14:36.

76. Matthew 3:8.

77. Edward L. Kimball, "The History of the LDS Temple Admission Standards," *Journal of Mormon History* 24.1 (1998): 140.

78. James R. Clark, comp., *Messages of the First Presidency of the Church of Jesus Christ of Latter-day Saints* (Salt Lake City, UT: Bookcraft, 1966), 3:63.

79. Clark, *Messages*, 141.

80. Cited in Devery S. Anderson, *The Development of LDS Temple Worship, 1846–2000: A Documentary History* (Salt Lake City, UT: Signature, 2011), 83.

81. Diary of Heber J. Grant, 5 May and 30 June 1898. Cited in Thomas G. Alexander, "The Word of Wisdom: From Principle to Requirement," *Dialogue* 14.3 (Autumn 1981): 78.

82. *Instructions to Presidents of Stakes, Bishops, and Clerks* (Salt Lake City, UT: Deseret News Press, 1900).

83. Clark, *Messages*, 5:111.

84. Kimball, "History," 142.

85. "Tithe," *EJ* 15:1155.

86. Genesis 14:20.

87. Genesis 28:22.

88. Malachi 3:10.

89. Deuteronomy 14:22–29.

90. "Tithes," *NCE* 14:92.

91. "Tithes," *NCE* 14:92.

92. Martin Luther, "How Christians Should Regard Moses," *Martin Luther's Basic Theological Writings*, Timothy F. Lull, ed. (Minneapolis: Fortress Press, 2005), 129.

93. Martin Luther, "The Sacrament of the Body and Blood of Christ-Against the Fanatics," trans. Frederick C. Ahrens, in *Luther's Works: Word and Sacrament*, II, ed. Abdel Ross Wentz (Philadelphia: Fortress Press, 1959), 36:356.

94. *ICR*, III.vii.5, pp. 452–53.

95. "The Use of Money," *SJW* 349–51.

96. *EMS* 1.10 (March 1832): 146 (Moses 7:18, PGP).

97. BC 52:20 (D&C 49:20).

98. *JD* 16:156.

99. *JSP-D1*, 251 (D&C 42:30–31).

100. Minute Book 2, 6–7 December 1837, in *JSP-D6*, forthcoming; http://www .josephsmithpapers.org/paper-summary/minute-book-2/92.

101. Thomas B. Marsh to Joseph Smith, 15 February 1838, in *JSP-D6*, forthcoming; http:// www.josephsmithpapers.org/paper-summary/letter-from-thomas-b-marsh-15-february-1838/2.

102. 1844 D&C 107 (D&C 119:1).

103. Joseph Smith to Edward Partridge and the Church, ca. 22 March 1839, in *JSP-D6*, forthcoming; http://www.josephsmithpapers.org/paper-summary/letter-to-edward-partridge-and-the-church-circa-22-march-1839/5.

104. High Council Meeting Minutes, 6 March 1840, in *MHC* C-1, 205.

105. High Council Meeting Minutes, 6 March 1840, in *MHC* C-1, 162.

106. At this time, in lieu of a functioning temple, ordinances were being performed in the "endowment house." *CDBY* 5:2995.

107. 1844 D&C 107:1 (D&C 119:4).

108. Reynolds Cahoon to Newell K. Whitney, 24 July 1838, in *JSP-D6*, forthcoming.

109. 1835 D&C 80 (D&C 89).

110. Lester Bush, "The Word of Wisdom in Early Nineteenth-Century Perspective," *Dialogue* 14.3 (Autumn 1981): 52.

111. Bush, "Word," 56.

112. 1835 D&C 80:heading (D&C 89:2).

113. George Q. Cannon, "Editorial Thoughts," *JI* 26.7 (1 April 1891): 219.

114. George Q. Cannon, "Editorial Thoughts," *JI* 32.24 (15 December 1897): 753–54.

115. *CDBY* 3:1536.

116. *CDBY* 5:2689; 5:3143.

117. "I did not eat meat at that time," he said, referring to his time working as a printer. *CDBY* 5:2952.

118. 1876 D&C 77:2.

119. *JD* 5:70.

120. Journal History, 5 May 1898, *Minutes*.

121. "Adam and Eve ate fruits and vegetables, not animal flesh," and that practice will "be restored." *JD* 20:18.

122. Journal History, 11 March 1897, *Minutes*.

123. *JD* 4:335.

124. *JD* 12:44.

125. "Taking Life Unnecessarily," *JI* 34.19 (1 October 1899): 592.

126. BC 52:20 (D&C 49:21).

127. *JST* Genesis 9:11, p. 630. The exception was "for meat, to save your lives."

128. *T&S* 3.15 (1 June 1842): 801.

129. For a time in the 1960s and 1970s, leaders too concluded that caffeine was the reason for the prohibition, and allowed "the drinking of a beverage made from the coffee bean, from

which all caffeine and deleterious drugs have been removed." Joseph L. Anderson, 8 January 1965, Secretary to the First Presidency. New Mormon Studies CD-ROM (Salt Lake City, UT: Signature Books, 1998).

130. Under the heading of "Cola Drinks," an official LDS publication stated: "The leaders of the Church have advised, and we do now specifically advise, against use of any drink containing harmful habit-forming drugs." Priesthood Bulletin, February 1972, 4. Cited in *CR* (April 1975): 102. And it should be noted that food services do not provide caffeinated drinks at the church's Brigham Young University. See Peggy Fletcher Stack, "Need Caffeine? New Business Delivers at Mormon-Owned BYU," *Salt Lake Tribune*, 3 December 2013. Online version.

131. Minutes of Kirtland High Council, 20 February 1834 (*KCMB* 33); Leonard Rich was "called in question for transgressing the Word of Wisdom" in February 1834 (*KCMB* 23). Noncompliance was also one of several charges leveled at the Missouri stake presidency in 1838. *JSP-D6*, forthcoming; http://www.josephsmithpapers.org/paper-summary/history-1838-1856-volume-b-1-1-september-1834-2-november-1838/243.

132. *MHC* B-2, 759.

133. Minutes, 26 July 1838, *JSP-D6*, forthcoming; http://www.josephsmithpapers.org/paper-summary/journal-march-september-1838/46.

134. *CDBY* 5:2999.

135. *CR* (October 1908): 5.

136. *CR* (October 1908): 10, 11.

137. Clark, *Messages*, 6:172.

138. This is a partial commentary on Matthew 23:1–12, in *New Interpreters Bible* (Nashville: Abingdon Press, 1994), 8:431.

139. Leviticus 20:10, 15; 18:22; Romans 1:26–27 is the most emphatic prohibition against same-sex relations, though some dispute the reading: "Men, giving up natural intercourse with women, . . . committed shameless acts with men."

140. Adrian Hastings et al., ed., *The Oxford Companion to Christian Thought* (New York: Oxford University Press, 2000), 660–61.

141. The number comes from a survey of more than 400,000 people by Amy Adamczyk and Brittany Hayes. Reported in Kevin Hartnett, "Which Religions Have the Most Premarital Sex?" *Boston Globe*, 3 March 2013, https://www.bostonglobe.com/ideas/2013/03/03/which-religions-have-most-premarital-sex/whTrXNIukf5nFRk9UlZ64I/story.html.

142. Nolan Feeney, "3 Other Christian Denominations that Allow Gay Marriage," *Time*, 18 March 2015, http://time.com/3749253/churches-gay-marriage/.

143. See both Christian Smith and Melinda Lundquist Denton, *Soul Searching: The Religious and Spiritual Lives of American Teenagers* (New York: Oxford University Press, 2005); and Christian Smith with Patricia Snell, *Souls in Transition: The Religious and Spiritual Lives of Emerging Adults* (New York: Oxford University Press, 2009).

144. *MHC* E-1, 1669, 1673; 1876 D&C 132:19, 63.

145. C. S. Lewis, *Letters*, ed. Walter Hooper (New York: Houghton Mifflin, 2003), 349.

146. Alma 39:5; Jacob 3:6.

147. This was a principal task of Terryl L. Givens, *Wrestling the Angel: The Foundations of Mormon Thought—Cosmos, God, Humanity* (New York: Oxford University Press, 2015). See also the classic treatment by Stephen E. Robinson, *Are Mormons Christian?* (Salt Lake City, UT: Deseret, 2010).

148. *Elders Journal* 1.3 (July 1838): 44.

149. From a discourse Smith delivered in Washington, DC, on 5 February 1840, and reported by Matthew Davis. *JSP-D7*, forthcoming; http://www.josephsmithpapers.org/paper-summary/history-1838-1856-volume-c-1-2-november-1838-31-july-1842/186.

150. Elder Dallin H. Oaks, "Another Testament of Jesus Christ," speech delivered at Brigham Young University, 6 June 1993, https://speeches.byu.edu/talks/dallin-h-oaks_another-testament-jesus-christ/.

151. Edward L. Kimball, "The History of the LDS Temple Admission Standards," *Journal of Mormon History* 24.1 (1998): 143.

152. Jarom 1:11.

153. Genesis 15:17.

154. Hebrews 10:20 *KJV*.

INDEX